M000266340

# Law and Politics in The Supreme Court

## Cases and Readings

### Revised, Second Edition

Susan E. Lawrence

 **KENDALL/HUNT PUBLISHING COMPANY**
4050 Westmark Drive   Dubuque, Iowa 52002

Cover art by Susan E. Lawrence.

Copyright © 1993, 2000 by Susan E. Lawrence

Library of Congress Catalog Card Number: 99-68674

ISBN 0-7872-6732-5

All rights reserved. No part of this publication may be reproduced,
stored in a retrieval system, or transmitted, in any form or by any
means, electronic, mechanical, photocopying, recording, or otherwise,
without the prior written permission of the copyright owner.

Printed in the United States of America
10  9  8  7  6  5  4  3  2

# ★ *Contents* ★

## 10. Checks on Supreme Court Decision Making: . . . . . . . . . . 493 Balancing Liberty, Constitutionalism, and Democracy

## 11. The Right to Privacy: Law and/or Politics? . . . . . . . . . . . . . . . 517

## 12. Balancing Liberty, Constitutionalism, and Democracy . . . . . . . . . . 647 in Theories of Constitutional Interpretation: Views from the Bench

# ★  *Preface*  ★

One of the great themes of American politics is the idea of law as a check on government power. The American system of liberal, constitutional, democracy is built on the belief that law can govern politics, yet we also know that politics shapes law. The American system of liberal, constitutional, democracy is built on the belief that law can be enforced against government, yet we also know that it is government that has a monopoly on the legitimate use of force to enforce law. The American system of liberal, constitutional, democracy is built on the belief that the people are the sovereign and entitled to rule as the majority sees fit; yet we also believe that individuals have rights which no government—democratic or not—may legitimately invade. These are the paradoxes of constitutionalism. These are the problems of *law* and *politics*.

This reader is designed for a mid-level course focusing on the U.S. Supreme Court as a governing institution. It is designed to facilitate an analysis of the Supreme Court as both a political and a legal institution in American politics through an examination of the processes of and participants in Supreme Court decision-making. It is structured by a focus on the recurring tension the Court faces in balancing the United States' complementary and competing commitments to liberty, constitutionalism, and republican democracy.

This reader is *not* meant to be a primer on constitutional law/doctrine per se; rather, it uses cases (the work product of the Court) to illustrate and explicate the processes of Supreme Court decision-making and the Court's role, historically and currently, in American political development. It takes the Court, as an institution with distinct norms, structures, histories, and institutional constraints, seriously. I use it with other texts that focus on judicial behavior and process—in particular, Lawrence Baum's classic *The Supreme Court*[1]—to provide context, substance, and richness. The materials herein can be used to explore, illustrate, and at times challenge, the implications and meaning of the findings of the judicial process approach to the study of Supreme Court decision-making. In short, the material here is designed to integrate constitutive approaches, political historical institutionalism, and judicial behaviorism in an exploration of the complex interaction between "law" and "politics" in a liberal constitutional democracy.

That said, this reader does consist primarily, though not exclusively, of Supreme Court cases. These cases have been selected to illustrate various aspects of the judicial process. Because this reader was designed for a course on judicial process rather than doctrinal development, I have been especially careful to include information from *U.S. Reports* on the attorneys and interest groups participating in these cases. I have also retained portions of the opinions that place the case in a political and historical context although they may not be central to a doctrinal analysis of the decision.

Unlike most texts that bury the Constitution in an appendix, this volume begins with that central document. It is followed by a short chapter that explains how to brief Supreme Court cases and why students should brief cases, or at least read cases as if they were going to brief them. Chapter 3 functions as an "overture," providing two pairs of cases—the flag salute cases and the flag burning cases—that raise a wide variety of questions about Supreme Court decision-making and its role in American politics. As such, they provide a useful referent throughout the rest of the text. Indeed, I would argue that one cannot really understand or explain the Court's work in these two pairs of cases without thoroughly understanding the many influences on Supreme Court decision-making explored in the following chapters. Hence, together, chapters 1, 2, and 3 provide an introduction to "Law and Politics."

Chapter 4 explores legal reasoning as a distinctive mode of argumentation. Irrespective of whether or not law and legal reasoning determine judicial decision making (a source of never ending debate among judicial scholars), legal reasoning remains the method of argumentation—the mode of rhetoric—judges use to explain and justify their decisions in the written opinions they issue. After a brief excerpt from Edward Levi's classic *An Introduction to Legal Reasoning,* and a playful illustration of reasoning by analogy, five classic equal protection cases involving issues of race, gender, and wealth are presented in order to stimulate discussion about how the law classifies and how judicial decisions are defended using a method of legal reasoning that relies on analogy. Chapter 5 puts judicial review in a historical and political context. It begins with an excerpt from Locke, The Declaration of Independence, and the Articles of Confederation to provide students with a basis for thinking about the Constitution as both a social contract and a series of political compromises. Those *Federalist Papers* that justify the structure and role of the Court in our constitutional system provide the transition to the cases that established judicial review as mechanism for enforcing the Constitution against government, both national and state.

From there, this volume rapidly moves to a modern view of the judicial process and the participants in that process. Chapter 6 provides an overview of the American court system, rates of escalation of disputes and appeals, and the procedural steps that proceed the Supreme Court's issuance of a written opinion. Chapter 7 begins our look at participants in Supreme Court decision-making by looking at the litigation that led up to, and followed, *Brown* v. *Board of Education* (1954). In addition to the obvious intrinsic importance of these cases, along with those in Chapter 4, this Chapter serves the dual purpose of introducing students to interest group litigation (an increasingly important aspect of the Court's work) and providing a concrete example of the development of legal doctrine through incremental change, reversal of past precedent, and routine application of established precedent. Chapter 8 focuses on the selection of Supreme Court Justices, the other major participant in Supreme Court decision-making. Chapter 9 allows an examination of how law and politics interact to effect the decision-making of the Justices once on the Court. This section focuses on the Court's various attempts to define "liberty" in the 14th Amendment due process clause (i.e., as liberty to contract, as a basis for incorporation of the Bill of Rights, and later in Chapter 12 as the "right to privacy") to explore the debate over judicial activism versus judicial restraint, and its political ramifications, including the failed Court-packing plan. Balancing Chapter 9's highlighting of executive checks on Supreme Court decision-making, Chapter 10 focuses on Congressional checks on Supreme Court decision-making.

Chapter 11 provides the modern right to privacy cases as illustrations of the intricate interweaving of law and politics explored in previous chapters. These cases again raise all the paradoxes flowing from our competing commitments to liberty, constitutionalism, and republican democracy. Are these cases instances of constitutional interpretation or judicial legislation? Are the decisions in these cases based in law or politics—or both? In conclusion, Chapter 12 allows two of the leading justices of the late 20th century to speak, in their own words, about how the Constitution should be interpreted and what the role of the Court should be in our liberal, constitutional, democracy. The eloquent voices of William H. Rehnquist and William J. Brennan again pose the questions with which this volume began. While the materials presented in this volume have not provided any easy answers, my hope is that they have left us better equipped to wrestle with these constitutive questions of American politics.

Like many Supreme Court opinions, not to mention American politics itself, this volume asks the reader to juggle many ideas at once. In particular, I use classic materials to make a wide variety of points. In choosing materials that illustrate aspects of the judicial process in American politics and the interplay of law and politics, I have striven to select those that are worth reading in their own right. Given the inherent, many layered, significance of the materials included in this volume, some may question its orginization. It follows neither a strict chronological nor doctrinal sequence; yet, in that my focus is on the processes of Supreme Court decision-making and its institutional and political context, I think its organization makes pedagogic sense. Of course, it goes without saying, that instructors are free to assign materials in a different order than they are presented here; indeed, at times I do so myself And, while outside the page limits of this work, a selection of cases on separation of powers, reapportionment and voting rights, and federalism, would provide an appropriate supplement to this volume.

This volume of readings grows out of nearly fifteen years of teaching, and revising, the Law and Politics course at Rutgers University. I am deeply grateful to the many undergraduates who developed this course with me. In more ways than they know, they have shaped both this volume and its editor. I also owe a debt of gratitude to the outstanding graduate students who have served as teaching apprentices and discussion section leaders for this course over the years: Ed Angelina, Jeff Becker, Deirdre Condit, Rose Corrigan, Kim Edens, Chip Hamlin, Jen Kirkpatrick, Chip Krieder, Carolyn Nestor, David Redlawsk, Rick Rose, Judithanne Scourfield, Greg Vafis, and Matt Voorhees. Michael Besso provided research assistance. My special thanks goes to Michael Paris, my colleague who has shared the duty and pleasure of teaching Law and Politics at Rutgers. He graciously adopted the first edition of this reader, and his helpful commentary on it challenged me to rethink many of my choices about what to add and what to subtract. This is a better volume, and 790:247 Law and Politics is a better course, for his wisdom. This book is dedicated to those students, past and future, who have joined our quest to understand how the Court goes about performing its unique role in the American system of liberal, constitutional, democracy.

## Notes

1. Lawrence Baum, *The Supreme Court, 6th ed.*, (Washington, D.C.: CQ Press, 1998).

# The Constitution
# of the United States of America

The Constitution serves as the governing charter of the United States of America. It gives, defines, divides, and limits our government's power. Written in Philadelphia in 1787 by a convention of delegates from 12 of the 13 states, and ratified by specially elected conventions in each of the states, the Constitution went into effect in 1789. During the state ratifying conventions there were repeated calls for a Bill of Rights, a request that Congress honored in its first session. Under the procedures outlined in Article V, the first ten amendments were ratified by the states and added to the Constitution in 1791. Over the years, an additional seventeen amendments have been added to the Constitution. Probably the most important ones are the Thirteenth, Fourteenth, and Fifteenth Amendments, passed in the wake of the Civil War. These three amendments abolished slavery, required the states to provide all citizens due process and equal protection of the laws, and guaranteed that neither race, color, nor previous condition of servitude would be used to deny any citizen the right to vote. Strangely enough, the most recent amendment to the Constitution was proposed by the first Congress along with the Bill of Rights amendments. This final amendment, which limits Congressional pay raises, was not ratified by two-thirds of the states until 1992 when it became the Twenty-Seventh Amendment.

The United States Constitution is the oldest written constitution still in effect and it has served as a model for many other nations as they have sought to establish liberal, democratic regimes. Its endurance is a testament to the wisdom of the founders and the strength of the American character.

# THE CONSTITUTION OF THE UNITED STATES OF AMERICA

We the People of the United States, in Order to form a more perfect Union, establish justice, insure domestic Tranquility, provide for the common defence, promote the general Welfare, and secure the Blessings of Liberty to ourselves and our Posterity, do ordain and establish this Constitution for the United States of America.

# ARTICLE I.

**SECTION 1.** All legislative Powers herein granted shall be vested in a Congress of the United States, which shall consist of a Senate and House of Representatives.

**SECTION 2.** The House of Representatives shall be composed of Members chosen every second Year by the People of the several States, and the Electors in each State shall have the Qualifications requisite for Electors of the most numerous Branch of the State Legislature.

No Person shall be a Representative who shall not have attained to the Age of twenty five Years, and been seven Years a Citizen of the United States, and who shall not, when elected, be an Inhabitant of that State in which he shall be chosen.

Representatives and direct Taxes shall be apportioned among the several States which may be included within this Union, according to their respective Numbers, which shall be determined by adding to the whole Number of free Persons, including those bound to Service for a Term of Years, and excluding Indians not taxed, three fifths of all other Persons. The actual Enumeration shall be made within three Years after the first Meeting of the Congress of the United States, and within every subsequent Term of ten Years, in such Manner as they shall by Law direct. The Number of Representatives shall not exceed one for every thirty Thousand, but each State shall have at Least one Representative; and until such enumeration shall be made, the State of New Hampshire shall be entitled to choose three, Massachusetts eight, Rhode Island and Providence Plantations one, Connecticut five, New-York six, New Jersey four, Pennsylvania eight, Delaware one, Maryland six, Virginia ten, North Carolina five, South Carolina five, and Georgia three.

When vacancies happen in the Representation from any State, the Executive Authority thereof shall issue Writs of Election to fill such Vacancies.

The House of Representatives shall chuse their Speaker and other Officers; and shall have the sole Power of Impeachment.

**SECTION 3.** The Senate of the United States shall be composed of two Senators from each State, chosen by the Legislature thereof, for six Years; and each Senator shall have one Vote.

Immediately after they shall be assembled in Consequence of the first Election, they shall be divided as equally as may be into three Classes. The Seats of the Senators of the first Class shall be vacated at the Expiration of the second Year, of the second Class at the Expiration of the fourth Year, and of the third Class at the Expiration of the sixth Year, so that one third may be chosen every second Year; and if Vacancies happen by Resignation, or otherwise, during the Recess of the Legislature of any State, the Executive thereof may make temporary Appointments until the next Meeting of the Legislature, which shall then fill such Vacancies.

No Person shall be a Senator who shall not have attained to the Age of thirty Years, and been nine Years a Citizen of the United States, and who shall not, when elected, be an Inhabitant of that State for which he shall be chosen.

The Vice President of the United States shall be President of the Senate, but shall have no Vote, unless they be equally divided.

The Senate shall chuse their other Officers, and also a President pro tempore, in the Absence of the Vice President, or when he shall exercise the Office of President of the United States.

The Senate shall have the sole Power to try all Impeachments. When sitting for that Purpose, they shall be on Oath or Affirmation. When the President of the United States is tried the Chief justice shall preside: And no Person shall be convicted without the Concurrence of two thirds of the Members present.

Judgment in Cases of Impeachment shall not extend further than to removal from Office, and disqualification to hold and enjoy any Office of honor, Trust or Profit under the United States: but the Party convicted shall nevertheless be liable and subject to Indictment, Trial, Judgment and Punishment, according to Law.

**SECTION 4.** The Times, Places and Manner of holding Elections for Senators and Representatives, shall be prescribed in each State by the Legislature thereof; but the Congress may at any time by Law make or alter such Regulations, except as to the Places of chusing Senators.

The Congress shall assemble at least once in every Year, and such Meeting shall be on the first Monday in December, unless they shall by Law appoint a different Day.

**SECTION 5.** Each House shall be the Judge of the Elections, Returns and Qualifications of its own Members, and a Majority of each shall constitute a Quorum to do Business; but a smaller Number may adjourn from day to day, and may be authorized to compel the Attendance of absent Members, in such Manner, and under such Penalties as each House may provide.

Each House may determine the Rules of its Proceedings, punish its Members for disorderly Behaviour, and, with the Concurrence of two thirds, expel a Member.

Each House shall keep a Journal of its Proceedings, and from time to time publish the same, excepting such Parts as may in their Judgment require Secrecy; and the Yeas and Nays of the Members of either House on any question shall, at the Desire of one fifth of those Present, be entered on the Journal.

Neither House, during the Session of Congress, shall, without the Consent of the other, adjourn for more than three days, nor to any other Place than that in which the two Houses shall be sitting.

**SECTION 6.** The Senators and Representatives shall receive a Compensation for their Services, to be ascertained by Law, and paid out of the Treasury of the United States. They shall in all Cases, except Treason, Felony and Breach of the Peace, be privileged from Arrest during their Attendance at the Session of their respective Houses, and in going to and returning from the same; and for any Speech or Debate in either House, they shall not be questioned in any other Place.

No Senator or Representative shall, during the Time for which he was elected, be appointed to any civil Office under the Authority of the United States, which shall have been created, or the Emoluments whereof shall have been encreased during such time; and no Person holding any Office under the United States, shall be a Member of either House during his Continuance in Office.

**SECTION 7.** All Bills for raising Revenue shall originate in the House of Representatives; but the Senate may propose or concur with amendments as on other Bills.

Every Bill which shall have passed the House of Representatives and the Senate, shall, before it become a Law, be presented to the President of the United States; If he approve he shall sign it, but if not he shall return it, with his Objections to that House in which it shall have originated, who shall enter the Objections at large on their Journal, and proceed to reconsider it. If after such Reconsideration two thirds of that House shall agree to pass the Bill, it shall be sent, together with the Objections, to the other House, by which it shall likewise be reconsidered, and if approved by two thirds of that House, it shall become a Law. But in all such Cases the Votes of both Houses shall be determined by Yeas and Nays, and the Names of the Persons voting for and against the Bill shall be entered on the Journal of each House respectively. If any Bill shall not be returned by the President within ten Days (Sunday excepted) after it shall have been presented to him, the Same shall be a Law, in like Manner as if he had signed it, unless the Congress by their Adjournment prevent its Return, in which Case it shall not be a Law.

Every Order, Resolution, or Vote to which the Concurrence of the Senate and House of Representatives may be necessary (except on a question of Adjournment) shall be presented to the President of the United States; and before the Same shall take Effect, shall be approved by him, or being disapproved by him, shall be repassed by two thirds of the Senate and House of Representatives, according to the Rules and Limitations prescribed in the Case of a Bill.

SECTION 8. The Congress shall have Power To lay and collect Taxes, Duties, Imposts and Excises, to pay the Debts and provide for the common Defence and general Welfare of the United States; but all Duties, Imposts and Excises shall be uniform throughout the United States;

To borrow Money on the credit of the United States;

To regulate Commerce with foreign Nations, and among the several States, and with the Indian Tribes;

To establish an uniform Rule of Naturalization, and uniform Laws on the subject of Bankruptcies throughout the United States;

To coin Money, regulate the Value thereof, and of foreign Coin, and fix the Standard of Weights and Measures;

To provide for the Punishment of counterfeiting the Securities and current Coin of the United States;

To establish Post Offices and post Roads;

To promote the Progress of Science and useful Arts, by securing for limited Times to Authors and Inventors the exclusive Right to their respective Writings and Discoveries;

To constitute Tribunals inferior to the supreme Court;

To define and punish Piracies and Felonies committed on the high Seas, and Offences against the Law of Nations;

To declare War, grant Letters of Marque and Reprisal, and make Rules concerning Captures on Land and Water;

To raise and support Armies, but no Appropriation of Money to that Use shall be for a longer Term than two Years;

To provide and maintain a Navy;

To make Rules for the Government and Regulation of the land and naval Forces;

To provide for calling forth the Militia to execute the Laws of the Union, suppress Insurrections and repel Invasions;

To provide for organizing, arming, and disciplining, the Militia, and for governing such Part of them as may be employed in the Service of the United States, reserving to the States respectively, the Appointment of the Officers, and the Authority of training the Militia according to the discipline prescribed by Congress;

To exercise exclusive Legislation in all Cases whatsoever, over such District (not exceeding ten Miles square) as may, by Cession of particular States, and the Acceptance of Congress, become the Seat of the Government of the United States, and to exercise like Authority over all Places purchased by the Consent of the Legislature of the State in which the Same shall be, for the Erection of Forts, Magazines, Arsenals, dock-Yards, and other needful Buildings; And

To make all Laws which shall be necessary and proper for carrying into Execution the foregoing Powers, and all other Powers vested by this Constitution in the Government of the United States, or in any Department or Officer thereof.

**SECTION 9.** The Migration or Importation of such Persons as any of the States now existing shall think proper to admit, shall not be prohibited by the Congress prior to the Year one thousand eight hundred and eight, but a Tax or duty may be imposed on such Importation, not exceeding ten dollars for each Person.

The Privilege of the Writ of Habeas Corpus shall not be suspended, unless when in Cases of Rebellion or Invasion the public Safety may require it.

No Bill of Attainder or ex post facto Law shall be passed.

No Capitation, or other direct, Tax shall be laid, unless in Proportion to the Census or Enumeration herein before directed to be taken.

No Tax or Duty shall be laid on Articles exported from any State.

No Preference shall be given by any Regulation of Commerce or Revenue to the Ports of one State over those of another; nor shall Vessels bound to, or from, one State, be obliged to enter, clear or pay Duties in another.

No Money shall be drawn from the Treasury, but in Consequence of Appropriations made by Law; and a regular Statement and Account of the Receipts and Expenditures of all public Money shall be published from time to time.

No Title of Nobility shall be granted by the United States: And no Person holding any Office of Profit or Trust under them, shall, without the Consent of the Congress, accept of any present, Emolument, Office, or Title, of any kind whatever, from any King, Prince or foreign State.

**SECTION 10.** No State shall enter into any Treaty, Alliance, or Confederation; grant Letters of Marque and Reprisal; coin Money; emit Bills of Credit; make any Thing but gold and silver Coin a Tender in Payment of Debts; pass any Bill of Attainder, ex post facto Law, or Law impairing the Obligation of Contracts, or grant any Title of Nobility.

No State shall, without the Consent of the Congress, lay any Imposts or Duties on Imports or Exports, except what may be absolutely necessary for executing its inspection Laws: and the net Produce of all Duties and Imposts, laid by any State on Imports or Exports, shall be for the Use of the Treasury of the United States; and all such Laws shall be subject to the Revision and Controul of the Congress.

No State shall, without the Consent of Congress, lay any Duty of Tonnage, keep Troops, or Ships of War in time of Peace, enter into any Agreement or Compact with another State, or with a foreign Power, or engage in War, unless actually invaded, or in such imminent Danger as will not admit of delay.

# ARTICLE II.

**SECTION 1.** The executive Power shall be vested in a President of the United States of America. He shall hold his Office during the Term of four Years, and, together with the Vice President, chosen for the same Term, be elected, as follows:

Each State shall appoint, in such Manner as the Legislature thereof may direct, a Number of Electors, equal to the whole Number of Senators and Representatives to which the State may be entitled in the Congress: but no Senator or Representative, or Person holding an Office of Trust or Profit under the United States, shall be appointed an Elector.

The Electors shall meet in their respective States, and vote by Ballot for two Persons, of whom one at least shall not be an Inhabitant of the same State with themselves. And they shall make a List of all the Persons voted for, and of the Number of Votes for each; which List they shall sign and certify, and transmit sealed to the Seat of the Government of the United States, directed to the President of the Senate. The President of the Senate shall, in the Presence of the Senate and House of Representatives, open all the Certificates, and the Votes shall then be counted. The Person having the greatest Number of Votes shall be the President, if such Number be a Majority of the whole Number of Electors appointed; and if there be more than one who have such Majority, and have an equal Number of Votes, then the House of Representatives shall immediately chuse by Ballot one of them for President; and if no Person have a Majority, then from the five highest on the List the said House shall in like Manner chuse the President. But in chusing the President, the Votes shall be taken by States, the Representation from each State having one Vote; a quorum for this Purpose shall consist of a Member or Members from two thirds of the States, and a Majority of all the States shall be necessary to a Choice. In every Case, after the Choice of the President, the Person having the greatest Number of Votes of the Electors shall be the Vice President. But if there should remain two or more who have equal Votes, the Senate shall chuse from them by Ballot the Vice President.

The Congress may determine the Time of chusing the Electors, and the Day on which they shall give their Votes; which Day shall be the same throughout the United States.

No Person except a natural born Citizen, or a Citizen of the United States, at the time of the Adoption of this Constitution, shall be eligible to the Office of President; neither shall any Person be eligible to that Office who shall not have attained to the Age of thirty five Years, and been fourteen Years a Resident within the United States.

In Case of the Removal of the President from Office, or of his Death, Resignation, or Inability to discharge the Powers and Duties of the said Office, the Same shall devolve on the Vice President, and the Congress may by Law provide for the Case of Removal, Death, Resignation or Inability, both of the President and Vice President, declaring what Officer shall then act as President, and such Officer shall act accordingly, until the Disability be removed, or a President shall be elected.

The President shall, at stated Times, receive for his Services, a Compensation, which shall neither be encreased nor diminished during the Period for which he shall have been elected, and he shall not receive within that Period any other Emolument from the United States, or any of them.

Before he enter on the Execution of his Office, he shall take the following Oath or Affirmation:—"I do solemnly swear (or affirm) that I will faithfully execute the Office of President of the United States, and will to the best of my Ability, preserve, protect and defend the Constitution of the United States."

**SECTION 2.** The President shall be Commander in Chief of the Army and Navy of the United States, and of the Militia of the several States, when called into the actual Service of the United States; he may require the Opinion, in writing, of the principal Officer in each of the executive Departments, upon any Subject relating to the Duties of their respective Offices, and he shall have Power to grant Reprieves and Pardons for Offences against the United States, except in Cases of Impeachment.

He shall have Power, by and with the Advice and Consent of the Senate, to make Treaties, provided two thirds of the Senators present concur; and he shall nominate, and by and with the Advice and Consent of the Senate, shall appoint Ambassadors, other public Ministers and Consuls, Judges of the supreme Court, and all other Officers of the United States, whose Appointments are not herein otherwise provided for, and which shall be established by Law: but the Congress may by Law vest the Appointment of such inferior Officers, as they think proper, in the President alone, in the Courts of Law, or in the Heads of Departments.

The President shall have Power to fill up all Vacancies that may happen during the Recess of the Senate, by granting Commissions which shall expire at the End of their next Session.

**SECTION 3.** He shall from time to time give to the Congress Information of the State of the Union, and recommend to their Consideration such Measures as he shall judge necessary and expedient; he may, on extraordinary Occasions, convene both Houses, or either of them, and in Case of Disagreement between them, with Respect to the Time of Adjournment, he may adjourn them to such Time as he shall think proper; he shall receive Ambassadors and other public Ministers; he shall take Care that the Laws be faithfully executed, and shall Commission all the Officers of the United States.

**SECTION 4.** The President, Vice President and all Civil Officers of the United States, shall be removed from Office on Impeachment for, and Conviction of, Treason, Bribery, or other high Crimes and Misdemeanors.

# ARTICLE III.

**SECTION 1.** The judicial Power of the United States, shall be vested in one supreme Court, and in such inferior Courts as the Congress may from time to time ordain and establish. The Judges, both of the supreme and inferior Courts, shall hold their Offices during good Behaviour, and shall, at stated Times, receive for their Services, a Compensation, which shall not be diminished during their Continuance in Office.

**SECTION 2.**   The judicial Power shall extend to all Cases, in Law and Equity, arising under this Constitution, the Laws of the United States, and Treaties made, or which shall be made, under their Authority;—to all Cases affecting Ambassadors, other public Ministers and Consuls;—to all Cases of admiralty and maritime jurisdiction;—to Controversies to which the United States shall be a Party;—to Controversies between two or more States;—between a State and Citizens of another State;—between Citizens of different States;—between Citizens of the same State claiming Lands under Grants of different States, and between a State, or the Citizens thereof, and foreign States, Citizens or Subjects.

In all Cases affecting Ambassadors, other public Ministers and Consuls, and those in which a State shall be Party, the Supreme Court shall have original jurisdiction. In all the other Cases before mentioned, the supreme Court shall have appellate jurisdiction, both as to Law and Fact, with such Exceptions, and under such Regulations as the Congress shall make.

The Trial of all Crimes, except in Cases of Impeachment, shall be by Jury; and such Trial shall be held in the State where the said Crimes shall have been committed; but when not committed within any State, the Trial shall be at such Place or Places as the Congress may by Law have directed.

**SECTION 3.**   Treason against the United States, shall consist only in levying War against them, or in adhering to their Enemies, giving them Aid and Comfort. No Person shall be convicted of Treason unless on the Testimony of two Witnesses to the same overt Act, or on Confession in open Court.

The Congress shall have Power to declare the Punishment of Treason, but no Attainder of Treason shall work Corruption of Blood, or Forfeiture except during the Life of the Person attained.

# ARTICLE IV.

**SECTION 1.**   Full Faith and Credit shall be given in each State to the public Acts, Records, and judicial Proceedings of every other State. And the Congress may by general Laws prescribe the Manner in which such Acts, Records and Proceedings shall be proved, and the Effect thereof.

**SECTION 2.**   The Citizens of each State shall be entitled to all Privileges and Immunities of Citizens in the several States.

A Person charged in any State with Treason, Felony, or other Crime, who shall flee from Justice, and be found in another State, shall on Demand of the executive Authority of the State from which he fled, be delivered up, to be removed to the State having Jurisdiction of the Crime.

No Person held to Service or Labour in one State, under the Laws thereof, escaping into another, shall, in Consequence of any Law or Regulation therein, be discharged from such Service or Labour, but shall be delivered up on Claim of the Party to whom such Service or Labour may be due.

**SECTION 3.** New States may be admitted by the Congress into this Union; but no new State shall be formed or erected within the Jurisdiction of any other State; nor any State be formed by the Junction of two or more States, or Parts of States, without the Consent of the Legislatures of the States concerned as well as of the Congress.

The Congress shall have Power to dispose of and make all needful Rules and Regulations respecting the Territory or other Property belonging to the United States; and nothing in this Constitution shall be so construed as to Prejudice any Claims of the United States, or of any particular State.

**SECTION 4.** The United States shall guarantee to every State in this Union a Republican Form of Government, and shall protect each of them against Invasion; and on Application of the Legislature, or of the Executive (when the Legislature cannot be convened) against domestic Violence.

# ARTICLE V.

The Congress, whenever two thirds of both Houses shall deem it necessary, shall propose Amendments to this Constitution, or, on the Application of the Legislatures of two thirds of the several States, shall call a Convention for proposing Amendments, which, in either Case, shall be valid to all Intents and Purposes, as Part of this Constitution, when ratified by the Legislatures of three fourths of the several States, or by Conventions in three fourths thereof, as the one or the other Mode of Ratification may be proposed by the Congress; Provided that no Amendment which may be made prior to the Year One thousand eight hundred and eight shall in any Manner affect the first and fourth Clauses in the Ninth Section of the first Article; and that no State, without its Consent, shall be deprived of its equal Suffrage in the Senate.

# ARTICLE VI.

All Debts contracted and Engagements entered into, before the Adoption of this Constitution, shall be as valid against the United States under this Constitution, as under the Confederation.

This Constitution, and the Laws of the United States which shall be made in Pursuance thereof, and all Treaties made, or which shall be made, under the Authority of the United States, shall be the supreme Law of the Land; and the Judges in every State shall be bound thereby, any Thing in the Constitution or Laws of any State to the Contrary notwithstanding.

The Senators and Representatives before mentioned, and the Members of the several State Legislatures, and all executive and judicial Officers, both of the United States and of the several States, shall be bound by Oath or Affirmation, to support this Constitution; but no religious Test shall ever be required as a Qualification to any Office or public Trust under the United States.

# ARTICLE VII.

The Ratification of the Conventions of nine States, shall be sufficient for the Establishment of this Constitution between the States so ratifying the Same.

# ARTICLES IN ADDITION TO, AND AMENDMENT OF, THE CONSTITUTION OF THE UNITED STATES OF AMERICA, PROPOSED BY CONGRESS, AND RATIFIED BY THE SEVERAL STATES, PURSUANT TO THE FIFTH ARTICLE OF THE ORIGINAL CONSTITUTION.

## AMENDMENT I [1791].

Congress shall make no law respecting an establishment of religion, or prohibiting the free exercise thereof; or abridging the freedom of speech, or of the press; or the right of the people peaceably to assemble, and to petition the Government for a redress of grievances.

# AMENDMENT II [1791].

A well regulated Militia, being necessary to the security of a free State, the right of the people to keep and bear Arms, shall not be infringed.

# AMENDMENT III [1791].

No Soldier shall, in time of peace be quartered in any house, without the consent of the Owner, nor in time of war, but in a manner to be prescribed by law.

# AMENDMENT IV [1791].

The right of the people to be secure in their persons, houses, papers, and effects, against unreasonable searches and seizures, shall not be violated, and no Warrants shall issue, but upon probable cause, supported by Oath or affirmation, and particularly describing the place to be searched, and the persons or things to be seized.

# AMENDMENT V [1791].

No person shall be held to answer for a capital, or otherwise infamous crime, unless on a presentment or indictment of a Grand Jury, except in cases arising in the land or naval forces, or in the Militia, when in actual service in time of War or public danger; nor shall any person be subject for the same offence to be twice put in jeopardy of life or limb; nor shall be compelled in any criminal case to be a witness against himself, nor be deprived of life, liberty, or property, without due process of law; nor shall private property be taken for public use, without just compensation.

# AMENDMENT VI [1791].

In all criminal prosecutions, the accused shall enjoy the right to a speedy and public trial, by an impartial jury of the State and district wherein the crime shall have been committed, which district shall have been previously ascertained by law, and to be informed of the nature and cause of the accusation; to be confronted with the witnesses against him; to have compulsory process for obtaining Witnesses in his favor, and to have the Assistance of Counsel for his defence.

## AMENDMENT VII [1791].

In Suits at common law, where the value in controversy shall exceed twenty dollars, the right of trial by jury shall be preserved, and no fact tried by a jury, shall be otherwise re-examined in any Court of the United States, than according to the rules of the common law.

## AMENDMENT VIII [1791].

Excessive bail shall not be required, nor excessive fines imposed, nor cruel and unusual punishments inflicted.

## AMENDMENT IX [1791].

The enumeration in the Constitution, of certain rights, shall not be construed to deny or disparage others retained by the people.

## AMENDMENT X [1791].

The powers not delegated to the United States by the Constitution, nor prohibited by it to the States, are reserved to the States respectively, or to the people.

## AMENDMENT XI [1798].

The Judicial power of the United States shall not be construed to extend to any suit in law or equity, commenced or prosecuted against one of the United States by Citizens of another State, or by Citizens or Subjects of any Foreign State.

## AMENDMENT XII [1804].

The Electors shall meet in their respective states and vote by ballot for President and Vice-President, one of whom, at least, shall not be an inhabitant of the same state with themselves; they shall name in their ballots the person voted for as President, and in distinct ballots the person voted for as Vice-President, and they shall make distinct lists of all persons voted for as President, and of all persons voted for as Vice-President, and of the number of votes for each, which lists they shall sign and certify, and transmit sealed to the seat of the government of the United States, directed to the President of the Senate;—The President of the Senate shall, in the presence of the Senate and House of Representatives, open all the certificates and the votes shall then be counted;—The person having the greatest number of votes for President, shall be the President, if such number be a majority of the whole number of Electors appointed; and if no person have such majority, then from the persons having the highest numbers not exceeding three on the list of those voted for as President, the House of Representatives shall choose immediately, by ballot, the President. But in choosing the President, the votes shall be taken by states, the representation from each state having one vote; a quorum for this purpose shall consist of a member or members from two-thirds of the states, and a majority of all the states shall be necessary to a choice. And if the House of Representatives shall not choose a President whenever the right of choice shall devolve upon them, before the fourth day of March next following, then the Vice-President shall act as President, as in the case of the death or other constitutional disability of the President, The person having the greatest number of votes as Vice-President, shall be the Vice-President, if such number be a majority of the whole number of Electors appointed, and if no person have a majority, then from the two highest numbers on the list, the Senate shall choose the Vice-President; a quorum for the purpose shall consist of two-thirds of the whole number of Senators, and a majority of the whole number shall be necessary to a choice. But no person constitutionally ineligible to the office of President shall be eligible to that of Vice-President of the United States.

## AMENDMENT XIII [1865].

**SECTION 1.** Neither slavery nor involuntary servitude, except as a punishment for crime whereof the party shall have been duly convicted, shall exist within the United States, or any place subject to their jurisdiction.

**SECTION 2.** Congress shall have power to enforce this article by appropriate legislation.

## AMENDMENT XIV [1868].

**SECTION 1.** All persons born or naturalized in the United States and subject to the jurisdiction thereof, are citizens of the United States and of the State wherein they reside. No State shall make or enforce any law which shall abridge the privileges or immunities of citizens of the United States; nor shall any State deprive any person of life, liberty, or property, without due process of law; nor deny to any person within its jurisdiction the equal protection of the laws.

**SECTION 2.** Representatives shall be apportioned among the several States according to their respective numbers, counting the whole number of persons in each State, excluding Indians not taxed. But when the right to vote at any election for the choice of electors for President and Vice-President of the United States, Representatives in

Congress, the Executive and Judicial officers of a State, or the members of the Legislature thereof, is denied to any of the male inhabitants of such State, being twenty-one years of age, and citizens of the United States, or in any way abridged, except for participation in rebellion, or other crime, the basis of representation therein shall be reduced in the proportion which the number of such male citizens shall bear to the whole number of male citizens twenty-one years of age in such State.

**SECTION 3.** No person shall be a Senator or Representative in Congress, or elector of President and Vice-President, or hold any office, civil or military, under the United States, or under any State, who, having previously taken an oath, as a member of Congress, or as an officer of the United States, or as a member of any State legislature, or as an executive or judicial officer of any State, to support the Constitution of the United States, shall have engaged in insurrection or rebellion against the same, or given aid or comfort to the enemies thereof. But Congress may by a vote of two-thirds of each House, remove such disability.

**SECTION 4.** The validity of the public debt of the United States, authorized by law, including debts incurred for payment of, pensions and bounties for services in suppressing insurrection or rebellion, shall not be questioned. But neither the United States nor any State shall assume or pay any debt or obligation incurred in aid of insurrection or rebellion against the United States, or any claim for the loss of emancipation of any slave; but all such debts, obligations and claims shall be held illegal and void.

**SECTION 5.** The Congress shall have power to enforce, by appropriate legislation, the provisions of this article.

# AMENDMENT XV [1870].

**SECTION 1.** The right of citizens of the United States to vote shall not be denied or abridged by the United States or by any State on account of race, color, or previous condition of servitude.

**SECTION 2.** The Congress shall have power to enforce this article by appropriate legislation.

# AMENDMENT XVI [1913].

The Congress shall have power to lay and collect taxes on incomes, from whatever source derived, without apportionment among the several States, and without regard to any census or enumeration.

# AMENDMENT XVII [1913].

The Senate of the United States shall be composed of two Senators from each State, elected by the people thereof, for six years; and each Senator shall have one vote. The electors in each State shall have the qualifications requisite for electors of the most numerous branch of the State legislatures.

When vacancies happen in the representation of any State in the Senate, the executive authority of such State shall issue writs of election to fill such vacancies: Provided, That the legislature of any State may empower the executive thereof to make temporary appointments until the people fill the vacancies by election as the legislature may direct.

This amendment shall not be so construed as to affect the election or term of any Senator chosen before it becomes valid as part of the Constitution.

# AMENDMENT XVIII [1919].

**SECTION 1.** After one year from the ratification of this article the manufacture, sale, or transportation of intoxicating liquors within, the importation thereof into, or the exportation thereof from the United States and all territory subject to the jurisdiction thereof for beverage purposes is hereby prohibited.

**SECTION 2.** The Congress and the several States shall have concurrent power to enforce this article by appropriate legislation.

**SECTION 3.** This article shall be inoperative unless it shall have been ratified as an amendment to the Constitution by the legislatures of the several States, as provided in the Constitution, within seven years from the date of the submission hereof to the States by the Congress.

# AMENDMENT XIX [1920].

The right of citizens of the United States to vote shall not be denied or abridged by the United States or by any State on account of sex.

Congress shall have power to enforce this article by appropriate legislation.

# AMENDMENT XX [1933].

**SECTION 1.** The terms of the President and Vice President shall end at noon on the 20th day of January, and the terms of Senators and Representatives at noon on the 3d day of January, of the years in which such terms would have ended if this article had not been ratified; and the terms of their successors shall then begin.

**SECTION 2.** The Congress shall assemble at least once in every year, and such meeting shall begin at noon on the 3d day of January, unless they shall by law appoint a different day.

**SECTION 3.** If, at the time fixed for the beginning of the term of the President, the President elect shall have died, the Vice President elect shall become President. If a President shall not have been chosen before the time fixed for the beginning of his term, or if the President elect shall have failed to qualify, then the Vice President elect shall act as President until a President shall have qualified; and the Congress may by law provide for the case wherein neither a President elect nor a Vice President elect shall have qualified, declaring who shall then act as President, or the manner in which one who is to act shall be selected, and such person shall act accordingly until a President or Vice President shall have qualified.

**SECTION 4.** The Congress may by law provide for the case of the death of any of the persons from whom the House of Representatives may choose a President whenever the right of choice shall have devolved upon them, and for the case of the death of any of the persons from whom the Senate may choose a Vice President whenever the right of choice shall have devolved upon them.

**SECTION 5.** Sections 1 and 2 shall take effect on the 15th day of October following the ratification of this article.

**SECTION 6.** This article shall be inoperative unless it shall have been ratified as an amendment to the Constitution by the legislatures of three-fourths of the several States within seven years from the date of its submission.

# AMENDMENT XXI [1933].

**SECTION 1.** The eighteenth article of amendment to the Constitution of the United States is hereby repealed.

**SECTION 2.** The transportation or importation into any State, Territory, or possession of the United States for delivery or use therein of intoxicating liquors, in violation of the laws thereof, is hereby prohibited.

**SECTION 3.** This article shall be inoperative unless it shall have been ratified as an amendment to the Constitution by conventions in the several States, as provided in the Constitution, within seven years from the date of the submission hereof to the States by the Congress.

# AMENDMENT XXII [1951].

**SECTION 1.** No person shall be elected to the office of the President more than twice, and no person who has held the office of President, or acted as President, for more than two years of a term to which some other person was elected President shall be elected to the office of the President more than once. But this Article shall not apply to any person holding the office of President when this Article was proposed by the Congress, and shall not prevent any person who may be holding the office of President, or acting as President, during the term within which this Article becomes operative from holding the office of President or acting as President during the remainder of such term.

**SECTION 2.** This article shall be inoperative unless it shall have been ratified as an amendment to the Constitution by the legislatures of three-fourths of the several States within seven years from the date of its submission to the States by the Congress.

# AMENDMENT XXIII [1961].

**SECTION 1.** The District constituting the seat of Government of the United States shall appoint in such manner as the Congress may direct:

A number of electors of President and Vice President equal to the whole number of Senators and Representatives in Congress to which the District would be entitled if it were a State, but in no event more than the least populous State; they shall be in addition to those appointed by the States, but they shall be considered, for the purposes of the election of President and Vice President, to be electors appointed by a State; and they shall meet in the District and perform such duties as provided by the twelfth article of amendment.

**SECTION 2.** The Congress shall have power to enforce this article by appropriate legislation.

# AMENDMENT XXIV [1964].

**SECTION 1.** The right of citizens of the United States to vote in any primary or other election for President or Vice President, for electors for President or Vice President, or for Senator or Representative in Congress, shall not be denied or abridged by the United States or any State by reason of failure to pay any poll tax or other tax.

**SECTION 2.** The Congress shall have power to enforce this article by appropriate legislation.

# AMENDMENT XXV [1967].

**SECTION 1.** In case of the removal of the President from office or of his death or resignation, the Vice President shall become President.

**SECTION 2.** Whenever there is a vacancy in the office of the Vice President, the President shall nominate a Vice President who shall take office upon confirmation by a majority vote of both Houses of Congress.

**SECTION 3.** Whenever the President transmits to the President pro tempore of the Senate and the Speaker of the House of Representatives his written declaration that he is unable to discharge the powers and duties of his office, and until he transmits to them a written declaration to the contrary, such powers and duties shall be discharged by the Vice President as Acting President.

**SECTION 4.** Whenever the Vice President and a majority of either the principal officers of the executive departments or of such other body as Congress may by law provide, transmit to the President pro tempore of the Senate and the Speaker of the House of Representatives their written declaration that the President is unable to discharge the powers and duties of his office, the Vice President shall immediately assume the powers and duties of the office as Acting President.

Thereafter, when the President transmits to the President pro tempore of the Senate and the Speaker of the House of Representatives his written declaration that no inability exists, he shall resume the powers and duties of his office unless the Vice President and a majority of either the principal officers of the executive department or of such other body as Congress may by law provide, transmit within four days to the President pro tempore of the Senate and the Speaker of the House of Representatives their written declaration that the President is unable to discharge the powers and duties of his office. Thereupon Congress shall decide the issue, assembling within forty-eight hours for that purpose if not in session. If the Congress, within twenty-one days after receipt of the latter written declaration, or, if Congress is not in session, within twenty-one days after Congress is required to assemble, determined by two-thirds vote of both Houses that the President is unable to discharge the powers and duties of his office, the Vice President shall continue to discharge the same as Acting President; otherwise, the President shall resume the powers and duties of his office.

# AMENDMENT XXVI [1971].

**SECTION 1.** The right of citizens of the United States, who are eighteen years of age or older, to vote shall not be denied or abridged by the United States or by any State on account of age.

**SECTION 2.** The Congress shall have power to enforce this article by appropriate legislation.

# AMENDMENT XXVI [1992].

No law varying the compensation for the services of the Senators and Representatives shall take effect until an election of Representatives shall have intervened.

# Reading Supreme Court Cases

$\mathcal{T}$he U.S. Supreme Court has become an important interpreter of the United States Constitution. The Court's interpretations can be found in the "opinions" the Justices write explaining the Court's decisions resolving conflicts between individuals or between individuals and government. Majority opinions, and concurring opinions, are the Justices' attempts to persuade the reader that the Court has made the correct, or at least a good, decision. Dissenting opinions are the Justices' attempts to do the opposite. Students of the Court disagree over whether the Justices' opinions represent the reasoning that led to the decision or are merely post-decision rationalizations. Either way, the tradition of issuing written opinions insures that the Court's decisions are defensible through rational argumentation based in law, even if the law, alone, does not "explain" judicial decisions or determine case outcomes.

A number of famous Supreme Court cases appear in this volume. They have been edited directly from the official publication of U.S. Supreme Court opinions, *U.S. Reports.* Cases appear in *Law and Politics* in the same format as they do in the official bound volumes issued by the Court itself, although in *Law and Politics* some portions of the opinions have been omitted. Consequently, the format in which the cases are presented here is somewhat different than that used in most casebooks; and to further complicate the matter, the Court itself has used different formats during different historical eras, and those have been followed here. While this may cause a bit of confusion, its purpose is to provide you with the opportunity to read edited cases as they would appear if you were to go to *U.S. Reports,* directly. This should ease the reading of cases directly out of *U.S. Reports* as you continue to explore Supreme Court decision-making on your own.

Reading the cases as presented here, and as presented in *U.S. Reports,* requires paying close attention to what the different sections of the case are. Often, the cases begin with what is called a "syllabus" of the decision, usually presented in a smaller type face. This portion is prepared by the Reporter of the U.S. Supreme Court and summarizes the case and recounts its judicial history. This is sometimes followed by a "Statement of the Case." The attorneys representing each party are listed by name, along with any amicus curiae filers—either in the text or in a footnote. Finally, the actual *opinion of the Court* will begin, introduced by the authoring Justice's name. The opinion of the Court is followed by any concurring and/or dissenting opinions. All these different sections of the case are labeled. Justices not specifically listed as writing or joining a dissenting opinion (or recusing themselves), have voted with the majority. In short, all of the above can be summarized in the simple adage: "Look before you read."

This Chapter explains how to read and study a Supreme Court opinion by writing a "brief" of the case.

## HBC: HOW (AND WHY) TO BRIEF A SUPREME COURT CASE

### Susan E. Lawrence

Writing briefs of Supreme Court cases serves two important purposes. First, the actual preparation of a brief focuses one's reading so that one gains a thorough understanding of the case. By isolating the salient facts of the case, formulating a statement of the legal question raised by the case—and the Court's answer to that question, and summarizing the Justices' reasoning justifying that answer, one moves from simply reading the case, to actually analyzing it—a prerequisite to any serious critique. Life-time readers of Supreme Court opinions have the briefing process running "on automatic pilot" in their heads every time they read a Court opinion; and ultimately, as with everything else in life, one only learns how to write a good brief through practice and reflecting on the experience. Second, briefs, once composed, provide an invaluable study aid. A well-prepared brief presents the elements of the case in a usable form and allows one to reacquaint one's self with the case without returning to the full Court opinion. These purposes are accomplished, in part, by following a standard, uniform format in writing briefs. This format is described below and is used in the sample brief that follow these directions. Please refer to this sample brief as you read.

All briefs must contain the following eight sections (or seven, if there are no concurring and/or dissenting opinions), in the order listed here:

1.  The case **CITATION**
2.  The **FACTS** of the case
3.  The **ISSUE** or issues
4.  A summary of the **REASONING** in the majority opinion
5.  The **DECISION**
6.  The **RULE** of the case
7.  A summary **of CONCURRING AND/OR DISSENTING OPINIONS**, if any, and
8.  The **STUDENT'S NOTE AND COMMENTS** on the case (this portion is **mandatory**)

Writing a brief is as much a process of *reading* as of writing and it requires at least three close readings of the case. Begin by reading the case through to get the general idea of what is going on and where the Court is ending up. Read the concurring and dissenting opinions as well; they often contain important information that will clarify parts of the majority opinion for the reader. Read the case again, marking passages you will want to use in composing the various sections of the brief. Then, pick up your pen, or fire up your keyboard, and begin the actual process of writing a brief. Read your brief looking for brevity and clarity—would you be able to understand the case if you picked up this brief six months from now? Briefs should be *brief*—concise, perhaps 1 1/2 or 2 single spaced pages in a standard size font; but, they should also contain all the salient information about the case in a condensed form.[1]

## CITATION

The citation consists of the name of the case, appropriate references to the place where it is published and the date. Thus, *Marbury* v. *Madison*, 1 Cranch 137 (1803), or *Baker* v. *Carr*, 369 U.S. 186; 82 S. Ct. 691; 7 L. Ed. 2d 663 (1962) constitutes a correct citation.

Supreme Court cases found in casebooks such as this one are excerpts drawn from *U.S. Reports*, the official government publication of Supreme Court opinions. The original and full version of the case is found in *U.S. Reports*. The first set of numbers before "U.S." directs one to the appropriate volume of *U.S. Reports* and the second set of numbers after "U.S. " directs one to the first page of the case in that volume. These references to volume and page number should be followed by the year the case was decided, presented in parentheses.

In the early days of the Court (for example, when *Marbury* v. *Madison* was decided), references were to the official reporter of the Court, such as Dallas, Cranch, Wheaton,

Peters, etc., so those names are used rather than "U.S." After 1874, the citation to the official *United States Report* is simply "volume number—U.S.—page number," starting with volume 91. Thus, in the examples cited above, the original opinion in *Marbury* v. *Madison* is found in volume 1 of Cranch at page 137; the original of *Baker* v. *Carr* is found in volume 369 of the official *United States Reports* at page 186.

Today, in addition to the official reports, there are two commercial firms which publish "reproductions" of the official reports. The second group of numbers and letters (82 S. Ct. 691) refers to the *Supreme Court Reporter* published by West Publishing Company. The third group refers to *the Lawyer's Edition of U.S. Reports* published by the Lawyers' Cooperative Publishing Company. Cases reproduced directly from *U.S. Reports* only provide the official *U.S. Reports* citation and that is sufficient in the brief. Docket numbers should be used for very recent cases issued as a "slip opinions"; such cases have not yet been published in the bound volumes of U.S. Reports and therefore lack an official citation number.[2]

Note that in writing case names, the names of the two parties are italicized or underlined, but the "v." (which stands for 'versus') is NOT italicized or underlined. Lawyers and judges—anyone learned in the law—never uses "vs." for 'versus' in a case name; a simple "v." is always used.

The official name of a case indicates the posture of the parties to the case. The name listed before the "v." in a case name is the petitioner/appellant, i.e., the party that lost in the lower court and is now asking the Supreme Court to reverse the lower court's decision. The name listed after the "v." is the respondent/appellee, i.e., the party that won in the lower court and is urging the Supreme Court to uphold the lower court's decision. Note that upholding the lower court's decision is not necessarily the same as upholding the statute being challenged. Also note that the petitioner appellant is not necessarily the plaintiff in the case (i.e., the party that initially filed the case in the lower court) and that the respondent/appellee is not necessarily the defendant in the original case (i.e., the party against whom the case was filed in the lower court.)

## FACTS

Every case arises out of some specific concrete situation—an actual controversy. These facts are usually provided early in the Court's majority opinion; but, sometimes the salient facts in the case are scattered throughout the majority, concurring, and dissenting opinions. Sometimes they will be laid out for you; other times, you will have to dig for them.

In a brief, one does not need to recount the whole story surrounding the case; rather, a brief should only include *material facts*. Material facts are those facts which *if they had been different* might have caused the case to be decided another way. This means that one cannot write the **FACTS** section of the brief without first understanding what the Court decided and why. The law, as it is interpreted and applied in the case, determines what facts are important or *material*. This section of the brief should summarize the *material facts* so that when a similar case arises, one could easily compare the facts in the two cases to see if the precedent set in the briefed case would apply. For example, in *Roe* v. *Wade*, 410 U.S. 113 (1973), neither Jane Roe's marital status, religious affiliation, nor race, are relevant in the Court's reasoning. In contrast, in *Planned Parenthood of Missouri* v. *Danforth*, 428 U.S. 52 (1976), the woman's marital status is relevant to the Court's reasoning and is a *material fact*. In *Brown* v. *Board of Education*, 347 U.S. 483 (1954), Linda Brown's race is relevant to the Court's reasoning and constitutes a *material fact*; in *Minersville* v. *Gobitis*, 310 U.S. 586 (1940), Lillian Gobitis' religious affiliation is relevant to the Court's reasoning and constitutes a *material fact*; McCulloch's gender is not *material*; Roe's is.

Also, included under the statement of facts, there should be a record of the *judicial history* of the case, if the case excerpt includes it. The *judicial history* of a case is an account of which lower courts heard the case before it reached the Supreme Court and what they decided. Remember, with a few minor exceptions, the Supreme Court is an appellate court, not a court of original jurisdiction (i.e. a trial court). Usually the Supreme Court is reviewing a case that has already been heard by at least one other court.

## ISSUE

This portion of the brief is a statement of the legal question decided by the Court in the case. The focus is on the broad legal/constitutional issue decided by the case rather than on the resolution of the specific controversy between the plaintiff and the defendant The **ISSUE** should be framed as **a single-sentence question** and should include (1) a statement of the **government action** that is being challenged and (2) the **specific provision of the constitution** claimed to be violated by the challenged government action. It is not useful to refer to the government action being challenged simply by naming a statute; rather, it will be more helpful to briefly state what the statute does. For example, reference to "the Fair Labor Standards Act of 1938" does not provide the brief reader with the information s/he needs, whereas "congressional regulation of the wages and hours of employees in local manufacturing" does. Nor is it useful to simply ask if the challenged government action is 'constitutional'; rather, it is much more helpful to ask if it violates, for example, Article 1, Sec. 8, para 3 (the commerce clause).

Stating the issue is not a simple matter and it is the key to understanding the entire case. Sometimes the opinion will state the issue, or issues, clearly, although sometimes the majority opinion will seem to state the issue and then proceed to write an opinion that addresses a different issue! *Marbury* v. *Madison,* 1 Cranch 137 (1803) is the classic example of this rhetorical strategy. The issue included in the brief should be the one that the Court's opinion actually addresses—not red herring issues thrown in for rhetorical effect. Usually, you will need to dig for the issue yourself. The section of the course or of the casebook in which the case appears should give you a clue as to the likely constitutional issue in the case. At times, you might find it necessary to go back and revise your formulation of the issue as you gain a fuller understanding of the case in the process of completing the other sections of the brief. Formulation of the issue is often the most challenging portion of writing a brief and involves a skill that can only be honed through attentive practice.

## REASONING

This section is a summary of the majority's reasoning in the case, condensed into a workable and recallable form. It should always begin with *the name of the majority opinion writer.*

What one wants in this portion of the brief is the basic argument of the Court—the major premises and lines of reasoning used by the Court, and the conclusions of the Court on the issues raised. In other words, why did the Court accept one line of reasoning and reject others? How did the Court's reasoning lead to the result? The goal is to analyze the case so that the extraneous materials—those materials that are not absolutely fundamental to an understanding of the case—are left out while those points that are basic and essential to an understanding of how the Court justifies its decision are included. It is usually easiest to retain some of the Court's own language and in a brief it is not necessary to use quotation marks when doing so. However, the REASONING section of a brief will always turn out to be too long and will not really help the writer understand the case if there is not substantial effort put into condensing (not merely chopping up and copying) the Court's reasoning and translating it into the brief writer's own words.

The REASONING section should be written in the first person; in other words, you should assume that you are the author of the Court's opinion and you are now preparing a summary of your longer opinion. One strategy that works well in attempting to distill down what is central in the Court's reasoning and what the major and minor premises are, is to attempt to reconstruct the outline that the Justice "must" have used in writing the opinion.

In summarizing and condensing the Court's reasoning, there will be a lot more to cut when you are working from the Court's full opinion than when you are working from an excerpt in a casebook where the editor has already eliminated much of the Court's opinion for you.

# DECISION

This portion of the brief tells the reader what the Court decided in terms of the disposition of the specific case before it. It usually consists of one word or phrase: "affirmed," "reversed," or something along the lines of "reversed (or vacated) and remanded for further proceedings not inconsistent with this opinion." Usually, though not always, the Court opinion itself will end with such a word or phrase, sometimes printed in italics.

"Affirmed" means that the lower court's decision stands and that the petitioner/appellant has lost. "Reversed" means that the lower court's decision is overturned and that the petitioner/appellant has won. "Reversed and remanded" means that the Supreme Court is reversing the lower court's specific ruling, but it is sending the case back to the lower court so that the lower court can re-decide the case in light of the guidance provided in the Supreme Court's opinion. "Vacated and remanded" means basically the same thing except that technically the lower court's decision has been set aside as void rather than overturned. The Supreme Court is particularly likely to use remand orders when reviewing decisions of state courts rather than lower federal courts. The feeling is that remands demonstrate respect for the dual sovereignty of state governments and their courts.

# RULE

This, along with the ISSUE, is the most important part of the brief. The RULE of the case is the general principle of law that the Court sets forth in the process of deciding the specific case. It is the answer to the question presented in the ISSUE portion of the brief. If the ISSUE has been well-crafted, formulating the RULE is fairly simple. Basically, the RULE should restate the ISSUE in a statement form rather than as an interrogatory, incorporating any controlling facts or legal doctrines developed in the case. Like the ISSUE, the RULE should include (1) a statement of the **government action** that is being challenged and (2) the **specific provision of the constitution** that the Court decides is/is not violated by the challenged government action. In addition, the RULE will often include some indication of the doctrine or standard the Court develops to justify its conclusion that the government practice does/does not violate the constitution.

## DISSENTING AND/OR CONCURRING OPINIONS (IF ANY)

In addition to the opinion of the Court, the reasoning of the Justices writing concurring and/or dissenting opinions must be condensed and summarized. Each concurring and/or dissenting opinion should begin with the authoring Justice's name. (Note that sometimes other Justices will join a concurring and/or dissenting opinion—sometimes even when they have also written their own separate opinion.)

Justices write concurring opinions when they agree with the specific decision the Court reached in relation to the individual litigants, but they disagree with the reasoning presented in the majority opinion. Justices write dissenting opinions when they disagree with both the majority's specific decision and its reasoning. (Justices not specifically listed as writing or joining a dissenting opinion (or recusing themselves), have voted with the majority.) In summarizing concurring and dissenting opinions, the primary focus should be on where the Justice disagrees with the majority. Often, reading the concurring and/or dissenting opinions will help in understanding the majority opinion.

Fundamentally, concurring and/or dissenting opinions illustrate that law, constitutional language, and legal reasoning do not provide one, single, correct answer to any given controversy; yet, the law and legal reasoning do shape and constrain what kinds of arguments can be made and what range of alternatives can be considered.

## STUDENTS NOTES AND COMMENTS ON THE CASE

This may be the second most important section of a brief. It is here that you should present your own views on the case, raise any questions about the Court's reasoning, and place the case in a historical, political, and doctrinal context.

**Finally**, as with all writing, standard conventions of spelling and grammar should be observed. Proofreading and spell checks are always expected. In briefing cases, as with most things, skill and ease come with practice. The point is not to write a "perfect" brief the first time you try, but rather to learn from the experience of briefing a number of Court cases. Once the mental process of briefing a case is mastered, no Supreme Court decision need ever seem a mystery again. And, equally important, the 'brief mind-set' will improve comprehension and analytical skills in reading all types of expository writing.

## *Notes*

1.  Whether you use long hand or type, you might find it useful to double-space. The "right" length for a brief varies with each case and is something one simply develops a feel for through experience. Basically, briefs tend to come out the "right" length when the writer stays focused on identifying the most important points in the Court's argument and condensing the material rather than simply recopying the Court's language; however, should you find that you have produced a 4 or 5 or 6 page brief, recheck that you have focused only the most important points and have condensed the Court's argument using your own words.

2.  There are numerous electronic sources of Supreme Court opinions now available, and one suspects that they will continue to multiply. These sources still provide the publication information described above as the official citation for a Supreme Court case.

Name_____

# Minersville School District. Bd. of Ed. of Minersville School District v. Gobitis
# 310 U.S. 586 (1940)

**FACTS**: Lillian Gobitis (12) and William Gobitis (10), Jehovah's Witnesses, were expelled from the Minersville public schools for refusing to salute the flag as required by the Minersville School Board policy. (Jehovah's Witnesses believe that such a gesture violates the commands of the Scripture). The Gobitis children were faced with possible criminal prosecution for truancy. The District Court and the Court of Appeals found the mandatory flag salute unconstitutional, holding for Gobitis.

**ISSUE**:  Does a local school board's requirement that students salute the flag over the students' sincere conscientious religious objections violate the free exercise of religion clause of the First Amendment [as incorporated as a bar on state action through the Fourteenth Amendment]?

**REASONING**:  Frankfurter: The First Amendment guarantees religious freedom by prohibiting the establishment of a state religion and by securing to every sect the free exercise of its faith. The scope of this precious right is only brought into question here because the conscience of the individual has collided with the felt necessities of society.

The religious liberty which the Constitution protects has never excluded legislation of general scope not directed against doctrinal loyalties of particular sects. The Court has upheld numerous general laws in their application to those who refused obedience from religious conviction because those laws were manifestations of specific powers of government deemed by the legislature essential to secure and maintain that orderly, tranquil, and free society without which religious toleration itself is unattainable.

The flag salute is designed to promote national cohesion which is the paramount interest of government, an interest inferior to none in the hierarchy of legal values. National unity is the basis of national security. The flag is the symbol of our national unity and the 'binding tie of cohesive sentiment' is the ultimate foundation of a free society.

School authorities may require students to salute the flag as part of their attempt to awaken in the child's mind considerations as to the significance of the flag contrary to those implanted by the parent. The school may rightfully refuse to exempt conscientious dissidents in an effort to achieve school discipline and prevent the casting of doubts in the minds of other children which may weaken the effect of the exercise.

An ordered society dedicated to the preservation of freedom may in self-protection use the educational process for inculcating those almost unconscious feelings which bind men together in a comprehending loyalty to the nation, whatever other lesser differences they may have.

To the legislatures, no less than to courts, is committed to the guardianship of deeply-cherished liberties.

**DECISION**: Reversed.

**RULE:**  A local school board's attempt to promote national unity through a requirement that students salute the flag over the students' sincere religious objections does not violate the free exercise of religion clause of the First Amendment [as incorporated as a bar on state action through the 14th Amendment].

**DISSENTING:** Stone: This law does more than suppress freedom of speech and more than prohibit free exercise of religion. This law seeks to coerce these children to express a sentiment which they do not believe and which violates their deepest religious convictions.

Constitutional guarantees of personal liberty are not always absolute. Government may compel military service despite religious objections. It may suppress religious practices dangerous to morals and inimical to public safety, health, and good order. But it is a long step, which I am not prepared to take, to the position that government may, as a supposed educational  measure and as a means of disciplining the young, compel public affirmations which violate their religious conscience.

There are other ways to promote national unity. While flag salutes may promote national unity when voluntarily given, it is another matter to claim that compulsory expression in violation of religious convictions plays such an important role in national unity as to leave school boards free to exact it despite the constitutional guarantees of freedom of religion.

It is no answer to leave it to the democratic process because that surrenders the protection of constitutional liberty to popular will.

**NOTES & COMMENTS:** [*just one example of the type of discussion that is appropriate here*] Justice Frankfurter's majority opinion relies solely on the First Amendment free exercise of religion clause, while Justice Stone's dissenting opinion invokes both the free exercise and the freedom of speech clauses of the First Amendment. Justice Stone believes that the mandatory flag salute violates both the prohibition on government interfering with the free exercise of religion and with freedom of speech. Justice Frankfurter never addresses the freedom of speech issue. "I was not sure whether I should include 'freedom of speech' in the issue; ultimately I decided to stick with the majority's approach and only include 'free exercise.'"

The *Minersville* v. *Gobitis* decision was handed down in 1940. World War II had begun in 1939 and the United States entered the war in December 1941. World War II made patriotism seem particularly important; but it also revealed the dangers of the kind of blind nationalism Nazism promoted.

I think that the First Amendment free exercise clause does mean that schools and other government officials cannot legitimately require students to violate their own religious beliefs. But, I also agree with Justice Frankfurter's argument that we cannot have everybody deciding for themselves what laws they are and are not going to obey. What I do not understand is why saluting the flag and saying the pledge of allegiance was seen as so important to the stability of our nation. I am also concerned about the dicta in Justice Frankfurter's opinion that suggests that it is perfectly fine for the states to "indoctrinate" students contrary to the wishes and beliefs of their parents. I think that I would concur with Justice Stone's dissenting opinion in this case.

# An Introduction to Law and Politics in the Supreme Court: Of Liberty, Constitutionalism, and Democracy

*I* n 1776 Betsy Ross stitched together the American flag, constituting our most widely recognized national symbol out of scraps of cloth. Over the years, the states and Congress have passed a myriad of laws prescribing precise directions for respectful treatment of the 'stars and bars.' In 1892, a publication called the *Youth's Companion* first printed what we now know as the Pledge of Allegiance: "I pledge allegiance to the flag of the United States of America and to the republic for which it stands, one nation, indivisible, with liberty and justice for all." In 1942, Congress adopted the Pledge of Allegiance as Section 7 of the U.S. Flag Code, adding "under God" in 1954.

There may be no better example of the intricate interweaving of law and politics, and the competing claims of liberty, constitutionalism, and democracy, than the two pairs of Supreme Court cases that make up this chapter. In the first pair, *Minersville School District* v. *Gobitis* (1940) and *West Virginia Board of Education* v. *Barnette* (1943) the Court first upheld, and then struck down, state and local requirements that school children salute the flag and recite the Pledge of Allegiance. In the second pair, *Texas* v. *Johnson* (1989) and *U.S.* v. *Eichman* (1990), the Supreme Court struck down first a state law prohibiting flag burning and then a similar federal statute passed in response to the *Texas* v. *Johnson* decision. In all four of these cases, the Justices relied on the First Amendment to support their arguments. Yet, in each of these pairs of cases, it was politics and political controversy that brought the issues back to the Court a second time. In the flag salute cases, the Court abruptly changed its mind and overruled *Gobitis* just three years after it was handed down. In the flag burning cases, the Court held firm, reconfirming its *Texas* v. *Johnson* argument a year later in *Eichman*. And, in all four of these cases, the Justices' arguments recast the dispute between an individual and government as a conflict between our commitments to liberty, constitutionalism, and democracy. In so doing, the Justices reveal different views on the proper role of the Supreme Court in the American political system.

The Justices' competing arguments in these cases help us think about conflicts in our polity in a principled way, relying on reasoning rather than passions. And, the Court's arguments in these cases illustrate how the various Justices construct arguments and how they use both the text of the Constitution and the precedents to argue for divergent conclusions. While these are all useful achievements, they still beg the question of *why* the Court decides as it does.

This volume of readings explores the judicial decision-making process and the factors that influence it. These cases begin to illustrate the role of many of those factors: the law, the Court's environment, and the Court's personnel. Is the Court's reversal in *Barnette* more explicable once one knows more about the historical and political context? For instance, more than 170 leading newspapers and almost all law reviews and journals condemned the *Gobitis* decision. The *Gobitis* decision seemed to unleash a great deal of violence against Jehovah's Witnesses, defended in the name of patriotism. Some Jehovah's Witnesses who refused to salute the flag were adjudged juvenile delinquents and sent to reformatories. A year after the *Gobitis* decision, the U.S. entered World War II and took up arms against Nazi Germany, a regime that glorified blind patriotism, vilified difference, and used an upheld arm flag salute quite similar to the one commonly used in American school houses of the day.[1] On the Court, two members of the *Gobitis* majority had resigned and been replaced by two new Justices by 1943; and Justice Stone, the lone dissenter in *Gobitis*, was promoted to Chief Justice in 1941. In the *Gobitis* decision, the 8 Justice majority rested its argument on the First Amendment free exercise clause; in the *Barnette* decision, the six Justice majority rested its argument on the First Amendment freedom of speech clause. Does any of this matter in explaining Supreme Court decision-making? What information would you want to know to construct an explanation of the Supreme Court's failure to give in to the opponents of its *Texas* v. *Johnson* decision, instead reaffirming it the following year in *U.S.* v. *Eichman?*

## *Notes*

1. Some information taken from Irving Dillard, "The Flag Salute Cases," in *Quarrels that Have Shaped the Constitution*, ed. by John A. Garraty (New York: *Harper & Row, Publishers*, 1987).

# Minersville School District, Board of Education of Minersville School District, et al. v. Gobitis et al.

## 310 U.S. 586

## Certiorari to the Circuit Court of Appeals for the Third Circuit.

### No. 690. Argued April 25, 1940.—Decided June 3, 1940.

. . . *Mr. Joseph W. Henderson*, with whom *Messrs. John B. McGurl, Thomas F. Mount,* and *George M. Brodhead, Jr.* were on the brief, for petitioners.

. . . *Messrs. Joseph F. Rutherford* and *George K. Gardner* argued the cause, and with the former *Mr. Hayden Covington,* was on the brief, for respondents.

. . . MR. JUSTICE FRANKFURTER delivered the opinion of the Court.

A grave responsibility confronts this Court whenever in course of litigation it must reconcile the conflicting claims of liberty and authority. But when the liberty invoked is liberty of conscience, and the authority is authority to safeguard the nation's fellowship, judicial conscience is put to its severest test. Of such a nature is the present controversy.

Lillian Gobitis, aged twelve, and her brother William, aged ten, were expelled from the public schools of Minersville, Pennsylvania, for refusing to salute the national flag as part of a daily school exercise. The local Board of Education required both teachers and pupils to participate in this ceremony. The ceremony is a familiar one. The right hand is placed on the breast and the following pledge recited in unison: "I pledge allegiance to my flag, and to the Republic for which it stands; one nation indivisible, with liberty and justice for all." While the words are spoken, teachers and pupils extend their right hands in salute to the flag. The Gobitis family are affiliated with "Jehovah's

Witnesses" for whom the Bible as the Word of God is the supreme authority. The children had been brought up conscientiously to believe that such a gesture of respect for the flag was forbidden by command of Scripture.

The Gobitis children were of an age for which Pennsylvania makes school attendance compulsory. Thus they were denied a free education, and their parents had to put them into private schools. To be relieved of the financial burden thereby entailed, their father, on behalf of the children and in his own behalf, brought this suit. He sought to enjoin the authorities from continuing to exact participation in the flag-salute ceremony as a condition of his children's attendance at the Minersville school. After trial of the issues, Judge Maris gave relief in the District Court, 24 F. Supp. 271, on the basis of a thoughtful opinion at a preliminary stage of the litigation, 21 F. Supp. 581; his decree was affirmed by the Circuit Court of Appeals, 108 F. 2d 683. Since this decision ran counter to several *per curiam* dispositions of this Court, we granted *certiorari* to give the matter full consideration. 309 U.S. 645. By their able submissions, the Committee on the Bill of Rights of the American Bar Association and the American Civil Liberties Union, as friends of the Court, have helped us to our conclusion.

We must decide whether the requirement of participation in such a ceremony, exacted from a child who refuses upon sincere, religious grounds, infringes without due process of law the liberty guaranteed by the Fourteenth Amendment.

Centuries of strife over the erection of particular dogmas as exclusive or all-comprehending faiths led to the inclusion of a guarantee for religious freedom in the Bill of Rights. The First Amendment, and the Fourteenth through its absorption of the First, sought to guard against repetition of those bitter religious struggles by prohibiting the establishment of a state religion and by securing to every sect the free exercise of its faith. So pervasive is the acceptance of this precious right that its scope is brought into question, as here, only when the conscience of individuals collides with the felt necessities of society.

Certainly the affirmative pursuit of one's convictions about the ultimate mystery of the universe and man's relation to it is placed beyond the reach of law. Government may not interfere with organized or individual expression of belief or disbelief. Propagation of belief—or even of disbelief—in the supernatural is protected, whether in church or chapel, mosque or synagogue, tabernacle or meeting-house. Likewise the Constitution assures generous immunity to the individual from imposition of penalties for offending, in the course of his own religious activities, the religious views of others, be they a minority or those who are dominant in government. *Cantwell* v. *Connecticut, ante,* p. 296

But the manifold character of man's relations may bring his conception of religious duty into conflict with the secular interests of his fellow-men. When does the constitutional guarantee compel exemption from doing what society thinks necessary for the promotion of some great common end, or from a penalty for conduct which appears dangerous to the general good? To state the problem is to recall the truth that no single principle can answer all of life's complexities. The right to freedom of religious belief, however dissident and however obnoxious to the cherished beliefs of others— even of a majority—is itself the denial of an absolute. But to affirm that the freedom to follow conscience has itself no limits in the life of a society would deny that very plurality of principles which, as a matter of history, underlies protection of toleration. Our present task, then, as so often the case with courts, is to reconcile two rights in order to prevent either from destroying the other. But, because in safeguarding conscience we are dealing with interests so subtle and so dear, every possible leeway should be given to the claims of religious faith.

In the judicial enforcement of religious freedom we are concerned with a historic concept. The religious liberty which the Constitution protects has never excluded legislation of general scope not directed against doctrinal loyalties of particular sects. Judicial nullification of legislation cannot be justified by attributing to the framers of the Bill of Rights views for which there is no historic warrant. Conscientious scruples have not, in the course of the long struggle for religious toleration, relieved the individual from obedience to a general law not aimed at the promotion or restriction of religious beliefs. The mere possession of religious convictions which contradict the relevant concerns of a political society does not relieve the citizen from the discharge of political responsibilities. The necessity for this adjustment has again and again been recognized. In a number of situations the exertion of political authority has been sustained, while basic considerations of religious freedom have been left inviolate. *Reynolds* v. *United States*, 98 U.S. 145; *Davis* v. *Beason*, 133 U.S. 333; *Selective Draft Law Cases*, 245 U.S. 366; *Hamilton* v. *Regents*, 293 U.S. 245. In all these cases the general laws in question, upheld in their application to those who refused obedience from religions conviction, were manifestations of specific powers of government deemed by the legislature essential to secure and maintain that orderly, tranquil, and free society without which religious toleration itself is unattainable. . . . the question remains whether school children, like the Gobitis children, must be excused from conduct required of all the other children in the promotion of national cohesion. We are dealing with an interest inferior to none in the hierarchy of legal values. National unity is the basis of national security. To deny the legislature the right to select appropriate means for its attainment presents a totally different order of problem from that of the propriety of subordinating the possible ugliness of littered streets to the free expression of opinion through distribution of handbills. Compare *Schneider* v. *State*, 308 U.S. 147.

Situations like the present are phases of the profoundest problem confronting a democracy—the problem which Lincoln cast in memorable dilemma: "Must a government of necessity be too *strong* for the liberties of its people, or too weak to maintain its own existence?" No mere textual reading or logical talisman can solve the dilemma. And when the issue demands judicial determination, it is not the personal notion of judges of what wise adjustment requires which must prevail. . . . The ultimate foundation of a free society is the binding tie of cohesive sentiment. Such a sentiment is fostered by all those agencies of the mind and spirit which may serve to gather up the traditions of a people, transmit them from generation to generation, and thereby create that continuity of a treasured common life which constitutes a civilization. "We live by symbols." The flag is the symbol of our national unity, transcending all internal differences, however large, within the framework of the Constitution. This Court has had occasion to say that ". . . the flag is the symbol of the Nation's power, the emblem of freedom in its truest, best sense. . . . it signifies government resting on the consent of the governed; liberty regulated by law; the protection of the weak against the strong; security against the exercise of arbitrary power; and absolute safety for free institutions against foreign aggression." *Halter* v. *Nebraska*, 205 U.S. 34, 43. And see *United States* v. *Gettysburg Electric Ry. Co.*, 160 U.S. 668.

The case before us must be viewed as though the legislature of Pennsylvania had itself formally directed the flag-salute for the children of Minersville; had made no exemption for children whose parents were possessed of conscientious scruples like those of the Gobitis family; and had indicated its belief in the desirable ends to be secured by having its public school children share a common experience at those periods of development when their minds are supposedly receptive to its assimilation, by an exercise appropriate in time and place and setting, and one designed to evoke in them appreciation of the nation's hopes and dreams, its sufferings and sacrifices. The precise issue, then, for us to decide is whether the legislatures of the various states and the authorities in a thousand counties and school districts of this country are barred from determining the appropriateness of various means to evoke that in a unifying sentiment without which there can ultimately be no liberties, civil or religious. . . .

The wisdom of training children in patriotic impulses by those compulsions which necessarily pervade so much of the educational process is not for our independent judgment. Even were we convinced of the folly of such a measure, such belief would be no proof of its unconstitutionality. For ourselves, we might be tempted to say that the deepest patriotism is best engendered by giving unfettered scope to the most crotchety beliefs. Perhaps it is best, even from the standpoint of those interests which ordinances like the one under review seek to promote, to give to the least popular sect leave from conformities like those here in issue. But the courtroom is not the arena for debating issues of educational policy. It is not our province to choose among competing considerations in the subtle process of securing effective loyalty to the traditional ideals of democracy, while respecting at the same time individual idiosyncrasies among a people so diversified in racial origins and religious allegiances. So to hold would in effect make us the school board for the country. That authority has not been given to this Court, nor should we assume it.

We are dealing here with the formative period in the development of citizenship. Great diversity of psychological and ethical opinion exists among us concerning the best way to train children for their place in society. Because of these differences and because of reluctance to permit a single, iron-cast system of education to be imposed upon a nation compounded of so many strains, we have held that, even though public education is one of our most cherished democratic institutions, the Bill of Rights bars a state from compelling all children to attend the public schools. *Pierce* v. *Society of Sisters*, 268 U.S. 510. But, it is a very different thing for this Court to exercise censorship over the conviction of legislatures that a particular program or exercise will best promote in the minds of children who attend the common schools an attachment to the institutions of their country.

What the school authorities are really asserting is the right to awaken in the child's mind considerations as to the significance of the flag contrary to those implanted by the parent. In such an attempt the state is normally at a disadvantage in competing with the parent's authority, so long—and this is the vital aspect of religious toleration— as parents are unmolested in their right to counteract by their own persuasiveness the wisdom and rightness of those loyalties which the state's educational system is seeking to promote. Except where the transgression of constitutional liberty is too plain for argument, personal freedom is best maintained—so long as the remedial channels of the democratic process remain open and unobstructed—when it is ingrained in a people's habits and not enforced against popular policy by the coercion of adjudicated law. That the flag-salute is an allowable portion of a school program for those who do not invoke conscientious scruples is surely not debatable. But for us to insist that, though the ceremony may be required, exceptional immunity must be given to dissidents, is to maintain that there is no basis for a legislative judgment that such an exemption might introduce elements of difficulty into the school discipline, might cast doubts in the minds of the other children which would themselves weaken the effect of the exercise.

The preciousness of the family relation, the authority and independence which give dignity to parenthood, indeed the enjoyment of all freedom, presuppose the kind of ordered society which is summarized by our flag. A society which is dedicated to the preservation of these ultimate values of civilization may in self-protection utilize the educational process for inculcating those almost unconscious feelings which bind men together in a comprehending loyalty, whatever may be their lesser differences and difficulties. . . .

Judicial review, itself a limitation on popular government, is a fundamental part of our constitutional scheme. But to the legislature no less than to courts is committed the guardianship of deeply-cherished liberties. See *Missouri, K. & T. Ry. Co.* v. *May*, 194 U.S. 267, 270. Where all the effective means of inducing political changes are left free from interference, education in the abandonment of foolish legislation is itself a training in liberty. To fight out the wise use of legislative authority in the forum of public opinion and before legislative assemblies rather than to transfer such a contest to the judicial arena, serves to vindicate the self-confidence of a free people.

*Reversed.*

MR. JUSTICE MCREYNOLDS concurs in the result.

MR. JUSTICE STONE, dissenting:

I think the judgment below should be affirmed.

Two youths, now fifteen and sixteen years of age, are by the judgment of this Court held liable to expulsion from the public schools and to denial of all publicly supported educational privileges because of their refusal to yield to the compulsion of a law which commands their participation in a school ceremony contrary to their religious convictions. They and their father are citizens and have not exhibited by any action or statement of opinion, any disloyalty to the Government of the United States. They are ready and willing to obey all its laws which do not conflict with what they sincerely believe to be the higher commandments of God. It is not doubted that these convictions are religious, that they are genuine, or that the refusal to yield to the compulsion of the law is in good faith and with all sincerity. It would be a denial of their faith as well as the teachings of most religions to say that children of their age could not have religious convictions.

The law which is thus sustained is unique in the history of Anglo-American legislation. It does more than suppress freedom of speech and more than prohibit the free exercise of religion, which concededly are forbidden by the First Amendment and are violations of the liberty guaranteed by the Fourteenth. For by this law the state seeks to coerce these children to express a sentiment which, as they interpret it, they do not entertain, and which violates their deepest religious convictions.

Concededly the constitutional guaranties of personal liberty are not always absolutes. Government has a right to survive and powers conferred upon it are not necessarily set at naught by the express prohibitions of the Bill of Rights. It may make war and raise armies. To that end it may compel citizens to give military service, *Selective Draft Law Cases*, 245 U.S. 366, and subject them to military training despite their religious objections. *Hamilton* v. *Regents*, 293 U.S. 245. It may suppress religious practices dangerous to morals, and presumably those also which are inimical to public safety, health and good order. *Davis* v. *Beason*, 133 U.S. 333. But it is a long step, and one which I am unable to take, to the position that government may, as a supposed educational measure and as a means of disciplining the young, compel public affirmations which violate their religious conscience.

The very fact that we have constitutional guaranties of civil liberties and the specificity of their command where freedom of speech and of religion are concerned require some accommodation of the powers which government normally exercises, when no question of civil liberty is involved, to the constitutional demand that those liberties be protected against the action of government itself. . . .

In these cases it was pointed out that where there are competing demands of the interests of government and of liberty under the Constitution, and where the performance of governmental functions is brought into conflict with specific constitutional restrictions, there must, when that is possible, be reasonable accommodation between them so as to preserve the essentials of both and that it is the function of courts to determine whether such accommodation is reasonably possible. . . . So here, even if we believe that such compulsions will contribute to national unity, there are other ways to teach loyalty and patriotism which are the sources of national unity, than by compelling the pupil to affirm that which he does not believe and by commanding a form of affirmance which violates his religious convictions. Without recourse to such compulsion the state is free to compel attendance at school and require teaching by instruction and study of all in our history and in the structure and organization of our government, including the guaranties of civil liberty which tend to inspire patriotism and love of country. . . .

History teaches us that there have been but few infringements of personal liberty by the state which have not been justified, as they are here, in the name of righteousness and the public good, and few which have not been directed, as they are now, at politically helpless minorities. The framers were not unaware that under the system which they created most governmental curtailments of personal liberty would have the support of a legislative judgment that the public interest would be better served by its curtailment than by its constitutional protection. . . . And while such expressions of loyalty, when voluntarily given, may promote national unity, it is quite another matter to say that their compulsory expression by children in violation of their own and their parents' religious convictions can be regarded as playing so important a part in our national unity as to leave school boards free to exact it despite the constitutional guarantee of freedom of religion. . . . I am not persuaded that we should refrain from passing upon the legislative judgment "as long as the remedial channels of the democratic process remain open and unobstructed." This seems to me no less than the surrender of the constitutional protection of the liberty of small minorities to the popular will. . . . I am not prepared to say that the right of this small and helpless minority, including children having a strong religious conviction, whether they understand its nature or not, to refrain from an expression obnoxious to their religion, is to be overborne by the interest of the state in maintaining discipline in the schools.

---

**Minersville v. Gobitis**, 310 U.S. 586 (1940) 8–1
*editor's note.*
*Opinion authors are in bold; () indicates the party of appointing president. If the party of the justice differs from that of appointing president, then the party of the justice is listed second after the slash.*

| MAJORITY | CONCURRING | DISSENTING |
|---|---|---|
| **Frankfurter** (d/i) | McReynolds (d) | **Stone** (r) |
| Hughes (r) | | |
| Roberts (r) | | |
| Black (d) | | |
| Reed (d) | | |
| Douglass (d) | | |
| Murphy (d) | | |

# West Virginia State Board of Education et al. v. Barnette et al.

## 319 U.S. 624

## Appeal from the District Court of the United States for the Southern District of West Virginia.

### No. 591. Argued March 11, 1943—Decided June 14, 1943.

*Mr. W. Holt Wooddell,* Assistant Attorney General of West Virginia, with whom *Mr. Ira J. Partlow* was on the brief, for appellants.

*Mr. Hayden C. Covington* for appellees.

Briefs of *amici curiae* were filed on behalf of the Committee on the Bill of Rights, of the American Bar Association, consisting of *Messrs. Douglas Arant, Julius Birge, William D. Campbell, Zechariah Chafee, Jr., L. Stanley Ford, Abe Fortas, George I. Haight, H. Austin Hauxhurst, Monte M. Lemann, Alvin Richards, Earl F. Morris, Burton W. Musser,* and *Basil O'Connor;* and by *Messrs. Osmond K. Fraenkel, Arthur Garfield Hays,* and *Howard B. Lee,* on behalf of the American Civil Liberties Union, urging affirmance; and by *Mr. Ralph B. Gregg,* on behalf of the American Legion, urging reversal.

MR. JUSTICE JACKSON delivered the opinion of the Court.

Following the decision by this Court on June 3, 1940, in *Minersville School District* v. *Gobitis,* 310 U.S. 586, the West Virginia legislature amended its statutes to require all schools therein to conduct courses of instruction in history, civics, and in the Constitutions of the United States and of the State "for the purpose of teaching, fostering and perpetuating the ideals, principles and spirit of Americanism, and increasing the knowledge of the organization and machinery of the government." Appellant Board of Education was directed, with advice of the State Superintendent of Schools to "prescribe the courses of study covering these subjects" for public schools. The Act made it the duty of private, parochial and denominational schools to prescribe courses of study "similar to those required for the public schools."

The Board of Education on January 9, 1942, adopted a resolution containing recitals taken largely from the Court's *Gobitis* opinion and ordering that the salute to the flag become "a regular part of the program of activities in the public schools," that all teachers and pupils "shall be required to participate in the salute honoring the Nation represented by the Flag; provided, however, that refusal to salute the Flag be regarded as an act of insubordination, and shall be dealt with accordingly."

The resolution originally required the "commonly accepted salute to the flag" which it defined. Objections to the salute as "being too much like Hitler's" were raised by the Parent and Teachers Association, the Boy and Girl Scouts, the Red Cross, and the Federation of Women's Clubs. Some modification appears to have been made in deference to these objections, but no concession was made to Jehovah's Witnesses. What is now required is the "stiff-arm" salute, the saluter to keep the right hand raised with palm turned up while the following is repeated: "I pledge allegiance to the Flag of the United States of America and to the Republic for which it stands; one Nation, indivisible, with liberty and justice for all."

Failure to conform is "insubordination" dealt with by expulsion. Readmission is denied by statute until compliance. Meanwhile the expelled child is "unlawfully absent" and may be proceeded against as a delinquent. His parents or guardians are liable to prosecution, and if convicted are subject to fine not exceeding $50 and jail term not exceeding thirty days.

Appellees, citizens of the United States and of West Virginia, brought suit in the United States District Court for themselves and others similarly situated asking its injunction to restrain enforcement of these laws and regulations against Jehovah's Witnesses. The Witnesses are an unincorporated body teaching that the obligation imposed by law of God is superior to that of laws enacted by temporal government. Their religious beliefs include a literal version of Exodus, Chapter 20, verses 4 and 5, which says: "Thou shalt not make unto thee any graven image, or any likeness of anything that is in heaven above, or that is in the earth beneath, or that is in the water under the earth; thou shalt not bow down thyself to them nor serve them." They consider that the flag, is an "image" within this command. For this reason they refuse to salute it.

Children of this faith have been expelled from school and are threatened with exclusion for no other cause. Officials threaten to send them to reformatories maintained for criminally inclined juveniles. Parents of such children have been prosecuted and are threatened with prosecutions for causing delinquency. . . .

This case calls upon us to reconsider a precedent decision, as the Court throughout its history often has been required to do. Before turning to the *Gobitis* case, however, it is desirable to notice certain characteristics by which this controversy is distinguished.

The freedom asserted by these appellees does not bring them into collision with rights asserted by any other individual. It is such conflicts which most frequently require intervention of the State to determine where the rights of one end and those of another begin. But the refusal of these persons to participate in the ceremony does not interfere with or deny rights of others to do so. Nor is there any question in this case that their behavior is peaceable and orderly. The sole conflict is between authority and rights of the individual. The State asserts power to condition access to public education on making a prescribed sign and profession and at the same time to coerce attendance by punishing both parent and child. The latter stand on a right of self-determination in matters that touch individual opinion and personal attitude.

As the present CHIEF JUSTICE said in dissent in the *Gobitis* case, the State may "require teaching by instruction and study of all in our history and in the structure and organization of our government, including the guaranties of civil liberty, which tend to inspire patriotism and love of country." 310 U.S. at 604. Here, however, we are dealing with a compulsion of students to declare a belief. They are not merely made acquainted with the flag salute so that they may be informed as to what it is or even what it means. The issue here is whether this slow and easily neglected route to aroused loyalties constitutionally may be short-cut by substituting a compulsory salute and slogan. . . .

There is no doubt that, in connection with the pledges, the flag salute is a form of utterance. Symbolism is a primitive but effective way of communicating ideas. The use of an emblem or flag to symbolize some system, idea, institution, or personality, is a short cut from mind to mind. Causes and nations, political parties, lodges and ecclesiastical groups seek to knit the loyalty of their followings to a flag or banner, a color or design. . . .

It is also to be noted that the compulsory flag salute and pledge requires affirmation of a belief and an attitude of mind. It is not clear whether the regulation contemplates that pupils forego any contrary convictions of their own and become unwilling converts to the prescribed ceremony or whether it will be acceptable if they simulate assent by words without belief and by a gesture barren of meaning. It is now a commonplace that censorship or suppression of expression of opinion is tolerated by our Constitution only when the expression presents a clear and present danger of action of a kind the State is empowered to prevent and punish. It would seem that involuntary affirmation could be commanded only on even more immediate and urgent grounds than silence. But here the power of compulsion is invoked without any allegation that remaining passive during a flag salute ritual creates a clear and present danger that would justify an effort even to muffle expression. To sustain the compulsory flag salute we are required to say that a Bill of Rights which guards the individuals' right to speak his own mind, left it open to public authorities to compel him to utter what is not in his mind. . . .

Hence validity of the asserted power to force an American citizen publicly to profess any statement of belief or to engage in any ceremony of assent to one, presents questions of power that must be considered independently of any idea we may have as to the utility of the ceremony in question.

Nor does the issue as we see it turn on one's possession of particular religious views or the sincerity with which they are held. While religion supplies appellees' motive for enduring the discomforts of making the issue in this case, many citizens who do not share these religious views hold such a compulsory rite to infringe constitutional liberty of the individual. It is not necessary to inquire whether non-conformist beliefs will exempt from the duty to salute unless we first find power to make the salute a legal duty.

The *Gobitis* decision, however, assumed, as did the argument in that case and in this, that power exists in the State to impose the flag salute discipline upon school children in general. The Court only examined and rejected a claim based on religions beliefs of immunity from an unquestioned general rule. The question which underlies the flag salute controversy is whether such a ceremony so touching matters of opinion and political attitude may be imposed upon the individual by official authority under powers committed to any political organization under our Constitution. We examine rather than assume existence of this power and, against this broader definition of issues in this case, reexamine specific grounds assigned for the *Gobitis* decision.

1.  It was said that the flag-salute controversy confronted the Court with "the problem which Lincoln cast in memorable dilemma: 'Must a government of necessity be too strong for the liberties of its people, or too weak to maintain its own existence?' " and that the answer must be in favor of strength. *Minersville School District* v. *Gobitis, supra,* at 596.

We think these issues may be examined free of pressure or restraint growing out of such considerations.

It may be doubted whether Mr. Lincoln would have thought that the strength of government to maintain itself would be impressively vindicated by our confirming power of the State to expel a handful of children from school. Such oversimplification, so handy in political debate, often lacks the precision necessary to postulates of judicial reasoning. If validly applied to this problem, the utterance cited would resolve every issue of power in favor of those in authority and would require us to override every liberty thought to weaken or delay execution of their policies.

Government of limited power need not be anemic government. Assurance that rights are secure tends to diminish fear and jealousy of strong government, and by making us feel safe to live under it makes for its better support. Without promise of a limiting Bill of Rights it is doubtful if our Constitution could have mustered enough strength to enable its ratification. To enforce those rights today is not to choose weak government over strong government. It is only to adhere as a means of strength to individual freedom of mind in preference to officially disciplined uniformity for which history indicates a disappointing and disastrous end. . . .

2. It was also considered in the *Gobitis* case that functions of educational officers in States, counties and school districts were such that to interfere with their authority "would in effect make us the school board for the country." *Id.* at 598.

The Fourteenth Amendment, as now applied to the States, protects the citizen against the State itself and all of its creatures—Boards of Education not excepted. . . . There are village tyrants as well as village Hampdens, but none who acts under color of law is beyond reach of the Constitution.

3. The *Gobitis* opinion reasoned that this is a field "where courts possess no marked and certainly no controlling competence," that it is committed to the legislatures as well as the courts to guard cherished liberties and that it is constitutionally appropriate to "fight out the wise use of legislative authority in the forum of public opinion and before legislative assemblies rather than to transfer such a contest to the judicial arena," since all the "effective means of inducing political changes are left free." *Id.* at 597–598, 600.

The very purpose of a Bill of Rights was to withdraw certain subjects from the vicissitudes of political controversy, to place them beyond the reach of majorities and officials and to establish them as legal principles to be applied by the courts. One's right to life, liberty, and property, to free speech, a free press, freedom of worship and assembly, and other fundamental rights may not be submitted to vote; they depend on the outcome of no elections. . . .

But we act in these matters not by authority of our competence but by force of our commissions. We cannot, because of modest estimates of our competence in such specialties as public education, withhold the judgment that history authenticates as the function of this Court when liberty is infringed.

4. Lastly, and this is the very heart of the *Gobitis* opinion, it reasons that "National unity is the basis of national security," that the authorities have "the right to select appropriate means for its attainment," and hence reaches the conclusion that such compulsory measures toward "national unity" are constitutional. *Id.* at 595. Upon the verity of this assumption depends our answer in this case.

National unity as an end which officials may foster by persuasion and example is not in question. The problem is whether under our Constitution compulsion as here employed is a permissible means for its achievement.

Struggles to coerce uniformity of sentiment in support of some end thought essential to their time and country have been waged by many good as well as by evil men. Nationalism is a relatively recent phenomenon but at other times and places the ends have been racial or territorial security, support of a dynasty or regime, and particular plans for saving souls. As first and moderate methods to attain unity have failed, those bent on its accomplishment must resort to an ever-increasing severity. As governmental pressure toward unity becomes greater, so strife becomes more bitter as to whose unity it shall be. Probably no deeper division of our people could proceed from any provocation than from finding it necessary to choose what doctrine and whose program public educational officials shall compel youth to unite in embracing. Ultimate futility of such attempts to compel coherence is the lesson of every such effort from the Roman drive to stamp out Christianity as a disturber of its pagan unity, the Inquisition, as a means to religious and dynastic unity, the Siberian exiles as a means to Russian unity, down to the fast failing efforts of our present totalitarian enemies. Those who begin coercive elimination of dissent soon find themselves exterminating dissenters. Compulsory unification of opinion achieves only the unanimity of the graveyard.

It seems trite but necessary to say that the First Amendment to our Constitution was designed to avoid these ends by avoiding these beginnings. There is no mysticism in the American concept of the State or of the nature or origin of its authority. We set up government by consent of the governed, and the Bill of Rights denies those in power any legal opportunity to coerce that consent. Authority here is to be controlled by public opinion, not public opinion by authority.

The case is made difficult not because the principles of its decision are obscure but because the flag involved is our own. Nevertheless, we apply the limitations of the Constitution with no fear that freedom to be intellectually and spiritually diverse or even contrary will disintegrate the social organization. To believe that patriotism will not flourish if patriotic ceremonies are voluntary and spontaneous instead of a compulsory routine is to make an unflattering estimate of the appeal of our institutions to free minds. We can have intellectual individualism and the rich cultural diversities that we owe to exceptional minds only at the price of occasional eccentricity and abnormal attitudes. When they are so harmless to others or to the State as those we deal with here, the price is not too great. But freedom to differ is not limited to things that do not matter much. That would be a mere shadow of freedom. The test of its substance is the right to differ as to things that touch the heart of the existing order.

If there is any fixed star in our constitutional constellation, it is that no official, high or petty, can prescribe what shall be orthodox in politics, nationalism, religion, or other matters of opinion or force citizens to confess by word or act their faith therein. If there are any circumstances which permit an exception, they do not now occur to us.

We think the action of the local authorities in compelling the flag salute and pledge transcends constitutional limitations on their power and invades the sphere of intellect and spirit which it is the purpose of the First Amendment to our Constitution to reserve from all official control.

The decision of this Court in *Minersville School District* v. *Gobitis* and the holdings of those few *per curiam* decisions which preceded and foreshadowed it are overruled, and the judgment enjoining enforcement of the West Virginia Regulation is

*Affirmed.*

MR. JUSTICE ROBERTS and MR. JUSTICE REED adhere to the views expressed by the Court in *Minersville School District* v. *Gobitis*, 310 U.S. 586, and are of the opinion that the judgment below should be reversed.

MR. JUSTICE BLACK and MR. JUSTICE DOUGLAS, concurring:

We are substantially in agreement with the opinion just read, but since we originally joined with the Court in the *Gobitis* case, it is appropriate that we make a brief statement of reasons for our change of view.

Reluctance to make the Federal Constitution a rigid bar against state regulation of conduct thought inimical to the public welfare was the controlling influence which moved us to consent to the *Gobitis* decision. Long reflection convinced us that although the principle is sound, its application in the particular case was wrong. *Jones* v. *Opelika*, 316 U.S. 584, 623. We believe that the statute before us fails to accord full scope to the freedom of religion secured to the appellees by the First and Fourteenth Amendments. . . .

No well-ordered society can leave to the individuals an absolute right to make final decisions, unassailable by the State, as to everything they will or will not do. The First Amendment does not go so far. Religious faiths, honestly held, do not free individuals from responsibility to conduct themselves obediently to laws which are either imperatively necessary to protect society as a whole from grave and pressingly imminent dangers for which, without any general prohibition, merely regulate time, place or manner of religious activity. Decision as to the constitutionality of particular laws which strike at the substance of religious tenets and practices must be made by this

Court. The duty is a solemn one, and in meeting it we cannot say that a failure, because of religious scruples, to assume a particular physical position and to repeat the words of a patriotic formula creates a grave danger to the nation. Such a statutory exaction is a form of test oath, and the test oath has always been abhorrent in the United States.

Words uttered under coercion are proof of loyalty to nothing but self-interest. Love of country must spring from willing hearts and free minds, inspired by a fair administration of wise laws enacted by the people's elected representatives within the bounds of express constitutional prohibitions. These laws must, to be consistent with the First Amendment, permit the widest toleration of conflicting viewpoints consistent with a society of free men.

Neither our domestic tranquillity in peace nor our martial effort in war depend on compelling little children to participate in a ceremony which ends in nothing for them but a fear of spiritual condemnation. If, as we think, their fears are groundless, time and reason are the proper antidotes for their errors. The ceremonial, when enforced against conscientious objectors, more likely to defeat than to serve its high purpose, is a handy implement for disguised religious persecution. As such, it is inconsistent with our Constitution's plan and purpose.

MR. JUSTICE MURPHY, concurring:

I agree with the opinion of the Court and join in it.

. . . A reluctance to interfere with considered state action, the fact that the end sought is a desirable one, the emotion aroused by the flag as a symbol for which we have fought and are now fighting again,—all of these are understandable. But there is before us the right of freedom to believe, freedom to worship one's Maker according to the dictates of one's conscience, a right which the Constitution specifically shelters. Reflection has convinced me that as a judge I have no loftier duty or responsibility than to uphold that spiritual freedom to its farthest reaches.

. . . Without wishing to disparage the purposes and intentions of those who hope to inculcate sentiments of loyalty and patriotism by requiring a declaration of allegiance as a feature of public education, or unduly belittle the benefits that may accrue therefrom, I am impelled to conclude that such a requirement is not essential to the maintenance of effective government and orderly society. . . .

MR. JUSTICE FRANKFURTER, dissenting:

One who belongs to the most vilified and persecuted minority in history is not likely to be insensible to the freedom guaranteed by our Constitution. Were my purely personal attitude relevant I should wholeheartedly associate myself with the general libertarian views in the Court's opinion, representing as they do the thought and action of a lifetime. But as judges we are neither Jew nor Gentile, neither Catholic nor agnostic. We owe equal attachment to the Constitution and are equally bound by our judicial obligations whether we derive our citizenship from the earliest or the latest immigrants to these shores. As a member of this Court I am not justified in writing my private notions of policy into the Constitution, no matter how deeply I may cherish them or how mischievous I may deem their disregard. The duty of a judge who must decide which of two claims before the Court shall prevail, that of a State to enact and enforce laws within its general competence, or that of an individual to refuse obedience because of the demands of his conscience, is not that of the ordinary person. It can never be emphasized too much that one's own opinion about the wisdom or evil of a law should be excluded altogether when one is doing one's duty on the bench. The only opinion of our own even looking in that direction that is material is our opinion whether legislators could in reason have enacted such a law. In the light of all the circumstances, including the history of this question in this Court, it would require more daring than I possess to deny that reasonable legislators could have taken the action which is before us for review. Most unwillingly, therefore, I must differ from my brethren with regard to legislation like this. I cannot bring my mind to believe that the "liberty" secured by the Due Process Clause gives this Court authority to deny to the State of West Virginia the attainment of that which we all recognize as a legitimate legislative end, namely, the promotion of good citizenship, by employment of the means here chosen. . . .

The constitutional protection of religious freedom terminated disabilities, it did not create new privileges. It gave religious equality, not civil immunity. Its essence is freedom from conformity to religious dogma, not freedom from conformity to law because of religious dogma. Religious loyalties may be exercised without hindrance from the state, not the state may not exercise that which except by leave of religious loyalties is within the domain of temporal power. Otherwise each individual could set up his own censor against obedience to laws conscientiously deemed for the public good by those whose business it is to make laws.

The prohibition against any religious establishment by the government placed denominations on an equal footing—it assured freedom from support by the government to any mode of worship and the freedom of individuals to support any mode of worship. Any person may therefore believe or disbelieve what he pleases. He may practice what he will in his own house of worship or publicly within the limits of public order. But the lawmaking authority is not circumscribed by the variety of religious beliefs, otherwise the constitutional guaranty would be not a protection of the free exercise of religion but a denial of the exercise of legislation.

The essence of the religious freedom guaranteed by our Constitution is therefore this: no religion shall either receive the state's support or incur its hostility. Religion is outside the sphere of political government. This does not mean that all matters on which religious organizations or beliefs may pronounce are outside the sphere of government. . . .

Parents have the privilege of choosing which schools they wish their children to attend. And the question here is whether the state may make certain requirements that seem to it desirable or important for the proper education of those future citizens who go to schools maintained by the states, or whether the pupils in those schools may be relieved from those requirements if they run counter to the consciences of their parents.

When dealing with religious scruples we are dealing with an almost numberless variety of doctrines and beliefs entertained with equal sincerity by the particular groups for which they satisfy man's needs in his relation to the mysteries of the universe. There are in the United States more than 250 distinctive established religious denominations. In the State of Pennsylvania there are 120 of these, and in West Virginia as many as 65. But if religious scruples afford immunity from civic obedience to laws, they may be invoked by the religious beliefs of any individual even though he holds no membership in any sect or organized denomination. Certainly this Court cannot be called upon to determine what claims of conscience should be recognized and what should be rejected as satisfying the "religion" which the Constitution protects. That would indeed resurrect the very discriminatory treatment of religion which the Constitution sought forever to forbid.

I am fortified in my view of this case by the history of the flag salute controversy in this Court. Five times has the precise question now before us been adjudicated. Four times the Court unanimously found that the requirement of such a school exercise was not beyond the powers of the states. Indeed in the first three cases to come before the Court the constitutional claim now sustained was deemed so clearly unmeritorious that this Court dismissed the appeals for want of a substantial federal question. *Leoles* v. *Landers*, 302 U.S. 656; *Hering* v. *State Board of Education*, 303 U.S. 624; *Gabrielli* v. *Knickerbocker*, 306 U.S. 621. In the fourth case the judgment of the district court upholding the state law was summarily affirmed on the authority of the earlier cases. *Johnson* v. *Deerfield*, 306 U.S. 621. The fifth case, *Minersville District* v. *Gobitis*, 310 U.S. 586, was brought here because the decision of the Circuit Court of Appeals for the Third Circuit ran counter to our rulings. They were reaffirmed after full consideration, with one Justice dissenting.

What may be even more significant than this uniform recognition of state authority is the fact that every Justice—thirteen in all—who has hitherto participated in judging this matter has at one or more times found no constitutional infirmity in what is now condemned. Only the two Justices sitting for the first time on this matter have not heretofore found this legislation inoffensive to the "liberty" guaranteed by the Constitution. And among the justices who sustained this measure were outstanding judicial leaders in the zealous enforcement of constitutional safeguards of civil liberties—men like Chief Justice Hughes, Mr. Justice Brandeis, and Mr. Justice Cardozo, to mention only those no longer on the Court.

One's conception of the Constitution cannot be severed from one's conception of a judge's function in applying it. The Court has no reason for existence if it merely reflects the pressures of the day. Our system is built on the faith that men set apart for this special function, freed from the influences of immediacy and from the deflections of worldly ambition, will become able to take a view of longer range than the period of responsibility entrusted to Congress and legislatures. We are dealing with matters as to which legislators and voters have conflicting views. Are we as judges to impose our strong convictions on where wisdom lies? That which three years ago had seemed to five successive Courts to lie within permissible areas of legislation is now outlawed by the deciding shift of opinion of two Justices. What reason is there to believe that they or their successors may not have another view a few years hence? Is that which was deemed to be of so fundamental a nature as to be written into the Constitution to endure for all times to be the sport of shifting winds of doctrine? Of course, judicial opinions, even as to questions of constitutionality, are not immutable. As has been true in the past, the Court will from time to time reverse its position. But I believe that never before these Jehovah's Witnesses cases (except for minor deviations subsequently retraced) has this Court overruled decisions so as to restrict the powers of democratic government. Always heretofore, it has withdrawn narrow views of legislative authority so as to authorize what formerly it had denied.

---

**West Virginia State Board of Education v. Barnette**, 319 U.S. 624 (1943) 6–3
*editor's note.*
*Opinion authors are in bold; () indicates the party of appointing president. If the party of the justice differs from that of appointing president, then the party of the justice is listed second after the slash.*

| MAJORITY | CONCURRING | DISSENTING |
|---|---|---|
| **Jackson** (d) | **Black** (d) | **Roberts** (r) |
| Stone (r) | Douglas (d) | Reed (d) |
| Rutledge (d) | **Murphy** (d) | **Frankfurter** (d/i) |

# Texas v. Johnson

## 491 U.S. 397

## Certiorari to the Court of Criminal Appeals of Texas

### No. 88–155. Argued March 21, 1989—Decided July 21, 1989

*Kathi Alyce Drew* argued the cause for petitioner. With her on the briefs were *John Vance* and *Dolena T. Westergard.*

*William M. Kunstler* argued the cause for respondent. With him on the brief was *David D. Cole.*

JUSTICE BRENNAN delivered the opinion of the Court.

After publicly burning an American flag as a means of political protest, Gregory Lee Johnson was convicted of desecrating a flag in violation of Texas law. This case presents the question whether his conviction is consistent with the First Amendment. We hold that it is not.

## — I —

While the Republican National Convention was taking place in Dallas in 1984, respondent Johnson participated in a political demonstration dubbed the "Republican War Chest Tour." As explained in literature distributed by the demonstrators and in speeches made by them, the purpose of this event was to protest the policies of the Reagan administration and of certain Dallas-based corporations. The demonstrators marched through the Dallas streets, chanting political slogans and stopping at several corporate locations to stage "die-ins" intended to dramatize the consequences of nuclear war. On several occasions they spray-painted the walls of buildings and overturned potted plants, but Johnson himself took no part in such activities. He did, however, accept an American flag handed to him by a fellow protester who had taken it from a flag pole outside one of the targeted buildings.

The demonstration ended in front of Dallas City Hall, where Johnson unfurled the American flag, doused it with kerosene, and set it on fire. While the flag burned, the protesters chanted, "America, the red, white, and blue, we spit on you." After the demonstrators dispersed, a witness to the flag burning collected the flag's remains and buried them in his backyard. No one was physically injured or threatened with injury, though several witnesses testified that they had been seriously offended by the flag burning.

Of the approximately 100 demonstrators, Johnson alone was charged with a crime. The only criminal offense with which he was charged was the desecration of a venerated object in violation of Tex. Penal Code Ann. § 42.09(a)(3) (1989).[1] After a trial, he was convicted, sentenced to one year in prison, and fined $2,000. The Court of Appeals for the Fifth District of Texas at Dallas affirmed Johnson's conviction, 706 S. W. 2d 120 (1986), but the Texas Court of Criminal Appeals reversed, 755 S. W. 2d 92 (1988), holding that the State could not, consistent with the First Amendment, punish Johnson for burning the flag in these circumstances. . . .

Johnson was convicted of flag desecration for burning the flag rather than for uttering insulting words. This fact somewhat complicates our consideration of his conviction under the First Amendment. We must first determine whether Johnson's burning of the flag constituted expressive conduct, permitting him to invoke the First Amendment in challenging his conviction. . . .

The First Amendment literally forbids the abridgment only of "speech," but we have long recognized that its protection does not end at the spoken or written word. While we have rejected "the view that an apparently limitless variety of conduct can be labeled 'speech' whenever the person engaging in the conduct intends thereby to express an idea," *United States* v. *O'Brien, supra,* at 376, we have acknowledged that conduct may be "sufficiently imbued with elements of communication to fall within the scope of the First and Fourteenth Amendments," *Spence, supra,* at 409.

In deciding whether particular conduct possesses sufficient communicative elements to bring the First Amendment into play, we have asked whether "[a]n intent to convey a particularized message was present, and [whether] the likelihood was great that the message would be understood by those who viewed it." 418 U.S., at 410–411. Hence, we have recognized the expressive nature of students' wearing of black armbands to protest American military involvement in Vietnam, *Tinker* v. *Des Moines Independent Community School Dist.,* 393 U.S. 503, 505 (1969); of a sit-in by blacks in a "whites only" area to protest segregation, *Brown* v. *Louisiana,* 383 U.S. 131, 141–142 (1966); of the wearing of American military uniforms in a dramatic presentation criticizing American involvement in Vietnam, *Schacht* v. *United States,* 398 U.S. 58 (1970); and of picketing about a wide variety of causes, see, *e.g., Food Employees* v. *Logan Valley Plaza,* 391 U.S. 308, 313–314 (1968); *United States* v. *Grace,* 461 U.S. 171, 176 (1983).

Especially pertinent to this case are our decisions recognizing the communicative nature of conduct relating to flags. Attaching a peace sign to the flag, *Spence, supra,* at 409–410; refusing, to salute the flag, *Barnette,* 319 U.S., at 632; and displaying a red flag, *Stromberg* v. *California* 283 U.S. 359, 368–369 (1931), we have held, all may find shelter under the First Amendment. See also *Smith* v. *Goguen,* 415 U.S. 566, 588 (1974) (WHITE, J., concurring in judgment) (treating flag "contemptuously" by wearing pants with small flag sewn into their seat is expressive conduct). That we have had little difficulty identifying an expressive element in conduct relating to flags should not be surprising. The very purpose of a national flag is to serve as a symbol of our country; it is, one might say, "the visible manifestation of two hundred years of nationhood.". . .

Pregnant with expressive content, the flag as readily signifies this Nation as does the combination of letters found in "America."

We have not automatically concluded, however, that any action taken with respect to our flag is expressive. Instead, in characterizing such action for First Amendment purposes, we have considered the context in which it occurred. . . .

The State of Texas conceded for purposes of its oral argument in this case that Johnson's conduct was expressive conduct, Tr. of Oral Arg. 4, and this concession seems to us as prudent as was Washington's in *Spence.* Johnson burned an American flag as part—indeed, as the culmination of a political demonstration that coincided with the convening of the Republican Party and its renomination of Ronald Reagan for President. The expressive, overtly political nature of this conduct was both intentional and overwhelmingly apparent. At his trial, Johnson explained his reasons for burning the flag as follows: "The American Flag was burned as Ronald Reagan was being renominated as President. And a more powerful statement of symbolic speech, whether you agree with it or not, couldn't have been made at that time. It's quite a just position [juxtaposition]. We had new patriotism and no patriotism." 5 Record 656. In these circumstances, Johnson's burning of the flag was conduct "sufficiently imbued with elements of communication," *Spence,* 418 U.S., at 409, to implicate the First Amendment.

The government generally has a freer hand in restricting expressive conduct than it has in restricting the written or spoken word. See *O'Brien,* 391 U.S. at 376–377; *Clark* v. *Community for Creative Non-Violence,* 468 U.S. 288, 293 (1984); *Dallas* v. *Stanglin,* 490 U.S. 19, 25 (1989). It may not, however, proscribe particular conduct *because* it has expressive elements. "[W]hat might be termed the more generalized guarantee of freedom of expression makes the communicative nature of conduct an inadequate *basis* for singling out that conduct for proscription. A law *directed at* the communicative nature of conduct must, like a law directed at speech itself, be justified by the substantial showing of need that the First Amendment requires." *Community for Creative Non-Violence* v. *Watt,* 227 U.S. App D. C. 19, 55–56, 703 F. 2d 586, 622–623 (1983) (SCALIA, J., dissenting) (emphasis in original), rev'd *sub nom. Clark* v. *Community for Creative Non-Violence, supra.* It is, in short, not simply the verbal or nonverbal nature of the expression, but the governmental interest at stake, that helps to determine whether a restriction on that expression is valid.

Thus, although we have recognized that where " 'speech' and 'nonspeech' elements are combined in the same course of conduct, a sufficiently important governmental interest in regulating the non-speech element can justify incidental limitations on First Amendment freedoms.". . .

In order to decide whether *O'Brien's* test applies here, therefore, we must decide whether Texas has asserted an interest in support of Johnson's conviction that is unrelated to the suppression of expression. If we find that an interest asserted by the State is simply not implicated on the facts before us, we need not ask whether *O'Brien's* test applies. See *Spence, supra,* at 414, n. 8. The State offers two separate interests to justify this conviction: preventing breaches of the peace and preserving the flag as a symbol of nationhood and national unity. We hold that the first interest is not implicated on this record and that the second is related to the suppression of expression.

Texas claims that its interest in preventing breaches of the peace justifies Johnson's conviction for flag desecration. However, no disturbance of the peace actually occurred or threatened to occur because of Johnson's burning of the flag. Although the State stresses the disruptive behavior of the protestors during their march toward City Hall, Brief for Petitioner 34–36, it admits that "no actual breach of the peace occurred at the time of the flagburning or in response to the flagburning." *Id.,* at 34. The State's emphasis on the protestors' disorderly actions prior to arriving at City Hall is not only somewhat surprising given that no charges were brought on the basis of this conduct, but it also fails to show that a disturbance of the peace was a likely reaction to *Johnson's* conduct. The only evidence offered by the State at trial to show the reaction to Johnson's actions was the testimony of several persons who had been seriously offended by the flag burning. *Id.,* at 6–7.

The State's position, therefore, amounts to a claim that an audience that takes serious offense at particular expression is necessarily likely to disturb the peace and that the expression may be prohibited on this basis. Our precedents do not countenance such a presumption. On the contrary, they recognize that a principal "function of free speech under our system of government is to invite dispute. It may indeed best serve its high purpose when it induces a condition of unrest, creates dissatisfaction with conditions as they are, or even stirs people to anger.". . .

Thus, we have not permitted the government to assume that every expression of a provocative idea will incite a riot, but have instead required careful consideration of the actual circumstances surrounding such expression, asking whether the expression "is directed to inciting or producing imminent lawless action and is likely to incite or produce such action." *Brandenburg* v. *Ohio*, 395 U.S. 444, 447 (1969) (reviewing circumstances surrounding rally and speeches by Ku Klux Klan). To accept Texas' arguments that it need only demonstrate "the potential for a breach of the peace," Brief for Petitioner 37, and that every flag burning necessarily possesses that potential, would be to eviscerate our holding in *Brandenburg*. This we decline to do.

Nor does Johnson's expressive conduct fall within that small class of "fighting words" that are "likely to provoke the average person to retaliation, and thereby cause a breach of the peace." *Chaplinsky* v. *New Hampshire,* 315 U.S. 568, 574 (1942). No reasonable onlooker would have regarded Johnson's generalized expression of dissatisfaction with the policies of the Federal Government as a direct personal insult or an invitation to exchange fisticuffs. See *id.,* at 572–573; *Cantwell* v. *Connecticut,* 310 U.S. 296, 309 (1940); *FCC* v. *Pacifica Foundation, supra,* at 745 (opinion of STEVENS, J.).

We thus conclude that the State's interest in maintaining order is not implicated on these facts. The State need not worry that our holding will disable it from preserving the peace. We do not suggest that the First Amendment forbids a State to prevent "imminent lawless action." *Brandenburg, supra,* at 447. And, in fact, Texas already has a statute specifically prohibiting breaches of the peace, Tex. Penal Code Ann. § 42.01 (1989), which tends to confirm that Texas need not punish this flag desecration in order to keep the peace. See *Boos* v. *Barry*, 485 U.S., at 327–329.

# B

The State also asserts an interest in preserving the flag as a symbol of nationhood and national unity. In *Spence,* we acknowledged that the government's interest in preserving the flag's special symbolic value "is directly related to expression in the context of activity" such as affixing a peace symbol to a flag. 418 U.S., at 414, n. 8. We are equally persuaded that this interest is related to expression in the case of Johnson's burning of the flag. The State, apparently, is concerned that such conduct will lead people to believe either that the flag does not stand for nationhood and national unity, but instead reflects other, less positive concepts, or that the concepts reflected in the flag do not in fact exist, that is, that we do not enjoy unity as a Nation. These concerns blossom only when a person's treatment of the flag communicates some message, and thus are related "to the suppression of free expression" within the meaning of *O'Brien.* We are thus outside of *O'Brien's* test altogether.

It remains to consider whether the State's interest in preserving the flag as a symbol of nationhood and national unity justifies Johnson's conviction.

As in *Spence,* "[w]e are confronted with a case of prosecution for the expression of an idea through activity," and "[a]ccordingly, we must examine with particular care the interests advanced by [petitioner] to support its prosecution." 418 U.S., at 411. Johnson was not, we add, prosecuted for the expression of just any idea; he was prosecuted for his expression of dissatisfaction with the policies of this country, expression situated at the core of our First Amendment values. See, *e.g., Boos v. Barry, supra,* at 318; *Frisby v. Schultz,* 487 U.S. 474, 479 (1988).

Moreover, Johnson was prosecuted because he knew that his politically charged expression would cause "serious offense." If he had burned the flag as a means of disposing of it because it was dirty or torn, he would not have been convicted of flag desecration under this Texas law: federal law designates burning as the preferred means of disposing of a flag "where it is in such condition that it is no longer a fitting emblem for display," 36 U. S. C. § 176(k), and Texas has no quarrel with this means of disposal. Brief for Petitioner 45. The Texas law is thus not aimed at protecting the physical integrity of the flag in all circumstances, but is designed instead to protect it only against impairments that would cause serious offense to others." Texas concedes as much: "Section 42.09(b) reaches only those severe acts of physical abuse of the flag carried out in a way likely to be offensive. The statute mandates intentional or knowing abuse, that is, the kind of mistreatment that is not innocent, but rather is intentionally designed to seriously offend other individuals." *Id.,* at 44.

Whether Johnson's treatment of the flag violated Texas law thus depended on the likely communicative impact of his expressive conduct. Our decision in *Boos* v. *Barry, supra,* tells us that this restriction on Johnson's expression is content based. In Boos, we considered the constitutionality of a law prohibiting "the display of any sign within 500 feet of a foreign embassy if that sign tends to bring that foreign government into 'public odium' or 'public disrepute.' " *Id.,* at 315. Rejecting the argument that the law was content neutral because it was justified by "our international law obligation to shield diplomats from speech that offends their dignity," *id.,* at 320, we held that "[t]he emotive impact of speech on its audience is not 'secondary effect' " unrelated to the content of the expression itself. *Id.,* at 321 (plurality opinion); see also *id.,* at 334 (BRENNAN, J., concurring in part and concurring in judgment).

According to the principles announced in Boos, Johnson's political expression was restricted because of the content of the message he conveyed. We must therefore subject the State's asserted interest in preserving the special symbolic character of the flag to "the most exacting scrutiny." *Boos* v. *Barry,* 485 U.S., at 321.

Texas argues that its interest in preserving the flag as a symbol of nationhood and national unity survives this close analysis. Quoting extensively from the writings of this Court chronicling the flag's historic and symbolic role in our society, the State emphasizes the "special place" reserved for the flag in our Nation. Brief for Petitioner 22, quoting *Smith* v. *Goguen,* 415 U.S., at 601 (REHNQUIST, J., dissenting). The State's argument is not that it has an interest simply in maintaining the flag as a symbol of *something,* no matter what it symbolizes; indeed, if that were the State's position, it would be difficult to see how that interest is endangered by highly symbolic conduct such as Johnson's. Rather, the State's claim is that it has an interest in preserving the flag as a symbol of *nationhood* and *national unity,* a symbol with a determinate range of meanings. Brief for Petitioner 20–24. According to Texas, if one physically treats the flag in a way that would tend to cast doubt on either the idea that nationhood and national unity actually exists, the message conveyed thereby is a harmful one and therefore may be prohibited.

If there is a bedrock principle underlying the First Amendment, it is that the government may not prohibit the expression of an idea simply because society finds the idea itself offensive or disagreeable. See, *e.g., Hustler Magazine* v. *Falwell,* 485 U.S., at 55–56; *City Council of Los Angeles* v. *Taxpayers for Vincent,* 466 U.S. 789, 804 (1984); *Bolger* v. *Youngs Drug Products Corp.,* 463 U.S. 60, 65, 72 (1983); *Carey* v. *Brown,* 447 U.S. 455, 462–463 (1980); FCC v. *Pacifica Foundation,* 438 U.S., at 745–746; *Young* v. *American Mini Theatres, Inc.,* 427 U.S. 50, 63–65, 67–68 (1976) (plurality opinion); *Buckley* v. *Valeo,* 424 U.S. 1, 16–17 (1976); *Grayned* v. *Rockford,* 408 U.S. 104, 115 (1972); *Police Dept. of Chicago* v. *Mosley,* 408 U.S. 92, 95 (1972); *Bachellar* v. *Maryland,* 397 U.S. 564, 567 (1970); *O'Brien,* 391 U.S., at 382; *Brown* v. *Louisiana,* 383 U.S., at 142–143; *Stromberg* v. *California,* 283 U.S., at 368–369.

We have not recognized an exception to this principle even where our flag has been involved. In *Street* v. *New York,* 394 U.S. 576 (1969), we held that a State may not criminally punish a person for uttering words critical of the flag. Rejecting the argument that the conviction could be sustained on the ground that Street had "failed to show the respect for our national symbol which may properly be demanded of every citizen," we concluded that "the constitutionally guaranteed 'freedom to be intellectually . . . diverse or even contrary,' and the 'right to differ as to things that touch the heart of the existing order,' encompass the freedom to express publicly one's opinions about our flag, including those opinions which are defiant or contemptuous." *Id.,* at 593, quoting *Barnette,* 319 U.S., at 642. Nor may the government, we have held, compel conduct that would evince respect for the flag. "To sustain the compulsory flag salute we are required to say that a Bill of Rights which guards the individual's right to speak his own mind, left it open to public authorities to compel him to utter what is not in his mind." *Id.,* at 634.

In holding in *Barnette* that the Constitution did not leave this course open to the government, JUSTICE JACKSON described one of our society's defining principles in words deserving of their frequent repetition: "If there is any fixed star in our constitutional constellation, it is that no official, high or petty, can prescribe what shall be orthodox in polities, nationalism, religion, or other matters of opinion or force citizens to confess by word or act their faith therein.". . .

In short, nothing in our precedents suggests that a State may foster its own view of the flag by prohibiting expressive conduct relating to it. To bring its argument outside our precedents, Texas attempts to convince us that even if its interest in preserving the flag's symbolic role does not allow it to prohibit words or some expressive conduct critical of the flag, it does permit it to forbid the outright destruction of the flag. The State's argument cannot depend here on the distinction between written or spoken words and nonverbal conduct. That distinction, we have shown, is of no moment where the nonverbal conduct is expressive, as it is here, and where the regulation of that conduct is related to expression, as it is here. See *supra* at 402–403. In addition, both *Barnette* and *Spence* involved expressive conduct, not only verbal communication, and both found that conduct protected.

Texas' focus on the precise nature of Johnson's expression, moreover, misses the point of our prior decisions: their enduring lesson, that the government may not prohibit expression simply because it disagrees with its message, is not dependent on the particular mode in which one chooses to express an idea. If we were to hold that a State may forbid flag burning wherever it is likely to endanger the flag's symbolic role, but allow it wherever burning a flag promotes that role—as where, for example, a person ceremoniously burns a dirty flag—we would be saying that when it comes to impairing the flag's physical integrity, the flag itself may be used as a symbol—as a substitute for the written or spoken word or a "short cut from mind to mind" only in one direction. We would be permitting a State to "prescribe what shall be orthodox" by saying that one may burn the flag to convey one's attitude toward it and its referents only if one does not endanger the flag's representation of nationhood and national unity.

We never before have held that the Government may ensure that a symbol be used to express only one view of that symbol or its referents. Indeed, in *Schacht* v. *United States,* we invalidated a federal statute permitting an actor portraying a member of one of our armed forces to " 'wear the uniform of that armed force if the portrayal does not tend to discredit that armed force.' " 398 U.S., at 60, quoting 10 U.S. C. §772(f). This proviso, we held, "which leaves Americans free to praise the war in Vietnam but can send persons like Schacht to prison for opposing it, cannot survive in a country which has the First Amendment." *Id.*, at 63.

We perceive no basis on which to hold that the principle underlying our decision in *Schacht* does not apply to this case. To conclude that the government may permit designated symbols to be used to communicate only a limited set of messages would be to enter territory having no discernible or defensible boundaries. Could the government, on this theory, prohibit the burning of state flags? Of copies of the Presidential seal? Of the Constitution? In evaluating these choices under the First Amendment, how would we decide which symbols were sufficiently special to warrant this unique status? To do so, we would be forced to consult our own political preferences, and impose them on the citizenry, in the very way that the First Amendment forbids us to do. See *Carey* v. *Brown,* 447 U.S., at 466–467.

There is, moreover, no indication—either in the text of the Constitution or in our cases interpreting it—that a separate juridical category exists for the American flag alone. Indeed, we would not be surprised to learn that the persons who framed our Constitution and wrote the Amendment that we now construe were not known for their reverence for the Union Jack. The First Amendment does not guarantee that other concepts virtually sacred to our Nation as a whole—such as the principle that discrimination on the basis of race is odious and destructive—will go unquestioned in the marketplace of ideas. See *Brandenburg* v. *Ohio,* 395 U.S. 444 (1969). We decline, therefore, to create for the flag an exception to the joust of principles protected by the First Amendment.

It is not the State's ends, but its means, to which we object. It cannot be gainsaid that there is a special place reserved for the flag in this Nation, and thus we do not doubt that the government has a legitimate interest in making efforts to "preserv[e] the national flag as an unalloyed symbol of our country." *Spence,* 418 U. S., at 412. We reject the suggestion, urged at oral argument by counsel for Johnson, that the government lacks "any state interest whatsoever" in regulating the manner in which the flag may be displayed. Tr. of Oral Arg. 38. Congress has, for example, enacted precatory regulations describing the proper treatment of the flag, see 36 U.S.C. §§ 173–177, and we cast no doubt on the legitimacy of its interest in making such recommendations. To say that the government has an interest in encouraging proper treatment of the flag, however, is not to say that it may criminally punish a person for burning a flag as a means of political protest. "National unity as an end which officials may foster by persuasion and example is not in question. The problem is whether under our Constitution compulsion as here employed is a permissible means for its achievement." *Barnette,* 319 U. S., at 640.

We are fortified in today's conclusion by our conviction that forbidding criminal punishment for conduct such as Johnson's will not endanger the special role played by our flag or the feelings it inspires. To paraphrase JUSTICE HOLMES, we submit that nobody can suppose that this one gesture of an unknown man will change our Nation's attitude towards its flag. See *Abrams* v. *United States*, 250 U.S. 616, 628 (1919) (HOLMES, J., dissenting). Indeed, Texas' argument that the burning of an American flag " 'is an act having a high likelihood to cause a breach of the peace,' " Brief for Petitioner 31, quoting *Sutherland* v. *DeWulf*, 323 F. Supp. 740, 745 (SD Ill. 1971) (citation omitted), and its statute's implicit assumption that physical mistreatment of the flag will lead to "serious offense," tend to confirm that the flag's special role is not in danger; if it were, no one would riot or take offense because a flag had been burned.

We are tempted to say, in fact, that the flag's deservedly cherished place in our community will be strengthened, not weakened, by our holding today. Our decision is a reaffirmation of the principles of freedom and inclusiveness that the flag best reflects, and of the conviction that our toleration of criticism such as Johnson's is a sign and source of our strength. Indeed, one of the proudest images of our flag, the one immortalized in our own national anthem, is of the bombardment it survived at Fort McHenry. It is the Nation's resilience, not its rigidity, that Texas sees reflected in the flag—and it is that resilience that we reassert today.

The way to preserve the flag's special role is not to punish those who feel differently about these matters. It is to persuade them that they are wrong. "To courageous, self-reliant men, with confidence in the power of free and fearless reasoning applied through the processes of popular government, no danger flowing from speech can be deemed clear and present, unless the incidence of the evil apprehended is so imminent that it may befall before there is opportunity for full discussion. If there be time to expose through discussion the falsehood and fallacies, to avert the evil by the processes of education, the remedy to be applied is more speech, not enforced silence." *Whitney* v. *California*, 274 U.S. 357, 377 (1927) (BRANDEIS, J., concurring). And, precisely because it is our flag that is involved, one's response to the flag burner may exploit the uniquely persuasive power of the flag itself. We can imagine no more appropriate response to burning a flag than waving one's own, no better way to counter a flag burner's message than by saluting the flag that burns, no surer means of preserving the dignity even of the flag that burned than by—as one witness here did according it's remains a respectful burial. We do not consecrate the flag by punishing its desecration, for in doing so we dilute the freedom that this cherished emblem represents.

Johnson was convicted for engaging in expressive conduct. The State's interest in preventing breaches of the peace does not support his conviction because Johnson's conduct did not threaten to disturb the peace. Nor does the State's interest in preserving the flag as a symbol of nationhood and national unity justify his criminal conviction for engaging in political expression. The judgment of the Texas Court of Criminal Appeals is therefore

*Affirmed.*

JUSTICE KENNEDY, concurring.

I write not to qualify the words JUSTICE BRENNAN chooses so well, for he says with power all that is necessary to explain our ruling. I join his opinion without reservation, but with a keen sense that this case, like others before us from time to time, exacts its personal toll. This prompts me to add to our pages these few remarks.

The case before us illustrates better than most that the judicial power is often difficult in its exercise. We cannot here ask another Branch to share responsibility, as when the argument is made that a statute is flawed or incomplete. For we are presented with a clear and simple statute to be judged against a pure command of the Constitution. The outcome can be laid at no door but ours.

The hard fact is that sometimes we must make decisions we do not like. We make them because they are right, right in the sense that the law and the Constitution, as we see them, compel the result. And so great is our commitment to the process that, except in the rare case, we do not pause to express distaste for the result, perhaps for fear of undermining a valued principle that dictates the decision. This is one of those rare cases.

Our colleagues in dissent advance powerful arguments why respondent may be convicted for his expression, reminding us that among those who will be dismayed by our holding will be some who have had the singular honor of carrying the flag in battle. And I agree that the flag holds a lonely place of honor in an age when absolutes are distrusted and simple truths are burdened by unneeded apologetics.

With all respect to those views, I do not believe the Constitution gives us the right to rule as the dissenting Members of the Court urge, however painful this judgment is to announce. Though symbols often are what we ourselves make of them, the flag is constant in expressing beliefs Americans share, beliefs in law and peace and that freedom which sustains the human spirit. The case here today forces recognition of the costs to which those beliefs commit us. It is poignant but fundamental that the flag protects those who hold it in contempt.

For all the record shows, this respondent was not a philosopher and perhaps did not even possess the ability to comprehend how repellent his statements must be to the Republic itself. But whether or not he could appreciate the enormity of the offense he gave, the fact remains that his acts were speech, in both the technical and the fundamental meaning of the Constitution. So I agree with the Court that he must go free.

CHIEF JUSTICE REHNQUIST, with whom JUSTICE WHITE and JUSTICE O'CONNOR join, dissenting.

In holding this Texas statute unconstitutional, the Court ignores Justice Holmes' familiar aphorism that "a page of history is worth a volume of logic." *New York Trust Co. v. Eisner*, 256 U.S. 345, 349 (1921). For more than 200 years, the American flag has occupied a unique position as the symbol of our Nation, a uniqueness that justifies a governmental prohibition against flag burning in the way respondent Johnson did here. . . .

The flag symbolizes the Nation in peace as well as in war. It signifies our national presence on battleships, airplanes, military installations, and public buildings from the United States Capitol to the thousands of county courthouses and city halls throughout the country. Two flags are prominently placed in our courtroom. Countless flags are placed by the graves of loved ones each year on what was first called Decoration Day, and is now called Memorial Day. The flag is traditionally placed on the casket of deceased members of the Armed Forces, and it is later given to the deceased's family. 10 U.S.C. §§ 1481, 1482. Congress has provided that the flag be flown at half-staff upon the death of the President, Vice President, and other government officials "as a mark of respect to their memory." 36 U.S.C. § 175(m). The flag identifies United States merchant ships, 22 U.S.C. § 454, and "[t]he laws of the Union protect our commerce wherever the flag of the country may float." *United States* v. *Guthrie*, 17 How. 284, 309 (1855).

No other American symbol has been as universally honored as the flag. In 1931, Congress declared "The Star-Spangled Banner" to be our national anthem. 36 U.S.C. § 170. In 1949, Congress declared June 14th to be Flag Day. § 157. In 1987, John Philip Sousa's "The Stars and Stripes Forever" was designated as the national march. Publ. L. 101–186, 101 Stat. 1286. Congress has also established "The Pledge of Allegiance to the Flag" and the manner of its deliverance. 36 U.S.C. § 172. The flag has appeared as the principal symbol on approximately 33 United States postal stamps and in the design of at least 43 more, more times than any other symbol. United States Postal Service, Definitive Mint Set 15 (1988).

Both Congress and the States have enacted numerous laws regulating misuse of the American flag. Until 1967, Congress left the regulation of misuse of the flag up to the States. Now, however, Title 18 U.S.C. § 700(a) provides that:

> "Whoever knowingly casts contempt upon any flag of the United States by publicly mutilating, defacing, defiling, burning, or trampling upon it shall be fined not more than $1,000 or imprisoned for not more than one year, or both."

Congress has also prescribed, *inter alia,* detailed rules for the design of the flag, 4 U.S.C § 1, the time and occasion of flag's display, 36 U.S.C. § 174, the position and manner of its display, § 175, respect for the flag, § 176, and conduct during hoisting, lowering and passing of the flag, § 177. With the exception of Alaska and Wyoming, all of the States now have statues prohibiting the burning of the flag. Most of the state statues are patterned after the Uniform Flag Act of 1917, which in § 3 provides: "No person shall publicly mutilate, deface, define, defy, trample upon, or by word or act cast contempt upon any such flag, standard, color, ensign or shield." Proceedings of National Conference of Commissioners on Uniform State Laws 323–324 (1917). Most were passed by the States at about the time of World War I. Rosenblatt, Flag Desecration Statues: History and Analysis, 1972 Wash. U. L. Q. 193, 197.

The American flag, then, throughout more than 200 years of our history, has come to be the visible symbol embodying our Nation. It does not represent the views of any particular political party, and it does not represent any particular political philosophy. The flag is not simply another "idea" or "point of view" competing for recognition in the marketplace of ideas. Millions and millions of Americans regard it with an almost mystical reverence regardless of what sort of social, political, or philosophical beliefs they may have. I cannot agree that the First Amendment invalidates the Act of Congress, and the laws of 48 of the 50 States, which make criminal the public burning of the flag. . . .

But the Court insists that the Texas statute prohibiting the public burning of the American flag infringes on respondent Johnson's freedom of expression. Such freedom, of course, is not absolute. See *Schenck* v. *United States,* 249 U.S. 47 (1919). In *Chaplinsky* v. *New Hampshire,* 315 U.S. 568 (1942), a unanimous Court said:

> "Allowing the broadest scope to the language and purpose of the Fourteenth Amendment, it is well understood that the right of free speech is not absolute at all times and under all circumstances. There are certain well-defined and narrowly limited classes of speech, the prevention and punishment of which have never been thought to raise any Constitutional problem. These include the lewd and obscene, the profane, the libelous, and the insulting or 'fighting' words—those which by their very utterance inflict injury or tend to incite an immediate breach of the peace. It has been well observed that such utterances are no essential part of any exposition of ideas, and are of such slight social value as a step to truth that any benefit that may be derived from them is clearly outweighed by the social interest in order and morality." *Id.,* at 571–572 (footnotes omitted).

The Court upheld Chaplinsky's conviction under a state statute that made it unlawful to "address any offensive, derisive or annoying word to any person who is lawfully in any street or other public place." *Id.,* at 569. Chaplinsky had told a local marshal,' "You are a God damned racketeer" and a "damned Fascist and the whole government of Rochester are Fascists or agents of Fascists." ' " *Ibid.*

Here it may equally well be said that the public burning of the American flag by Johnson was no essential part of any exposition of ideas, and at the same time it had a tendency to incite a breach of the peace. Johnson was free to make any verbal denunciation of the flag that he wished; indeed, he was free to burn the flag in private. He could publicly burn other symbols of the Government or effigies of political leaders. He did lead a march through the streets of Dallas, and conducted a rally in front of the Dallas City Hall. He engaged in a "die-in" to protest nuclear weapons. He shouted out various slogans during the march, including: "Reagan, Mondale which will it be? Either one means World War III"; "Ronald Reagan, killer of the hour, Perfect example of U.S. power"; and "red, white and blue, we spit on you, you stand for plunder, you will go under." Brief for Respondent 3. For none of these acts was he arrested or prosecuted; it was only when he proceeded to burn publicly an American flag stolen from its rightful owner that he violated the Texas statute.

The Court could not, and did not, say that Chaplinsky's utterances were not expressive phrases—they clearly and succinctly conveyed an extremely low opinion of the addressee. The same may be said of Johnson's public burning of the flag in this case; it obviously did convey Johnson's bitter dislike of his country. But his act, like Chaplinsky's provocative words, conveyed nothing that could not have been conveyed and was not conveyed just as forcefully in a dozen different ways. As with "fighting words," so with flag burning, for purposes of the First Amendment: It is "no essential part of any exposition of ideas, and [is] of such slight social value as a step to truth that any benefit that may be derived from [it] is clearly outweighed" by the public interest in avoiding a probable breach of the peace. The highest courts of several States have upheld state statutes prohibiting the public burning of the flag on the grounds that it is so inherently inflammatory that it may cause a breach of public order. . . .

The result of the Texas statute is obviously to deny one in Johnson's frame of mind one of many means of "symbolic speech." Far from being a case of "one picture being worth a thousand words," flag burning is the equivalent of an inarticulate grunt or roar that, it seems fair to say, is most likely to be indulged in not to express any particular idea, but to antagonize others. Only five years ago we said in *City Council of Los Angeles* v. *Taxpayers for Vincent,* 466 U.S. 789 812 (1984), that "the First Amendment does not guarantee the right to employ every conceivable method of communication at all times, and in all places." The Texas statute deprived Johnson of only one rather inarticulate symbolic form of protest—a form of protest that was profoundly offensive to many—and left him with a full panoply of other symbols and every conceivable form of verbal expression to express his deep disapproval of national policy. Thus, in no way can it be said that Texas is punishing him because his hearers—or any other group of people—were profoundly opposed to the message that he sought to convey. Such opposition is no proper basis for restricting speech or expression under the First Amendment. It was Johnson's use of this particular symbol, and not the idea that he sought to convey by it or by his many other expressions, for which he was punished.

Our prior cases dealing with flag desecration statutes have left open the question that the Court resolves today. In *Street* v. *New York*, 394 U.S. 576, 579 (1969), the defendant burned a flag in the street, shouting "We don't need no damned flag" and, "[i]f they let that happen to Meredith we don't need an American flag." The Court ruled that since the defendant might have been convicted solely on the basis of his words, the conviction could not stand, but it expressly reserved the question whether a defendant could constitutionally be convicted for burning the flag. *Id.*, at 581.

Chief justice Warren, in dissent, stated: "I believe that the States and Federal Government do have the power to protect the flag from acts of desecration and disgrace. . . . [I]t is difficult for me to imagine that, had the Court faced this issue, it would have concluded otherwise." *Id.*, at 605. JUSTICES BLACK and FORTAS also expressed their personal view that a prohibition on flag burning did not violate the Constitution. See *id.*, at 610 (Black, J., dissenting) ("It passes my belief that anything in the Federal Constitution bars a State from making the deliberate burning of the American Flag an offense"); *id.*, at 615–617 (FORTAS, J., dissenting) ("[T]he States and the Federal Government have the power to protect the flag from acts of desecration committed in public. . . . [T]he flag is a special kind of personality. Its use is traditionally and universally subject to special rules and regulation. . . . A person may 'own' a flag, but ownership is subject to special burdens and responsibilities. A flag may be property, in a sense; but it is property burdened with peculiar obligations and restrictions. Certainly . . . these special conditions are not *per se* arbitrary or beyond governmental power under our Constitution"). . . .

But the Court today will have none of this. The uniquely deep awe and respect for our flag felt by virtually all of us are bundled off under the rubric of "designated symbols," *ante*, at 417, that the First Amendment prohibits the government from "establishing." But the government has not "established" this feeling; 200 years of history have done that. The government is simply recognizing as a fact the profound regard for the American flag created by that history when it enacts statutes prohibiting the disrespectful public burning of the flag. . . .

Surely one of the high purposes of a democratic society is to legislate against conduct that is regarded as evil and profoundly offensive to the majority of people—whether it be murder, embezzlement, pollution, or flag burning.

Our Constitution wisely places limits on powers of legislative majorities to act, but the declaration of such limits by this Court "is, at all times, a question of much delicacy, which ought seldom, if ever, to be decided in the affirmative, in a doubtful case." *Fletcher* v. *Peck*, 6 Cranch 87, 128 (1810) (MARSHALL, C.J.). Uncritical extension of constitutional protection to the burning of the flag risks the frustration of the very purpose for which organized governments are instituted. The Court decides that the American flag is just another symbol, about which not only must opinions pro and con be tolerated, but for which the most minimal public respect may not be enjoined. The government may conscript men into the Armed Forces where they must fight and perhaps die for the flag, but the government may not prohibit the public burning of the banner under which they fight. I would uphold the Texas statute as applied in this case.

JUSTICE STEVENS, dissenting.

As the Court analyzes this case, it presents the question whether the State of Texas, or indeed the Federal Government, has the power to prohibit the public desecration the American flag. The question is unique. In my judgment rules that apply to a host of other symbols, such as state flags, armbands, or various privately promoted emblems of political or commercial identify, are not necessarily controlling. Even if flag burning could be considered just another species of symbolic speech under the logical application of the rules that the Court has developed in its interpretation of the First Amendment in other contexts, this case has an intangible dimension that makes those rules inapplicable.

A country's flag is a symbol of more than "nationhood and national unity." *Ante*, at 407, 410, 443, and n. 9. 417, 420. It also signifies the ideas that characterize the society that has chosen that emblem as well as the special history that has animated the growth and power of those ideas. The fleurs-de-lis and the tricolor both symbolized "nationhood and national unity," but they had vastly different meanings. The message conveyed by some flags—the swastika, for example—may survive long after it has outlived its usefulness as a symbol of regimented unity in a particular nation.

So it is with the American flag. It is more than a proud symbol of the courage, the determination, and the gifts of nature that transformed 13 fledgling Colonies into a world power. It is a symbol of freedom, of equal opportunity, of religious tolerance, and of good will for other peoples who share our aspirations. The symbol carries its message to dissidents both at home and abroad who may have no interest at all in our national unity or survival.

The value of the flag as a symbol cannot be measured. Even so, I have no doubt that the interest in preserving that value for the future is both significant and legitimate.

Conceivably that value will be enhanced by the Court's conclusion that our national commitment to free expression is so strong that even the United States as ultimate guarantor of that freedom is without power to prohibit the desecration of its unique symbol. But I am unpersuaded. The creation of a federal right to post bulletin boards and graffiti on the Washington Monument might enlarge the market for free expression, but at a cost I would not pay. Similarly, in my considered judgment, sanctioning the public desecration of the flag will tarnish its value—both for those who cherish the ideas for which it waves and for those who desire to don the robes of martyrdom by burning it. That tarnish is not justified by the trivial burden on free expression occasioned by requiring that an available, alternative mode of expression—including uttering words critical of the flag, see *Street v. New York*, 394 U.S. 576 (1969— be employed.

It is appropriate to emphasize certain propositions that are not implicated by this case. The statutory prohibition of flag desecration does not "prescribe what shall be orthodox in politics, nationalism, religion, or other matters of opinion or force citizens to confess by word or act their faith therein." West *Virginia Board of Education* v. *Barnette*, 319 U. S. 624, 642 (1943). The statute does not compel any conduct or any profession of respect for any idea or any symbol.

Nor does the statute violate "the government's paramount obligation of neutrality in its regulation of protected communication." *Young* v. *American Mini Theatres, Inc.*, 427 U.S. 50, 70 (1976) (plurality opinion). The content of respondent's message has no relevance whatsoever to the case. The concept of "desecration" does not turn on the substance of the message the actor intends to convey, but rather on whether those who view the act will take serious offense. Accordingly, one intending to convey a message of respect for the flag by burning it in a public square might nonetheless be guilty of desecration if he knows that others—perhaps simply because they misperceive the intended message will be seriously offended. Indeed, even if the actor knows that all possible witnesses will understand that he intends to send a message of respect, he might still be guilty of desecration if he also knows that this understanding does not lessen the offense taken by some of those witnesses. Thus, this is not a case in which the fact that "it is the speaker's opinion that gives offense" provides a special "reason for according it constitutional protection," *FCC* v. *Pacifica Foundation*, 438 U.S. 726, 745 (1978) (plurality opinion). The case has nothing to do with "disagreeable ideas," see *ante*, at 409. It involves disagreeable conduct that, in my opinion, diminishes the value of an important national asset.

The Court is therefore quite wrong in blandly asserting that respondent "was prosecuted for his expression of dissatisfaction with the policies of this country, expression situated at the core of our First Amendment values." *Ante*, at 411. Respondent was prosecuted because of the method he chose to express his dissatisfaction with those policies. Had he chosen to spray-paint or perhaps convey with a motion picture projector—his message of dissatisfaction on the facade of the Lincoln Memorial, there would be no question about the power of the Government to prohibit his means of expression. The prohibition would be supported by the legitimate interest in preserving the quality of an important national asset. Though the asset at stake in this case is intangible, given its unique value, the same interest supports a prohibition on the desecration of the American flag.

The ideas of liberty and equality have been an irresistible force in motivating leaders like Patrick Henry, Susan B. Anthony, and Abraham Lincoln, schoolteachers like Nathan Hale and Booker T. Washington, the Philippine Scouts who fought at Bataan, and the soldiers who scaled the bluff at Omaha Beach. If those ideas are worth fighting for—and our history demonstrates that they are—it cannot be true that the flag that uniquely symbolizes their power is not itself worthy of protection from unnecessary desecration.

*I respectfully dissent.*

## Notes

\* Briefs of *amici curiae* urging reversal were filed for the Legal Affairs Council by *Wyatt B. Durrette, Jr.,* and *Bradley B. Cavedo;* and for the Washington Legal Foundation by *Daniel J. Popeo* and *Paul D. Kamenar.*

Briefs of *amici curiae* urging affirmance were filed for the American Civil Liberties Union et al. by *Peter Linzer, James C. Harrington,* and *Steven R. Shapiro;* for the Christic Institute et al. by *James C. Goodale;* and for Jasper Johns et al. by *Robert G. Sugarman* and *Gloria C. Phares.*

1. Tex. Penal Code Ann. § 42.09 (1989) provides in full:

"§ 42.09. Desecration of Venerated Object

"(a) A person commits an offense if he intentionally or knowingly desecrates:

"(1) a public monument:

"(2) a place of worship or burial; or

"(3) a state or national flag.

"(b) For purposes of this section, 'desecrate' means deface, damage or otherwise physically mistreat in a way that the actor knows will seriously offend one or more persons likely to observe or discover his action.

"(c) An offense under this section is a Class A misdemeanor."

**Texas v. Johnson**, 491 U.S. 397 (1989) 5–4
*editor's note.*
*Opinion authors are in bold; () indicates the party of appointing president. If the party*
*of the justice differs from that of appointing president, then the party of the justice is*
*listed second after the slash.*

| MAJORITY | CONCURRING | DISSENTING |
|---|---|---|
| **Brennan** (r/d) | **Kennedy** (r) | **Rehnquist** (r) |
| Marshall (d) | | White (d) |
| Blackmun (r) | | O'Connor (r) |
| Scalia (r) | | **Stevens** (r) |

# United States v. Eichman et al.

## 496 U.S. 310

## Appeal from the District Court for the District of Columbia

### No. 89–1433. Argued May 14, 1990—Decided June 11, 1990*

JUSTICE BRENNAN delivered the opinion of the Court.

In these consolidated appeals, we consider whether appellees' prosecution for burning a United States flag in violation of the Flag Protection Act of 1989 is consistent with the First Amendment. Applying our recent decision in *Texas v. Johnson*, 491 U. S.—(1989), the District Courts held that the Act cannot constitutionally be applied to appellees. We affirm.

## — I —

In No. 89–1433, the United States prosecuted certain appellees for violating the Flag Protection Act of 1989, 103 Stat. 777, 18 U.S.C.A. § 700 (Supp. 1990), by knowingly setting fire to several United States flags on the steps of the United States Capitol while protesting various aspects of the Government's domestic and foreign policy. In No. 89–1434, the United States prosecuted other appellees for violating the Act by knowingly setting fire to a United States flag while protesting the Act's passage. In each case, the respective appellees moved to dismiss the flag-burning charge on the ground that the Act, both on its face and as applied, violates the First Amendment. Both the United States District Court for the Western District of Washington, F. Supp. (1990), and the United States District Court for the District of Columbia, 731—F. Supp. 1123—(1990), following *Johnson, supra* held the Act unconstitutional as applied to appellees and dismissed the charges. The United States appealed both decisions directly to this Court pursuant to 18 U.S.C.A. § 700(d) (Supp 1990). We noted probable jurisdiction and consolidated the two cases. 494 U.S.—(1990).

Last Term in *Johnson,* we held that a Texas statute criminalizing the desecration of venerated objects, including the United States flag, was unconstitutional as applied to an individual who had set such a flag on fire during a political demonstration. . . .

After our decision in *Johnson,* Congress passed the Flag Protection Act of 1989.[1] The Act provides in relevant part:

> "(a)(1) Whoever knowingly mutilates, defaces, physically defiles, burns, maintains on the floor or ground, or tramples upon any flag of the United States shall be fined under this title or imprisoned for not more than one year or both.

> "(2) This subsection does not prohibit any conduct consisting of the disposal of a flag when it has become worn or soiled.

> "(b) As used in this section, the term "flag of the United States' means any flag of the United States, or any part thereof, made of any substance, of any size, in a form that is commonly displayed." 18 U.S.C.A. § 700 (Supp. 1990).

The Government concedes in this case, as it must, that appellees' flag-burning constituted expressive conduct, Brief for United States 28; see *Johnson, supra,* at —, but invites us to reconsider our rejection in *Johnson* of the claim that flag-burning as a mode of expression, like obscenity or "fighting words," does not enjoy the full protection of the First Amendment. Cf. *Chaplinsky* v. *New Hampshire,* 315 U.S. 568, 572 (1942). This we decline to do.[2] The only remaining question is whether the Flag Protection Act is sufficiently distinct from the Texas statute that it may constitutionally be applied to proscribe appellees' expressive conduct.

The Government contends that the Flag Protection Act is constitutional because, unlike the statute addressed in *Johnson,* the Act does not target expressive conduct on the basis of the content of its message. The Government asserts an interest in "protect[ing] the physical integrity of the flag under all circumstances" in order to safeguard the flag's identity " 'as the unique and unalloyed symbol of the Nation.' " Brief for United States 28, 29. The Act proscribes conduct (other than disposal) that damages or mistreats a flag, without regard to the actor's motive, his intended message, or the likely effects of his conduct on onlookers. By contrast, the Texas statute expressly prohibited only those acts of physical flag desecration "that the actor knows will seriously offend" onlookers, and the former federal statute prohibited only those acts of desecration that "cas[t] contempt upon" the flag.

Although the Flag Protection Act contains no explicit content-based limitation on the scope of prohibited conduct, it is nevertheless clear that the Government's asserted *interest is* "related 'to the suppression of free expression,' " 491 U.S., at —, and concerned with the content of such expression. The Government's interest in protecting the "physical integrity" of a privately owned flag rests upon a perceived need to preserve the flag's status as a symbol of our Nation and certain national ideals. But the mere destruction or disfigurement of a particular physical manifestation of the symbol, without more, does not diminish or otherwise affect the symbol itself in any way. For example, the secret destruction of a flag in one's own basement would not threaten the flag's recognized meaning. Rather, the Government's desire to preserve the flag as a symbol for certain national ideals is implicated "only when a person's treatment of the flag communicates [a] message" to others that is inconsistent with those ideals. *Id.*, at —.

Moreover, the precise language of the Act's prohibitions confirms Congress' interest in the communicative impact of flag destruction. The Act criminalizes the conduct of anyone who "knowingly mutilates, defaces, physically defiles, burns, maintains on the floor or ground, or tramples upon any flag.' " 18 U.S.C.A. § 700(a)(1) (Supp. 1990). Each of the specified terms—with the possible exception of "burns"—unmistakably connotes disrespectful treatment of the flag and suggests a focus on those acts likely to damage the flag's symbolic value. And the explicit exemption in § 700(a)(2) for disposal of "worn or soiled" flags protects certain acts traditionally associated with patriotic respect for the flag.

As we explained in *Johnson, supra,* at — – — " [I]f we were to hold that a State may forbid flag-burning wherever it is likely to endanger the flag's symbolic role, but allow it wherever burning a flag promotes that role—as where, for example, a person ceremoniously burns a dirty flag—we would be . . . permitting a State to 'prescribe what shall be orthodox' by saying that one may burn the flag to convey one's attitude toward it and its referents only if one does not endanger the flag's representation of nationhood and national unity." Although Congress cast the Flag Protection Act in somewhat broader terms than the Texas statute at issue in *Johnson*, the Act still suffers from the same fundamental flaw: it suppresses expression out of concern for its likely communicative impact. Despite the Act's wider scope, its restriction on expression cannot be " 'justified without reference to the content of the regulated speech.' " *Boos,* 485 U.S., at 320 (citation omitted); see *Spence* v. *Washington,* 418 U.S. 405, 414, nn. 8, 9 (1974) (State's interest in protecting flag's symbolic value is directly related to suppression of expression and thus *O'Brien* test is inapplicable even where statute declared "simply . . . that *nothing* may be affixed to or superimposed on a United States flag"). The Act therefore must be subjected to "the most exacting scrutiny," *Boos, supra,* at 321, and for the reasons stated in *Johnson, supra,* at — – —, the Government's interest cannot justify its infringement on First Amendment rights. We decline the Government's invitation to reassess this conclusion in light of Congress' recent recognition of a purported "national consensus" favoring a prohibition on flag-burning. Brief for United States 27. Even assuming such a consensus exists, any suggestion that the Government's interest in suppressing speech becomes more weighty as popular opposition to that speech grows is foreign to the First Amendment.

" 'National unity as an end which officials may foster by persuasion and example is not in question.' " *Johnson, supra,* at —, quoting *West Virginia Board of Education* v. *Barnette,* 319 U.S. 624, 640 (1943). Government may create national symbols, promote them, and encourage their respectful treatment. But the Flag Protection Act goes well beyond this by criminally proscribing expressive conduct because of its likely communicative impact.

We are aware that desecration of the flag is deeply offensive to many. But the same might be said, for example, of virulent ethnic and religious epithets, see *Terminiello* v. *Chicago,* 337 U.S. 1 (1949), vulgar repudiations of the draft, see *Cohen* v. *California,* 403 U.S. 15 (1971), and scurrilous caricatures, see *Hustler Magazine, Inc.* v. *Falwell,* 485 U.S. 46 (1988). "If there is a bedrock principle underlying the First Amendment, it is that the Government may not prohibit the expression of an idea simply because society finds the idea itself offensive or disagreeable." *Johnson, supra,* at —. Punishing desecration of the flag dilutes the very freedom that makes this emblem so revered, and worth revering. The judgments are

*Affirmed.*

JUSTICE STEVENS, with whom THE CHIEF JUSTICE, JUSTICE WHITE and JUSTICE O'CONNOR join, dissenting.

The Court's opinion ends where proper analysis of the issue should begin. Of course "the Government may not prohibit the expression of an idea simply because society finds the idea itself offensive or disagreeable." *Ante,* at 7. None of us disagrees with that proposition. But it is equally well settled that certain methods of expression may be prohibited if (a) the prohibition is supported by a legitimate societal interest that is unrelated to suppression of the ideas the speaker desires to express; (b) the prohibition does not entail any interference with the speaker's freedom to express those ideas by other means; and (c) the interest in allowing the speaker complete freedom of choice among alternative methods of expression is less important than the societal interest supporting the prohibition.

Contrary to the position taken by counsel for the flag burners in *Texas* v. *Johnson,* 491 U.S. —(1989), it is now conceded that the Federal Government has a legitimate interest in protecting the symbolic value of the American flag. Obviously that value cannot be measured, or even described, with any precision. It has at least these two components: in times of national crisis, it inspires and motivates the average citizen to make personal sacrifices in order to achieve societal goals of overriding importance; at all times, it serves as a reminder of the paramount importance of pursuing the ideals that characterize our society.

The first question the Court should consider is whether the interest in preserving the value of that symbol is unrelated to suppression of the ideas that flag burners are trying to express. In my judgment the answer depends, at least in part, on what those ideas are. A flag burner might intend various messages. The flag burner may wish simply to convey hatred, contempt, or sheer opposition directed at the United States. This might be the case if the flag were burned by an enemy during time of war. A flag burner may also, or instead, seek to convey the depth of his personal conviction about some issue, by willingly provoking the use of force against himself. In so doing, he says that "my disagreement with certain policies is so strong that I am prepared to risk physical harm (and perhaps imprisonment) in order to call attention to my views." This second possibility apparently describes the expressive conduct of the flag burners in these cases. Like the protesters who dramatized their opposition to our engagement in Vietnam by publicly burning their draft cards—and who were punished for doing so—their expressive conduct is consistent with affection for this country and respect for the ideals that the flag symbolizes. There is at least one further possibility: a flag burner may intend to make an accusation against the integrity of the American people who disagree with him. By burning the embodiment of America's collective commitment to freedom and equality, the flag burner charges that the majority has forsaken that commitment—that continued respect for the flag is nothing more than hypocrisy. Such a charge may be made even if the flag burner loves the country and zealously pursues the ideals that the country claims to honor.

The idea expressed by a particular act of flag burning is necessarily dependent on the temporal and political context in which it occurs. In the 1960's it may have expressed opposition to the country's Vietnam policies, or at least to the compulsory draft. In *Texas* v. *Johnson,* it apparently expressed opposition to the platform of the Republican Party. In these cases, the respondents have explained that it expressed their opposition to racial discrimination, to the failure to care for the homeless, and of course to statutory prohibitions of flag burning. In any of these examples, the protestors may wish both to say that their own position is the only one faithful to liberty and equality, and to accuse their fellow citizens of hypocritical indifference to—or even of a selfish departure—from the ideals which the flag is supposed to symbolize. The ideas expressed by flag burners are thus various and often ambiguous.

The Government's legitimate interest in preserving the symbolic value of the flag is, however, essentially the same regardless of which of many different ideas may have motivated a particular act of flag burning. As I explained in my dissent in *Johnson,* 491 U. S., at — – —, the flag uniquely symbolizes the ideas of liberty, equality, and tolerance—ideas that Americans have passionately defended and debated throughout our history. The flag embodies the spirit of our national commitment to those ideals. The message thereby transmitted does not take a stand upon our disagreements, except to say that those disagreements are best regarded as competing interpretations of shared ideals. It does not judge particular policies, except to say that they command respect when they are enlightened by the spirit of liberty and equality. To the world, the flag is our promise that we will continue to strive for these ideals. To us, the flag is a reminder both that the struggle for liberty and equality is unceasing, and that our obligation of tolerance and respect for all of our fellow citizens encompasses those who disagree with us—indeed, even those whose ideas are disagreeable or offensive.

Thus, the Government may—indeed, it should—protect the symbolic value of the flag without regard to the specific content of the flag burner's speech. The prosecution in this case does not depend upon the object of the defendants' protest. It is, moreover, equally clear that the prohibition does not entail any interference with the speaker's freedom to express his or her ideas by other means. It may well be true that other means of expression may be less effective in drawing attention to those ideas, but that is not itself a sufficient reason for immunizing flag burning. Presumably a gigantic fireworks display or a parade of nude models in a public park might draw even more attention to a controversial message, but such methods of expression are nevertheless subject to regulation.

This case therefore comes down to a question of judgment. Does the admittedly important interest in allowing every speaker to choose the method of expressing his or her ideas that he or she deems most effective and appropriate outweigh the societal interest in preserving the symbolic value of the flag? This question, in turn, involves three different judgments: (1) The importance of the individual interest in selecting the preferred means of communication; (2) the importance of the national symbol; and (3) the question whether tolerance of flag burning will enhance or tarnish that value. The opinions in *Texas* v. *Johnson* demonstrate that reasonable judges may differ with respect to each of these judgments.

The individual interest is unquestionably a matter of great importance. Indeed, it is one of the critical components of the idea of liberty that the flag itself is intended to symbolize. Moreover, it is buttressed by the societal interest in being alerted to the need for thoughtful response to voices that might otherwise go unheard. The freedom of expression protected by the First Amendment embraces not only the freedom to communicate particular ideas, but also the right to communicate them effectively. That right, however, is not absolute—the communicative value of a well-placed bomb in the Capitol does not entitle it to the protection of the First Amendment.

Burning the flag is not, of course, equivalent to burning a public building. Assuming that the protester is burning his own flag, it causes no physical harm to other persons or to their property. The impact is purely symbolic, and it is apparent that some thoughtful persons believe that impact, far from depreciating the value of the symbol, will actually enhance its meaning. I most respectfully disagree. Indeed, what makes this case particularly difficult for me is what I regard as the damage to the symbol that has already occurred as a result of this Court's decision to place its stamp of approval on the act of flag burning. A formerly dramatic expression of protest is now rather commonplace. . . .

The symbolic value of the American flag is not the same today as it was yesterday. Events during the last three decades have altered the country's image in the eyes of numerous Americans, and some now have difficulty understanding the message that the flag conveyed to their parents and grandparents—whether born abroad and naturalized or native born. Moreover, the integrity of the symbol has been compromised by those leaders who seem to advocate compulsory worship of the flag even by individuals whom it offends, or who seem to manipulate the symbol of national purpose into a pretext for partisan disputes about meaner ends. And, as I have suggested, the residual value of the symbol after this Court's decision in *Texas* v. *Johnson* is surely not the same as it was a year ago.

Given all these considerations, plus the fact that the Court today is really doing nothing more than reconfirming what it has already decided, it might be appropriate to defer to the judgment of the majority and merely apply the doctrine of *stare decisis* to the case at hand. That action, however, would not honestly reflect my considered judgment concerning the relative importance of the conflicting interests that are at stake. I remain persuaded that the considerations identified in my opinion *Texas* v. *Johnson* are of controlling importance in this case as well.

Accordingly, I respectfully dissent.

## *Notes*

1. The Act replaced the then-existing federal flag-burning statute, which Congress perceived might be unconstitutional in light of *Johnson.* Former 18 U.S. C. § 700(a) prohibited "knowingly cast[ing] contempt upon any flag of the United States by publicly mutilating, defacing, defiling, burning, or trampling upon it."

2. We deal here with concededly political speech and have not occasion to pass on the validity of laws regulating commercial exploitation of the image of the United States flag. See *Texas* v. *Johnson,* 491 U.S.—,—, n. 10(1989); cf. *Halter* v. *Nebraska,* 205 U.S. 34 (1907).

---

**U.S. v. Eichman**, 496 U.S. 310 (1990) 5–4

*editor's note.*

*Opinion authors are in bold; () indicates the party of appointing president. If the party of the justice differs from that of appointing president, then the party of the justice is listed second after the slash.*

| MANORITY | CONCURRING | DISSENTING |
|---|---|---|
| **Brennan** (r/d) | | **Stevens** (r) |
| Marshall (d) | | Rehnquist (r) |
| Blackmun (r) | | White (d) |
| Scalia (r) | | O'Connor (r) |
| Kennedy (r) | | |

---

# *Legal Reasoning and Constitutionalism:*

## *Judging Classifications and Analogies Under the Equal Protection Clause—When Is It Legitimate to Classify Based on Race, Gender, or Wealth?*

*W*hen judges decide cases, and thereby make public policy, they employ legal reasoning to persuade us that they have reached the right, or at least a good, decision. The tradition of issuing written opinions articulating the legal reasoning that justifies a result is one of the judicial norms and practices that influences judicial decision-making. The norm that judges are supposed to defend their decisions using legal reasoning no doubt places some constraints on the free play of judicial policy preferences, even though the method of legal reasoning rarely determines a single correct result in any particular case.

Legal reasoning is basically a system of decision by analogy. Stare decisis, or let the decision stand, is a basic rule of legal reasoning in the American system. This means that, by and large, judges rely on precedents in deciding a case. The basic question before the judge is whether the current fact situation is sufficiently analogous to the fact situations in previous cases to require that the later case be decided in the same way as the former case. In the excerpt from Edward H. Levi's classic book, *An Introduction to Legal Reasoning*, that follows, Levi describes the three steps to legal reasoning as "similarity is seen between cases; next the rule of law inherent in the first case is announced; then the rule of law is made applicable to the second case." He adds, "Thus it cannot be said that the legal process is the application of known rules to diverse facts. Yet it is a system of rules; the rules are discovered in the process of determining similarity or difference . . . Therefore it appears that the kind of reasoning involved in the legal process is one in which the classification changes as the classification is made."[1] Law as a system of classification based in analogy can be seen in the selection from the 1996 Old Farmer's Almanac that follows Levi. In *Nix* v. *Hedden* (1893) the Supreme Court joins in this playful discussion of fruits and vegetables.

Legal reasoning, stare decisis, and the use of precedent reflect one of our conceptions of justice: that similarly situated people should be treated similarly. The question for the judge becomes which people are similarly enough situated to require that they be treated the same. In the five equal protection cases that follow, one can see the Court engaged in the process of legal reasoning. In *Brown* v. *Bd. of Education* (1954) the Court found that classifications based on race are inherently suspect and therefore unconstitutional under the equal protection clause. In essence, the Court found that in the realm of public education African-Americans and whites should be treated similarly. The question arises again in the context of affirmative action in medical school admissions in *Regents of the University of California* v. *Bakke* (1978) where the Court addresses the question of whether classifying based on race for benign and remedial purposes is like classifying based on race for segregationist purposes. In *Frontiero* v. *Richardson* (1973) the Court asks whether gender is analogous to race for the purposes of applying the equal protection clause; in other words, is discrimination against women like discrimination against African-Americans? In *San Antonio Independent School District* v. *Rodriquez* (1973) the Justices engage in a debate about the parameters and scope of "suspect classifications" under the equal protection clause. What general rules can be derived from the analogies to explain what characteristics make a classification similar enough to race to be forbidden, under what circumstance? Is wealth a "suspect class" analogous to race? The Supreme Court addresses this in the context of rejecting a challenge to property-tax-based school financing. But, it is worth noting that many state courts have relied on state constitutions to come to the opposite conclusion. Finally, a fifth circuit federal Court of Appeals decision, *Hopwood* v. *Texas*, 78 F.3d 932, cert. denied 116 S. Ct. 2581 (1996) again examines the question of whether "whiteness" is analogous to "blackness" in the context of affirmative action admissions policies.

## Notes

1.   Edward H. Levi, An *Introduction to Legal Reasoning* (University of Chicago Press, 1949), pp. 3–4.

## AN INTRODUCTION TO LEGAL REASONING
### (Chicago: University of Chicago Press, 1949) pp. 1–18.
#### *Edward Levi*

This is an attempt to describe generally the process of legal reasoning in the field of case law and in the interpretation of statutes and of the Constitution. It is important that the mechanism of legal reasoning should not be concealed by its pretense. The

From *An Introduction to Legal Reasoning* pp. 1–8 by Edward H. Levi. Copyright © 1949 by University of Chicago Press. Reprinted by permission.

pretense is that the law is a system of known rules applied by a judge; the pretense has long been under attack.[1] In an important sense legal rules are never clear, and, if a rule had to be clear before it could be imposed, society would be impossible. The mechanism accepts the differences of view and ambiguities of words. It provides for the participation of the community in resolving the ambiguity by providing a forum for the discussion of policy in the gap of ambiguity. On serious controversial questions, it makes it possible to take the first step in the direction of what otherwise would be forbidden ends. The mechanism is indispensable to peace in a community.

The basic pattern of legal reasoning is reasoning by example.[2] It is reasoning from case to case. It is a three-step process described by the doctrine of precedent in which a proposition descriptive of the first case is made into a rule of law and then applied to a next similar situation. The steps are these: similarity is seen between cases; next the rule of law inherent in the first case is announced; then the rule of law is made applicable to the second case. This is a method of reasoning necessary for the law, but it has characteristics which under other circumstances might be considered imperfections.

These characteristics become evident if the legal process is approached as though it were a method of applying general rules of law to diverse facts—in short, as though the doctrine of precedent meant that general rules, once properly determined, remained unchanged, and then were applied, albeit imperfectly, in later cases. If this were the doctrine, it would be disturbing to find that the rules change from case to case and are remade with each case. Yet this change in the rules is the indispensable dynamic quality of law. It occurs because the scope of a rule of law, and therefore its meaning, depends upon a determination of what facts will be considered similar to those present when the rule was first announced. The finding of similarity or difference is the key step in the legal process.

The determination of similarity or difference is the function of each judge. Where case law is considered, and there is no statute, he is not bound by the statement of the rule of law made by the prior judge even in the controlling case. The statement is mere dictum, and this means that the judge in the present case may find irrelevant the existence or absence of facts which prior judges thought important.[3] It is not what the prior judge intended that is of any importance; rather it is what the present judge, attempting to see the law as a fairly consistent whole, thinks should be the determining classification. In arriving at his result he will ignore what the past thought important; he will emphasize facts which prior judges would have thought made no difference. It is not alone that he could not see the law through the eyes of another, for he could at least try to do so. It is rather that the doctrine of dictum forces him to make his own decision.[4]

Thus it cannot be said that the legal process is the application of known rules to diverse facts. Yet it is a system of rules; the rules are discovered in the process of determining similarity or difference. But if attention is directed toward the finding of similarity or difference, other peculiarities appear. The problem for the law is: When will it be just to treat different cases as though they were the same? A working legal system must therefore be willing to pick out key similarities and to reason from them to the justice of applying a common classification. The existence of some facts in common brings into play the general rule. If this is really reasoning, then by common standards, thought of in terms of closed systems, it is imperfect unless some overall rule has announced that this common and ascertainable similarity is to be decisive. But no such fixed prior rule exists. It could be suggested that reasoning is not involved at all; that is, that no new insight is arrived at through a comparison of cases. But reasoning appears to be involved; the conclusion is arrived at through a process and was not immediately apparent. It seems better to say there is reasoning, but it is imperfect.[5]

Therefore it appears that the kind of reasoning involved in the legal process is one in which the classification changes as the classification is made. The rules change as the rules are applied. More important, the rules arise out of a process which, while comparing fact situations, creates the rules and then applies them. But this kind of reasoning is open to the charge that it is classifying things as equal when they are somewhat different, justifying the classification by rules made up as the reasoning or classification proceeds. In a sense all reasoning is of this type,[6] but there is an additional requirement which compels the legal process to be this way. Not only do new situations arise, but in addition peoples' wants change. The categories used in the legal process must be left ambiguous in order to permit the infusion of new ideas. And this is true even where legislation or a constitution is involved. The words used by the legislature or the constitutional convention must come to have new meanings. Furthermore, agreement on any other basis would be impossible. In this manner the laws come to express the ideas of the community and even when written in general terms, in statute or constitution, are molded for the specific case.

But attention must be paid to the process. A controversy as to whether the law is certain, unchanging, and expressed in rules, or uncertain, changing, and only a technique for deciding specific cases misses the point. It is both. Nor is it helpful to dispose of the process as a wonderful mystery possibly reflecting a higher law, by which the law can remain the same and yet change. The law forum is the most explicit demonstration of the mechanism required for a moving classification system. The folklore of law may choose to ignore the imperfections in legal reasoning,[7] but the law forum itself has taken care of them.

What does the law forum require? It requires the presentation of competing examples. The forum protects the parties and the community by making sure that the competing analogies are before the court. The rule which will be created arises out of a process in which if different things are to be treated as similar, at least the differences have been urged.[8] In this sense the parties as well as the court participate in the lawmaking. In this sense, also, lawyers represent more than the litigants.

Reasoning by example in the law is a key to many things. It indicates in part the hold which the law process has over the litigants. They have participated in the lawmaking. They are bound by something they helped to make. Moreover, the examples or analogies urged by the parties bring into the law the common ideas of the society. The ideas have their day in court, and they will have their day again. This is what makes the hearing fair, rather than any idea that the judge is completely impartial, for of course he cannot be completely so. Moreover, the hearing in a sense compels at least vicarious participation by all the citizens, for the rule which is made, even though ambiguous, will be law as to them.

Reasoning by example shows the decisive role which the common ideas of the society and the distinctions made by experts can have in shaping the law. The movement of common or expert concepts into the law may be followed. The concept is suggested in arguing difference or similarity in a brief, but it wins no approval from the court. The idea achieves standing in the society. It is suggested again to a court. The court this time reinterprets the prior case and in doing so adopts the rejected idea. In subsequent cases, the idea is given further definition and is tied to other ideas which have been accepted by courts. It is now no longer the idea which was commonly held in the society. It becomes modified in subsequent cases. Ideas first rejected but which gradually have won acceptance now push what has become a legal category out of the system or convert it into something which may be its opposite. The process is one in which the ideas of the community and of the social sciences, whether correct or not, as they win acceptance in the community, control legal decisions. Erroneous ideas, of course, have played an enormous part in shaping the law. An idea, adopted by a court, is in a superior position to influence conduct and opinion in the community; judges, after all, are rulers. And the adoption of an idea by a court reflects the power structure in the community. But reasoning by example will operate to change the idea after it has been adopted.

Moreover, reasoning by example brings into focus important similarity and difference in the interpretation of case law, statutes, and the constitution of a nation. There is a striking similarity. It is only folklore which holds that a statute if clearly written can be completely unambiguous and applied as intended to a specific case. Fortunately or otherwise, ambiguity is inevitable in both statute and constitution as well as with case law. Hence reasoning by example operates with all three. But there are important differences. What a court says is dictum, but what a legislature says is a statute. The reference of the reasoning changes. Interpretation of intention when dealing with a statute is the way of describing the attempt to compare cases on the basis of the standard thought to be common at the time the legislation was passed. While this is the attempt, it may not initially accomplish any different result than if the standard of the judge had been explicitly used. Nevertheless, the remarks of the judge are directed toward describing a category set up by the legislature. These remarks are different from ordinary dicta. They set the course of the statute, and later reasoning in subsequent cases is tied to them. As a consequence, courts are less free in applying a statute than in dealing with case law. The current rationale for this is the notion that the legislature has acquiesced by legislative silence in the prior, even though erroneous, interpretation of the court. But the change in reasoning where legislation is concerned seems an inevitable consequence of the division of function between court and legislature, and, paradoxically, a recognition also of the impossibility of determining legislative intent. The impairment of a court's freedom in interpreting legislation is reflected in frequent appeals to the constitution as a necessary justification for overruling cases even though these cases are thought to have interpreted the legislation erroneously.

Under the United States experience, contrary to what has sometimes been believed when a written constitution of a nation is involved, the court has greater freedom than it has with the application of a statute or case law. In case law, when a judge determines what the controlling similarity between the present and prior case is, the case is decided. The judge does not feel free to ignore the results of a great number of cases which he cannot explain under a remade rule. And in interpreting legislation, when the prior interpretation, even though erroneous, is determined after a comparison of facts to cover the case, the case is decided. But this is not true with a constitution. The constitution sets up the conflicting ideals of the community in certain ambiguous categories.[9] These categories bring along with them satellite concepts covering the areas of ambiguity. It is with a set of these satellite concepts that reasoning by example must work. But no satellite concept, no matter how well developed, can prevent the court from shifting its course, not only by realigning cases which impose certain restrictions, but by going beyond realignment back to the over-all ambiguous category written into the document. The constitution, in other words, permits the court to be inconsistent. The freedom is concealed either as a search for the intent of the framers or as a proper understanding of a living instrument, and sometimes as both. But this does not mean that reasoning by example has any less validity in this field.

## *Notes*

1. The controlling book is Frank, Law and the Modern Mind (1936).
2. "Clearly then to argue by example is neither like reasoning from part to whole, nor like reasoning from whole to part, but rather reasoning from part to part, when both particulars are subordinate to the same term and one of them is known. It differs from induction, because induction starting from all the particular cases proves . . . that the major term belongs to the middle and does not apply the syllogistic conclusion to the minor term, whereas argument by example does make this application and does not draw its proof from all the particular cases." Aristotle, Analytica Priora 69a (McKeon ed., 1941).
3. But cf. Goodhart, Determining the Ratio Decidendi of a Case, 40 Yale J. 161 (1930).
4. Cf. Mead, The Philosophy of the Act 81, 92–102 (1938)
5. The logical fallacy is the fallacy of the undistributed middle or the fallacy of assuming the antecedent is true because the consequent has been affirmed.
6. Dewey, Logic, The Theory of Inquiry, Ch. 6 (1938); cf. Pareto, The Mind and Society § 894 (1935); Arnold, The Folklore of Capitalism, Ch. 7 (1937).

7. "That the law can be obeyed even when it grows is often more than the legal profession itself can grasp." Cohen and Nagel, An Introduction to Logic and Scientific Method 371 (1934); see Stone, The Province and Function of Law 140–206 (1946).

8. The reasoning may take this form: A falls more appropriately in B than in C. It does so because A is more like D which is of B than it is like E which is of C. Since A is in B and B is in G (legal concept), then A is in G. But perhaps C is in G also. If so, then B is in a decisively different segment of G, because B is like H which is in G and has a different result from C.

9. Compare Myrdal, An American Dilemma, Ch. 1 (1944); Dicey, Law of the Constitution 126. 146 (9th ed. 1939).

# LAW AND THE CREATION OF CATEGORIES
### The Old Farmer's 1996 Almanac

## IS IT A FRUIT? OR IS IT A VEGETABLE? (AND DOES IT MATTER?)
### A Game of Botany, Cooking, and Common Sense by Georgia Orcutt

There was a time not so very long ago when schoolteachers and other people of authority frequently spoke of doing things "according to Hoyle." If, as a small child, you were caught misbehaving, chances are Mr. Hoyle's sense of rightness was invoked by a governing adult.

Hoyle, in fact, was an Englishman who spent a good part of his life prescribing rules and regulations for all sorts of indoor games. He died in 1769. And we sorely miss him today, as we set out to play a game that might be easier if we could simply refer to his rules to settle any disputes that might occur. The game is called "Fruit or Vegetable?"

The object of this exercise is educational in nature. As you make your choices, think about the differences between fruits and vegetables. How do they grow, what parts of the plant do you eat? Since we don't have Mr. Hoyle's rules to follow, we'll use reference books to guide us through several versions of the game. These are *The New Garden Encyclopedia* (A) and *Wyman's Gardening Encyclopedia* (B).

Now let's get started. Read through the list below and decide whether each food mentioned is a fruit or a vegetable. In the space provided to the left of each item, write V next to those that you think of as vegetables and F next to those that you think of as fruits. (Use a pencil with an eraser.)

| | | | | |
|---|---|---|---|---|
| __Apple | __Artichoke | __Asparagus | __Avocado | __ Bean (String) |
| __Beet | __Broccoli | __Brussels Sprouts | __Cabbage | __Carrot |
| __Cauliflower | __Celery | __Corn | __Cucumber | __Eggplant |
| __Grape | __Lettuce | __Onion . | __Parsnip | __Pea |
| __Peach | __Pear | __Pepper | __Plum | __Potatoe |
| __Radish | __Rasberry | __Squash | __Tomatoe | __Watermelon |

From *The Old Farmer's Almanac* by Georgia Orcutt. Copyright © 1996 by Yankee Publishing Inc., Dublin, NH. Reprinted by permission.

Now that you've categorized these familiar fruits and vegetables, let's consider several ways to judge your answers.

## THE BOTANICALLY CORRECT VERSION

If you've ever taken a botany course, you know that every part of a plant, whether fruit or vegetable, has a name. There's a science to it all, the sort of thing Mr. Hoyle would appreciate. So let's look at some definitions. "Botanically and strictly, fruit is the ripened ovary of a flower, including its contents and any closely adhering parts. Examples are cucumber, pepper, tomato, apple, plum raspberry" (see source A). Or even more to the point, fruit is the "the seed-bearing product of a plant" (source B).

According to the botanists, the parts of squash, eggplant, watermelon, cucumber, and pepper that we eat are actually very large berries, so we are correct to call them fruit. With this light to guide us, we can safely determine that avocado, string bean, grape, peach, and pear are also, of course, fruit. Corn and peas also have seeds, so we may as well include them. Maybe we ought to rename that plot out back the fruit garden.

Wait, you wail. You've never called a cucumber or a string bean or a squash a fruit in your life, and you're not about to start now. You don't *like* that version of the game.

Maybe it's time to consider fruits and vegetables from the cook's point of view.

## THE CULINARY VERSION

Let's play another way, starting with a definition for vegetable as "any plant whose edible part is used in some culinary way, as distinguished from a 'fruit,' which is used as a dessert" (source A).

Look back over that list one more time and think about how you would prepare those foods in your kitchen. What is dessert and what isn't? Surely asparagus is a vegetable, apple a fruit, avocado goes in salads so that must be a vegetable, artichokes, beans, broccoli, Brussels sprouts are surely vegetables . . . is this starting to feel better? Now carrots we bake in carrot cake, so they must be fruit. That sets us to thinking about squash pie, so we'll call squash a fruit, too.

What's that you're yelling? You want to play by some other rules? There is another possibility.

## COMMON SENSE VERSION

In the name of sportsmanship, let's consider one more way to look at fruits and vegetables. "According to L.H. Bailey, a vegetable is 'in horticultural usage, an edible herbaceous plant or part thereof that is commonly used for culinary purposes.' In common usage, the fruits of the tomato, cucumber, squash, etc., are considered as vegetables, grown with other vegetables in the home garden, although of course each one is a seed-bearing organ and hence, under strict usage of the language, might be considered a fruit" (source B). It is also, as popularly understood, any plant cultivated for its edible parts. This loose definition includes roots (beet, carrot), tubers (potato), stems (celery), leaves (lettuce), flower buds and heads (cauliflower), fruits (tomato), and seeds (peas, corn) (source A).

Looking back to the list, we can easily slip into familiar habits: artichoke, asparagus, avocado, bean, beet, broccoli, Brussels sprouts, cabbage, carrot, cauliflower, celery, corn, cucumber, eggplant, lettuce, onion parsnip, pea, pepper, potato, radish, squash, and tomato are vegetables; all the others are fruits.

In other words, if you call it a vegetable, and your neighbor calls it a vegetable, and your local grocer calls it a vegetable, then it must be a vegetable. You like the sound of this? Fine with us. And deep in our hearts, we suspect that's the best way to play, according to Hoyle.

## IN THE EYES OF THE LAW

*In 1893 the U.S. Supreme Court decided that a tomatoe was a vegetable!*

While it may seem frivolous to ponder the differences between fruits and vegetables, more than 100 years ago the tomato's status became legal fodder for the U.S. Supreme Court in the case of Nix v. Hedden.

In 1887 a businessman importing tomatoes from the West Indies tried to sue the Port of New York to recover back duties he'd been forced to pay to bring his produce into the country. He was, in fact, trying to elude a tariff imposed on vegetables by claiming that tomatoes were fruits. (Fruits were not subject to the tariff.)

He fought hard, and his case spiraled up through the judicial system until it reached the Supreme Court in 1893. Definitions of fruits and vegetables from several dictionaries were read at the trial, and two professional fruit and vegetable sellers who served as witnesses for the plaintiff were asked to reflect on the matter. The Court's decision: Tomatoes are "vegetables" and not "fruit" within the meaning of the Tariff Act of March 3, 1883.

In the opinion of the court, "Botanically speaking, tomatoes are the fruit of a vine, just as are cucumbers, squashes, beans, and peas. But in the common language of the people, whether sellers or consumers of provisions, all these are vegetables, which are grown in kitchen gardens, and which whether eaten cooked or raw, are, like potatoes, carrots, parsnips, turnips, beets, cauliflower, cabbage, celery, and lettuce, usually served at dinner in, with, or after the soup, fish, or meats which constitute the principal part of the repast, and not, like fruits generally, as dessert."

# Nix v. Hedden

## [304 U.S. 304 (1893)]

## Error to the Circuit Court of the United States for the Southern District of New York

### No. 137. Submitted April 24, 1893. —Decided May 10, 1893.

This was an action, brought February 4, 1887, against the collector of the port of New York, to recover back duties, paid under protest, on tomatoes imported by the plaintiff from the West Indies in the spring of 1886. . . .

*Mr. Edwin B. Smith* for plaintiff in error.

*Mr. Assistant Attorney General Maury* for defendant in error.

Mr. Justice Gray, after stating the case, delivered the opinion of the court.

The single question in this case is whether tomatoes, considered as provisions, are to be classed as "vegetables" or as "fruit," within the meaning of the Tariff Act of 1883.

The only witnesses called at the trial testified that neither "vegetables" nor "fruit" had any special meaning in trade or commerce, different from that given in the dictionaries; and that they had the same meaning in trade to-day that they had in March, 1883.

The passages cited from the dictionaries define the word "fruit" as the seed of plants, or that part of plants which contains the seed, and especially the juicy, pulpy products of certain plants, covering and containing the seed. These definitions have no tendency to show that tomatoes are "fruit," as distinguished from "vegetables," in common speech, or within the meaning of the Tariff Act.

There being no evidence that the words "fruit" and "vegetables" have acquired any special meaning in trade or commerce, they must receive their ordinary meaning. Of that meaning the court is bound to take judicial notice, as it does in regard to all words in our own tongue; and upon such a question dictionaries are admitted, not as evidence, but only as aids to the memory and understanding of the court.

Botanically speaking, tomatoes are the fruit of a vine, just as are cucumbers, squashes, beans and peas. But in the common language of the people, whether sellers or consumers of provisions, all these are vegetables, which are grown in kitchen gardens, and which, whether eaten cooked or raw, are, like potatoes, carrots, parsnips, turnips, beets, cauliflower, cabbage, celery and lettuce, usually served at dinner in, with or after the soup, fish or meats which constitute the principal part of the repast, and not, like fruits generally, as dessert.

The attempt to class tomatoes with fruit is not unlike a recent attempt to class beans as seeds, of which Mr. Justice Bradley, speaking for this court, said: "We do not see why they be classified as seeds, any more than walnuts should be so classified. Both are seeds in the language of botany or natural history, but not in commerce nor in common parlance. On the other hand, in speaking generally of provisions, beans may well be included under the term 'vegetables.' As an article of food on our tables, whether baked or boiled, or forming the basis of soup, they are used as a vegetable, as well when ripe as when green. This is the principal use to which they are put. Beyond the common knowledge of which we have on this subject, very little evidence is necessary, or can be produced." *Robertson* v *Salomon*, 130 U.S. 412, 414.

*Judgment affirmed.*

---

**Nix v. Hedden**, 304 U.S. 304 (1893) 9–0
*editor's note.*
*Opinion authors are in bold; () indicates the party of appointing president. If the party of the justice differs from that of appointing president, then the party of the justice is listed second after the slash.*

| MAJORITY | CONCURRING | DISSENTING |
|---|---|---|
| **Gray** (r) | | |
| Fuller (d) | | |
| Blatchford | | |
| Lamar (d) | | |
| Brown (r) | | |
| Shiras (r) | | |
| Brewer (r) | | |
| Harlan (r) | | |
| Field (r/d) | | |

# Brown et al. v. Board of Education of Topeka et al.

## 347 U.S. 483

## No. 1. Appeal from the United States District Court for the District of Kansas.*

Argued December 9, 1952.—Reargued December 8, 1953.—
Decided May 17, 1954.

### Syllabus of Decision

Segregation of white and Negro children in the public schools of a State solely on the basis of race, pursuant to state laws permitting or requiring such segregation, denies to Negro children the equal protection of the laws guaranteed by the Fourteenth Amendment even though the physical facilities and other "tangible" factors of white and Negro schools may be equal.

(a) The history of the Fourteenth Amendment is inconclusive as to its intended effect on public education.
(b) The question presented in these cases must be determined, not on the basis of conditions existing when the Fourteenth Amendment was adopted, but in the light of the full development of public education and its present place in American life throughout the Nation.
(c) Where a State has undertaken to provide an opportunity for an education in its public schools, such an opportunity is a right which must be made available to all on equal terms.
(d) Segregation of children in public schools solely on the basis of race deprives children of the minority group of equal educational opportunities, even though the physical facilities and other "tangible" factors may be equal.
(e) The "separate but equal" doctrine adopted in *Plessy* v. *Ferguson*, 163 U.S. 537, has no place in the field of public education.
(f) The cases are restored to the docket for further argument on specified questions relating to the forms of the decrees.

*Robert L. Carter* argued the cause for appellants in No. 1 on the original argument and on the reargument. *Thurgood Marshall* argued the cause for appellants in No. 2 on the original argument and *Spottswood W. Robinson, III,* for appellants in No. 4 on the original argument, and both argued the causes for appellants in Nos. 2 and 4 on the reargument. *Louis L. Redding* and *Jack Greenberg* argued the cause for respondents in No. 10 on the original argument and *Jack Greenberg* and *Thurgood Marshall* on the reargument.

On the briefs were *Robert L. Carter, Thurgood Marshall, Spottswood W. Robinson, III, Louis L. Redding, Jack Greenberg, George E.C. Hayes, William R. Ming, Jr., Constance Baker Motley, James M. Nabrit, Jr., Charles S. Scott, Frank D. Reeves, Harold R. Boulware* and *Oliver W. Hill* for appellants in Nos. 1, 2 and 4 and respondents in No. 10; *George M. Johnson* for appellants in Nos. 1, 2 and 4; and *Loren Miller* for appellants in Nos. 2 and 4. *Arthur D. Shores* and *A. T. Walden* were on the Statement as to jurisdiction and a brief opposing a Motion to Dismiss or Affirm in No. 2.

*Paul E. Wilson,* Assistant Attorney General of Kansas, argued the cause for appellees in No. 1 on the original argument and on the reargument. With him on the briefs was *Harold R. Fatzer,* Attorney General.

*John W. Davis* argued the cause for appellees in No. 2 on the original argument and for appellees in Nos. 2 and 4 on the reargument. With him on the briefs in No. 2 were *T. C. Callison,* Attorney General of South Carolina, *Robert McC. Figg, Jr., S.E. Rogers, William R. Meagher* and *Taggart Whipple.*

*J. Lindsay Almond, Jr.,* Attorney General of Virginia, and *T. Justin Moore* argued the cause for appellees in No. 4 on the original argument and for appellees in Nos. 2 and 4 on the reargument. On the briefs in No. 4 were *J. Lindsay Almond, Jr.,* Attorney General, and *Henry T. Wickham,* Special Assistant Attorney General, for the State of Virginia, and *T. Justin Moore, Archibald G. Robertson, John W. Riely* and *T. Justin Moore, Jr.* for the Prince Edward County School Authorities, appellees.

*H. Albert Young,* Attorney General of Delaware, argued the cause for petitioners in No. 10 on the original argument and on the reargument. With him on the briefs was *Louis J. Finger,* Special Deputy Attorney General.

By special leave of Court, *Assistant Attorney General Rankin,* argued the cause for the United States on the reargument, as *amicus curiae,* urging reversal in Nos. 1, 2 and 4 and affirmance in No. 10. With him on the brief were *Attorney General Brownell, Philip Elman, Leon Ulman, William J. Lamont* and *M. Magdelena Schoch. James P. McGranery,* then Attorney General, and *Philip Elman* filed a brief for the United States on the original argument, as *amicus curiae,* urging reversal in Nos. 1, 2 and 4 and affirmance in No. 10.

Briefs of *amici curiae* supporting appellants in No. 1 were filed by *Shad Polier, Will Maslow* and *Joseph B. Robison* for the American Jewish Congress; by *Edwin J. Lukas, Arnold Forster, Arthur Garfield Hays, Frank E. Karelsen, Leonard Haas, Saburo Kido* and *Theodore Leskes* for the American Civil Liberties Union et al.; and by *John Ligtenberg* and

*Selma M. Borchardt* for the American Federation of Teachers. Briefs of *amici curiae* supporting appellants in No. 1 and respondents in No. 10 were filed by *Arthur J. Goldberg* and *Thomas E. Harris* for the Congress of Industrial Organizations and by *Phineas Indritz* for the American Veterans Committee, Inc.

MR. CHIEF JUSTICE WARREN delivered the opinion of the Court.

These cases come to us from the States of Kansas, South Carolina, Virginia, and Delaware. They are premised on different facts and different local conditions, but a common legal question justifies their consideration together in this consolidated opinion.[1]

In each of the cases, minors of the Negro race, through their legal representatives, seek the aid of the courts in obtaining admission to the public schools of their community on a nonsegregated basis. In each instance, they had been denied admission to schools attended by white children under laws requiring or permitting segregation according to race. This segregation was alleged to deprive the plaintiffs of the equal protection of the laws under the Fourteenth Amendment. In each of the cases other than the Delaware case, a three-judge federal district court denied relief to the plaintiffs on the so-called "separate but equal" doctrine announced by this Court in *Plessy* v. *Ferguson*, 163 U.S. 537 [1896]. Under that doctrine, equality of treatment is accorded when the races are provided substantially equal facilities, even though these facilities be separate. In the Delaware case, the Supreme Court of Delaware adhered to that doctrine, but ordered that the plaintiffs be admitted to the white schools because of their superiority to the Negro schools.

The plaintiffs contend that segregated public schools are not "equal" and cannot be made "equal," and that hence they are deprived of the equal protection of the laws. Because of the obvious importance of the question presented, the Court took jurisdiction.[2] Argument was heard in the 1952 Term, and reargument was heard this Term on certain questions propounded by the Court.[3]

Reargument was largely devoted to the circumstances surrounding the adoption of the Fourteenth Amendment in 1868. It covered exhaustively consideration of the Amendment in Congress, ratification by the states, then existing practices in racial segregation, and the views of proponents and opponents of the Amendment. This discussion and our own investigation convince us that, although these sources cast some light, it is not enough to resolve the problem with which we are faced. At best, they are inconclusive. The most avid proponents of the post-War Amendments undoubtedly intended them to remove all legal distinctions among "all persons born or naturalized in the United States." Their opponents, just as certainly, were antagonistic to both the letter and the spirit of the Amendments and wished them to have the most limited effect. What others in Congress and the state legislatures had in mind cannot be determined with any degree of certainty.

An additional reason for the inconclusive nature of the Amendment's history, with respect to segregated schools, is the status of public education at that time.[4] In the South, the movement toward free common schools, supported by general taxation, had not yet taken hold. Education of white children was largely in the hands of private groups. Education of Negroes was almost nonexistent, and practically all of the race were illiterate. In fact, any education of Negroes was forbidden by law in some states. Today, in contrast, many Negroes have achieved outstanding success in the arts and sciences as well as in the business and professional world. It is true that public school education at the time of the Amendment had advanced further in the North, but the effect of the Amendment on Northern States was generally ignored in the congressional debates. Even in the North, the conditions of public education did not approximate those existing today. The curriculum was usually rudimentary; ungraded schools were common in rural areas; the school term was but three months a year in many states; and compulsory school attendance was virtually unknown. As a consequence, it is not surprising that there should be so little in the history of the Fourteenth Amendment relating to its intended effect on public education.

In the first cases in this Court construing the Fourteenth Amendment, decided shortly after its adoption, the Court interpreted it as proscribing all state-imposed discriminations against the Negro race.[5] The doctrine of "separate but equal" did not make its appearance in this Court until 1896 in the case of *Plessy* v. *Ferguson* [1896], involving not education but transportation.[6] American courts have since labored with the doctrine for over half a century. In this Court, there have been six cases involving the "separate but equal" doctrine in the field of public education.[7] In *Cumming* v. *County Board of Education*, 175 U.S. 528 [1899], and *Gong Lum* v. *Rice,* 275 U.S. 78 [1927], the validity of the doctrine itself was not challenged.[8] In more recent cases, all on the graduate school level, inequality was found in that specific benefits enjoyed by white students were denied to Negro students of the same educational qualifications. *Missouri ex rel. Gaines* v. *Canada,* 305 U.S. 337 [1938], *Sipuel* v. *Oklahoma,* 332 U.S. 631 [1948], *Sweatt* v. *Painter,* 339 U.S. 629 [1950], *McLaurin* v. *Oklahoma State Regents,* 339 U.S. 637 [1950]. In none of these cases was it necessary to re-examine the doctrine to grant relief to the Negro plaintiff. And in *Sweatt* v. *Painter, supra,* the Court expressly reserved decision on the question whether *Plessy* v. *Ferguson* should be held inapplicable to public education.

In the instant cases, that question is directly presented. Here, unlike *Sweatt* v. *Painter,* there are findings below that the Negro and white schools involved have been equalized, or are being equalized, with respect to buildings, curricula, qualifications and salaries of teachers, and other "tangible" factors.[9] Our decision, therefore, cannot turn on merely a comparison of these tangible factors in the Negro and white schools involved in each of the cases. We must look instead to the effect of segregation itself on public education.

In approaching this problem, we cannot turn the clock back to 1868 when the Amendment was adopted, or even to 1896 when *Plessy* v. *Ferguson* was written. We must consider public education in the light of its full development and its present place in American life throughout the Nation. Only in this way can it be determined if segregation in public schools deprives these plaintiffs of the equal protection of the laws.

Today, education is perhaps the most important function of state and local governments. Compulsory school attendance laws and the great expenditures for education both demonstrate our recognition of the importance of education to our democratic society. It is required in the performance of our most basic public responsibilities, even service in the armed forces. It is the very foundation of good citizenship. Today it is a principal instrument in awakening the child to cultural values, in preparing him for later professional training, and in helping him to adjust normally to his environment. In these days, it is doubtful that any child may reasonably be expected to succeed in life if he is denied the opportunity of an education. Such an opportunity, where the state has undertaken to provide it, is a right which must be made available to all on equal terms.

We come then to the question presented: Does segregation of children in public schools solely on the basis of race, even though the physical facilities and other "tangible" factors may be equal, deprive the children of the minority group of equal educational opportunities? We believe that it does.

In *Sweatt* v. *Painter*, in finding that a segregated law school for Negroes could not provide them equal educational opportunities, this Court relied in large part on "those qualities which are incapable of objective measurement but which make for greatness in a law school." In *McLaurin* v. *Oklahoma State Regents*, the Court, in requiring that a Negro admitted to a white graduate school be treated like all other students, again resorted to intangible considerations: ". . . his ability to study, to engage in discussions and exchange views with other students, and, in general, to learn his profession." Such considerations apply with added force to children in grade and high schools. To separate them from others of similar age and qualifications solely because of their race generates a feeling of inferiority as to their status in the community that may affect their hearts and minds in a way unlikely ever to be undone. The effect of this separation on their educational opportunities was well stated by a finding in the Kansas case by a court which nevertheless felt compelled to rule against the Negro plaintiffs:

Segregation of white and colored children in public schools has a detrimental effect upon the colored children. The impact is greater when it has the sanction of the law; for the policy of separating the races is usually interpreted as denoting the inferiority of the negro group. A sense of inferiority affects the motivation of a child to learn. Segregation with the sanction of law, therefore, has a tendency to [retard] the educational and mental development of negro children and to deprive them of some of the benefits they would receive in a racial[ly] integrated school System.[10]

Whatever may have been the extent of psychological knowledge at the time of *Plessy* v. *Ferguson,* this finding is amply supported by modern authority.[11] Any language in *Plessy* v. *Ferguson* contrary to this finding is rejected.

We conclude that in the field of public education the doctrine of "separate but equal" has no place. Separate educational facilities are inherently unequal. Therefore, we hold that the plaintiffs and others similarly situated for whom the actions have been brought are, by reason of the segregation complained of, deprived of the equal protection of the laws guaranteed by the Fourteenth Amendment. This disposition makes unnecessary any discussion whether such segregation also violates the Due Process Clause of the Fourteenth Amendment.[12]

Because these are class actions, because of the wide applicability of this decision, and because of the great variety of local conditions, the formulation of decrees in these cases presents problems of considerable complexity. On reargument, the consideration of appropriate relief was necessarily subordinated to the primary question—the constitutionality of segregation in public education. We have now announced that such segregation is a denial of the equal protection of the laws. In order that we may have the full assistance of the parties in formulating decrees, the cases will be restored to the docket, and the parties are requested to present further argument on Questions 4 and 5 previously propounded by the Court for the reargument this Term.[13] The Attorney General of the United States is again invited to participate. The Attorneys General of the states requiring or permitting segregation in public education will also be permitted to appear as *amici curiae* upon request to do so by September 15, 1954, and submission of briefs by October 1, 1954.[14]

*It is so ordered.*

## Notes

\* Together with No. 2, *Briggs et al.* v. *Elliott et al.*, on appeal from the United States District Court for the Eastern District of South Carolina, argued December 9–10, 1952, reargued December 7–8, 1953; No. 4, *Davis et al.* v. *County School Board of Prince Edward County, Virginia, et al.*, on appeal from the United States District Court for the Eastern District of Virginia, argued December 10, 1952, reargued December 7–8, 1953; and No. 10, *Gebhart et al.* v. *Belton* *et al.,* on certiorari to the Supreme Court of Delaware, argued December 11, 1952, reargued December 9, 1953.

1.   In the Kansas case, *Brown* v. *Board of Education,* the plaintiffs are Negro children of elementary school age residing in Topeka. They brought this action in the United States District Court for the District of Kansas to enjoin enforcement of a Kansas statute which permits, but does not require, cities of more than 15,000 population to maintain separate school facilities for Negro and white students. Kan. Gen. Stat. § 72–1724 (1949). Pursuant to that authority, the Topeka Board of Education elected to establish segregated elementary schools. Other public schools in the community, however, are operated on a nonsegregated basis. The three-judge District Court, convened under 28 U.S.C. §§ 2281 and 2284, found that segregation in public education has a detrimental effect upon Negro children, but denied relief on the ground that the Negro and white schools were substantially equal with respect to buildings, transportation, curricula, and educational qualifications of teachers. 98 F. Supp. 797. The case is here on direct appeal under 28 U.S.C. § 1253.

In the South Carolina case, *Briggs* v. *Elliott,* the plaintiffs are Negro children of both elementary and high school age residing in Clarendon County. They brought this action in the United States District Court for the Eastern District of South Carolina to enjoin enforcement of provisions in the state constitution and statutory code which require the segregation of Negroes and whites in public schools. S.C. Const., Art. XI, § 7; S.C. Code § 5377 (1942). The three-judge District Court, convened under 28 U.S.C. §§ 2281 and 2284, denied the requested relief. The court found that the Negro schools were inferior to the white schools and ordered the defendants to begin immediately to equalize the facilities. But the court sustained the validity of the contested provisions and denied the plaintiffs admission to the white schools during the equalization program. 98 F. Supp. 529. This Court vacated the District Court's judgment and remanded the case for the purpose of obtaining the court's views on a report filed by the defendants concerning the progress made in the equalization program. 342 U.S. 350. On remand, the District Court found that substantial equality had been achieved except for buildings and that the defendants were proceeding to rectify this inequality as well. 103 F. Supp. 920. The case is again here on direct appeal under 28 U.S.C. § 1253.

In the Virginia case, *Davis* v. *County School Board,* the plaintiffs are Negro children of high school age residing in Prince Edward County. They brought this action in the United States District Court for the Eastern District of Virginia to enjoin enforcement of provisions in the state constitution and statutory code which require the segregation of Negroes and whites in public schools. Va. Const., § 140; Va. Code § 22–221 (1950). The three-judge District Court, convened under 28 U.S.C. §§ 2281 and 2284, denied the requested relief. The court found the Negro school inferior in physical plant, curricula, and transportation, and ordered the defendants forthwith to provide substantially equal curricula and transportation and to "proceed with all reasonable diligence and dispatch to remove" the inequality in physical plant. But, as in the South Carolina case, the court sustained the validity of the contested provisions and denied the plaintiffs admission to the white schools during the equalization program. 103 F. Supp. 337. The case is here on direct appeal under 28 U.S.C. § 1253.

In the Delaware case, *Gebhart* v. *Belton,* the plaintiffs are Negro children of both elementary and high school age residing in New Castle County. They brought this action in the

Delaware Court of Chancery to enjoin enforcement of provisions in the state constitution and statutory code which require the segregation of Negroes and whites in public schools. Del. Const., Art. X, § 2; Del. Rev. Code § 2631 (1935). The Chancellor gave judgment for the plaintiffs and ordered their immediate admission to schools previously attended only by white children, on the ground that the Negro schools were inferior with respect to teacher training, pupil-teacher ratio, extracurricular activities, physical plant, and time and distance involved in travel. 87 A. 2d 862. The Chancellor also found that segregation itself results in an inferior education for Negro children (see note 10, *infra*), but did not rest his decision on that ground. *Id.*, at 865. The Chancellor's decree was affirmed by the Supreme Court of Delaware, which intimated, however, that the defendants might be able to obtain a modification of the decree after equalization of the Negro and white schools had been accomplished. 91 A. 2d 137, 152. The defendants, contending only that the Delaware courts had erred in ordering the immediate admission of the Negro plaintiffs to the white schools, applied to this Court for certiorari. The writ was granted, 344 U.S. 891. The plaintiffs, who were successful below, did not submit a cross-petition.

2.  344 U.S. 1, 141, 89 1.

3.  345 U.S. 972. The Attorney General of the United States participated both Terms as *amicus curiae*.

4.  For a general study of the development of public education prior to the Amendment, see Butts and Cremin, A History of Education in American Culture (1953), Pts. I, II; Cubberley, Public Education in the United States (1934 ed.), cc. II–XII. School practices current at the time of the adoption of the Fourteenth Amendment are described in Butts and Cremin, *supra,* at 269–275; Cubberley, *supra,* at 288–339, 408–431; Knight, Public Education in the South (1922), cc. VIII, IX. See also H. Ex. Doc. No. 315, 41st Cong., 2d Sess. (1871). Although the demand for free public schools followed substantially the same pattern in both the North and the South, the development in the South did not begin to gain momentum until about 1850, some twenty years after that in the North. The reasons for the somewhat slower development in the South (*e. g.,* the rural character of the South and the different regional attitudes toward state assistance) are well explained in Cubberley, *supra,* at 408–423. In the country as a whole, but particularly in the South, the War virtually stopped all progress in public education. *Id.*, at 427–428. The low status of Negro education in all sections of the country, both before and immediately after the War, is described in Beale, A History of Freedom of Teaching in American Schools (1941), 112–132, 175–195. Compulsory school attendance laws were not generally adopted until after the ratification of the Fourteenth Amendment, and it was not until 1918 that such laws were in force in all the states. Cubberley, *supra,* at 563–565.

5.  *Slaughter House Cases*, 16 Wall. 36, 67–72 (1873); *Strauder* v. *West Virginia*, 100 U.S. 303, 307–308 (1880):

    "It ordains that no State shall deprive any person of life, liberty, or property, without due process of law, or deny to any person within its jurisdiction the equal protection of the laws. What is this but declaring that the law in the States shall be the same for the black as for the white; that all persons, whether colored or white, shall stand equal before the laws of the States, and, in regard to the colored race, for whose protection the amendment was primarily designed, that no discrimination shall be made against them by law because of their color? The words of the amendment, it is true, are prohibitory, but they contain a necessary implication of a positive immunity, or right, most valuable to the colored race,—the right, to exemption from unfriendly legislation against them distinctively as colored,—exemption from legal discriminations, implying inferiority in civil society, lessening the security of their enjoyment of the rights which others enjoy, and discriminations which are steps towards reducing them to the condition of a subject race."

See also *Virginia* v. *Rives*, 100 U.S. 313, 318 (1880); *Ex parte Virginia*, 100 U.S. 339, 344–345 (1880).

6. The doctrine apparently originated in *Roberts* v. *City of Boston*, 59 Mass. 198, 206 (1850), upholding school segregation against attack as being violative of a state constitutional guarantee of equality. Segregation in Boston public schools was eliminated in 1855. Mass. Acts 1855, c. 256. But elsewhere in the North segregation in public education has persisted in some communities until recent years. It is apparent that such segregation has long been a nationwide problem, not merely one of sectional concern.

7. See also *Berea College* v. *Kentucky*, 211 U.S. 45 (1908).

8. In the *Cumming* case, Negro taxpayers sought an injunction requiring the defendant school board to discontinue the operation of a high school for white children until the board resumed operation of a high school for Negro children. Similarly, in the *Gong Lum* case, the plaintiff, a child of Chinese descent, contended only that state authorities had misapplied the doctrine by classifying him with Negro children and requiring him to attend a Negro school.

9. In the Kansas case, the court below found substantial equality as to all such factors. 98 F. Supp. 797, 798. In the South Carolina case, the court below found that the defendants were proceeding "promptly and in good faith to comply with the court's decree." 103 F. Supp. 920, 921. In the Virginia case, the court below noted that the equalization program was already "afoot and progressing" (103 F. Supp. 337, 341); since then, we have been advised, in the Virginia Attorney General's brief on reargument, that the program has now been completed. In the Delaware case, the court below similarly noted that the state's equalization program was well under way. 91 A. 2d 137, 149.

10. A similar finding was made in the Delaware case: "I conclude from the testimony that in our Delaware society, State-imposed segregation in education itself results in the Negro children, as a class, receiving educational opportunities which are substantially inferior to those available to white children otherwise similarly situated." 87 A. 2d 862, 865.

11. K. B. Clark, Effect of Prejudice and Discrimination on Personality Development (Midcentury White House Conference on Children and Youth, 1950); Witmer and Kotinsky, Personality in the Making (1952), c. VI; Deutscher and Chein, The Psychological Effects of Enforced Segregation: A Survey of Social Science Opinion, 26 J. Psychol. 259 (1948); Chein, What are the Psychological Effects of Segregation Under Conditions of Equal Facilities?, 3 Int. J. Opinion and Attitude Res. 229 (1949); Brameld, Educational Costs, in Discrimination and National Welfare (MacIver, ed., 1949), 44–48; Frazier, The Negro in the United States (1949), 674–681. And see generally Myrdal, An American Dilemma (1944).

12. See *Bolling* v. *Sharpe, post,* p. 497, concerning the Due Process Clause of the Fifth Amendment.

13. "4. Assuming it is decided that segregation in public schools violates the Fourteenth Amendment

    "(a) would a decree necessarily follow providing that, within the limits set by normal geographic school districting, Negro children should forthwith be admitted to schools of their choice, or

    "(b) may this Court, in the exercise of its equity powers, permit an effective gradual adjustment to be brought about from existing segregated systems to a system not based on color distinctions?

    "5. On the assumption on which questions 4 (a) and (b) are based, and assuming further that this Court will exercise its equity powers to the end described in question 4 (b),

    "(a) should this Court formulate detailed decrees in these cases;

    "(b) if so, what specific issues should the decrees reach;

    "(c) should this Court appoint a special master to hear evidence with a view to recommending specific terms for such decrees;

    "(d) should this Court remand to the courts of first instance with directions to frame decrees in these cases, and if so what general directions should the decrees of this Court include and what procedures should the courts of first instance follow in arriving at the specific terms of more detailed decrees?"

14. See Rule 42, Revised Rules of this Court (effective July 1, 1954).

---

**Brown v. Bd. of Education**, 347 U.S. 483 (1954) 9–0
editor's note
*Opinion authors are in bold; () indicates the party of apointing president. If the party of the justice differs from that of appointing president, then the party of the justice is listed second after the slash.*

| MAJORITY | CONCURRING | DISSENTING |
|---|---|---|
| **Warren** (r) | | |
| Black (d) | | |
| Reed (d) | | |
| Frankfurter (d/1) | | |
| Douglas (d) | | |
| Jackson (d) | | |
| Burton (d) | | |
| Clark (d) | | |
| Minton (d) | | |

# Regents of the University of California v. Bakke

## 438 U.S. 265

## Certiorari to the Supreme Court of California

No. 76811. Argued October 12, 1977—Decided June 28, 1978.

## Syllabus of Decision

The Medical School of the University of California at Davis (hereinafter Davis) had two admissions programs for the entering class of 100 students—the regular admissions program and the special admissions program. Under the regular procedure, candidates whose overall undergraduate grade point averages fell below 2.5 on a scale of 4.0 were summarily rejected. About one out of six applicants was then given an interview, following which he was rated on a scale of 1 to 100 by each of the committee members (five in 1973 and six in 1974), his rating based on the interviewers' summaries, his overall grade point average, his science courses grade point average, his Medical College Admissions Test (MCAT) scores, letters of recommendations, extracurricular activities, and other biographical data, all of which resulted in a total "benchmark score." The full admissions committee then made offers of admission on the basis of their review of the applicant's file and his score, considering and acting upon applications as they were received. The committee chairman was responsible for placing names on a waiting list and had discretion to include persons with "special skills." A separate committee, a majority of whom were members of minority groups, operated the special admissions program. The 1973 and 1974 application forms, respectively, asked candidates whether they wished to be considered as "economically and/or educationally disadvantaged" applicants and members of a "minority group" (blacks, Chicanos, Asians, American Indians). If an applicant of a minority group was found to be "disadvantaged," he would be rated in a manner similar to the one employed by the general admissions committee. Special candidates, however, did not have to meet the 2.5 grade point cutoff and were not ranked against candidates in the general admissions process. About one-fifth of the special applicants were invited for interviews in 1973 and 1974, following which they were given benchmark scores, and the top choices were then given to the general admissions committee which could reject special candidates for failure to meet course requirements or other specific deficiencies. The special committee continued to recommend candidates until 16 special admission selections had been made. During a four-year period 63 minority students were admitted to Davis under the special program and 44 under the general program. No disadvantaged whites were admitted under the special program, though many applied. Respondent, a white male, applied to Davis in 1973 and 1974, in both years being considered only under the general admissions program. Though he had a 468 out of 500 score in 1973, he was rejected since no general applicants with scores less than 470 were being accepted after respondent's application, which was filed late in the year, had been processed and completed. At that time four special admission slots were still unfilled. In 1974 respondent applied early, and though he had a total score of 549 out of 600, he was again rejected. In neither year was his name placed on the discretionary waiting list. In both years special applicants were admitted with significantly lower scores than respondent's. After his second rejection, respondent filed this action in state court for mandatory, injunctive, and declaratory relief to compel his admission to Davis, alleging that the special admissions program operated to exclude him on the basis of his race in violation of the Equal Protection Clause of the Fourteenth Amendment, a provision of the California Constitution, and § 601 of Title VI of the Civil Rights Act of 1964, which provides, *inter alia* that no person shall on the ground of race or color be excluded from participating in any program receiving federal financial assistance. Petitioner cross-claimed for a declaration that the special program operated as a racial quota, because minority applicants in that program were rated only against one another, and 16 places in the class of 100 were reserved for them. Declaring that petitioner could not take race into account in making admissions decisions, the program was held to violate the Federal and State Constitutions and Title VI. Respondent's admission was not ordered, however, for lack of proof that he would have been admitted but for the special program. The California Supreme Court, applying a strict-scrutiny standard, concluded that the special admissions program was not the least restrictive means of achieving the goals of the admittedly compelling state interests of integrating the medical profession and increasing the number of doctors willing to serve minority patients. Without passing on the state constitutional or federal statutory grounds the court held that petitioner's special admissions program violated the Equal Protection Clause. Since petitioner could not satisfy its burden of demonstrating that respondent, absent the special program, would not have been admitted, the court ordered his admission to Davis.

Held: The judgment below is affirmed insofar as it orders respondent's admission to Davis and invalidates petitioner's special admissions program, but is reversed insofar as it prohibits petitioner from taking race into account as a factor in its future admission decisions.

18 Cal. 3d 34, 553 P. 2d 1152, affirmed in part and reversed in part.

*Archibald Cox* argued the cause for petitioner. With him on the briefs were *Paul J. Mishkin, Jack B. Owens,* and *Donald L. Reidhaar.*

*Reynold H. Colvin* argued the cause and filed briefs for respondent.

*Solicitor General McCree* argued the cause for the United States as *amicus curiae.* With him on the briefs were *Attorney General Bell, Assistant Attorney General Days, Deputy Solicitor General Wallace, Brian K. Landsberg, Jessica Dunsay Silver, Mariam R. Eisenstein,* and *Vincent F. O'Rourke.* *

MR. JUSTICE POWELL announced the judgment of the Court.

For the reasons stated in the following opinion, I believe that so much of the judgment of the California court as holds petitioner's special admissions program unlawful and directs that respondent be admitted to the Medical School must be affirmed. For the reasons expressed in a separate opinion, my Brothers THE CHIEF JUSTICE, MR. JUSTICE STEWART, MR. JUSTICE REHNQUIST, AND MR. JUSTICE STEVENS concur in this judgment.

I also conclude for the reasons stated in the following opinion that the portion of the court's judgment enjoining petitioner from according any consideration to race in its admissions process must be reversed. For reasons expressed in separate opinions, my Brothers MR. JUSTICE BRENNAN, MR. JUSTICE WHITE, MR. JUSTICE MARSHALL, AND MR. JUSTICE BLACKMUN concur in this judgment.

*Affirmed in part and reversed in part.*

— I —

The Medical School of the University of California at Davis opened in 1968 with an entering class of 50 students. In 1971, the size of the entering class was increased to 100 students, a level at which it remains. No admissions program for disadvantaged or minority students existed when the school opened, and the first class contained three Asians but no blacks, no Mexican-Americans, and no American Indians. Over the next two years, the faculty devised a special admissions program to increase the representation of "disadvantaged" students in each Medical School Class. The special program consisted of a separate admissions system operating in coordination with the regular admissions process.

From the year of the increase in class size 1971—through 1974, the special program resulted in the admission of 21 black students, 30 Mexican-Americans, and 12 Asians, for a total of 63 minority students. Over the same period, the regular admissions program produced 1 black, 6 Mexican-Americans, and 37 Asians, for a total of 44 minority students. Although disadvantaged whites applied to the special program in large numbers, none received an offer of admission through that process. Indeed, in 1974, at least, the special committee explicitly considered only "disadvantaged" special applicants who were members of one of the designated minority groups. Record 171.

Allan Bakke is a white male who applied to the Davis Medical School in both 1973 and 1974.

After the second rejection, Bakke filed the instant suit in the Superior Court of California.

En route to this crucial battle over the scope of judicial review, the parties fight a sharp preliminary action over the proper characterization of the special admissions program. Petitioner prefers to view it as establishing a "goal" of minority representation in the Medical School. Respondent, echoing the courts below, labels it a racial quota.[3]

This semantic distinction is beside the point: The special admissions program is undeniably a classification based on race and ethnic background. To the extent that there existed a pool of at least minimally qualified minority applicants to fill the 16 special admissions seats, white applicants could compete only for 84 seats in the entering class, rather than the 100 open to minority applicants. Whether this limitation is described as a quota or a goal, it is a line drawn on the basis of race and ethnic status.

The guarantees of the Fourteenth Amendment extend to all persons. Its language is explicit: "No State shall . . . deny to any person within its jurisdiction the equal protection of the laws." It is settled beyond question that the "rights created by the first section of the Fourteenth Amendment are, by its terms, guaranteed to the individual. The rights established are personal rights." *Shelley* v. *Kraemer*, supra, at 22. Accord, *Missouri ex rel. Gaines* v. *Canada*, supra, at 351; *McCabe* v. *Atchinson, T. & S. F. R. Co.*, 235 U.S. 151, 161–162 (1914). The guarantee of equal protection cannot mean one thing when applied to one individual and something else when applied to a person of another color. If both are not accorded the same protection, then it is not equal.

Nevertheless, petitioner argues that the court below erred in applying strict scrutiny to the special admissions program because white males, such as respondent, are not a "discrete and insular minority" requiring extraordinary protection from the majoritarian political process. *Carolene Products Co.*, supra, at 152–153, n. 4. This rationale, however, has never been invoked in our decisions as a prerequisite to subjecting racial or ethnic distinctions to strict scrutiny. Nor has this Court held that discreteness and insularity constitute necessary preconditions to a holding that a particular classification is invidious. See, *e.g.*, *Skinner* v. *Oklahoma ex rel. Williamson*, 316 U.S. 535, 541 (1942); *Carrington* v. *Rash*, 380 U.S. 89, 94–97 (1965). These characteristics may be relevant in deciding whether or not to add new types of classifications to the list of "suspect" categories or whether a particular classification survives close examination. See, *e.g.*, *Massachusetts Board of Retirement* v. *Murgia*, 427 U.S. 307, 313 (1976) (age); *San Antonio Independent School Dist.* v. *Rodriguez*, 411 U.S. 1, 28 (1973) (wealth); *Graham* v. *Richardson*,

403 U.S. 365, 372 (1971) (aliens). Racial and ethnic classifications, however, are subject to stringent examination without regard to these additional characteristics. . . .

Racial and ethnic distinctions of any sort are inherently suspect and thus call for the most exacting judicial examination.

# B

This perception of racial and ethnic distinctions is rooted in our Nation's constitutional and demographic history. The Court's initial view of the Fourteenth Amendment was that its "one pervading purpose" was "the freedom of the slave race, the security and firm establishment of that freedom, and the protection of the newly-made freeman and citizen from the oppressions of those who had formerly exercised dominion over him." *Slaughter-House Cases*, 16 Wall. 36, 71 (1873). The Equal Protection Clause, however, was "[v]irtually strangled in infancy by post-civil-war judicial reactionism." It was relegated to decades of relative desuetude.

It was only as the era of substantive due process came to a close, see, *e.g.*, *Nebbia* v. *New York*, 291 U.S. 502 (1934); *West Coast Hotel Co.* v. *Parrish*, 300 U.S. 379 (1937), that the Equal Protection Clause began to attain a genuine measure of vitality, see, *e.g.*, *United States* v. *Carolene Products*, 304 U.S. 144 (1938); *Skinner* v. *Oklahoma ex rel. Williamson*, *supra*.

By that time it was no longer possible to peg the guarantees of the Fourteenth Amendment to the struggle for equality of one racial minority. During the dormancy of the Equal Protection Clause, the United States had become a Nation of minorities. Each had to struggle—and to some extent struggles still—to overcome the prejudices not of a monolithic majority, but of a "majority" composed of various minority groups of whom it was said perhaps unfairly in many cases—that a shared characteristic was a willingness to disadvantage other groups. As the Nation filled with the stock of many lands, the reach of the Clause was gradually extended to all ethnic groups seeking protection from official discrimination. See *Strauder* v. *West Virginia*, 100 U.S. 303, 308 (1880) (Celtic Irishmen) (dictum); *Yick Wo* v. *Hopkins*, 118 U.S. 356 (1886) (Chinese); *Truax* v. *Raich*, 239 U.S. 33, 41 (1915) (Austrian resident aliens); *Korematsu, supra* (Japanese); *Hernandez* v. *Texas*, 347 U.S. 475 (1954) (Mexican-Americans). The guarantees of equal protection, said the Court in *Yick Wo*, "are universal in their application, to all persons within the territorial jurisdiction, without regard to any differences of race, of color, or of nationality; and the equal protection of the laws is a pledge of the protection of equal laws." 118 U.S., at 369.

Although many of the Framers of the Fourteenth Amendment conceived of its primary function as bridging the vast distance between members of the Negro race and the white "majority," *Slaughter-House Cases, supra,* the Amendment itself was framed in universal terms, without reference to color, ethnic origin, or condition of prior servitude.

Over the past 30 years, this Court has embarked upon the crucial mission of interpreting the Equal Protection Clause with the view of assuring to all persons "the protection of equal laws," *Yick Wo, supra,* at 369, in a Nation confronting a legacy of slavery and racial discrimination. See, *e.g., Shelley* v. *Kraemer,* 334 U.S. 1 (1948); *Brown* v. *Board of Education,* 347 U.S. 483 (1954); *Hills* v. *Gautreaux,* 425 U.S. 284 (1976). Because the landmark decisions in this area arose in response to the continued exclusion of Negroes from the mainstream of American society, they could be characterized as involving discrimination by the "majority" white race against the Negro minority. But they need not be read as depending upon that characterization for their results. It suffices to say that "[o]ver the years, this Court has consistently repudiated '[d]istinctions between citizens solely because of their ancestry' as being 'odious to a free people whose institutions are founded upon the doctrine of equality.'" *Loving* v. *Virginia,* 388 U.S. 1, 11 (1967), quoting *Hirabayashi,* 320 U.S., at 100.

Petitioner urges us to adopt for the first time a more restrictive view of the Equal Protection Clause and hold that discrimination against members of the white "majority" cannot be suspect if its purpose can be characterized as "benign." The clock of our liberties, however, cannot be turned back to 1868. *Brown* v. *Board o Education, supra,* at 492; accord. *Loving* v. *Virginia, supra,* at 9. It is far too late to argue that the guarantee of equal protection to *all* persons permits the recognition of special wards entitled to a degree of protection greater than that accorded others. "The Fourteenth Amendment is not directed solely against discrimination due to a 'two-class theory'—that is, based upon differences between 'white' and Negro." *Hernandez,* 347 U.S., at 478.

Once the artificial line of a "two-class theory" of the Fourteenth Amendment is put aside, the difficulties entailed in varying the level of judicial review according to a perceived "preferred" status of a particular racial or ethnic minority are intractable. The concepts of "majority" and "minority" necessarily reflect temporary arrangements and political judgments. As observed above, the white "majority" itself is composed of various minority groups, most of which can lay claim to a history of prior discrimination at the hands of the State and private individuals. Not all of these groups can receive preferential treatment and corresponding judicial tolerance of distinctions drawn in terms of race and nationality, for then the only "majority" left would be a new minority of white Anglo-Saxon Protestants. There is no principled basis for deciding which groups would merit "heightened judicial solicitude" and which would not. Courts would be asked to evaluate the extent of the prejudice and consequent harm suffered by various minority groups. Those whose societal injury is thought to exceed some arbitrary level of tolerability then would be entitled to preferential classifications at the expense of individuals belonging to other groups. Those classifications would be free from exacting judicial scrutiny. As these preferences began to have their desired effect, and the consequences of past discrimination were undone, new judicial rankings would be necessary. The kind of variable sociological and political analysis necessary to produce such rankings simply does not lie within the judicial competence—even if they otherwise were politically feasible and socially desirable.

Moreover, there are serious problems of justice connected with the idea of preference itself. First, it may not always be clear that a so-called preference is in fact benign. Courts may be asked to validate burdens imposed upon individual members of a particular group in order to advance the group's general interest. See *United Jewish Organizations* v. *Carey*, 430 U.S., at 172–173 (Brennan, J., concurring in part). Nothing in the Constitution supports the notion that individuals may be asked to suffer otherwise impermissible burdens in order to enhance the societal standing of their ethnic groups. Second, preferential programs may only reinforce common stereotypes holding that certain groups are unable to achieve success without special protection based on a factor having no relationship to individual worth. See *DeFunis* v. *Odegaard*, 416 U.S. 312, 343 (1974) (Douglas, J., dissenting). Third, there is a measure of inequity in forcing innocent persons in respondent's position to bear the burdens of redressing grievances not of their making.

By hitching the meaning of the Equal Protection Clause to these transitory considerations, we would be holding, as a constitutional principle, that judicial scrutiny of classifications touching on racial and ethnic background may vary with the ebb and flow of political forces. Disparate constitutional tolerance of such classifications well may serve to exacerbate racial and ethnic antagonisms rather than alleviate them. *United Jewish Organizations, supra,* at 173–174 (Brennan, J., concurring in part) . . .

If it is the individual who is entitled to judicial protection against classifications based upon his racial or ethnic background because such distinctions impinge upon personal rights, rather than the individual only because of his membership in a particular group, then constitutional standards may be applied consistently. Political judgments regarding the necessity for the particular classification may be weighed in the constitutional balance, *Korematsu* v. *United States*, 323 U.S. 214 (1944), but the standard of justification will remain constant. This is as it should be, since those political judgments are the product of rough compromise struck by contending groups within the democratic process. When they touch upon an individual's race or ethnic background, he is entitled to a judicial determination that the burden he is asked to bear on that basis is precisely tailored to serve a compelling governmental interest. The Constitution guarantees that right to every person regardless of his background. *Shelley* v. *Kraemer,* 334 U.S., at 22; *Missouri ex rel. Gaines* v. *Canada,* 305 U.S., at 351.

# C

Petitioner contends that on several occasions this Court has approved preferential classifications without applying the most exacting scrutiny. . . .

Nor is petitioner's view as to the applicable standard supported by the fact that gender based classifications are not subjected to this level of scrutiny. *E.g., Califano* v. *Webster,* 430 U.S. 313, 316–317 (1977); *Craig* v. *Boren,* 429 U.S. 190, 211 n. (1976) (Powell, J., concurring). Gender-based distinctions are less likely to create the analytical and practical problems present in preferential programs premised on racial or ethnic criteria. With respect to gender there are only two possible classifications. The incidence of the burdens imposed by preferential classifications is clear. There are no rival groups which can claim that they, too, are entitled to preferential treatment. Classwide questions as to the group suffering previous injury and groups which fairly can be burdened are relatively manageable for reviewing courts. See, *e.g., Califano* v. *Goldfarb,* 430 U.S. 199, 212–217 (1977); *Weinberger* v. *Wiesenfeld,* 420 U.S. 636, 645 (1975). The resolution of these same questions in the context of racial and ethnic preferences presents far more complex and intractable problems than gender-based classifications. More importantly, the perception of racial classifications as inherently odious stems from a lengthy and tragic history that gender-based classifications do not share. In sum, the Court has never viewed such classifications as inherently suspect or as comparable to racial or ethnic classifications for the purpose of equal protection analysis. . . .

In this case, unlike *Lau* and *United Jewish Organizations,* there has been no determination by the legislature or a responsible administrative agency that the University engaged in a discriminatory practice requiring remedial efforts. Moreover the operation of petitioner's special admissions program is quite different from the remedial measures approved in those cases. It prefers the designated minority groups at the expense of other individuals who are totally foreclosed from competition for the 16 special admissions seats in every Medical School class. Because of that foreclosure, some individuals are excluded from enjoyment of a state-provided benefit—admission to the Medical School—they otherwise would receive. When a classification denies an individual opportunities or benefits enjoyed by others solely because of his race or ethnic background, it must be regarded as suspect. *E.g., McLaurin* v. *Oklahoma State Regents,* 339 U.S., at 641–642.

## — IV —

We have held that in "order to justify the use of a suspect classification, a State must show that its purpose or interest is both constitutionally permissible and substantial, and that its use of the classification is 'necessary . . . to the accomplishment' of its purpose or the safeguarding of its interest." *In re Griffiths*, 413 U.S. 717, 721–722 (1973) (footnotes omitted); *Loving* v. *Virginia*, 388 U.S., at 11; *McLaughlin* v. *Florida*, 379 U.S. 184, 196 (1964). The special admissions program purports to serve the purposes of: (i) "reducing the historic deficit of traditionally disfavored minorities in medical schools and in the medical profession," Brief for Petitioner 32; (ii) countering the effects of societal discrimination; (iii) increasing the number of physicians who will practice in communities currently underserved; and (iv) obtaining the educational benefits that flow from an ethnically diverse student body. It is necessary to decide which, if any, of these purposes is substantial enough to support the use of a suspect classification.

## A

If petitioner's purpose is to assure within its student body some specified percentage of a particular group merely because of its race or ethnic origin, such a preferential purpose must be rejected not as insubstantial but as facially invalid. Preferring members of any one group for no reason other than race or ethnic origin is discrimination for its own sake. This the Constitution forbids. *E.g.*, *Loving* v. *Virginia*, supra, at 11; *McLaughlin* v. *Florida*, supra, at 196; *Brown* v. *Board of Education*, 347 U.S. 483 (1954).

## B

The State certainly has a legitimate and substantial interest in ameliorating, or eliminating where feasible, the disabling effects of identified discrimination. The line of school desegregation cases, commencing with *Brown*, attests to the importance of this state goal and the commitment of the judiciary to affirm all lawful means toward its attainment. In the school cases, the States were required by court order to redress the wrongs worked by specific instances of racial discrimination. That goal was far more focused than the remedying of the effects of "societal discrimination," an amorphous concept of injury that may be ageless in its reach into the past.

We have never approved a classification that aids persons perceived as members of relatively victimized groups at the expense of other innocent individuals in the absence of judicial, legislative, or administrative findings of constitutional or statutory violations. See, e.g., *Teamsters* v. *United States*, 431 U.S. 324, 367–376 (1977); *United Jewish Organizations*, 430 U.S., at 155–156; *South Carolina* v. *Katzenbach*, 383 U.S. 301, 308 (1966). After such findings have been made, the governmental interest in preferring members of the injured groups at the expense of others is substantial, since the legal rights of the victims must be vindicated. In such a case, the extent of the injury and the consequent remedy will have been judicially, legislatively, or administratively defined. . . .

Petitioner does not purport to have made, and is in no position to make, such findings. Its broad mission is education, not the formulation of any legislative policy or the adjudication of particular claims of illegality. . . .

Hence, the purpose of helping certain groups whom the faculty of the Davis Medical School perceived as victims of "societal discrimination" does not justify a classification that imposes disadvantages upon persons like respondent, who bear no responsibility for whatever harm the beneficiaries of the special admissions program are thought to have suffered. To hold otherwise would be to convert a remedy heretofore reserved for violations of legal rights into a privilege that all institutions throughout the Nation could grant at their pleasure to whatever groups are perceived as victims of societal discrimination. That is a step we have never approved. Cf. *Pasadena City Board of Education* v. *Spangler*, 427 U.S. 424 (1976).

## C

Petitioner identifies, as another purpose of its program, improving the delivery of health care services to communities currently underserved. It may be assumed that in some situations a State's interest in facilitating the health care of its citizens is sufficiently compelling to support the use of a suspect classification. But there is virtually no evidence in the record indicating that petitioner's special admissions program is either needed or geared to promote that goal. The court below addressed this failure of proof:

> The University concedes it cannot assure that minority doctors who entered under the program, all of whom expressed an "interest" in practicing in a disadvantaged community, will actually do so. It may be correct to assume that some of them will carry out this intention, and that it is more likely they will practice in minority communities than the average white doctor. (See Sandalow, *Racial Preferences in Higher Education: Political Responsibility and the Judicial Role* (1975) 42 U. Chi. L. Rev. 653, 688.) Nevertheless, there are more precise and reliable ways to identify applicants who are genuinely interested in the medical problems of minorities than by race. An applicant of whatever race who has demonstrated his concern for disadvantaged minorities in the past and who declares that practice in such a community is his primary professional goal would be more likely to contribute to alleviation of the medical shortage than one who is chosen entirely on the basis of race and disadvantage. In short, there is no empirical data to demonstrate that any one race

is more selflessly socially oriented or by contrast that another is more selfishly acquisitive. 18 Cal. 3d, at 56, 553 P. 2d, at 1167.

Petitioner simply has not carried its burden of demonstrating that it must prefer members of particular ethnic groups over all other individuals in order to promote better health-care delivery to deprived citizens. Indeed, petitioner has not shown that its preferential classification is likely to have any significant effect on the problem.

# D

The fourth goal asserted by petitioner is the attainment of a diverse student body. This clearly is a constitutionally permissible goal for an institution of higher education. Academic freedom, though not a specifically enumerated constitutional right, long has been viewed as a special concern of the First Amendment. The freedom of a university to make its own judgments as to education includes the selection of its student body. . . .

The atmosphere of "speculation, experiment and creation"—so essential to the quality of higher education—is widely believed to be promoted by a diverse student body. As the Court noted in *Keyishian*, it is not too much to say that the "nation's future depends upon leaders trained through wide exposure" to the ideas and mores of students as diverse as this Nation of many peoples.

Thus, in arguing that its universities must be accorded the right to select those students who will contribute the most to the "robust exchange of ideas," petitioner invokes a countervailing constitutional interest, that of the First Amendment. In this light, petitioner must be viewed as seeking to achieve a goal that is of paramount importance in the fulfillment of its mission.

It may be argued that there is greater force to these views at the undergraduate level than in a medical school where the training is centered primarily on professional competency. But even at the graduate level, our tradition and experience lend support to the view that the contribution of diversity is substantial. . . .

Physicians serve a heterogeneous population. An otherwise qualified medical student with a particular background—whether it be ethnic, geographic, culturally advantaged or disadvantaged—may bring to a professional school of medicine experiences, outlooks, and ideas that enrich the training of its student body and better equip its graduates to render with understanding their vital service to humanity.

Ethnic diversity, however, is only one element in a range of factors a university properly may consider in attaining the goal of a heterogeneous student body. Although a university must have wide discretion in making the sensitive judgments as to who should be admitted, constitutional limitations protecting individual rights may not be disregarded. Respondent urges—and the courts below have held—that petitioner's dual admissions program is a racial classification that impermissibly infringes his rights under the Fourteenth Amendment. As the interest of diversity is compelling in the context of a university's admissions program, the question remains whether the program's racial classification is necessary to promote this interest. In *re Griffiths,* 413 U.S., at 721–722.

## — V —

## A

It may be assumed that the reservation of a specified number of seats in each class for individuals from the preferred ethnic groups would contribute to the attainment of considerable ethnic diversity in the student body. But petitioner's argument that this is the only effective means of serving the interest of diversity is seriously flawed. In a most fundamental sense the argument misconceives the nature of the state interest that would justify consideration of race or ethnic background. It is not an interest in simple ethnic diversity, in which a specified percentage of the student body is in effect guaranteed to be members of selected ethnic groups, with the remaining percentage an undifferentiated aggregation of students. The diversity that furthers a compelling state interest encompasses a far broader array of qualifications and characteristics of which racial or ethnic origin is but a single though important element. Petitioner's special admissions program focused *solely* on ethnic diversity, would hinder rather than further attainment of genuine diversity.

Nor would the state interest in genuine diversity be served by expanding petitioner's two-track system into a multitrack program with a prescribed number of seats set aside for each identifiable category of applicants. Indeed, it is inconceivable that a university would thus pursue the logic of petitioner's two-track program to the illogical end of insulating each category of applicants with certain desired qualifications from competition with all other applicants.

The experience of other university admissions programs, which take race into account in achieving the educational diversity valued by the First Amendment, demonstrates that the assignment of a fixed number of places to a minority group is not a necessary means toward that end. An illuminating example is found in the Harvard College program:

"In recent years Harvard College has expanded the concept of diversity to include students from disadvantaged economic, racial and ethnic groups. Harvard College now recruits not only Californians or Louisianans but also blacks and Chicanos and other minority students. . . .

"In Practice, this new definition of diversity has meant that race has been a factor in some admission decisions. When the Committee on Admissions reviews the large middle group of applicants who are 'admissible' and deemed capable of doing good work in their courses, the race of an applicant may tip the balance in his favor just as geographic origin or a life spent on a farm may tip the balance in other candidates' cases. A farm boy from Idaho can bring something to Harvard College that a Bostonian cannot offer. Similarly, a black student can usually bring something that a white person cannot offer. . . . [See Appendix hereto.]

"In Harvard College admissions the Committee has not set target-quotas for the number of blacks, or of musicians, football players, physicists or Californians to be admitted in a given year. . . . But that awareness [of the necessity of including more than a token number of black students] does not mean that the Committee sets a minimum number of blacks or of people from west of the Mississippi who are to be admitted. It means only that in choosing among thousands of applicants who are not only 'admissible' academically but have other strong qualities, the Committee, with a number of criteria in mind, pays some attention to distribution among many types and categories of students." App. to Brief for Columbia University, Harvard University, Stanford University, and the University of Pennsylvania, as *Amici Curiae* 2–3.

In such an admissions program, race or ethnic background may be deemed a "plus" in a particular applicant's file, yet it does not insulate the individual from comparison with all other candidates for the available seats. The file of a particular black applicant may be examined for his potential contribution to diversity without the factor of race being decisive when compared, for example, with that of an applicant identified as an Italian-American if the latter is thought to exhibit qualities more likely to promote beneficial educational pluralism. Such qualities could include exceptional personal talents, unique work or service experience, leadership potential, maturity, demonstrated compassion, a history of overcoming disadvantage, ability to communicate with the poor, or other qualifications deemed important. In short, an admissions program operated in this way is flexible enough to consider all pertinent elements of diversity in light of the particular qualifications of each applicant, and to place them on the same footing for consideration, although not necessarily according them the same weight. Indeed, the weight attributed to a particular quality may vary from year to year depending upon the 'mix' both of the student body and the applicants for the incoming class.

This kind of program treats each applicant as an individual in the admissions process. The applicant who loses out on the last available seat to another candidate receiving a "plus" on the basis of ethnic background will not have been foreclosed from all consideration for that seat simply because he was not the right color or had the wrong surname. It would mean only that his combined qualifications, which may have included similar nonobjective factors, did not outweigh those of the other applicant. His qualifications would have been weighed fairly and competitively, and he would have no basis to complain of unequal treatment under the Fourteenth Amendment.

It has been suggested that an admissions program which considers race only as one factor is simply a subtle and more sophisticated—but no less effective means of according racial preference than the Davis program. A facial intent to discriminate, however, is evident in petitioner's preference program and not denied in this case. No such facial infirmity exists in an admissions program where race or ethnic background is simply one element to be weighed fairly against other elements in the selection process. "A boundary line," as MR. JUSTICE FRANKFURTER remarked in another connection, "is none the worse for being narrow." *McLeod* v. *Dilworth*, 322 U.S. 327, 329 (1944). And a court would not assume that a university, professing to employ a facially nondiscriminatory admissions policy, would operate it as a cover for the functional equivalent of a quota system. In short, good faith would be presumed in the absence of a showing to the contrary in the manner permitted by our cases. See, *e.g., Arlington Heights* v. *Metropolitan Housing Dev. Corp.*, 429 U.S. 252 (1977); *Washington* v. *Davis*, 426 U.S. 229 (1976); *Swain* v. *Alabama*, 380 U.S. 202 (1965).

# B

In summary, it is evident that the Davis special admissions program involves the use of an explicit racial classification never before countenanced by this Court. It tells applicants who are not Negro, Asian, or Chicano that they are totally excluded from a specific percentage of the seats in an entering class. No matter how strong their qualifications, quantitative and extracurricular, including their own potential for contribution to educational diversity, they are never afforded the chance to compete with applicants from the preferred groups for the special admission seats. At the same time, the preferred applicants have the opportunity to compete for every seat in the class.

The fatal flaw in petitioner's preferential program is its disregard of individual rights as guaranteed by the Fourteenth Amendment. *Shelley* v. *Kraemer*, 334 U.S., at 22. Such rights are not absolute. But when a State's distribution of benefits or imposition of burdens hinges on ancestry or the color of a person's skin, that individual is entitled to a demonstration that the challenged classification is necessary to promote a substantial state interest. Petitioner has failed to carry this burden. For this reason, that portion of the California court's judgment holding petitioner's special admissions program invalid under the Fourteenth Amendment must be affirmed.

## C

In enjoining petitioner from ever considering the race of any applicant, however, the courts below failed to recognize that the State has a substantial interest that legitimately may be served by a properly devised admissions program involving the competitive consideration of race and ethnic origin. For this reason, so much of the California court's judgment as enjoins petitioner from any consideration of the race of any applicant must be reversed.

## — VI —

With respect to respondent's entitlement to an injunction directing his admission to the Medical School, petitioner has conceded that it could not carry its burden of proving that, but for the existence of its unlawful special admissions program, respondent still would not have been admitted. Hence, respondent is entitled to the injunction, and that portion of the judgment must be affirmed. . . .

Opinion of MR. JUSTICE BRENNAN, MR. JUSTICE WHITE, MR. JUSTICE MARSHALL, and MR. JUSTICE BLACKMUN, concurring in the judgment in part and dissenting in part.

The Court, today, in reversing in part the judgment of the Supreme Court of California, affirms the constitutional power of Federal and State Governments to act affirmatively to achieve equal opportunity for all. The difficulty of the issue presented—whether government may use race-conscious programs to redress the continuing effects of past discrimination—and the mature consideration which each of our Brethren has brought to it have resulted in many opinions, no single one speaking for the Court. But this should not and must not mask the central meaning of today's opinions: Government may take race into account when it acts not to demean or insult any racial group, but to remedy disadvantages cast on minorities by past racial prejudice, at least when appropriate findings have been made by judicial, legislative, or administrative bodies with competence to act in this area. . . .

Since we conclude that the affirmative admissions program at the Davis Medical School is constitutional, we would reverse the judgment below in all respects. Mr. justice Powell agrees that some uses of race in university admissions are permissible and, therefore, he joins with us to make five votes reversing the judgment below insofar as it prohibits the University from establishing race-conscious programs in the future.

Our Nation was founded on the principle that "all Men are created equal." Yet candor requires acknowledgment that the Framers of our Constitution, to forge the 13 Colonies into one Nation, openly compromised this principle of equality with its antithesis: slavery. The consequences of this compromise are well known and have aptly been called our "American Dilemma." Still, it is well to recount how recent the time has been, if it has yet come, when the promise of our principles has flowered into the actuality of equal opportunity for all regardless of race or color.

The Fourteenth Amendment, the embodiment in the Constitution of our abiding belief in human equality, has been the law of our land for only slightly more than half its 200 years. And for half of that, the Equal Protection Clause of the Amendment was largely moribund so that, as late as 1927, MR. JUSTICE HOLMES could sum up the importance of that Clause by remarking that it was the "last resort of constitutional arguments." *Buck* v. *Bell,* 274 U.S. 200, 208 (1927). Worse than desuetude, the Clause was early turned against those whom it was intended to set free, condemning them to a "separate but equal" status before the law, a status always separate but seldom equal. Not until 1954—only 24 years ago—was this odious doctrine interred by our decision in *Brown* v. *Board of Education,* 347 U.S. 483 (*Brown I*), and its progeny, which proclaimed that separate schools and public facilities of all sorts were inherently unequal and forbidden under our Constitution. Even then inequality was not eliminated with "all deliberate speed." *Brown* v. *Board of Education,* 349 U.S. 294 (1955). In 1968 and again in 1971, for example, we were forced to remind school boards of their obligation to eliminate racial discrimination root and branch. And a glance at our docket and at dockets of lower courts will show that even today officially sanctioned discrimination is not a thing of the past.

Against this background, claims that law must be "color-blind" or that the datum of race is no longer relevant to public policy must be seen as aspiration rather than as description of reality. This is not to denigrate aspiration; for reality rebukes us that race has too often been used by those who would stigmatize and oppress minorities. Yet we cannot—and, as we shall demonstrate, need not under our Constitution or Title VI, which merely extends the constraints of the Fourteenth Amendment to private parties who receive federal funds—let color blindness become myopia which masks the reality that many "created equal" have been treated within our lifetimes as inferior both by the law and by their fellow citizens. . . .

# — III —

# A

The assertion of human equality is closely associated with the proposition that differences in color or creed, birth or status, are neither significant nor relevant to the way in which persons should be treated. Nonetheless, the position that such factors must be "constitutionally an irrelevance," *Edwards* v. *California*, 314 U.S. 160, 185 (1941) (Jackson, J., concurring), summed up by the shorthand phrase "[o]ur Constitution is color-blind," *Plessy* v. *Ferguson*, 163 U.S. 537, 559 (1896) (Harlan, J., dissenting), has never been adopted by this Court as the proper meaning of the Equal Protection Clause. Indeed, we have expressly rejected this proposition on a number of occasions.

Our cases have always implied that an "overriding statutory purpose," *McLaughlin* v. *Florida*, 379 U.S. 184, 192 (1964), could be found that would justify racial classifications. See, *e.g.*, *ibid.*; *Loving* v. *Virginia*, 388 U.S. 1, 11 (1967); *Korematsu* v. *United States*, 323 U.S. 214, 216 (1944); *Hirabayashi* v. *United States*, 320 U.S. 81, 100–101 (1943).

. . . We conclude, therefore, that racial classifications are not per se invalid under the Fourteenth Amendment. Accordingly, we turn to the problem of articulating what our role should be in reviewing state action that expressly classifies by race. . . .

Unquestionable we have held that a government practice or statute which restricts "fundamental rights" or which contains "suspect classifications" is to be subjected to "strict scrutiny" and can be justified only if it furthers a compelling government purpose and even then, only if no less restrictive alternative is available. See, *e.g., San Antonio Independent School District* v. *Rodriguez*, 411 U.S. 1, 16–17 (1973); *Dunn* v. *Blumstein*, 405 U.S. 330 (1972). But no fundamental right is involved here. See *San Antonio, supra,* at 29–36. Nor do whites as a class have any of the "traditional indicia of suspectness: the class is not saddled with such disabilities, or subjected to such a history of purposeful unequal treatment, or relegated to such a position of political powerlessness as to command extraordinary protection from the majoritarian political process." *Id.,* at 28; see *United States* v. *Carolene Products Co.,* 304 U.S. 144, 152n. 4 (1938).

Moreover, if the University's representations are credited, this in not a case where racial classifications are "irrelevant and therefore prohibited." *Hirabayashi, supra,* at 100. Nor has anyone suggested that the University's purposes contravene the cardinal principle that racial classifications that stigmatize—because they are drawn on the presumption that one race is inferior to another or because they put the weight of government behind racial hatred and separatism—are invalid without more. . . .

On the other hand, . . . "The mere recitation of a benign, compensatory purpose is not an automatic shield which protects against any inquiry into the actual purposes underlying a statutory scheme." *Califano* v. *Webster*, 430 U.S. 313, 317 (1977), quoting *Weinberger* v. *Wiensenfeld*, 420 U.S. 636, 648 (1975). Instead, a number of considerations—developed in gender-discrimination cases but which carry even more force when applied to racial classifications—lead us to conclude that racial classifications designed to further remedial purposes "must serve important governmental objectives and must be substantially related to achievement of those objectives.'" *Califano* v. *Webster*, supra, at *317*, quoting *Craig* v. *Boren*, 429 U.S. 190, 197 (1976).

First, race, like, "gender-based classifications too often [has] been inexcusably utilized to stereotype and stigmatize politically powerless segments of society." *Kahn* v. *Shevin*, 416 U.S. 351, 357 (1974) (dissenting opinion). While a carefully tailored statute designed to remedy past discrimination could avoid these vices, see *Califano* v. *Webster, supra; Schlesinger* v. *Ballard*, 419 U.S. 498 (1975); *Kahn* v. *Shevin, supra*, we nonetheless have recognized that the line between honest and thoughtful appraisal of the effects of past discrimination and paternalistic stereotyping is not so clear and that a statute based on the latter is patently capable of stigmatizing all women with a badge of inferiority. Cf. *Schlesinger* v. *Ballard, supra*, at 508; *UJO, supra*, at *174*, and n. 3 (opinion concurring in part); *Califano* v. *Goldfarb*, 430 U.S. 199, 223 (1977) (Stevens, J., concurring in judgment). See also *Stanton* v. *Stanton*, 421 U.S. 7, 14–15 (1975). State programs designed ostensibly to ameliorate the effects of past racial discrimination obviously create the same hazard of stigma, since they may promote racial separatism and reinforce the views of those who believe that members of racial minorities are inherently incapable of succeeding on their own. See *UJO, supra*, at 172 (opinion concurring in part); *ante*, at 298 (opinion of POWELL, J.).

Second, race, like gender and illegitimacy, see *Weber* v. *Aetna Casualty & Surety Co.*, 406 U.S. 164 (1972), is an immutable characteristic which its possessors are powerless to escape or set aside. While a classification is not per se invalid because it divides classes on the basis of an immutable characteristic, see *supra*, at 355–356, it is nevertheless true that such divisions are contrary to our deep belief that "legal burdens should bear some relationship to individual responsibility or wrongdoing," *Weber, supra*, at 175; *Frontiero* v. *Richardson*, 411 U.S. 677, 686 (1973) (opinion of BRENNAN, WHITE, AND MARSHALL, JJ.), and that advancement sanctioned, sponsored, or approved by the State should ideally be based on individual merit or achievement, or at the least on factors within the control of an individual. See *UJO*, 430 U.S., at 173 (opinion concurring in part); *Kotch* v. *Board of River Port Pilot Comm'rs*, 330 U.S. 552, 566 (1947) (Rutledge, J., dissenting).

Because this principle is so deeply rooted it might be supposed that it would be considered in the legislative process and weighed against the benefits of programs preferring individuals because of their race. But this is not necessarily so: The "natural consequence of our governing processes [may well be] that the most 'discrete and insular' of whites . . . will be called upon to bear the immediate, direct costs of benign discrimination." *UJO, supra,* at 174 (opinion concurring in part). Moreover, it is clear from our cases that there are limits beyond which majorities may not go when they classify on the basis of immutable characteristics. See, *e. g., Weber, supra.* Thus, even if the concern for individualism is weighed by the political process, that weighing cannot waive the personal rights of individuals under the Fourteenth Amendment. See *Lucas v. Colorado General Assembly,* 377 U.S. 713, 736 (1964).

In sum, because of the significant risk that racial classifications established for ostensibly benign purposes can be misused, causing effects not unlike those created by invidious classifications, it is inappropriate to inquire only whether there is any conceivable basis that might sustain such a classification. Instead, to justify such a classification an important and articulated purpose for its use must be shown. In addition, any statute must be stricken that stigmatizes any group or that singles out those least well represented in the political process to bear the brunt of a benign program. Thus, our review under the Fourteenth Amendment should be strict—not "'strict' in theory and fatal in fact," because it is stigma that causes fatality—but strict and searching nonetheless.

## — IV —

Davis' articulated purpose of remedying the effects of past societal discrimination is, under our cases, sufficiently important to justify the use of race-conscious admissions programs where there is a sound basis for concluding that minority underrepresentation is substantial and chronic, and that the handicap of past discrimination is impeding access of minorities to the Medical School.

## A

. . . relief does not require as a predicate proof that recipients of preferential advancement have been individually discriminated against; it is enough that each recipient is within a general class of persons likely to have been the victims of discrimination. See id., at 357–362. Nor is it an objection to such relief that preference for minorities will upset the settled expectations of nonminorities. See *Franks, supra.* In addition, we have held that Congress, to remove barriers to equal opportunity, can and has required employers to use test criteria that fairly reflect the qualifications of minority applicants vis-à-vis nonminority applicants, even if this means interpreting the qualifications of an applicant in light of his race. See *Albemarle Paper Co.* v. *Moody,* 422 U.S. 405, 435 (1975).[1]

These cases cannot be distinguished simply by the presence of judicial findings of discrimination, for race-conscious remedies have been approved where such findings have not been made. *McDaniel* v. *Barresi, supra;* UJO; see *Califano* v. *Webster,* 430 U.S. 313 (1977); *Schlesinger* v. *Ballard,* 419 U.S. 498 (1975); *Kahn* v. *Shevin,* 416 U.S. 351 (1974). See also *Katzenbach* v. *Morgan,* 384 U.S. 641 (1966). Indeed, the requirement of a judicial determination of a constitutional or statutory violation as a predicate for race conscious remedial actions would be self-defeating. Such a requirement would severely undermine efforts to achieve voluntary compliance with the requirements of law. And our society and jurisprudence have always stressed the value of voluntary efforts to further the objectives of the law. Judicial intervention is a last resort to achieve cessation of illegal conduct or the remedying of its effects rather than a prerequisite to action. . . .

Moreover, the presence or absence of past discrimination by universities or employers is largely irrelevant to resolving respondent's constitutional claims. The claims of those burdened by the race-conscious actions of a university or employer who has never been adjudged in violation of an anti-discrimination law are not any more or less entitled to deference than the claims of the burdened nonminority workers in *Franks* v. *Bowman Transportation Co., supra,* in which the employer had violated Title VII, for in each case the employees are innocent of past discrimination.

We therefore conclude that Davis' goal of admitting minority students disadvantaged by the effects of past discrimination is sufficiently important to justify use of race-conscious admissions criteria.

# B

Properly construed, therefore, our prior cases unequivocally show that a state government may adopt race-conscious programs if the purpose of such programs is to remove the disparate racial impact its actions might otherwise have and if there is reason to believe that the disparate impact is itself the product of past discrimination, whether its own or that of society at large. There is no question that Davis' program is valid under this test.

Certainly, on the basis of the undisputed factual submissions before this Court, Davis had a sound basis for believing that the problem of underrepresentation of minorities was substantial and chronic and that the problem was attributable to handicaps imposed on minority applicants by past and present racial discrimination. Until at least 1973, the practice of medicine in the country was, in fact, if not in law, largely the prerogative of whites. In 1950, for example, while Negroes constituted 10% of the total population, Negro physicians constituted only 2.2% of the total number of physicians. The overwhelming majority of these, moreover, were educated in two predominantly

Negro medical schools, Howard and Meharry. By 1970, the gap between the proportion of Negroes in medicine and their proportion in the population had widened: The number of Negroes employed in medicine remained frozen at 2.2% while the Negro population had increased to 11.1%. The number of Negro admittees to predominantly white medical schools, moreover, had declined in absolute numbers during the years 1955 to 1964. Odegaard 19.

Moreover, Davis had very good reason to believe that the national pattern of underrepresentation of minorities in medicine would be perpetuated if it retained a single admissions standard. For example, the entering classes in 1968 and 1969, the years in which such a standard was used, included only 1 Chicano and 2 Negroes out of the 50 admittees for each year. Nor is there any relief from this pattern of underrepresentation in the statistics for the regular admissions program in later years.

Davis clearly could conclude that the serious and persistent underrepresentation of minorities in medicine depicted by these statistics is the result of handicaps under which minority applicants labor as a consequence of a background of deliberate, purposeful discrimination against minorities in education and in society generally, as well as in the medical profession. From the inception of our national life, Negroes have been subjected to unique legal disabilities impairing access to equal educational opportunity. Under slavery, penal sanctions were imposed upon anyone attempting to educate Negroes. After enactment of the Fourteenth Amendment the States continued to deny Negroes equal educational opportunity, enforcing a strict polity of segregation that itself stamped Negroes as inferior, *Brown I*, 347 U.S. 483 (1954), that relegated minorities to inferior educational institutions, and that denied them intercourse in the mainstream of professional life necessary to advancement. See *Sweatt* v. *Painter*, 339 U.S. 629 (1950). Segregation was not limited to public facilities, moreover, but was enforced by criminal penalties against private action as well. Thus, as late as 1908, this Court enforced a state criminal conviction against a private college for teaching Negroes together with whites. *Berea College* v. *Kentucky*, 211 U.S. 45. See also *Plessy* v. *Ferguson*, 163 U.S. 537 (1896).

*Green* v. *County School Board*, 391 U.S. 430 (1968), gave explicit recognition to the fact that the habit of discrimination and cultural tradition of race prejudice cultivated by centuries of legal slavery and segregation were not immediately dissipated when *Brown I, supra*, announced the constitutional principle that equal educational opportunity and participation in all aspects of American life could not be denied on the basis of race. Rather, massive official and private resistance prevented, and to a lesser extent still prevents, attainment of equal opportunity in education at all levels and in the professions. The generation of minority students applying to Davis Medical School since it opened in 1968—most of whom were born before or about the time of *Brown I* was decided—clearly have been victims of this discrimination. Judicial decrees recognizing discrimination in public education in California testify to the fact of widespread discrimination suffered by California-born minority applicants; many minority group members living in California, moreover, were born and reared in school districts in Southern States segregated by law. Since separation of schoolchildren by race "generates a feeling of inferiority as to their status in the community that may affect their hearts and minds in a way unlikely ever to be undone," *Brown I, supra,* at 494, the conclusion is inescapable that applicants to medical school must be few indeed who endured the effects of *de jure* segregation, the resistance to *Brown I,* or the equally debilitating pervasive private discrimination, cf. *Reitman* v. *Mulkey,* 387 U.S. 369 (1967), and yet come to the starting line with an education equal to whites.

# C

The second prong of our test—whether the Davis program stigmatizes any discrete group or individual and whether race is reasonably used in light of the program's objectives is clearly satisfied by the Davis program.

It is not even claimed that Davis' program in any way operates to stigmatize or single out any discrete and insular or even any identifiable, nonminority group. Nor will harm comparable to that imposed upon racial minorities by exclusion or separation on grounds of race be the likely result of the program. It does not, for example, establish an exclusive preserve for minority students apart from and exclusive of whites. Rather, its purpose is to overcome the effects of segregation by bringing the races together. True, whites are excluded from participation in the special admissions program, but this fact only operates to reduce the number of whites to be admitted in the regular admissions program in order to permit admission of a reasonable percentage—less than their proportion of the California population—of otherwise underrepresented qualified minority applicants.

Nor was Bakke in any sense stamped as inferior by the Medical School's rejection of him. Indeed, it is conceded by all that he satisfied those criteria regarded by the school as generally relevant to academic performance better than most of the minority members who were admitted. Moreover, there is absolutely no basis for concluding that Bakke's rejection as a result of Davis' use of racial preference will affect him throughout his life in the same way as the segregation of the Negro schoolchildren in *Brown I* would have affected them. Unlike discrimination against racial minorities, the use of racial preferences for remedial purposes does not inflict a pervasive injury upon individual whites in the sense that wherever they go or whatever they do there is a significant likelihood that they will be treated as second-class citizens because of their color. This distinction does not mean that the exclusion of a white resulting from the preferential use of race is not sufficiently serious to require justification; but it does mean that the injury inflicted by such a policy is not distinguishable from disadvantages caused by a wide range of government actions, none of which has ever been thought impermissible for that reason alone.

In addition, there is simply no evidence that the Davis program discriminates intentionally or unintentionally against any minority group which it purports to benefit. The program does not establish a quota in the invidious sense of a ceiling on the number of minority applicants to be admitted. Nor can the program reasonably be regarded as stigmatizing the program's beneficiaries or their race as inferior. The Davis program does not simply advance less qualified applicants; rather, it compensates applicants, who it is uncontested are fully qualified to study medicine, for educational disadvantages which it was reasonable to conclude were a product of state-fostered discrimination. Once admitted, these students must satisfy the same degree requirements as regularly admitted students; they are taught by the same faculty in the same classes; and their performance is evaluated by the same standards by which regularly admitted students are judged. Under these circumstances, their performance and degrees must be regarded equally with the regularly admitted students with whom they compete for standing. Since minority graduates cannot justifiably be regarded as less well qualified than nonminority graduates by virtue of the special admissions program, there is no reasonable basis to conclude that minority graduates at schools using such programs would be stigmatized as inferior by the existence of such programs.

# D

We disagree with the lower courts' conclusion that the Davis program's use of race was unreasonable in light of its objectives. First, as petitioner argues, there are no practical means by which it could achieve its ends in the foreseeable future without the use of race conscious measures. With respect to any factor (such as poverty or family educational background) that may be used as a substitute for race as an indicator of past discrimination, whites greatly outnumber racial minorities simply because whites make up a far larger percentage of the total population and therefore far outnumber minorities in absolute terms at every socioeconomic level. For example, of a class of recent medical school applicants from families with less than $10,000 income, at least 71% were white. Of all 1970 families headed by a person not a high school graduate which included related children under 18, 80% were white and 20% were racial minorities. Moreover, while race is positively correlated with differences in GPA and MCAT scores, economic disadvantage is not. Thus, it appears that economically disadvantaged whites do not score less well than economically advantaged whites, while economically advantaged blacks score less well than do disadvantaged whites. These statistics graphically illustrate that the University's purpose to integrate its classes by compensating for past discrimination could not be achieved by a general preference for the economically disadvantaged or the children of parents of limited education unless such groups were to make up the entire class.

Second, the Davis admissions program does not simply equate minority status with disadvantage. Rather, Davis considers on an individual basis each applicant's personal history to determine whether he or she has likely been disadvantaged by racial discrimination. The record makes clear that only minority applicants likely to have been isolated from the mainstream of American life are considered in the special program; other minority applicants are eligible only through the regular admissions program. True, the procedure by which disadvantage is detected is informal, but we have never insisted that educators conduct their affairs through adjudicatory proceedings, and such insistence here is misplaced. A case-by-case inquiry into the extent to which each individual applicant has been affected, either directly or indirectly, by racial discrimination, would seem to be, as a practical matter, virtually impossible, despite the fact that there are excellent reasons for concluding that such effects generally exist. When individual measurement is impossible or extremely impractical, there is nothing to prevent a State from using categorical means to achieve its ends, at least where the category is closely related to the goal. Cf. *Gaston County* v. *United States*, 395 U.S. 285, 295–296 (1969); *Katzenbach* v. *Morgan*, 384 U.S. 641 (1966). And it is clear from our cases that specific proof that a person has been victimized by discrimination is not a necessary predicate to offering him relief where the probability of victimization is great. See *Teamsters* v. *United States*, 431 U.S. 324 (1977).

# E

Finally, Davis' special admissions program cannot be said to violate the Constitution simply because it has set aside a predetermined number of places for qualified minority applicants rather than using minority status as a positive factor to be considered in evaluating the applications of disadvantaged minority applicants. For purposes of constitutional adjudication, there is no difference between the two approaches. In any admissions program which accords special consideration to disadvantaged racial minorities, a determination of the degree of preference to be given is unavoidable, and any given preference that results in the exclusion of a white candidate is no more or less constitutionally acceptable than a program such as that at Davis. Furthermore, the extent of the preference inevitably depends on how many minority applicants the particular school is seeking to admit in any particular year so long as the number of qualified minority applicants exceeds that number. There is no sensible, and certainly no constitutional, distinction between, for example, adding a set number of points to the admissions rating of disadvantaged minority applicants as an expression of the preference with the expectation that this will result in the admission of an approximately determined number of qualified minority applicants and setting a fixed number of places for such applicants as was done here.

The "Harvard" program, see *ante*, at 316–318, as those employing it readily concede, openly and successfully employs a racial criterion for the purpose of ensuring that some of the scarce places in institutions of higher education are allocated to disadvantaged minority students. That the Harvard approach does not also make public the extent of the preference and the precise workings of the system while the Davis program employs a specific, openly stated number, does not condemn the latter plan for purposes of Fourteenth Amendment adjudication. It may be that the Harvard plan is more acceptable to the public than is the Davis "quota." If it is, any State, including California, is free to adopt it in preference to a less acceptable alternative, just as it is generally free, as far as the Constitution is concerned, to abjure granting any racial preferences in its admissions program. But there is no basis for preferring a particular preference program simply because in achieving the same goals that the Davis Medical School is pursuing, it proceeds in a manner that is not immediately apparent to the public.

## — V —

Accordingly, we would reverse the judgment of the Supreme Court of California holding the Medical School's special admissions program unconstitutional and directing respondent's admission, as well as that portion of the judgment enjoining the Medical School for according any consideration to race in the admissions process.

MR. JUSTICE WHITE.

I write separately concerning the question of whether Title VI of the Civil Rights Act of 1964, 42 U.S.C. § 2000d *et seq.*, provides for a private cause of action. . . . my views with respect to the equal protection issue, are included in the joint opinion that my Brothers Brennan, Marshall, and Blackmun and I have filed.[2]

MR. JUSTICE MARSHALL.

I agree with the judgment of the Court only insofar as it permits a university to consider the race of an applicant in making admissions decisions. I do not agree that petitioner's admissions program violates the Constitution. For it must be remembered that, during most of the past 200 years, the Constitution as interpreted by this Court did not prohibit the most ingenious and pervasive forms of discrimination against the Negro. Now, when a State acts to remedy the effects of the legacy of discrimination, I cannot believe that this same Constitution stands as a barrier.

# — I —

## A

Three hundred and fifty years ago, the Negro was dragged to this country in chains to be sold into slavery. Uprooted from his homeland and thrust into bondage for forced labor, the slave was deprived of all legal rights. It was unlawful to teach him to read; he could be sold away from his family and friends at the whim of his master; and killing or maiming him was not a crime. The system of slavery brutalized and dehumanized both master and slave.[1]

The denial of human rights was etched into the American Colonies' first attempts at establishing self-government. When the colonists determined to seek their independence from England, they drafted a unique document cataloguing their grievances against the King and proclaiming as "self-evident" that "all men are created equal" and are endowed "with certain unalienable Rights," including those to "Life, Liberty and the pursuit of Happiness." The self-evident truths and the unalienable rights were intended, however, to apply only to white men. An earlier draft of the Declaration of Independence, submitted by Thomas Jefferson to the Continental Congress, had included among the charges against the King that

> he has waged cruel war against human nature itself, violating its most sacred rights of life and liberty in the persons of a distant people who never offended him, captivating and carrying them into slavery in another hemisphere, or to incur miserable death in their transportation thither." Franklin 88.

The Southern delegation insisted that the charge be deleted; the colonists themselves were implicated in the slave trade, and inclusion of this claim might have made it more difficult to justify the continuation of slavery once the ties to England were severed. Thus, even as the colonists embarked on a course to secure their own freedom and equality, they ensured perpetuation of the system that deprived a whole race of those rights.

The implicit protection of slavery embodied in the Declaration of Independence was made explicit in the Constitution, which treated a slave as being equivalent to three-fifths of a person for purposes of apportioning representatives and taxes among the States. Art. 1, § 2. The Constitution also contained a clause ensuring that the "Migration or Importation" of slaves into the existing States would be legal until at least 1808, Art. I. § 9, and a fugitive slave clause requiring that when a slave escaped to another State, he must be returned on the claim of the master, Art. IV, § 2. In their declaration of the principles that were to provide the cornerstone of the new Nation, therefore, the

Framers made it plain that "we the people," for whose protection the Constitution was designed, did not include those whose skins were the wrong color. As Professor John Hope Franklin has observed, Americans "proudly accepted the challenge and responsibility of their new political freedom by establishing the machinery and safeguards that insured the continued enslavement of blacks." Franklin 100.

The individual States likewise established the machinery to protect the system of slavery through the promulgation of the Slave Codes, which were designed primarily to defend the property interest of the owner in his slave. The position of the Negro slave as mere property was confirmed by this Court in *Dred Scott* v. *Sandford*, 19 How. 393 (1857), holding that the Missouri Compromise—which prohibited slavery in the portion of the Louisiana Purchase Territory north of Missouri—was unconstitutional because it deprived slave owners of their property without due process. The Court declared that under the Constitution a slave was property, and "[t]he right to traffic in it, like an ordinary article of merchandise and property, was guaranteed to the citizens of the United States. . . ." *Id.*, at 451. The Court further concluded that Negroes were not intended to be included as citizens under the Constitution, but were "regarded as beings of an inferior order. . . . altogether unfit to associate with the white race, either in social or political relations; and so far inferior, that they had no rights which the white man was bound to respect. . . ." *Id.*, at 407.

# B

The status of the Negro as property was officially erased by his emancipation at the end of the Civil War. But the long awaited emancipation, while freeing the Negro from slavery, did not bring him citizenship or equality in any meaningful way. Slavery was replaced by a system of "laws which imposed upon the colored race onerous disabilities and burdens, and curtailed their rights in the pursuit of life, liberty, and property to such an extent that their freedom was of little value." *Slaughter-House Cases*, 16 Wall. 36, 70 (1873). Despite the passage of the Thirteenth, Fourteenth, and Fifteenth Amendments, the Negro was systematically denied the rights those Amendments were supposed to secure. The combined actions and inactions of the State and Federal Governments maintained Negroes in a position of legal inferiority for another century after the Civil War.

The Southern States took the first steps to re-enslave the Negroes. Immediately following the end of the Civil War, many of the provisional legislatures passed Black Codes, similar to the Slave Codes, which, among other things, limited the rights of Negroes to own or rent property and permitted imprisonment for breach of employment contracts. Over the next several decades, the South managed to disenfranchise the Negroes in spite of the Fifteenth Amendment by various techniques, including poll taxes, deliberately complicated balloting processes, property and literacy qualifications, and finally the white primary.

Congress responded to the legal disabilities being imposed in the Southern States by passing the Reconstruction Acts and the Civil Rights Acts. Congress also responded to the needs of the Negroes at the end of the Civil War by establishing the Bureau of Refugees, Freedmen, and Abandoned Lands, better known as the Freedmen's Bureau, to supply food, hospitals, land, and education to the newly freed slaves. Thus, for a time it seemed as if the Negro might be protected from the continued denial of his civil rights and might be relieved of the disabilities that prevented him from taking his place as a free and equal citizen.

That time, however, was short-lived. Reconstruction came to a close, and, with the assistance of this Court, the Negro was rapidly stripped of his new civil rights. In the words of C. Vann Woodward: "By narrow and ingenious interpretation [the Supreme Court's] decisions over a period of years had whittled away a great part of the authority presumably given the government for protection of civil rights." Woodward 139.

The Court began by interpreting the Civil War Amendments in a manner that sharply curtailed their substantive protections. See, *e.g., Slaughter-House Cases, supra; United States v. Reese,* 92 U.S. 214 (1876); *United States v. Cruikshank,* 92 U.S. 542 (1876). Then in the notorious *Civil Rights Cases,* 109 U.S. 3 (1883), the Court strangled Congress' efforts to use its power to promote racial equality. In those cases the court invalidated sections of the Civil Rights Act of 1875 that made it a crime to deny equal access to "inns, public conveyances, theatres and other places of public amusement." *Id.,* at 10. According to the Court, the Fourteenth Amendment gave Congress the power to proscribe only discriminatory action by the State. The Court ruled that the Negroes who were excluded from public places suffered only an invasion of their social rights at the hands of private individuals, and Congress had no power to remedy that. *Id.,* at 24–25. "When a man has emerged from slavery, and by the aid of beneficent legislation has shaken off the inseparable concomitants of that state," the Court concluded, "there must be some stage in the progress of his elevation when he takes the rank of a mere citizen, and ceases to be the special favorite of the laws. . . ." *Id.,* at 25. As Mr. Justice Harlan noted in dissent, however the Civil War Amendments and Civil Rights Acts did not make the Negroes the "special favorite" of the laws but instead "sought to accomplish in reference to that race . . .—what had already been done in every State of the Union for the white race to secure and protect rights belonging to them as freemen and citizens; nothing more." *Id.,* at 61.

The Court's ultimate blow to the Civil War Amendments and to the equality of Negroes came in *Plessy* v. *Ferguson,* 163 U.S. 537 (1896). In upholding a Louisiana law that required railway companies to provide "equal but separate" accommodations for white and Negroes, the Court held that the Fourteenth Amendment was not intended "to abolish distinctions based upon color, or to enforce social, as distinguished from political equality, or a commingling of the two races upon terms unsatisfactory to either." *Id.*, at 544. Ignoring totally the realities of the positions of the two races, the Court remarked:

> "We consider the underlying fallacy of the plaintiff's argument to consist in the assumption that the enforced separation of the two races stamps the colored race with a badge of inferiority. If this be so, it is not by reason of anything found in the act, but solely because the colored race chooses to put that construction upon it." *Id.*, at 551.

MR. JUSTICE HARLAN's dissenting opinion recognized the bankruptcy of the Court's reasoning. He noted that the "real meaning" of the legislation was "that colored citizens are so inferior and degraded that they cannot be allowed to sit in public coaches occupied by white citizens." *Id.*, at 560. He expressed his fear that if like laws were enacted in other States, "the effect would be in the highest degree mischievous." *Id.*, at 563. Although slavery would have disappeared, the States would retain the power "to interfere with the full enjoyment of the blessings of freedom; to regulate civil rights, common to all citizen, upon the basis of race; and to place in a condition of legal inferiority a large body of American citizens. . . ." *Ibid.*

The fears of MR. JUSTICE HARLAN were soon to be realized. In the wake of *Plessy,* many States expanded their Jim Crow laws, which had up until that time been limited primarily to passenger trains and schools. The segregation of the races was extended to residential areas, parks, hospitals, theaters, waiting rooms, and bathrooms. There were even statutes and ordinances which authorized separate phone booths for Negroes and whites, which required that textbooks used by children of one race be kept separate from those used by the other, and which required that Negro and white prostitutes be kept in separate districts. In 1898, after *Plessy,* the Charleston News and Courier printed a parody of Jim Crow laws:

> "If there must be Jim Crow cars on the railroads, there should be Jim Crow cars on the street railways. Also on all passenger boats. . . . If there are to be Jim Crow cars, moreover, there should be Jim Crow waiting saloons at all stations, and Jim Crow eating houses. . . . There should be Jim Crow sections of the jury box, and a separate Jim Crow dock and witness stand in every court—and a Jim Crow Bible for colored witnesses to kiss.'" Woodward 68.

The irony is that before many years had passed, with the exception of the Jim Crow witness stand, "all the improbable applications of the principle suggested by the editor in derision had been put into practice—down to and including the Jim Crow Bible." *Id.*, at 69.

In many of the Northern States, the Negro was denied the right to vote, prevented from serving on juries, and excluded from theaters, restaurants, hotels, and inns. Under President Wilson, the Federal Government began to require segregation in Government buildings; desks of Negro employees were curtained off; separate bathrooms and separate tables in the cafeterias were provided; and even the galleries of the Congress were segregated. When his segregationist policies were attacked, President Wilson responded that segregation was not humiliating but a benefit'" and that he was "'rendering [the Negroes] more safe in their possession of office and less likely to be discriminated against.'" Kluger 91.

The enforced segregation of the races continued into the middle of the 20th century. In both World Wars, Negroes were for the most part confined to separate military units; it was not until 1948 that an end to segregation in the military was ordered by President Truman. And the history of the exclusion of Negro children from white public schools is too well known and recent to require repeating here. That Negroes were deliberately excluded from public graduate and professional schools—and thereby denied the opportunity to become doctors, lawyers, engineers, and the like—is also well established. It is of course true that some of the Jim Crow laws (which the decisions of this Court had helped to foster) were struck down by this Court in a series of decisions leading up to *Brown* v. *Board of Education,* 347 U.S. 483 (1954). See, *e.g., Morgan* v. *Virginia,* 328 U.S. 373 (1946); *Sweatt* v. *Painter,* 339 U.S. 629 (1950); *McLaurin* v. *Oklahoma State Regents,* 339 U.S. 647 (1950). Those decisions, however, did not automatically end segregation, nor did they move Negroes from a position of legal inferiority to one of equality. The legacy of years of slavery and of years of second-class citizenship in the wake of emancipation could not be so easily eliminated.

## — II —

The position of the Negro today in America is the tragic but inevitable consequence of centuries of unequal treatment. Measured by any benchmark of comfort or achievement, meaningful equality remains a distant dream for the Negro.

A Negro child today has a life expectancy which is shorter by more than five years than that of a white child. The Negro child's mother is over three times more likely to die of complications in childbirth, and the infant mortality rate for Negroes is nearly twice that for whites. The median income of the Negro family is only 60% that of the median of a white family, and the percentage of Negroes who live in families with incomes below the poverty line is nearly four times greater than that of whites.

When the Negro child reaches working age, he finds that America offers him significantly less than it offers his white counterpart. For Negro adults, the unemployment rate is twice that of whites, and the unemployment rate for Negro teenagers is nearly three times that of white teenagers. A Negro male who completes four years of college can expect a median annual income of merely $110 more than a white male who has only a high school diploma. Although Negroes represent 11.5% of the population, they are only 1.2% of the lawyers and judges, 2% of the physicians, 2.3% of the dentists, 1.1% of the engineers and 2.6% of the college and university professors.

The relationship between those figures and the history of unequal treatment afforded to the Negro cannot be denied. At every point from birth to death the impact of the past is reflected in the still disfavored position of the Negro.

In light of the sorry history of discrimination and its devastating impact on the lives of Negroes, bringing the Negro into the mainstream of American life should be a state interest of the highest order. To fail to do so is to ensure that American will forever remain a divided society.

— III —

I do not believe that the Fourteenth Amendment requires us to accept that fate. Neither its history nor our past cases lend any support to the conclusion that a university may not remedy the cumulative effects of society's discrimination by giving consideration to race in an effort to increase the number and percentage of Negro doctors.

A

... It is plain that the Fourteenth Amendment was not intended to prohibit measures designed to remedy the effects of the Nation's past treatment of Negroes. ...

Since the Congress that considered and rejected the objections to the 1866 Freedmen's Bureau Act concerning special relief to Negroes also proposed the Fourteenth Amendment, it is inconceivable that the Fourteenth Amendment was intended to prohibit all race-conscious relief measures. It "would be a distortion of the policy manifested in that amendment, which was adopted to prevent state legislation designed to perpetuate discrimination on the basis of race or color," *Railway Mail Assn.* v. *Corsi*, 326 U.S. 88, 94 (1945), to hold that it barred state action to remedy the effects of that discrimination. Such a result would pervert the intent of the Framers by substituting abstract equality for the genuine equality the Amendment was intended to achieve.

— IV —

While I applaud the judgment of the Court that a university may consider race in its admissions process, it is more than a little ironic that, after several hundred years of class-based discrimination against Negroes, the Court is unwilling to hold that a class-based remedy for that discrimination is permissible. In declining to so hold, today's judgment ignores the fact that for several hundred years Negroes have been discriminated against, not as individuals, but rather solely because of the color of their skins. It is unnecessary in 20th century America to have individual Negroes demonstrate that they have been victims of racial discrimination; the racism of our society has been so pervasive that none, regardless of wealth or position, has managed to escape its impact. The experience of Negroes in America has been different in kind, not just in degree, from that of other ethnic groups. It is not merely the history of slavery alone but also that a whole people were marked as inferior by the law. And that mark has endured. The dream of America as the great melting pot has not been realized for the Negro; because of his skin color he never even made it into the pot.

These differences in the experience of the Negro make it difficult for me to accept that Negroes cannot be afforded greater protection under the Fourteenth Amendment where it is necessary to remedy the effects of past discrimination.

It is because of a legacy of unequal treatment that we now must permit the institutions of this society to give consideration to race in making decisions about who will hold the position of influence, affluence, and prestige in America. For far too long, the doors to those positions have been shut to Negroes. If we are ever to become a fully integrated society, one in which the color of a person's skin will not determine the opportunities available to him or her, we must be willing to take steps to open those doors. I do not believe that anyone can truly look into America's past and still find that a remedy for the effects of that past is impermissible.

It has been said that this case involves only the individual, Bakke, and this University. I doubt, however, that there is a computer capable of determining the number of persons and institutions that may be affected by the decision in this case. For example, we are told by the Attorney General of the United States that at least 27 federal agencies have adopted regulations requiring recipients of federal funds to take *"affirmative action* to overcome the effects of conditions which resulted in limiting participation . . . by persons of a particular race, color, or national origin." Supplemental Brief for United States as *Amicus Curiae* 16 (emphasis added). I cannot even guess the number of state and local governments that have set up affirmative-action programs, which may be affected by today's decision.

I fear that we have come full circle. After the Civil War our Government started several "affirmative action" programs. This Court in the *Civil Rights Cases* and *Plessy* v. *Ferguson* destroyed the movement toward complete equality. For almost a century no action was taken, and this nonaction was with the tacit approval of the courts. Then we had *Brown* v. *Board of Education* and the Civil Rights Acts of Congress, followed by numerous affirmative-action programs. Now, we have this Court again stepping in, this time to stop affirmative-action programs of the type used by the University of California.

MR. JUSTICE BLACKMUN.

I participate fully, of course, in the opinion, *ante,* p. 324, that bears the names of my Brothers Brennan, White, Marshall, and myself. I add only some general observations that hold particular significance for me, and then a few comments on equal protection. . . .

I yield to no one in my earnest hope that the time will come when an "affirmative action" program is unnecessary and is, in truth, only a relic of the past. I would hope that we could reach this stage within a decade at the most. But the story of *Brown* v. *Board of Education,* 347 U.S. 483 (1954), decided almost a quarter of a century ago, suggests that that hope is a slim one. At some time, however, beyond any period of what some would claim is only transitional inequality, the United States must and will reach a stage of maturity where action along this line is no longer necessary. Then persons will be regarded as persons, and discrimination of the type we address today will be an ugly feature of history that is instructive but that is behind us.

The number of qualified, indeed highly qualified, applicants for admission to existing medical schools in the United States far exceeds the number of places available. Wholly apart from racial and ethnic considerations, therefore, the selection process inevitably results in the denial of admission to many *qualified* persons, indeed, to far more than the number of those who are granted admission. . . .

One theoretical solution to the need for more minority members in higher education would be to enlarge our graduate schools. Then all who desired and were qualified could enter, and talk of discrimination would vanish. Unfortunately, this is neither feasible nor realistic. The vast resources that apparently would be required simply are not available. And the need for more professional graduates, in the strict numerical sense, perhaps has not been demonstrated at all.

It is somewhat ironic to have us so deeply disturbed over a program where race is an element of consciousness, and yet to be aware of the fact, as we are, that institutions of higher learning, albeit more on the undergraduate than the graduate level, have given conceded preferences up to a point to those possessed of athletic skills, to the children of alumni, to the affluent who may bestow their largess on the institutions, and to those having connections with celebrities, the famous, and the powerful. . . .

I suspect that it would be impossible to arrange an affirmative-action program in a racially neutral way and have it successful. To ask that this be so is to demand the impossible. In order to get beyond racism, we must first take account of race. There is no other way. And in order to treat some persons equally, we must treat them differently. We cannot—we dare not—let the Equal Protection Clause perpetuate racial supremacy.

MR. JUSTICE STEVENS, with whom THE CHIEF JUSTICE BURGER, MR. JUSTICE STEWART, and MR. JUSTICE REHNQUIST join, concurring in the judgment in part and dissenting in part.

It is always important at the outset to focus precisely on the controversy before the Court. . . .

## — II —

Both petitioner and respondent have asked us to determine the legality of the University's special admissions program by reference to the Constitution. Our settled practice, however, is to avoid the decision of a constitutional issue if a case can be fairly decided on a statutory ground. "If there is one doctrine more deeply rooted than any other in the process of constitutional adjudication, it is that we ought not to pass on questions of constitutionality . . . unless such adjudications is unavoidable." *Spector Motor Co.* v. *McLaughlin,* 323 U.S. 101, 105. The more important the issue, the more force there is to this doctrine. In this case, we are presented with a constitutional question of undoubted and unusual importance. Since, however, a dispositive statutory claim was raised at the very inception of this case, and squarely decided in the portion of the trial court judgment affirmed by the California Supreme Court, it is our plain duty to confront it. Only if petitioner should prevail on the statutory issue would it be necessary to decide whether the University's admissions program violated the Equal Protection Clause of the Fourteenth Amendment.

## — III —

Section 601 of the Civil Rights Act of 1964, 78 Stat. 252, 42 U.S.C. §2000d, provides:

"No person in the United States shall, on the ground of race, color, or national origin, be excluded from participation in, be denied the benefits of, or be subjected to discrimination under any program or activity receiving Federal financial assistance." . . .

As with other provisions of the Civil Rights Act, Congress' expression of its policy to end racial discrimination may independently proscribe conduct that the Constitution does not. However, we need not decide the congruence—or lack of congruence—of the controlling statute and the Constitution since the meaning of the Title VI ban on exclusion is crystal clear: Race cannot be the basis of excluding anyone from participation in a federally funded program.

The University's special admissions program violated Title VI of the Civil Rights Act of 1964 by excluding Bakke from the Medical School because of his race. It is therefore our duty to affirm the judgment ordering Bakke admitted to the University.

Accordingly, I concur in the Court's judgment insofar as it affirms the judgment of the Supreme Court of California. To the extent that it purports to do anything else, I respectfully dissent.

## *Notes*

\* Briefs of amici curiae urging reversal were filed by *Slade Gorton*, Attorney General, and *James B. Wilson*, Senior Assistant General, for the State of Washington et al.; by *E. Richard Larson, Joel M. Gora, Charles C. Marson, Sanford Jay Rosen, Fred Okrand, Norman Dorsen, Ruth Bader Ginsburg,* and *Frank Askin* for the American Civil Liberties Union et al.; by *Edgar S. Cahn, Jean Camper Cahn,* and *Robert S. Catz* for the Antioch School of Law; by *William Jack Chow* for the Asian American Bar Assn. of the Greater Bay Area; by *A. Kenneth Pye, Robert B. McKay, David E. Feller,* and *Ernest Gellhorn* for the Association of American Law Schools; by *John Holt Meyers* for the Association of American Medical Colleges; by *Jerome B. Falk* and *Peter Roos* for the Bar Assn. of San Francisco et al.; by *Ephraim Margolin* for the Black Law Students Assn. at the University of California, Berkeley School of Law; by *John T. Baker* for the Black Law Students Union of Yale University Law School; by *Annamay T. Sheppard* and *Jonathan M. Hyman* for the Board of Governors of Rutgers, State University of New Jersey, et al.; by *Robert J. Willey* for the Cleveland State University Chapter of the Black American Law Students Assn.; by *John Mason Harding, Albert J. Rosenthal, Daniel Steiner, Iris Brest, James v. Siena, Louis H. Pollak,* and *Michael I. Sovern* for Columbia University et al.; by *Herbert O. Reid* for Howard University; by *Harry B. Reese* and *L. Orin Slagle* for the Law School Admission Council; by *Albert E. Jenner, Jr., Stephen J. Pollak, Burke Marshall, Norman Redlich, Robert A. Murphy,* and *William E. Caldwell* for the Lawyers' Committee for Civil Rights Under Law; by *Alice Daniel* and *James E. Coleman, Jr.,* for the Legal Services Corp.; by *Nathaniel R. Jones, Nathaniel S. Colley,* and *Stanley Goodman* for the National Assn. for the Advancement of Colored People; by *Jack Greenberg, James M. Nabrit III, Charles S. Ralston, Eric Shnapper,* and *David E. Kendall* for the NAACP Legal Defense and Educational Fund, Inc.; by *Stephen V. Bomse* for the National Assn. of Minority Contractors et al.; by *Richard R. Sobol, Marian Wright Edelman, Stephen P. Berzon,* and *Joseph L. Rauh, Jr.,* for the National Council of Churches of Christ in the United States et al.; by *Barbara A. Morris, Joan Bertin Lowy,* and *Diana H. Greene* for the National Employment Law Project, Inc.; by *Herbert O. Reid* and *J. Clay Smith, Jr.,* for the National Medical Assn., Inc., et al.: by *Robert Hermann* for the Puerto Rican Legal Defense and Education Fund et al.; by *Robert Allen Sedler, Howard Lesnick,* and *Arval A. Morris* for the Society of American Law Teachers; for the American Medical Student Assn.; and for the Council on Legal Education Opportunity.

Briefs of *amici curiae* urging affirmance were filed by *Lawrence A. Poltrock* and *Wayne B. Giampietro* for the American Federation of Teachers; by *Abraham S. Goldstein, Nathan Z. Dershowitz, Arthur J. Gajarsa, Thaddeus L. Kowalski, Anthony J. Fornelli, Howard L. Greenberger, Samuel Rabinove, Themis N. Anastos, Julian E. Kulas,* and *Alan M. Dershowitz* for the American Jewish Committee et al.; by *McNeill Stokes* and *Ira J. Smotherman, Jr.,* for the American Subcontractors Assn.; by *Philip B. Kurland, Daniel D. Polsby, Larry M. Lavinsky, Arnold Forster, Dennis Rapps, Anthony J. Fornelli, Leonard Greenwald,* and *David I. Ashe* for the Anti-Defamation League of B'nai B'rith et al.; by *Charles G. Bakaly* and *Lawrence B. Kraus* for the Chamber of Commerce of the United States; by *Roger A. Clark, Jerome K. Tankel,* and *Glen R. Murphy* for the Fraternal Order of Police et al.; by *Judith R. Cohn* for the Order Sons of Italy in America; by *Ronald A. Zumbrun, John H. Findley,* and *William F. Harvey* for the Pacific Legal Foundation; by *Benjamin Vinar* and *David I. Caplan* for the Queens Jewish Community Council et al.; and by *Jennings P. Felix* for Young Americans for Freedom.

Briefs of *amici curiae* were filed by *Matthew W. Finkin* for the American Assn. of University Professors; by *John W. Finley, Jr., Michael Blinick, John Cannon, Leonard J. Theberge,* and *Edward H. Dowd* for the Committee on Academic Nondiscrimination and Integrity et al.; by *Kenneth C. McGuiness, Robert E. Williams, Douglas S. McDowell,* and *Ronald M. Green* for the Equal Employment Advisory Council; by *Charles E. Wilson* for the Fair Employment Practice Comm'n of California; by *Mario G. Obledo* for Jerome A. Lackner, Director of the Department of Health of California, et al.; by *Vilma S. Martinez, Peter D. Roos,* and *Ralph Santiago Abscal* for the Mexican American Legal Defense and Educational Fund, et al.; by *Eva S. Goodwin* for the National Assn. of Affirmative Action Officers; by *Lennox S. Hinds* for the National Conference of Black Lawyers; by *David Ginsburg* for the National Fund for Minority Engineering Students; by *A. John Wabaunsee, Walter R. EchoHawk,* and *Thomas W. Fredericks* for the Native American Law Students of the University of California at Davis et al.; by *Joseph A. Broderick, Calvin Brown, LeMarquis Dejarmon, James E. Ferguson II, Harry E. Groves, John H. Harmon, William A. Marsh, Jr.,* and *James W. Smith* for the North Carolina Assn. of Black Lawyers; by *Leonard F. Walentynowicz* for the Polish American Congress et al.; by *Daniel M. Luevano* and *John E. McDermott* for the UCLA Black Law Students Assn. et al.; by *Henry A. Waxman pro se;* by *Leo Branton, Jr., Ann Fagan Ginger, Sam Rosewein,* and *Laurence R. Sperber* for Price M. Cobbs, M.D., et al.; by *John S. Nolan* for Ralph J. Galliano; and by *Daniel T. Spitler* for Timothy J. Hoy.

1. In *Albemarle,* we approved "differential validation" of employment tests. See 422 U.S., at 435. That procedure requires that an employer must ensure that a test score of, for example, 50 for a minority job applicant means the same thing as a score of 50 for a non-minority applicant. By implication, were it determined that a test score of 50 for a minority corresponded in "potential for employment" to a 60 for whites, the test could not be used consistently with Title VII unless the employer hired minorities with scores of 50 even though he might not hire nonminority applicants with scores above 50 but below 60. Thus, it is clear that employers, to ensure equal opportunity, may have to adopt race-conscious hiring practices.

2. I also join Parts I, III-A, and V-C of Mr. Justice Powell's opinion.

3. Petitioner defines "quota" as a requirement which must be met but can never be exceeded, regardless of the quality of the minority applicants. Petitioner declares that there is no

"floor" under the total number of minority students admitted; completely unqualified students will not be admitted simply to meet a "quota." Neither is there a "ceiling," since an unlimited number could be admitted through the general admissions process. On this basis the special admissions program does not meet petitioner's definition of a quota.

The court below found—and petitioner does not deny—that white applicants could not compete for the 16 places reserved solely for the special admissions program. 18 Cal.3d, at 44, 553 P. 2d, at 1159. Both courts below characterized this as a "quota" system.

---

**Regents of the University of California v. Bakke**, 438 U.S. 265 (1978) 5–4
*editor's note.*
*Opinion authors are in bold; () indicates the party of appointing president. If the party of the justice differs from that of appointing president, then the party of the justice is listed second after the slash.*

| MAJORITY | CONCURRING | DISSENTING |
|---|---|---|
| **Powell** (d) | *(in part and dissenting in part\*)* | *(in part and concurring in part# )* |
| | **Stevens** (r) | **Brennan** (r/d) |
| | Burger (r) | **White** (d) |
| | Stewart (r) | **Marshall** (d) |
| | Rehnquist (r) | **Blackmun** (r) |

\*These four justices *agreed* with Powell's holding that the University of California, Davis special admissions program is unconstitutional and Bakke must be admitted. But, these four justices *disagree* with Powell's holding that race may be taken into account as a factor in future admissions decisions.

#These four justices *disagree* with Powell's holding that the University of California, Davis special admissions program is unconstitutional and Bakke must be admitted. But, these four justices *agree* with Powell's holding that race may be taken into account as a factor in future admissions decisions.

# Frontiero et vir v. Richardson, Secretary of Defense, et al.

## 411 U.S. 677

## Appeal from the United States District Court for the Middle District of Alabama

No. 71–1694. Argued January 17, 1973—Decided May 14, 1973

*Joseph J. Levin, Jr.,* argued the cause for appellants. With him on the brief was *Morris S. Dees, Jr.*

*Samuel Huntington* argued the cause for appellees. On the brief were *Solicitor General Griswold, Assistant Attorney General Wood,* and *Mark L. Evans.*

*Ruth Bader Ginsburg* argued the cause for the American Civil Liberties Union as *amicus curiae* urging reversal. With her on the brief was *Melvin L. Wulf.*

MR. JUSTICE BRENNAN announced the judgment of the Court and an opinion in which MR. JUSTICE DOUGLAS, MR. JUSTICE WHITE, and MR. JUSTICE MARSHALL join.

The question before us concerns the right of a female member of the uniformed services[1] to claim her spouse as a "dependent" for the purposes of obtaining increased quarters allowances and medical and dental benefits under 37 U.S.C. §§ 401, 403, and 10 U.S.C. §§ 1072, 1076, on an equal footing with male members. Under these statutes, a serviceman may claim his wife as a "dependent" without regard to whether she is in fact dependent upon him for any part of her support. 37 U.S.C. § 401 (1); 10 U.S.C. § 1072 (2) (A). A servicewoman, on the other hand, may not claim her husband as a "dependent" under these programs unless he is in fact dependent upon her for over one-half of his support. 37 U.S.C. § 401; 10 U.S.C. § 1072 (2)(C).

Thus, the question for decision is whether this difference in treatment constitutes an unconstitutional discrimination against servicewomen in violation of the Due Process Clause of the Fifth Amendment. A three-judge District Court for the Middle District of Alabama, one judge dissenting, rejected this contention and sustained the constitutionality of the provisions of the statutes making this distinction. 341 F. Supp. 201 (1972). We noted probable jurisdiction. 409 U.S. 840 (1972). We reverse. . . .

Appellant Sharron Frontiero, a lieutenant in the United States Air Force, sought increased quarters allowances, and housing and medical benefits for her husband, appellant Joseph Frontiero, on the ground that he was her "dependent." Although such benefits would automatically have been granted with respect to the wife of a male member of the uniformed services, appellant's application was denied because she failed to demonstrate that her husband was dependent on her for more than one-half of his support. Appellants then commenced this suit, contending that, by making this distinction, the statutes unreasonably discriminate on the basis of sex in violation of the Due Process Clause of the Fifth Amendment. In essence, appellants asserted that the discriminatory impact of the statutes is twofold: first, as a procedural matter, a female member is required to demonstrate her spouse's dependency, while no such burden is imposed upon male members; and, second, as a substantive matter, a male member who does not provide more than one-half of his wife's support receives benefits, while a similarly situated female member is denied such benefits. Appellants therefore sought a permanent injunction against the continued enforcement of these statutes and an order directing the appellees to provide Lieutenant Frontiero with the same housing and medical benefits that a similarly situated male member would receive.

Although the legislative history of these statutes sheds virtually no light on the purposes underlying the differential treatment accorded male and female members, a majority of the three-judge District Court surmised that Congress might reasonably have concluded that, since the husband in our society is generally the "bread winner" in the family—and the wife typically the "dependent" partner—" it would be more economical to require married female members claiming husbands to prove actual dependency than to extend the presumption of dependency to such members." 341 F. Supp., at 207. Indeed, given the fact that approximately 99% of all members of the uniformed services are male, the District Court speculated that such differential treatment might conceivably lead to a "considerable saving of administrative expense and manpower." *Ibid.*

— **II** —

At the outset, appellants contend that classifications based upon sex, like classifications based upon race, alienage, and national origin, are inherently suspect and must therefore be subjected to close judicial scrutiny. We agree and, indeed, find at least implicit support for such an approach in our unanimous decision only last Term in *Reed* v. *Reed,* 404 U.S. 71 (1971).

In *Reed,* the Court considered the constitutionality of an Idaho statute providing that, when two individuals are otherwise equally entitled to appointment as administrator of an estate, the male applicant must be preferred to the female . . . the Court held the statutory preference for male applicants unconstitutional. In reaching this result, the Court implicitly rejected appellee's apparently rational explanation of the statutory scheme, and concluded that, by ignoring the individual qualifications of particular applicants, the challenged statute provided "dissimilar treatment for men and women who are . . . similarly situated." 404 U. S., at 77. The Court therefore held that, even though the State's interest in achieving administrative efficiency "is not without some legitimacy," "[t]o give a mandatory preference to members of either sex over members of the other, merely to accomplish the elimination of hearings on the merits, is to make the very kind of arbitrary legislative choice forbidden by the [Constitution] . . . . *Id.,* at 76. This departure from "traditional" rational-basis analysis with respect to sex-based classifications is clearly justified.

There can be no doubt that our Nation has had a long and unfortunate history of sex discrimination. Traditionally, such discrimination was rationalized by an attitude of "romantic paternalism" which, in practical effect, put women, not on a pedestal, but in a cage. Indeed, this paternalistic attitude became so firmly rooted in our national consciousness that, 100 years ago, a distinguished Member of this Court was able to proclaim:

> "Man is, or should be, woman's protector and defender. The natural and proper timidity and delicacy which belongs to the female sex evidently unfits it for many of the occupations of civil life. The constitution of the family organization, which is founded in the divine ordinance, as well as in the nature of things, indicates the domestic sphere as that which properly belongs to the domain and functions of womanhood. The harmony, not to say identity, of interests and views which belong, or should belong, to the family institution is repugnant to the idea of a woman adopting a distinct and independent career from that of her husband. . . .

> ". . . The paramount destiny and mission of woman are to fulfil the noble and benign offices of wife and mother. This is the law of the Creator." *Bradwell* v. *State,* 16 Wall. 130, 141 (1873) (Bradley, J., concurring).

As a result of notions such as these, our statute books gradually became laden with gross, stereotyped distinctions between the sexes and, indeed, throughout much of the 19th century the position of women in our society was, in many respects, comparable to that of blacks under the pre-Civil War slave codes. Neither slaves nor women could hold office, serve on juries, or bring suit in their own names, and married women traditionally were denied the legal capacity to hold or convey property or to serve as legal guardians of their own children. See generally L. Kanowitz, Women and the Law: The Unfinished Revolution 5–6 (1969); G. Myrdal, An American Dilemma 1073 (20th anniversary ed. 1962). And although blacks were guaranteed the right to vote in 1870, women were denied even that right—which is itself "preservative of other basic civil and political rights"—until adoption of the Nineteenth Amendment half a century later.

It is true, of course, that the position of women in America has improved markedly in recent decades. Nevertheless, it can hardly be doubted that, in part because of the high visibility of the sex characteristic, women still face pervasive, although at times more subtle, discrimination in our educational institutions, in the job market and, perhaps most conspicuously, in the political arena.[2] See generally K. Amundsen, The Silenced Majority: Women and American Democracy (1971); The President's Task Force on Women's Rights and Responsibilities, A Matter of Simple Justice (1970).

Moreover, since sex, like race and national origin, is an immutable characteristic determined solely by the accident of birth, the imposition of special disabilities upon the members of a particular sex because of their sex would seem to violate "the basic concept of our system that legal burdens should bear some relationship to individual responsibility . . . ." *Weber* v. *Aetna Casualty & Surety Co.*, 406 U.S. 164, 175 (1972). And what differentiates sex from such nonsuspect statuses as intelligence or physical disability, and aligns it with the recognized suspect criteria, is that the sex characteristic frequently bears no relation to ability to perform or contribute to society. As a result, statutory distinctions between the sexes often have the effect of invidiously relegating the entire class of females to inferior legal status without regard to the actual capabilities of its individual members.

We might also note that, over the past decade, Congress has itself manifested an increasing sensitivity to sex-based classifications. . . . Thus, Congress itself has concluded that classifications based upon sex are inherently invidious, and this conclusion of a coequal branch of Government is not without significance to the question presently under consideration. Cf. *Oregon* v. *Mitchell*, 400 U.S. 112, 240, 248–249 (1970) (opinion of BRENNAN, WHITE, and MARSHALL, JJ.); *Katzenbach* v. *Morgan*, 384 U.S. 641, 648–649 (1966).

With these considerations in mind, we can only conclude that classifications based upon sex, like classifications based upon race, alienage, or national origin, are inherently suspect, and must therefore be subjected to strict judicial scrutiny. Applying the analysis mandated by that stricter standard of review, it is clear that the statutory scheme now before us is constitutionally invalid.

# — III —

The sole basis of the classification established in the challenged statutes is the sex of the individuals involved. Thus, under 37 U.S.C. §§ 401, 403, and 10 U.S.C. §§ 1072, 1076, a female member of the uniformed services seeking to obtain housing and medical benefits for her spouse must prove his dependency in fact, whereas no such burden is imposed upon male members. In addition, the statutes operate so as to deny benefits to a female member, such as appellant Sharron Frontiero, who provides less than one-half of her spouse's support, while at the same time granting such benefits to a male member who likewise provides less than one-half of his spouse's support. Thus, to this extent at least, it may fairly be said that these statutes command "dissimilar treatment for men and women who are . . . similarly situated." *Reed* v. *Reed,* 404 U. S., at 77.

Moreover, the Government concedes that the differential treatment accorded men and women under these statutes serves no purpose other than mere "administrative convenience." In essence, the Government maintains that, as an empirical matter, wives in our society frequently are dependent upon their husbands, while husbands rarely are dependent upon their wives. Thus, the Government argues that Congress might reasonably have concluded that it would be both cheaper and easier simply conclusively to presume that wives of male members are financially dependent upon their husbands, while burdening female members with the task of establishing dependency in fact.[3]

The Government offers no concrete evidence, however, tending to support its view that such differential treatment in fact saves the Government any money. In order to satisfy the demands of strict judicial scrutiny, the Government must demonstrate, for example, that it is actually cheaper to grant increased benefits with respect to *all* male members, than it is to determine which male members are in fact entitled to such benefits and to grant increased benefits only to those members whose wives actually meet the dependency requirement. Here, however, there is substantial evidence that, if put to the test, many of the wives of male members would fail to qualify for benefits. And in light of the fact that the dependency determination with respect to the husbands of female members is presently made solely on the basis of affidavits, rather than through the more costly hearing process, the Government's explanation of the statutory scheme is, to say the least, questionable.

In any case, our prior decisions make clear that, although efficacious administration of governmental programs is not without some importance, "the Constitution recognizes higher values than speed and efficiency." *Stanley* v. *Illinois,* 405 U.S. 645, 656 (1972). And when we enter the realm of "strict judicial scrutiny," there can be no doubt that "administrative convenience" is not a shibboleth, the mere recitation of which dictates constitutionality. See *Shapiro* v. *Thompson*, 394 U.S. 618 (1969); *Carrington* v. *Rash*, 380 U.S. 89 (1965). On the contrary, any statutory scheme which draws a sharp line between the sexes, *solely* for the purpose, of achieving administrative convenience, necessarily commands "dissimilar treatment for men and women who are ... similarly situated," and therefore involves the "very kind of arbitrary legislative choice forbidden by the [Constitution] . . . ." Reed v. *Reed*, 404 U. S., at 77, 76. We therefore conclude that, by according differential treatment to male and female members of the uniformed services for the sole purpose of achieving administrative convenience, the challenged statutes violate the Due Process Clause of the Fifth Amendment insofar as they require a female member to prove the dependency of her husband.

*Reversed.*

MR. JUSTICE STEWART concurs in the judgment, agreeing that the statutes before us work an invidious discrimination in violation of the Constitution. *Reed* v. *Reed*, 404 U.S. 71.

MR. JUSTICE REHNQUIST dissents for the reasons stated by Judge Rives in his opinion for the District Court, *Frontiero* v. *Laird*, 341 F. Supp. 201 (1972).

MR. JUSTICE POWELL, with whom THE CHIEF JUSTICE and MR. JUSTICE BLACKMUN join, concurring in the judgment.

I agree that the challenged statutes constitute an unconstitutional discrimination against servicewomen in violation of the Due Process Clause of the Fifth Amendment, but I cannot join the opinion of Mr. Justice Brennan, which would hold that all classifications based upon sex, "like classifications based upon race, alienage, and national origin," are "inherently suspect and must therefore be subjected to close judicial scrutiny." *Ante*, at 682. It is unnecessary for the Court in this case to characterize sex as a suspect classification, with all of the far-reaching implications of such a holding. *Reed* v. *Reed*, 404 U.S. 71 (1971), which abundantly supports our decision today, did not add sex to the narrowly limited group of classifications which are inherently suspect. In my view, we can and should decide this case on the authority of *Reed* and reserve for the future any expansion of its rationale.

There is another, and I find compelling, reason for deferring a general categorizing of sex classifications as invoking the strictest test of judicial scrutiny. The Equal Rights Amendment, which if adopted will resolve the substance of this precise question, has been approved by the Congress and submitted for ratification by the States. If this Amendment is duly adopted, it will represent the will of the people accomplished in the manner prescribed by the Constitution. By acting prematurely and unnecessarily, as I view it, the Court has assumed a decisional responsibility at the very time when state legislatures, functioning within the traditional democratic process, are debating the proposed Amendment. It seems to me that this reaching out to pre-empt by judicial action a major political decision which is currently in process of resolution does not reflect appropriate respect for duly prescribed legislative processes.

There are times when this Court, under our system, cannot avoid a constitutional decision on issues which normally should be resolved by the elected representatives of the people. But democratic institutions are weakened, and confidence in the restraint of the Court is impaired, when we appear unnecessarily to decide sensitive issues of broad social and political importance at the very time they are under consideration within the prescribed constitutional processes.

## *Notes*

1. The "uniformed services" include the Army, Navy, Air Force, Marine Corps, Coast Guard, Environmental Science Services Administration, and Public Health Service. 37 U.S.C. § 101 (3); 10 U.S.C. § 1072 (1).

2. It, is true, of course, that when viewed in the abstract, women do not constitute a small and powerless minority. Nevertheless, in part because of past discrimination, women are vastly underrepresented in this Nation's decisionmaking councils. There has never been a female President, nor a female member of this Court. Not a single woman presently sits in the United States Senate, and only 14 women hold seats in the House of Representatives. And, as appellants point out, this underrepresentation is present throughout all levels of our State and Federal Government. See Joint Reply Brief of Appellants and American Civil Liberties Union (Amicus *Curiae)* 9.

3. It should be noted that these statutes are not in any sense designed to rectify the effects of past discrimination against women. See *Gruenwald* v. *Gardner,* 390 F. 2d 591 (CA2), cert. denied, 393 U.S. 982 (1968); ef. *Jones* v. *Alfred H. Mayer Co.,* 392 U.S. 409 (1968); *South Carolina* v. *Katzenbach,* 383 U.S. 301 (1966). On the contrary, these statutes seize upon a group— women—who have historically suffered discrimination in employment, and rely on the effects of this past discrimination as a justification for heaping on additional economic disadvantages. Cf. *Gaston County* v. *United States.* 395 U.S. 285. 296–297 (1969).

**Frontiero, v. Richardson,** 411 U.S. 677 (1973) 8–1

*editor's note.*

*Opinion authors are in bold; () indicates the party of appointing president. If the party of the justice differs from that of appointing president, then the party of the justice is listed second after the slash.*

| MAJORITY | CONCURRING | DISSENTING |
|---|---|---|
| **Brennan** (r/d) | **Stewart** (r) | Rehnquist (r) |
| Douglas (d) | **Powell** (r/d) | |
| White (d) | Burger (r) | |
| Marshall (d) | Blackmun (r) | |

# San Antonio Independent School District et al.,

## Appellants,

## v.

# Demetrio P. Rodriguez et al.

411 U.S. 1

[No. 71–1332]

Argued October 12, 1972. Decided March 21, 1973.

reh den 411 US 959,

*Charles Alan Wright,* argued the cause and, with *Crawford C. Martin,* Attorney General of Texas, *Nola White,* First Assistant Attorney General, *Alfred Walker,* Executive Assistant Attorney General, *J.C. Davis* and *Pat Bailey,* Assistant Attorneys General, and *Samuel D. McDaniel* filed briefs for appellants.

*Arthur Gochman* argued the cause and, with *Mario Obledo* filed a brief for appellees.

*George F. Kugler, Jr.*, Attorney General, pro se, and *Stephen Skillman*, Assistant Attorney General, filed a brief for the Attorney General of New Jersey as amicus curiae urging reversal; *George W. Liebmann* and *Shale D. Stiller*, joined by *Francis B. Burch*, Attorney General of Maryland, *Henry R. Lord*, Deputy Attorney General, *E. Stephen Derby*, Assistant Attorney General, *William J. Baxley*, Attorney General of Alabama, *Gary K. Nelson*, Attorney General of Arizona, *James G. Bond*, Assistant Attorney General, *Evelle J. Younger*, Attorney General of California, *Elizabeth Palmer*, Assistant Attorney General, *Edward M. Belasco*, Deputy Attorney General, *Duke W. Dunbar*, Attorney General of Colorado, *Robert K. Killian*, Attorney General of Connecticut, *F. Michael Ahern*, Assistant Attorney General, *W. Anthony Park*, Attorney General of Idaho, *James R. Hargis*, Deputy Attorney General, *Theodore L. Sendak*, Attorney General of Indiana, *Charles M. Wells, Harry T. Ice, Richard C. Turner*, Attorney General of Iowa, *George W. Murray*, Assistant Attorney General, *Vern Miller*, Attorney General of Kansas, *Matthew J. Dowd* and *John C. Johnson*, Assistant Attorneys General, *Ed W. Hancock*, Attorney General of Kentucky, *Carl T. Miller*, Assistant Attorney General, *William J. Guste, Jr.*, Attorney General of Louisiana, *James S. Erwin*, Attorney General of Maine, *George West*, Assistant Attorney General, *Robert H. Quinn*, Attorney General of Massachusetts, *Lawrence T. Bench*, Assistant Attorney General, *Charles F. Clippert, William M. Saxton, Robert B. Webster, A. F. Summer*, Attorney General of Mississippi, *Martin R. McLendon*, Assistant Attorney General, *John Danforth*, Attorney General of Missouri, *D. Brook Bartlett*, Assistant Attorney General, *Clarence A. H. Meyer*, Attorney General of Nebraska, *Harold Mosher*, Assistant Attorney General, *Warren B. Rudman*, Attorney General of New Hampshire, *Louis J. Lefkowitz*, Attorney General of New York, *Robert B. Morgan*, Attorney General of North Carolina, *Burley B. Mitchell, Jr.*, Assistant Attorney General, *Helgi Johanneson*, Attorney General of North Dakota, *Gerald Vandewalle*, Assistant Attorney General, *Lee Johnson*, Attorney General of Oregon, *Daniel R. McLeod*, Attorney General of South Carolina, *G. Lewis Argoe, Jr.*, Assistant Attorney General, *Gordon Mydland*, Attorney General of South Dakota, *C.J. Kelly*, Assistant Attorney General, *David M. Pack*, Attorney General of Tennessee, *Milton P. Rice*, Deputy Attorney General, *Vernon B. Romney*, Attorney General of Utah, *Robert B. Hansen*, Deputy Attorney General, *James M. Jeffords*, Attorney General of Vermont, *Chauncey H. Browning, Jr.*, Attorney General of West Virginia, *Victor A. Barone*, Assistant Attorney General, *Robert W. Warren*, Attorney General of Wisconsin, and *Betty R. Brown*, Assistant Attorney General, filed a brief for Montgomery County, Maryland, as amicus curiae urging reversal; and *John D. Maharg* and *James W. Briggs* filed a brief for Richard M. Clowes, Superintendent of Schools of the County of Los Angeles, et al. as amici curiae urging reversal.

*David Bonderman* and *Peter Van N. Lockwood* filed a brief for *Wendell Anderson*, Governor of Minnesota, et al. as amici curiae urging affirmance; *Robert R. Coffman* filed a brief for Wilson Riles, Superintendent of Public Instruction of California, et al.

as amici curiae urging affirmance; *Roderick M. Hills* filed a brief for Houston I. Flournoy, Controller of California as amicus curiae urging affirmance; *Ramsey Clark, John Silard, David C. Long, George L. Russell, Jr., Harold J. Ruvoldt, Jr., J. Albert Woll, Thomas E. Harris, John Ligtenberg, A. L. Zwerdling,* and *Stephen I. Schlossberg* filed a brief for the Mayor and City Council of Baltimore et al. as amici curiae urging affirmance; *George H. Spencer* filed a brief for San Antonio Independent School District as amicus curiae urging affirmance; *Norman Dorsen, Marvin M. Karpatkin, Melvin L. Wulf, Paul S. Berger, Joseph B. Robison, Arnold Forster,* and *Stanley P. Hebert* filed a brief for the American Civil Liberties Union et al. as amici curiae urging affirmance; *Jack Greenberg, James M. Nabrit III, Norman J. Chachkin,* and *Abramham Sofaer* filed a brief for the NAACP Legal Defense and Educational Fund, Inc. as amicus curiae urging affirmance; *Stephen J. Pollak, Ralph J. Moore, Jr., Richard M. Sharp, and David Rubin* filed a brief for the National Education Association, et al. as amici curiae urging affirmance; and *John E. Coons* filed a brief for John Serrano, Jr., et al. as amici curiae urging affirmance.

*Lawrence E. Walsh, Victor W. Bouldin, Richard B. Smith,* and *Guy M. Struve* filed a brief for the Republic National Bank of Dallas et al. as amici curiae; *Joseph R. Cortese, Joseph Guandolo, Bryce Huguenin, Manly W. Mumford, Joseph H. Johnson, Jr., Joseph Rudd, Fred H. Rosenfeld, Herschel H. Friday, George Herrington, Harry T. Ice, Cornelius W. Grafton, Fred G. Benton, Jr., Eugene E. Huppenbauer, Jr., Harold B. Judell, Robert B. Fizzell, John B. Dawson, George J. Fagin, Howard A. Rankin, Huger Sinkler, Robert W. Spence, Hobby H. McCall, James R. Ellis,* and *William J. Kiernan, Jr.,* filed a brief for Bond Counsel as amicus curiae.

MR. JUSTICE POWELL delivered the opinion of the Court.

This suit attacking the Texas system of financing public education was initiated by Mexican-American parents whose children attend the elementary and secondary schools in the Edgewood Independent School District, an urban school district in San Antonio, Texas. They brought a class action on behalf of school children throughout the State who are members of minority groups or who are poor and reside in school districts having a low property tax base. Named as defendants[1] were the State Board of Education, the Commissioner of Education, the State Attorney General, and the Bexar County (San Antonio) Board of Trustees. [A three-judge district court] rendered its judgment in a per curiarn opinion holding the Texas school finance system unconstitutional under the Equal Protection Clause of the Fourteenth Amendment. The State appealed . . . For the reasons stated in this opinion, we reverse the decision of the District Court.

## — I —

The first Texas State Constitution, promulgated upon Texas' entry into the Union in 1845, provided for the establishment of a system of free schools.[2] Early in its history, Texas adopted a dual approach to the financing of its schools, relying on mutual participation by the local school districts and the State. As early as 1883, the state constitution was amended to provide for the creation of local school districts empowered to levy ad valorem taxes with the consent of local taxpayers for the "erection . . . of school buildings" and for the "further maintenance of public free schools." Such local funds as were raised were supplemented by funds distributed to each district from the State's Permanent and Available School Funds. . . .

Until recent times, Texas was a predominantly rural State and its population and property wealth were spread relatively evenly across the State. Sizable differences in the value of assessable property between local school districts became increasingly evident as the State became more industrialized and as rural-to-urban population shifts became more pronounced. The location of commercial and industrial property began to play a significant role in determining the amount of tax resources available to each school district. These growing disparities in population and taxable property between districts were responsible in part for increasingly notable differences in levels of local expenditure for education.

The school district in which appellees reside, the Edgewood Independent School District, has been compared throughout this litigation with the Alamo Heights Independent School District. This comparison between the least and most affluent districts in the San Antonio area serves to illustrate the manner in which the dual system of finance operates and to indicate the extent to which substantial disparities exist despite the State's impressive progress in recent years. Edgewood is one of seven public school districts in the metropolitan area. Approximately 22,000 students are enrolled in its 25 elementary and secondary schools. The district is situated in the core-city sector of San Antonio in a residential neighborhood that has little commercial or industrial property. The residents are predominantly of Mexican-American descent: approximately 90% of the student population is Mexican-American and over 6% is Negro. The average assessed property value per pupil is $5,960—the lowest in the metropolitan area—and the median family income ($4,686) is also the lowest. At an equalized tax rate of $1.05 per $100 of assessed property—the highest in the metropolitan area—the district contributed $26 to the education of each child for the 1967–1968 school year above its Local Fund Assignment for the Minimum Foundation Program. The Foundation Program contributed $222 per pupil for a state-local total of $248. Federal funds added another $108 for a total of $356 per pupil. . . .

Alamo Heights is the most affluent school district in San Antonio. Its six schools, housing approximately 5,000 students, are situated in a residential community quite unlike the Edgewood District. The school population is predominantly "Anglo," having only 18% Mexican-Americans and less than 1% Negroes. The assessed property value per pupil exceeds $49,000, and the median family income is $8,001. In 1967–1968 the local tax rate of $.85 per $100 of valuation yielded $333 per pupil over and above its contribution to the Foundation Program. Coupled with the $225 provided from that Program, the district was able to supply $558 per student. Supplemented by a $36 per pupil grant from federal sources, Alamo Heights spent $594 per pupil.

. . . [S]ubstantial interdistrict disparities in school expenditures found by the District Court to prevail in San Antonio and in varying degrees throughout the State still exist. And it was these disparities, largely attributable to differences in the amounts of money collected through local property taxation, that led the District Court to conclude that Texas' dual system of public school financing violated the Equal Protection Clause. The District Court held that the Texas system discriminates on the basis of wealth in the manner in which education is provided for its people. Finding that wealth is a "suspect" classification and that education is a "fundamental" interest, the District Court held that the Texas system could be sustained only if the State could show that it was premised upon some compelling state interest. On this issue the court concluded that " [n]ot only are defendants unable to demonstrate compelling state interests . . . they fail even to establish a reasonable basis for these classifications." . . .

This, then, establishes the framework for our analysis. We must decide, first, whether the Texas system of financing public education operates to the disadvantage of some suspect class or impinges upon a fundamental right explicitly or implicitly protected by the Constitution, thereby requiring strict judicial scrutiny. If so, the judgment of the District Court should be affirmed. If not, the Texas scheme must still be examined to determine whether it rationally furthers some legitimate, articulated state purpose and therefore does not constitute an invidious discrimination in violation of the Equal Protection Clause of the Fourteenth Amendment.

— II —

. . . oral argument suggests, however, at least three ways in which the discrimination claimed here might be described. The Texas system of school financing might be regarded as discriminating (1) against "poor" persons whose incomes fall below some identifiable level of poverty or who might be characterized as functionally "indigent," or (2) against those who are relatively poorer than others, or (3) against all those who, irrespective of their personal incomes, happen to reside in relatively poorer school districts. Our task must be to ascertain whether, in fact, the Texas system has been shown to discriminate on any of these possible bases and, if so, whether the resulting classification may be regarded as suspect.

The precedents of this Court provide the proper starting point. The individuals, or groups of individuals, who constituted the class discriminated against in our prior cases shared two distinguishing characteristics: because of their impecunity they were completely unable to pay for some desired benefit, and as a consequence, they sustained an absolute deprivation of a meaningful opportunity to enjoy that benefit. . . .

Only appellees' first possible basis for describing the class disadvantaged by the Texas school-financing system—discrimination against a class of definably "poor" persons—might arguably meet the criteria established in these prior cases. Even a cursory examination, however, demonstrates that neither of the two distinguishing characteristics of wealth classifications can be found here. First, in support of their charge that the system discriminates against the "poor," appellees have made no effort to demonstrate that it operates to the peculiar disadvantage of any class fairly definable as indigent, or as composed of persons whose incomes are beneath any designated poverty level. Indeed, there is reason to believe that the poorest families are not necessarily clustered in the poorest property districts.

Defining "poor" families as those below the Bureau of the Census "poverty level," the Connecticut study found, not surprisingly, that the poor were clustered around commercial and industrial areas—those same areas that provide the most attractive sources of property tax income for school districts. Whether a similar pattern would be discovered in Texas is not known, but there is no basis on the record in this case for assuming that the poorest people—defined by reference to any level of absolute impecunity—are concentrated in the poorest districts.

Second, neither appellees nor the District Court addressed the fact that, unlike each of the foregoing cases, lack of personal resources has not occasioned an absolute deprivation of the desired benefit. The argument here is not that the children in districts having relatively low assessable property values are receiving no public education; rather, it is that they are receiving a poorer quality education than that available to children in districts having more assessable wealth. Apart from the unsettled and disputed question whether the quality of education may be determined by the amount of money expended for it, a sufficient answer to appellees' argument is that, at least where wealth is involved, the Equal Protection Clause does not require absolute equality or precisely equal advantages. Nor, indeed, in view of the infinite variables affecting the educational process, can any system assure equal quality of education except in the most relative sense. Texas asserts that the Minimum Foundation Program provides an "adequate" education for all children in the State. By providing 12 years of free public-school education, and by assuring teachers, books, transportation, and operating funds, the Texas Legislature has endeavored to "guarantee, for the welfare of the state as a whole, that all people shall have at least an adequate program of education. This is what is meant by 'A Minimum Foundation Program of Education.'" The State repeatedly asserted in its briefs in this Court that it has fulfilled this desire and that it now assures "every child in every school district an adequate education." No proof was offered at trial persuasively discrediting or refuting the State's assertion.

For these two reasons—the absence of any evidence that the financing system discriminates against any definable category of "poor" people or that it results in the absolute deprivation of education—the disadvantaged class is not susceptible of identification in traditional terms:

As suggested above, appellees and the District Court may have embraced a second or third approach, the second of which might be characterized as a theory of relative or comparative discrimination based on family income. Appellees sought to prove that a direct correlation exists between the wealth of families within each district and the expenditures therein for education. That is, along a continuum, the poorer the family the lower the dollar amount of education received by the family's children. . . .

If, in fact, these correlations could be sustained, then it might be argued that expenditures on education—equated by appellees to the quality of education—are dependent on personal wealth. Appellees' comparative-discrimination theory would still face serious unanswered questions, including whether a bare positive correlation or some higher degree of correlation is necessary to provide a basis for concluding that the financing system is designed to operate to the peculiar disadvantage of the comparatively poor, and whether a class of this . . . size and diversity could ever claim the special protection accorded "suspect" classes. These questions need not be addressed in this case, however, since appellees' proof fails to support their allegations or the District Court's conclusions. . . . It is evident that, even if the conceptual questions were answered favorably to appellees, no factual basis exists upon which to found a claim of comparative wealth discrimination.

This brings us, then, to the third way in which the classification scheme might be defined—*district* wealth discrimination. Since the only correlation indicated by the evidence is between district property wealth and expenditures, it may be argued that discrimination might be found without regard to the individual income characteristics of district residents. Assuming a perfect correlation between district properly wealth and expenditures from top to bottom, the disadvantaged class might be viewed as encompassing every child in every district except the district that has the most assessable wealth and spends the most on education. Alternatively as suggested in Mr. Justice Marshall's dissenting opinion, the class might be defined more restrictively to include children in districts with assessable property which falls below the statewide average, or median, or below some other artificially defined level.

However described, it is clear that appellees' suit asks this Court to extend its most exacting scrutiny to review a system that allegedly discriminates against a large, diverse, and amorphous class, unified only by the common factor of residence in districts that happen to have less taxable wealth than other districts. The system of alleged discrimination and the class it defines have none of the traditional indicia of suspectness: the class is not saddled with such disabilities, or subjected to such a history of purposeful unequal treatment, or relegated to such a position of political powerlessness as to command extraordinary protection from the majoritarian political process.

We thus conclude that the Texas system does not operate to the peculiar disadvantage of any suspect class. But in recognition of the fact that this Court has never heretofore held that wealth discrimination alone provides an adequate basis for invoking strict scrutiny appellees have not relied solely on this contention. They also assert that the State's system impermissibly interferes with the exercise of a "fundamental" right and that accordingly the prior decisions of this Court require the application of the strict standard of judicial review. . . . It is this question—whether education is a fundamental right, in the sense that it is among the rights and liberties protected by the Constitution—which has so consumed the attention of courts and commentators in recent years.

# B

In *Brown* v. *Board of Education*, (1954), a unanimous Court recognized that "education is perhaps the most important function of state and local governments.". . . This theme, expressing an abiding respect for the vital role of education in a free society, may be found in numerous opinions of Justices of this Court writing both before and after Brown was decided. . . .

Nothing this Court holds today in any way detracts from our historic dedication to public education. We are in complete agreement with the conclusion of the three-judge panel below that "the grave significance of education both to the individual and to our society" cannot be doubted. But the importance of a service performed by the State does not determine whether it must be regarded as fundamental for purposes of examination under the Equal Protection Clause. . . . [I]f the degree of judicial scrutiny of state legislation fluctuated depending on a majority's view of the importance of the interest affected, we would have gone "far toward making this Court a 'super-legislature.'" We would, indeed, then be assuming a legislative role and one for which the Court lacks both authority and competence. . . . [S]ocial importance is not the critical determinant for subjecting state legislation to strict scrutiny. . . . The lesson of these [past] cases in addressing the question now before the Court is plain. It is not the province of this Court to create substantive constitutional rights in the name of guaranteeing equal protection of the laws. Thus, the key to discovering whether education is "fundamental" is not to be found in comparisons of the relative societal significance of education as opposed to subsistence or housing. Nor is it to be found by weighing whether education is as important as the right to travel. Rather, the answer lies in assessing whether there is a right to education explicitly or implicitly guaranteed by the Constitution. . . . Education, of course, is not among the rights afforded explicit protection under our Federal Constitution. Nor do we find any basis for saying it is implicitly so protected. As we have said, the undisputed importance of education will not alone cause this Court to depart from the usual standard for removing a State's social and economic legislation. It is appellees' contention, however, that education is distinguishable from other services and benefits provided by the State because it bears a peculiarly close relationship to other rights and liberties accorded protection under the Constitution. Specifically, they insist that education is itself a fundamental personal right because it is essential to the effective exercise of First Amendment freedoms and to intelligent utilization of the right to vote. In asserting a nexus between speech and education, appellees urge that the right to speak is meaningless unless the speaker is capable of articulating his thoughts intelligently and persuasively. The "marketplace of ideas" is an empty forum for those lacking basic communicative tools. Likewise, they argue that the corollary right to receive information becomes little more than a hollow privilege when the recipient has not been taught to read, assimilate, and utilize available knowledge.

A similar line of reasoning is pursued with respect to the right to vote. Exercise of the franchise, it is contended, cannot be divorced from the educational foundation of the voter. The electoral process, if reality is to conform to the democratic ideal, depends on an informed electorate: a voter cannot cast his ballot intelligently unless his reading skills and thought processes have been adequately developed.

We need not dispute any of these propositions. The Court has long afforded zealous protection against unjustifiable governmental interference with the individual's rights to speak and to vote. Yet we have never presumed to possess either the ability or the authority to guarantee to the citizenry the most *effective* speech or the most *informed* electoral choice. That these may be desirable goals of a system of freedom of expression and of a representative form of government is not to be doubted. These are indeed goals to be pursued by a people whose thoughts and beliefs are freed from governmental interference. But they are not values to be implemented by judicial intrusion into otherwise legitimate state activities.

Even if it were conceded that some identifiable quantum of education is a constitutionally protected prerequisite to the meaningful exercise of either right, we have no indication that the present levels of educational expenditure in Texas provide an education that falls short. Whatever merit appellees' argument might have if a State's financing system occasioned an absolute denial of educational opportunities to any of its children, that argument provides no basis for finding an interference with fundamental rights where only relative differences in spending levels are involved and where—as is true in the present case—no charge fairly could be made that the system fails to provide each child with an opportunity to acquire the basic minimal skills necessary for the enjoyment of the rights of speech and of full participation in the political process.

Furthermore, the logical limitations on appellees' nexus theory are difficult to perceive. How, for instance, is education to be distinguished from the significant personal interests in the basics of decent food and shelter? Empirical examination might well buttress an assumption that the ill-fed, ill-clothed, and illhoused are among the most ineffective participants in the political process, and that they derive the least enjoyment from the benefits of the First Amendment.

We have carefully considered each of the arguments supportive of the District Court's finding that education is a fundamental right or liberty and have found those arguments unpersuasive. In one further respect we find this a particularly inappropriate case in which to subject state action to strict judicial scrutiny. The present case, in another basic sense, is significantly different from any of the cases in which the Court has applied strict scrutiny to state or federal legislation touching upon constitutionally protected rights. Each of our prior cases involved legislation which "deprived," "infringed," or "interfered" with the free exercise of some such fundamental personal right or liberty. . . . A critical distinction between those cases and the one now before us lies in what Texas is endeavoring to do with respect to education. . . .

Every step leading to the establishment of the system Texas utilizes today—including the decisions permitting localities to tax and expend locally, and creating and continuously expanding state aid was implemented in an effort to *extend* public education and to improve its quality. Of course, every reform that benefits some more than others may be criticized for what it fails to accomplish. But we think it plain that, in substance, the thrust of the Texas system is affirmative and reformatory and, therefore, should be scrutinized under judicial principles sensitive to the nature of the State's efforts and to the rights reserved to the States under the Constitution.

# C

It should be clear, for the reasons stated above and in accord with the prior decisions of this Court, that this is not a case in which the challenged state action must be subjected to the searching judicial scrutiny reserved for laws that create suspect classifications or impinge upon constitutionally protected rights.

We need not rest our decision, however, solely on the inappropriateness of the strict-scrutiny test. A century of Supreme Court adjudication under the Equal Protection Clause affirmatively supports the application of the traditional standard of review, which requires only that the State's system be shown to bear some rational relationship to legitimate state purposes. This case represents far more than a challenge to the manner in which Texas provides for the education of its children. We have here nothing less than a direct attack on the way in which Texas has chosen to raise and disburse state and local tax revenues. . . .

[T]he Justices of this Court lack both the expertise and the familiarity with local problems so necessary to the making of wise decisions with respect to the raising and disposition of public revenues. . . .

No scheme of taxation, whether the tax is imposed on property, income, or purchases of goods and services, has yet been devised which is free of all discriminatory impact. In such a complex arena in which no perfect alternatives exist, the Court does well not to impose too rigorous a standard of scrutiny lest all local fiscal schemes become subjects of criticism under the Equal Protection Clause.

In addition to matters of fiscal policy, this case also involves the most persistent and difficult questions of educational policy, another area in which this Court's lack of specialized knowledge and experience counsels against premature interference with the informed judgments made at the state and local levels. . . . On even the most basic questions in this area the scholars and educational experts are divided. Indeed, one of the major sources of controversy concerns the extent to which there is a demonstrable correlation between educational expenditures and the quality of education. . . .

. . . The foregoing considerations buttress our conclusion that Texas' system of public school finance is an inappropriate candidate for strict judicial scrutiny. These same considerations are relevant to the determination whether that system, with its conceded imperfections, nevertheless bears some rational relationship to a legitimate state purpose. It is to this question that we next turn our attention.

# — III —

. . . The greatest interdistrict disparities, however, are attributable to differences in the amount of assessable property available within any district. Those districts that have more property, or more valuable property, have a greater capability for supplementing state funds. In large measure, these additional local revenues are devoted to paying higher salaries to more teachers. Therefore, the primary distinguishing attributes of schools in property-affluent districts are lower pupil-teacher ratios and higher salary schedules.

. . . Because of differences in expenditure levels occasioned by disparities in property tax income, appellees claim that children in less affluent districts have been made the subject of invidious discrimination. The District Court found that the State had failed even "to establish a reasonable basis" for a system that results in different levels of per-pupil expenditure. We disagree.

In its reliance on state as well as local resources, the Texas system is comparable to the systems employed in virtually every other State. The power to tax local property for educational purposes has been recognized in Texas at least since 1883. When the growth of commercial and industrial centers and accompanying shifts in population began to create disparities in local resources, Texas undertook a program calling for a considerable investment of state funds. . . .

Their efforts were devoted to establishing a means of guaranteeing a minimum statewide educational program without sacrificing the vital element of local participation. The Texas system of school finance is responsive to these two forces. While assuring a basic education for every child in the State, it permits and encourages a large measure of participation in and control of each district's schools at the local level. In an era that has witnessed a consistent trend toward centralization of the functions of government, local sharing of responsibility for public education has survived.

. . . In part, local control means, . . . the freedom to devote more money to the education of one's children. Equally important, however, is the opportunity it offers for participation in the decisionmaking process that determines how those local tax dollars will be spent. Each locality is free to tailor local programs to local needs. Pluralism also affords some opportunity for experimentation, innovation, and a healthy competition for educational excellence. An analogy to the Nation-State relationship in our federal system seems uniquely appropriate.

. . . Appellees suggest that local control could be preserved and promoted under other financing systems that resulted in more equality in educational expenditures. While it is no doubt true that reliance on local property taxation for school revenues provides less freedom of choice with respect to expenditures for some districts than for others, the existence of "some inequality" in the manner in which the State's rationale is achieved is not alone a sufficient basis for striking down the entire system. . . . It may not be condemned simply because it imperfectly effectuates the State's goals. Nor must the financing system fail because, as appellees suggest, other methods of satisfying the State's interest, which occasion "less drastic" disparities in expenditures, might be conceived. Only where state action impinges on the exercise of fundamental constitutional rights or liberties must it be found to have chosen the least restrictive alternative. . . .

Appellees further urge that the Texas system is unconstitutionally arbitrary because it allows the availability of local taxable resources to turn on "happenstance." They see no justification for a system that allows, as they contend, the quality of education to fluctuate on the basis of the fortuitous positioning of the boundary lines of political subdivisions and the location of valuable commercial and industrial property. But any scheme of local taxation—indeed the very existence of identifiable local government units requires the establishment of jurisdictional boundaries that are inevitably arbitrary. It is equally inevitable that some localities are going to be blessed with more taxable assets than others. Nor is local wealth a static quantity. Changes in the level of taxable wealth within any district may result from any number of events, some of which local residents can and do influence. For instance, commercial and industrial enterprises may be encouraged to locate within a district by various actions—public and private.

Moreover, if local taxation for local expenditures were an unconstitutional method of providing for education then it might be an equally impermissible means of providing other necessary services customarily financed largely from local property taxes, including local police and fire protection, public health and hospitals, and public utility facilities of various kinds. We perceive no justification for such a severe denigration of local property taxation and control as would follow from appellees' contentions. It has simply never been within the constitutional prerogative of this Court to nullify statewide measures for financing public services merely because the burdens or benefits thereof fall unevenly depending upon the relative wealth of the political subdivisions in which citizens live.

In sum, to the extent that the Texas system of school financing results in unequal expenditures between children who happen to reside in different districts, we cannot say that such disparities are the product of a system that is so irrational as to be invidiously discriminatory. Texas has acknowledged its shortcomings and has persistently endeavored—not without some success to ameliorate the differences in levels of expenditures without sacrificing the benefits of local participation. The Texas plan is not the result of hurried, ill-conceived legislation. It certainly is not the product of purposeful discrimination against any group or class. On the contrary, it is rooted in decades of experience in Texas and elsewhere, and in major part is the product of responsible studies by qualified people. In giving substance to the presumption of validity to which the Texas system is entitled . . . it is important to remember that at every stage of its development it has constituted a "rough accommodation" of interests in an effort to arrive at practical and workable solutions. . . . One also must remember that the system here challenged is not peculiar to Texas or to any other State. In its essential characteristics, the Texas plan for financing public education reflects what many educators for a half century have thought was an enlightened approach to a problem for which there is no perfect solution. We are unwilling to assume for ourselves a level of wisdom superior to that of legislators, scholars, and educational authorities in 50 States, especially where the alternatives proposed are only recently conceived and nowhere yet tested. The constitutional standard under the Equal Protection Clause is whether the challenged state action rationally furthers a legitimate state purpose or interest. . . . We hold that the Texas plan abundantly satisfies this standard. . . .

The complexity of these problems is demonstrated by the lack of consensus with respect to whether it may be said with any assurance that the poor, the racial minorities, or the children in overburdened core-city school districts would be benefited by abrogation of traditional modes of financing education. Unless there is to be a substantial increase in state expenditures on education across the board—an event the likelihood of which is open to considerable question—these groups stand to realize gains in terms of increased per-pupil expenditures only if they reside in districts that presently spend at relatively low levels, i. e., in those districts that would benefit from the redistribution of existing resources. Yet, recent studies have indicated that the poorest families are not invariably clustered in the most impecunious school districts. Nor does it now appear that there is any more than a random chance that racial minorities are concentrated in property-poor districts. . . .

These practical considerations, of course, play no role in the adjudication of the constitutional issues presented here. But they serve to highlight the wisdom of the traditional limitations on this Court's function. The consideration and initiation of fundamental reforms with respect to state taxation and education are matters reserved for the legislative processes of the various States, and we do no violence to the values of federalism and separation of powers by staying our hand. We hardly need add that this Court's action today is not to be viewed as placing its judicial imprimatur on the status quo. The need is apparent for reform in tax systems which may well have relied too long and too heavily on the local property tax. And certainly innovative thinking as to public education, its methods, and its funding is necessary to assure both a higher level of quality and greater uniformity of opportunity. These matters merit the continued attention of the scholars who already have contributed much by their challenges. But the ultimate solutions must come from the lawmakers and from the democratic pressures of those who elect them.

*Reversed.*

MR. JUSTICE STEWART, concurring.

The method of financing public schools in Texas, as in almost every other State, has resulted in a system of public education that can fairly be described as chaotic and unjust. It does not follow, however, and I cannot find, that this system violates the Constitution of the United States. I join the opinion and judgment of the Court because I am convinced that any other course would mark an extraordinary departure from principled adjudication under the Equal Protection Clause of the Fourteenth Amendment. . . .

Unlike other provisions of the Constitution, the Equal Protection Clause confers no substantive rights and creates no substantive liberties. The function of the Equal Protection Clause, rather, is simply to measure the validity of *classifications* created by state laws.

There is hardly a law on the books that does not affect some people differently from others. But the basic concern of the Equal Protection Clause is with state legislation whose purpose or effect is to create discrete and objectively identifiable classes. And with respect to such legislation, it has long been settled that the Equal Protection Clause is offended only by laws that are invidiously discriminatory only by classifications that are wholly arbitrary or capricious. . . . This settled principle of constitutional law was compendiously stated in MR. CHIEF JUSTICE WARREN's opinion for the Court in *McGowan v. Maryland*, 366 US 420, 425–426, in the following words:

> "Although no precise formula has been developed, the Court has held that the Fourteenth Amendment permits the States a wide scope of discretion in enacting laws which affect some groups of citizens differently than others. The constitutional safeguard is offended only if the classification rests on grounds wholly irrelevant to the achievement of the State's objective. State legislatures are presumed to have acted within their constitutional power despite the fact that, in practice, their laws result in some inequality. A statutory discrimination will not be set aside if any state of facts reasonably may be conceived to justify it."

This doctrine is no more than a specific application of one of the first principles of constitutional adjudication—the basic presumption of the constitutional validity of a duly enacted state or federal law.

Under the Equal Protection Clause, this presumption of constitutional validity disappears when a State has enacted legislation whose purpose or effect is to create classes based upon criteria that, in a constitutional sense, are inherently "suspect." Because of the historic purpose of the Fourteenth Amendment, the prime example of such a "suspect" classification is one that is based upon race. See, e. g., *Brown v. Board of Education*, 347 US 483. But there are other classifications that, at least in some settings, are also "suspect"—for example, those based upon national origin, alienage, indigency, or illegitimacy.

Moreover, apart from the Equal Protection Clause, a state law that impinges upon a substantive right or liberty created or conferred by the constitution is, of course presumptively invalid, whether, or not the law's purpose or effect is to create any classifications. For example, a law that provided that newspapers could be published only by people who had resided in the State for five years could be superficially viewed as invidiously discriminating against an identifiable class in violation of the Equal Protection Clause. But, more basically, such a law would be invalid simply because it abridged the freedom of the press. Numerous cases in this Court illustrate this principle.

In refusing to invalidate the Texas system of financing its public schools, the Court today applies with thoughtfulness and understanding the basic principles I have so sketchily summarized. First, as the Court points out, the Texas system has hardly created the kind of objectively identifiable classes that are cognizable under the Equal Protection Clause. Second, even assuming the existence of such discernible categories, the classifications are in no sense based upon constitutionally "suspect" criteria. Third, the Texas system does not rest "on grounds wholly irrelevant to the achievement of the State's objective." Finally, the Texas system impinges upon no substantive constitutional rights or liberties. It follows, therefore, under the established principle reaffirmed in MR. CHIEF JUSTICE WARREN's opinion for the Court in *McGowan v. Maryland*, *supra*, that the judgment of the District Court must be reversed.

MR. JUSTICE BRENNAN, dissenting.

Although I agree with my Brother White that the Texas statutory scheme is devoid of any rational basis, and for that reason is violative of the Equal Protection Clause, I also record my disagreement with the Court's rather distressing assertion that a right may be deemed "fundamental" for the purposes of equal protection analysis only if it is "explicitly or implicitly guaranteed by the Constitution."

. . . As my Brother Marshall convincingly demonstrates, our prior cases stand for the proposition that "fundamentality" is, in large measure, a function of the right's importance in terms of the effectuation of those rights which are in fact constitutionally guaranteed. (Thus, "[a]s the nexus between the specific constitutional guarantee and the nonconstitutional interest draws closer, the nonconstitutional interest becomes more fundamental and the degree of judicial scrutiny applied when the interest is infringed on a discriminatory basis must be adjusted accordingly."

Here, there can be no doubt that education is inextricably linked to the right to participate in the electoral process and to the rights of free speech and association guaranteed by the First Amendment. This being so, any classification affecting education must be subjected to strict judicial scrutiny, and since even the State concedes that the statutory scheme now before us cannot pass constitutional muster under this stricter standard of review, I can only conclude that the Texas school financing scheme is constitutionally invalid.

MR. JUSTICE WHITE, with whom MR. JUSTICE DOUGLAS and MR. JUSTICE BRENNAN join, dissenting.

The Texas public schools are financed through a combination of state funding, local property tax revenue, and some federal funds. Concededly, the system yields wide disparity in per-pupil revenue among the various districts. In a typical year, for example, the Alamo Heights district had total revenues of $594 per pupil, while the Edgewood district had only $356 per pupil. The majority and the State concede, as they must, the existence of major disparities in spendable funds. But the State contends that the disparities do not invidiously discriminate against children and families in districts such as Edgewood, because the Texas scheme is designed "to provide an adequate education for all, with local autonomy to go beyond that as individual school districts desire and are able . . . . It leaves to the people of each district the choice whether to go beyond the minimum and, if so, by how much." The majority advances this rationalization: "While assuring a basic education for every child in the State, it permits and encourages a large measure of participation in and control of each district's schools at the local level."

I cannot disagree with the proposition that local control and local decisionmaking play an important part in our democratic system of government. Much may be left to local option, and this case would be quite different if it were true that the Texas system, while insuring minimum educational expenditures in every district through state funding, extended a meaningful option to all local districts to increase their per-pupil expenditures and so to improve their children's education to the extent that increased funding would achieve that goal. The system would then arguably provide a rational and sensible method of achieving the stated aim of preserving an area for local initiative and decision.

The difficulty with the Texas system, however, is that it provides a meaningful option to Alamo Heights and like school districts but almost none to Edgewood and those other districts with a low per-pupil real estate tax base. In these latter districts, no matter how desirous parents are of supporting their schools with greater revenues, it is impossible to do so through the use of the real estate property tax. In these districts, the Texas system utterly fails to extend a realistic choice to parents because the property tax, which is the only revenue-raising mechanism extended to school districts, is practically and legally unavailable. . . .

In order to equal the highest yield in any other Bexar County district, Alamo Heights would be required to tax at the rate of 68¢ per $100 of assessed valuation. Edgewood would be required to tax at the prohibitive rate of $5.76 per $100. But state law places a $1.50 per $100 ceiling on the maintenance tax rate, a limit that would surely be reached long before Edgewood attained an equal yield. Edgewood is thus precluded in law, as well as in fact, from achieving a yield even close to that of some other districts.

The Equal Protection Clause permits discriminations between classes but requires that the classification bear some rational relationship to a permissible object sought to be attained by the statute. It is not enough that the Texas system before us seeks to achieve the valid, rational purpose of maximizing local initiative; the means chosen by the State must also be rationally related to the end sought to be achieved.

Neither Texas nor the majority heeds this rule. If the State aims at maximizing local initiative and local choice, by permitting school districts to resort to the real property tax if they choose to do so, it utterly fails in achieving its purpose in districts with property tax bases so low that there is little if any opportunity for interested parents, rich or poor, to augment school district revenues. Requiring the State to establish only that unequal treatment is in furtherance of a permissible goal, without also requiring the State to show that the means chosen to effectuate that goal are rationally related to its achievement, makes equal protection analysis no more than an empty gesture. In my view, the parents and children in Edgewood, and in like districts, suffer from an invidious discrimination violative of the Equal Protection Clause.

This does not, of course, mean that local control may not be a legitimate goal of a school financing system. Nor does it mean that the State must guarantee each district an equal per-pupil revenue from the state school-financing system.

. . . On the contrary, it would merely mean that the State must fashion a financing scheme which provides a rational basis for the maximization of local control, if local control is to remain a goal of the system, and not a scheme with "different treatment be[ing] accorded to persons placed by a statute into different classes on the basis of criteria wholly unrelated to the objective of that statute." . . .

There is no difficulty in identifying the class that is subject to the alleged discrimination and that is entitled to the benefits of the Equal Protection Clause. I need go no farther than the parents and children in the Edgewood district, who are plaintiffs here and who assert that they are entitled to the same choice as Alamo Heights to augment local expenditures for schools but are denied that choice by state law. This group constitutes a class sufficiently definite to invoke the protection of the Constitution. They are as entitled to the protection of the Equal Protection Clause as were the voters in allegedly unrepresented counties in the reapportionment cases. . . . At the very least, the law discriminates against those children and their parents who live in districts where the per-pupil tax base is sufficiently low to make impossible the provision of comparable school revenues by resort to the real property tax which is the only device the State extends for this purpose.

MR. JUSTICE MARSHALL, with whom MR. JUSTICE DOUGLAS concurs, dissenting.

The Court today decides, in effect, that a State may constitutionally vary the quality of education which it offers its children in accordance with the amount of taxable wealth located in the school districts within which they reside. . . . the majority's holding can only be seen as a retreat from our historic commitment to equality of educational opportunity and as unsupportable acquiescence in a system which deprives children in their earliest years of the chance to reach their full potential as citizens. The Court does this despite the absence of any substantial justification for a scheme which arbitrarily channels educational resources in accordance with the fortuity of the amount of taxable wealth within each district.

In my judgment, the right of every American to an equal start in life, so far as the provision of a state service as important as education is concerned, is far too vital to permit state discrimination on grounds as tenuous as those presented by this record. Nor can I accept the notion that it is sufficient to remit these appellees to the vagaries of the political process which, contrary to the majority's suggestion, has proved singularly unsuited to the task of providing a remedy for this discrimination. I, for one, am unsatisfied with the hope of an ultimate "political" solution sometime in the indefinite future while, in the meantime, countless children unjustifiably receive inferior educations that "may affect their hearts and minds in a way unlikely ever to be undone." *Brown* v. *Board of Education.* 347 US 483, 494, (1954). I must therefore respect fully dissent.

— I —

. . . When the Texas financing scheme is taken as a whole, I do not think it can be doubted that it produces a discriminatory impact on substantial numbers of the school age children of the State of Texas.

# A

... The necessary effect of the Texas local property tax is, in short, to favor property-rich districts and to disfavor property-poor ones.

The seriously disparate consequences of the Texas local property tax, when that tax is considered alone, are amply illustrated by data presented to the District Court by appellees. ...

It is clear, moreover, that the disparity of per-pupil revenues cannot be dismissed as the result of lack of local effort—that is, lower tax rates by property-poor districts. To the contrary, the data presented below indicate that the poorest districts tend to have the highest tax rates and the richest districts tend to have the lowest tax rates. Yet, despite the apparent *extra* effort being made by the poorest districts, they are unable even to begin to match the richest districts in terms of the production of local revenues.

... Nor are these funding variations corrected by the other aspects of the Texas financing scheme. ... [T]he majority continually emphasizes how much state aid has, in recent years, been given to property-poor Texas school districts. What the Court fails to emphasize is the cruel irony of how much more state aid is being given to property-rich Texas school districts on top of their already substantial local property tax revenues. ... There can, moreover, be no escaping the conclusion that the local property tax which is dependent upon taxable district property wealth is an essential feature of the Texas scheme for financing public education.

# B

The appellants do not deny the disparities in educational funding caused by variations in taxable district property wealth. They do contend, however, that whatever the differences in per-pupil spending among Texas districts, there are no discriminatory consequences for the children of the disadvantaged districts. They recognize that what is at stake in this case is the quality of the public education provided Texas children in the districts in which they live. But appellants reject the suggestion that the quality of education in any particular district is determined by money—beyond some minimal level of funding which they believe to be assured every Texas district by the Minimum Foundation School Program. In their view, there is simply no denial of equal educational opportunity to any Texas school children as a result of the widely varying per-pupil spending power provided districts under the current financing scheme.

In my view, though, even an unadorned restatement of this contention is sufficient to reveal its absurdity. Authorities concerned with educational quality no doubt disagree as to the significance of variations in per-pupil spending. . . . We sit, however, not to resolve disputes over educational theory but to enforce our Constitution. It is an inescapable fact that if one district has more funds available per pupil than another district, the former will have greater choice in educational planning than will the latter. In this regard, I believe the question of discrimination in educational quality must be deemed to be an objective one that looks to what the State provides its children, not to what the children are able to do with what they receive. That a child forced to attend an underfunded school with poorer physical facilities, less experienced teachers, larger classes, and a narrower range of courses than a school with substantially more funds—and thus with greater choice in educational planning—may nevertheless excel is to the credit of the child, not the State . . . Indeed, who can ever measure for such a child the opportunities lost and the talents wasted for want of a broader, more enriched education? Discrimination in the opportunity to learn that is afforded a child must be our standard. . . . In fact, if financing variations are so insignificant to educational quality, it is difficult to understand why a number of our country's wealthiest school districts, which have no legal obligation to argue in support of the constitutionality of the Texas legislation, have nevertheless zealously pursued its cause before this Court.

The consequences, in terms of objective educational input, of the variations in district funding caused by the Texas financing scheme are apparent from the data introduced before the District Court. . . . For constitutional purposes, I believe this situation, which is directly attributable to the Texas financing scheme, raises a grave question of state-created discrimination in the provision of public education. . . .

Alternatively, the appellants and the majority may believe that the Equal Protection Clause cannot be offended by substantially unequal state treatment of persons who are similarly situated so long as the State provides everyone with some unspecified amount of education which evidently is "enough." The basis for such a novel view is far from clear. It is, of course, true that the Constitution does not require precise equality in the treatment of all persons. . . . But this Court has never suggested that because some "adequate" level of benefits is provided to all, discrimination in the provision of services is therefore constitutionally excusable. The Equal Protection Clause is not addressed to the minimal sufficiency but rather to the unjustifiable inequalities of state action. It mandates nothing less than that "all persons similarly circumstanced shall be treated alike." . . .

Even if the Equal Protection Clause encompassed some theory of constitutional adequacy, discrimination in the provision of educational opportunity would certainly seem to be a poor candidate for its application. Neither the majority nor appellants inform us how judicially manageable standards are to be derived for determining how much education is "enough" to excuse constitutional discrimination. One would think that the majority would heed its own fervent affirmation of judicial self-restraint before undertaking the complex task of determining at large what level of education is constitutionally sufficient. . . .

In my view, then, it is inequality—not some notion of gross inadequacy—of educational opportunity that raises a question of denial of equal protection of the laws. I find any other approach to the issue unintelligible and without directing principle. Here appellees have made a substantial showing of wide variations in educational funding and the resulting educational opportunity afforded to the school children of Texas. This discrimination is, in large measure, attributable to significant disparities in the taxable wealth of local Texas school districts. This is a sufficient showing to raise a substantial question of discriminatory state action in violation of the Equal Protection Clause.

## C

Despite the evident discriminatory effect of the Texas financing scheme, both the appellants and the majority raise substantial questions concerning the precise character of the disadvantaged class in this case. . . . In light of the data introduced before the District Court, the conclusion that the schoolchildren of property-poor districts constitute a sufficient class for our purposes seems indisputable to me. . . . Texas has chosen to provide free public education for all its citizens, and it has embodied that decision in its constitution. Yet, having established public education for its citizens, the State, as a direct consequence of the variations in local property wealth endemic to Texas' financing scheme, has provided some Texas schoolchildren with substantially less resources for their education than others. Thus, while on its face the Texas scheme may merely discriminate between local districts, the impact of that discrimination falls directly upon the children whose educational opportunity is dependent upon where they happen to live. Consequently, the District Court correctly concluded that the Texas financing scheme discriminates, from a constitutional perspective, between school children on the basis of the amount of taxable property located within their local districts. . . .

. . . [A]s the District Court concluded, that consistent with the guarantee of equal protection of the laws, "the quality of public education may not be a function of wealth, other than the wealth of the state as a whole." Under such a principle, the children of a district are excessively advantaged if that district has more taxable property per pupil than the average amount of taxable property per pupil considering the State as a whole. By contrast, the children of a district are disadvantaged if that district has less taxable property per pupil than the state average. . . . Whether this discrimination, against the schoolchildren of property-poor districts, inherent in the Texas financing scheme, is violative of the Equal Protection Clause is the question to which we must now turn.

## — II —

To avoid having the Texas financing scheme struck down because of the interdistrict variations in taxable property wealth, the District Court determined that it was insufficient for appellants to show merely that the State's scheme was rationally related to some legitimate state purpose; rather, the discrimination inherent in the scheme had to be shown necessary to promote a "compelling state interest" in order to withstand constitutional scrutiny. The basis for this determination was twofold: first, the financing scheme divides citizens on a wealth basis, a classification which the District Court viewed as highly suspect; and second, the discriminatory scheme directly affects what it considered to be a "fundamental interest," namely, education.

This Court has repeatedly held that state discrimination which either adversely affects a "fundamental interest," or is based on a distinction of a suspect character, must be carefully scrutinized to ensure that the scheme is necessary to promote a substantial, legitimate state interest.

The majority today concludes, however, that the Texas scheme is not subject to such a strict standard of review under the Equal Protection Clause. Instead, in its view, the Texas scheme must be tested by nothing more than that lenient standard of rationality which we have traditionally applied to discriminatory state action in the context of economic and commercial matters. By so doing the Court avoids the telling task of searching for a substantial state interest which the Texas financing scheme, with its variations in taxable district property wealth, is necessary to further. I cannot accept such an emasculation of the Equal Protection Clause in the context of this case.

## A

To begin, I must once more voice my disagreement with the Court's rigidified approach to equal protection analysis. The Court apparently seeks to establish today that equal protection cases fall into one of two neat categories which dictate the appropriate standard of review—strict scrutiny or mere rationality. But this Court's decisions in the field of equal protection defy such easy categorization. A principled reading of what this Court has done reveals that it has applied a spectrum of standards in reviewing discrimination allegedly violative of the Equal Protection Clause. This spectrum clearly comprehends variations in the degree of care with which the Court will scrutinize particular classifications, depending, I believe, on the constitutional and societal importance of the interest adversely affected and the recognized invidiousness of the basis upon which the particular classification is drawn. I find in fact that many of the Court's recent decisions embody the very sort of reasoned approach to equal protection analysis for which I previously argued—that is, an approach in which "concentration [is] placed upon the character of the classification in question, the relative importance to individuals in the class discriminated against of the governmental benefits that they do not receive, and the asserted state interests in support of the classification."

I therefore cannot accept the majority's labored efforts to demonstrate that fundamental interests, which call for strict scrutiny of the challenged classification, encompass only established rights which we are somehow bound to recognize from the text of the Constitution itself. To be sure, some interests which the Court has deemed to be fundamental for purposes of equal protection analysis are themselves constitutionally protected rights. Thus, discrimination against the guaranteed right of freedom of speech has called for strict judicial scrutiny. Further, every citizen's right to travel interstate, although nowhere expressly mentioned in the Constitution, has long been recognized as implicit in the premises underlying that document: the right "was conceived from the beginning to be a necessary concomitant of the stronger Union the Constitution created." Consequently, the Court has required that a state classification affecting the constitutionally protected right to travel must be "shown to be necessary to promote a *compelling* governmental interest." But it will not do to suggest that the "answer" to whether an interest is fundamental for purposes of equal protection analysis is *always* determined by whether that interest "is a right . . . explicitly or implicitly guaranteed by the Constitution."

I would like to know where the Constitution guarantees the right to procreate, *Skinner* v. *Oklahoma*, 316 US 535, 541, (1942), or the right to vote in state elections, e. g., *Reynolds* v. *Sims*, 377 US 533, (1964), or the right to an appeal from a criminal conviction, e. g., *Griffin* v. *Illinois*, 351 US 12, 100 (1956). These are instances in which, due to the importance of the interests at stake, the Court has displayed a strong concern with the existence of discriminatory state treatment. But the Court has never said or indicated that these are interests which independently enjoy full blown constitutional protection.

Thus, in *Buck* v. *Bell*, 274 US 200, (1927), the Court refused to recognize a substantive constitutional guarantee of the right to procreate. Nevertheless, in *Skinner* v. *Oklahoma*, *supra*, at 541, 86 L Ed 1655, the Court, without impugning the continuing validity of *Buck* v. *Bell,* held that "strict scrutiny" of state discrimination affecting procreation "is essential," for "[m]arriage and procreation are fundamental to the very existence and survival of the race." Recently, in *Roe* v. *Wade*, 410 US 113, the importance of procreation has indeed been explained on the basis of its intimate relationship with the constitutional right of privacy which we have recognized. Yet the limited stature thereby accorded any "right" to procreate is evident from the fact that at the same time the Court reaffirmed its initial decision in *Buck* v. *Bell*. See *Roe* v. *Wade*, *supra*, at 154, 35 L Ed 2d 147.

Similarly, the right to vote in state elections has been recognized as a "fundamental political right," because the Court concluded very early that it is "preservative of all rights." *Yick Wo* v. *Hopkins*, 118 US 356, 370, (1886); For this reason, "this Court has made clear that a citizen has a *constitutionally protected right* to participate in elections *on an equal basis with other citizens in the jurisdiction.*" *Dunn* v. *Blumstein*, 405 US, at 336, (emphasis added). The final source of such protection from inequality in the provision of the state franchise is, of course, the Equal Protection Clause. Yet it is clear that whatever degree of importance has been attached to the state electoral process when unequally distributed, the right to vote in state elections has itself never been accorded the stature of an independent constitutional guarantee. Or See *Oregon* v. *Mitchell*, 400 US 112, (1970); . . .

Finally, it is likewise "true that a State is not required by the Federal Constitution to provide appellate courts or a right to appellate review at all." *Griffin* v. *Illinois*, 351 US, at 18. Nevertheless, discrimination adversely affecting access to an appellate process which a State has chosen to provide has been considered to require close judicial scrutiny. See, e. g., *Griffin* v. *Illinois*, *Douglas* v. *California*, 372 US 353, (1963).

The majority is, of course, correct when it suggests that the process of determining which interests are fundamental is a difficult one. But I do not think the problem is insurmountable. And I certainly do not accept the view that the process need necessarily degenerate into an unprincipled, subjective "picking-and-choosing" between various interests or that it must involve this Court in creating "substantive constitutional rights in the name of guaranteeing equal protection of the laws." Although not all fundamental interests are constitutionally guaranteed, the determination of which interests are fundamental should be firmly rooted in the text of the Constitution. The task in every case should be to determine the extent to which constitutionally guaranteed rights are dependent on interests not mentioned in the Constitution. As the nexus between the specific constitutional guarantee and the nonconstitutional interest draws closer, the nonconstitutional interest becomes more fundamental and the degree of judicial scrutiny applied when the interest is infringed on a discriminatory basis must be adjusted accordingly. Thus, it cannot be denied that interests such as procreation, the exercise of the state franchise, and access to criminal appellate processes are not fully guaranteed to the citizen by our Constitution. But these interests have nonetheless been afforded special judicial consideration in the face of discrimination because they are, to some extent, interrelated with constitutional guarantees. Procreation is now understood to be important because of its interaction with the established constitutional right of privacy. The exercise of the state franchise is closely tied to basic civil and political rights inherent in the First Amendment. And access to criminal appellate processes enhances the integrity of the range of rights implicit in the Fourteenth Amendment guarantee of due process of law. Only if we closely protect the related interests from state discrimination do we ultimately ensure the integrity of the constitutional guarantee itself. This is the real lesson that must be taken from our previous decisions involving interests deemed to be fundamental. . . .

A similar process of analysis with respect to the invidiousness of the basis on which a particular classification is drawn has also influenced the Court as to the appropriate degree of scrutiny to be accorded any particular case. The highly suspect character of classifications based on race,[3] nationality,[4] or alienage[5] is well established. The reasons why such classifications call for close judicial scrutiny are manifold. Certain racial and ethnic groups have frequently been recognized as "discrete and insular minorities" who are relatively powerless to protect their interests in the political process. See *Graham* v. *Richardson*, 403 US, at 372, cf. *United States* v. *Carolene Products Co.* 304 US 144, 152–153, n 4, (1938). Moreover, race, nationality, or alienage is "in most circumstances irrelevant" to any constitutionally acceptable legislative purpose, *Hirabayashi* v. *United States*, 320 US 81. *McLaughlin* v. *Florida*, 379 US, at 192. Instead, lines drawn on such bases are frequently the reflection of historic prejudices rather than legislative rationality. It may be that all of these considerations, which make for particular judicial solicitude in the face of discrimination on the basis of race, nationality, or alienage, do not coalesce—or at least not to the same degree—in other forms of discrimination. Nevertheless, these considerations have undoubtedly influenced the care with which the Court has scrutinized other forms of discrimination.

In *James* v. *Strange*, 407 US 128, (1972), the Court held unconstitutional a state statute which provided for recoupment from indigent convicts of legal defense fees paid by the State.

Similarly, in *Reed* v. *Reed*, 404 US 71, (1971), the Court, in striking down a state statute which gave men preference over women when persons of equal entitlement apply for assignment as an administrator of a particular estate, resorted to a more stringent standard of equal protection review than that employed in cases involving commercial matters. The Court indicated that it was testing the claim of sex discrimination by nothing more than whether the line drawn bore "a rational relationship to a state objective," which it recognized as a legitimate effort to reduce the work of probate courts in choosing between competing applications for letters of administration. Accepting such a purpose, the Idaho Supreme Court had thought the classification to be sustainable on the basis that the legislature might have reasonably concluded that, as a rule, men have more experience than women in business matters relevant to the administration of estate. This Court, however, concluded that "[t]o give a mandatory preference to members of either sex over members of the other, merely to accomplish the elimination of hearings on the merits, is to make the very kind of arbitrary legislative choice forbidden by the Equal Protection Clause of the Fourteenth Amendment. . . "

. . . *James* and *Reed* can only be understood as instances in which the particularly invidious character of the classification caused the Court to pause and scrutinize with more than traditional care the rationality of state discrimination. Discrimination on the basis of past criminality and on the basis of sex posed for the Court the specter of forms of discrimination which it implicitly recognized to have deep social and legal roots without necessarily having any basis in actual differences. Still, the Court's sensitivity to the invidiousness of the basis for discrimination is perhaps most apparent in its decisions protecting the interests of children born out of wedlock from discriminatory state action. See *Weber* v. *Aetna Casualty & Surety Co.*, 406 US 164, (1972) *Levy* v. *Louisiana*, 391 US 68, (1968).

In Weber, the Court struck down a portion of a state workmen's compensation statute that related unacknowledged illegitimate children of the deceased to a lesser status with respect to benefits than that occupied by legitimate children of the deceased. The Court acknowledged the true nature of its inquiry in cases such as these: "What legitimate state interest does the classification promote? What fundamental personal rights might the classification endanger?" . . . Status of birth, like the color of one's skin, is something which the individual cannot control, and should generally be irrelevant in legislative considerations. Yet illegitimacy has long been stigmatized by our society Hence, discrimination on the basis of birth—particularly when it affects innocent children—warrants special judicial consideration.

In summary it seems to me inescapably clear that this Court has consistently adjusted the care with which it will review state discrimination in light of the constitutional significance of the interests affected and the invidiousness of the particular classification. In the context of economic interests, we find that discriminatory state action is almost always sustained, for such interests are generally far removed from constitutional guarantees. Moreover, "[t]he extremes to which the Court has gone in dreaming up rational bases for state regulation in that area may in many instances be ascribed to a healthy revulsion from the Court's earlier excesses in using the Constitution to protect interests that have more than enough power to protect themselves in the legislative halls." But the situation differs markedly when discrimination against important individual interests with constitutional implications and against particularly disadvantaged or powerless classes is involved. The majority suggests, however, that a variable standard of review would give this Court the appearance of a "super-legislature." I cannot agree. Such an approach seems to me a part of the guarantees of our Constitution and of the historic experiences with oppression of and discrimination against discrete, powerless minorities which underlie that document. . . .

Nevertheless, the majority today attempts to force this case into the same category for purposes of equal protection analysis as decisions involving discrimination affecting commercial interests. By so doing, the majority singles this case out for analytic treatment at odds with what seems to me to be the clear trend of recent decisions in this Court, and thereby ignores the constitutional importance of the interest at stake and the invidiousness of the particular classification, factors that call for far more than the lenient scrutiny of the Texas financing scheme which the majority pursues. Yet if the discrimination inherent in the Texas scheme is scrutinized with the care demanded by the interest and classification present in this case, the unconstitutionality of that scheme is unmistakable.

# B

Since the Court now suggests that only interests guaranteed by the Constitution are fundamental for purposes of equal protection analysis, and since it rejects the contention that public education is fundamental, it follows that the Court concludes that public education is not constitutionally guaranteed. It is true that this Court has never deemed the provision of free public education to be required by the Constitution. . . . Nevertheless, the fundamental importance of education is amply indicated by the prior decisions of this Court, by the unique status accorded public education by our society, and by the close relationship between education and some of our most basic constitutional values.

The special concern of this Court with the educational process of our country is a matter of common knowledge. Undoubtedly, this Court's most famous statement on the subject is that contained in *Brown* v. *Board of Education*, 347 US, at 493,

> "Today, education is perhaps the most important function of state and local governments. Compulsory school attendance laws and the great expenditures for education both demonstrate our recognition of the importance of education to our democratic society. It is required in the performance of our most basic public responsibilities, even service in the armed forces. It is the very foundation of good citizenship. Today it is a principal instrument in awakening the child to cultural values, in preparing him for later professional training, and in helping him to adjust normally to his environment. . . ."

[I]n 48 of our 50 States the provision of public education is mandated by the state constitution.[6] No other state function is so uniformly recognized[7] as an essential element of our society's well-being. In large measure, the explanation for the special importance attached to education must rest, on the facts that "some degree of education is necessary to prepare citizens to participate effectively and intelligently in our open political system . . . ," and that "education prepares individuals to be self-reliant and self-sufficient participants in society." Both facets of this observation are suggestive of the substantial relationship which education bears to guarantees of our Constitution.

Education directly affects the ability of a child to exercise his First Amendment interests, both as a source and as a receiver of information and ideas, whatever interests he may pursue in life. . . .

Of particular importance is the relationship between education and the political process. . . . Education serves the essential function of instilling in our young an understanding of and appreciation for the principles and operation of our governmental processes. . . . But of most immediate and direct concern must be the demonstrated effect of education on the exercise of the franchise by the electorate. The right to vote in federal elections is conferred by Art 1, § 2, and the Seventeenth Amendment of the Constitution, and access to the state franchise has been afforded special protection because it is "preservative of other basic civil and political rights," *Reynolds* v. *Sims*, 377 US, at 562. Data from the Presidential Election of 1968 clearly demonstrates a direct relationship between participation in the electoral process and level of educational attainment; and, as this Court recognized in *Gaston County* v. *United States*, 395 US 285, 296, (1969), the quality of education offered may influence a child's decision to "enter or remain in school." It is this very sort of intimate relationship between a particular personal interest and specific constitutional guarantees that has heretofore caused the Court to attach special significance, for purposes of equal protection analysis, to individual interests such as procreation and the exercise of the state franchise.

While ultimately disputing little of this, the majority seeks refuge in the fact that the Court has "never presumed to possess either the ability or the authority to guarantee to the citizenry the most *effective* speech or the most *informed* electoral choice." This serves only to blur what is in fact at stake. With due respect, the issue is neither provision of the most *effective* speech nor of the most *informed* vote. Appellees do not now seek the best education Texas might provide. They do seek, however, an end to state discrimination resulting from the unequal distribution of taxable district property wealth that directly impairs the ability of some districts to provide the same educational opportunity that other districts can provide with the same—or even substantially less tax effort. The issue is, in other words, one of discrimination that affects the quality of the education which Texas has chosen to provide its children; and, the precise question here is what importance should attach to education for purposes of equal protection analysis of that discrimination. As this Court held in *Brown* v. *Board of Education*, 347 US, at 493, the opportunity of education, "where the state has undertaken to provide it, is a right which must be made available to all on equal terms." The factors just considered, including the relationship between education and the social and political interests enshrined within the Constitution, compel us to recognize the fundamentality of education and to scrutinize with appropriate care the bases for state discrimination affecting equality of educational opportunity in Texas' school districts—a conclusion which is only strengthened when we consider the character of the classification in this case.

# C

The District Court found that in discriminating between Texas schoolchildren on the basis of the amount of taxable property wealth located in the district in which they live, the Texas financing scheme created a form of wealth discrimination. This Court has frequently recognized that discrimination on the basis of wealth may create a classification of a suspect character and thereby call for exacting judicial scrutiny. . . . The majority, however, considers any wealth classification in this case to lack certain essential characteristics which it contends are common to the instances of wealth discrimination that this Court has heretofore recognized. We are told that in every prior case involving a wealth classification, the members of the disadvantaged class have "shared two distinguishing characteristics: because of their impecunity they were completely unable to pay for some desired benefit, and as a consequence, they sustained an absolute deprivation of a meaningful opportunity to enjoy that benefit." . . .

This is not to say that the form of wealth classification in this case does not differ significantly from those recognized in the previous decisions of this Court. Our prior cases have dealt essentially with discrimination on the basis of personal wealth. Here, by contrast, the children of the disadvantaged Texas school districts are being discriminated against not necessarily because of their personal wealth or the wealth of their families, but because of the taxable property wealth of the residents of the district in which they happen to live. The appropriate question, then, is whether the same degree of judicial solicitude and scrutiny that has previously been afforded wealth classifications is warranted here. As the Court points out, no previous decision has deemed the presence of just a wealth classification to be sufficient basis to call forth rigorous judicial scrutiny of allegedly discriminatory state action. . . .

That wealth classifications alone have not necessarily been considered to bear the same high degree of suspectness as have classifications based on, for instance, race or alienage may be explainable on a number of grounds. The "poor" may not be seen as politically powerless as certain discrete and insular minority groups. Personal poverty may entail much the same social stigma as historically attached to certain racial or ethnic groups. But personal poverty is not a permanent disability; its shackles may be escaped. Perhaps most importantly, though, personal wealth may not necessarily share the general irrelevance as a basis for legislative action that race or nationality is recognized to have. While the "poor" have frequently been a legally disadvantaged group, it cannot be ignored that social legislation must frequently take cognizance of the economic status of our citizens. Thus, we have generally gauged the invidiousness of wealth classifications with an awareness of the importance of the interests being affected and the relevance of personal wealth to those interests.

When evaluated with these considerations in mind, it seems to me that discrimination on the basis of group wealth in this case likewise calls for careful judicial scrutiny. First, it must be recognized that while local district wealth may serve other interests, it bears no relationship whatsoever to the interest of Texas school children in the educational opportunity afforded them by the State of Texas. . . . Discrimination on the basis of group wealth may not, to be sure, reflect the social stigma frequently attached to personal poverty. Nevertheless, insofar as group wealth discrimination involves wealth over which the disadvantaged individual has no significant control, it represents in fact a more serious basis of discrimination than does personal wealth. For such discrimination is no reflection of the individual's characteristics or his abilities. And thus—particularly in the context of a disadvantaged class composed of children—we have previously treated discrimination on a basis which the individual cannot control as constitutionally disfavored.

The disability of the disadvantaged class in this case extends as well into the political processes upon which we ordinarily rely as adequate for the protection and promotion of all interests. Here legislative reallocation of the State's property wealth must be sought in the face of inevitable opposition from significantly advantaged districts that have a strong vested interest in the preservation of the status quo, a problem not completely dissimilar to that faced by underrepresented districts prior to the Court's intervention in the process of reapportionment, see *Baker* v. *Carr,* 369 US 186, (1962).

Nor can we ignore the extent to which, in contrast to our prior decisions, the State is responsible for the wealth discrimination in this instance. Griffin, Douglas, Williams, Tate, and our other prior cases have dealt with discrimination on the basis of indigency which was attributable to the operation of the private sector. But we have no such simple de facto wealth discrimination here. The means for financing public education in Texas are selected and specified by the State. It is the State that has created local school districts, and tied educational funding to the local property tax and thereby to local district wealth. At the same time, governmentally imposed land use controls have undoubtedly encouraged and rigidified natural trends in the allocation of particular areas for residential or commercial use, and thus determined each district's amount of taxable property wealth. In short, this case, in contrast to the Court's previous wealth discrimination decisions, can only be seen as "unusual in the extent to which governmental action is the cause of the wealth classifications."

In the final analysis, then, the invidious characteristics of the group wealth classification present in this case merely serve to emphasize the need for careful judicial scrutiny of the State's justifications for the resulting inter district discrimination in the educational opportunity afforded to the schoolchildren of Texas.

# D

The nature of our inquiry into the justifications for state discrimination is essentially the same in all equal protection cases: We must consider the substantiality of the state interests sought to be served, and we must scrutinize the reasonableness of the means by which the State has sought to advance its interests. Differences in the application of this test are, in my view, a function of the constitutional importance of the interests at stake and the invidiousness of the particular classification. In terms of the asserted state interests, the Court has indicated that it will require, for instance, a "compelling," or a "substantial" or "important," state interest to justify discrimination affecting individual interests of constitutional significance. Whatever the differences, if any, in these descriptions of the character of the state interest necessary to sustain such discrimination, basic to each is, I believe, a concern with the legitimacy and the reality of the asserted state interests. Thus, when interests of constitutional importance are at stake, the Court does not stand ready to credit the State's classification with any conceivable legitimate purpose, but demands a clear showing that there are legitimate state interests which the classification was in fact intended to serve. Beyond the question of the adequacy of the State's purpose for the classification, the Court traditionally has become increasingly sensitive to the means by which a State chooses to act as its action affects more directly interests of constitutional significance. . . . Thus, by now, "less restrictive alternatives" analysis is firmly established in equal protection jurisprudence. . . . It seems to me that the range of choice we are willing to accord the State in selecting the means by which it will act, and the care with which we scrutinize the effectiveness of the means which the State selects, also must reflect the constitutional importance of the interest affected and the invidiousness of the particular classification. Here both the nature of the interest and the classification dictate close judicial scrutiny of the purposes which Texas seeks to serve with its present educational financing scheme and of the means it has selected to serve that purpose.

The only justification offered by appellants to sustain the discrimination in educational opportunity caused by the Texas financing scheme is local educational control. . . .

At the outset, I do not question that local control of public education, as an abstract matter, constitutes a very substantial state interest. For on this record, it is apparent that the State's purported concern with local control is offered primarily as an excuse rather than as a justification for interdistrict inequality.

In Texas, statewide laws regulate in fact the most minute details of local public education. . . . It ignores reality to suggest—as the Court does, that the local property tax element of the Texas financing scheme reflects a conscious legislative effort to provide school districts with local fiscal control. If Texas had a system truly dedicated to local fiscal control, one would expect the quality of the educational opportunity provided in each district to vary with the decision of the voters in that district as to the level of sacrifice they wish to make for public education. In fact, the Texas scheme produces precisely the opposite result. Local school districts cannot choose to have the best education in the State by imposing the highest tax rate. Instead, the quality of the educational opportunity offered by any particular district is largely determined by the amount of taxable property located in the district—a factor over which local voters can exercise no control. . . . [T]he property-poor districts making the highest tax effort obtained the lowest per-pupil yield. . . .

In my judgment, any substantial degree of scrutiny of the operation of the Texas financing scheme reveals that the State has selected means wholly inappropriate to secure its purported interest in assuring its school districts local fiscal control. . . . If, for the sake of local education control, this Court is to sustain interdistrict discrimination in the educational opportunity afforded Texas school children it should require that the State present something more than the mere sham now before us.

## — III —

In conclusion, it is essential to recognize that an end to the wide variations in taxable district property wealth inherent in the Texas financing scheme would entail none of the untoward consequences suggested by the Court or by the appellants

First, affirmance of the District Court's decisions would hardly sound the death knell for local control of education. . . . took the course which is most likely to make true local control over educational decisionmaking a reality for *all* Texas school districts.

Nor does the District Court's decision even necessarily eliminate local control of educational funding. The District Court struck down nothing more than the continued interdistrict wealth discrimination inherent in the present property tax. Both centralized and decentralized plans for educational funding not involving such interdistrict discrimination have been put forward. The choice among these or other alternatives would remain with the State, not with the federal courts. . . .

The Court seeks solace for its action today in the possibility of legislative reform. The Court's suggestions of legislative redress and experimentation will doubtless be of great comfort to the schoolchildren of Texas' disadvantaged districts, but considering the vested interests of wealthy school districts in the preservation of the status quo, they are worth little more. The possibility of legislative action is, in all events, no answer to this Court's duty under the Constitution to eliminate unjustified state discrimination. . . .

I believe that the wide disparities in taxable district property wealth inherent in the local property tax element of the Texas financing scheme render that scheme violative of the Equal Protection Clause.[8]

I would therefore affirm the judgment of the District Court.

## Notes

1. The San Antonio Independent School District, whose name this case still bears, was one of seven school districts in the San Antonio metropolitan area that were originally named as defendants. After a pretrial conference, the District Court issued an order dismissing the school districts from the case. Subsequently, the San Antonio Independent School District joined in the plaintiffs' challenge to the State's school finance system and filed an amicus curiae brief in support of that position in this Court.

2. Tex Const, Art X, § 1 (1846):
   "A general diffusion of knowledge being essential to the preservation of the rights and liberties of the people, it shall be the duty of the Legislature of this State to make suitable provision for the support and maintenance of public schools."

   Id., § 2:
   "The Legislature shall as early as practicable establish free schools throughout the State, and shall furnish means for their support, by taxation on property . . . ."

3. See. e.g., *McLaughlin v. Florida*, 379 US 184, (1964); *Loving v. Virginia*, 388 US 1, 9, (1967).

4. See *Oyama v. California*, 332 US 633, (1948); *Korematsu v. United States*, 323 US 214 (1944).

5. See *Graham v. Richardson*, 403 US 365, (1971).

6. See Brief of the National Education Association et al. as amici curiae App A. All 48 of the 50 States which mandate public education also have compulsory attendance laws which require school attendance for eight years or more. Id., at 20–21.

7. Prior to this Court's decision in *Brown v. Board of Education*, 347 US 483, 98 L Ed 873, 74 S Ct 686 (1964), every State had a constitutional provision directing the establishment of a system of public schools. But after Brown, South Carolina repealed its constitutional provision, and Mississippi made its constitutional provision discretionary with the state legislature.

8. Of course, nothing in the Court's decision today should inhibit further review of state educational funding schemes under state constitutional provisions. See *Milliken v. Green*, 389 Mich 1, 203 NW2d 467 (1972), rehearing granted, Jan 1973): *Robinson v. Cahill*, 118 NJ Super 223, 287 A2d 187, 119 NJ Super 40, 289 A2d 659 (1972); cf. *Serrano v. Priest*, 5 Cal 3d 584, 487 P2d 1241 (1971).

**San Antonio Independent School District v. Rodriguez,** 411 U.S. 1 (1973) 5–4
*editor's note.*
*Opinion authors are in bold; () indicates the party of appointing president. If the party of the justice differs from that of appointing president, then the party of the justice is listed second after the slash.*

| MAJORITY | CONCURRING | DISSENTING |
|---|---|---|
| **Powell** (r/d) | **Stewart** (r) | **Brennan** (r/d) |
| Burger (r) | | **White** (d) |
| Blackmun (r) | | Douglas (d) |
| Rehnquist (r) | | **Marshall** (d) |

# Cheryl J. Hopwood, et al.,

### Plaintiffs—Appellants,

## v.

# State of Texas, et al.,

### Defendants—Appellees.

[78 F3d 932 (1996)]
Nos. 94–50569, 94–50664.

## United States Court of Appeals, Fifth Circuit.

March 18, 1996.
Rehearing and Rehearing En Banc Denied
April 4, 1996, 1996 WL 268347.

Janell M. Byrd, NAACP Legal Defense & Educational Fund, Inc., Washington, DC, Theodore M. Shaw, Norman J. Chachkin, NAACP Legal Defense & Educational Fund, Inc., New York City, Anthony P. Griffin, Galveston, TX, for appellants in No. 94–50569.

Dennis D. Parker, New York City, for TMLS—proposed intervenor.

Terral Ray Smith, Steven W. Smith, Small, Craig & Werkenthin, Austin, TX, for Elliott & Rogers.

Michael E. Rosman, Vincent A. Mulloy, Ctr. for Individual Rights, Washington, DC, for Cheryl Hopwood et al.

Harry M. Reasoner, Vinson & Elkins, Houston, TX, Barry D. Burgdorf, Vinson & Elkins, Austin, TX, R. Scott Placek, Houston, TX, Samuel Issacharoff, Charles Alan Wright, Univ. of Texas School of Law, Austin, TX, Betty R. Owens, Houston, TX, Javier Aguilar, Spec. Asst. Atty. Gen., Austin, TX, Allan Van Fleet, Houston, TX, for State of Texas et al.

Steven W. Smith, Austin, TX, Terral R. Smith, Austin, TX, for Appellants, Elliott & Rogers.

Theodore B. Olson, Washington DC, Michael E. Rosman, Ctr. for Ind. Rights, Washington, DC, Joseph A. Wallace, Elkins, West VA, for Hopwood and Douglas W. Carvell.

Javier Aguilar, Austin, TX, Harry M. Reasoner, Betty R. Owens, Houston, TX, Barry D. Burgdorf, Vinson & Elkins, Austin, TX, Dana C. Livingston, Manuel Lopez, Allan Van Fleet, Houston, TX, R. Scott Placek, Austin, TX, Samuel Issacharoff, Charles Alan Wright, Austin, TX, for State of Texas et al.

Janell M. Byrd, Anthony P. Griffin, Washington, DC, Theodore M. Shaw, Norman J. Chachkin, New York City, Myles V. Lynk, Washington, DC, for amicus curiae TMLS.

Albert H. Kauffman, John R. Vasquez, San Antonio, TX, for amicus curiae MALDEF.

Appeals from the United States District Court for the Western District of Texas.

Before SMITH, WIENER and DEMOSS, Circuit Judges.

JERRY E. SMITH, Circuit Judge:

With the best of intentions, in order to increase the enrollment of certain favored classes of minority students, the University of Texas School of Law ("the law school") discriminates in favor of those applicants by giving substantial racial preferences in its admissions program. The beneficiaries of this system are blacks and Mexican Americans, to the detriment of whites and non-preferred minorities. The question we decide today in No. 94–50664 is whether the Fourteenth Amendment permits the school to discriminate in this way.

We hold that it does not. The law school has presented no compelling justification, under the Fourteenth Amendment or Supreme Court precedent, that allows it to continue to elevate some races over others, even for the wholesome purpose of correcting perceived racial imbalance in the student body. "Racial preferences appear to 'even the score' . . . only if one embraces the proposition that our society is appropriately viewed as divided into races, making it right that an injustice rendered in the past to a black man should be compensated for by discriminating against a white." *City of Richmond v. J.A. Croson Co.*, 488 U.S. 469, 528, 109 S.Ct. 706, 740, 102 L.Ed.2d 854 (1989) (Scalia, J., concurring in the judgment).

As a result of its diligent efforts in this case, the district court concluded that the law school may continue to impose racial preferences. *See Hopwood v. Texas*, 861 F. Supp. 551 (W.D.Tex. 1994). In No. 94–50664, we reverse and remand, concluding that the law school may not use race as a factor in law school admissions. . . .

— I —

A

The University of Texas School of Law is one of the nation's leading law schools, consistently ranking in the top twenty. . . . Accordingly, admission to the law school is fiercely competitive, with over 4,000 applicants a year competing to be among the approximately 900 offered admission to achieve an entering class of about 500 students. Many of these applicants have some of the highest grades and test scores in the country.

Numbers are therefore paramount for admission. In the early 1990's the law school largely based its initial admissions decisions upon an applicant's so-called Texas Index ("TI") number, a composite of undergraduate grade point average ("GPA") and Law School Aptitude Test ("LSAT") score. The law school used this number as a matter of administrative convenience in order to rank candidates and to predict, roughly, one's probability of success in law school. Moreover, the law school relied heavily upon such numbers to estimate the number of offers of admission it needed to make in order to fill its first-year class.

Of course, the law school did not rely upon numbers alone. The admissions office necessarily exercised judgment in interpreting the individual scores of applicants, taking into consideration factors such as the strength of a student's undergraduate education, the difficulty of his major, and significant trends in his own grades and the undergraduate grades at his respective college (such as grade inflation). Admissions personnel also considered what qualities each applicant might bring to his law school class. Thus, the law school could consider an applicant's background, life experiences, and outlook. Not surprisingly, these hard-to-quantify factors were especially significant for marginal candidates.

Because of the large number of applicants and potential admissions factors, the TI's administrative usefulness was its ability to sort candidates. For the class entering in 1992—the admissions group at issue in this case—the law school placed the typical applicant in one of three categories according to his TI scores: "presumptive admit," "presumptive deny," or a middle "discretionary zone." An applicant's TI category determined how extensive a review his application would receive.

Most, but not all, applicants in the presumptive admit category received offers of admission with little review. Professor Stanley Johanson, the Chairman of the Admissions Committee, or Dean Laquita Hamilton, the Assistant Dean for Admissions, reviewed these files and downgraded only five to ten percent to the discretionary zone because of weaknesses in their applications, generally a noncompetitive major or a weak undergraduate education.

Applicants in the presumptive denial category also received little consideration. Similarly, these files would be reviewed by one or two professors, who could upgrade them if they believed that the TI score did not adequately reflect potential to compete at the law school. Otherwise, the applicant was rejected.

Applications in the middle range were subjected to the most extensive scrutiny. For applicants other than blacks and Mexican Americans, the files were bundled into stacks of thirty, which were given to admissions subcommittees consisting of three members of the full admissions committee. Each subcommittee member, in reviewing the thirty files, could case a number of votes—typically from nine to eleven[1]—among the thirty files. Subject to the chairman's veto, if a candidate received two or three votes, he received an offer; if he garnered one vote, he was put on the waiting list; those with no votes were denied admission.

Blacks and Mexican Americans were treated differently from other candidates, however. First, compared to whites and non-preferred minorities,[2] the TI ranges that were used to place them into the three admissions categories were lowered to allow the law school to consider and admit more of them. In March 1992, for example, the presumptive TI admissions score for resident whites and non-preferred minorities was 199. Mexican Americans and blacks needed a TI of only 189 to be presumptively admitted.[3] The difference in the presumptive-deny ranges is even more striking. The presumptive denial score for "nonminorities" was 192; the same score for blacks and Mexican Americans was 179.

While these cold numbers may speak little to those unfamiliar with the pool of applicants, the results demonstrate that the difference in the two ranges was dramatic. According to the law school, 1992 resident white applicants had a *mean* GPA of 3.53 and an LSAT of 164. Mexican Americans scored 3.27 and 158; blacks scored 3.25 and 157. The category of "other minority" achieved a 3.56 and 160.

These disparate standards greatly affected a candidate's chance of admission. For example, by March 1992, because the presumptive *denial* score for whites was TI of 192 or lower, and the presumptive *admit* TI for minorities was 189 or higher, a minority candidate with a TI of 189 or above almost certainly would be *admitted*, even though his score was considerably below the level at which a white candidate almost certainly would be *rejected*. Out of the pool of resident applicants who fell within this range (189–192 inclusive), 100% of blacks and 90% of Mexican Americans, but only 6% of whites, were offered admission.

The stated purpose of this lowering of standards was to meet an "aspiration" of admitting a class consisting of 10% Mexican Americans and 5% blacks, proportions roughly comparable to the percentages of those races graduating from Texas colleges. The law school found meeting these "goals" difficult, however, because of uncertain acceptance rates and the variable quality of the applicant pool. In 1992, for example, the entering class contained 41 blacks and 55 Mexican Americans, respectively 8% and 10.7% of the class.

In addition to maintaining separate presumptive TI levels for minorities and whites, the law school ran a segregated application evaluation process. Upon receiving an application form, the school color-coded it according to race. If a candidate failed to designate his race, he was presumed to be in a nonpreferential category. Thus, race was always an overt part of the review of any applicant's file.

The law school reviewed minority candidates within the applicable discretionary range differently from whites. Instead of being evaluated and compared by one of the various discretionary zone subcommittees, black and Mexican American applicants' files were reviewed by a minority subcommittee of three, which would meet and discuss every minority candidate. Thus, each of these candidates' files could get extensive review and discussion. And while the minority subcommittee reported summaries of files to the admissions committee as a whole, the minority subcommittee's decisions were "virtually final."

Finally, the law school maintained segregated waiting lists, dividing applicants by race and residence. Thus, even many of those minority applicants who were not admitted could be set aside in "minority-only" waiting lists. Such separate lists apparently helped the law school maintain a pool of potentially acceptable, but marginal, minority candidates.

# B

Cheryl Hopwood, Douglas Carvell, Kenneth Elliott, and David Rogers (the "plaintiffs") applied for admission to the 1992 entering law school class. All four were white residents of Texas and were rejected.

The plaintiffs were considered as discretionary zone candidates. Hopwood, with a GPA of 3.8 and an LSAT of 39 (equivalent to a three-digit LSAT of 160), had a TI of 199, a score barely within the presumptive-admit category for resident whites, which was 199 and up. She was dropped into the discretionary zone for resident whites (193 to 198) however, because Johanson decided her educational background overstated the strength of her GPA. Carvell, Elliott, and Rogers had TI's of 197, at the top end of that discretionary zone. Their applications were reviewed by admissions subcommittees, and each received one or no vote.

# — II —

The plaintiffs sued primarily under the Equal Protection Clause of the Fourteenth Amendment; they also claimed derivative statutory violations of 42 U.S.C. §§ 1981 and 1983 and of title VI of the Civil Rights Act of 1964, 42 U.S.C. § 2000d ("title VI").[4] The plaintiffs' central claim is that they were subjected to unconstitutional racial discrimination by the law school's evaluation of their admissions applications. They sought injunctive and declaratory relief and compensatory and punitive damages.

After a bench trial, the district court held that the school had violated the plaintiffs' equal protection rights. 861 F.Supp. at 579. The plaintiffs' victory was pyrrhic at best, however, as the court refused to enjoin the law school from using race in admissions decisions or to grant damages beyond a one-dollar nominal award to each plaintiff. The district court, however, did grant declaratory relief and ordered that the plaintiffs be allowed to apply again without paying the requisite fee.

The district court began by recognizing the proper constitutional standard under which to evaluate the admissions program: strict scrutiny. As it was undisputed that the school had treated applicants disparately based upon the color of their skin, the court asked whether the law school process (1) served a compelling government interest and (2) was narrowly tailored to the achievement of that goal. . . .

The court held, however, that differential treatment was not allowed where candidates of different races were not compared at some point in the admission process. Thus, the court struck down the school's use of separate admissions committees for applications in the discretionary zone. . . . The court then found that the defendants had proffered a legitimate, non-discriminatory reason for denying the plaintiffs admission and that the plaintiffs had not met their burden of showing that they would have been admitted but for the unlawful system. . . . To pass muster under the court's reasoning, the law school simply had to have one committee that at one time during the process reviewed all applications and did not establish separate TI numbers to define the presumptive denial categories. In other words, if the law school applied the same academic standards, but had commingled the minority review in the discretionary zone with the review of whites, its program would not have been struck down. The same admissions result would occur, but the process would be "fair." . . .

## — III —

The central purpose of the Equal Protection Clause "is to prevent the States from purposefully discriminating between individuals on the basis of race." . . . It seeks ultimately to render the issue of race irrelevant in governmental decisionmaking. . . .

Accordingly, discrimination based upon race is highly suspect. . . . Hence, "[p]referring members of any one group for no reason other than race or ethnic origin is discrimination for its own sake. This the Constitution forbids." *Regents of Univ. of Cal. v. Bakke*, 438 U.S. 265, 307, (1978) (opinion of Powelll, J.); *see also Loving v. Virginia*, 388 U.S. 1. 11, (1967); *Brown v. Board of Educ.*, 347 U.S. 483, 493–94, (1954). These equal protection maxims apply to all races. *Adarand Constructors v. Peña*, — U.S. ——, ——, 132 L. Ed.2d 158 (1995).

In order to preserve these principles, the Supreme Court recently has required that any governmental action that expressly distinguishes between persons on the basis of race be held to the most exacting scrutiny. *See, e.g., id*, at ——, 115 S.Ct. at 2113; *Loving*, 388 U.S. at 11. Furthermore, there is now absolutely no doubt that courts are to employ strict scrutiny when evaluating all racial classifications, including those characterized by their proponents as "benign" or "remedial." . . .

Under the strict scrutiny analysis, we ask two questions: (1) Does the racial classification serve a compelling government interest, and (2) is it narrowly tailored to the achievement of that goal? *Adarand*, —— U.S. at ——, ——, 115 S.Ct. at 2111, 2117. As the *Adarand* Court emphasized, strict scrutiny ensures that "courts will consistently give racial classifications . . . detailed examination both as to ends and as to means."

Finally, when evaluating the proffered governmental interest for the specific racial classification, to decide whether the program in question narrowly achieves that interest, we must recognize that "the rights created by . . . the Fourteenth Amendment are, by its terms, guaranteed to the individual. The rights established are personal rights." *Shelley v. Kraemer*, 334 U.S. 1, 22, (1948). Thus, the Court consistently has rejected arguments conferring benefits on a person based solely upon his membership in a specific class of persons.

With these general principles of equal protection in mind, we turn to the specific issue of whether the law school's consideration of race as a factor in admissions violates the Equal Protection Clause. The district court found both a compelling remedial and a nonremedial justification for the practice.

First, the court approved of the non-remedial goal of having a diverse student body, reasoning that "obtaining the educational benefits that flow from a racially and ethnically diverse student body remains a sufficiently compelling interest to support the use of racial classifications." Second, the court determined that the use of racial classifications could be justified as a remedy for the "present effects at the law school of past discrimination in both the University of Texas system and the Texas educational system as a whole."

# A

## 1

Justice Powell's separate opinion in *Bakke* provided the original impetus for recognizing diversity as a compelling state interest in higher education. . . .

While Justice Powell found the program unconstitutional under the Equal Protection Clause and affirmed Bakke's admission, Justice Stevens declined to reach the constitutional issue and upheld Bakke's admission under title VI. Justice Powell also concluded that the California Supreme Court's proscription of the consideration of race in admissions could not be sustained. This became the judgment of the Court, as the four-Justice opinion by Justice Brennan opined that racial classifications designed to serve remedial purposes should receive only intermediate scrutiny. These Justices would have upheld the admissions program under this intermediate scrutiny, as it served the substantial and benign purpose of remedying past societal discrimination.

Hence, Justice Powell's opinion has appeared to represent the "swing vote," and though, in significant part, it was joined by no other Justice, it has played a prominent role in subsequent debates concerning the impact of *Bakke*. . . .

Justice Powell speculated that a program in which "race or ethnic background may be deemed a 'plus' in a particular applicant's file, yet does not insulate the individual from comparison with all the other candidates for the available seats," might pass muster. . . .

Under this conception of the Fourteenth Amendment, a program that considered a host of factors that include race would be constitutional, even if an applicant's race "tipped the scales" among qualified applicants. What a school could not do is to refuse to compare applicants of different races or establish a strict quota on the basis of race. In sum, Justice Powell found the school's program to be an unconstitutional "quota" system, but he intimated that the Constitution would allow schools to continue to use race in a wide-ranging manner.

## 2

. . . We agree with the plaintiffs that any consideration of race or ethnicity by the law school for the purpose of achieving a diverse student body is not a compelling interest under the Fourteenth Amendment. Justice Powell's argument in *Bakke* garnered only his own vote and has never represented the view of a majority of the Court in *Bakke* or any other case. Moreover, subsequent Supreme Court decisions regarding education state that non-remedial state interests will never justify racial classifications. Finally, the classification of persons on the basis of race for the purpose of diversity frustrates, rather than facilitates, the goals of equal protection.

Justice Powell's view in *Bakke* is not binding precedent on this issue. While he announced the judgment, no other Justice joined in that part of the opinion discussing the diversity rationale. In *Bakke* the word "diversity" is mentioned nowhere except in Justice Powell's single-Justice opinion. In fact, the four-Justice opinion, which would have upheld the special admissions program under intermediate scrutiny, implicitly rejected Justice Powell's position. *See* 438 U.S. at 326 n. 1, 98 S.Ct. at 2766 n. 1 (Brennan, White, Marshall, and Blackmun JJ., concurring in the judgment in part and dissenting). . . .

Thus, only one Justice concluded that race could be used solely for the reason of obtaining a heterogeneous student body. As the *Adarand* Court states, the *Bakke* Court did not express a majority view and is questionable as binding precedent. —— U.S. at ——, 115 S.Ct. at 2109 . . . No case since *Bakke* has accepted diversity as a compelling state interest under a strict scrutiny analysis.

Indeed, recent Supreme Court precedent shows that the diversity interest will not satisfy strict scrutiny. Foremost, the Court appears to have decided that there is essentially only one compelling state interest to justify racial classifications: remedying past wrongs. In *Croson*, 488 U.S. at 493, 109 S.Ct. at 722 (plurality opinion), the Court flatly stated that "[u]nless [racial classifications] are strictly reserved for remedial settings, they may in fact promote notions of racial inferiority and lead to a politics of racial hostility." . . .

In short, there has been no indication from the Supreme Court, other than Justice Powell's lonely opinion in *Bakke*, that the state's interest in diversity constitutes a compelling justification for governmental race-based discrimination. Subsequent Supreme Court caselaw strongly suggests, in fact, that it is not.

Within the general principles of the Fourteenth Amendment, the use of race in admissions for diversity in higher education contradicts, rather than furthers, the aims of equal protection. Diversity fosters, rather than minimizes, the use of race. It treats minorities as a group, rather than as individuals. It may further remedial purposes but, just as likely, may promote improper racial stereotypes, thus fueling racial hostility.

The use of race, in and of itself, to choose students simply achieves a student body that looks different. Such a criterion is no more rational on its own terms than would be choices based upon the physical size or blood type of applicants. Thus, the Supreme Court has long held that governmental actors cannot justify their decisions solely because of race. . . .

Accordingly, we see the caselaw as sufficiently established that the use of ethnic diversity simply to achieve racial heterogeneity, even as part of the consideration of a number of factors, is unconstitutional. Were we to decide otherwise, we would contravene precedent that we are not authorized to challenge.

While the use of race *per se* is prescribed, state-supported schools may reasonably consider a host of factors—some of which may have some correlation with race—in making admissions decisions. The federal courts have no warrant to intrude on those executive and legislative judgments unless the distinctions intrude on specific provisions of federal law or the Constitution.

A university may properly favor one applicant over another because of his ability to play the cello, make a downfield tackle, or understand chaos theory. An admissions process may also consider an applicant's home state or relationship to school alumni. Law schools specifically may look at things such as unusual or substantial extracurricular activities in college, which may be atypical factors affecting undergraduate grades. Schools may even consider factors such as whether an applicant's parents attended college or the applicant's economic and social background.[5]

For this reason, race often is said to be justified in the diversity context, not on its own terms, but as a proxy for other characteristics that institutions of higher education value but that do not raise similar constitutional concerns. Unfortunately, this approach simply replicates the very harm that the Fourteenth Amendment was designed to eliminate.

The assumption is that a certain individual possesses characteristics by virtue of being a member of a certain racial group. This assumption, however, does not withstand scrutiny. . . .

To believe that a person's race controls his point of view is to stereotype him. The Supreme Court, however, "has remarked a number of times, in slightly different contexts, that it is incorrect and legally inappropriate to impute to women and minorities 'a different attitude about such issues as the federal budget, school prayer, voting, and foreign relations.'" . . .

"Social scientists may debate how peoples' thoughts and behavior reflect their background, but the Constitution provides that the government may not allocate benefits or burdens among individuals based on the assumption that race or ethnicity determines how they act or think." *Metro Broadcasting*, 497 U.S. at 602, 110 S.Ct. at 3029 (O'Connor, J., dissenting).

Instead, individuals, with their own conceptions of life, further diversity of viewpoint. Plaintiff Hopwood is a fair example of an applicant with a unique background. She is the now-thirty-two-year-old wife of a member of the Armed Forces stationed in San Antonio and, more significantly, is raising a severely handicapped child. Her circumstance would bring a different perspective to the law school. The school might consider this an advantage to her in the application process, or it could decide that her family situation would be too much of a burden on her academic performance.

We do not opine on which way the law school should weigh Hopwood's qualifications; we only observe that "diversity" can take many forms. To foster such diversity, state universities and law schools and other governmental entities must scrutinize applicants individually, rather than resorting to the dangerous proxy of race.

The Court also has recognized that government's use of racial classifications serves to stigmatize. *See, e.g., Brown v. Board of Educ.*, 347 U.S. 483, (1954) (observing that classification on the basis of race "generates a feeling of inferiority"). While one might argue that the stigmatization resulting from so-called "benign" racial classifications is not as harmful as that arising from invidious ones, the current Court has now retreated from the idea that so-called benign and invidious classifications may be distinguished. As the plurality in *Croson* warned, "[c]lassifications based on race carry the danger of stigmatic harm. Unless they are reserved for remedial settings, they may in fact promote notions of racial inferiority and lead to the politics of racial hostility."

Finally, the use of race to achieve diversity undercuts the ultimate goal of the Fourteenth Amendment: the end of racially-motivated state action. Justice Powell's conception of race as a "plus" factor would allow race always to be a potential factor in admissions decisionmaking. While Justice Blackmun recognized the tension inherent in using race-conscious remedies to achieve a race-neutral society, nevertheless accepted it as necessary. *Bakke*, 438 U.S. at 405, 98 S.Ct. at 2806. Several Justices who, unlike Justices Powell and Blackmun, are still on the Court, have now renounced toleration of this tension, however. . . .

In sum, the use of race to achieve a diverse student body, whether as a proxy for permissible characteristics, simply cannot be a state interest compelling enough to meet the steep standard of strict scrutiny. These latter factors may, in fact, turn out to be substantially correlated with race, but the key is that race itself not be taken into account. Thus, that portion of the district court's opinion upholding the diversity rationale is reversibly flawed.

## B

We now turn to the district court's determination that "the remedial purpose of the law school's affirmative action program is a compelling government objective." . . .

In contrast to its approach to the diversity rationale, a majority of the Supreme Court has held that a state actor may racially classify where it has "strong basis in the evidence for its conclusion that remedial action was necessary."

Because a state does not have a compelling state interest in remedying the present effects of past *societal* discrimination, however, we must examine the district court's legal determination that the relevant governmental entity is the system of education within the state as a whole. Moreover, we also must review the court's identification of what types of present effects of past discrimination, if proven, would be sufficient under strict scrutiny review. Finally, where the state actor puts forth a remedial justification for its racial classifications, the district court must make a "factual determination" as to whether remedial action is necessary. We review such factual rulings for clear error.

## 1

The Supreme Court has "insisted upon some showing of prior discrimination by the governmental unit involved before allowing limited use of racial classifications in order to remedy such discrimination." . . .

Applying the teachings of *Croson* and *Wygant*, we conclude that the district court erred in expanding the remedial justification to reach all public education within the State of Texas. The Supreme Court repeatedly has warned that the use of racial remedies must be carefully limited, and a remedy reaching all education within a state addresses a putative injury that is vague and amorphous. It has "no logical stopping point."

The district court's holding employs no viable limiting principle. If a state can "remedy" the present effects of past discrimination in its primary and secondary schools, it also would be allowed to award broad-based preferences in hiring, government contracts, licensing, and any other state activity that in some way is affected by the educational attainment of the applicants. This very argument was made in *Croson* and rejected: . . .

Strict scrutiny is meant to ensure that the purpose of a racial preference is remedial. Yet when one state actor begins to justify racial preferences based upon the actions of other state agencies, the remedial actor's competence to determine the existence and scope of the harm—and the appropriate reach of the remedy—is called into question. . . . Thus, one justification for limiting the remedial powers of a state actor is that the specific agency involved is best able to measure the harm of its past discrimination.

Here, however, the law school has no comparative advantage in measuring the present effects of discrimination in primary and secondary schools in Texas. Such a task becomes even more improbable where, as here, benefits are conferred on students who attended out-of-state or private schools for such education. Such boundless "remedies" raise a constitutional concern beyond mere competence. In this situation, an inference is raised that the program was the result of racial social engineering rather a desire to implement a remedy. . . .

Even if, *arguendo*, the state is the proper government unit to scrutinize, the law school's admissions program would not withstand our review. For the admissions scheme to pass constitutional muster, the State of Texas, through its legislature, would have to find that past segregation has present effects; it would have to determine the magnitude of those present effects; and it would need to limit carefully the "plus" given to applicants to remedy that harm. A broad program that sweeps in all minorities with a remedy that is in no way related to past harms cannot survive constitutional scrutiny. Obviously, none of those predicates has been satisfied here.

In sum, for purposes of determining whether the law school's admissions system properly can act as a remedy for the present effects of past discrimination, we must identify the law school as the relevant alleged past discriminator. The fact that the law school ultimately may be subject to the directives of others, such as the board of regents, the university president, or the legislature, does not change the fact that the relevant putative discriminator in this case is still the law school. In order for any of these entities to direct a racial preference program at the law school, it must be because of past wrongs at that school.

**2**

Next, the relevant governmental discriminator must prove that there are present effects of past discrimination of the type that justify the racial classifications at issue. . . . Moreover, as part of showing that the alleged present effects of past discrimination in fact justify the racial preference program at issue, the law school must show that it adopted the program specifically to remedy the identified present effects of the past discrimination. . . . While the school once did practice *de jure* discrimination in denying admissions to blacks, the Court in *Sweatt v. Painter*, 339 U.S. 629, 70 S.Ct. 848, 94 L.Ed. 1114 (1950), struck down the law school's program. Any other discrimination by the law school ended in the 1960's. *Hopwood*, 861 F.Supp. at 555.

By the late 1960's, the school had implemented its first program designed to recruit minorities, *id.* at 557, and it now engages in an extensive minority recruiting program that includes a significant amount of scholarship money. The vast majority of the faculty, staff, and students at the law school had absolutely nothing to do with any discrimination that the law school practiced in the past.

In such a case, one cannot conclude that a hostile environment is the present effect of past discrimination. Any racial tension at the law school is contributed to, rather than alleviated by, the overt and prevalent consideration of race in admissions.

Even if the law school's alleged current lingering reputation in the minority community—and the perception that the school is a hostile environment for minorities—were considered to be the present effects of past discrimination, rather than the result of societal discrimination, they could not constitute compelling state interests justifying the use of racial classifications in admissions. A bad reputation within the minority community is alleviated not by the consideration of race in admissions, but by school action designed directly to enhance its reputation in that community.

Minority students who are aided by the law school's racial preferences have already made the decision to apply, despite the reputation. And, while prior knowledge that they will get a "plus" might make potential minorities more likely to apply, such an inducement does nothing, *per se*, to change any hostile environment. As we have noted, racial preferences, if anything, can compound the problem of a hostile environment.

The law school wisely concentrates only on the second effect the district court identified: underrepresentation of minorities because of past discrimination. The law school argues that we should consider the prior discrimination by the State of Texas and its educational system rather than of the law school. The school contends that this prior discrimination by the state had a direct effect on the educational attainment of the pool of minority applicants and that the discriminatory admissions program was implemented partially discharge the school's duty of eliminating the vestiges of past segregation. . . . [P]ast discrimination in education, other than at the law school, cannot justify the present consideration of race in law school admissions. . . .

In sum, the law school has failed to show a compelling state interest in remedying the present effects of past discrimination sufficient to maintain the use of race in its administrations system. Accordingly, it is unnecessary for us to examine the district court's determination that the law school's admissions program was not narrowly tailored to meet the compelling interests that the district court erroneously perceived.

## — IV —

While the district court declared the admissions program unconstitutional, it granted the plaintiffs only limited relief. They had requested injunctive relief ordering that they be admitted to the law school, compensatory and punitive damages, and prospective injunctive relief preventing the school from using race as a factor in admissions.

### A

. . . In the event that the law school is unable to show (by a preponderance of the evidence) that a respective plaintiff would not have been admitted to the law school under a constitutional admissions system, the court is to award to that plaintiff any equitable and/or monetary relief it deems appropriate.

Obviously if the school proves that a plaintiff would not have gained admittance to the law school under a race-blind system, that plaintiff would not be entitled to an injunction admitting him to the school. On the other hand, the law school's inability to establish a plaintiff's non-admissions—if that occurs on remand—opens a panoply of potential relief, depending in part upon what course that plaintiff's career has taken since trial in mid-1994. It then would be up to the district court, in its able discretion, to decide whether money damages can substitute for an order of immediate admission—relief that would ring hollow for a plaintiff for whom an education at the law school now is of little or no benefit.

## B

The plaintiffs argue that, because they proved a constitutional violation, and further violations were likely to result, the district court erred in denying them prospective injunctive relief. . . .

According to the district court, the school had abandoned the admissions procedure—consisting of the separate minority subcommittee—that was used in 1992, 1993, and 1994. The court reasoned that, as a new procedure was developed for 1995, a prospective injunction against the school was inappropriate. We conclude, however, that, while the district court may have been correct in deciding that the new procedure eliminates the constitutional flaws that the district court identified in the 1992 system, there is no indication that the new system will cure the additional constitutional defects we now have explained.

The new system utilizes a small "administrative admissions group" and does not use presumptive admission and denial scores. *See Hopwood*, 861 F.Supp. at 582 n. 87. Most significantly, there is no indication that in employing the new plan, the law school will cease to consider race *per se* in making its admissions decisions. To the contrary, as the district court recognized, the law school continues to assert that overt racial preferences are necessary to the attainment of its goals. *See Hopwood*, 861 F.Supp. at 578–75.

The district court has already granted some equitable relief: It directed that the plaintiffs be permitted to re-apply to the law school without incurring further administrative costs. In accordance with this opinion, the plaintiffs are entitled to apply under a system of admissions that will not discriminate against anyone on the basis of race. . . .

It is not necessary, however, for us to order at this time that the law school be enjoined, as we are confident that the conscientious administration at the school, as well as its attorneys, will heed the directives contained in this opinion. If an injunction should be needed in the future, the district court, in its discretion, can consider its parameters without our assistance. Accordingly, we leave intact that court's refusal to enter an injunction.

## C

. . . [W]e agree with the district court that punitive damages are not warranted. We note, however, that if the law school continues to operate a disguised or overt racial classification system in the future, its actors could be subject to actual and punitive damages.

# — V —

. . .

# — VI —

In summary, we hold that the University of Texas School of Law may not use race as a factor in deciding which applicants to admit in order to achieve a diverse student body, to combat the perceived effects of a hostile environment at the law school, to alleviate the law school's poor reputation in the minority community, or to eliminate any present effects of past discrimination by actors other than the law school. Because the law school has proffered these justifications for its use of race in admissions, the plaintiffs have satisfied their burden of showing that they were scrutinized under an unconstitutional admissions system. The plaintiffs are entitled to reapply under an admissions system that invokes none of these serious constitutional infirmities. We also direct the district court to reconsider the question of damages, and we conclude that the proposed intervenors properly were denied intervention.

In No. 94–50664, the judgment is REVERSED and REMANDED for further proceedings in accordance with this opinion.

WIENER, Circuit Judge, specially concurring.

"We judge best when we judge least, particularly in controversial matters of high public interest." In this and every other appeal, we should decide only the case before us, and should do so on the narrowest possible basis. Mindful of this credo, I concur in part and, with respect, specially concur in part.

The sole substantive issue in this appeal is whether the admissions process employed by the law school for 1992 meets muster under the Equal Protection Clause of the Fourteenth Amendment. . . .

As to present effects, I concur in the panel opinion's analysis: Irrespective of whether the law school or the University of Texas system as a whole is deemed the relevant governmental unit to be tested, neither has established the existence of present effects of past discrimination sufficient to justify the use of a racial classification. As to diversity, however, I respectfully disagree with the panel opinion's conclusion that diversity can never be a compelling governmental interest in a public graduate school. Rather than attempt to decide that issue, I would take a considerably narrower path—and, I believe, a more appropriate one—to reach an equally narrow result: I would assume arguendo that diversity can be a compelling interest but conclude that the admissions process here under scrutiny was not narrowly tailored to achieve diversity.

# — I —

## THE LAW

### A. Equal Protection

The Equal Protection Clause provides that "[n]o State shall . . . deny to any person within its jurisdiction the equal protection of the laws." Accordingly, "all racial classifications, imposed by whatever federal, state, or local governmental actor, must be analyzed by a reviewing court under *strict scrutiny*." Racial classifications will survive strict scrutiny "only if they are narrowly tailored measures that further compelling governmental interests." Thus, strict scrutiny comprises two inquiries of equal valence: the "compelling interest" inquiry and the "narrow tailoring" inquiry. Moreover, these inquiries are conjunctive: To avoid constitutional nullity, a racial classification must satisfy *both* inquiries. Failure to satisfy either is fatal.

### B. Racial Classification

None dispute that the law school's admission process for 1992 employed a racial classification. . . . Thus, the law school's 1992 admissions process, like all racial classifications by the government, is subject to strict scrutiny.

### C. Strict Scrutiny

The law school contents that it employs a racially stratified admissions process to obtain, the educational benefits of a diverse student body. . . . My fellow panelists thus declare categorically that "*any* consideration of race or ethnicity by the law school for the purposes of achieving a diverse student body is not a compelling interest under the Fourteenth Amendment."

This conclusion may well be a defensible *extension* of recent Supreme Court precedent, an extension which in time may prove to be the Court's position. It admittedly has a simplifying appeal as an easily applied, bright-line rule proscribing any use of race as a determinant. Be that as it may, this position remains an extension of the law—one that, in my opinion, is both overly broad and unnecessary to the disposition of this case. I am therefore unable to concur in the majority's analysis.

My decision not to embrace the ratio decidendi of the majority opinion results from three premises: First, if *Bakke* is to be declared dead, the Supreme Court, not a three-judge panel of a circuit court, should make that pronouncement. Second, JUSTICE

O'CONNOR expressly states that *Adarand* is not the death knell of affirmative action—to which I would add, especially *not* in the framework of achieving diversity in public graduate schools. Third, we have no need to decide the thornier issue of compelling interest, as the narrowly tailored inquiry of strict scrutiny presents a more surgical and—it seems to me—more principled way to decide the case before us. I am nevertheless reluctant to proceed with a narrowly tailored inquiry without pausing to respond briefly to the panel opinion's treatment of diversity in the context of the compelling interest inquiry.

## D. Is Diversity A Compelling Interest?

Along its path to a per se ban on any consideration of race in attempting to achieve student body diversity, the panel opinion holds (or strongly implies) that remedying vestigial effects of past discrimination is the only compelling state interest that can ever justify racial classification. The main reason that I cannot go along with the panel opinion to that extent is that I do not read the applicable Supreme Court precedent as having held squarely and unequivocally either that remedying effects of past discrimination is the only compelling state interest that can ever justify racial classification, or conversely that achieving diversity in the student body of a public graduate or professional school can never be a compelling governmental interest. . . . I perceive no "compelling" reason to rush in where the Supreme Court fears—or at least declines—to tread. Instead, I would pretermit any attempt at a compelling interest inquiry and accept JUSTICE O'CONNOR's invitation to apply the Court's more discernible and less intrusive "narrow tailoring" precedent. Thus, for the purpose of this appeal I *assume*, without deciding, that diversity is a compelling interest, and proceed to the narrowly tailored inquiry.

## E. Test for Narrow Tailoring

When strictly scrutinizing a racial classification for narrow tailoring, the first question is "What is the purpose of this racial classification?" . . . The law school's purpose is diversity. Accordingly, I perceive the next question to be, "Was the law school's 1992 admissions process, with one TI range for blacks, another for Mexican Americans, and a third for other races, narrowly tailored to achieve diversity?" I conclude that it was not. Focusing as it does on blacks and Mexican Americans only, the law school's 1992 admissions process misconceived the concept of diversity, as did California's in the view of JUSTICE POWELL: Diversity which furthers a compelling state interest "encompasses a far broader array of qualifications and characteristics of which racial or ethnic origin is but a single though important element."

When the selective race-based preferences of the law school's 1992 admissions process are evaluated under justice Powell's broad, multi-faceted concept of diversity, that process fails to satisfy the requirements of the Constitution. The law school purported to accomplish diversity by ensuring an increase in the numbers of only blacks and Mexican Americans in each incoming class to produce percentages—virtually indistinguishable from quotas—of approximately five and ten percent, respectively. Yet blacks and Mexican Americans are but two among any number of racial or ethnic groups that could and presumably should contribute to genuine diversity. By singling out only those two ethnic groups, the initial stage of the law school's 1992 admissions process ignored altogether non-Mexican Hispanic Americans, Asian Americans, and Native Americans, to name but a few.

In this light, the limited racial effects of the law school's preferential admissions process, targeting exclusively blacks and Mexican Americans, more closely resembles a set aside or quota system for those two disadvantaged minorities than it does an academic admissions program narrowly tailored to achieve true diversity. I concede that the law school's 1992 admissions process would increase the percentages of black faces and brown faces in that year's entering class. But facial diversity is not true diversity, and a system thus conceived and implemented simply is not narrowly tailored to achieve diversity.

Accordingly, I would find that the law school's race-based 1992 admissions process was not narrowly tailored to achieve diversity and hold it constitutionally invalid on that basis. By so doing I would avoid the largely uncharted waters of a compelling interest analysis. Although I join my colleagues of the panel in their holding that the law school's 1992 admissions process fails to pass strict scrutiny, on the question of diversity I follow the solitary path of narrow tailoring rather than the primrose path of compelling interest to reach our common holding. . . .

## — III —

## CONCLUSION

. . . Thus I concur in the judgment of the panel opinion but, as to its conclusion on the issue of a strict scrutiny and its gloss on the order of remand, I disagree for the reasons I have stated and therefore concur specially.

### *Notes*

1. The number of votes would change over the course of the admissions season in order to achieve the appropriate number of offers.

2. As blacks and Mexican Americans were the only two minority categories granted preferential treatment in admissions, it is inaccurate to say that the law school conducted separate admissions programs for "minorities" and "non-minorities." While the law school applica-

tion form segregated racial and ethnic classification into seven categories—"Black/African American," "Mexican American," "Other Hispanic" (meaning non-Mexican descent), "White," and "Other (describe)"—only American blacks and Mexican Americans received the benefit of the separate admissions track.

Thus, for example, the law school decided that a black citizen of Nigeria would not get preferential treatment, but a resident alien from Mexico, who resided in Texas, would. Likewise, Asians, American Indians, Americans from El Salvador and Cuba, and many others did not receive a preference.

It is important to keep the composition of these categories in mind. For the sake of simplicity and readability, however, we sometimes will refer to two broad categories: "whites" (meaning Texas residents who were white and non-preferred minorities) and "minorities" (meaning Mexican Americans and black Americans).

3.  In March 1992, the resident Mexican American and black presumptive admit lines were in parity, but they had not started that way. The initial presumptive admit TI's were 196 for Mexican Americans and 192 for blacks. Thus, initially, blacks received preferential treatment over Mexican Americans by having a lower hurdle to cross to get into the discretionary zone. In March, Professor Johanson lowered the Mexican American TI in order to admit more of this group.

4.  Shortly before trial, apparently in response to the filing of this lawsuit, the law school modified its 1992 admissions practices to fit the district court's view of the proper constitutional system. *See id.* at 582 n. 87.

5.  The law school's admission program makes no distinction among black and Mexican American applicants in an effort to determine which of them, for example, may have been culturally or educationally disadvantaged.

---

**Hopwood v. Texas,** 78 R3d 932 (1996) 3–0
  U.S. Court of Appeals for the Fifth Circuit

| MAJORITY | CONCURRING | DISSENTING |
| --- | --- | --- |
| Smith | Weiner | |
| DeMoss | | |

# No. 95–1773, Texas, et al., Petitioners
# v. Cheryl J. Hopwood, et al.

## [116 S. Ct. 2581 (1996)]

## July 1, 1996. Petition for writ of certiorari to the United States Court of Appeals for the Fifth Circuit denied.

### Same case below, 78 F3d 932.

Opinion of JUSTICE GINSBURG, with whom JUSTICE SOUTER joins, respecting the denial of the petition for a writ of certiorari.

Whether it is constitutional for a public college or graduate school to use race or national origin as a factor in its admissions process is an issue of great national importance. The petition before us, however, does not challenge the lower courts' *judgments* that the particular admissions procedure used by the University of Texas Law School in 1992 was unconstitutional. Acknowledging that the 1992 admissions program "has long since been discontinued and will not be reinstated," Pet. for Cert. 28, the petitioners do not defend that program in this Court, see Reply to Brief in Opposition 1, 3; see also Brief for United States as *Amicus Curiae* 14, n. 13 ("We agree that the 1992 [admissions] policy was constitutionally flawed...."). Instead, petitioners challenge the *rationale* relied on by the Court of Appeals. "[T]his Court," however, "reviews judgments not opinions." *Chevron U.S. A. Inc.* v. *Natural Resources Defense Council, Inc.*, 467 US 837, 842, 81 L Ed 2d 694, 104 S Ct 2778 (1984) (footnote omitted). Accordingly, we must await a final judgment on a program genuinely in controversy before addressing the important question raised in this petition. See Reply to Brief in Opposition 2 ("[A]ll concede this record is inadequate to assess definitively" the constitutionality of the law school's current consideration of race in its admissions process).

From *The New York Times*, 3/23/96. Copyright © 1996 by The New York Times. Reprinted by permission.

# FOR 4 WHITES WHO SUED UNIVERSITY, RACE IS THE COMMON THREAD

## New York Times 2/23/96

### *Sam Howe Verhovek*

HOUSTON, March 22 — One is now the manager of a Relax the Back store in suburban Dallas. Another returned to her accounting job, a third went back to a work as a financial analyst with the state insurance department of Texas. And the fourth actually did go to law school, but not at the University of Texas.

What these four people have in common is that they all are white, and they all were rejected when they applied for admission to the University of Texas Law School in the early 1990's. And they all are the plaintiffs in a case that may be on its way to becoming a landmark in the nation's battle over affirmative action.

On Monday, a Federal appeals court, ruling largely in favor of the plaintiffs, struck down the law school's affirmative-action program for admissions and decreed that race should not be used as a factor in admissions. The ruling stunned universities across the nation with similar programs and led the University of Texas to suspend all admissions decisions for at least a week as it struggles to devise new guidelines.

The plaintiffs, the court suggested, could provide the university a broader definition of diversity. Judge Jerry E. Smith pointed in particular to the "unique background" of one plaintiff, Cheryl J. Hopwood, 32. Her father died when she was young, and she worked her way through high school and college; she has also been the mother of a severely handicapped child and a baby who died hours after birth.

"Individuals, with their own conceptions of life, further diversity of viewpoint," Judge Smith wrote. "Her circumstance would bring a different perspective to the law school."

Even as university officials warned that the decision could force them to cut the number of minority students by as much as one-half to two-thirds, the four plaintiffs hailed the ruling as a major victory for civil rights. All had argued in court that their qualifications were well above those of dozens of black and Hispanic applicants who were accepted.

"The purpose of the lawsuit is to make the University of Texas fulfill Dr. Martin Luther King's dream, which is to judge each person individually, not by the color of their skin but by the content of their character," David Rogers, the plaintiff who is now a store manager in Arlington, said in an interview.

Mr. Rogers, 32, said that after his rejection he believed that he had been a victim of discrimination. He said he was pleased that the court's ruling would allow the plaintiffs to reapply for admission under a system that gives no preference to minority applicants, and said he intended to compete for a spot at the Austin campus in fall 1997.

"This whole business of affirmative action flies in the face of the Civil War amendments, which say Congress shall make no laws regarding race," he said.

The university is still considering an appeal, and the Texas case is widely viewed as the one that may wind up in the Supreme Court, where the Justices could rule on whether race-based preference systems in admissions should be dismantled altogether.

How the four white applicants came to be plaintiffs in the case is a story that begins in 1992, after their applications were rejected and after a lawyer in Austin, Steven W. Smith, filed a request under the Texas Open Records Act as part of his own investigation into what he believed was reverse discrimination.

As part its admissions procedures, the law school ranked all applicants on something known as the Texas Index, largely a product of grades and test scores. Mr. Smith obtained the names of dozens of applicants with relatively high index scores who were not admitted. He then mailed letters to them.

The four plaintiffs did not know one another beforehand, and Mr. Rogers said they were not in close contact. Ms. Hopwood has moved to Columbia, Md., where she has continued work as an accountant.

The two other plaintiffs are Kenneth Elliott, who is in his early 30's and who returned to work at the insurance department, and Douglas Wade Carvell, who is in his mid-20's and who is now a law and business student at Southern Methodist University in Dallas.

Michael Rosman, general counsel for the Center for Individual Rights, a libertarian group in Washington that helped the plaintiffs with the appeal, said he believed that Ms. Hopwood, the wife of a military serviceman, still wanted to go to law school, but he did not know where. Messages left at the phone number for a Hopwood listed in Columbia have not been returned.

In an August 1995 article in Rolling Stone magazine, Ms. Hopwood was quoted as saying: "Affirmative action should be used to help disadvantaged people of whatever background. You can find injustice anywhere. The fact that I have one severely handicapped child and another one died is an injustice. But nobody's helping me." The handicapped child, Tara, has since died.

Mr. Rogers, who said he had a nearly 3.8 grade-point average as an undergraduate at the University of Houston, is confident he will be admitted in a colorblind system. "I'm not asking for set-asides for white people," he said. "I'm asking that the university not consider race at all."

# Establishing A Liberal, Constitutional, Democracy and Inventing the Power of Judicial Review

*T*he United States governmental system was designed as a liberal, constitutional, democracy. It is *liberal* in that it incorporates the notion that individuals have rights that proceed the establishment of government and that limit the legitimate exercises of government power. It is *constitutional* in that these boundaries are laid out in a written document which gives, defines, divides, and limits government's power. It is a *democracy* in that it is based on the notion that the people are sovereign and that government should be accountable to the people. More specifically, it is a *republican* democracy in that people rule through electorally accountable representatives.

This chapter begins with excerpts from John Locke, the famous 17th century social contract theorist who had a profound influence on the American founding fathers. Locke explains why humans form governments, what the proper purposes of government are, and what the people can do when government exceeds its rightful scope. Jefferson draws on these notions in the Declaration of Independence which sets out the American conception of natural rights, and lists King George's violations of the implicit social contract. Many have suggested that the U.S. Constitution, which opened this volume, serves as our Lockean social contract; but, unlike Locke, the framers devised mechanisms, short of revolution, for insuring that government abides by the social contract that gave birth to it. Among these devices are separation of powers, federalism, regular periodic elections, and judicial review. But, the framers were not utopian drafters of some sort of ideal social contract; rather, the framers were well aware of the necessity of compromise and the hard experience of real political life, particularly the unfortunate weaknesses of the Articles of Confederation. And, the battle over ratification of the Constitution, our supreme law, was equally political.

In defending the Constitution in a series of articles published in New York newspapers during the ratifying conventions, Alexander Hamilton described and explained what the role of the judiciary was to be in interpreting and enforcing the new Constitution, suggesting a power of judicial review. His articles are reprinted here as *Federalist Papers* 78, 79, 80, and 81.

The Supreme Court's first significant use of this power of judicial review to overturn a federal statute came in *Marbury* v. *Madison* (1803). John Garraty's article places the *Marbury* case in a political and historical context and it is followed by excerpts from Justice Marshall's opinion in *Marbury*, much of which was foreshadowed by Hamilton's argument in *Federalist* 78. While the Supreme Court's power to declare a statute passed by the national Congress unconstitutional has remained controversial, the Supreme Court has declared relatively few federal statutes void. The Court has been much more active in declaring state laws unconstitutional.[1] *McCulloch* v. *Maryland* (1819) provides an early example of this use of the Court's power; it is especially interesting because it involves a conflict between a federal statute and a state statute so that while the Court declares a Maryland state statute unconstitutional in *McCulloch* it also declares a federal statute constitutional under a fairly broad reading of Congress's Article I powers. Indeed, the primary activity of the U.S. Supreme Court during the last 200 years has been to declare legislative acts, both national and state, constitutional. But, it is the Court's power to declare laws unconstitutional that gives the Court's power to declare laws constitutional meaning.

## Notes

1. The first case in which the new U.S. Supreme Court declared a state law unconstitutional is *Fletcher* v. *Peck*, 6 Cranch (10 U.S.) 87 (1810). In that case, the Supreme Court held that the Georgia legislature's attempt to revoke land grants made by a previous, corrupt, legislature violated the Contracts Clause of the Constitution.

2. From 1789 up through 1996, the U.S. Supreme Court has only declared 135 federal statutes and 1233 state statutes unconstitutional. Lawrence Baum, *The Supreme Court*, 6th edition (Washington, D.C., CQ Press, 1998), Chapter 5.

# SECOND TREATISE OF CIVIL GOVERNMENT

*John Locke*

## OF THE STATE OF NATURE

To understand political power aright, and derive it from its original, we must consider what estate all men are naturally in, and that is, a state of perfect freedom to order their actions, and dispose of their possessions and persons as they think fit, within the bounds of the laws of Nature, without asking leave or depending upon the will of any other man.

A state also of equality, wherein all the power and jurisdiction is reciprocal, no one having more than another, there being nothing more evident than that creatures of the same species and rank, promiscuously born to all the same advantages of Nature, and the use of the same faculties, should also be equal one amongst another, without subordination or subjection, unless the lord and master of them all should, by any manifest declaration of his will, set one above another, and confer on him, by an evident and clear appointment, an undoubted right to dominion and sovereignty. . . .

But though this be a state of liberty, yet it is not a state of license; though man in that state have an uncontrollable liberty to dispose of his person or possessions, yet he had not liberty to destroy himself, or so much as any creature in his possession, but where some nobler use than its bare preservation calls for it. The state of Nature has a law of Nature to govern it, which obliges every one, and reason, which is that law, teaches all mankind who will but consult it, that being all equal and independent, no one ought to harm another in his life, health, liberty or possessions. . . . And, being furnished with like faculties, sharing all in one community of Nature, there cannot be supposed any such subordination among us that may authorize us to destroy one another, as if we were made for one another's uses, as the inferior ranks of creatures are for ours. Every one as he is bound to preserve himself, and not to quit his station wilfully, so by the like reason, when his own preservation comes not in competition, ought he as much as he can to preserve the rest of mankind, and not unless it be to do justice on an offender, take away or impair the life, or what tends to the preservation of the life, the liberty, health, limb, or goods of another.

And that all men may be restrained from invading others' rights, and from doing hurt to one another, and the law of Nature be observed, which willeth the peace and preservation of all mankind, the execution of the law of Nature is in that state put into every man's hands, whereby every one has a right to punish the transgressors of that law to such a degree as may hinder its violation. For the law of Nature would, as all, other laws that concern men in this world, be in vain if there were nobody that in the state of Nature had a power to execute that law, and thereby preserve the innocent and restrain offenders; and if any one in the state of Nature may punish another for any evil he has done, every one may do so. For in that state of perfect equality, where naturally there is no superiority or jurisdiction of one over another, what any may do in prosecution of that law, every one must needs have a right to do.

And thus, in the state of Nature, one man comes by a power over another, but yet no absolute or arbitrary power to use a criminal, when he has got him in his hands, according to the passionate heats or boundless extravagancy of his own will, but only to retribute to him so far as calm reason and conscience dictate, what is proportionate to his transgression, which is so much as may serve for reparation and restraint. . . .

Every offence that can be committed in the state of Nature may, in the state of Nature, be also punished equally, and as far forth, as it may, in a commonwealth. For—though it would be beside my present purpose to enter here into the particulars of the law of Nature, or its measures of punishment, yet it is certain there is such a law, and that too as intelligible and plain to a rational creature and a studier of that law as the positive laws of commonwealths, nay, possibly plainer; as much as reason is easier to be understood than the fancies and intricate contrivances of men, following contrary and hidden interests put into words. . . .

## OF THE ENDS OF POLITICAL SOCIETY AND GOVERNMENT

If man in the state of Nature be so free as has been said, if he be absolute lord of his own person and possessions, equal to the greatest and subject to nobody, why will he part with his freedom, this empire, and subject himself to the dominion and control of any other power? To which it is obvious to answer, that though in the state of Nature he hath such a right, yet the enjoyment of it is very uncertain and constantly exposed to the invasion of others; for all being kings as much as he, every man his equal, and the greater part no strict observers of equity and justice, the enjoyment of the property he has in this state is very unsafe, very insecure. This makes him willing to quit this condition which, however free, is full of fears and continual dangers; and it is not without reason that he seeks out and is willing to join in society with others who are already united, or have a mind to unite for the mutual preservation of their lives, liberties, and estates, which I call by the general name—property.

The great and chief end, therefore, of men uniting into commonwealths, and putting themselves under government, is the preservation of their property; to which in the state of Nature there are many things wanting.

Firstly, there wants an established, settled, known law, received and allowed by common consent to be the standard of right and wrong, and the common measure to decide all controversies between them. For though the law of Nature be plain and intelligible to all rational creatures, yet men, being biased by their interest, as well as ignorant for want of study of it, are not apt to allow of it as a law binding to them in the application of it to their particular cases.

Secondly, in the state of Nature there wants a known and indifferent judge, with authority to determine all differences according to the established law. For every one in that state being both judge and executioner of the law of Nature, men being partial to themselves, passion and revenge is very apt to carry them too far, and with too much heat in their own cases, as well as negligence and unconcernedness, make them too remiss in other men's.

Thirdly, in the state of Nature there often wants power to back and support the sentence when right, and to give it due execution. They who by any injustice offended will seldom fail where they are able by force to make good their injustice. Such resistance many times makes the punishment dangerous, and frequently destructive to those who attempt it.

Thus mankind, notwithstanding all the privileges of the state of Nature, being but in an ill condition while they remain in it are quickly driven into society. Hence it comes to pass, that we seldom find any number of men live any time together in this state. The inconveniences that they are therein exposed to by the irregular and uncertain exercise of the power every man has of punishing the transgressions of others, make them take sanctuary under the established laws of government, and therein seek the preservation of their property. It is this makes them so willingly give up every one his single power of punishing to be exercised by such alone as shall be appointed to it amongst them, and by such rules as the community, or those authorized by them to that purpose, shall agree on. And in this we have the original right and rise of both the legislative and executive power as well as of the governments and societies themselves.

For in the state of Nature to omit the liberty he has of innocent delights, a man has two powers. The first is to do whatsoever he thinks fit for the preservation of himself and others within the permission of the law of Nature; by which law, common to them all, he and all the rest of mankind are one community, make up one society distinct from all other creatures, and were it not for the corruption and viciousness of degenerate men, there would be no need of any other, no necessity that men should separate from this great and natural community, and associate into lesser combinations. The other power a man has in the state of Nature is the power to punish the crimes committed against that law. Both these he gives up when he joins in a private, if I may so call it, or particular political society, and incorporates into any commonwealth separate from the rest of mankind.

The first power—viz., of doing whatsoever he thought fit for the preservation of himself and the rest of mankind, he gives up to be regulated by laws made by the society, so far forth as the preservation of himself and the rest of that society shall require; which laws of the society in many things confine the liberty he had by the law of Nature.

Secondly, the power of punishing he wholly gives up, and engages his natural force, which he might before employ in the execution of the law of Nature, by his own single authority, as he thought fit, to assist the executive power of the society as the law thereof shall require. For being now in a new state, wherein he is to enjoy many conveniences from the labor, assistance, and society of others in the same community, as well as protection from its whole strength, he is to part also with as much of his natural liberty, in providing for himself, as the good, prosperity, and safety of the society shall require, which is not only necessary but just, since the other members of the society do the like.

But though men when they enter into society give up the equality, liberty, and executive power they had in the state of Nature into the hands of the society, to be so far disposed of by the legislative as the good of the society shall require, yet it being only with an intention in every one the better to preserve himself, his liberty and property (for no rational creature can be supposed to change his condition with an intention to be worse), the power of the society or legislative constituted by them can never be supposed to extend farther than the common against those three defects above mentioned that made the state of Nature so unsafe and uneasy. And so, whoever has the legislative or supreme power of any commonwealth, is bound to govern by established standing laws, promulgated and known to the people, and not by extemporary decrees, by indifferent and upright judges, who are to decide controversies by those laws; and to employ the force of the community at home only in the execution of such laws, or abroad to prevent or redress foreign injuries and secure the community from inroads and invasion. And all this to be directed to no other end but the peace, safety, and public good of the people.

## OF THE EXTENT OF THE LEGISLATIVE POWER

The great end of men's entering into society being the enjoyment of their properties in peace and safety, and the great instrument and means of that being the laws established in that society, the first and fundamental positive law of all commonwealths is the establishing of the legislative power, as the first and fundamental natural law, which is to govern even the legislative itself, is the preservation of the society and (as far as will consist with the public good) of every person in it. This legislative is not only the supreme power of the commonwealth, but sacred and unalterable in the hands where the community have once placed it. Nor can any edict of anybody else, in what form soever conceived, or by what power soever backed, have the force and obligation of a law which has not its sanction from that legislative which the public has chosen and appointed; for without this the law could not have that which is absolutely necessary to its being a law, the consent of the society, over whom nobody can have a power to make laws but by their own consent and by authority received from them. . . .

These are the bounds which the trust that is put in them by the society and the law of God and Nature have set to the legislative power of every commonwealth, in all forms of government. First: They are to govern by promulgated established laws, not to be varied in particular cases, but to have one rule for rich and poor, for the favorite at Court and the countryman at plough. Secondly: These laws also ought to be designed for no other end ultimately but the good of the people. Thirdly: They must not raise taxes on the property of the people without the consent of the people given by themselves or their deputies. And this properly concerns only such governments where the legislative is always in being, or at least where the people have not reserved any part of the legislative to deputies, to be from time to time chosen by themselves. Fourthly: Legislative neither must nor can transfer the power of making laws to anybody else, or place it anywhere but where the people have. . . .

## OF THE DISSOLUTION OF GOVERNMENT

The constitution of the legislative [authority] is the first and fundamental act of society, whereby provision is made for the continuation of their union under the direction of persons and bonds of laws, made by persons authorized thereunto, by the consent and appointment of the people, without which no one man, or number of men, amongst them can have authority of making laws that shall be binding to the rest. When any one, or more, shall take upon them to make laws whom the people have not appointed so to do, they make laws without authority, which the people are not therefore bound to obey; by which means they come again to be out of subjection, and may constitute to themselves a new legislative, as they think best, being in full liberty to resist the force of those who, without authority, would impose anything upon them. . . .

Whosoever uses force without right—as every one does in society who does it without law—puts himself into a state of war with those against whom he so uses it, and in that state all former ties are cancelled, all other rights cease, and every one has a right to defend himself, and to resist the aggressor. . . .

Here it is like the common question will be made: Who shall be judge whether the prince or legislative act contrary to their trust? This, perhaps, ill-affected and factious men may spread amongst the people, when the prince only makes use of his due prerogative. To this I reply, The people shall be judge; for who shall be judge whether his trustee or deputy acts well and according to the trust reposed in him, but he who deputes him and must, by having deputed him, have still a power to discard him when he fails in his trust? If this be reasonable in particular cases of private men, why should it be otherwise in that of the greatest moment, where the welfare of millions is concerned and also where the evil, if not prevented, is greater, and the redress very difficult, dear, and dangerous? . . .

To conclude. The power that every individual gave the society when he entered into it can never revert to the individuals again, as long as the society lasts, but will always remain in the community; because without this there can be no community—no commonwealth, which is contrary to the original agreement; so also when the society hath placed the legislative in any assembly of men, to continue in them and their successors, with direction and authority for providing such successors, the legislative can never revert to the people whilst that government lasts; because, having provided a legislative with power to continue for ever, they have given up their political power to the legislative, and cannot resume it. But if they have set limits to the duration of their legislative, and made this supreme power in any person or assembly only temporary; or else when, by the miscarriages of those in authority, it is forfeited; upon the forfeiture of their rulers, or at the determination of the time set, it reverts to the society, and the people have a right to act as supreme, and continue the legislative in themselves or place it in a new form, or new hands, as they think good.

# THE DECLARATION OF INDEPENDENCE

## In CONGRESS, July 4, 1776.
## A DECLARATION

### The REPRESENTATIVES of the UNITED STATES OF AMERICA,
### In GENERAL CONGRESS assembled.

When in the Course of human Events, it becomes necessary for one People to dissolve the Political Bands which have connected them with another, and to assume among the Powers of the Earth, the separate and equal Station to which the Laws of Nature and of Nature's God entitle them, a decent Respect to the Opinions of Mankind requires that they should declare the causes which impel them to the Separation.

We hold these Truths to be self-evident, that all Men are created equal, that they are endowed by their Creator with certain unalienable Rights, that among these are Life, Liberty, and the Pursuit of Happiness—That to secure these Rights, Governments are instituted among Men, deriving their just Powers from the Consent of the Governed, that whenever any Form of Government becomes destructive of these Ends, it is the Right of the People to alter or to abolish it, and to institute new Government, laying its Foundation on such Principles, and organizing its Powers in such Form, as to them shall seem most likely to effect their Safety and Happiness. Prudence, indeed, will dictate that Governments long established should not be changed for light and transient Causes; and accordingly all Experience hath shewn, that Mankind are more disposed to suffer, while Evils are sufferable, than to right themselves by abolishing the Forms to which they are accustomed. But when a long Train of Abuses and Usurpations, pursuing invariably the same Object, evinces a Design to reduce them under absolute Despotism, it is their Right, it is their Duty, to throw off such Government, and to provide new Guards for their future Security. Such has been the patient Sufferance of these Colonies; and such is now the Necessity which constrains them to alter their former Systems of Government. The History of the present King of Great-Britain is a History of repeated Injuries and Usurpations, all having in direct Object the Establishment of an absolute Tyranny over these States. To prove this, let Facts be submitted to a candid World.

He has refused his Assent to Laws, the most wholesome and necessary for the public Good.

He has forbidden his Governors to pass Laws of immediate and pressing Importance, unless suspended in their Operation till his Assent should be obtained; and when so suspended, he has utterly neglected to attend to them.

He has refused to pass other Laws for the Accommodation of large Districts of People, unless those People would relinquish the Right of Representation in the Legislature, a Right inestimable to them, and formidable to Tyrants only.

He has called together Legislative Bodies at Places unusual, uncomfortable, and distant from the Depository of their public Records, for the sole Purpose of fatiguing them into Compliance with his Measures.

He has dissolved Representative Houses repeatedly, for opposing with manly Firmness his Invasions on the Rights of the People.

He has refused for a long Time, after such Dissolutions, to cause others to be elected; whereby the Legislative Powers, incapable of Annihilation, have returned to the People at large for their exercise; the State remaining in the mean time exposed to all the Dangers of Invasion from without, and Convulsions within.

He has endeavoured to prevent the Population of these States; for that Purpose obstructing the Laws for Naturalization of Foreigners; refusing to pass others to encourage their Migrations hither, and raising the Conditions of new Appropriations of Lands.

He has obstructed the Administration of Justice, by refusing his Assent to Laws for establishing Judiciary Powers.

He has made Judges dependent on his Will alone, for the Tenure of their Offices, and the Amount and Payment of their Salaries.

He has erected a Multitude of new Offices, and sent hither Swarms of Officers to harrass our People, and eat out their Substance.

He has kept among us, in Times of Peace, Standing Armies, without the consent of our Legislatures.

He has affected to render the Military independent of and superior to the Civil Power.

He has combined with others to subject us to a Jurisdiction foreign to our Constitution, and unacknowledged by our Laws; giving his Assent to their Acts of pretended Legislation:

For quartering large Bodies of Armed Troops among us:

For protecting them, by a mock Trial, from Punishment for any Murders which they should commit on the Inhabitants of these States:

For cutting off our Trade with all Parts of the World:

For imposing Taxes on us without our Consent:

For depriving us, in many Cases, of the Benefits of Trial by Jury:

For transporting us beyond Seas to be tried for pretended Offences:

For abolishing the free System of English Laws in a neighbouring Province, establishing therein an arbitrary Government, and enlarging its Boundaries, so as to render it at once an Example and fit Instrument for introducing the same absolute Rule into these Colonies:

For taking away our Charters, abolishing our most valuable Laws, and altering fundamentally the Forms of our Governments:

For suspending our own Legislatures, and declaring themselves invested with Power to legislate for us in all Cases whatsoever.

He has abdicated Government here, by declaring us out of his Protection and waging War against us.

He has plundered our Seas, ravaged our Coasts, burnt our Towns, and destroyed the Lives of our People.

He is, at this Time, transporting large Armies of foreign Mercenaries to compleat the Works of Death, Desolation, and Tyranny, already begun with circumstances of Cruelty and Perfidy, scarcely paralleled in the most barbarous Ages, and totally unworthy the Head of a civilized Nation.

He has constrained our fellow Citizens taken Captive on the high Seas to bear Arms against their Country, to become the Executioners of their Friends and Brethren, or to fall themselves by their Hands.

He has excited domestic Insurrections amongst us, and has endeavoured to bring on the Inhabitants of our Frontiers, the merciless Indian Savages, whose known Rule of Warfare, is an undistinguished Destruction, of all Ages, Sexes and Conditions.

In every stage of these Oppressions we have Petitioned for Redress in the most humble Terms: Our repeated Petitions have been answered only by repeated Injury. A Prince, whose Character is thus marked by every act which may define a Tyrant, is unfit to be the Ruler of a free People.

Nor have we been wanting in Attentions to our British Brethren. We have warned them from Time to Time of Attempts by their Legislature to extend an unwarrantable Jurisdiction over us. We have reminded them of the Circumstances of our Emigration and Settlement here. We have appealed to their native Justice and Magnanimity, and we have conjured them by the Ties of our common Kindred to disavow these Usurpations, which, would inevitably interrupt our Connections and Correspondence. They too have been deaf to the Voice of Justice and of Consanguinity. We must, therefore, acquiesce in the Necessity, which denounces our Separation, and hold them, as we hold the rest of Mankind, Enemies in War, in Peace, Friends.

We, therefore, the Representatives of the UNITED STATES OF AMERICA, in General Congress, Assembled, appealing to the Supreme Judge of the World for the Rectitude of our Intentions, do, in the Name, and by Authority of the good People of these Colonies, solemnly Publish and Declare, That these United Colonies are, and of Right out to be, Free and Independent States; that they are absolved from all Allegiance to the British Crown, and that all political Connection between them and the State of Great-Britain, is and ought to be totally dissolved; and that as Free and Independent States, they have full Power to levy War, conclude Peace, contract Alliances, establish Commerce, and to do all other Acts and Things which Independent States may of right do. And for the support of this Declaration, with a firm Reliance on the Protection of divine Providence, we mutually pledge to each other our Lives, our Fortunes, and our sacred Honor.

*Signed by Order and in Behalf of the Congress,*
*JOHN HANCOCK, President.*

Attest.
CHARLES THOMSON, Secretary.

# SIGNERS OF THE DECLARATION OF INDEPENDENCE

### According to the Authenticated List Printed by Order of Congress of January 18, 1777

## *John Hancock.*

| | | | |
|---|---|---|---|
| **New-Hampshire.** | Josiah Bartlett, Wm. Whipple, Matthew Thornton. | **Delaware.** | Caesar Rodney, Geo. Read, (Tho M:Kean.) |
| **Massachusetts Bay.** | Saml. Adams, John Adams, Robt. Treat Paine, Elbridge Gerry. | **Maryland.** | Samuel Chase, Wm. Paca, Thos. Stone, Charles Carroll, of Carrollton. |
| **Rhode-Island and Providence, &c.** | Step. Hopkins, William Ellery, | **Virginia.** | George Wythe Richard Henry Lee, Ths. Jefferson, Benja. Harrison, Thos. Nelson, jr. Francis Lightfoot Lee, Carter Braxton. |
| **Connecticut.** | Roger Sherman, Saml. Huntington, Wm. Williams, Oliver Wolcott. | | |
| **New-York.** | Wm. Floyd Phil. Livingston, Frans. Lewis, Lewis Morris. | **North-Carolina.** | Wm. Hooper, Joseph Hewes, John Penn. |
| **New-Jersey.** | Richd. Stockton, Jno. Witherspoon, Fras. Hopkinson, John Hart, Abra. Clark. | **South-Carolina.** | Edward Rutledge, Thos. Heyward. junr. Thomas Lynch, junr. Arthur Middleton. |
| **Pennsylvania.** | Robt. Morris, Benjamin Rush, Benja. Franklin, John Morton, Geo. Clymer, Jas. Smith, Geo. Taylor, James Wilson, Geo. Ross. | **Georgia.** | Button Gwinnett, Lyman Hall, Geo. Walton. |

# THE ARTICLES OF CONFEDERATION
## November 15, 1777

*Articles of Confederation and Perpetual Union between the states of New-Hampshire, Massachusetts-bay, RhodeIsland and Providence Plantations, Connecticut, New-York, New-Jersey, Pennsylvania, Delaware, Maryland, Virginia, North Carolina, South-Carolina and Georgia.*

**ARTICLE I.**   The Stile of this confederacy shall be "**The United States of America.**"

**ARTICLE II.**   Each state retains its sovereignty, freedom, and independence, and every Power, Jurisdiction and right, which is not by this confederation expressly delegated to the United States, in Congress assembled.

**ARTICLE III.**   The said states hereby severally enter into a firm league of friendship with each other, for their common defence, the security of their Liberties, and their mutual and general welfare, binding themselves to assist each other, against all force offered to, or attacks made upon them, or any of them, on account of religion, sovereignty, trade, or any other pretence whatever.

**ARTICLE IV.**   The better to secure and perpetuate mutual friendship and intercourse among the people of the different states in this union, the free inhabitants of each of these states, paupers, vagabonds and fugitives from justice excepted, shall be entitled to all privileges and immunities of free citizens in the several states; and the people of each state shall have free ingress and regress to and from any other state, and shall enjoy therein all the privileges of trade and commerce, subject to the same duties, impositions and restrictions as the inhabitants thereof respectively, provided that such restriction shall not extend so far as to prevent the removal of property into any state, to any other state, of which the Owner is an inhabitant; provided also that no imposition, duties or restriction shall be laid by any state, on the property of the united states, or either of them.

If any person guilty of, or charged with treason, felony, or other high misdemeanor in any state, shall flee from Justice, and be found in any of the united states, he shall, upon demand of the Governor or executive power, of the state from which he fled, be delivered up and removed to the state having jurisdiction of his offence.

Full faith and credit shall be given in each of these states to the records, acts and judicial proceedings of the courts and magistrates of every other state.

**ARTICLE V.** For the more convenient management of the general interests of the united states, delegates shall be annually appointed in such manner as the legislature of each state shall direct, to meet in Congress on the first Monday in November, in every year, with a power reserved to each state, to recall its delegates, or any of them, at any time within the year, and to send others in their stead, for the remainder of the Year.

No state shall be represented in Congress by less than two, nor by more than seven Members; and no person shall be capable of being a delegate for more than three years in any term of six years; nor shall any person, being a delegate, be capable of holding any office under the united states, for which he, or another for his benefit receives any salary, fees, or emolument of any kind.

Each state shall maintain its own delegates in a meeting of the states, and while they act as members of the committee of the states.

In determining questions in the united states in Congress assembled, each state shall have one vote.

Freedom of speech and debate in Congress shall not be impeached or questioned in any Court, or place out of Congress, and the members of congress shall be protected in their persons from arrests and imprisonments, during the time of their going to and from, and attendance on congress, except for treason, felony, or breach of the peace.

**ARTICLE VI.** No state, without the Consent of the united states in congress assembled, shall send any embassy to, or receive any embassy from, or enter into any conference, agreement, alliance or treaty with any King prince or state; nor shall any person holding any office of profit or trust under the united states, or any of them, accept any present, emolument, office or title of any kind whatsoever from any king, prince or foreign state; nor shall the united states in congress assembled, or any of them, grant any title of nobility.

No two or more states shall enter into any treaty, confederation or alliance whatever between them, without the consent of the united states in congress assembled, specifying accurately the purposes for which the same is to be entered into, and how long it shall continue.

No state shall lay any imposts or duties, which may interfere with any stipulations in treaties, entered into by the united states in congress assembled, with any king, prince or state, in pursuance of any treaties already proposed by congress, to the courts of France and Spain.

No vessels of war shall be kept up in time of peace by any state, except such number only, as shall be deemed necessary by the united states in congress assembled, for the defence of such state, or its trade; nor shall any body of forces be kept up by any state, in time of peace, except such number only, as in the judgment of the united states, in congress assembled, shall be deemed requisite to garrison the forts necessary for the defense of such state; but every state shall always keep up a well regulated and disciplined militia, sufficiently armed and accoutred, and shall provide and constantly have ready for use, in public stores, a due number of field pieces and tents, and a proper quantity of arms, ammunition and camp equipage.

No state shall engage in any war without the consent of the united states in congress assembled, unless each state be actually invaded by enemies, or shall have received certain advice of a resolution being formed by some nation of Indians to invade such state, and the danger is so imminent as not to admit of a delay till the united states in congress assembled can be consulted; nor shall any state grant commissions to any ships or vessels of war, or letters of marque or reprisal, except it be after a declaration of war by the united states in congress assembled, and then only against the kingdom or state and the subjects thereof, against which war has been declared, and under such regulations as shall be established by the united states in congress assembled, unless such state be infested by pirates, in which case vessels of war may be fitted out for that occasion, and kept so long as the danger shall continue, or until the united states in congress assembled, shall determine otherwise.

**ARTICLE VII.** When landforces are raised by any state for the common defense, all officers of or under the rank of colonel, shall be appointed by the legislature of each state respectively, by whom such forces shall be raised, or in such manner as such state shall direct, and all vacancies shall be filled up by the State which first made the appointment.

**ARTICLE VIII.** All charges of war, and all other expences that shall be incurred for the common defence or general welfare, and allowed by the united states in congress assembled, shall be defrayed out of a common treasury, which shall be supplied by the several states in proportion to the value of all land within each state, granted to or surveyed for any person, as such land and the buildings and improvements thereon shall be estimated according to such mode as the united states in congress assembled, shall from time to time direct and appoint.

The taxes for paying that proportion shall be laid and levied by the authority and direction of the legislatures of the several states within the time agreed upon by the united states in congress assembled.

**ARTICLE IX.** The united states in congress assembled, shall have the sole and exclusive right and power of determining on peace and war, except in the cases mentioned in the sixth article—of sending and receiving ambassadors—entering into treaties and alliances, provided that no treaty of commerce shall be made whereby the legislative power of the respective states shall be restrained from imposing such imposts and duties on foreigners as their own people are subjected to, or from prohibiting the exportation or importation of any species of goods or commodities, whatsoever—of establishing rules for deciding in all cases, what captures on land or water shall be legal, and in what manner prizes taken by land or sea forces in the service of the united states shall be divided or appropriated—of granting letters of marque and reprisal in times of peace—appointing courts for the trial of piracies and felonies committed on the high seas and establishing courts for receiving and determining finally appeals in all cases of captures, provided that no members of congress shall be appointed a judge in any of the said courts.

The united states in congress assembled shall also be the last resort on appeal in all disputes and differences now subsisting or that hereafter may arise between two or more states concerning boundary, jurisdiction or any other cause whatever; which authority shall always be exercised in the manner following. Whenever the legislative or executive authority or lawful agent of any state in controversy with another shall present a petition to congress stating the matter in question and praying for a hearing, notice thereof shall be given by order of congress to the legislative or executive authority of the other state in controversy, and a day assigned for the appearance of the parties by their lawful agents, who shall then be directed to appoint by joint consent, commissioners or judges to constitute a court for hearing and determining the matter in question: but if they cannot agree, congress shall name three persons out of each of the united states, and from the list of such persons each party shall alternately strike out one, the petitioners beginning, until the number shall be reduced to thirteen; and from that number not less than seven, nor more than nine names as congress shall direct, shall in the presence of congress be drawn out by lot, and the persons whose names shall be so drawn or any five of them, shall be commissioners or judges, to hear and finally determine the controversy, so always as a major part of the judges who shall hear the cause shall agree in the determination: and if either party shall neglect to attend at the day appointed, without showing reasons, which congress shall judge sufficient, or being present refuse to strike, the congress shall proceed to nominate three persons out of each state, and the secretary of congress shall strike in behalf of such party absent or refusing; and the judgment and sentence of the court to be appointed, in the manner before prescribed, shall be final and conclusive; and if any of the parties shall refuse to submit to the authority of such court, or to appear or defend their claim or cause, the court shall nevertheless proceed to pronounce sentence, or judgment, which shall in like manner be final and decisive, the judgment or sentence and other proceedings being in either case transmitted to congress, and lodged among the acts of congress for the security of the parties concerned: provided that every commissioner, before he sits in judgment, shall take an oath to be administered by one of the judges of the supreme or superior court of the state, where the case will be tried, "well and truly to hear and determine the matter in question, according to the best of his judgment, without favour, affection or hope of reward": provided also, that no state shall be deprived of territory for the benefit of the united states.

All controversies concerning the private right of soil claimed under different grants of two or more states, whose jurisdictions as they may respect such lands, and the states which passed such settlement of jurisdiction, shall on the petition of either party to the congress of the united states, be finally determined as near as may be in the same manner as is before prescribed for deciding disputes respecting territorial jurisdiction between different states.

The united states in congress assembled shall also have the sole and exclusive right and power of regulating the alloy and value of coin struck by their own authority, or by that of the respective states—fixing the standard of weights and measures throughout the united states—regulating the trade and managing all affairs with the Indians, not members of any of the states, provided that the legislative right of any state within its own limits be not infringed or violated—establishing or regulating post-offices from one state to another, throughout all the united states, and exacting such postage on the papers passing through the same as may be requisite to defray the expenses of the said office—appointing all the officers of the land forces, in the service of the united states, excepting regimental officers—appointing all the officers of the naval forces, and commissioning all officers whatever in the service of the united states—making rules for the government and regulation of the said land and naval forces, and directing their operations.

The united states in congress assembled shall have authority to appoint a committee, to sit in the recess of congress, to be denominated "A Committee of the States," and to consist of one delegate from each state; and to appoint such other committees and civil officers as may be necessary for managing the general affairs of the united states under their direction—to appoint one of their number to preside, provided that no person be allowed to serve in the office of president more than one year in any term of three years; to ascertain the necessary sums of money to be raised for the service of the united states, and to appropriate and apply the same for defraying the public expences—to borrow money, or emit bills on the credit of the united states, transmitting every half year to the respective states an account of the sums of money so borrowed or emitted,—to build and equip a navy—to agree upon the number of land forces, and to make requisitions from each state for its quota, in proportion to the number of white inhabitants in such state; which requisition shall be binding, and thereupon the legislature of each state shall appoint the regimental officers, raise the men and cloath, arm and equip them in a soldier like manner, at the expence of the united states; and the officers and men so cloathed, armed and equipped shall march to the place appointed, and within the time agreed on by the united states in congress assembled: But if the united states in congress assembled shall, on consideration of circumstances judge proper that any state should not raise men, or should raise a smaller number than its quota, and that any other state should raise a greater number of men than the quota thereof, such extra men shall be raised, officered, cloathed, armed and equipped in the same manner as the quota of such state, unless the legislature of such state shall judge that such extra number cannot be safely spared out of the same, in which case they shall raise officer, cloath, arm and equip as many of such extra number as they judge can be safely spared. And the officers and men so cloathed, armed and equipped, shall march to the place appointed, and within the time agreed on by the united states in congress assembled.

The united states in congress assembled shall never engage in a war, nor grant letters of marque and reprisal in time of peace, nor enter into any treaties or alliances, nor coin money, nor regulate the value thereof, nor ascertain the sums and expences necessary for the defense and welfare of the united states, or any of them, nor emit bills, nor borrow money on the credit of the united states, nor appropriate money, nor agree upon the number of vessels of war, to be built or purchased, or the number of land or sea forces to be raised, nor appoint a commander in chief of the army or navy, unless nine states assent to the same: nor shall a question on any other point, except for adjourning from day to day be determined, unless by a majority of the united states in congress assembled.

The congress of the united states shall have power to adjourn at any time within the year, and to any place within the united states, so that no period of adjustment be for a longer duration than the space of six Months, and shall publish the Journal of their proceedings monthly, except such parts thereof relating to treaties, alliances or military operations, as in their judgment require secrecy; and the yeas and nays of the delegates of each state on any question shall be entered on the journal, when it is desired by any delegate; and the delegates of a state, or any of them, at his or their request shall be furnished with a transcript of the said journal, except such parts as are above excepted, to lay before the legislatures of the several states.

**ARTICLE XI.** Canada acceding to this confederation, and joining in the measures of the united states, shall be admitted into, and entitled to all the advantages of this union: but no other colony shall be admitted into the same, unless such admission be agreed to by nine states.

**ARTICLE XII.** All bills of credit emitted, monies borrowed and debts contracted by, or under the authority of congress, before the assembling of the united states, in pursuance of the present confederation, shall be deemed and considered as a charge against the united states, for payment and satisfaction whereof the said united states, and the public faith are hereby solemnly pledged.

**ARTICLE XIII.** Every state shall abide by the determinations of the united states in congress assembled, on all questions which by this confederation are submitted to them. And the Articles of this confederation shall be inviolably observed by every state, and the union shall be perpetual; nor shall any alteration at any time hereafter be made in any of them; unless such alteration be agreed to in a congress of the united states, and be afterwards confirmed by the legislature of every state.

And Whereas it hath pleased the Great Governor of the World to incline the hearts of the legislatures we respectively represent in congress, to approve of, and to authorize us to ratify the said articles of confederation and perpetual union. Know Ye that we the undersigned delegates, by virtue of the power and authority to us given for that purpose, do by these presents, in the name and in behalf of our respective constituents, fully and entirely ratify and confirm each and every of the said articles of confederation and perpetual union, and all and singular the matters and things therein contained: And we do further solemnly plight and engage the faith of our respective constituents, that they shall abide by the determinations of the united states in congress assembled, on all questions, which by the said confederation are submitted to them. And that the articles thereof shall be inviolably observed by the states we respectively represent, and that the union shall be perpetual. In Witness wherof we have hereunto set our hands in Congress. Done at Philadelphia in the state of Pennsylvania the ninth day of July, in the Year of our Lord one Thousand seven Hundred and Seventy-eight, and in the third year of the independence of America.

| | |
|---|---|
| *Josiah Bartlett,* | On the part & behalf of the State of |
| *John Wentworth, jun,* | New Hampshire |
| *August 8th, 1778,* | |
| | |
| *John Hancock,* | |
| *Samuel Adams,* | |
| *Elbridge Gerry,* | On the part and behalf of the State of |
| *Francis Dana,* | Massachusetts Bay |
| *James Lovell,* | |
| *Samuel Holten,* | |
| | |
| *William Ellery,* | On the part and behalf of the State of |
| *Henry Marchant,* | Rhode-Island and Providence Plantations |
| *John Collins,* | |

Roger Sherman,
Samuel Huntington,
Oliver Wolcott,
Titus Hosmer,
Andrew Adams,

On the part and behalf of the State of
Connecticut

Ja^s Duane,
Fra: Lewis,
W^m Duer,
Gouv^r Morris,

On the part and behalf of the State of
New York

Jn^o Witherspoon,
Nath^l Scudder,

On the Part and in Behalf of the State of
New Jersey, November 26th, 1778.

Robert Morris,
Daniel Roberdeau,
Jon. Bayard Smith,
William Clingar,
Joseph Reed,
    22d July, 1778

On the part and behalf of the State of
Pennsylvania

Tho^s McKean
    Feb^r 22d, 1779,
John Dickinson,
    May 5th, 1779,
Nicholas Van Dyke,

On the part & behalf of the State of
Delaware

John Hanson,
    March 1, 1781,
Daniel Carroll, do

On the part and behalf of the State of
Maryland

Richard Henry Lee,
John Banister,
Thomas Adams,
Jn^o. Harvie,
Francis Lightfoot Lee,

On the Part and Behalf of the State of
Virginia

John Penn,
    July 21st 1778,
Corn^s Harnett,
Jn^o. Willams,

On the part and behalf of the State of
North Carolina

*Henry Laurens,*
*William Henry Drayton,*
*Jn°. Mathews,*
*Rich^d Hutson,*
*Tho^s Heyward, jun^r.*

On the part and on behalf of the State of
South Carolina

*Jn° Walton,*
   *24th July, 1778,*
*Edw^d Telfair,*
*Edw^d Langworthy,*

On the part and behalf of the State of
Georgia

## *Note*

The text reproduced here was adopted by the Continental Congress on July 9, 1778, after nine of the thirteen state legislatures had ratified the document sent to them the previous November. Except for the last paragraph and the signatures, the text is from Merrill Jensen, *The Articles of Confederation* (Madison: University of Wisconsin Press, 1966), 263–70. The final paragraph and signatures of an otherwise identical text is included because it shows who had ratified by July 9, 1778, and the dates of later state ratifications. The text is taken from Thorpe, *Federal and State Constitutions,* 9–17.

# CREATING THE CONSTITUTION: UTOPIAN OR PRAGMATIC? AND, THE CONSTITUTION CREATED: AN OUTLINE

*Susan E. Lawrence*

A. Creating the Constitution: Utopian or Pragmatic?
   1. Historical Background
   2. Political Problems
      a. no prestige
      b. land titles
      c. fiscal problems
      d. economic and trade problems
      e. foreign affairs
   3. The Convention
   4. Ratification—Opponents & Proponents

B. The Constitution Created
   1. Structure
   2. Addressing the Problems
   3. Limits on Government Power
   4. Creating and Justifying the Judiciary

Constitutions perform the role of a social contract. They establish government and limit its power. Generally they are ratified by the people or their representatives.

In looking at the origins of our Constitution, we can see that though the founders were products of the Lockean tradition, the actual forging of the constitution was the result of political problems and political compromises. As the framers met in Philadelphia in the summer of 1787, they set out not only to construct a new government for the nation, but to solve or respond to very real political problems facing the United States.

## HISTORICAL BACKGROUND

After the Declaration of Independence, the 13 new states were governed by two continental Congresses. The first met on Sept. 5, 1774 and the second adjourned Feb. 28, 1781.

They were succeeded by the Articles of Confederation Congress which ran from 1781 to 1789. Each state was represented in the Congress and any ONE state could block any action. The national government consisted only of the Congress—no executive or courts. It exercised external sovereignty, but had very little internal power—no power to tax, to regulate commerce, or to levy tariffs.

## POLITICAL PROBLEMS:

Problems Under the Articles of Confederation that Precipitated the Constitutional Convention of 1787

1.  **No Prestige:** Prestige of the Confederation Congress declined to such a degree that some states no longer sent delegates. Quorums could not be obtained for lengthy periods of time. The quality of the delegates suffered. Given the limited powers of the Articles of Confederation Congress, there was not much to do when the country was not engaged in war. Consequently, the national government was ineffectual. Also, they found that attempting to run the government by committee, without an executive or a judiciary, did not work.

2.  **Land Titles/Disputes**: Conflicting claims to land titles between states and conflicting border claims. No body/institution had the power to resolve these conflicts. Several times these disputes escalated into "shooting wars." The states were particularly divided over conflicting claims to the trans-Appalachian West. Congress eventually took control over all of it and passed the Northwest Ordinance of 1787, which provided for a three stage transition from territorial government to statehood. Established the precedent of treating new territories, not as conquered provinces, but as future states.
    Unclear procedures for admitting new states, especially those carved out of the original 13—Kentucky, Vermont, and Tennessee. The Articles of Confederation specifically listed the states, rather than the people, as the contracting parties to the Articles of Confederation Constitution. These states were ultimately admitted under the new Constitution (Art. 4, Sec. 3).

3.  **Fiscal Problems:** Money problems. The major problem was a $40 million war debt that the Articles of Confederation Congress had promised to pay to Britain in the Peace Treaty of 1783. Congress had no power to tax. The national government acquired money through (1) pleading for money from the states or (2) in theory, amending the Art. of Confederation to allow the national government to levy taxes. However, under the Art. of Confederation, amendments had to get unanimous approval—any one state could block the adoption of an amendment.

4.  **Economic and Trade Problems**: Congress had no power to regulate interstate or foreign commerce.

    • The British were unloading goods on the American market and stifling the growth of American industries. Britain had blocked U.S. trade with the British empire, thus the states had no market for their goods. This resulted in an economic depression.

- States were erecting tariffs against each other, thus restricting trade and adding to the depression. The development of steam navigation led to a desire for a system of canals, but they couldn't get the states to meet to work out cooperation.
- There was no uniform national currency. The state currencies were extremely unstable. There were significant debtor-creditor problems. Hard coins were in short supply; the states were issuing paper money that depreciated in value rapidly. Mortgage foreclosures reached record highs. Many people were placed in debtors' prison or sold into service.

This all led to massive public discontent which escalated into violence in July 1786 in Shays Rebellion.

*Shay's Rebellion:* Farmers had taken out loans in paper money. There was rampant inflation. The Massachusetts legislature passed a bill requiring that the loans be repaid in hard currency. The farmers did not have hard currency. The courts were foreclosing on mortgages and repossessing farms. Shay, and a band of followers, tried to forcibly shut down the courts. The state sent in troops. Shooting ensued. This was very scary to the monied interests in the country.

5. **Foreign Affairs**: While this was the one area in which the Articles of Confederation Congress was supposed to have some power; this area clearly revealed the impotence of the Articles of Confederation Congress in practice.

- The British were not complying with the Peace Treaty of 1783. Britain refused to withdraw troops from frontier posts and their presence made it impossible for the U.S. to obtain peace with the Indians. The U.S. did not have the military strength to pacify the Indians or take on the British troops.
- The states refused to comply with the Peace Treaty showing the impotence of the national government. They put up obstacles preventing the collection of pre-War debts owed to British creditors. The states confiscated British loyalists' property, in violation of the Treaty.

The US government was powerless to enforce the treaty, either against Britain or the states. This made it impossible to negotiate with Britain for better trade provisions.

The Articles of Confederation Congress was unable to negotiate a treaty with Spain to insure the free navigation of the Mississippi. This was a crushing economic blow to western settlers who used the Mississippi to ship farm produce to Eastern cites.

The Art. of Confederation Congress was unable to respond to the enslavement of American mariners by the Barbary States (Algiers, Tripoli, Tunis, and Morocco). The U.S. was too impoverished to meet the blackmail demands or build the navy needed to protect her commerce.

## Specific Precipitating Event to the Calling of the Constitutional Convention:

Call for a meeting of the states to discuss canal building, especially from the headwaters of the Ohio to one of the rivers following into the Atlantic. (George Washington was President of the Potomac Navigation Co. and had a particular interest in such a canal). Only NY, NJ, Delaware, Penn, and Va showed up—such a canal required the concurrence, at least, of Maryland, Penn, and Delaware). At this meeting, Madison proposed that a convention of all the states be called to discuss commercial conditions. The Articles of Confederation Congress called a convention "for the sole and express purpose of revising the Articles of Confederation and reporting to Congress and the several legislatures such alterations and provisions therein."

At this constitutional convention, a majority of the delegates agreed that the national government needed to be strengthened. Only NY sent an Anti-Federalist delegation. (RI did not send a delegation at all.) It became clear early on, that the delegates were not simply going to revise the Art. of Confederation; rather, they were going to start from scratch.

The constitutional convention was the Second Revolution. Unlike the first revolution, it was not primarily concerned with preserving individual rights and liberties. Rather, it was concerned with setting up a government that could function effectively and address the public/common problems facing the nation. This is a common post-revolution phenomena—the first revolution begins as a quest for liberty/freedom, but excess leads to a desire for order. The danger is that a new repressive order will be instituted, making the first revolution meaningless.

At the convention, the delegates made a series of *political compromises*:

- between small and large states: bicameral legislature established, with one house based on proportionate representation and one house based on state representation.
- between slave and free states: (1) 3/5ths compromise: slaves would be counted as 3/5ths of a person for purposes of taxes and representation (2) trade compromise: the south agreed to congressional power to pass navigation acts; the north agreed to prohibit congressional interference with the importation of slaves for 20 years.*
- between those who wanted the President to be elected by congress and those who wanted him elected by the people or the states: electoral college—each state could make its own decision on how to select electors (shortly after 1789, nearly all states choose electors by popular election).

The convention avoided directly dealing with the issue of who would have the power to declare state laws unconstitutional, although they clearly agreed that the federal government should be able to do so. They considered giving the power to Congress or to a Council of Revision composed of the President and the Supreme Court. Compromise between the states' righters and potential opponents at the ratifying conventions and those who wanted a strong national government led them to leave the creation of lower federal courts to Congress and to add the Supremacy Clause in Article 6 making the Constitution, the laws, and treaties of the U.S. supreme over state laws. (Under the Articles of Confederation, state courts had not been enforcing federal laws that they thought were contrary to their own constitutions.) In 1789, Congress passed the Judiciary Act which established the federal judiciary and provided for appeals from state courts to federal courts—hence the federal judiciary acquired the power to declare state laws unconstitutional.

There was *agreement* on (both initially and finally):

- congressional power to levy and collect taxes
- congressional power to regulate foreign and interstate commerce
- congressional power to pay debts
- congressional power to provide for the common defense and general welfare of the U.S.
- the prohibition on the issue of paper money by the states.

## RATIFICATION

The convention delegates choose not to submit the constitution to the Articles of Confederation Congress for approval, since they were actually proposing an entirely new government. They declared that ratification by 9 states would be sufficient for the establishment and ratification of the new constitution. They by-passed the state legislature and submitted it directly to the people who voted for delegates to the state ratifying conventions.

### Supporters of the Constitution:
1. commercial and manufacturing interests
2. people around the main arteries of commerce—urban
3. creditors
4. Revolutionary War officers
5. professional men

## Opponents: Anti-Federalists

1. states' righters—believed that individual rights were safer in hands of state governments because state governments were closer to the people.
2. agrarians—rural interests
3. paper money men
4. debtors
5. other special interests

   Opponents concentrated their attack on the Constitution on the absence of safeguards for civil liberties. In the Virginia ratifying conventions James Madison promised to propose a Bill of Rights as amendments to the Constitution in the first Congress.

   Congress passed the Bill of Rights on Sept. 25, 1789. NJ was the first state to ratify it on Nov. 20, 1789. Va. became the necessary tenth ratifier on Dec. 15, 1791.

Supporters of the Constitution, in an attempt to convince NY to ratify the constitution, published a series of articles beginning Oct. 27,1787. By May 1788, they had been collected as *The Federalist Papers*.

Delaware ratified first—Dec. 7, 1787. New Hampshire became the ninth ratifier on June 21, 1788. Four days later Va. ratified and then NY saw the futility of a 'no' vote and ratified.

## HOW THE CONSTITUTION ADDRESSED THE POLITICAL PROBLEMS THAT PRECIPITATED ITS WRITING

1. **Low Prestige**: Created a more powerful government; prestige often follows power. Created an executive to solve the problems stemming from attempting to run a government by committee. Established a separate judicial branch.

2. **Land Titles/Disputes**: Created the federal judiciary independent of state governments to resolve disputes. Established a procedure for admitting new states.

3. **Fiscal Problems**: Gave Congress the power to tax and borrow, to lay duties, to coin money and regulate its value.

4. **Economic and Trade Problems**: Most of Congress' enumerated powers address these problems, especially the power to regulate commerce, both foreign and interstate; establish bankruptcy laws; coin money and regulate its value; establish tariffs; limit states' power to do these things, and forbid states from impairing the obligation of contracts.

5. **Foreign Affairs**: Congress' enumerated powers: define and punish piracy; declare war; raise and support armies and a navy. States are forbidden from engaging in foreign affairs. President is made commander and chief of the army and navy and given treaty-making power. The federal courts are given jurisdiction in all cases involving ambassadors, etc.

## HOW DOES THE CONSTITUTION LIMIT POLITICAL POWER?

1. **Separation of Powers**:  Three separate co-equal branches with checks and balances. Separate institutions sharing power. Based on political theory of Montesquieu. Make power check (or counter balance) power and thereby limit the government's ability to act—to impede the liberty of autonomous individuals.

2. **Federalism**: State and national governments are each supreme within their own sphere of action. Each U.S. citizen is controlled by both the state and the federal/national government. The national government has direct power over the people; it does not have to go through the states. State and federal governments share some powers: *CONCURRENT POWERS* (ex: tax). Under the supremacy clause, when the two level of governments' exercise of concurrent powers conflict, federal law trumps. Some powers are given exclusively to one level: *EXCLUSIVE POWERS*. (ex: only national government can sign treaties and coin money; only state governments can exercise police powers [regulate for the health, safety and morals of the citizenry]).

3. **Regular Periodic Elections**: The people, or their representatives in the states, control the staffing of the federal government. When federal government office holders are abusing or mis-using their power, the people can "throw the rascals out."

4. **Judicial Review and the Bill of Rights**: The Bill of Rights was added to the Constitution in 1791. It limits the national government's power in relation to individuals; it protects individual rights from over zealous majorities. It is left primarily up to the courts to enforce the Bill of Rights as a limit on government action, although all branches of the national government are bound to abide by it in their actions. Judicial review is a mechanism for the enforcement of the Constitution on government, both by determining whether government action is authorized by the Constitution and by determining whether the government has violated the limitations on government power found in the Constitution, such as the Bill of Rights.

## *Notes*

\* In 1808, Congress passed legislation prohibiting Americans from participating in the African slave trade. Slavery, itself, was not outlawed until ratification of the Thirteenth Amendment to the Constitution in 1865, after the Civil War.

# THE FEDERALIST NO. 78

*Alexander Hamilton*

## TO THE PEOPLE OF THE STATE OF NEW YORK

WE PROCEED NOW to an examination of the judiciary department of the proposed government.

In unfolding the defects of the existing Confederation, the utility and necessity of a federal judicature have been clearly pointed out. It is the less necessary to recapitulate the considerations there urged, as the propriety of the institution in the abstract is not disputed; the only questions which have been raised being relative to the manner of constituting it, and to its extent. To these points, therefore, our observations shall be confined.

The manner of constituting it seems to embrace these several objects: 1st. The mode of appointing the judges. 2d. The tenure by which they are to hold their places. 3d. The partition of the judiciary authority between different courts, and their relations to each other.

**FIRST.** As to the mode of appointing the judges; this is the same with that of appointing the officers of the Union in general, and has been so fully discussed in the two last numbers, that nothing can be said here which would not be useless repetition.

**SECOND.** As to the tenure by which the judges are to hold their places: this chiefly concerns their duration in office; the provisions for their support; the precautions for their responsibility.

According to the plan of the convention, all judges who may be appointed by the United States are to hold their offices *during good behavior;* which is conformable to the most approved of the State constitutions, and among the rest, to that of this State. Its propriety having been drawn into question by the adversaries of that plan, is no light symptom of the rage for objection, which disorders their imaginations and judgements. The standard of good behavior for the continuance in office of the judicial magistracy, is certainly one of the most valuable of the modern improvements in the practice of government. In a monarchy it is an excellent barrier to the despotism of the prince; in a republic it is a no less excellent barrier to the encroachments and oppressions of the representative body. And it is the best expedient which can be devised in any government, to secure a steady, upright, and impartial administration of the laws.

Whoever attentively considers the different departments of power must perceive, that, in a government in which they are separated from each other, the judiciary from the nature of its functions, will always be the least dangerous to the political rights of the Constitution; because it will be least in a capacity to annoy or injure them. The executive not only dispenses the honors, but holds the sword of the community. The legislature not only commands the purse, but prescribes the rules by which the duties and rights of every citizen are to be regulated. The judiciary, on the contrary, has no influence over either the sword or the purse; no direction either of the strength or of the wealth of the society; and can take no active resolution whatever. It may truly be said to have neither FORCE NOR WILL, but merely judgment; and must ultimately depend upon the aid of the executive arm even for the efficacy of its judgments.

This simple view of the matter suggests several important consequences. It proves incontestably, that the judiciary is beyond comparison the weakest of the three departments of power;* that it can never attack with success either of the other two; and that all possible care is requisite to enable it to defend itself against their attacks. It equally proves, that though individual oppression may now and then proceed from the courts of justice, the general liberty of the people can never be endangered from that quarter; I mean so long as the judiciary remains truly distinct from both the legislature and the Executive. For I agree, that "there is no liberty if the power of judging be not separated from the legislative and executive powers."[1] And it proves, in the last place, that as liberty can have nothing to fear from the judiciary alone, but would have every thing to fear from its union with either of the other departments; that as all the effects of such a union must ensue from a dependence of the former on the latter, notwithstanding a nominal and apparent separation; that as, from the natural feebleness of the judiciary, it is in continual jeopardy of being overpowered, awed, or influenced by its coordinate branches; and that as nothing can contribute so much to its firmness and independence as permanency in office, this equality may therefore be justly regarded as an indispensable ingredient in its constitution, and, in a great measure, as the citadel of the public justice and the public security.

The complete independence of the courts of justice is peculiarly essential in a limited Constitution. By a limited Constitution, I understand one which contains certain specified exceptions to the legislative authority; such, for instance, as that it shall pass no bills of attainder, no *ex-post-facto* laws, and the like. Limitations of this kind can be preserved in practice no other way than through the medium of courts of justice, whose duty it must be to declare all acts contrary to the manifest tenor of the Constitution void. Without this, all the reservations of particular rights or privileges would amount to nothing.

Some perplexity respecting the rights of the courts to pronounce legislative acts void, because contrary to the constitution, has arisen from an imagination that the doctrine would imply a superiority of the judiciary to the legislative power. It is urged that the authority which can declare the acts of another void, must necessarily be superior to the one whose acts may be declared void. As this doctrine is of great importance in all the American constitutions, a brief discussion of the ground on which it rests cannot be unacceptable.

There is no position which depends on clearer principles, than that every act of a delegated authority, contrary to the tenor of the commission under which it is exercised, is void. No legislative act, therefore, contrary to the Constitution, can be valid. To deny this, would be to affirm, that the deputy is greater than his principal; that the servant is above his master; that the representatives of the people are superior to the people themselves; that men acting by virtue of powers, may do not only what their powers do not authorize, but what they forbid.

If it be said that the legislative body are themselves the constitutional judges of their own powers, and that the construction they put upon them is conclusive upon the other departments, it may be answered, that this cannot be the natural presumption, where it is not to be collected from any particular provisions in the Constitution. It is not otherwise to be supposed, that the Constitution could intend to enable the representatives of the people to substitute their *will* to that of their constituents. It is far more rational to suppose, that the courts were designed to be an intermediate body between the people and the legislature, in order, among other things, to keep the latter within the limits assigned to their authority. The interpretation of the laws is the proper and peculiar province of the courts. A constitution is, in fact, and must be regarded by the judges, as a fundamental law. It therefore belongs to them to ascertain its meaning, as well as the meaning of any particular act proceeding from the legislative body. If there should happen to be an irreconcilable variance between the two, that which has the superior obligation and validity ought, of course, to be preferred; or, in other words, the Constitution ought to be preferred to the statute, the intention of the people to the intention of their agents.

Nor does this conclusion by any means suppose a superior of the judicial to the legislative power. It only supposes that the power of the people is superior to both; and that where the will of the legislature, declared in its statutes, stand in opposition to that of the people, declared in the Constitution, the judges ought to be governed by the latter rather than the former. They ought to regulate their decisions by the fundamental laws, rather than by those which are not fundamental.

This exercise of judicial discretion, in determining between two contradictory laws, is exemplified in a familiar instance. It not uncommonly happens, that there are two statutes existing at one time, clashing in whole or in part with each other, and neither of them containing any repealing clause or expression. In such a case, it is the province of the courts to liquidate and fix their meaning and operation. So far as they can, by any fair construction, be reconciled to each other, reason and law conspire to dictate that this should be done; where this is impracticable, it becomes a matter of necessity to give effect to one, in exclusion of the other. The rule which has obtained in the courts for determining their relative validity is, that the last in order of time shall be preferred to the first. But this is a mere rule of construction, not derived from any positive law, but from the nature and reason of the thing. It is a rule not enjoined upon the courts by legislative provision, but adopted by themselves, as consonant to truth and propriety, for the direction of their conduct as interpreters of the law. They thought it reasonable, that between the interfering acts of an *equal* authority, that which was the last indication of its will should have the preference.

But in regard to the interfering acts of a superior and subordinate authority, of an original and derivative power, the nature and reason of the thing indicate the converse of that rule as proper to be followed. They teach us that the prior act of a superior ought to be preferred to the subsequent act of an inferior and subordinate authority; and that accordingly, whenever a particular statute contravenes the Constitution, it will be the duty of the judicial tribunals to adhere to the latter and disregard the former.

It can be of no weight to say that the courts, on the pretence of a repugnancy, may substitute their own pleasure to the constitutional intentions of the legislature. This might as well happen in the case of two contradictory statutes; or it might as well happen in every adjudication upon any single statute. The courts must declare the sense of the law; and if they should be disposed to exercise WILL instead of JUDG-MENT, the consequence would equally be the substitution of their pleasure to that of the legislative body. The observation, if it prove any thing, would prove that there ought to be no judges distinct from that body.

If, then, the courts of justice are to be considered as the bulwarks of a limited Constitution against legislative encroachments, this consideration will afford a strong argument for the permanent tenure of judicial offices, since nothing will contribute so much as this to that independent spirit in the judges which must be essential to the faithful performance of so arduous a duty.

This independence of the judges is equally requisite to guard the Constitution and the rights of individuals from the effects of those ill humors, which the arts of designing men, or the influence of particular conjunctures, sometimes disseminate among the people themselves, and which, though they speedily give place to better information, and more deliberate reflection, have a tendency, in the meantime, to occasion dangerous innovations in the government, and serious oppressions of the minor party in the community. Though I trust the friends of the proposed Constitution will never concur with its enemies,[2] in questioning that fundamental principle of republican government, which admits the right of the people to alter or abolish the established Constitution, whenever they find it inconsistent with their happiness, yet it is not to be inferred from this principle, that the representatives of the people, whenever a momentary inclination happens to lay hold of a majority of their constituents, incompatible with the provisions in the existing Constitution, would, on that account, be justifiable in a violation of those provisions; or that the courts would be under a greater obligation to connive at infractions in this shape, than when they had proceeded wholly from the cabals of the representative body. Until the people have, by some solemn and authoritative act, annulled or changed the established form, it is binding upon themselves collectively, as well as individually; and no presumption, or even knowledge, of their sentiments, can warrant their representatives in a departure from it, prior to such an act. But it is easy to see, that it would require an uncommon portion of fortitude in the judges to do their duty as faithful guardians of the Constitution, where legislative invasions of it had been instigated by the major voice of the community.

But it is not with a view to infractions of the Constitution only, that the independence of the judges may be an essential safeguard against the effects of occasional ill humors in the society. These sometimes extend no farther than to the injury of the private rights of particular classes of citizens, by unjust and partial laws. Here also the firmness of the judicial magistracy is of vast importance in mitigating the severity and confining the operation of such laws. It not only serves to moderate the immediate mischiefs of those which may have been passed but it operates as a check upon the legislative body in passing them; who, perceiving that obstacles to the success of iniquitous intention are to be expected from the scruples of the courts, are in a manner compelled, by the very motives of the injustice they mediate, to qualify their attempts. This is a circumstance calculated to have more influence upon the character of our governments, than but a few may be aware of. The benefits of the integrity and moderation of the judiciary have already been felt in more States than one; and though they may have displeased those whose sinister expectations they may have disappointed, they must have commanded the esteem and applause of all the virtuous and disinterested. Considerate men, of every description, ought to prize whatever will tend to beget or fortify that temper in the courts; as no man can be sure that he may not be to-morrow the victim of a spirit of injustice, by which he may be a gainer today. And every man must now feel, that the inevitable tendency of such a spirit is to sap the foundations of public and private confidence, and to introduce in its stead universal distrust and distress.

That inflexible and uniform adherence to the rights of the Constitution, and of individuals, which we perceive to be indispensable in the courts of justice, can certainly not be expected from judges who hold their offices by a temporary commission. Periodical appointments, however regulated, or by whomsoever made, would, in some way or other, be fatal to their necessary independence. If the power of making them was committed either to the Executive or legislature, there would be danger of an improper complaisance to the branch which possessed it; if to both, there would be an unwillingness to hazard the displeasure of either; if to the people, or to persons chosen by them for the special purpose, there would be too great a disposition to consult popularity, to justify a reliance that nothing would be consulted *but* the Constitution and the laws.

There is yet a further and weightier reason for the permanency of the judicial offices, which is deducible from the nature of the qualifications they require. It has been frequently remarked, with great propriety, that a voluminous code of laws is one of the inconveniences necessarily connected with the advantages of a free government. To avoid an arbitrary discretion in the courts, it is indispensable that they should be bound down by strict rules and precedents, which serve to define and point out their duty in every particular case that comes before them; and it will readily be conceived from the variety of controversies which grow out of the folly and wickedness of mankind, that the records of those precedents must unavoidably swell to a very considerable bulk, and must demand long and laborious study to acquire a competent knowledge of them. Hence it is, that there can be but few men in the society who will have sufficient skill in the laws to qualify them for the stations of judges. And making the proper deductions for the ordinary depravity of human nature, the number must be still smaller of those who unite the requisite integrity with the requisite knowledge. These considerations apprise us, that the government can have no great option between fit character; and that a temporary duration in office, which would naturally discourage such characters from quitting a lucrative line of practice to accept a seat on the bench, would have a tendency to throw the administration of justice into hands less able, and less well qualified, to conduct it with utility and dignity. In the present circumstances of this country, and in those in which it is likely to be for a long time to come, the disadvantages of this score would be greater than they may at first sight appear: but it must be confessed, that they are far inferior to those which present themselves under the other aspects of the subject.

Upon the whole, there can be no room to doubt that the convention acted wisely in copying from the models of those constitutions which have established *good behavior* as the tenure of their judicial offices, in point of duration; and that so far from being blamable on this account, their plan would have been inexcusably defective, if it had wanted this important feature of good government. The experience of Great Britain affords an illustrious comment on the excellence of the institution.

*PUBLIUS.*

## Notes

\* The celebrated Montesquieu, speaking of them, says: "Of the three powers above mentioned, the judiciary is next to nothing."—"Spirit of Laws," vol. i., page 186.—PUBLIUS

1. *Idem*, page 181.—PUBLIUS

2. *Vide* "Protest of the Minority of the Convention of Pennsylvania," Martin's Speech, etc.—PUBLIUS

# THE FEDERALIST NO. 79

### Alexander Hamilton

## TO THE PEOPLE OF THE STATE OF NEW YORK

Next to permanency in office, nothing can contribute more to the independence of the judges than a fixed provision for their support. The remark made in relation to the President is equally applicable here. In the general course of human nature, a power over a man's subsistence amounts to a power over his will. And we can never hope to see realized in practice, the complete separation of the judicial from the legislative power, in any system which leaves the former dependent for pecuniary resources on the occasional grants of the latter. The enlightened friends to good government in every State, have seen cause to lament the want of precise and explicit precautions in the State constitutions on this head. Some of these indeed have declared that permanent\* salaries should be established for the judges; but the experiment has in some instances shown that such expressions are not sufficiently definite to preclude legislative evasions. Something still more positive and unequivocal has been evinced to be requisite. The plan of the convention accordingly has provided that the judges of the United States "shall at *stated times* receive for their services a compensation which shall not be *diminished* during their continuance in office."

This, all circumstances considered, is the most eligible provision that could have been devised. It will readily be understood that the fluctuations in the value of money and in the state of society rendered a fixed rate of compensation in the Constitution inadmissible. What might be extravagant to-day, might in half a century become penurious and inadequate. It was therefore necessary to leave it to the discretion of the legislature to vary its provisions in conformity to the variations in circumstances, yet under such restrictions as to put it out of the power of that body to change the condition of the individual for the worse. A man may then be sure of the ground upon which he stands, and can never be deterred from his duty by the apprehension of being placed in a less eligible situation. The clause which has been quoted combines both advantages. The salaries of judicial officers may from time to time be altered, as occasion shall require, yet so as never to lessen the allowance with which any particular judge comes into office, in respect to him. It will be observed that a difference has been made by the convention between the compensation of the President and of the judges. That of the former can neither be increased nor diminished; that of the latter can only not be diminished. This probably arose from the difference in the duration of the respective offices. As the President is to be elected for no more than four years, it can rarely happen that an adequate salary, fixed at the commencement of that period, will not continue to be such to its end. But with regard to the judges, who, if they behave properly, will be secured in their places for life, it may well happen, especially in the early stages of the government, that a stipend, which would be very sufficient at their first appointment, would become too small in the progress of their service.

This provision for the support of the judges bears every mark of prudence and efficacy; and it may be safely affirmed that, together with the permanent tenure of their offices, it affords a better prospect of their independence than is discoverable in the constitutions of any of the States in regard to their own judges.

The precautions for their responsibility are comprised in the article respecting impeachments. They are liable to be impeached for malconduct by the House of Representatives, and tried by the Senate; and, if convicted, may be dismissed from office, and disqualified for holding any other. This is the only provision on the point which is consistent with the necessary independence of the judicial character, and is the only one which we find in our own Constitution in respect to our own judges.

The want of a provision for removing the judges on account of inability has been a subject of complaint. But all considerate men will be sensible that such a provision would either not be practiced upon or would be more liable to abuse than calculated to answer any good purpose. The mensuration of the faculties of the mind has, I believe, no place in the catalogue of known arts. An attempt to fix the boundary between the regions of ability and inability, would much oftener give scope to personal and party attachments and enmities than advance the interests of justice or the public good. The results, except in the case of insanity, must for the most part be arbitrary; and insanity, without any formal or express provision, may be safely pronounced to be a virtual disqualification.

The constitution of New York, to avid investigations that must forever be vague and dangerous, has taken a particular age as the criterion of inability. No man can be a judge beyond sixty. I believe there are few at present who do not disapprove of this provision. There is no station, in relation to which it is less proper than to that of a judge. The deliberating and comparing faculties generally preserve their strength much beyond that period in men who survive it; and when, in addition to this circumstance, we consider how few there are who outlive the season of intellectual vigor, and how improbable it is that any considerable portion of the bench, whether more or less numerous, should be in such a situation at the same time, we shall be ready to conclude that limitations of this sort have little to recommend them. In a republic where fortunes are not affluent, and pensions not expedient, the dismission of men from stations in which they have served their country long and usefully, on which they depend for subsistence, and from which it will be too late to resort to any other occupation for a livelihood, ought to have some better apology to humanity than is to be found in the imaginary danger of a superannuated bench.

PUBLIUS.

## Note

\* *Vide* "Constitution of Massachusetts," chapter 2, section 1, article 13.—PUBLIUS

# THE FEDERALIST NO. 80

## Alexander Hamilton

## TO THE PEOPLE OF THE STATE OF NEW YORK

To JUDGE with accuracy of the proper extent of the federal judicature, it will be necessary to consider, in the first place, what are its proper objects.

It seems scarcely to admit of controversy, that the judiciary authority of the Union ought to extend to these several descriptions of cases: 1st, to all those which arise out of the laws of the United States, passed in pursuance of their just and constitutional powers of legislation; 2d, to all those which concern the execution of the provisions expressly contained in the articles of Union; 3d, to all those in which the United States are a party; 4th, to all those which involve the PEACE of the CONFEDERACY, whether they relate to the intercourse between the United States and foreign nations, or to that between the States themselves; 5th, to all those which originate on the high seas, and are of admiralty or maritime jurisdiction; and, lastly, to all those in which the State tribunals cannot be supposed to be impartial and unbiased.

The first point depends upon this obvious consideration, that there ought always to be a constitutional method of giving efficacy to constitutional provisions. What, for instance, would avail restrictions on the authority of the State legislatures, without some constitutional mode of enforcing the observance of them? The States, by the plan of the convention, are prohibited from doing a variety of things, some of which are incompatible with the interests of the Union, and others with the principles of good government. The imposition of duties on imported articles, and the emission of paper money, are specimens of each kind. No man of sense will believe, that such prohibitions would be scrupulously regarded, without some effectual power in the government to restrain or correct the infractions of them. This power must either be a direct negative on the State laws, or an authority in the federal courts to overrule such as might be in manifest contravention of the articles of Union. There is no third course that I can imagine. The latter appears to have been thought by the convention preferable to the former, and, I presume, will be most agreeable to the States.

As to the second point, it is impossible, by any argument or comment, to make it clearer than it is in itself. If there are such things as political axioms, the propriety of the judicial power of a government being coextensive with its legislative, may be ranked among the number. The mere necessity of uniformity in the interpretation of the national laws, decides the question. Thirteen independent courts of final jurisdiction over the same causes, arising upon the same laws, is a hydra in government from which nothing but contradiction and confusion can proceed.

Still less need be said in regard to the third point. Controversies between the nation and its members or citizens, can only be properly referred to the national tribunals. Any other plan would be contrary to reason, to precedent, and to decorum.

The fourth point rests on this plain proposition, that the peace of the WHOLE ought not to be left at the disposal of a PART. The Union will undoubtedly be answerable to foreign powers for the conduct of its members. And the responsibility for an injury ought ever to be accompanied with the faculty of preventing it. As the denial or perversion of justice by the sentences of courts, as well as in any other manner, is with reason classed among the just causes of war, it will follow that the federal judiciary ought to have cognizance of all causes in which the citizens of other countries are concerned. This is not less essential to the preservation of the public faith, than to the security of the public tranquillity. A distinction may perhaps be imagined between cases arising upon treaties and the laws of nations and those which may stand merely on the footing of the municipal law. The former kind may be supposed proper for the federal jurisdiction, the latter for that of the States. But it is at least problematical, whether an unjust sentence against a foreigner, where the subject of controversy was wholly relative to the lex loci, would not, if unredressed, be an aggression upon his sovereign, as well as one which violated the stipulations of a treaty or the general law of nations. And a still greater objection to the distinction would result from the immense difficulty, if not impossibility, of a practical discrimination between the cases of one complexion and those of the other. So great a proportion of the cases in which foreigners are parties, involve national questions, that it is by far most safe and most expedient to refer all those in which they are concerned to the national tribunals.

The power of determining causes between two States, between one State and the citizens of another, and between the citizens of different States, is perhaps not less essential to the peace of the Union than that which has been just examined. History gives us a horrid picture of the dissensions and private wars which distracted and desolated Germany prior to the institution of the Imperial Chamber by Maximilian, towards the close of the fifteenth century; and informs us, at the same time, of the vast influence of that institution in appeasing the disorders and establishing the tranquillity of the empire. This was a court invested with authority to decide finally all differences among the members of the Germanic body.

A method of terminating territorial disputes between the States, under the authority of the federal head, was not unattended to, even in the imperfect system by which they have been hitherto held together. But there are many other sources, besides interfering claims of boundary, from which bickerings and animosities may spring up among the members of the Union. To some of these we have been witnesses in the course of our past experience. It will readily be conjectured that I allude to the fraudulent laws which have been passed in too many of the States. And though the proposed Constitution establishes particular guards against the repetition of those instances which have heretofore made their appearance, yet it is warrantable to apprehend that the spirit which produced them will assume new shapes that could not be foreseen nor specifically provided against. Whatever practices may have a tendency to disturb the harmony between the States, are proper objects of federal superintendence and control.

It may be esteemed the basis of the Union, that "the citizens of each State shall be entitled to all the privileges and immunities of citizens of the several States." And if it be a just principle that every government *ought to possess the means of executing its own provisions by its own authority,* it will follow, that in order to the inviolable maintenance of that equality of privileges and immunities to which the citizens of the Union will be entitled, the national judiciary ought to preside in all cases in which one State or its citizens are opposed to another State or its citizens. To secure the full effect of so fundamental a provision against all evasion and subterfuge, it is necessary that its construction should be committed to that tribunal which, having no local attachments, will be likely to be impartial between the different States and their citizens, and which, owing its official existence to the Union, will never be likely to feel any bias inauspicious to the principles on which it is founded.

The fifth point will demand little animadversion. The most bigoted idolizers of State authority have not thus far shown a disposition to deny the national judiciary the cognizances of maritime causes. These so generally depend on the laws of nations, and so commonly affect the rights of foreigners, that they fall within the considerations which are relative to the public peace. The most important part of them are, by the present Confederation, submitted to federal jurisdiction.

The reasonableness of the agency of the national courts in cases in which the State tribunals cannot be supposed to be impartial, speaks for itself. No man ought certainly to be a judge in his own cause, or in any cause in respect to which he has the least interest or bias. The principle has no inconsiderable weight in designating the federal courts as the proper tribunals for the determination of controversies between different States and their citizens. And it ought to have the same operation in regard to some cases between citizens of the same State. Claims to land under grants of different States, founded upon adverse pretensions of boundary, are of this description. The courts of neither of the granting States could be expected to be unbiased. The laws may have even prejudged the question, and tied the courts down to decisions in favor of the grants of the State to which they belonged. And even where this had not been done, it would be natural that the judges, as men, should feel a strong predilection to the claims of their own government.

Having thus laid down and discussed the principles which ought to regulate the constitution of the federal judiciary, we will proceed to test, by these principles, the particular powers of which, according to the plan of the convention, it is to be composed. It is to comprehend "all cases in law and equity arising under the Constitution, the laws of the United States, and treaties made, or which shall be made, under their authority; to all cases affecting ambassadors, other public ministers, and consuls; to all cases of admiralty and maritime jurisdiction; to controversies to which the United States shall be a party; to controversies between two or more States; between a State and citizens of another State; between citizens of different States; between citizens of the same State claiming lands and grants of different States; and between a State or the citizens thereof and foreign states, citizens, and subjects." This constitutes the entire mass of the judicial authority of the Union. Let us now review it in detail. It is, then, to extend:

**FIRST.** To all cases in law and equity, *arising under the Constitution* and *the laws of the United States.* This corresponds with the two first classes of causes, which have been enumerated, as proper for the jurisdiction of the United States. It has been asked, what is meant by "cases arising under the Constitution," in contradistinction from those "arising under the laws of the United States"? The difference has been already explained. All the restrictions upon the authority of the State legislatures furnish examples of it. They are not, for instance, to emit paper money; but the interdiction results from the Constitution, and will have no connection with any law of the United States. Should paper money, notwithstanding, be emitted, the controversies concerning it would be cases arising under the Constitution and not the laws of the United States, in the ordinary signification of the terms. This may serve as a sample of the whole.

It has also been asked, what need of the word "equity"? What equitable causes can grow out of the Constitution and laws of the United States? There is hardly a subject of litigation between individuals, which may not involve those ingredients of *fraud, accident, trust,* or *hardship,* which would render the matter an object of equitable rather than of legal jurisdiction, as the distinction is known and established in several of the States. It is the peculiar province, for instance, of a court of equity to relieve against what are called hard bargains: these are contracts in which, though there may have been no direct fraud or deceit, sufficient to invalidate them in a court of law, yet there may have been some undue and unconscionable advantage taken of the necessities of misfortunes of one of the parties, which a court of equity would not tolerate. In such cases, where foreigners were concerned on either side, it would be impossible for the federal judicatories to do justice without an equitable as well as a legal jurisdiction. Agreements to convey lands claimed under the grants of different States, may afford another example of the necessity of an equitable jurisdiction in the federal courts. This reasoning may not be so palpable in those States where the formal and technical distinction between LAW and EQUITY is not maintained, as in this State, where it is exemplified by every day's practice.

The judiciary authority of the Union is to extend:

**SECOND.** To treaties made, or which shall be made, under the authority of the United States, and to all cases affecting ambassadors, other public ministers, and consuls. These belong to the fourth class of the enumerated cases, as they have an evident connection with the preservation of the national peace.

**THIRD.** To cases of admiralty and maritime jurisdiction. These form, altogether, the fifth of the enumerated classes of causes proper for the cognizance of the national courts.

**FOURTH.** To controversies to which the United States shall be a party. These constitute the third of those classes.

**FIFTH.** To controversies between two or more States; between a State and citizens of another State; between citizens of different States. These belong to the fourth of those classes, and partake, in some measure, of the nature of the last.

**SEVENTH.** To cases between a State and the citizens thereof, the foreign States, citizens, or subjects. These have been already explained to belong to the fourth of the enumerated classes, and have been shown to be, in a peculiar manner, the proper subjects of the national judicature.

From this review of the particular powers of the federal judiciary, as marked out in the Constitution, it appears that they are all conformable to the principles which ought to have governed the structure of that department, and which were necessary to the perfection of the system. If some partial inconveniences should appear to be connected with the incorporation of any of them into the plan, it ought to be recollected that the national legislature will have ample authority to make such *exceptions*, and to prescribe such regulations as will be calculated to obviate or remove these inconveniences. The possibility of particular mischiefs can never be viewed, by a well-informed mind, as a solid objection to a general principle, which is calculated to avoid general mischiefs and to obtain general advantages.

*PUBLIUS.*

# THE FEDERALIST NO. 81

*Alexander Hamilton*

## TO THE PEOPLE OF THE STATE OF NEW YORK

Let us now return to the partition of the judiciary authority between different courts, and their relations to each other,

"The judicial power of the United States is" (by the plan of the convention) "to be vested in one Supreme Court, and in such inferior courts as the Congress may, from time to time, ordain and establish."

That there ought to be one court of supreme and final jurisdiction, is a proposition which is not likely to be contested. The reasons for it have been assigned in another place, and are too obvious to need repetition. The only question that seems to have been raised concerning it, is, whether it ought to be a distinct body or a branch of the legislature. The same contradiction is observable in regard to this matter which has been remarked in several other cases. The very men who object to the Senate as a court of impeachments, on the ground of an improper intermixture of powers, advocate, by implication at least, the propriety of vesting the ultimate decision of all causes, in the whole or in a part of the legislative body.

The arguments, or rather suggestions, upon which this charge is founded, are to this effect: The authority of the proposed Supreme Court of the United States, which is to be a separate and independent body, will be superior to that of the legislature. The power of construing the laws according to the *spirit* of the Constitution, will enable that court to mould them into whatever shape it may think proper; especially as its decisions will not be in any manner subject to the revision or correction of the legislative body. This is as unprecedented as it is dangerous. In Britain, the judicial power, in the last resort, resides in the House of Lords, which is a branch of the legislature; and this part of the British government has been imitated in the State constitutions in general. The Parliament of Great Britain, and the legislatures of the several States, can at any time rectify, by law, the exceptionable decisions of their respective courts. But the errors and usurpations of the Supreme Court of the United States will be uncontrollable and remediless. This, upon examination, will be found to be made up altogether of false reasoning upon misconceived fact.

In the first place, there is not a syllable in the plan under consideration which *directly* empowers the national courts to construe the laws according to the spirit of the Constitution, or which gives them any greater latitude in this respect than may be claimed by the courts of every State. I admit, however, that the Constitution ought to be the standard of construction for the laws, and that wherever there is an evident opposition, the laws ought to give place to the Constitution. But this doctrine is not deducible from any circumstance peculiar to the plan of the convention, but from the general theory of a limited Constitution; and as far as it is true, is equally applicable to most, if not to all the State governments. There can be no objection, therefore, on this account, to the federal judicature which will not lie against the local judicatures in general, and which will not serve to condemn every constitution that attempts to set bounds to legislative discretion.

But perhaps the force of the objection may be thought to consist in the particular organization of the Supreme Court; in its being composed of a distinct body of magistrates, instead of being one of the branches of the legislature, as in the government of Great Britain and that of the State. To insist upon this point, the authors of the objection must renounce the meaning they have labored to annex to the celebrated maxim, requiring a separation of the departments of power. It shall, nevertheless, be conceded to them, agreeably to the interpretation given to that maxim in the course of these papers, that it is not violated by vesting the ultimate power of judging in a *part* of the legislative body. But though this be not an absolute violation of that excellent rule, yet it verges so nearly upon it, as on this account alone to be less eligible than the mode preferred by the convention. From a body which had even a partial agency in passing bad laws, we could rarely expect a disposition to temper and moderate them in the application. The same spirit which had operated in making them, would be too apt in interpreting them; still less could it be expected that men who had infringed the Constitution in the character of legislators, would be disposed to repair the breach in the character of judges. Nor is this all. Every reason which recommends the tenure of good behavior for judicial offices, militates against placing the judiciary power, in the last resort, in a body composed of men chosen for a limited period. There is an absurdity in referring the determination of causes, in the first instance to judges of permanent standing; in the last, to those of a temporary and mutable constitution. And there is a still greater absurdity in subjecting the decisions of men, selected for their knowledge of the laws, acquired by long and laborious study, to the revision and control of men who, for want of the same advantage, cannot but be deficient in that knowledge. The members of the legislature will rarely be chosen with a view to those qualifications which fit men for the stations of judges; and as, on this account, there will be great reason to apprehend all the ill consequences of defective information, so, on account of the natural propensity of such bodies to party divisions, there will be no less reason to fear that the pestilential breath of faction may poison the fountains of justice. The habit of being continually marshalled on opposite sides will be too apt to stifle the voice both of law and of equity.

These considerations teach us to applaud the wisdom of those States who have committed the judicial power, in the last resort, not to a part of the legislature, but to distinct and independent bodies of men. Contrary to the supposition of those who have represented the plan of the convention, in this respect, as novel and unprecedented, it is but a copy of the constitutions of New Hampshire, Massachusetts, Pennsylvania, Delaware, Maryland, Virginia, North Carolina, South Carolina, and Georgia; and the preference which has been given to those models is highly to be commended.

It is not true, in the second place, that the Parliament of Great Britain, or the legislatures of the particular States, can rectify the exceptionable decisions of their respective courts, in any other sense than might be done by a future legislature of the United States. The theory, neither of the British, nor the State constitutions, authorizes the revisal of a judicial sentence by a legislative act. Nor is there any thing in the proposed Constitution, more than in either of them by which it is forbidden. In the former, as well as in the latter, the impropriety of the thing, on the general principles of law and reason, is the sole obstacle. A legislature, without exceeding its province, cannot reverse a determination once made in a particular case; though it may prescribe a new rule for future cases. This is the principle, and it applies in all its consequences, exactly in the same manner and extent, to the State governments, as to the national governments now under consideration. Not the least difference can be pointed out in any view of the subject.

It may in the last place be observed that the supposed danger of judiciary encroachments on the legislative authority, which has been upon many occasions reiterated is in reality a phantom. Particular misconstructions and contraventions of the will of the legislature may now and then happen; but they can never be so extensive as to amount to an inconvenience, or in any sensible degree to affect the order of the political system. This may be inferred with certainty, from the general nature of the judicial power, from the objects to which it relates, from the manner in which it is exercised, from its comparative weakness, and from its total incapacity to support its usurpations by force. And the inference is greatly fortified by the consideration of the important constitutional check which the power of instituting impeachments in one part of the legislative body, and of determining upon them in the other, would give to that body upon the members of the judicial department. This is alone a complete security. There never can be danger that the judges, by a series of deliberate usurpations on the authority of the legislature, would hazard the united resentment of the body intrusted with it, while this body was possessed of the means of punishing their presumption, by degrading them from their stations. While this ought to remove all apprehensions on the subject, it affords, at the same time, a cogent argument for constituting the Senate a court for the trial of impeachments.

Having now examined, and, I trust, removed the objections to the distinct and independent organization of the Supreme Court, I proceed to consider the propriety of the power of constituting inferior courts,[1] and the relations which will subsist between these and the former.

The power of constituting inferior courts is evidently calculated to obviate the necessity of having recourse to the Supreme Court in every case of federal cognizance. It is intended to enable the national government to institute or *authorize,* in each State of district of the United States, a tribunal competent to the determination of matters of national jurisdiction within its limits.

But why, it is asked, might not the same purpose have been accomplished by the instrumentality of the State courts? This admits the different answers. Though the fitness and competency of those courts should be allowed in the utmost latitude, yet the substance of the power in question may still be regarded as a necessary part of the plan, if it were only to empower the national legislature to commit to them the cognizance of causes arising out of the national Constitution. To confer the power of determining such causes upon the existing courts of the several States, would perhaps be as much "to constitute tribunals," as to create new courts with the like power. But ought not a more direct and explicit provision to have been made in favor of the State courts? There are, in my opinion, substantial reasons against such a provision: the most discerning cannot foresee how far the prevalency of a local spirit may be found to disqualify the local tribunals for the jurisdiction of national causes; whilst every man may discover, that courts constituted like those of some of the States would be improper channels of the judicial authority of the Union. State judges, holding their offices during pleasure, or from year to year, will be too little independent to be relied upon for an inflexible execution of the national laws. And if there was a necessity for confiding the original cognizance of causes arising under those laws to them, there would be a correspondent necessity for leaving the door of appeal as wide as possible. In proportion to the grounds of confidence in, or distrust of, the subordinate tribunals, ought to be the facility or difficulty of appeals. And well satisfied as I am of the propriety of the appellate jurisdiction, in the several classes of causes to which it is extended by the plan of the convention, I should consider every thing calculated to give, in practice, and *unrestrained course* to appeals, as a source of public and private inconvenience.

I am not sure, but that it will be found highly expedient and useful, to divide the United States into four or five or half a dozen districts; and to institute a federal court in each district, in lieu of one in every State. The judges of these courts, with the aid of the State judges, may hold circuits for the trial of causes in the several parts of the respective districts. Justice through them may be administered with ease and despatch; and appeals may be safely circumscribed within a narrow compass. This plan appears to me at present the most eligible of any that could be adopted; and in order to it, it is necessary that the power of constituting inferior courts should exist in the full extent in which it is to be found in the proposed Constitution.

These reasons seem sufficient to satisfy a candid mind, that the want of such a power would have been a great defect in the plan. Let us now examine in what manner the judicial authority is to be distributed between the supreme and the inferior courts of the Union.

The Supreme Court is to be invested with original jurisdiction, only "in cases affecting ambassadors, other public ministers, and consuls, and those in which a STATE shall be a party." Public ministers of every class are the immediate representatives of their sovereigns. All questions in which they are concerned are so directly connected with the public peace, that, as well for the preservation of this, as out of respect to the sovereignties they represent, it is both expedient and proper that such questions should be submitted in the first instance to the highest judicatory of the nation. Though consuls have not in strictness a diplomatic character, yet as they are the public agents of the nations to which they belong, the same observation is in a great measure applicable to them. In cases in which a State might happen to be a party, it would ill suit its dignity to be turned over to an inferior tribunal.

Though it may rather be a digression from the immediate subject of this paper, I shall take occasion to mention here a supposition which has excited some alarm upon very mistaken grounds. It has been suggested that an assignment of the public securities of one State to the citizens of another, would enable them to prosecute that State in the federal courts for the amount of those securities; a suggestion which the following considerations prove to be without foundation.

It is inherent in the nature of sovereignty not to be amenable to the suit of an individual *without its consent.* This is the general sense, and the general practice of mankind; and the exemption, as one of the attributes of sovereignty, is now enjoyed by the government of every State in the Union. Unless, therefore, there is a surrender of this immunity in the plan of the convention, it will remain with the States, and the danger intimated must be merely ideal. The circumstances which are necessary to produce an alienation of State sovereignty were discussed in considering the article of taxation, and need not be repeated here. A recurrence to the principles there established will satisfy us, that there is no color to pretend that the State governments would, by the adoption of that plan, be divested of the privilege of paying their own debts in their own way, free from every constraint but that which flows from the obligations of good faith. The contracts between a nation and individuals are only binding on the conscience of the sovereign, and have no pretensions to a compulsive force. They confer no right of action, independent of the sovereign will. To what purpose would it be to authorize suits against States for the debts they owe? How could recoveries be enforced? It is evident, it could not be done without waging war against the contracting State; and to ascribe to the federal courts, by mere implication, and in destruction of a pre-existing right of the State governments, a power which would involve such a consequence, would be altogether forced and unwarrantable.

Let us resume the train of our observations. We have seen that the original jurisdiction of the Supreme Court would be confined to two classes of causes, and those of a nature rarely to occur. In all other cases of federal cognizance, the original jurisdiction would appertain to the inferior tribunals; and the Supreme Court would have nothing more than an appellate jurisdiction, "with such *exceptions* and under such *regulations* as the Congress shall make."

The propriety of this appellate jurisdiction has been scarcely called in question in regard to matters of law; but the clamors have been loud against it as applied to matters of fact. Some well-intentioned men in this State, deriving their notions from the language and forms which obtain in our courts, have been induced to consider it as an implied supersedure of the trial by jury, in favor of the civil-law mode of trial, which prevails in our courts of admiralty, probate, and chancery. A technical sense has been affixed to the term "appellate," which, in our law parlance, is commonly used in reference to appeals in the course of the civil law. But if I am not misinformed, the same meaning would not be given to it in any part of New England. There an appeal from one jury to another, is familiar both in language and practice, and is even a matter of course, until there have been two verdicts on one side. The word "appellate," therefore, will not be understood in the same sense in New England as in New York, which shows the impropriety of a technical interpretation derived from the jurisprudence of any particular State. The expression, taken in the abstract, denotes nothing more than the power of one tribunal to review the proceedings of another, either as to the law or fact, or both. The mode of doing it may depend on ancient custom or legislative provision (in a new government it must depend on the latter), and may be with or without the aid of a jury, as may be judged advisable. If, therefore, the reexamination of a fact once determined by a jury, should in any case be admitted under the proposed Constitution, it may be so regulated as to be done by a second jury, either by remanding the cause to the court below for a second trial of the fact, or by directing an issue immediately out of the Supreme Court.

But it does not follow that the reexamination of a fact once ascertained by a jury, will be permitted in the Supreme Court. Why may not it be said, with the strictest propriety, when a writ of error is brought from an inferior to a superior court of law in this State, that the latter has jurisdiction of the fact as well as the law? It is true it cannot institute a new inquiry concerning the fact, but it takes cognizance of it as it appears upon the record, and pronounces the law arising upon it.[2] This is jurisdiction of both fact and law; nor is it even possible to separate them. Though the common-law courts of this State ascertain disputed facts by a jury, yet the unquestionable have jurisdiction of both fact and law; and accordingly when the former is agreed in the pleadings, they have no recourse to a jury, but proceed at once to judgment. I contend, therefore, on this ground, that the expressions, "appellate jurisdiction, both as to law and fact," do not necessarily imply a reexamination in the Supreme Court of facts decided by juries in the inferior courts.

The following train of ideas may well be imagined to have influenced the convention, in relation to this particular provision. The appellate jurisdiction of the Supreme Court (it may have been argued) will extend to causes determinable in different modes, some in the course of the COMMON LAW, others in the course of the CIVIL LAW. In the former, the revision of the law only will be, generally speaking, the proper province of the Supreme Court; in the latter, the reexamination of the fact is agreeable to usage, and in some cases, of which prime causes are an example, might be essential to the preservation of the public peace. It is therefore necessary that the appellate jurisdiction should, in certain cases, extend in the broadest sense to matters of fact. It will not answer to make an express exception of cases which shall have been originally tried by a jury, because in the courts of some of the States *all causes* are tried in this mode[3]; and such an exception would preclude the revision of matters of fact, as well where it might be proper, as where it might be improper. To avoid all inconveniences, it will be safest to declare generally, that the Supreme Court shall possess appellate jurisdiction both as to law and *fact,* and that this jurisdiction shall be subject to such *exceptions* and regulations as the national legislature may prescribe. This will enable the government to modify it in such a manner as will best answer the ends of public justice and security.

This view of the matter, at any rate, puts it out of all doubt that the supposed *abolition* of the trial by jury, by the operation of this provision, is fallacious and untrue. The legislature of the United States would certainly have full power to provide, that in appeals to the Supreme Court there should be no reexamination of facts where they had been tried in the original causes by juries. This would certainly be an authorized exception; but if, for the reason already intimated, it should be thought too extensive, it might be qualified with a limitation to such causes only as are determinable at common law in that mode of trial.

The amount of the observations hitherto made on the authority of the judicial department is this: that it has been carefully restricted to those causes which are manifestly proper for the cognizance of the national judicature; that in the partition of this authority a very small portion of original jurisdiction has been preserved to the Supreme Court, and the rest consigned to the subordinate tribunals; that the Supreme Court will possess an appellate jurisdiction, both as to law and fact, in all cases referred to them, both subject to any *exceptions* and *regulations* which may be thought advisable; that this appellate jurisdiction does, in no case, *abolish* the trial by jury; and that an ordinary degree of prudence and integrity in the national councils will insure us solid advantages from the establishment of the proposed judiciary, without exposing us to any of the inconveniences which have been predicted from that source.

*PUBLIUS.*

## Notes

1. This power has been absurdly represented as intended to abolish all the county courts in the several States, which are commonly called inferior courts. But the expressions of the Constitution are to constitute "tribunals INFERIOR TO THE SUPREME COURT"; and the evident design of the provision is to enable the institution of local courts, subordinate to the Supreme, either in States or larger districts. It is ridiculous to imagine that county courts were in contemplation.—PUBLIUS

2. This word is composed of JUS and DICTIO, *juris dictio*, or a speaking and pronouncing of the law. —PUBLIUS

3. I hold that the States will have concurrent jurisdiction with the subordinate federal judicatories, in many cases of federal cognizance as will be explained in my next paper.—PUBLIUS

# THE CASE OF THE MISSING COMMISSIONS

*John A. Garraty*

## Marbury v. Madison, 1 Cranch 137

*Paradoxically, the first of our controversies and in some respects the most important rose from by far the least significant of cases and the meanest of motives. It is a tale of narrow partisanship, clashing ambitions, and a man seeking the humble office of justice of the peace for the District of Columbia.*

It was the evening of March 3, 1801, his last day in office, and President John Adams was in a black and bitter mood. Assailed by his enemies, betrayed by some of his most trusted friends, he and his Federalist party had gone down to defeat the previous November before the forces of Thomas Jefferson. His world seemed to have crumbled about his doughty shoulders.

Conservatives of Adams's persuasion were convinced that Thomas Jefferson was a dangerous radical. He would, they thought, in the name of individual liberty and states' rights import the worst excesses of the French Revolution, undermine the very foundations of American society, and bring the proud edifice of the national government, so laboriously erected under Washington and Adams, tumbling to the ground. Jefferson was a "visionary," Chief Justice Oliver Ellsworth had said. With him as President, "there would be no national energy." Secretary of State John Marshall, an ardent believer in a powerful central government, feared that Jefferson would "sap the fundamental principles of government." Others went so far as to call Jefferson a "howling atheist."

Adams himself was not quite so disturbed as some, but he was deeply troubled. "What course is it we steer?" he had written to an old friend after the election. "To what harbor are we bound?" Now on the morrow Jefferson was to be inaugurated, and Adams was so disgruntled that he was unwilling to remain for the ceremonies, the first to be held in the new capital on the Potomac. At the moment, however, John Adams was still President of the United States, and not about to abandon what he called "all virtuous exertion" in the pursuit of his duty. Sitting at his desk in the damp, drafty, still

"The Case of the Missing Commissions" from QUARRELS THAT HAVE SHAPED THE CONSTITUTION by John A. Garraty. Copyright @1987 by Harper & Row, Publishers, Inc. Reprinted by permission of Harper-Collins Publishers, Inc.

unfinished sandstone "palace" soon to be known as the White House, he was writing his name on official papers in his large, quavering hand.

The documents he was signing were mostly commissions appointing various staunch Federalists to positions in the national judiciary, but the President did not consider his actions routine. On the contrary: he believed he was saving the Republic itself. Jefferson was to be President and his Democratic Republicans would control Congress, but the courts, thank goodness, would be beyond his control. As soon as the extent of Jefferson's triumph was known, Adams had determined to make the judiciary a stronghold of Federalism. Responding enthusiastically to his request, the lame-duck Congress had established sixteen new circuit judgeships (and a host of marshals, attorneys, and clerks as well). It had also given the President authority to create as many justices of the peace for the new District of Columbia as he saw fit, and—to postpone the evil day when Jefferson would be able to put one of his sympathizers on the Supreme Court—it provided that when the next vacancy occurred it should not be filled, thus reducing the Court from six justices to five.[1]

In this same period between the election and Jefferson's inauguration, Chief Justice Ellsworth, who was old and feeble, had resigned, and Adams had replaced him with Secretary of State Marshall. John Marshall was primarily a soldier and politician; he knew relatively little of the law. But he had a powerful mind, and, as Adams reflected, his "reading of the science" was "fresh in his head." He was also but forty-five years of age, and vigorous. A more forceful opponent of Jeffersonian principles would have been hard to find.

Marshall had been confirmed by the Senate on January 27, and without resigning as secretary of state he had begun at once to help Adams strengthen the judicial branch of the government. Perforce they had worked rapidly, for time was short. The new courts were authorized by Congress on February 13; within two weeks Adams had submitted a full slate of officials for confirmation by the Senate. The new justices of the peace for the District of Columbia were authorized on February 27; within three days Adams had submitted for confirmation the names of no less than forty-two justices for that sparsely populated region. The Federalist Senate had done its part nobly too, pushing through the necessary confirmations with dispatch. Now, in the lamplight of his last night in Washington, John Adams was affixing his signature to the commissions appointing these "midnight justices" to office.

Working with his customary diligence, Adams completed his work by nine o'clock, and went off to bed for the last time as President of the United States, presumably with a clear conscience. The papers were carried to the State Department, where Secretary Marshall was to affix to each the Great Seal of the United States and see to it that the documents were then dispatched to the new appointees. But Marshall, a Virginian with something of the easygoing carelessness about detail that is said to be characteristic of Southerners, failed to complete this routine task. All the important new circuit judgeships were taken care of, and most of the other appointments as well. But in the bustle of last-minute arrangements, the commissions of the new District of Columbia justices of the peace went astray. As a result of this slipup, and entirely without anyone's having planned it, a fundamental principle of the Constitution—affecting the lives of countless millions of future Americans—was to be forever established. Because *Secretary of State* Marshall made his last mistake, *Chief Justice* Marshall was soon to make the first—and in some respects the greatest—of his decisions.

It is still not entirely clear what happened to the missing commissions on the night of March 3. To help with the rush of work, Adams had borrowed two State Department clerks, Jacob Wagner and Daniel Brent. Among his other tasks that fateful night, Brent prepared a list of the forty-two new justices and gave it to another clerk, who "filled up" the appropriate blank commissions. As fast as batches of these were made ready, Brent took them to Adams's office, where he turned them over to William Smith Shaw, the President's private secretary. After Adams had signed them, Brent brought them back to the State Department, where Marshall was supposed to attach the Great Seal. Evidently Marshall did seal these documents, but he did not trouble to make sure that they were delivered to the appointees. As he later said: "I did not send out the commissions because I apprehended such . . . to be completed when signed & sealed." He admitted that he would have sent them out in any case "but for the extreme hurry of the time & the absence of Mr. Wagner who had been called on by the President to act as his private secretary."

March 4 dawned and Jefferson, who does not seem to have digested the significance of Adams's partisan appointments at this time, prepared to take the oath of office and deliver his brilliant inaugural address. His mood, as the speech indicated, was friendly and conciliatory. He even asked Chief Justice Marshall, who administered the inaugural oath, to stay on briefly as secretary of state while the new administration was getting established.

That morning it would still have been possible to deliver the commissions. As a matter of fact, a few actually were delivered, although quite by chance. Marshall's brother James (whom Adams had just made circuit judge for the District of Columbia) was disturbed by rumors that there was going to be a riot in Alexandria in connection with the inaugural festivities. Feeling the need of some justices of the peace in case trouble developed, he went to the State Department and picked up a batch of the commissions. He signed a receipt for them, but "finding that he could not conveniently carry the whole," he returned several, crossing out the names of these from the receipt. Among the ones returned were those appointing William Harper and Robert Townshend Hooe. By failing to deliver these commissions, Judge James M. Marshall unknowingly enabled Harper and Hooe, obscure men, to win for themselves a small claim to legal immortality.

The new President was eager to mollify the Federalists, but when he realized the extent to which they had packed the judiciary with his "most ardent political enemies," he was indignant. Adams's behavior, he said at the time, was an "outrage on decency," and some years later, when passions had cooled a little, he wrote sorrowfully: "I can say with truth that one act of Mr. Adams' life, and only one, ever gave me a moment's personal displeasure. I did consider his last appointments to office as personally unkind." When he discovered the J.P. commissions in the State Department, he decided at once not to allow them to be delivered.

James Madison, the new secretary of state, was not yet in Washington. So Jefferson called in his attorney general, a Massachusetts lawyer named Levi Lincoln, whom he had designated acting secretary. Giving Lincoln a new list of justices of the peace, he told him to put them "Into a general commission" and notify the men of their selection.

In truth, Jefferson acted with remarkable forbearance. He reduced the number of justices to thirty, fifteen each for Washington and Alexandria counties. But only seven of his appointees were new men; the rest he chose from among the forty-two names originally submitted by Adams. (One of Jefferson's choices was Thomas Corcoran, father of W. W. Corcoran, the banker and philanthropist who founded the Corcoran Gallery of Art.) Lincoln prepared the general commissions, one for each county, and notified the appointees. Then, almost certainly, he destroyed the original commissions signed by Adams.

For some time thereafter Jefferson did very little about the way Adams had packed the judiciary. Indeed, despite his famous remark that officeholders seldom die and never resign, he dismissed relatively few persons from the government service. For example, the State Department clerks, Wagner and Brent, were permitted to keep their jobs. The new President learned quickly how hard it was to institute basic changes in a going organization. "The great machine of society" could not easily be moved, he admitted, adding that it was impossible "to advance the notions of a whole people suddenly to ideal right." Soon some of his more impatient supporters, like John Randolph of Roanoke, were grumbling about the President's moderation.

But Jefferson was merely biding his time. Within a month of the inauguration he conferred with Madison at Monticello and made the basic decision to try to abolish the new system of circuit courts. Aside from removing the newly appointed marshals and attorneys, who served at the pleasure of the chief executive, little could be done until the new Congress met in December. Then, however, he struck. In his annual message he urged the "contemplation" by Congress of the Judiciary Act of 1801. To direct the lawmakers' thinking, he submitted a statistical report showing how few cases the federal courts had been called upon to deal with since 1789. In January, 1802, a repeal bill was introduced; after long debate it passed early in March, thus abolishing the jobs of the new circuit judges.

Some of the deposed jurists petitioned Congress for "relief," but their plea was coldly rejected. Since these men had been appointed for life, the Federalists claimed that the Repeal Act was unconstitutional, but to prevent the Supreme Court from quickly so declaring, Congress passed another bill abolishing the June term of the Court and setting the second Monday of February, 1803, for its next session. By that time, the Jeffersonians reasoned, the old system would be dead beyond resurrection.

This assault on the courts thoroughly alarmed the conservative Federalists; to them the foundations of stable government seemed threatened if the "independence" of the judiciary could be thus destroyed. No one was more disturbed than the new Chief Justice, John Marshall, nor was anyone better equipped by temperament and intellect to resist it. Headstrong but shrewd, contemptuous of detail and of abstractions but a powerful logician, he detested Jefferson, to whom he was distantly related, and the President fully returned his dislike.

In the developing conflict Marshall operated at a disadvantage that a modern Chief Justice would not have to face. The Supreme Court had none of the prestige and little of the accepted authority it now possesses. Few cases had come before it, and none of much importance. A prominent newspaper of the day referred to the chief justiceship, with considerable truth, as a "sinecure." Before appointing Marshall, Adams had offered the chief justiceship to John Jay, the first man to hold the post. Jay had resigned from the Court in 1795 to become governor of New York. He refused reappointment, saying the Court lacked "energy, weight, and dignity." One of the reasons Marshall had accepted the post was his belief that it would afford him ample leisure for writing the biography of his hero, George Washington. Indeed, in the grandiose plans for the new capital, no thought had been given to housing the Supreme Court, so that when Marshall took office in 1801 the judges had to meet in the office of the clerk of the Senate, a small room on the first floor of what is now the North Wing of the Capitol.

Nevertheless, Marshall struck out at every opportunity against the power and authority of the new President. But the opportunities were few. In one case, he refused to allow a presidential message to be read into the record on the ground that this would bring the President into the Court in violation of the principle of separation of powers. In another, he ruled that Jefferson's action in a ship seizure case was illegal. But these were matters of small importance. When he tried to move more boldly, his colleagues would not sustain him. He was ready to declare the Judicial Repeal Act unconstitutional, but none of the deposed circuit court judges would bring a case to court.

Marshall also tried to persuade his associates that it was unconstitutional for Supreme Court Justices to ride the circuit, as they must again do since the lower courts had been abolished. But although they agreed with his legal reasoning, they refused to go along because, they said, years of acquiescence in the practice lent sanction to the law requiring it. Thus frustrated, Marshall was eager for any chance to attack his enemy, and when a case that was to be known as *Marbury* v. *Madison* came before the Court in December 1801, he took it up with gusto.

William Marbury, a forty-one-year-old Washingtonian, was one of the justices of the peace for the District of Columbia whose commissions Jefferson had held up. Originally from Annapolis, he had moved to Washington to work as an aide to the first secretary of the navy, Benjamin Stoddert. It was probably his service to this staunch Federalist that earned him the appointment by Adams. Together with one Dennis Ramsay and Messrs. Harper and Hooe, whose commissions James Marshall had *almost* delivered, Marbury was asking the Court to issue an order (a writ of mandamus) requiring Secretary of State Madison to hand over their "missing" commissions. Marshall willingly assumed jurisdiction and issued a rule calling upon Madison to show cause at the next term of the Supreme Court why such a writ should not be drawn. Clearly here was an opportunity to get at the President through one of his chief agents, to assert the authority of the Court over the executive branch of the government.

This small controversy quickly became a matter of great moment both to the administration and to Marshall. The decision to do away with the June term of the Court was made in part to give Madison more time before having to deal with Marshall's order. The abolition of the circuit courts and the postponement of the next Supreme Court session to February 1803 made Marshall even more determined to use the Marbury case to attack Jefferson. Of course, Marshall was embarrassingly involved in this case, since his carelessness was the cause of its very existence. He ought to have disqualified himself, but his fighting spirit was aroused, and he was in no mood to back out.

On the other hand, the Jeffersonians, eager to block any judicial investigation of executive affairs, used every conceivable mode of obstruction to prevent the case from being decided. Madison ignored Marshall's order. When Marbury and Ramsay called on the secretary to inquire whether their commissions had been duly signed (Hooe and Harper could count on the testimony of James Marshall to prove that theirs had been attended to), he gave them no satisfactory answer. When they asked to *see* the documents, Madison referred them to the clerk, Jacob Wagner. He, in turn, would only say that the commissions were not then in the State Department files.

Unless the plaintiffs could prove that Adams had appointed them their case would collapse. Frustrated at the State Department, they turned to the Senate for help. A friendly senator introduced a motion calling upon the secretary of the Senate to produce the record of the action in an executive session on their nominations. But the motion was defeated after an angry debate on January 31, 1803. Thus tempers were hot when the Court finally met on February 9 to deal with the case.

In addition to Marshall, only Justices Bushrod Washington and Samuel Chase were on the bench, and the chief justice dominated the proceedings. The almost childishly obstructive tactics of the administration witnesses were no match for his fair but forthright management of the hearing. The plaintiffs' lawyer was Charles Lee, an able advocate and brother of "Light-Horse Harry" Lee; he had served as attorney general under both Washington and Adams. He was a close friend of Marshall, and his dislike of Jefferson had been magnified by the repeal of the Judiciary Act of 1801, for he was another of the circuit court judges whose "midnight" appointments repeal had canceled.

Lee's task was to prove that the commissions had been completed by Adams and Marshall, and to demonstrate that the Court had authority to compel Madison to issue them. He summoned Wagner and Brent, and when they objected to being sworn in because "they were clerks in the Department of State, and not bound to disclose any facts relating to the business or transactions in the office," he argued that in addition to their "confidential" duties as agents of the President, the secretary and his deputies had duties "of a public nature" delegated to them by Congress. They must testify about these public matters, just as, in a suit involving property, a clerk in the land office could be compelled to state whether or not a particular land patent was on file.

Marshall agreed and ordered the clerks to testify. They then disclosed many of the details of what had gone on in the President's "palace" and in the State Department on the evening of March 3, 1801. But they claimed to be unsure of the fate of the particular commissions of the plaintiffs.

Next Lee called Attorney General Levi Lincoln. He too objected strenuously to testifying. He demanded that Lee submit his questions in writing so that he might consider carefully his obligations both to the Court and to the President before making up his mind. He also suggested that it might be necessary for him to exercise his constitutional right (under the Fifth Amendment) to refuse to give evidence that might "criminate" him. Lee then wrote out four questions. After studying them, Lincoln asked to be excused from answering, but the Justices ruled against him. Still hesitant, the attorney general asked for time to consider his position further, and Marshall agreed to an overnight adjournment.

The next day, the tenth of February, Lincoln offered to answer all of Lee's questions but the last: What had he done with the commissions? He had seen "a considerable number of commissions signed and sealed, but could not remember—he claimed—whether the plaintiffs' were among them. He did not know if Madison had ever seen these documents, but was certain that *he* had not given them to the Secretary. On the basis of this last statement, Marshall ruled that the embarrassing question as to what Lincoln had done with the commissions was irrelevant; he excused Lincoln from answering it.

Despite these reluctant witnesses, Lee was able to show conclusively through affidavits submitted by another clerk and by James Marshall that the commissions had been signed and sealed. In his closing argument he stressed the significance of the case as a test of the principle of judicial independence. "The emoluments or the dignity of the office," he said, "are no objects with the applicants." This was undoubtedly true; the positions were unimportant and two years of the five-year terms had already expired. As Jefferson later pointed out, the controversy itself had become "a moot case" by 1803. But Marshall saw it as a last-ditch fight against an administration campaign to make lackeys of all federal judges, while Jefferson looked at it as an attempt by the Federalist-dominated judiciary to usurp the power of the executive.

In this controversy over principle, Marshall and the Federalists were of necessity the aggressors. The administration boycotted the hearings. After Lee's summation, no government spokesman came forward to argue the other side, Attorney General Lincoln coldly announcing that he "had received no instructions to appear." With his control over Congress, Jefferson was content to wait for Marshall to act. If he overreached himself, the Chief Justice could be impeached. If he backed down, the already trifling prestige of his court would be further reduced.

Marshall had acted throughout with characteristic boldness; quite possibly it was he who had persuaded the four aggrieved justices of the peace to press their suit in the first place. But now his combative temperament seemed to have driven him too far. As he considered the Marbury case after the close of the hearings, he must have realized this himself, for he was indeed in a fearful predicament. However sound his logic and just his cause, he was on dangerous ground. Both political partisanship and his sense of justice prompted him to issue the writ sought by Marbury and his fellows, but what effect would the mandamus produce? Madison almost certainly would ignore it and Jefferson would back him up. No power but public opinion could make the Executive Department obey an order of the Court. Since Jefferson was riding the crest of a wave of popularity, to issue the writ would be an act of futile defiance; it might even trigger impeachment proceedings against Marshall that, if successful, would destroy him and reduce the Court to servility.

Yet what was the alternative? To find against the petitioners would be to abandon principle and surrender abjectly to Jefferson. This a man of Marshall's character simply could not consider. Either horn of the dilemma threatened disaster; that it was disaster of his own making could only make the Chief Justice's discomfiture the more complete.

But at some point between the close of the hearings on February 11 and the announcement of his decision on the twenty-fourth, Marshall found a way out. It was an inspired solution, surely the cleverest of his long career. It provided a perfect escape from the dilemma, which probably explains why he was able to persuade the associate justices to agree to it despite the fact that it was based on questionable legal logic. The issue, Marshall saw, involved a conflict between the Court and the President, the problem being how to check the President without exposing the Court to his might. Marshall's solution was to state vigorously the justice of the plaintiffs' cause and to condemn the action of the Executive, but to deny the Court's power to provide the plaintiffs with relief.

Marbury and his associates were legally entitled to their commissions, Marshall announced. In withholding them Madison was acting "in plain violation" of the law of the land. But the Supreme Court could not issue a writ of mandamus because the provision of the Judiciary Act of 1789 authorizing the Court to issue such writs was unconstitutional. In other words, Congress did not have the legal right to give that power to the Court!

So far as it concerned the Judiciary Act, modern commentators agree that Marshall's decision was based on a very weak argument. The Act of 1789 stated (section 13) that the Supreme Court could issue the writ to "persons holding office under the authority of the United States." This law had been framed by experts thoroughly familiar with the Constitution, including William Paterson, who now sat by Marshall's side on the Supreme Bench. The justices had issued the writ in earlier cases without questioning section 13 for a moment. But Marshall now claimed that the Court could not issue a mandamus except in cases that came to it on *appeal* from a lower court, since, under the Constitution, the Court was specifically granted original jurisdiction only over "cases affecting ambassadors, other public ministers and consuls, and those in which a state shall be a party." The Marbury case had *originated* in the Supreme Court; since it did not involve a diplomat or a state, any law that gave the Court the right to decide it was unauthorized.

This was shaky reasoning because the Constitution does not say the Court may exercise original jurisdiction *only* in such cases. But Marshall was on solid ground when he went on to argue that "the constitution controls any legislative act repugnant to it," which he called "one of the fundamental principles of our society." The Constitution is "the *supreme* law of the land," he emphasized. Since it is "the duty of the judicial department to say what the law is," the Supreme Court must overturn any law of Congress that violates the Constitution. "A law repugnant to the constitution," he concluded, "is void." By this reasoning section 13 of the Act of 1789 simply ceased to exist and without it the Court could not issue the writ of mandamus. By thus denying himself authority, Marshall found the means to flay his enemies without exposing himself to their wrath.

Although this was the first time the Court had declared an act of Congress unconstitutional, its right to do so had not been seriously challenged by most authorities. Even Jefferson accepted the principle, claiming only that the executive as well as the judiciary could decide questions of constitutionality. Jefferson was furious over what he called the "twistifications" of Marshall's gratuitous opinion in *Marbury* v. *Madison,* but his anger was directed at the Chief Justice's stinging criticisms of his behavior, not at the constitutional doctrine Marshall had enunciated.

Even in 1803, the idea of judicial review had had a long history in America. The concept of natural law (the belief that certain principles of right and justice transcend the laws of mere men) was thoroughly established in American thinking. It is seen, for example, in Jefferson's statement in the Declaration of Independence that men "are endowed by their Creator" with "unalienable" rights. Although not a direct precedent for Marshall's decision, the colonial practice of "disallowance," whereby laws had been ruled void on the ground that local legislatures had exceeded their powers in passing them, illustrates the belief that there is a limit to legislative power and that courts may determine when it has been overstepped.

More specifically, Lord Coke had declared early in the seventeenth century that "the common law will controul acts of Parliament." One of the chief legal apologists of the American Revolution, James Otis, had drawn upon this argument a century and a half later in his famous denunciation of the Writs of Assistance. In the 1780s courts in New Jersey, New York, Rhode Island, and North Carolina had exercised judicial review over the acts of state legislatures. The debates at the Constitutional Convention and some of the *Federalist Papers* (especially No. 78) indicated that most of the Founding Fathers accepted the idea of judicial review as already established. The Supreme Court, in fact, had considered the constitutionality of an act of Congress before—when it upheld a federal tax law in 1796—and it had encountered little questioning of its right to do so. All these precedents, when taken together with the fact that the section of the Act of 1789 nullified by Marshall's decision was of minor importance, explain why no one paid much attention to this part of the decision.

Thus the "case of the missing commissions" passed into history, seemingly a fracas of slight significance. When it was over, Marbury and his frustrated colleagues disappeared into the obscurity whence they had arisen.[2] In the partisan struggle for power between Marshall and Jefferson, the incident was of secondary importance. The real showdown came later in the impeachment proceedings against Justice Chase and the treason trial of Aaron Burr. In the long run, Marshall won his fight to preserve the independence and integrity of the federal judiciary, but generally speaking, the Courts have not been able to exert much influence over the appointive and dismissal powers of the President. Even the enunciation of the Court's power to void acts of Congress wrought no immediate change in American life. Indeed, more than half a century passed before another federal law was overturned.

Nevertheless, this squabble over some small political plums was of vital importance. For with the expansion of the federal government into new areas of activity in more recent times, the power of the Supreme Court to nullify acts of Congress has been repeatedly employed, with profound effects upon our social, economic, and political life. At various times income tax, child labor, wage and hours laws, and many other types of legislation have been thrown out by the Court, and always, in the last analysis, its right to do so has depended upon the decision John Marshall made to escape from a dilemma of his own making. The irony is that in 1803 no one—not even the great Chief Justice himself—realized how tremendously significant the case of the missing commissions would one day become.

## Notes

1.  The Constitution says nothing about the number of Justices on the Court; its size is left to Congress. Originally six, the membership was enlarged to seven in 1807, and to nine in 1837. Briefly during the Civil War the bench held ten; the number was set at seven again in 1867 and in 1869 returned to nine, where it has remained.

2.  Marbury became president of a Georgetown bank in 1814 and died in 1835.

# MARBURY v. MADISON, (1803): A CHRONOLOGY

## Adapted from Burton, "Marbury v. Madison: The Cornerstone of Constitutional Law," in Choper, *The Supreme Court and Its Justices.*

1789: First Judiciary Act passed. Sec. 13 gave the Supreme Court original jurisdiction in mandamus cases.

1800: Presidential Election—conducted in accordance with Art. II, Sec. 1—replaced by the 12th Amendment in 1804.

|  |  | *Electoral Votes* |
|---|---|---|
| FEDERALISTS: | President Adams (Incumbent) | 65 |
|  | Pinckney | 64 |
| ANTI-FEDERALISTS: | Jefferson | 73 |
|  | Burr | 73 |
|  | Jay | 1 |

Feb. 17, 1801: On the 36th ballot, the House of Representatives (with each state casting one vote) elected Jefferson as President.

Jan. 20, 1801: Adams appointed John Marshall (his Secretary of State) to the Chief Justiceship of the Supreme Court. He replaced C. J. Ellsworth who resigned to become minister to France. (John Jay, who had been the first Chief Justice, declined reappointment. Marshall joined 5 other Federalists on the Supreme Court: Cushing, Paterson, Chase (all appointed by G. Washington) and Bushrod and Moore (appointed by Adams.)

Jan 27, 1801: John Marshall confirmed as Chief Justice by the Senate.

Feb. 2, 1801: Supreme Court met in Washington for the first time.

Feb. 4, 1801: John Marshall assumed duties of Chief Justice, while still serving, without salary, as Secretary of State.

Feb. 13, 1801: Congress passed the Circuit Court Bill creating 16 new judgeships to staff the Circuit Courts (replaced S. Ct. Justices who had been 'riding circuit' to sit on the Circuit Courts)

Feb. 27, 1801: Congress passed the District of Columbia Organic Act. Provided for 42 new justices of the peace to be appointed by President Adams for 5 year terms to serve in Washington and Alexandria. Also, reduced the number of Supreme Court Justices from 6 to 5 at the next retirement.

March 2, 1801: 16 Federalists circuit judges confirmed by the Senate.

March 3, 1801: the 42 justices of the peace appointed by the President were confirmed by the Senate. The commissions were signed by President Adams and sealed by Sec. of State John Marshall. His brother, James Marshall, delivered some of the commissions, but not Marbury's.

March 4, 1801: John Marshall, as Chief Justice, swore Jefferson in as President of the United States.

Jefferson appointed James Madison as Secretary of State.

Dec. 1801: The Supreme Court met. The Marbury litigation started. The Supreme Court ordered Jefferson's Sec. of State, James Madison to show cause as to why a writ of mandamus should not issue on the 4th day of the next term. The Court expected that the next term would be in June 1802.

> Congress, with the obvious purpose of preventing the Supreme Court from deciding this case so soon, abolished the June Term of the Supreme Court and prescribed Annual Terms meeting in February.

Jan 6. 1802: Senator Breckenridge of Kentucky (an Anti-Federalist) introduced a bill repealing the Circuit Court Act of 1801 and abolishing the 16 new judgeships Adams had filled with Federalists.

March 31, 1802: Repeal of the Circuit Court Act of 1801 became law. Passed the Senate 16–15 and the House 59–32. The Circuit Court judges protested to Congress. The Anti-Federalists knew that the Supreme Court might declare the repealer unconstitutional; but, in fact, the Supreme Court Justices acquiesced and resumed their Circuit Court duties. [Indeed, the Supreme Court Justices were not relieved of Circuit Court duty until the 1890s].

Feb. 24, 1803: *Marbury* v. *Madison* was heard and decided. Justices Cushing and Moore did not participate. The Court consisted of Marshall, Paterson, Chase and Washington.

> Size of Supreme Court:
> originally six members;
> 1807 enlarged to seven;
> 1837 to nine;
> briefly during the Civil War—ten;
> 1867—seven;
> 1869 to the present—nine members of the Supreme Court.

March 1803: week after Marbury, the Supreme Court decided *Stuart* v. *Laird*, 1 Cranch 299 which upheld the constitutionality of the 1802 repealer of the Circuit Court Act of 1801.

Feb. 4, 1805: House of Representatives voted a bill of impeachment against Justice Samuel Chase—the charges were largely related to his conduct on the Circuit Court.

March 1, 1805: Majority of the Senate acquitted Chase on 5 of 8 counts and failed to get 2/3rds on the other 3 counts.

# William Marbury v. James Madison

I Cranch 137
February, 1803

At the last term, viz. December term, 1801, William Marbury, Dennis Ramsay, Robert Townsend Hooe, and William Harper, by their counsel, Charles Lee, esq. late attorney general of the United States, severally moved the court for a rule to James Madison, secretary of state of the United States, to show cause why a mandamus should not issue commanding him to cause to be delivered to them respectively their several commissions as justices of the peace in the district of Columbia. This motion was supported by affidavits of the following facts; that notice of this motion had been given to Mr. Madison; that Mr. Adams, the late president of the United States, nominated the applicants to the senate for their advice and consent to be appointed justices of the peace of the district of Columbia; that the senate advised and consented to the appointments; that commissions in due form were signed by the said president appointing them justices, etc. and that the seal of the United States was in due form affixed to the said commissions by the secretary of state; that the applicants have requested Mr. Madison to deliver them their said commissions, who has not complied with that request; and that their said commissions are withheld from them; that the applicants have made application to Mr. Madison as secretary of state of the United States at his office, for information whether the commissions were signed, and sealed as aforesaid; that explicit and satisfactory information has not been given in answer to that enquiry, either by the secretary of state or any officer in the department of state; that application has been made to the secretary of the Senate for a certificate of the nomination of the applicants, and of the advice and consent of the senate, who has declined giving such a certificate; whereupon a rule was laid to show cause on the 4th day of this term. This rule having been duly served, . . .

Afterwards on the 24th of February the following opinion of the court was delivered by the Chief Justice.

MR. CHIEF JUSTICE MARSHALL delivered the opinion of the Court.

At the last term on the affidavits then read and filed with the clerk, a rule was granted in this case, requiring the secretary of state to show cause why a mandamus should not issue, directing him to deliver to William Marbury his commission as a justice of the peace for the county of Washington in the district of Columbia.

No cause has been shown, and the present motion is for a mandamus. The peculiar delicacy of the case, the novelty of some of its circumstances, and the real difficulty attending the points which occur in it, require a complete exposition of the principles, on which the opinion to be given by the court, is founded. . . .

In the order in which the court has viewed this subject, the following questions have been considered and decided.

**1st.** Has the applicant a right to the commission he demands?

**2ndly**. If he has a right, and that right has been violated, do the laws of his country afford him a remedy?

**3rdly.** If they do afford him a remedy, is it a *mandamus* issuing from this court?

The first object of enquiry is,

**1st.** Has the applicant a right to the commission he demands?

His right originates in an act of congress passed in February 1801, concerning the district of Columbia.

After dividing the district into two counties, the 11th section of this law, enacts, "that there shall be appointed in and for each of the said counties, such number of discreet persons to be justices of the peace as the president of the United States shall, from time to time, think expedient, to continue in office for five years."

It appears, from the affidavits, that in compliance with this law, a commission for William Marbury as a justice of peace for the county of Washington, was signed by John Adams, then president of the United States; after which the seal of the United States was affixed to it; but the commission has never reached the person for whom it was made out.

In order to determine whether he is entitled to this commission, it becomes necessary to enquire whether he has been appointed to the office. For if he has been appointed, the law continues him in office for five years, and he is entitled to the possession of those evidences of office, which, being completed, became his property. . . .

Some point of time must be taken when the power of the executive over an officer, not removeable at his will, must cease. That point of time must be when the constitutional power of appointment has been exercised. And this power has been exercised when the last act, required from the person possessing the power, has been performed. This last act is the signature of the commission. . . .

The signature, which gives force and effect to the commission, is conclusive evidence that the appointment is made.

The commission being signed, the subsequent duty of the secretary of state is prescribed by law, and not to be guided by the will of the President. He is to affix the seal of the United States to the commission, and is to record it.

This is not a proceeding which may be varied, if the judgment of the executive shall suggest one more eligible; but is a precise course accurately marked out by law and is to be strictly pursued. It is the duty of the secretary of state to conform to the law, and in this he is an officer of the United States, bound to obey the laws. He acts in this respect, as has been very properly stated at the bar, under the authority of law, and not by the instructions of the President. It is a ministerial act which the law enjoins on a particular officer for a particular purpose. . . .

It is therefore decidedly the opinion of the court, that when a commission has been signed by the President, the appointment is made; and that the commission is complete, when the seal of the United States has been affixed to it by the secretary of state. . . .

Mr. Marbury, then, since his commission was signed by the President, and sealed by the secretary of state, was appointed; and as the law creating the office, gave the officer a right to hold for five years, independent of the executive, the appointment was not revocable; but vested in the officer legal rights, which are protected by the laws of his country.

To withhold his commission, therefore, is an act deemed by the court not warranted by law, but violative of a vested legal right.

This brings us to the second enquiry; which is,

**2ndly.** If he has a right, and that right has been violated, do the laws of his country afford him a remedy?

The very essence of civil liberty certainly consists in the right of every individual to claim the protection of the laws, whenever he receives an injury. One of the first duties of government is to afford that protection. In Great Britain the king himself is sued in the respectful form of a petition, and he never fails to comply with the judgment of his court. . . .

The government of the United States has been emphatically termed a government of laws, and not of men. It will certainly cease to deserve this high appellation, if the laws furnish no remedy for the violation of a vested legal right. . . .

It is then the opinion of the court,

**1st.** That by signing the commission of Mr. Marbury, the president of the United States appointed him a justice of peace, for the county of Washington in the district of Columbia; and that the seal of the United States affixed thereto by the secretary of state, is conclusive testimony of the verity of the signature, and of the completion of the appointment; and that the appointment conferred on him a legal right to the office for the space of five years.

**2ndly.** That, having this legal title to the office, he has a consequent right to the commission; a refusal to deliver which, is a plain violation of that right, for which the laws of his country afford him a remedy.

It remains to be enquired whether,

**3rdly.** He is entitled to the remedy for which he applies.

This depends on,

**1st.** The nature of the writ applied for, and,

**2ndly.** The power of this court.

**1st.** The nature of the writ.

Blackstone, in the 3d volume of his commentaries, page 110, defines a mandamus to be, "a command issuing in the king's name from the court of king's bench, and directed to any person, corporation, or inferior court of judicature within the king's dominions, requiring them to do some particular thing therein specified, which appertains to their office and duty, and which the court of king's bench has previously determined, or at least supposes, to be consonant to right and justice." . . .

This writ, if awarded, would be directed to an officer of government, and its mandate to him would be, to use the words of Blackstone, "to do a particular thing therein specified, which appertains to his office and duty and which the court has previously determined, or at least supposes, to be consonant to right and justice." Or, in the words of Lord Mansfield, the applicant, in this case, has a right to execute an office of public concern, and is kept out of possession of that right.

These circumstances certainly concur in this case.

Still, to render the mandamus a proper remedy, the officer to whom it is to be directed, must be one to whom, on legal principles, such writ may be directed; and the person applying for it must be without any other specific and legal remedy.

**1st.** With respect to the officer to whom it would be directed. The intimate political relation, subsisting between the president of the United States and the heads of departments, necessarily renders any legal investigation of the acts of one of those high officers peculiarly irksome, as well as delicate; and excites some hesitation with respect to the propriety of entering into such investigation. Impressions are often received without much reflection or examination, and it is not wonderful that, in such a case as this, the assertion, by an individual, of his legal claims in a court of justice; to which claims it is the duty of that court to attend; should at first view be considered by some, as an attempt to intrude into the cabinet, and to intermeddle with the prerogatives of the executive.

It is scarcely necessary for the court to disclaim all pretensions to such a jurisdiction. An extravagance, so absurd and excessive, could not have been entertained for a moment. The province of the court is, solely, to decide on the rights of individuals, not to enquire how the executive, or executive officers, perform duties in which they have a discretion. Questions, in their nature political, or which are, by the constitution and laws, submitted to the executive, can never be made in this court. . . .

If one of the heads of departments commits any illegal act, under color of his office, by which an individual sustains an injury, it cannot be pretended that his office alone exempts him from being sued in the ordinary mode of proceeding, and being compelled to obey the judgment of the law. How then can his office exempt him from this particular mode of deciding on the legality of his conduct, if the case be such a case as would, were any other individual the party complained of, authorize the process?

It is not by the office of the person to whom the writ is directed, but the nature of the thing to be done that the propriety or impropriety of issuing a mandamus, is to be determined. Where the head of a department acts in a case, in which executive discretion is to be exercised; in which he is the mere organ of executive will; it is again repeated, that any application to a court to control, in any respect, his conduct, would be rejected without hesitation.

But where he is directed by law to do a certain act affecting the absolute rights of individuals, in the performance of which he is not placed under the particular direction of the President, and the performance of which, the President cannot lawfully forbid, and therefore is never presumed to have forbidden; as for example, to record a commission, or a patent for land, which has received all the legal solemnities; or to give a copy of such record; in such cases, it is not perceived on what ground the courts of the country are further excused from the duty of giving judgment, that right be done to an injured individual, than if the same services were to be performed by a person not the head of a department. . . .

It is true that the mandamus, now moved for, is not for the performance of an act expressly enjoined by statute.

It is to deliver a commission; on which subject the acts of Congress are silent. This difference is not considered as affecting the case. It has already been stated that the applicant has, to that commission, a vested legal right, of which the executive cannot deprive him. He has been appointed to an office, from which he is not removable at the will of the executive; and being so appointed, he has a right to the commission which the secretary has received from the president for his use. The act of congress does not indeed order the secretary of state to send it to him, but it is placed in his hands for the person entitled to it; and cannot be more lawfully withheld by him, than by any other person.

This, then, is a plain case for a mandamus, either to deliver the commission, or a copy of it from the record; and it only remains to be enquired,

Whether it can issue from this court.

The act to establish the judicial courts of the United States authorizes the Supreme Court "to issue writs of mandamus, in cases warranted by the principles and usages of law, to any courts appointed, or persons holding office, under the authority of the United States."

The secretary of state, being a person holding an office under the authority of the United States, is precisely within the letter of the description; and if this court is not authorized to issue a writ of mandamus to such an officer, it must be because the law is unconstitutional, and therefore absolutely incapable of conferring the authority, and assigning the duties which its words purport to confer and assign.

The constitution vests the whole judicial power of the United States in one supreme court, and such inferior courts as congress shall, from time to time, ordain and establish. This power is expressly extended to all cases arising under the laws of the United States; and consequently, in some form, may be exercised over the present case; because the right claimed is given by a law of the United States.

In the distribution of this power it is declared that "the supreme court shall have original jurisdiction in all cases affecting ambassadors, other public ministers and consuls, and those in which a state shall be a party. In all other cases, the supreme court shall have appellate jurisdiction."

It has been insisted, at the bar, that as the original grant of jurisdiction, to the supreme and inferior courts, is general, and the clause, assigning original jurisdiction to the supreme court, contains no negative or restrictive words; the power remains to the legislature, to assign original jurisdiction to that court in other cases than those specified in the article which has been recited; provided those cases belong to the judicial power of the United States.

If it had been intended to leave it in the discretion of the legislature to apportion the judicial power between the supreme and inferior courts according to the will of that body, it would certainly have been useless to have proceeded further than to have defined the judicial power, and the tribunals in which it should be vested. The subsequent part of the section is mere surplussage, is entirely without meaning, if such is to be the construction. If congress remains at liberty to give this court appellate jurisdiction, where the constitution has declared their jurisdiction shall be original; and original jurisdiction where the constitution has declared it shall be appellate; the distribution of jurisdiction, made in the constitution, is form without substance.

Affirmative words are often, in their operation, negative of other objects than those affirmed; and in this case, a negative or exclusive sense must be given to them or they have no operation at all.

It cannot be presumed that any clause in the constitution is intended to be without effect; and therefore such a construction is inadmissible, unless the words require it.

If the solicitude of the convention, respecting our peace with foreign powers, induced a provision that the supreme court should take original jurisdiction in cases which might be supposed to affect them; yet the clause would have proceeded no further than to provide for such cases, if no further restriction on the powers of congress had been intended. That they should have appellate jurisdiction in all other cases, with such exceptions as congress might make, is no restriction; unless the words be deemed exclusive of original jurisdiction.

When an instrument organizing fundamentally a judicial system, divides it into one supreme, and so many inferior courts as the legislature may ordain and establish; then enumerates its powers, and proceeds so far to distribute them, as to define the jurisdiction of the supreme court by declaring the cases in which it shall take appellate jurisdiction; the plain import of the words seems to be, that in one class of cases its jurisdiction is original, and not appellate; in the other it is appellate, and not original. If any other construction would render the clause inoperative, that is an additional reason for rejecting such other construction, and for adhering to their obvious meaning.

To enable this court then to issue a mandamus, it must be shown to be an exercise of appellate jurisdiction, or to be necessary to enable them to exercise appellate jurisdiction.

It has been stated at the bar that the appellate jurisdiction may be exercised in a variety of forms, and that if it be the will of the legislature that a mandamus should be used for that purpose, that will must be obeyed. This is true, yet the jurisdiction must be appellate, not original.

It is the essential criterion of appellate jurisdiction, that it revises and corrects the proceedings in a cause already instituted, and does not create that cause. Although, therefore, a mandamus may be directed to courts, yet to issue such a writ to an officer for the delivery of a paper, is in effect the same as to sustain an original action for that paper, and therefore seems not to belong to appellate, but to original jurisdiction. Neither is it necessary in such a case as this, to enable the court to exercise its appellate jurisdiction.

The authority, therefore, given to the supreme court, by the act establishing the judicial courts of the United States, to issue writs of mandamus to public officers, appears not to be warranted by the constitution; and it becomes necessary to enquire whether a jurisdiction, so conferred can be exercised.

The question, whether an act, repugnant to the constitution, can become the law of the land, is a question deeply interesting to the United States; but, happily, not of an intricacy proportioned to its interest. It seems only necessary to recognise certain principles, supposed to have been long and well established, to decide it.

That the people have an original right to establish, for their future government, such principles as, in their opinion, shall most conduce to their own happiness, is the basis, on which the whole American fabric has been erected. The exercise of this original right is a very great exertion; nor can it, nor ought it to be frequently repeated. The principles, therefore, so established, are deemed fundamental. And as the authority, from which they proceed, is supreme, and can seldom act, they are designed to be permanent.

This original and supreme will organizes the government, and assigns, to different departments, their respective powers. It may either stop here; or establish certain limits not to be transcended by those departments.

The government of the United States is of the latter description. The powers of the legislature are defined, and limited; and that those limits may not be mistaken, or forgotten, the constitution is written. To what purpose are powers limited, and to what purpose is that limitation committed to writing, if these limits may, at any time, be passed by those intended to be restrained? The distinction, between a government with limited and unlimited powers, is abolished, if those limits do not confine the persons on whom they are imposed, and if acts prohibited and acts allowed, are of equal obligation. It is a proposition too plain to be contested, that the constitution controls any legislative act repugnant to it; or that the legislature may alter the constitution by an ordinary act.

Between these alternatives there is no middle ground. The constitution is either a superior, paramount law, unchangeable by ordinary means, or it is on a level with ordinary legislative acts, and like other acts, is alterable when the legislature shall please to alter it.

If the former part of the alternative be true, then a legislative act contrary to the constitution is not law: if the latter part be true, then written constitutions are absurd attempts on the part of the people, to limit a power, in its own nature illimitable.

Certainly all those who have framed written constitutions contemplate them as forming the fundamental and paramount law of the nation, and consequently the theory of every such government must be, that an act of the legislature, repugnant to the constitution, is void.

This theory is essentially attached to a written constitution, and is consequently to be considered, by this court, as one of the fundamental principles of our society. It is not therefore to be lost sight of in the further consideration of this subject.

If an act of the legislature, repugnant to the constitution, is void, does it, notwithstanding its invalidity, bind the courts, and oblige them to give it effect? Or, in other words, though it be not law, does it constitute a rule as operative as if it was a law? This would be to overthrow in fact what was established in theory; and would seem, at first view, an absurdity too gross to be insisted on. It shall, however, receive a more attentive consideration.

It is emphatically the province and duty of the judicial department to say what the law is. Those who apply the rule to particular cases, must of necessity expound and interpret that rule. If two laws conflict with each other, the courts must decide on the operation of each.

So if a law be in opposition to the constitution; if both the law and the constitution apply to a particular case, so that the court must either decide that case conformably to the law, disregarding the constitution; or conformably to the constitution, disregarding the law; the court must determine which of these conflicting rules governs the case. This is of the very essence of judicial duty.

If then the courts are to regard the constitution; and the constitution is superior to any ordinary act of the legislature; the constitution, and not such ordinary act, must govern the case to which they both apply.

Those then who controvert the principle that the constitution is to be considered, in court, as a paramount law, are reduced to the necessity of maintaining that courts must close their eyes on the constitution, and see only the law.

This doctrine would subvert the very foundation of all written constitutions. It would declare that an act, which, according to the principles and theory of our government, is entirely void; is yet, in practice, completely obligatory. It would declare, that if the legislature shall do what is expressly forbidden, such act, notwithstanding the express prohibition, is in reality effectual. It would be giving to the legislature a practical and real omnipotence, with the same breath which professes to restrict their powers within narrow limits. It is prescribing limits, and declaring that those limits may be passed at pleasure.

That it reduces to nothing what we have deemed the greatest improvement on political institutions—a written constitution—would of itself be sufficient, in America, where written constitutions have been viewed with so much reverence, for rejecting the construction. But the peculiar expressions of the constitution of the United States furnish additional arguments in favour of its rejection.

The judicial power of the United States is extended to all cases arising under the constitution.

Could it be the intention of those who gave this power, to say that, in using it, the constitution should not be looked into? That a case arising under the constitution should be decided without examining the instrument under which it arises?

This is too extravagant to be maintained.

In some cases then, the constitution must be looked into by the judges. And if they can open it at all, what part of it are they forbidden to read, or to obey?

There are many other parts of the constitution which serve to illustrate this subject.

It is declared that "no tax or duty shall be laid on articles exported from any state." Suppose a duty on the export of cotton, of tobacco, or of flour; and a suit instituted to recover it. Ought judgment to be rendered in such a case? ought the judges to close their eyes on the constitution, and only see the law.

The constitution declares that "no bill of attainder or *ex-post-facto* law shall be passed."

If, however, such a bill should be passed and a person should be prosecuted under it; must the court condemn to death those victims whom the constitution endeavours to preserve?

"No person," says the constitution, "shall be convicted of treason unless on the testimony of two witnesses to the same overt act, or on confession in open court."

Here the language of the constitution is addressed especially to the courts. It prescribes, directly for them, a rule of evidence not to be departed from. If the legislature should change that rule, and declare one witness, or a confession out of court, sufficient for conviction, must the constitutional principle yield to the legislative act?

From these, and many other selections which might be made, it is apparent, that the framers of the constitution contemplated that instrument, as a rule for the government of courts, as well as of the legislature.

Why otherwise does it direct the judges to take an oath to support it? This oath certainly applies, in an especial manner, to their conduct in their official character. How immoral to impose it on them, if they were to be used as the instruments, and the knowing instruments, for violating what they swear to support!

The oath of office, too, imposed by the legislature, is completely demonstrative of the legislative opinion on this subject. It is in these words, "I do solemnly swear that I will administer justice without respect to persons, and do equal right to the poor and to the rich; and that I will faithfully and impartially discharge all the duties incumbent on me as . . . according to the best of my abilities and understanding, agreeably to *the constitution,* and laws of the United States."

Why does a judge swear to discharge his duties agreeably to the constitution of the United States, if that constitution forms no rule for his government? if it is closed upon him, and cannot be inspected by him?

If such be the real state of things, this is worse than solemn mockery. To prescribe, or to take this oath, becomes equally a crime.

It is also not entirely unworthy of observation, that in declaring what shall be the Supreme law of the land, the constitution itself is first mentioned; and not the laws of the United States generally, but those only which shall be made in pursuance of the constitution, have that rank.

Thus, the particular phraseology of the constitution of the United States confirms and strengthens the principle, supposed to be essential to all written constitutions, that a law repugnant to the constitution is void; and that *courts,* as well as other departments, are bound by that instrument.

The rule must be discharged.

---

**Marbury v. Madison**, 1 Cranch 137 (1803) 6–0
*editor's note.*
*Opinion authors are in bold; () indicates the party of appointing president. If the party of the justice differs from that of appointing president, then the party of the justice is listed second after the slash.*

| MAJORITY | CONCURRING | DISSENTING |
|---|---|---|
| **Marshall** (federalist) | | |
| Cushing (federalist) | | |
| Paterson (federalist | | |
| Chase (federalist) | | |
| Washington (federalist) | | |
| Moore (federalist) | | |

# McCulloch v. Maryland

## 4 Wheat. 316 (1819)

## BACKGROUND

In 1791, Congress chartered the First Bank of the United States after a full and bitter argument as to whether it had the power to do so. Nevertheless, the First Bank was never attacked in the courts as being unconstitutional and its charter expired in 1811. In 1816 the Second Bank of the United States was chartered. There was much opposition to the Bank, especially in the western and southern sections of the country. After several financial disasters were wrongly attributed to the national Bank; eight states passed statutes or constitutional amendments restricting the "activities of the Bank or imposing heavy burdens on it. The Maryland law at issue in this case was typical of the legislation passed by these eight states.

The Maryland statute forbade all banks not chartered by the state itself to issue bank notes save upon special stamped paper obtainable upon the payment of a very heavy tax. This requirement could be commuted by the payment of an annual tax to the state of $15,000. A penalty of $500 forfeiture was inflicted for each offense, an amount which in the case of the Baltimore branch of the Bank of the United States could have amounted to millions of dollars. McCulloch, the cashier (i.e. chief officer) of the national Bank branch in Baltimore, issued notes without complying with the state law, and this case was brought on behalf of the state of Maryland to recover the penalties. In the Maryland trial court, the case was decided against McCulloch and that decision was affirmed by the Maryland Court of Appeals.

The decision in this case was extremely controversial. Judge Roane of the Virginia court of appeals published a series of newspaper attacks upon the decision so bitter that Marshall was led to write a reply in his defense. (This exchange has been compiled and published as a book: Gerald Gunther, ed. John Marshall's Defense of *McCulloch* v. *Maryland* (Stanford: Stanford University Press, 1969)). The Virginia legislature passed a resolution urging that the Supreme Court be stripped of its power to pass upon cases to which states were parties. Ohio, which had previously passed a law taxing each branch of the Bank of the United States within its limits $50,000 a year, defied the Supreme Court and proceeded to collect the tax in spite of its decision. See *Osborn* v. *Bank of the United States,* 9 Wheat. 738 (1824). The attack on upon the Court in this case was directed in large part against the failure of the Court to invalidate the Act of Congress incorporating the Bank and not against the exercise of the judicial veto in declaring the state law unconstitutional. The decision was particularly offensive to the strict constructionists because it not only sustained the doctrine of implied powers of Congress, but it also recognized the binding effect of an implied limitation upon the states preventing them from interfering with the functioning of federal agencies.

In 1832 then President Jackson vetoed the recharter of the second national Bank and in 1836 the Bank went out of existence. (Adapted from Robert F. Cushman, *Cases in Constitutional Law* 4th edition (Englewood Cliffs, NJ. Prentice Hall, Inc., 1975).)

MR. CHIEF JUSTICE MARSHALL delivered the opinion of the Court.

In the case now to be determined, the defendant, a sovereign state, denies the obligation of a law enacted by the legislature of the Union, and the plaintiff, on his part, contests the validity of an act which has been passed by the legislature of that state. The constitution of our country, in its most interesting and vital parts, is to be considered; the conflicting powers of the government of the Union and of its members, as marked in that constitution, are to be discussed; and an opinion given, which may essentially influence the great operations of the government. No tribunal can approach such a question without a deep sense of its importance, and of the awful responsibility involved in its decision. But it must be decided peacefully, or remain a source of hostile legislation, perhaps of hostility of a still more serious nature; and if it is to be so decided, by this tribunal alone can the decision be made. On the Supreme Court of the United States has the constitution of our country devolved this important duty.

1. The first question made in the cause is, has Congress Power to incorporate a bank?

It has been truly said that this can scarcely be considered as an open question, entirely unprejudiced by the former proceedings of the nation respecting it. The principle now contested was introduced at a very early period of our history, has been recognized by many successive legislatures, and has been acted upon by the judicial department, in cases of peculiar delicacy, as a law of undoubted obligation. [The] power now contested was exercised by the first Congress elected under the present constitution. The bill for incorporating the bank of the United States did not steal upon an unsuspecting legislature, and pass unobserved. Its principle was completely understood, and was opposed with equal zeal and ability. After being resisted, first in the fair and open field of debate, and afterwards in the executive cabinet, with as much persevering talent as any measure has ever experienced, and being supported by arguments which convinced minds as pure and as intelligent as this country can boast, it became a law. The original act was permitted to expire; but a short experience of the embarrassments to which the refusal to revive it exposed the government, convinced those who were most prejudiced against the measure of its necessity, and induced the passage of the present law. It would require no ordinary share of intrepidity to assert that a measure adopted under these circumstances was a bold and plain usurpation, to which the constitution gave no countenance. These observations belong to the cause; but they are not made under the impression that, were the question entirely new, the law would be found irreconcilable with the constitution.

In discussing this question, the counsel for the State of Maryland have deemed it of some importance, in the construction of the constitution, to consider that instrument not as emanating from the people, but as the act of sovereign and independent states. The powers of the general government, it has been said, are delegated by the states, who alone are truly sovereign; and must be exercised in subordination to the states, who alone possess supreme dominion.

It would be difficult to sustain this proposition. The Convention which framed the constitution was indeed elected by the state legislatures. But the instrument, when it came from their hands, was a mere proposal, without obligation, or pretensions to it. It was reported to the then existing Congress of the United States, with a request that it might "be submitted to a convention of delegates, chosen in each State by the people thereof, under the recommendation of its legislature, for their assent and ratification." This mode of proceeding was adopted; and by the convention, by Congress, and by the state legislatures, the instrument was submitted to the people. They acted upon it in the only manner in which they can act safely, effectively, and wisely, on such a subject, by assembling in convention. It is true, they assembled in their several states—and where else should they have assembled? No political dreamer was ever wild enough to think of breaking down the lines which separate the states, and of compounding the American people into one common mass. Of consequence, when they act, they act in their states. But the measures they adopt do not, on that account, cease to be the measures of the people themselves, or become the measures of the state governments.

From these conventions the constitution derives its whole authority. The government proceeds directly from the people; is "ordained and established" in the name of the people; and is declared to be ordained, "in order to form a more perfect union, establish justice, ensure domestic tranquility, and secure the blessings of liberty to themselves and to their posterity." The assent of the states, in their sovereign capacity, is implied in calling a convention, and thus submitting that instrument to the people. But the people were at perfect liberty to accept or reject it; and their act was final. It required not the affirmance, and could not be negatived, by the state governments. The constitution, when thus adopted, was of complete obligation, and bound the State sovereignties.

[The] government of the Union, then (whatever may be the influence of this fact on the case), is, emphatically, and truly, a government of the people. In form and in substance it emanates from them. Its powers are granted by them, and are to be exercised directly on them, and for their benefit.

This government is acknowledged by all to be one of enumerated powers. The principle, that it can exercise only the powers granted to it, [is] now universally admitted. But the question respecting the extent of the powers actually granted, is perpetually arising, and will probably continue to arise, as long as our system shall exist. [If] any one proposition could command the universal assent of mankind, we might expect it would be this—that the government of the Union, though limited in its powers, is supreme within its sphere of action.

[Among] the enumerated powers, we do not find that of establishing a bank or creating a corporation. But there is no phrase in the instrument which, like the articles of confederation, excludes incidental or implied powers; and which requires that everything granted shall be expressly and minutely described. [The Articles of Confederation had provided that each state "retains" every power not "expressly delegated."] Even the 10th amendment, which was framed for the purpose of quieting the excessive jealousies which had been excited, omits the word "expressly," and declares only that the powers "not delegated to the United States, nor prohibited to the States, are reserved to the States or to the people"; thus leaving the question, whether the particular power which may become the subject of contest has been delegated to the one government, or prohibited to the other, to depend on a fair construction of the whole instrument. The men who drew and adopted this amendment had experienced the embarrassments resulting from the insertion of this word in the articles of confederation, and probably omitted it to avoid those embarrassments. A constitution, to contain an accurate detail of all the subdivisions of which its great powers will admit, and of all the means by which they may be carried into execution, would partake of the prolixity of a legal code, and could scarcely be embraced by the human mind. It would probably never be understood by the public. Its nature, therefore, requires, that only its great outlines should be marked, its important objects designated, and the minor ingredients which compose those objects be deduced from the nature of the objects themselves. That this idea was entertained by the framers of the American constitution, is not only to be inferred from the nature of the instrument, but from the language. Why else were some of the limitations, found in the ninth section of the 1st article, introduced? It is also, in some degree, warranted by their having omitted to use any restrictive term which might prevent its receiving a fair and just interpretation. In considering this question, then, we must never forget that it is a *constitution* we are expounding.

Although, among the enumerated powers of government, we do not find the word "bank," or "incorporation," we find the great powers to lay and collect taxes; to borrow money; to regulate commerce; to declare and conduct a war; and to raise and support armies and navies. The sword and the purse, all the external relations, and no inconsiderable portion of the industry of the nation, are entrusted to its government. It can never be pretended that these vast powers draw after them others of inferior importance, merely because they are inferior. [But] it may with great reason be contended, that a government, entrusted with such ample powers, on the due execution of which the happiness and prosperity of the nation so vitally depends, must also be entrusted with ample means for their execution. The power being given, it is the interest of the nation to facilitate its execution. It can never be their interest, and cannot be presumed to have been their intention, to clog and embarrass its execution by withholding the most appropriate means. Throughout this vast republic, from the St. Croix to the Gulf of Mexico, from the Atlantic to the Pacific, revenue is to be collected and expended, armies are to be marched and supported. The exigencies of the nation may require that the treasure raised in the north should be transported to the south, that raised in the east conveyed to the west, or that this order should be reversed. Is that construction of the constitution to be preferred which would render these operations difficult, hazardous, and expensive? Can we adopt that construction (unless the words imperiously require it) which would impute to the framers of that instrument, when granting these powers for the public good, the intention of impeding their exercise by withholding a choice of means? If, indeed, such be the mandate of the constitution, we have only to obey; but that instrument does not profess to enumerate the means by which the powers it confers may be executed; nor does it prohibit the creation of a corporation, if the existence of such a being be essential to the beneficial exercise of those powers. It is, then, the subject of fair inquiry, how far such means may be employed.

[The] government which has a right to do an act, and has imposed on it the duty of performing that act, must, according to the dictates of reason, be allowed to select the means; and those who contend that it may not select any appropriate means, that one particular mode of effecting the object is excepted, take upon themselves the burden of establishing that exception. [The] power of creating a corporation, though appertaining to sovereignty, is not, like the power of making war, or levying taxes, or of regulating commerce, a great substantive and independent power, which cannot be implied as incidental to other powers, or used as a means of executing them. It is never the end for which other powers are exercised, but a means by which other objects are accomplished. [The] power of creating a corporation is never used for its own sake, but for the purpose of effecting something else. No sufficient reason is, therefore, perceived, why it may not pass as incidental to those powers which are expressly given, if it be a direct mode of executing them.

But the constitution of the United States has not left the right of Congress to employ the necessary means, for the execution of the powers conferred on the government, to general reasoning. To its enumeration of Powers is added that of making "laws which shall be necessary and proper for carrying into execution the foregoing powers, and all other powers vested by this constitution, in the government of the United States, or in any department thereof." The counsel for the State of Maryland have urged various arguments, to prove that this clause, though in terms a grant of power, is not so in effect; but is really restrictive of the general right, which might otherwise be implied, of selecting means for executing the enumerated powers.

(The] argument on which most reliance is placed, is drawn from the peculiar language of this clause. Congress is not empowered by it to make all laws, which may have relation to the Powers conferred on the government, but such only as may be *"necessary and proper"* for carrying them into execution. The word *"necessary"* is considered as controlling the whole sentence, and as limiting the right to pass laws for the execution of the granted powers, to such as are indispensable, and without which the power would be nugatory. That it excludes the choice of means, and leaves to Congress, in each case, that only which is most direct and simple.

Is it true, that this is the sense in which the word "necessary" is always used? Does it always import an absolute physical necessity, so strong, that one thing, to which another may be termed necessary, cannot exist without that other? We think it does not. If reference be had to its use, in the common affairs of the world, or in approved authors, we find that it frequently imports no more than that one thing is convenient, or useful, or essential to another. To employ the means necessary to an end, is generally understood as employing any means calculated to produce the end, and not as being confirmed to those single means, without which the end would be entirely unattainable. [It] is essential to just construction, that many words which import something excessive should be understood in a more mitigated sense—in that sense which common usage justifies. The word "necessary" is of this description. It has not a fixed character peculiar to itself. It admits of all degrees of comparison. [A] thing may be necessary, very necessary, absolutely or indispensably necessary. To no mind would the same idea be conveyed by these several phrases. This comment on the word is well illustrated by the Passage cited at the bar, from the 10th section of the 1st article of the constitution. It is, we think, impossible to compare the sentence which prohibits a state from laying "imposts, or duties on imports or exports, except what may be *absolutely* necessary for executing its inspection laws," with that which authorizes Congress "to make all laws which shall be necessary and proper for carrying into execution" the Powers of the general government, without feeling a conviction that the convention understood itself to change materially the meaning of the word "necessary," by prefixing the word "absolutely." This word, then, like others, is used in various senses; and, in its construction, the subject, the context, the intention of the person using them, are all to be taken into view.

Let this be done in the case under consideration. The subject is the execution of those great powers on which the welfare of a nation essentially depends. It must have been the intention of those who gave these powers, to insure, as far as human prudence could insure, their beneficial execution. This could not be done by confining the choice of means to such narrow limits as not to leave it in the power of Congress to adopt any which might be appropriate, and which were conducive to the end. This provision is made in a constitution intended to endure for ages to come, and, consequently, to be adapted to the various crises of human affairs. To have prescribed the means by which government should, in all future time, execute its powers, would have been to change, entirely, the character of the instrument, and give it the properties of a legal code. It would have been an unwise attempt to provide, by immutable rules, for exigencies which, if foreseen at all, must have been seen dimly, and which can be best provided for as they occur. To have declared that the best means shall not be used, but those alone without which the power given would be nugatory, would have been to deprive the legislature of the capacity to avail itself of experience, to exercise its reason, and to accommodate its legislation to circumstances. If we apply this principle of construction to any of the powers of the government, we shall find it so pernicious in its operation that we shall be compelled to it.

[Take], for example, the power "to establish post offices and post roads." This power is executed by the single act of making the establishment. But, from this has been inferred the power and duty of carrying the mail along the post road, from one post office to another. And, from this implied power, has again been inferred the right to punish those who steal letters from the post office, or rob the mail. It may be said, with some plausibility, that the right to carry the mail, and to punish those who rob it, is not indispensably necessary to the establishment of a post office and post road. This right is indeed essential to the beneficial exercise of the power, but not indispensably necessary to its existence. So, of the punishment of the crimes of stealing or falsifying a record or process of a Court of the United States, or of perjury in such Court. To punish these offences is certainly conducive to the due administration of justice. But courts may exist, and may decide the causes brought before them, though such crimes escape punishment.

[If a] limited construction of the word "necessary" must be abandoned in order to punish, whence is derived the rule which would reinstate it, when the government would carry its powers into execution by means not vindictive in their nature? If the word "necessary" means "needful," "requisite," "essential," "conducive to," in order to let in the power of punishment for the infraction of law; why is it not equally comprehensive when required to authorize the use of means which facilitate the execution of the powers of government without the infliction of punishment?

In ascertaining the sense in which the word "necessary" is used in this clause of the constitution, we may derive some aid from that with which it is associated. Congress shall have power "to make all laws which shall be necessary and proper to carry into execution" the powers of the government. If the word "necessary" was used in that strict and rigorous sense for which the counsel for the State of Maryland contend, it would be an extraordinary departure from the usual course of the human mind, as exhibited in composition, to add a word, the only possible effect of which is to qualify that strict and rigorous meaning; to present to the mind the idea of some choice of means of legislation not straightened and compressed within the narrow limits for which gentlemen contend.

But the argument which most conclusively demonstrates the error of the construction contended for by the counsel for the State of Maryland, is founded on the intention of the Convention, as manifested in the whole clause. To waste time and argument in proving that, without it, Congress might carry its powers into execution, would be not much less idle than to hold a lighted taper to the sun. As little can it be required to prove, that in the absence of this clause, Congress would have some choice of means. That it might employ those which, in its judgment, would most advantageously effect the object to be accomplished. That any means adapted to the end, any means which tended directly to the execution of the constitutional powers of the government, were in themselves constitutional. This clause, as construed by the State of Maryland, would abridge, and almost annihilate this useful and necessary right of the legislature to select its means. That this could not be intended, is, we should think, had it not been already controverted, too apparent for controversy. We think so for the following reasons: 1st. The clause is placed among the powers of Congress, not among the limitations on those powers. 2nd. Its terms purport to enlarge, not to diminish the powers vested in the government. It purports to be an additional power, not a restriction on those already granted. No reason has been, or can be assigned for thus concealing an intention to narrow the discretion of the national legislature under words which purport to enlarge it.

[The] result of the most careful and attentive consideration bestowed upon this clause is, that if it does not enlarge, it cannot be construed to restrain the powers of Congress, or to impair the right of the legislature to exercise its best judgment in the selection of measures to carry into execution the constitutional powers of the government. If no other motive for its insertion can be suggested, a sufficient one is found in the desire to remove all doubts respecting the right to legislate on that vast mass of incidental powers which must be involved in the constitution, if that instrument be not a splendid bauble.

We admit, as all must admit, that the powers of the government are limited, and that its limits are not to be transcended. But we think the sound construction of the constitution must allow to the national legislature that discretion, with respect to the means by which the powers it confers are to be carried into execution, which will enable that body to perform the high duties assigned to it, in the manner most beneficial to the people. Let the end be legitimate, let it be within the scope of the constitution, and all means which are appropriate, which are plainly adapted to that end, which are not prohibited, but consist with the letter and spirit of the constitution, are constitutional.

[If] a corporation may be employed indiscriminately with other means to carry into execution the powers of the government, no particular reason can be assigned for excluding the use of a bank, if required for its fiscal operations. To use one, must be within the discretion of Congress, if it be an appropriate mode of executing the powers of government. That it is a convenient, a useful, and essential instrument in the prosecution of its fiscal operations, is not now a subject of controversy. All those who have been concerned in the administration of our finances, have concurred in repre-senting its importance and necessity; and so strongly have they been felt, that states-men of the first class, whose previous opinions against it had been confirmed by every circumstance which can fix the human judgment, have yielded those opinions to the exigencies of the nation. [But], were its necessity less apparent, none can deny its being an appropriate measure; and if it is, the degree of its necessity, as has been very justly observed, is to be discussed in another place. Should Congress, in the execution of its powers, adopt measures which are prohibited by the constitution; or should Congress, under the pretext of executing its powers, pass laws for the accomplishment of objects not entrusted to the government; it would become the painful duty of this tribunal, should a case requiring such a decision come before it, to say that such an act was not the law of the land. But where the law is not prohibited, and is really calculated to effect any of the objects entrusted to the government, to undertake here to inquire into the degree of its necessity, would be to pass the line which circumscribes the judicial department, and to tread on legislative ground. This court disclaims all pretensions to such a power.

After this declaration, it can scarcely be necessary to say that the existence of state banks can have no possible influence on the question. No trace is to be found in the constitution of an intention to create a dependence of the government of the Union on those of the states, for the execution of the great powers assigned to it. Its means are adequate to its ends; and on those means alone was it expected to rely for the accomplishment of its ends. To impose on it the necessity of resorting to means which it cannot control, which another government may furnish or withhold, would render its course precarious, the result of its measures uncertain, and create a dependence on other governments, which might disappoint its most important designs, and is incom-patible with the language of the constitution. But were it otherwise, the choice of means implies a right to choose a national bank in preference to state banks, and Congress alone can make the election.

After the most deliberate consideration, it is the unanimous and decided opinion of this Court, that the act to incorporate the Bank of the United States is a law made in pursuance of the constitution, and is a part of the supreme law of the land. The branches, proceeding from the same stock, and being conducive to the complete accomplishment of the object, are equally constitutional. [It] being the opinion of the Court, that the act incorporating the bank is constitutional; and that the power of establishing a branch in the State of Maryland might be properly exercised by the bank itself, we proceed to inquire—

2. Whether the State of Maryland may, without violating the constitution, tax that branch?

That the power of taxation is one of vital importance; that it is retained by the states; that it is not abridged by the grant of a similar power to the government of the Union; that it is to be concurrently exercised by the two governments: are truths which have never been denied. But, such is the paramount character of the constitution, that its capacity to withdraw any subject from the action of even this power, is admitted. The states are expressly forbidden to lay any duties on imports or exports, except what may be absolutely necessary for executing their inspection laws. If the obligation of this prohibition must be conceded, [the] same paramount character would seem to restrain, as it certainly may restrain, a state from such other exercise of this power, as is in its nature incompatible with, and repugnant to, the constitutional laws of the Union. [On] this ground the counsel for the bank place its claim to be exempted from the power of a State to tax its operations. There is no express provision for the case, but the claim has been sustained on a principle which so entirely pervades the constitution, is so intermixed with the materials which compose it, so interwoven with its web, so blended with its texture, as to be incapable of being separated from it, without rending it into shreds. This great principle is, that the constitution and the laws made in pursuance thereof are supreme; that they control the constitution and laws of the respective States, and cannot be controlled by them. From this, which may be almost termed an axiom, other propositions are deduced as corollaries, on the truth or error of which, and on their application to this case, the cause has been supposed to depend. These are, 1st. That a power to create implies a power to preserve. 2d. That a power to destroy, if wielded by a different hand, is hostile to, and incompatible with these powers to create and to preserve. 3d. That where this repugnancy exists, that authority which is supreme must control, not yield to that over which it is supreme.

[That] the power of taxing it by the states may be exercised so as to destroy it, is too obvious to be denied. But taxation is said to be an absolute power, which acknowledges no other limits than those expressly prescribed in the constitution, and like sovereign power of every other description, is intrusted to the discretion of those who use it. But the very terms of this argument admit, that the sovereignty of the state, in the article of taxation itself, is subordinate to, and may be controlled by the constitution of the United States. How far it has been controlled by that instrument must be a question of construction. In making this construction, no principle, not declared, can be admissible, which would defeat the legitimate operations of a supreme government. It is of the very essence of supremacy, to remove all obstacles to its action within its own sphere, and so to modify every power vested in subordinate governments, as to exempt its own operations from their own influence. This effect need not be stated in terms. It is so involved in the declaration of supremacy, so necessarily implied in it, that the expression of it could not make it more certain. We must, therefore, keep it in view, while construing the constitution.

The argument on the part of the State of Maryland is, not that the states may directly resist a law of Congress, but that they may exercise their acknowledged powers upon it, and that the constitution leaves them this right in the confidence that they will not abuse it. Before we proceed to examine this argument, and to subject it to the test of the constitution, we must be permitted to bestow a few considerations on the nature and extent of this original right of taxation, which is acknowledged to remain with the states. It is admitted that the power of taxing the people and their property is essential to the very existence of government, and may be legitimately exercised on the objects to which it is applicable, to the utmost extent to which the government may choose to carry it. The only security against the abuse of this power, is found in the structure of the government itself. In imposing a tax the legislature acts upon its constituents. This is in general a sufficient security against erroneous and oppressive taxation. [But] the means employed by the government of the Union have no such security, nor is the right of a state to tax them sustained by the same theory. Those means are not given by the people of a particular state, [but] by the people of all the states. They are given by all, for the benefit of all—and upon theory, should be subjected to that government only which belongs to all.

[We] find, then, on just theory, a total failure of this original right to tax the means employed by the government of the Union, for the execution of its powers. The right never existed, and the question whether it has been surrendered, cannot arise. But, waiving this theory for the present, let us resume the inquiry, whether this power can be exercised by the respective states, consistently with a fair construction of the constitution?

That the power to tax involves the power to destroy; that the power to destroy may defeat and render useless the power to create; that there is a plain repugnance, in conferring on one government a power to control the constitutional measures of another, which other, with respect to those very measures, is declared to be supreme over that which exerts the control, are propositions not to be denied. But all inconsistencies are to be reconciled by the magic of the word CONFIDENCE. Taxation, it is said, does not necessarily and unavoidably destroy. To carry it to the excess of destruction would be an abuse, to presume which, would banish that confidence which is essential to all government.

But is this a case of confidence? Would the people of any one state trust those of another with a power to control the most insignificant operations of their state government? We know they would not. Why, then, should we suppose that the people of any one state should be willing to trust those of another with a power to control the operations of a government to which they have confided their most important and most valuable interests? In the legislature of the Union alone, are all represented. The legislature of the Union alone, therefore, can be trusted by the people with the power of controlling measures which concern all, in the confidence that it will not be abused. This, then, is not a case of confidence, and we must consider it as it really is.

[If] we apply the principle for which the State of Maryland contends, to the constitution generally, we shall find it capable of changing totally the character of that instrument. We shall find it capable of arresting all the measures of the government, and of prostrating it at the foot of the states. [If] the states may tax one instrument, employed by the government in the execution of its powers, they may tax any and every other instrument. They may tax the mail; they may tax the mint; they may tax patent rights; they may tax the papers of the custom-house; they may tax judicial process; they may tax all the means employed by the government, to an excess which would defeat all the ends of government. [The American people] did not design to make their government dependent on the states.

[It] has also been insisted, that, as the power of taxation in the general and state governments is acknowledged to be concurrent, every argument which would sustain the right of the general government to tax banks chartered by the states, will equally sustain the right of the states to tax banks chartered by the general government. But the two cases are not on the same reason. The people of all the states have created the general government, and have conferred upon it the general power of taxation. The people of all the states, and the states themselves, are represented in Congress, and, by their representatives, exercise this power. When they tax the chartered institutions of the states, they tax their constituents; and these taxes must be uniform. But, when a state taxes the operations of the government of the United States, it acts upon institutions created, not by their own constituents, but by people over whom they claim no control. It acts upon the measures of a government created by others as well as themselves, for the benefit of others in common with themselves. The difference is that which always exist, and always must exist, between the action of the whole on a part, and the action of a part on the whole—between the laws of a government declared to be supreme, and those of a government which, when in opposition to those laws, is not supreme. But if the full application of this argument could be admitted, it might bring into question the right of Congress to tax the State banks, and could not prove the right of the States to tax the Bank of the United States.

[We conclude] that the states have no power, by taxation or otherwise, to retard, impede, burden, or in any manner control, the operations of the constitutional laws enacted by Congress to carry into execution the powers vested in the general government. [We) are unanimously of opinion, that the law passed by the legislature of Maryland, imposing a tax on the Bank of the United States, is unconstitutional and void.

This opinion does not deprive the states of any resources which they originally possessed. It does not extend to a tax paid by the real property of the bank, in common with the other real property within the state, nor to a tax imposed on the interest which the citizens of Maryland may hold in this institution, in common with other property of the same description through out the state. But this is a tax on the operations of the bank, and is, consequently, a tax on the operation of an instrument employed by the government of the Union to carry its powers into execution. Such a tax must be unconstitutional.

*Reversed.*

---

**McCulloch v. Maryland**, 4 Wheat. 316 (1819) 6–0
*editor's note.*
*Opinion authors are in bold; () indicates the party of appointing president. If the party of the justice differs from that of appointing president, then the party of the justice is listed second after the slash.*

| MAJORITY | CONCURRING | DISSENTING |
|---|---|---|
| **Marshall** (federalist) | | |
| Washington (federalist) | | |
| Johnson (r) | | |
| Livingston (r) | | |
| Duvall (r) | | |
| Story (r) | | |

# 6

# The Modern American Court Structure and System

The U.S. Supreme Court sits at the top of an extensive system of 50 state court systems and a national federal court system. As such, the Supreme Court is the 'court of last resort' in the American system of liberal, constitutional, democracy. Yet, very few legal conflicts ever make it to the Supreme Court; most cases are resolved at a much earlier step in the legal process. And, outside the institutional norm of stare decisis, which makes U.S. Supreme Court decisions the controlling precedents when they are relevant to deciding the case at hand, the Supreme Court exercises no supervisory role over the legal decisions of lower federal or state courts.[1]

The structure and functioning of our modern court system, or rather, our 51 modern court systems, can tell us much about the interaction of law and politics in the American system. The very fact that states retain their own court systems to hear claims based in state law is a result of the political contingencies shaping the development of our federal system under the Constitution of 1789. And, the need for political compromise at the convention led the framers to avoid several potentially controversial decisions. For example, Article III of the Constitution opens with "The judicial power of the United States, shall be vested in one supreme Court, and in such inferior Courts as the Congress may from time to time ordain and establish," leaving the divisive issue of the establishment of a system of federal trial courts to the first Congress. Indeed, that was the primary purpose of the Judiciary Act of 1789 whose Section 13 gained notoriety in the *Marbury* v. *Madison* (1803) case. Perhaps most importantly, the Supremacy Clause of Article VI stated, "This Constitution, and the Laws of the United States which shall be made in Pursuance thereof and all Treaties made, or which shall be made, under the Authority of the United States, shall be the supreme Law of the Land; and the Judges in every State shall be bound thereby, any Thing in the Constitution or Laws of any State to the Contrary notwithstanding"; but, left open the politically-charged question of whether state court judges or federal court judges would be the authoritative interpreter of the meaning of that supreme law—of the Constitution. The political importance of the structure and jurisdiction of judicial power in the new nation may be best evidenced by the speedy adoption of the Eleventh Amendment (1791) which limits the legal actions that can be brought against state governments in federal, rather than state, courts.

This chapter consists largely of annotated diagrams presenting information on the structure of the nation's fifty-one court systems. Each state is free to adopt its own system of courts; a generic picture is presented here, followed by a specific picture of the courts with jurisdiction in New Jersey providing one, concrete, example. Each state is free to adopt its own system of names for its courts, and some of their choices can be misleading to the unwary. For example, New York refers to its trial-level courts as New York Supreme Courts; Maryland refers to its highest appellate court as the Maryland Court of Appeals. Hence, assuming a state court's function from its name leads to many mistakes.

The primary system of federal trial and appellate courts is geographically based and it respects state borders. As one can see on the map of the federal court system, in constructing the U.S. District Courts and U.S. Court of Appeals, the district and circuit boundaries never divide a state. The chart that illustrates how few legal conflicts ever become Supreme Court cases presents trial and appeal rates in the federal court system. In addition, cases begun in state courts may be appealed directly to the U.S. Supreme Court, if, and *only if* the case (a) raises a substantial question of *federal* law and (b) the litigants have *exhausted all state remedies,* i.e. appealed through the state system, and, generally, received a decision from the state's highest appellate court. The U.S. Supreme Court may be the only court in the land that makes law for the entire country; but, proportionately speaking, it very seldom does so. As these materials demonstrate, judicial lawmaking is highly decentralized in the American system and the shape of its specific structures is embedded in politics.

Finally, as we embark on an examination of the interaction between law and politics once a case does reach the U.S. Supreme Court, the final figure in this chapter, "Trace A Case," outlines the procedural steps in the Supreme Court's decision-making process.

## *Notes*

1.   As head of the federal court system, the Supreme Court does exercise some administrative control over lower federal courts.

# AMERICAN COURT SYSTEM

## Generic State System

**State Supreme Court—highest appellate court**

In most states, these courts have discretionary jurisdiction

**Intermediate Appellate Court**

32 states have, 18 states do not have generally there is a right to one appeal

**County Court Trial Courts**

hear major criminal and civil cases

**Municipal Court**

traffic courts, cts. of small claims, night court, civil cases involving small amounts of money, minor criminal cases

**Justice of the Peace**

mostly found in rural areas. Minor civil matters, criminal misdemeanors

HEAR VIOLATIONS OF STATE LAW (federal constitutional questions, such as criminal procedure questions can be argued too.)

(1) must raise a substantial federal question, i.e., involving a federal statute or the federal constitution and (2) must have exhausted all state remedies.

## Federal System

**U.S. Supreme Court**

Makes law for nation

9 justices appointed for life

discretionary jurisdiction

4000–5000 petitions for a writ of certiorari filed each year

Less than 200 cases are accepted; the court hears oral argument and issues written opinions in about 100 per year.

**Courts of Appeal**

Makes law for circuit

Established in 1891

Formerly "Circuit Courts"
11 Courts of Appeals with at least 3 states in each circuit, plus the D.C. Court of Appeals and the U.S. Court of Appeals for the Federal Circuit which has no geographic designation (hears appeals from the U.S. Ct. of Claims and U.S. Court of Custom and Patent Appeals)
Total of 13 with 168 judges who sit in panels of 3 judges to hear cases.

right to appeal

**District Court**

Trial Courts
94 courts with 575 judges
Single judge with or without a jury

HEAR VIOLATIONS OF FEDERAL LAW

# MAJOR COURTS WITH JURISDICTION IN NEW JERSEY: A LOOK AT ONE STATE

## State System

hears cases involving violations of state law or N.J. Constitution

**Supreme Court of the State of New Jersey**

highest state appellate court; discretionary jurisdiction; cases must be "certified" by the Supreme Ct. of N.J. to be heard

↑

**Appellate Division of the New Jersey State Superior Court**

28 judges—intermediate appellate court; right to appeal ↑

**New Jersey State Superior Court of the Law or Chancery Division**

about 300 judges—county level trial courts; hears major criminal and civil cases; hears appeals from Municipal Ct.

↑

**Municipal Court**

about 500 judges—small claims court; traffic court; a few other specialized courts

(Justices of the Peace were abolished in N.J.'s 1947 Constitution)

## Federal System

hears cases involving violations of federal law or U.S. Constitution

**Supreme Court of the United States**

(highest appellate court in the nation; discretionary jurisdiction; hears appeals from Ct. of Appeals and Supreme Ct. of N.J. if case raises a "substantial federal question")

↑

**Court of Appeals for the Third Circuit**

intermediate appellate court; right to appeal; hears cases from NJ, PA, DE, Virgin Islands; sits in Philadelphia ↑

**United States District Court**

trial courts; sits in Newark, Trenton, and Camden

### Notes on the New Jersey State Court System

The Chief Justice of the Supreme Court of New Jersey heads the state judicial branch. Each N.J. judge is required to hold court during specific days and hours. They must submit weekly reports on the numbers of cases heard, decisions rendered, and other pertinent matters. By judicial rule, N.J. judges may not withhold a decision on a case for more than two weeks after it was heard. When necessary, judges are shifted from one court to another to help alleviate long delays or assist when a court's docket is unusually burdened. These are fairly stringent controls compared to other states.

In the summer of 1985, the National Conference of Chief Justices of State Courts praised New Jersey as having the most advanced court system in the country. The New Jersey courts have done an exemplary job in dealing with delay in the processing of cases—the number one problem facing courts today. New Jersey is in the vanguard of court reform, having instituted a number of new court management techniques.

Over half a million civil lawsuits are filed in N.J. courts annually. In New Jersey it takes from 18 months to 2 years for a civil suit to come to trial. In contrast, in Los Angeles it takes 5 years.

**Figure 6-2. District and Appellate Court Boundaries**

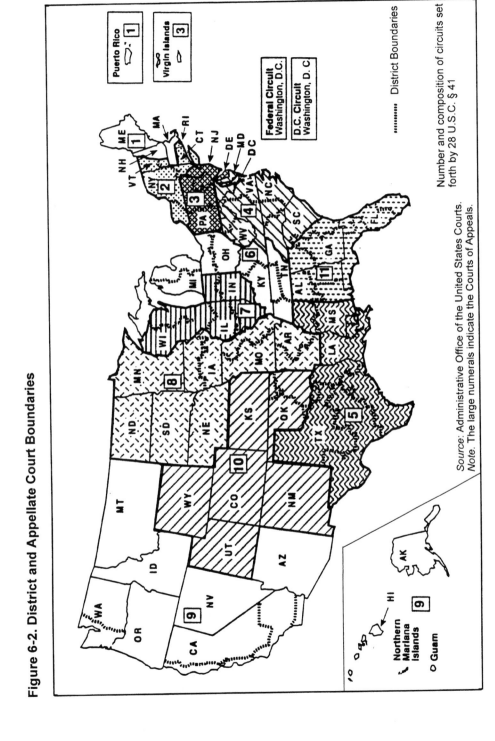

*Source:* Administrative Office of the United States Courts.
*Note:* The large numerals indicate the Courts of Appeals.

## THE FILTERING OF LAW VIOLATIONS OUT OF THE SYSTEM:

Out of every 100,000 grievances, how many get to the Supreme Court?

*Susan E. Lawrence*

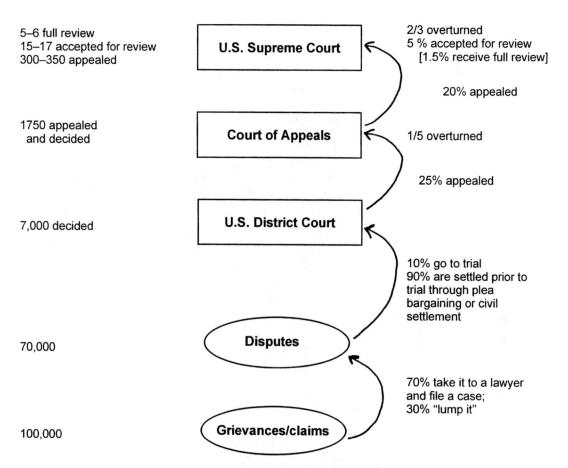

5–6 full review
15–17 accepted for review
300–350 appealed

**U.S. Supreme Court**

2/3 overturned
5 % accepted for review
[1.5% receive full review]

20% appealed

1750 appealed
and decided

**Court of Appeals**

1/5 overturned

25% appealed

7,000 decided

**U.S. District Court**

10% go to trial
90% are settled prior to
trial through plea
bargaining or civil
settlement

70,000

**Disputes**

70% take it to a lawyer
and file a case;
30% "lump it"

100,000

**Grievances/claims**

problems perceived as legal problems, i.e., viewed
as violations of some right or entitlement, caused
by a human agent, voiced to the offending party,
and susceptible of remedy.

Results: 0.016% of grievances are reviewed by the Supreme Court.
0.006% of grievances receive full review by the Supreme Court.

Source of data on grievances and disputes, Feistiner, William L.F., Richard Abel, and Austin Sarat,
"The Emergence and Transformation of Disputes: Naming, Blaming, Claiming..." *Law and Society
Review* 15 (1980–81): 631–654.

# TRACE A CASE
## Susan E. Lawrence

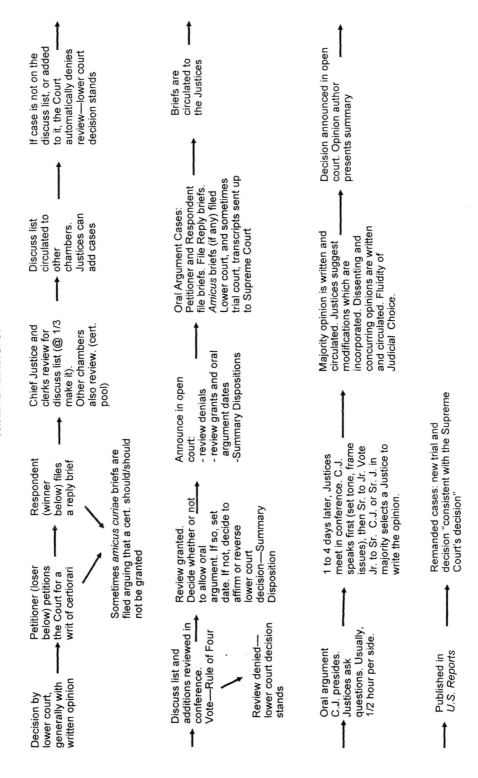

Decision by lower court, generally with written opinion

Petitioner (loser below) petitions the Court for a writ of certiorari

Respondent (winner below) files a reply brief

Sometimes *amicus curiae* briefs are filed arguing that a cert. should/should not be granted

Chief Justice and clerks review for discuss list (@ 1/3 make it). Other chambers also review. (cert. pool)

Discuss list circulated to other chambers. Justices can add cases

If case is not on the discuss list, or added to it, the Court automatically denies review—lower court decision stands

Discuss list and additions reviewed in conference. Vote—Rule of Four

Review denied— lower court decision stands

Review granted. Decide whether or not to allow oral argument. If so, set date. If not, decide to affirm or reverse lower court decision—Summary Disposition

Announce in open court:
- review denials
- review grants and oral argument dates
-Summary Dispositions

Oral Argument Cases: Petitioner and Respondent file briefs. File Reply briefs. *Amicus* briefs (if any) filed Lower court, and sometimes trial court, transcripts sent up to Supreme Court

Briefs are circulated to the Justices

Oral argument C.J. presides. Justices ask questions. Usually, 1/2 hour per side.

1 to 4 days later, Justices meet in conference. C.J. speaks first (set tone, frame issues), then Sr. to Jr. Vote Jr. to Sr. C.J. or Sr. J. in majority selects a Justice to write the opinion.

Majority opinion is written and circulated. Justices suggest modifications which are incorporated. Dissenting and concurring opinions are written and circulated. Fluidity of Judicial Choice.

Decision announced in open court. Opinion author presents summary

Published in *U.S. Reports*

Remanded cases: new trial and decision "consistent with the Supreme Court's decision"

# *Interest Groups in Court: Racial Equality Litigation Sets the Prototype*

*I*nterest groups have become an increasingly important participant in the judicial policy-making process. While pursuing their own policy goals through litigation, interest groups provide access to litigants who would otherwise be unable to participate in Supreme Court decision-making for either financial, political, or sociological reasons. Which legal claims the Court is asked to decide, and when, is highly dependent upon the politics surrounding the need for and extent of interest group litigation in our liberal, constitutional, democracy. One might argue that, while the role of the courts in our political process seems anomalous given the judges' and justices' insulation from the political process, interest group litigation interjects a dose of republican democracy in to Supreme Court decision-making.

Sporadic use of the courts by interest groups can be traced back to at least the turn of the century, but in recent decades group litigation has become a central feature of the adjudicatory policy-making process. Following the successful model set by the NAACP Legal Defense Fund culminating in *Brown* v. *Bd. of Education* (1954), many litigation-oriented interest groups and public interest law firms were established in the 1960s, 1970s, and 1980s. By the 1987 Court Term, interest groups were sponsoring 65.4 percent of the 132 cases the Supreme Court decided with a full opinion and filing amicus curiae briefs in 80 percent of these cases. During the 1987 Term, the Court received nearly 460 amicus curiae briefs signed by more than 1,600 interest groups and governmental interests.[1]

The NAACP's litigation campaign to overturn *Plessy* v. *Ferguson* (1896), which had declared that separate was not inherently unequal and that the requirement that African-Americans and whites sit in separate train cars did not violate the equal protection clause, provides the model of successful interest group use of the Court to obtain policy objectives not obtainable in the political branches. The NAACP, formed in 1909, presented a series of test cases to the Court in which the Court protected the rights of African-Americans in voting, housing, transportation, education, and juries.[2]

The NAACP's successful attack on segregation in education which led to the Court's decision in *Brown* v. *Bd. of Education* (1954) is its best known litigation campaign. The NAACP's first important victory in this area was *Missouri ex rel. Gaines* v. *Canada* (1938) in which the Court held that Missouri's failure to admit Gaines to the state's "white" law school and its failure to provide a "black" law school, instead merely offering to pay his tuition to a law school in another state, violated the equal protection clause of the Fourteenth Amendment. In *Spiuel* v. *Oklahoma* (1948), the Court ordered the state to provide an equal education in the state's law school to a black woman. Further chipping away at the "separate but equal" doctrine in education, the NAACP won a significant victory in *Sweatt* v. *Painter* (1950) when the Court held that Texas had to admit Sweatt, a black man, to the all white University of Texas law school rather than requiring him to attend the state's separate law school for blacks. The Court found that the two schools were not indeed equal and that therefore the state had not met the requirements of the "separate but equal" test. In *McLaurin* v. *Oklahoma State Regents* (1950) the Court held that blacks could not be segregated into separate seating arrangements within the classrooms, libraries, and cafeterias of a predominately white graduate school. Armed with these precedents from the relatively safe arena of law and graduate education, Thurgood Marshall, then lead counsel for the NAACP, set out to challenge school desegregation in public elementary schools. The result was *Brown* v. *Bd. of Education* (1954), the landmark decision that rejected *Plessy*'s "separate but equal" doctrine and held that the Kansas, Delaware, South Carolina, and Virginia systems of segregated public schooling were "inherently unequal" in violation of the Fourteenth Amendment's equal protection clause.[3] (See Chapter Four) The following year *"Brown* II" was handed down addressing the implementation issues the justices had set for reargument after their decision in *Brown* I. A series of memorandum cases were handed down in subsequent years extending *Brown*'s principle holding to beaches, buses, golf courses, and public parks; finally, in 1963, in *Johnson* v. *Virginia*, the Court explicitly expanded the *Brown* principle to all public facilities. The NAACP's attack on *Plessy* v. *Ferguson* reveals the Court's legal reasoning process at work; it is a concrete example of the development of legal doctrine through incremental change, reversal of past precedent, routine application and expansion of established precedent, and, in the affirmative action cases presented in Chapter Four, the continuing quest to define the principle itself.

*Brown* v. *Bd. of Education* (1954) is probably the single most important Supreme Court decision of the twentieth century, though scholars continue to disagree about exactly what role it played in changing race relations and the status of African-Americans in modern society. But, most agree that it was perceived as significant enough to encourage other groups disadvantaged in the political branches to turn to the Court in their quest for policy change. Over the decades since *Brown*, women's rights groups, religious organizations, and various other civil liberties and civil rights groups, as well as a growing number of conservative policy groups, have turned to the Court for social change and transformed the agendas and doctrines of the Court.

The final case in this chapter is *NAACP* v. *Button* (1963). Here, the Court takes explicit account of interest group litigation and provides it with first amendment protection. This is followed by an outline of interest group participation in Supreme Court decision-making. Throughout this volume, special care has been taken to include information on counsel in the case and amicus filers to demonstrate the scope of interest group activity in these cases.

## *Notes*

1. Lee Epstein, "Courts and Interest Groups," in *The American Courts: A Critical Assessment*, ed. John B. Gates and Charles A. Johnson (Washington, D.C.: CQ Press, 1991), p. 350.

2. Clement E. Vose, "Litigation as a Form of Pressure Group Activity," *The Annals of the American Academy* 319 (1958):20–31.

3. In a companion case, *Bollin* v. *Sharpe* (1954), the Court held that under the Fifth Amendment due process clause, segregated schools in the District of Columbia were also unconstitutional. For an excellent account of the NAACP's litigation campaign and the litigants involved in these cases see Richard Kluger, *Simple Justice* (New York: Vintage Books, 1977).

# Plessy v. Ferguson

## 163 U.S. 537 (1896)

## Error to the Supreme Court of the State of Louisiana

### No. 210. Argued April 18, 1896—Decided May 18, 1896.

*Mr. A. W. Tourgee* and *Mr. S. F. Phillips* for plaintiff in error. *Mr. F. D. McKenney* was on *Mr. Phillips's* brief.

*Mr. James C. Walker* filed a brief for plaintiff in error.

*Mr. Alexander Porter Morse* for defendant in error. *Mr. M. J. Cunningham*, Attorney General of the State of Louisiana, and *Mr. Lional Adams* were on his brief.

MR. JUSTICE BROWN, after stating the case, delivered the opinion of the court.

This case turns upon the constitutionality of an act of the General Assembly of the State of Louisiana, passed in 1890, providing for separate railway carriages for the white and colored races. Acts 1890, No. 111, p. 152.

The first section of the statute enacts "that all railway companies carrying passengers in their coaches in this State, shall provide equal but separate accommodations for the white, and colored races, by providing two or more passenger coaches for each passenger train, or by dividing the passenger coaches by a partition so as to secure separate accommodations: *Provided*, That this section shall not be construed to apply to street railroads. No person or persons, shall be admitted to occupy seats in coaches, other than, the ones, assigned, to them on account of the race they belong to."

By the second section it was enacted "that the officers of such passenger trains shall have power and are hereby required to assign each passenger to the coach or compartment used for the race to which such passenger belongs; any passenger insisting on going into a coach or compartment to which by race he does not belong, shall be liable to a fine of twenty-five dollars, or in lieu thereof to imprisonment for a period of not more than twenty days in the parish prison, and any officer of any railroad insisting on assigning a passenger to a coach or compartment other than the one set aside for the race to which said passenger belongs, shall be liable to a fine of twenty-five dollars, or in lieu thereof to imprisonment for a period of not more than twenty days in the parish prison; and should any passenger refuse to occupy the coach or compartment to which he or she is assigned by the officer of such railway, said officer shall have power to refuse to carry such passenger on his train, and for such refusal neither he nor the railway company which he represents shall be liable for damages in any of the courts of this State."

The third section provides penalties for the refusal or neglect of the officers, directors, conductors and employees of railway companies to comply with the act, with a proviso that "nothing in this act shall be construed as applying to nurses attending children of the other race." The fourth section is immaterial.

The information filed in the criminal District Court charged in substance that Plessy, being a passenger between two stations within the State of Louisiana, was assigned by officers of the company to the coach used for the race to which he belonged, but he insisted upon going into a coach used by the race to which he did not belong. Neither in the information nor plea was his particular race or color averred [declared].

The petition for the writ of prohibition averred [asserted] that petitioner was seven eighths Caucasian and one eighth African blood; that the mixture of colored blood was not discernible in him, and that he was entitled to every right, privilege and immunity secured to citizens of the United States of the white race; and that, upon such theory, he took possession of a vacant seat in a coach where passengers of the white race were accommodated, and was ordered by the conductor to vacate said coach and take a seat in another assigned to persons of the colored race, and having refused to comply with such demand he was forcibly ejected with the aid of a police officer, and imprisoned in the parish jail to answer a charge of having violated the above act.

The constitutionality of this act is attacked upon the ground that it conflicts both with the Thirteenth Amendment of the Constitution, abolishing slavery, and the Fourteenth Amendment, which prohibits certain restrictive legislation on the part of the States.

1. That it does not conflict with the Thirteenth Amendment, which abolished slavery and involuntary servitude, except as a punishment for crime, is too clear for argument. Slavery implies involuntary servitude—a state of bondage; the ownership of mankind as a chattel, or at least the control of the labor and services of one man for the benefit of another, and the absence of a legal right to the disposal of his own person, property and services. . . .

A statute which implies merely a legal distinction between the white and colored races—a distinction which is founded in the color of the two races, and which must always exist so long as white men are distinguished from the other race by color—has no tendency to destroy the legal equality of the two races, or reestablish a state of involuntary servitude. Indeed, we do not understand that the Thirteenth Amendment is strenuously relied upon by the plaintiff in error in this connection.

2. By the Fourteenth Amendment, all persons born or naturalized in the United States, and subject to the jurisdiction thereof, are made citizens of the United States and of the State wherein they reside; and the States are forbidden from making or enforcing any law which shall abridge the privileges or immunities of citizens of the United States, or shall deprive any person of life, liberty or property without due process of law, or deny to any person within their jurisdiction the equal protection of the laws. . . .

The object of the amendment was undoubtedly to enforce the absolute equality of the two races before the law, but in the nature of things it could not have been intended to abolish distinctions based upon color, or to enforce social, as distinguished from political equality, or a commingling of the two races upon terms unsatisfactory to either. Laws permitting, and even requiring, their separation in places where they are liable to be brought into contact do not necessarily imply the inferiority of either race to the other, and have been generally, if not universally, recognized as within the competency of the state legislatures in the exercise of their police power. The most common instance of this is connected with the establishment of separate schools for white and colored children, which has been held to be a valid exercise of the legislative power even by courts of States where the political rights of the colored race have been longest and most earnestly enforced.

Laws forbidding the intermarriage of the two races may be said in a technical sense to interfere with the freedom of contract, and yet have been universally recognized as within the police power of the State. *State* v. *Gibson*, 36 Indiana, 389.

The distinction between laws interfering with the political equality of the negro and those requiring the separation of the two races in schools, theatres and railway carriages has been frequently drawn by this court. . . .

[W]e think the enforced separation of the races, as applied to the internal commerce of the State, neither abridges the privileges or immunities of the colored man, deprives him of his property without due process of law, nor denies him the equal protection of the laws, within the meaning of the Fourteenth Amendment, . . .

[I]t is also suggested by the learned counsel for the plaintiff in error that the same argument that will justify the state legislature in requiring railways to provide separate accommodations for the two races will also authorize them to require separate cars to be provided for people whose hair is of a certain color, or who are aliens, or who belong to certain nationalities, or to enact laws requiring colored people to walk upon one side of the street, and white people upon the other, or requiring white men's houses to be painted white, and colored men's black, or their vehicles or business signs to be of different colors, upon the theory that one side of the street is as good as the other, or that a house or vehicle of one color is as good as one of another color. The reply to all this is that every exercise of the police power must be reasonable, and extend only to such laws as are enacted in good faith for the promotion of the public good, and not for the annoyance or oppression of a particular class. . . .

So far, then, as a conflict with the Fourteenth Amendment is concerned, the case reduces itself to the question whether the statute of Louisiana is a reasonable regulation, and with respect to this there must necessarily be a large discretion on the part of the legislature. In determining the question of reasonableness it is at liberty to act with reference to the established usages, customs and traditions of the people, and with a view to the promotion of their comfort, and the preservation of the public peace and good order. Gauged by this standard, we cannot say that a law which authorizes or even requires the separation of the two races in public conveyances is unreasonable, or more obnoxious to the Fourteenth Amendment than the acts of Congress requiring separate schools for colored children in the District of Columbia, the constitutionality of which does not seem to have been questioned, or the corresponding acts of state legislatures.

We consider the underlying fallacy of the plaintiff's argument to consist in the assumption that the enforced separation of the two races stamps the colored race with a badge of inferiority. If this be so, it is not by reason of anything found in the act, but solely because the colored race chooses to put that construction upon it. The argument necessarily assumes that if, as has been more than once the case, and is not unlikely to be so again, the colored race should become the dominant power in the state legislature, and should enact a law in precisely similar terms, it would thereby relegate the white race to an inferior position. We imagine that the white race, at least, would not acquiesce in this assumption. The argument also assumes that social prejudices may be overcome by legislation, and that equal rights cannot be secured to the negro except by an enforced commingling of the two races. We cannot accept this proposition. If the two races are to meet upon terms of social equality, it must be the result of natural affinities, a mutual appreciation of each other's merits and a voluntary consent of individuals. As was said by the Court of Appeals of New York in *People* v. *Gallagher*, 93 N. Y. 438, 448, "this end can neither be accomplished nor promoted by laws which conflict with the general sentiment of the community upon whom they are designed to operate. . . ."

Legislation is powerless to eradicate racial instincts or to abolish distinctions based upon physical differences, and the attempt to do so can only result in accentuating the

308 ★ *Interest Groups in Court*

difficulties of the present situation. If the civil and political rights of both races be equal one cannot be inferior to the other civilly or politically. If one race be inferior to the other socially, the Constitution of the United States cannot put them upon the same plane.

It is true that the question of the proportion of colored blood necessary to constitute a colored person, as distinguished from a white person, is one upon which there is a difference of opinion in the different States, some holding that any visible admixture of black blood stamps the person as belonging to the colored race, (*State* v. *Chavers*, 5 Jones, [N. C.] 1, p. 11); others that it depends upon the preponderance of blood, (*Gray* v. *State*, 4 Ohio, 354; *Monroe* v. *Collins*, 17 Ohio St. 665); and still others that the predominance of white blood must only be in the proportion of three fourths. (*People* v. *Dean*, 14 Michigan, 406; *Jones* v. *Commonwealth*, 80 Virginia, 538.) But these are questions to be determined under the laws of each State and are not properly put in issue in this case. Under the allegations of his petition it may undoubtedly become a question of importance whether, under the laws of Louisiana, the petitioner belongs to the white or colored race.

The judgment of the court below is, therefore,

*Affirmed.*

MR. JUSTICE HARLAN dissenting.

By the Louisiana statute, the validity of which is here involved, all railway companies carrying passengers in that State are required to have separate but equal accommodations for white and colored persons, . . .

Only "nurses attending children of the other race" are excepted from the operation of the statute. No exception is made of colored attendants traveling with adults. A white man is not permitted to have his colored servant with him in the same coach, even if his condition of health requires the constant, personal assistance of such servant. If a colored maid insists upon riding in the same coach with a white woman whom she has been employed to serve, and who may need her personal attention while traveling, she is subject to be fined or imprisoned for such an exhibition of zeal in the discharge of duty. . . .

Thus the State regulates the use of a public highway by citizens of the United States solely upon the basis of race.

However apparent the injustice of such legislation may be, we have only to consider whether it is consistent with the Constitution of the United States.

That a railroad is a public highway, and that the corporation which owns or operates it is in the exercise of public functions, is not, at this day, to be disputed. . . .

In respect of civil rights, common to all citizens, the Constitution of the United States does not, I think, permit any public authority to know the race of those entitled to be protected in the enjoyment of such rights. Every true man has pride of race, and under appropriate circumstances when the rights of others, his equals before the law, are not to be affected, it is his privilege to express such pride and to take such action based upon it as to him seems proper. But I deny that any legislative body or judicial tribunal may have regard to the race of citizens when the civil rights of those citizens are involved. Indeed, such legislation, as that here in question, is inconsistent not only with that equality of rights which pertains to citizenship, National and State, but with the personal liberty enjoyed by every one within the United States.

The Thirteenth Amendment does not permit the withholding or the deprivation of any right necessarily inhering in freedom. It not only struck down the institution of slavery as previously existing in the United States, but it prevents the imposition of any burdens or disabilities that constitute badges of slavery or servitude. It decreed universal civil freedom in this country. This court has so adjudged. But that amendment having been found inadequate to the protection of the rights of those who had been in slavery, it was followed by the Fourteenth Amendment, which added greatly to the dignity and glory of American citizenship, and to the security of personal liberty, by declaring that "all persons born or naturalized in the United States, and subject to the jurisdiction thereof, are citizens of the United States and of the State wherein they reside," and that "no State shall make or enforce any law which shall abridge the privileges or immunities of citizens of the United States; nor shall any State deprive any person of life, liberty or property without due process of law, nor deny to any person within its jurisdiction the equal protection of the laws." These two amendments, if enforced according to their true intent and meaning, will protect all the civil rights that pertain to freedom and citizenship. Finally, and to the end that no citizen should be denied, on account of his race, the privilege of participating in the political control of his country, it was declared by the Fifteenth Amendment that "the right of citizens of the United States to vote shall not be denied or abridged by the United States or by any State on account of race, color or previous condition of servitude."

These notable additions to the fundamental law were welcomed by the friends of liberty throughout the world. They removed the race line from our governmental systems. They had, as this court has said, a common purpose, namely, to secure "to a race recently emancipated, a race that through many generations have been held in slavery, all the civil rights that the superior race enjoy." They declared, in legal effect, this court has further said, "that the law in the States shall be the same for the black as for the white; that all persons, whether colored or white, shall stand equal before the laws of the States, and, in regard to the colored race, for whose protection the amendment was primarily designed, that no discrimination shall be made against them by law because of their color." . . .

It was said in argument that the statute of Louisiana does not discriminate against either race, but prescribes a rule applicable alike to white and colored citizens. But this argument does not meet the difficulty. Every one knows that the statute in question had its origin in the purpose, not so much to exclude white persons from railroad cars occupied by blacks, as to exclude colored people from coaches occupied by or assigned to white persons. . . . If a white man and a black man choose to occupy the same public conveyance on a public highway, it is their right to do so, and no government, proceeding alone on grounds of race, can prevent it without infringing the personal liberty of each.

It is one thing for railroad carriers to furnish, or to be required by law to furnish, equal accommodations for all whom they are under a legal duty to carry. It is quite another thing for government to forbid citizens of the white and black races from traveling in the same public conveyance, and to punish officers of railroad companies for permitting persons of the two races to occupy the same passenger coach. If a State can prescribe, as a rule of civil conduct, that whites and blacks shall not travel as passengers in the same railroad coach, why may it not so regulate the use of the streets of its cities and towns as to compel white citizens to keep on one side of a street and black citizens to keep on the other? Why may it not, upon like grounds, punish whites and blacks who ride together in street cars or in open vehicles on a public road or street? Why may it not require sheriffs to assign whites to one side of a court-room and blacks to the other? And why may it not also prohibit the commingling of the two races in the galleries of legislative halls or in public assemblages convened for the consideration of the political questions of the day? Further, if this statute of Louisiana is consistent with the personal liberty of citizens, why may not the State require the separation in railroad coaches of native and naturalized citizens of the United States, or of Protestants and Roman Catholics?

The answer given at the argument to these questions was that regulations of the kind they suggest would be unreasonable, and could not, therefore, stand before the law. Is it meant that the determination of questions of legislative power depends upon the inquiry whether the statute whose validity is questioned is, in the judgment of the courts, a reasonable one, taking all the circumstances into consideration? . . . There is a dangerous tendency in these latter days to enlarge the functions of the courts, by means of judicial interference with the will of the people as expressed by the legislature. Our institutions have the distinguishing characteristic that the three departments of government are coordinate and separate. Each must keep within the limits defined by the Constitution. And the courts best discharge their duty by executing the will of the law-making power, constitutionally expressed, leaving the results of legislation to be dealt with by the people through their representatives. . . . If the power exists to enact a statute, that ends the matter so far as the courts are concerned. The adjudged cases in which statutes have been held to be void, because unreasonable, are those in which the means employed by the legislature were not at all germane to the end to which the legislature was competent.

The white race deems itself to be the dominant race in this country. And so it is, in prestige, in achievements, in education, in wealth and in power. So, I doubt not, it will continue to be for all time, if it remains true to its great heritage and holds fast to the principles of constitutional liberty. But in the view of the Constitution, in the eye of the law, there is in this country no superior, dominant, ruling class of citizens. There is no caste here. Our Constitution is color-blind, and neither knows nor tolerates classes among citizens. In respect of civil rights, all citizens are equal before the law. The humblest is the peer of the most powerful. The law regards man as man, and takes no account of his surroundings or of his color when his civil rights as guaranteed by the supreme law of the land are involved. It is, therefore, to be regretted that this high tribunal, the final expositor of the fundamental law of the land, has reached the conclusion that it is competent for a State to regulate the enjoyment by citizens of their civil rights solely upon the basis of race.

In my opinion, the judgment this day rendered will, in time, prove to be quite as pernicious as the decision made by this tribunal in the *Dred Scott case*. It was adjudged in that case that the descendants of Africans who were imported into this country and sold as slaves were not included nor intended to be included under the word "citizens" in the Constitution, and could not claim any of the rights and privileges which that instrument provided for and secured to citizens of the United States; that at the time of the adoption of the Constitution they were "considered as a subordinate and inferior class of beings, who had been subjugated by the dominant race, and, whether emancipated or not, yet remained subject to their authority, and had no rights or privileges but such as those who held the power and the government might choose to grant them." The recent amendments of the Constitution, it was supposed, had eradicated these principles from our institutions. But it seems that we have yet, in some of the States, a dominant race—a superior class of citizens, which assumes to regulate the enjoyment of civil rights, common to all citizens, upon the basis of race. The present decision, it may well be apprehended, will not only stimulate aggressions, more or less brutal and irritating, upon the admitted rights of colored citizens, but will encourage the belief that it is possible, by means of state enactments, to defeat the beneficent purposes which the people of the United States had in view when they adopted the recent amendments of the Constitution, by one of which the blacks of this country were made citizens of the United States and of the States in which they respectively reside, and whose privileges and immunities, as citizens, the States are forbidden to abridge. Sixty millions of whites are in no danger from the presence here of eight millions of blacks. The destinies of the two races, in this country, are indissolubly linked together, and the interests of both require that the common government of all shall not permit the seeds of race hate to be planted under the sanction of law. What can more certainly arouse race hate, what more certainly create and perpetuate a feeling of distrust between these races, than state enactments, which, in fact, proceed on the ground that colored citizens are so inferior and degraded that they cannot be allowed to sit in public coaches occupied by white citizens? That, as all will admit, is the real meaning of such legislation as was enacted in Louisiana.

The sure guarantee of the peace and security of each race is the clear, distinct, unconditional recognition by our governments, National and State, of every right that inheres in civil freedom, and of the equality before the law of all citizens of the United States without regard to race. State enactments, regulating the enjoyment of civil rights, upon the basis of race, and cunningly devised to defeat legitimate results of the [civil] war, under the pretence of recognizing equality of rights, can have no other result than to render permanent peace impossible, and to keep alive a conflict of races, the continuance of which must do harm to all concerned. . . .

There is a race so different from our own that we do not permit those belonging to it to become citizens of the United States. Persons belonging to it are, with few exceptions, absolutely excluded from our country. I allude to the Chinese race. But by the statute in question, a Chinaman can ride in the same passenger coach with white citizens of the United States, while citizens of the black race in Louisiana, many of whom, perhaps, risked their lives for the preservation of the Union, who are entitled, by law, to participate in the political control of the State and nation, who are not excluded, by law or by reason of their race, from public stations of any kind, and who have all the legal rights that belong to white citizens, are yet declared to be criminals, liable to imprisonment, if they ride in a public coach occupied by citizens of the white race. It is scarcely just to say that a colored citizen should not object to occupying a public coach assigned to his own race. He does not object, nor, perhaps, would he object to separate coaches for his race, if his rights under the law were recognized. But he objects, and ought never to cease objecting to the proposition, that citizens of the white and black races can be adjudged criminals because they sit, or claim the right to sit, in the same public coach on a public highway.

The arbitrary separation of citizens, on the basis of race, while they are on a public highway, is a badge of servitude wholly inconsistent with the civil freedom and the equality before the law established by the Constitution. It cannot be justified upon any legal grounds.

If evils will result from the commingling of the two races upon public highways established for the benefit of all, they will be infinitely less than those that will surely come from state legislation regulating the enjoyment of civil rights upon the basis of race. We boast of the freedom enjoyed by our people above all other peoples. But it is difficult to reconcile that boast with a state of the law which, practically, puts the brand of servitude and degradation upon a large class of our fellow-citizens, our equals before the law. The thin disguise of "equal" accommodations for passengers in railroad coaches will not mislead any one, nor atone for the wrong this day done.

The result of the whole matter is, that while this court has frequently adjudged, and at the present term has recognized the doctrine, that a State cannot, consistently with the Constitution of the United States, prevent white and black citizens, having the required qualifications for jury service, from sitting in the same jury box, it is now solemnly held that a State may prohibit white and black citizens from sitting in the same passenger coach on a public highway, or may require that they be separated by a "partition," when in the same passenger coach. May it not now be reasonably expected that astute men of the dominant race, who affect to be disturbed at the possibility that the integrity of the white race may be corrupted, or that its supremacy will be imperilled, by contact on public highways with black people, will endeavor to procure statutes requiring white and black jurors to be separated in the jury box by a "partition," and that, upon retiring from the court room to consult as to their verdict, such partition, if it be a moveable one, shall be taken to their consultation room, and set up in such way as to prevent black jurors from coming too close to their brother jurors of the white race. If the "partition" used in the court room happens to be stationary, provision could be made for screens with openings through which jurors of the two races could confer as to their verdict without coming into personal contact with each other. I cannot see but that, according to the principles this day announced, such state legislation, although conceived in hostility to, and enacted for the purpose of humiliating citizens of the United States of a particular race, would be held to be consistent with the Constitution. . . .

I am of opinion that the statute of Louisiana is inconsistent with the personal liberty of citizens, white and black, in that State, and hostile to both the spirit and letter of the Constitution of the United States. If laws of like character should be enacted in the several States of the Union, the effect would be in the highest degree mischievous. Slavery, as an institution tolerated by law would, it is true, have disappeared from our country, but there would remain a power in the States, by sinister legislation, to interfere with the full enjoyment of the blessings of freedom; to regulate civil rights, common to all citizens, upon the basis of race; and to place in a condition of legal inferiority a large body of American citizens, now constituting a part of the political community called the People of the United States, for whom, and by whom through representatives, our government is administered. Such a system is inconsistent with the guarantee given by the Constitution to each State of a republican form of government, and may be stricken down by Congressional action, or by the courts in the discharge of their solemn duty to maintain the supreme law of the land, anything in the constitution or laws of any State to the contrary notwithstanding.

For the reasons stated, I am constrained to withhold my assent from the opinion and judgment of the majority.

MR. JUSTICE BREWER did not hear the argument or participate in the decision of this case.

---

**Plessy v. Ferguson,** 163 U.S. 537 (1896) 7–1*
*editor's note.*
*Opinion authors are in bold; () indicates the party of appointing president. If the party of the justice differs from that of appointing president, then the party of the justice is listed second after the slash.*

| MAJORITY | CONCURRING | DISSENTING |
| --- | --- | --- |
| **Brown** (r) | | Harlan (r) |
| Fuller (d) | | |
| White (d)Gray (r) | | |
| Peckham (d) | | |
| Shiras (r) | | |
| Field (r/d) | | |

 *Brewer (r) did not participate.

# Missouri ex rel. Gaines v. Canada, Registrar of the University of Missouri, et. al.

## 305 U.S. 337 (1938)

### Certiorari to the Supreme Court of Missouri

No. 57. Argued November 9, 1938—Decided December 12, 1938.

*Messrs. Charles H. Houston* and *Sidney R. Redmond*, with whom *Mr. Leon A. Ransom* was on the brief, for petitioner.

*Messrs. William S. Hogsett* and *Fred L. Williams*, with whom *Mr. Fred L. English* was on the brief, for respondents.

MR. CHIEF JUSTICE HUGHES delivered the opinion of the Court.

Petitioner Lloyd Gaines, a negro, was refused admission to the School of Law at the State University of Missouri. Asserting that this refusal constituted a denial by the State of the equal protection of the laws in violation of the Fourteenth Amendment of the Federal Constitution, petitioner brought this action for mandamus to compel the curators of the University to admit him. On final hearing, an alternative writ was quashed and a peremptory writ was denied by the Circuit Court. The Supreme Court of the State affirmed the judgment. 113 S. W. 2d 783. We granted certiorari, October 10, 1938.

Petitioner is a citizen of Missouri. In August, 1935, he was graduated with the degree of Bachelor of Arts at the Lincoln University, an institution maintained by the State of Missouri for the higher education of negroes. That University has no law school. Upon the filing of his application for admission to the law school of the University of Missouri, the registrar advised him to communicate with the president of Lincoln University and the latter directed petitioner's attention to § 9622 of the Revised Statutes of Missouri (1929), providing as follows:

"Sec. 9622. *May arrange for attendance at university of any adjacent state—Tuition fees.—* Pending the full development of the Lincoln university, the board of curators shall have the authority to arrange for the attendance of negro residents of the state of

Missouri at the university of any adjacent state to take any course or to study an subjects provided for at the state university of Missouri, and which are not taught at the Lincoln university and to pay the reasonable tuition fees for such attendance; *provided* that whenever the board of curators deem it advisable they shall have the power to open any necessary school or department. (Laws 1921, p. 86, § 7.)"

Petitioner was advised to apply to the State Superintendent of Schools for aid under that statute. It was admitted on the trial that petitioner's "work and credits at the Lincoln University would qualify him for admission to the School of Law of the University of Missouri if he were found otherwise eligible." He was refused admission upon the ground that it was "contrary to the constitution, laws and public policy of the State to admit a negro as a student in the University of Missouri." It appears that there are schools of law in connection with the state universities of four adjacent States, Kansas, Nebraska, Iowa and Illinois, where nonresident negroes are admitted. . . .

In answering petitioner's contention that this discrimination constituted a denial of his constitutional right, the state court has fully recognized the obligation of the State to provide negroes with advantages for higher education substantially equal to the advantages afforded to white students. The State has sought to fulfill that obligation by furnishing equal facilities in separate schools, a method the validity of which has been sustained by our decisions. *Plessy* v. *Ferguson,* . . . Respondent's counsel have appropriately emphasized the special solicitude of the State for the higher education of negroes as shown in the establishment of Lincoln University, a state institution well conducted on a plane with the University of Missouri so far as the offered courses are concerned. It is said that Missouri is a pioneer in that field and is the only State in the Union which has established a separate university for negroes on the same basis as the state university for white students. But, commendable as is that action, the fact remains that instruction in law for negroes is not now afforded by the State, either at Lincoln University or elsewhere within the State, and that the State excludes negroes from the advantages of the law school it has established at the University of Missouri.

It is manifest that this discrimination, if not relieved by the provisions we shall presently discuss, would constitute a denial of equal protection. . . . In the light of its [the state supreme court] ruling we must regard the question whether the provision for the legal education in other States of negroes resident in Missouri is sufficient to satisfy the constitutional requirement of equal protection, as the pivot upon which this case turns.

The state court stresses the advantages that are afforded by the law schools of the adjacent States,—Kansas, Nebraska, Iowa and Illinois,—which admit non-resident negroes. The court considered that these were schools of high standing where one desiring to practice law in Missouri can get "as sound, comprehensive, valuable legal education" as in the University of Missouri; that the system of education in the former is the same as that in the latter and is designed to give the students a basis for the practice of law in any State where the Anglo-American system of law obtains; that the law school of the University of Missouri does not specialize in Missouri law and that the course of study and the case books used in the five schools are substantially identical. Petitioner insists that for one intending to practice in Missouri there are special advantages in attending a law school there, both in relation to the opportunities for the particular study of Missouri law and for the observation of the local courts, and also in view of the prestige of the Missouri law school among the citizens of the State, his prospective clients. Proceeding with its examination of relative advantages, the state court found that the difference in distances to be traveled afforded no substantial ground of complaint and that there was an adequate appropriation to meet the full tuition fees which petitioner would have to pay.

We think that these matters are beside the point. The basic consideration is not as to what sort of opportunities other States provide, or whether they are as good as those in Missouri, but as to what opportunities Missouri itself furnishes to white students and denies to negroes solely upon the ground of color. The admissibility of laws separating the races in the enjoyment of privileges afforded by the State rests wholly upon the equality of the privileges which the laws give to the separated groups within the State. The question here is not of a duty of the State to supply legal training which it does supply, but of its duty when it provides such training to furnish it to the residents of the State upon the basis of an equality of right. By the operation of the laws of Missouri a privilege has been created for white law students which is denied to negroes by reason of their race. The white resident is afforded legal education within the State; the negro resident having the same qualifications is refused it there and must go outside the State to obtain it. That is a denial of the equality of legal right to the enjoyment of the privilege which the State has set up, and the provision for the payment of tuition fees in another State does not remove the discrimination.

The equal protection of the laws is "a pledge of the protection of equal laws." . . . That obligation is imposed by the Constitution upon the States severally as governmental entities,—each responsible for its own laws establishing the rights and duties of persons within its borders. It is an obligation the burden of which cannot be cast by one State upon another, and no State can be excused from performance by what another State may do or fail to do. That separate responsibility of each State within its own sphere is of the essence of statehood maintained under our dual system. It seems to be implicit in respondents' argument that if other States did not provide courses for legal education, it would nevertheless be the constitutional duty of Missouri when it supplied such courses for white students to make equivalent provision for negroes. But that plain duty would exist because it rested upon the State independently of the action of other States. We find it impossible to conclude that what otherwise would be an unconstitutional discrimination, with respect to the legal right to the enjoyment of opportunities within the State, can be justified by requiring resort to opportunities elsewhere. That resort may mitigate the inconvenience of the discrimination but cannot serve to validate it.

Nor can we regard the fact that there is but a limited demand in Missouri for the legal education of negroes as excusing the discrimination in favor of whites. . . . It is the individual who is entitled to the equal protection of the laws, . . .

Here, petitioner's right was a personal one. It was as an individual that he was entitled to the equal protection of the laws, and the State was bound to furnish him within its borders facilities for legal education substantially equal to those which the State there afforded for persons of the white race, whether or not other negroes sought the same opportunity. . . .

We are of the opinion . . . that petitioner was entitled to be admitted to the law school of the State University in the absence of other and proper provision for his legal training within the State.

The judgment of the Supreme Court of Missouri is reversed and the cause is remanded for further proceedings not inconsistent with this opinion.

*Reversed.*

Separate opinion of MR. JUSTICE MCREYNOLDS. [dissenting]

Considering the disclosures of the record, the Supreme Court of Missouri arrived at a tenable conclusion and its judgment should be affirmed. That court well understood the grave difficulties of the situation and rightly refused to upset the settled legislative policy of the State by directing a mandamus. . . .

For a long time Missouri has acted upon the view that the best interest of her people demands separation of whites and negroes in schools. Under the opinion just announced, I presume she may abandon her law school and thereby disadvantage her white citizens without improving petitioner's opportunities for legal instruction; or she may break down the settled practice concerning separate schools and thereby, as indicated by experience, damnify both races. Whether by some other course it may be possible for her to avoid condemnation is matter for conjecture.

The State has offered to provide the negro petitioner opportunity for study of the law—if perchance that is the thing really desired—by paying his tuition at some nearby school of good standing. This is far from unmistakable disregard of his rights and in the circumstances is enough to satisfy any reasonable demand for specialized training. It appears that never before has a negro applied for admission to the Law School and none has ever asked that Lincoln University provide legal instruction.

The problem presented obviously is a difficult and highly practical one. A fair effort to solve it has been made by offering adequate opportunity for study when sought in good faith. The State should not be unduly hampered through theorization inadequately restrained by experience. . . .

MR. JUSTICE BUTLER concurs in the above views.

---

**Missouri ex. Rel. Gaines, v. Canada, Registrar of the University of Missouri, et. al.,** 305 U.S. 337 (1938) 6–2

*editor's note.*

*Opinion authors are in bold; () indicates the party of appointing president. If the party of the justice differs from that of appointing president, then the party of the justice is listed second after the slash.*

| MAJORITY | CONCURRING | DISSENTING |
|---|---|---|
| **Hughes** (r) | | McReynolds (r) |
| Brandeis (d) | | Butler (r/d) |
| Stone (r) | | |
| Roberts (r) | | |
| Black (d) | | |
| Reed (d) | | |

---

**Please refer to** *Brown* **v.** *Board of Education,* 347 U.S. 483 (1954) [*Brown* I], **Chapter 4, herein.**

# Brown et al. v. Board of Education of Topeka et al.

## 349 U.S. 294 (1955)

## No. 1. Appeal from the United States District Court for the District of Kansas. *

(Reargued on the question of relief April 11–14, 1955.—Opinion and judgments announced May 31, 1955.

*Robert L. Carter* argued the cause for appellants in No. 1. *Spottswood W. Robinson, III,* argued the causes for appellants in Nos. 2 and 3. *George E. C. Hayes* and *James M. Nabrit, Jr.* argued the cause for petitioners in No. 4. *Louis L. Redding* argued the cause for respondents in No. 5. *Thurgood Marshall* argued the causes for appellants in Nos. 1, 2 and 3, petitioners in No. 4 and respondents in No. 5.

On the briefs were *Harold Boulware, Robert L. Carter, Jack Greenberg, Oliver W. Hill, Thurgood Marshall, Louis L. Redding, Spottswood W. Robinson, III, Charles S. Scott, William T. Coleman, Jr., Charles T. Duncan, George E. C. Hayes, Loren Miller, William R. Ming, Jr., Constance Baker Motley, James M. Nabrit, Jr., Louis H. Pollack* and *Frank D. Reeves* for appellants in Nos. 1, 2 and 3, and respondents in No. 5; and *George E. C. Hayes, James M. Nabrit, Jr., George M. Johnson, Charles W. Quick, Herbert O. Reid, Thurgood Marshall* and *Robert L. Carter* for petitioners in No. 4.

*Harold R. Fatzer*, Attorney General of Kansas, argued the cause for appellees in No. 1. With him on the brief was *Paul E. Wilson*, Assistant Attorney General. *Peter F. Caldwell* filed a brief for the Board of Education of Topeka, Kansas, appellee.

*S.E. Rogers* and *Robert McC.Figg, Jr.* argued the cause and filed a brief for appellees in No. 2.

*J. Lindsay Almond, Jr.*, Attorney General of Virginia, and *Archibald G. Robertson* argued the cause for appellees in No. 3. With them on the brief were *Henry T. Wickham*, Special Assistant to the Attorney General, *T. Justin Moore, John W. Riley* and *T. Justin Moore, Jr.*

*Milton D. Korman* argued the cause for respondents in No. 4. With him on the brief were *Vernon E. West, Chester H. Gray* and *Lyman J. Umstead.*

*Joseph Donald Craven*, Attorney General of Delaware, argued the cause for petitioners in No. 5. On the brief were *H. Albert Young*, then Attorney General, *Clarence W. Taylor*, Deputy Attorney General, and *Andrew D. Christie*, Special Deputy to the Attorney General.

In response to the Court invitation, 347 U.S. 483, 495–496, *Solicitor General Sobeloff* participated in the oral argument for the United States. With him on the brief were *Attorney General Brownell, Assistant Attorney General Rankin, Philip Elman, Ralph S. Spritzer* and *Alan S. Rosenthal.*

By invitation of the Court, 347 U. S. 483, 496, the following State officials presented their views orally as *amici curiae: Thomas J. Gentry*, Attorney General of Arkansas, with whom on the brief were *James L. Sloan*, Assistant Attorney General, and *Richard B. McCulloch*, Special Assistant Attorney General, and *Richard W. Ervin*, Attorney General of Florida, and *Ralph E. Odum*, Assistant Attorney General, both of whom were also on a brief. *C. Ferdinand Sybert*, Attorney General of Maryland, with whom on the brief were *Edward D. E. Rollins*, then Attorney General, *W. Giles Parker*, Assistant Attorney General, and *James H. Norris, Jr.*, Special Assistant Attorney General. *I. Beverly Lake*, Assistant Attorney General of North Carolina, with whom on the brief were *Harry McMullan*, Attorney General, and *T. Wade Bruton, Ralph Moody* and *Claude L. Love*, Assistant Attorneys General. *Mac Q. Williamson*, Attorney General of Oklahoma, who also filed a brief. *John Ben Shepperd*, Attorney General of Texas, and *Burnell Waldrep*, Assistant Attorney General, with whom on the brief were *Billy E. Lee, J. A. Amis, Jr., L. P. Lollar, J. Fred Jones, John Davenport, John Reeves* and *Will Davis.*

*Phineas Indritz* filed a brief for the American Veterans Committee, Inc., as *amicus curiae.*

MR. CHIEF JUSTICE WARREN delivered the opinion of the Court.

These cases were decided on May 17, 1954. The opinions of that date,[1] declaring the fundamental principle that racial discrimination in public education is unconstitutional, are incorporated herein by reference. All provisions of federal, state, or local law requiring or permitting such discrimination must yield to this principle. There remains for consideration the manner in which relief is to be accorded.

Because these cases arose under different local conditions and their disposition will involve a variety of local problems, we requested further argument on the question of relief. In view of the nationwide importance of the decision, we invited the Attorney General of the United States and the Attorney General of all states requiring or permitting racial discrimination in public education to present their views on that question. The parties, the United States, and the States of Florida, North Carolina,

Arkansas, Oklahoma, Maryland, and Texas filed briefs and participated in the oral argument.

These presentations were informative and helpful to the Court in its consideration of the complexities arising from the transition to a system of public education freed of racial discrimination. The presentations also demonstrated that substantial steps to eliminate racial discrimination in public schools have already been taken, not only in some of the communities in which these cases arose, but in some of the states appearing as *amici curiae*, and in other states as well. Substantial progress has been made in the District of Columbia and in the communities in Kansas and Delaware involved in this litigation. The defendants in the cases coming to us from South Carolina and Virginia are awaiting the decision of this Court concerning relief.

Full implementation of these constitutional principles may require solution of varied local school problems. School authorities have the primary responsibility for elucidating, assessing, and solving these problems; courts will have to consider whether the action of school authorities constitutes good faith implementation of the governing constitutional principles. Because of their proximity to local conditions and the possible need for further hearings, the courts which originally heard these cases can best perform this judicial appraisal. Accordingly, we believe it appropriate to remand the cases to those courts.

In fashioning and effectuating the decrees, the courts will be guided by equitable principles. Traditionally, equity has been characterized by a practical flexibility in shaping its remedies and by a facility for adjusting and reconciling public and private needs. These cases call for the exercise of these traditional attributes of equity power. At stake is the personal interest of the plaintiffs in admission to public schools as soon as practicable on a nondiscriminatory basis. To effectuate this interest may call for elimination of a variety of obstacles in making the transition to school systems operated in accordance with the constitutional principles set forth in our May 17, 1954, decision. Courts of equity may properly take into account the public interest in the elimination of such obstacles in a systematic and effective manner. But it should go without saying that the vitality of these constitutional principles cannot be allowed to yield simply because of disagreement with them.

While giving weight to these public and private considerations, the courts will require that the defendants make a prompt and reasonable start toward full compliance with our May 17, 1954, ruling. Once such a start has been made, the courts may find that additional time is necessary to carry out the ruling in an effective manner. The burden rests upon the defendants to establish that such time is necessary in the public interest and is consistent with good faith compliance at the earliest practicable date. To that end, the courts may consider problems related to administration, arising from the physical condition of the school plant, the school transportation system, personnel, revision of school districts and attendance areas into compact units to achieve a system of determining admission to the public schools on a nonracial basis, and revision of local laws and regulations which may be necessary in solving the foregoing problems. They will also consider the adequacy of any plans the defendants may propose to meet these problems and to effectuate a transition to a racially nondiscriminatory school system. During this period of transition, the courts will retain jurisdiction of these cases.

The judgments below, except that in the Delaware case, are accordingly reversed and the cases are remanded to the District Courts to take such proceedings and enter such orders and decrees consistent with this opinion as are necessary and proper to admit to public schools on a racially nondiscriminatory basis with all deliberate speed the parties to these cases. The judgment in the Delaware case—ordering the immediate admission of the plaintiffs to schools previously attended only by white children—is affirmed on the basis of the principles stated in our May 17, 1954, opinion, but the case is remanded to the Supreme Court of Delaware for such further proceedings as that Court may deem necessary in light of this opinion.

*It is so ordered.*

## Notes

\*    Together with No. 2, *Briggs et al.* v. *Elliott et al.*, on appeal from the United States District Court for the Eastern District of South Carolina; No. 3, *Davis et al.* v. *County School Board of Prince Edward County, Virginia, et al.*, on appeal from the United States District Court for the Eastern District of Virginia; No. 4, *Bolling et al.* v. *Sharpe et al.*, on certiorari to the United States Court of Appeals for the District of Columbia Circuit; and No. 5, *Gebhart et al.* v. *Belton et al.*, on certiorari to the Supreme Court of Delaware.

1.    347 U. S. 483; 347 U. S. 497.

**Brown v. Board of Education**, 349 U. S. 294 (1955) [*Brown* II] 9–0
*editor's note.*
*Opinion authors are in bold; () indicates the party of appointing president. If the party of the justice differs from that of appointing president, then the party of the justice is listed second after the slash.*

| MAJORITY | CONCURRING | DISSENTING |
| --- | --- | --- |
| **Warren** (r) | | |
| Black (d) | | |
| Reed (d) | | |
| Frankfurter (d/i) | | |
| Douglas (d) | | |
| Jackson (d) | | |
| Burton (d) | | |
| Clark (d) | | |
| Minton (d) | | |

# DECISIONS PER CURIAM

## Mayor and City Council of Baltimore City et al. v. Dawson et al.

### 350 U.S. 877 (1955)

Appeal from the United States Court of Appeals for the Fourth Circuit. *Per Curiam*: The motion to affirm is granted and the judgment is affirmed. *C. Ferdinand Sybert*, Attorney General of Maryland, *Norman P. Ramsey*, Deputy Attorney General, and *Ambrose T. Hartman*, Assistant Attorney General, for appellants. *Robert L. Carter, Thurgood Marshall* and *Jack Greenberg* for appellees. Reported below: 220 F. 2d. 386. [editor's note: public beaches]

## Holmes et al. v. City of Atlanta et al.

### 350 U.S. 879 (1955)

On petition for writ of certiorari to the United States Court of Appeals for the Fifth Circuit. *Per Curiam*: The petition for writ of certiorari is granted, the judgments both of the Court of Appeals and the District Court are vacated and the case is remanded to the District Court with directions to enter a decree for petitioners in conformity with *Mayor & City Council of Baltimore City* v. *Dawson, ante,* p. 877, decided this day. *Robert L. Carter, Thurgood Marshall* and *E. E. Moore* for petitioners. *J. C. Murphy* and *Henry L. Bowden* for respondents. Reported below: 223 F. 2d. 93. [editor's note: golf courses]

## Commissioners of Montgomery, Alabama, et al. v. Browder et al.; and Owen et al., Members of the Alabama Public Service Commission, et al. v. Browder et al.

### 352 U.S. 903 (1956)

Appeals from the United States District Court for the Middle District of Alabama. *Per Curiam:* The motion to affirm is granted and the judgment is affirmed. *Brown* v. *Board of Education,* 347 U. S. 483; *Mayor and City Council of Baltimore* v. *Dawson,* 350 U. S. 877; *Holmes* v. *Atlanta,* 350 U. S. 879.

*Walter J. Knabe* for appellants. *John Patterson,* Attorney General of Alabama, and *William N. McQueen* and *Gordon Madison,* Assistant Attorneys General, for appellants. *Robert L. Carter* and *Thurgood Marshall* for appellees. Reported below: 142 F. Supp. 707. [editor's note: buses]

## New Orleans City Park Improvement Association v. Detiege et al.

### 358 U. S. 54 (1958)

#### Appeal from the United States Court of Appeals for the Fifth Circuit.

#### No. 295. Decided October 20, 1958.

*252 F. 2d 122, affirmed.*

*Ed J. de Verges* for appellant.

Per Curiam

The judgment is affirmed. [editor's note: city parks]

# Johnson v. Virginia

## 373 U. S. 61 (1963)

## On Petition for Writ of Certiorari to the Supreme Court of Appeals of Virginia.

### No. 715. Decided April 29, 1963.

*Roland D. Ealey* and *Herman T. Benn* for petitioner.

*Reno S. Harp III*, Assistant Attorney General of Virginia, for respondent.

## PER CURIAM

The petition for a writ of certiorari is granted, the judgment of the Supreme Court of Appeals of Virginia is reversed, and the case is remanded for proceedings not inconsistent with this opinion.

The petitioner, Ford T. Johnson, Jr., was convicted of contempt of the Traffic Court of the City of Richmond, Virginia, and appealed his conviction to the Hustings Court, where he was tried without a jury and again convicted. The Supreme Court of Appeals of Virginia refused to grant a writ of error on the ground that the judgment appealed from was "plainly right," but the Chief Justice of that court stayed execution of the judgment pending disposition of this petition for certiorari.

The evidence at petitioner's trial in the Hustings Court is summarized in an approved statement of facts. According to this statement, the witnesses for the State testified as follows: The petitioner, a Negro, was seated in Traffic Court in a section reserved for whites, and when requested to move by the bailiff, refused to do so. The judge then summoned the petitioner to the bench and instructed him to be seated in the right-hand section of the courtroom, the section reserved for Negroes. The petitioner moved back in front of the counsel table and remained standing with his arms folded, stating that he preferred standing and indicating that he would not comply with the judge's order. Upon refusal to obey the judge's further direction to be seated, the petitioner was arrested for contempt. At no time did he behave in a boisterous or abusive manner, and there was no disorder in the courtroom. The State, in its Brief in Opposition filed in this Court, concedes that in the section of the Richmond Traffic Court reserved for spectators, seating space "is assigned on the basis of racial designation, the seats on one side of the aisle being for use of Negro citizens and the seats on the other side being for the use of white citizens."

It is clear from the totality of circumstances, and particularly the fact that the petitioner was peaceably seated in the section reserved for whites before being summoned to the bench, that the arrest and conviction rested entirely on the refusal to comply with the segregated seating requirements imposed in this particular courtroom. Such a conviction cannot stand, for it is no longer open to question that a State may not constitutionally require segregation of public facilities. See, *e.g., Brown* v. *Board of Education,* 347 U. S. 483; *Mayor and City Council of Baltimore* v. *Dawson,* 350 U. S. 877; *Turner* v. *Memphis,* 369 U. S. 350. State-compelled segregation in a court of justice is a manifest violation of the State's duty to deny no one the equal protection of its laws.

*Reversed and remanded.*

---

**Johnson v. Virginia**, 373 U.S. 61 (1963) 9–0
*editor's note.*
*Opinion authors are in bold; () indicates the party of appointing president. If the party of the justice differs from that of appointing president, then the party of the justice is listed second after the slash.*

## PER CURIAM OPINION

Warren (r)
Black (d)
Goldberg (d)
Brennan (r/d)
Douglass (d)
Clark (d)
White (d)
Stewart (r)
Harlan (r)

# National Association for the Advancement of Colored People v. Button, Attorney General of Virginia, et al.

## 371 U.S. 415

### Certiorari to the Supreme Court of Appeals of Virginia

No. 5. Argued November 8, 1961.—Restored to the calendar for reargument April 2, 1962,—Reargued October 9, 1962,—Decided January 14, 1963.

*Robert L. Carter* reargued the case for petitioner. With him on the briefs was *Frank D. Reeves.*

*Henry T. Wickham* reargued the case for respondents. With him on the brief was *David J. Mays.*

MR. JUSTICE BRENNAN delivered the opinion of the Court.

This case originated in companion suits by the National Association for the Advancement of Colored People, Inc., (NAACP), and the NAACP Legal Defense and Educational Fund, Inc. (Defense Fund), brought in 1957 in the United States District Court for the Eastern District of Virginia. The suits sought to restrain the enforcement of Chapters 31, 32, 33, 35 and 36 of the Virginia Acts of Assembly, 1956 Extra Session, on the ground that the statutes, as applied to the activities of the plaintiffs, violated the Fourteenth Amendment. . . .

There is no substantial dispute as to the facts; the dispute centers about the constitutionality under the Fourteenth Amendment of Chapter 33, as construed and applied by the Virginia Supreme Court of Appeals to include NAACP's activities within the statute's ban against "the improper solicitation of any legal or professional business."

The NAACP was formed in 1909 and incorporated under New York law as a nonprofit membership corporation in 1911. It maintains its headquarters in New York and presently has some 1,000 active unincorporated branches throughout the Nation. The corporation is licensed to do business in Virginia, and has 89 branches there. The Virginia branches are organized into the Virginia State Conference of NAACP Branches (the Conference), an unincorporated association, which in 1957 had some

13,500 members. The activities of the Conference are financed jointly by the national organization and the local branches from contributions and membership dues. NAACP policy, binding upon local branches and conferences, is set by the annual national convention.

The basic aims and purposes of NAACP are to secure the elimination of all racial barriers which deprive Negro citizens of the privileges and burdens of equal citizenship rights in the United States. To this end the Association engages in extensive educational and lobbying activities. It also devotes much of its funds and energies to an extensive program of assisting certain kinds of litigation on behalf of its declared purposes. For more than 10 years, the Virginia Conference has concentrated upon financing litigation aimed at ending racial segregation in the public schools of the Cornmonwealth.

The Conference ordinarily will finance only cases in which the assisted litigant retains an NAACP staff lawyer to represent him. The Conference maintains a legal staff of 15 attorneys, all of whom are Negroes and members of the NAACP. The staff is elected at the Conference's annual convention. Each legal staff member must agree to abide by the policies of the NAACP, which, insofar as they pertain to professional services, limit the kinds of litigation which the NAACP will assist. Thus the NAACP will not underwrite ordinary damages actions, criminal actions in which the defendant raises no question of possible racial discrimination, or suits in which the plaintiff seeks separate but equal rather than fully desegregated public school facilities. The staff decides whether a litigant, who may or may not be an NAACP member, is entitled to NAACP assistance. The Conference defrays all expenses of litigation in an assisted case, and usually, although not always, pays each lawyer on the case a per diem fee not to exceed $60, plus out-of-pocket expenses. The assisted litigant receives no money from the Conference or the staff lawyers. The staff member may not accept, from the litigant or any other source, any other compensation for his services in an NAACP-assisted case. None of the staff receives a salary or retainer from the NAACP; the per diem fee is paid only for professional services in a particular case. This per diem payment is smaller than the compensation ordinarily received for equivalent private professional work. The actual conduct of assisted litigation is under the control of the attorney, although the NAACP continues to be concerned that the outcome of the lawsuit should be consistent with NAACP's policies already described. A client is free at any time to withdraw from an action.

The members of the legal staff of the Virginia Conference and other NAACP or Defense Fund lawyers called in by the staff to assist are drawn into litigation in various ways. One is for an aggrieved Negro to apply directly to the Conference or the legal staff for assistance. His application is referred to the Chairman of the legal staff. The Chairman, with the concurrence of the President of the Conference, is authorized to agree to give legal assistance in an appropriate case. In litigation involving public school segregation, the procedure tends to be different. Typically, a local NAACP branch will invite a member of the legal staff to explain to a meeting of parents and children the legal steps necessary to achieve desegregation. The staff member will bring printed forms to the meeting authorizing him, and other NAACP or Defense Fund attorneys of his designation, to represent the signers in legal proceedings to achieve desegregation. On occasion, blank forms have been signed by litigants, upon the understanding that a member or members of the legal staff, with or without assistance from other NAACP lawyers, or from the Defense Fund, would handle the case. It is usual, after obtaining authorizations, for the staff lawyer to bring into the case the other staff members in the area where suit is to be brought, and sometimes to bring in lawyers from the national organization or the Defense Fund.[1] In effect, then, the prospective litigant retains not so much a particular attorney as the "firm" of NAACP and Defense Fund lawyers, which has a corporate reputation for expertness in presenting and arguing the difficult questions of law that frequently arise in civil rights litigation.

These meetings are sometimes prompted by letters and bulletins from the Conference urging active steps to fight segregation. The Conference has on occasion distributed to the local branches petitions for desegregation to be signed by parents and filed with local school boards, and advised branch officials to obtain, as petitioners, persons willing to "go all the way" in any possible litigation that may ensue. While the Conference in these ways encourages the bringing of lawsuits, the plaintiffs in particular actions, so far as appears, make their own decisions to become such.

Statutory regulation of unethical and nonprofessional conduct by attorneys has been in force in Virginia since 1849. These provisions outlaw, *inter alia*, solicitation of legal business in the form of "running" or "capping." Prior to 1956, however, no attempt was made to proscribe under such regulations the activities of the NAACP, which had been carried on openly for many years in substantially the manner described. In 1956, however, the legislature amended, by the addition of Chapter 33, the provisions of the Virginia Code forbidding solicitation of legal business by a "runner" or "capper" to include, in the definition of "runner" or "capper," an agent for an individual or organization which retains a lawyer in connection with an action to which it is not a party and in which it has no pecuniary right or liability. The Virginia Supreme Court of Appeals held that the chapter's purpose "was to strengthen the existing statutes to further control the evils of solicitation of legal business. . . ." 202 Va., at 154, 116 S.E. 2d, at 65. The court held that the activities of NAACP, the Virginia Conference, the Defense Fund, and the lawyers furnished by them fell within, and could constitutionally be proscribed by, the chapter's expanded definition of improper solicitation of legal business, and also violated Canons 35 and 47 of the American Bar Association's Canons of Professional Ethics, which the court had adopted in 1938. Specifically the court held that, under the expanded definition, such activities on the part of NAACP, the Virginia

Conference, and the Defense Fund constituted "fomenting and soliciting legal business in which they are not parties and have no pecuniary right or liability, and which they channel to the enrichment of certain lawyers employed by them, at no cost to the litigants and over which the litigants have no control." 202 Va., at 155; 116 S. E. 2d, at 66. . . .

Petitioner challenges the decision of the Supreme Court of Appeals on many grounds. But we reach only one: that Chapter 33 as construed and applied abridges the freedoms of the First Amendment, protected against state action by the Fourteenth. More specifically, petitioner claims that the chapter infringes the right of the NAACP and its members and lawyers to associate for the purpose of assisting persons who seek legal redress for infringements of their constitutionally guaranteed and other rights. . . .

We reverse the judgment of the Virginia Supreme Court of Appeals. We hold that the activities of the NAACP, its affiliates and legal staff shown on this record are modes of expression and association protected by the First and Fourteenth Amendments which Virginia may not prohibit, under its power to regulate the legal profession, as improper solicitation of legal business violative of Chapter 33 and the Canons of Professional Ethics.

We meet at the outset the contention that "solicitation" is wholly outside the area of freedoms protected by the First Amendment. To this contention there are two answers. The first is that a State cannot foreclose the exercise of constitutional rights by mere labels. The second is that abstract discussion is not the only species of communication which the Constitution protects; the First Amendment also protects vigorous advocacy, certainly of lawful ends, against governmental intrusion. *Thomas v. Collins*, 323 U. S. 516, 537; *Herndon v. Lowry*, 301 U. S. 242, 259–264. Cf. *Cantwell v. Connecticut*, 310 U. S. 296; *Stromberg v. California*, 283 U. S. 359, 369; *Terminiello v. Chicago*, 337 U. S. 1, 4. In the context of NAACP objectives, litigation is not a technique of resolving private differences; it is a means for achieving the lawful objectives of equality of treatment by all government, federal, state and local, for the members of the Negro community in this country. It is thus a forum of political expression. Groups which find themselves unable to achieve their objectives through the ballot frequently turn to the courts. Just as it was true of the opponents of New Deal legislation during the 1930s, for example, no less is it true of the Negro minority today. And under the conditions of modern government, litigation may well be the sole practicable avenue open to a minority to petition for redress of grievances.

We need not, in order to find constitutional protection for the kind of cooperative, organizational activity disclosed by this record, whereby Negroes seek through lawful means to achieve legitimate political ends, subsume such activity under a narrow, literal conception of freedom of speech, petition or assembly. For there is no longer any doubt that the First and Fourteenth Amendments protect certain forms of orderly group activity. . . .

The NAACP is not a conventional political party; but the litigation it assists, while serving to vindicate the legal rights of members of the American Negro community, at the same time and perhaps more importantly, makes possible the distinctive contribution of a minority group to the ideas and beliefs of our society. For such a group, association for litigation may be the most effective form of political association. . . .

We conclude that under Chapter 33, as authoritatively construed by the Supreme Court of Appeals, a person who advises another that his legal rights have been infringed and refers him to a particular attorney or group of attorneys (for example, to the Virginia Conference's legal staff) for assistance has committed a crime, as has the attorney who knowingly renders assistance under such circumstances. There thus inheres in the statute the gravest danger of smothering all discussion looking to the eventual institution of litigation on behalf of the rights of members of an unpopular minority. Lawyers on the legal staff or even mere NAACP members or sympathizers would understandably hesitate, at an NAACP meeting or on any other occasion, to do what the decree purports to allow, namely, acquaint "persons with what they believe to be their legal rights and . . . [advise] them to assert their rights by commencing or further prosecuting a suit. . . . " For if the lawyers, members or sympathizers also appeared in or had any connection with any litigation supported with NAACP funds contributed under the provision of the decree by which the NAACP is not prohibited "from contributing money to persons to assist them in commencing or further prosecuting such suits," they plainly would risk (if lawyers) disbarment proceedings and lawyers and nonlawyers alike, criminal prosecution for the offense of "solicitation," to which the Virginia court gave so broad and uncertain a meaning. It makes no difference whether such prosecutions or proceedings would actually be commenced. It is enough that a vague and broad statute lends itself to selective enforcement against unpopular causes. We cannot close our eyes to the fact that the militant Negro civil rights movement has engendered the intense resentment and opposition of the politically dominant white community of Virginia; litigation assisted by the NAACP has been bitterly fought. In such circumstances, a statute broadly curtailing group activity leading to litigation may easily become a weapon of oppression, however evenhanded its terms appear. Its mere existence could well freeze out of existence all such activity on behalf of the civil rights of Negro citizens.

It is apparent, therefore, that Chapter 33 as construed limits First Amendment freedoms. . . .

The second contention is that Virginia has a subordinating interest in the regulation of the legal profession, embodied in Chapter 33, which justifies limiting petitioner's First Amendment rights. Specifically, Virginia contends that the NAACP's activities in furtherance of litigation, being "improper solicitation" under the state statute, fall within the traditional purview of state regulation of professional conduct. However, the State's attempt to equate the activities of the NAACP and its lawyers with common-law barratry, maintenance and champerty, and to outlaw them accordingly, cannot obscure the serious encroachment worked by Chapter 33 upon protected freedoms of expression. The decisions of this Court have consistently held that only a compelling state interest in the regulation of a subject within the State's constitutional power to regulate can justify limiting First Amendment freedoms. Thus it is no answer to the constitutional claims asserted by petitioner to say, as the Virginia Supreme Court of Appeals has said, that the purpose of these regulations was merely to insure high professional standards and not to curtail free expression. For a State may not, under the guise of prohibiting professional misconduct, ignore constitutional rights. . . .

However valid may be Virginia's interest in regulating the traditionally illegal practices of barratry, maintenance and champerty, that interest does not justify the prohibition of the NAACP activities disclosed by this record. Malicious intent was of the essence of the common-law offenses of fomenting or stirring up litigation. And whatever may be or may have been true of suits against government in other countries, the exercise in our own as in this case, of First Amendment rights to enforce constitutional rights through litigation, as a matter of law, cannot be deemed malicious. . . . There has been no showing of a serious danger here of professionally reprehensible conflicts of interest which rules against solicitation frequently seek to prevent. This is so partly because no monetary stakes are involved, and so there is no danger that the attorney will desert or subvert the paramount interests of his client to enrich himself or an outside sponsor. And the aims and interests of NAACP have not been shown to conflict with those of its members and nonmember Negro litigants. . . .

Resort to the courts to seek vindication of constitutional rights is a different matter from the oppressive, malicious, or avaricious use of the legal process for purely private gain. Lawsuits attacking racial discrimination, at least in Virginia, are neither very profitable nor very popular. They are not an object of general competition among Virginia lawyers; the problem is rather one of an apparent dearth of lawyers who are willing to undertake such litigation. There has been neither claim nor proof that any assisted Negro litigants have desired, but have been prevented from retaining, the services of other counsel. We realize that an NAACP lawyer must derive personal satisfaction from participation in litigation on behalf of Negro rights, else he would hardly be inclined to participate at the risk of financial sacrifice. But this would not seem to be the kind of interest or motive which induces criminal conduct.

We conclude that although the petitioner has amply shown that its activities fall within the First Amendment's protections, the State has failed to advance any substantial regulatory interest, in the form of substantive evils flowing from petitioner's activities, which can justify the broad prohibitions which it has imposed. Nothing that this record shows as to the nature and purpose of NAACP activities permits an inference of any injurious intervention in or control of litigation which would constitutionally authorize the application of Chapter 33 to those activities. A *fortiori*, nothing in this record justifies a breadth and vagueness of the Virginia Supreme Court of Appeals decree.

A final observation is in order. Because our disposition is rested on the First Amendment as absorbed in the Fourteenth, we do not reach the consideration of race or racial discrimination which are the predicate of petitioner's challenge to the statute under the Equal Protection Clause. That the petitioner happens to be engaged in activities of expression and association on behalf of the rights of Negro children to equal opportunity is constitutionally irrelevant to the ground of our decision. The course of our decisions in the First Amendment area makes plain that its protections would apply as fully to those who would arouse our society against the objectives of the petitioner. See, *e.g.*, *Near* v. *Minnesota*, 283 U.S. 697; *Terminiello* v. *Chicago*, 337 U. S. 1; *Kunz* v. *New York*, 340 U. S. 290. For the Constitution protects expression and association without regard to the race, creed, or political or religious affiliation of the members of the group which invokes its shield, or to the truth, popularity, or social utility of the ideas and beliefs which are offered.

*Reversed.*

Mr. Justice Douglas, concurring.

While I join the opinion of the Court, I add a few words. This Virginia Act is not applied across the board to all groups that use this method of obtaining and managing litigation, but instead reflects a legislative purpose to penalize the N.A.A.C.P. because it promotes desegregation of the races. Our decision in *Brown* v. *Board of Education*, 347 U. S. 483, holding that maintenance of public schools segregated by race violated the Equal Protection Clause of the Fourteenth Amendment, was announced May 17, 1954. The amendments to Virginia's code, here in issue, were enacted in 1956. Arkansas, Florida, Georgia, Mississippi, South Carolina, and Tennessee also passed laws following our 1954 decision which brought within their barratry statutes attorneys paid by an organization such as the N.A.A.C.P. and representing litigants without charge.

The bill, here involved, was one of five that Virginia enacted "as parts of the general plan of massive resistance to the integration of schools of the state under the Supreme Court's decrees.". . .

MR. JUSTICE WHITE, concurring in part and dissenting in part.

I agree that as construed by the Virginia Supreme Court, Chapter 33 does not proscribe only the actual control of litigation after its commencement, that it does forbid, under threat of criminal punishment, advising the employment of particular attorneys, and that as so construed the statute is unconstitutional. . . . I concur in the judgment of the Court, but not in all of its opinion.

If we had before us, which we do not, a narrowly drawn statute proscribing only the actual day-to-day management and dictation of the tactics, strategy and conduct of litigation by a lay entity such as the NAACP, the issue would be considerably different, at least for me; for in my opinion neither the practice of law by such an organization nor its management of the litigation of its members or others is constitutionally protected. Both practices are well within the regulatory power of the State. In this regard I agree with my Brother HARLAN.

It is not at all clear to me, however, that the opinion of the majority would not also strike down such a narrowly drawn statute. To the extent that it would, I am in disagreement. . . .

MR. JUSTICE HARLAN, whom MR. JUSTICE CLARK and MR. JUSTICE STEWART join, dissenting.

No member of this Court would disagree that the validity of state action claimed to infringe rights assured by the Fourteenth Amendment is to be judged by the same basic constitutional standards whether or not racial problems are involved. No worse setback could befall the great principles established by *Brown* v. *Board of Education*, 347 U. S. 483, than to give fair-minded persons reason to think otherwise. With all respect, I believe that the striking down of this Virginia statute cannot be squared with accepted constitutional doctrine in the domain of state regulatory power over the legal profession.

— I —

At the outset the factual premises on which the Virginia Supreme Court of Appeals upheld the application of Chapter 33 to the activities of the NAACP in the area of litigation, as well as the scope of that court's holding, should be delineated.

*First,* the lawyers who participate in litigation sponsored by petitioner are, almost without exception, members of the legal staff of the NAACP Virginia State Conference. (It is, in fact, against Conference policy to give financial support to litigation not handled by a staff lawyer.) As such, they are selected by petitioner, are compensated by it for work in litigation (whether or not petitioner is a party thereto), and so long as they remain on the staff, are necessarily subject to its directions. As the Court recognizes, it is incumbent on staff members to agree to abide by NAACP policies.

*Second,* it is equally clear that the NAACP's directions, or those of its officers and divisions, to staff lawyers cover many subjects relating to the form and substance of litigation. Thus, in 1950, it was resolved at a Board of Directors meeting that:

> "Pleadings in all educational cases—the prayer in the pleading and proof be aimed at obtaining education on a non-segregated basis and that no relief other than that will be acceptable as such.

> Further, that all lawyers operating under such rule will urge their client and the branches of the Association involved to insist on this final relief."

The minutes of the meeting went on to state:

> "Mr. Weber inquired if this meant that the branches would be prohibited from starting equal facility cases and the Special Counsel said it did." . . .

In short, as these and other materials in the record show, the form of pleading, the type of relief to be requested, and the proper timing of suits have to a considerable extent, if not entirely, been determined by the Conference in coordination with the national office.

*Third,* contrary to the conclusion of the Federal District Court in the original federal proceeding, *NAACP v. Patty,* 159 F. Supp. 503, 508–509, the present record establishes that the petitioner does a great deal more than to advocate litigation and to wait for prospective litigants to come forward. In several instances, especially in litigation touching racial discrimination in public schools, specific directions were given as to the type of prospective forms to meetings for the purpose of obtaining signatures authorizing the prosecution of litigation in the name of the signer.

*Fourth,* there is substantial evidence indicating that the normal incidents of the attorney client relationship were often absent in litigation handled by staff lawyers and financed by petitioner. Forms signed by prospective litigants have on occasion not contained the name of the attorney authorized to act. In many cases, whether or not the form contained specific authorization to that effect, additional counsel have been brought into the action by staff counsel. There were several litigants who testified that at no time did they have any personal dealings with the lawyers handling their cases nor were they aware until long after the event that suits had been filed in their names. This is not to suggest that the petitioner has been shown to have plaintiffs under false pretenses or by inaccurate statements. But there is no basis for concluding that these were isolated incidents, or that petitioner's methods of operation have been such as to render these happenings out of the ordinary. . . .

At the same time the Virginia court demonstrated a responsible awareness of two important limitations on the State's power to regulate such conduct. The first of these is the long-standing recognition, incorporated in the Canons, of the different treatment to be accorded to those aiding the indigent in prosecuting or defending against legal proceedings. The second, which coupled with the first led the court to strike down Chapter 36 (*ante,* p. 418), is the constitutional right of any person to express his views, to disseminate those views to others, and to advocate action designed to achieve lawful objectives, which in the present case are also constitutionally due. Mindful of these limitations, the state court construed Chapter 33 not to prohibit petitioner and those associated with it from acquainting colored persons with what it believes to be their rights, or from advising them to assert those rights in legal proceedings, but only from "solicit[ing] legal business for their attorneys or any particular attorneys." Further, the court determined that Chapter 33 did not preclude petitioner from contributing money to persons to assist them in prosecuting suits, if the suits "have not been solicited by the appellants [the NAACP and Defense Fund] or those associated with them, and channeled by them to their attorneys or any other attorneys."

In my opinion the litigation program of the NAACP, as shown by this record, falls within an area of activity which a State may constitutionally regulate. . . .

Freedom of expression embraces more than the right of an individual to speak his mind. It includes also his right to advocate and his right to join with his fellows in an effort to make that advocacy effective. *Thomas* v. *Collins*, 323 U. S. 516; *NAACP* v. *Alabama*, 357 U. S. 449; *Bates* v. *Little Rock*, 361 U. S. 516. And just as it includes the right jointly to petition the legislature for redress of grievances, see *Eastern R. Presidents Conference* v. *Noerr Motor Freight, Inc.*, 365 U. S. 127, 137–138, so it must include the right to join together for purposes of obtaining judicial redress. We have passed the point where litigation is regarded as an evil that must be avoided if some accommodation short of a lawsuit can possibly be worked out. Litigation is often the desirable and orderly way of resolving disputes of broad public significance, and of obtaining vindication of fundamental rights. This is particularly so in the sensitive area of racial relationships.

But to declare that litigation is a form of conduct that may be associated with political expression does not resolve this case. Neither the First Amendment nor the Fourteenth constitutes an absolute bar to government regulation in the fields of free expression and association. This Court has repeatedly held that certain forms of speech are outside the scope of the protection of those Amendments, and that, in addition, "general regulatory statutes, not intended to control the content of speech but incidentally limiting its unfettered exercise," are permissible, "when they have been found justified by subordinating valid governmental interests." The problem in each such case is to weigh the legitimate interest of the State against the effect of the regulation on individual's rights.

But as we move away from speech alone and into the sphere of conduct—even conduct associated with speech or resulting from it—the area of legitimate governmental interest expands. A regulation not directly suppressing speech or peaceable assembly but having some impact on the form or manner of their exercise will be sustained if the regulation has a reasonable relationship to a proper governmental objective and does not unduly interfere with such individual rights. . . .

Turning to the present case, I think it evident that the basic rights in issue are those of the petitioner's members to associate, to discuss, and to advocate. Absent the gravest danger to the community, these rights must remain free from frontal attack or sup-pression, and the state court has recognized this in striking down Chapter 36 and in carefully limiting the impact of Chapter 33. But litigation, whether or not associated with the attempt to vindicate constitutional rights, is *conduct;* it is speech *plus*. Although the State surely may not broadly prohibit individuals with a common interest from joining together to petition a court for redress of their grievances, it is equally certain that the State may impose reasonable regulations limiting the permissible form of litigation and the manner of legal representation within its borders.

The interest which Virginia has here asserted is that of maintaining high professional standards among those who practice law within its borders. This Court has consistently recognized the broad range of judgments that a State may properly make in regulating any profession. See, *e.g. Dent* v. *West Virginia,* 129 U. S. 114; *Semler* v. *Oregon State Board of Dental Examiners,* 294 U. S. 608; *Williamson* v. *Lee Optical Co.,* 348 U. S. 483. But the regulation of professional standards for members of the bar comes to us with even deeper roots in history and policy since courts for centuries have possessed disciplinary powers incident to the administration. See *Cohen* v. *Hurley,* 366 U. S. 117, 123–124; *Konigsberg* v. *State Bar,* 366 U. S. 36; *Martin* v. *Walton,* 368 U. S. 25.

*First,* with regard to the claimed absence of the pecuniary element, it cannot well be suggested that the attorneys here are donating their services, since they are in fact compensated for their work. Nor can it tenably be argued that petitioner's litigating activities fall into the accepted category of aid to indigent litigants. The reference is presumably to the fact that petitioner itself is a nonprofit organization not motivated by desire for financial gain but by public interest and to the fact that no monetary stakes are involved in the litigation.

But a State's felt need for regulation of professional conduct may reasonably extend beyond mere "ambulance chasing." . . .

Underlying this impressive array of relevant precedent is the widely shared conviction that avoidance of improper pecuniary gain is not the only relevant factor in determining standards of professional conduct. Running perhaps even deeper is the desire of the profession, of courts, and of legislatures to prevent any interference with the uniquely personal relationship between lawyer and client and to maintain untrammeled by outside influences the responsibility which the lawyer owes to the courts he serves.

When an attorney is employed by an association or corporation to represent individual litigants, two problems arise, whether or not the association is organized for profit and no matter how unimpeachable its motives. The lawyer becomes subject to the control of a body that is not itself a litigant and that, unlike the lawyers it employs, is not subject to strict professional discipline as an officer of the court. In addition, the lawyer necessarily finds himself with a divided allegiance—to his employer and to his client—which may prevent full compliance with his basic professional obligations. . . .

*Second,* it is claimed that the interests of petitioner and its members are sufficiently identical to eliminate any "serious danger" of "professionally reprehensible conflicts of interests." *Ante,* p. 443. Support for this claim is sought in our procedural holding in *NAACP v. Alabama,* 357 U. S. 449, 458–459. But from recognizing, as in that case, that the NAACP has standing to assert the rights of its members when it is a real party in interest, it is plainly too large a jump to conclude that whenever individuals are engaged in litigation involving claims that the organization promotes, there cannot be any significant difference between the interests of the individual and those of the group.

The NAACP may be no more than the sum of the efforts and views infused in it by its members; but the totality of the separate interests of the members and others whose causes the petitioner champions, even in the field of race relations, may far exceed in scope and variety that body's views of policy, as embodied in litigating strategy and tactics. Thus it may be in the interest of the Association in every case to make a frontal attack on segregation, to press for an immediate breaking down of racial barriers, and to sacrifice minor points that may win a given case for the major points that may win other cases too. But in a particular litigation, it is not impossible that after authorizing action in his behalf, a Negro parent, concerned that a continued frontal attack could result in schools closed for years, might prefer to wait with his fellows a longer time for good-faith efforts by the local school board than is permitted by the centrally determined policy of the NAACP. Or he might see a greater prospect of success through discussion with local school authorities than through the litigation deemed necessary by the Association. The parent, of course, is free to withdraw his authorization, but is his lawyer, retained and paid by petitioner and subject to its directions on matters of policy, able to advise the parent with that undivided allegiance that is the hallmark of the attorney-client relation? I am afraid not. . . .

Where, the interests of the NAACP go well beyond the providing of competent counsel for the prosecution or defense of individual claims; they embrace broadly fixed substantive policies that may well often deviate from the immediate, or even long-range, desires to those who choose to accept its offers of legal representations. This serves to underscore the close interdependence between the State's condemnation of solicitation and its prohibition of the unauthorized practice of law by a lay organization.

*Third,* it is said that the practices involved here must stand on a different footing because the litigation that petitioner supports concerns the vindication of constitutionally guaranteed rights.

But surely state law is still the course of basic regulation of the legal profession, whether an attorney is pressing a federal or a state claim within its borders. See *In re Brotherhood of Railroad Trainmen, supra.* The true question is whether the State has taken action which unreasonably obstructs the assertion of federal rights. Here, it cannot be said that the underlying state policy is inevitably inconsistent with federal interests. The State has sought to prohibit the solicitation and sponsoring of litigation by those who have no standing to initiate that litigation themselves and who are not simply coming to the assistance of indigent litigants. . . .

There remains to be considered on this branch of the argument the question whether this particular exercise of state regulatory power bears a sufficient relation to the established and substantial interest of the State to overcome whatever indirect impact this statute may have on rights of free expression and association.

Chapter 33 as construed does no more than prohibit petitioner and those associated with it from soliciting legal business for its staff attorneys or, under a fair reading of the state court's opinion and amounting to the same thing, for "outside" attorneys who are subject to the Association's control in the handling of litigation which it refers to them. See pp. 466–468, *infra.* Such prohibitions bear a strong and direct relation to the area of legitimate state concern. . . .

The impact of such a prohibition on the rights of petitioner and its members to free expression and association cannot well be deemed so great as to require that it be struck down in the face of this substantial state interest.

*I would affirm.*

# *Notes*

1.  The Defense Fund, which is not involved in the present phase of the litigation, is a companion body to the NAACP. It is also a nonprofit New York corporation licensed to do business in Virginia, and has the same general purposes and policies as the NAACP. The Fund maintains a legal staff in New York City and retains regional counsel elsewhere, one of whom is in Virginia. Social scientists, law professors, and law students throughout the country donate their services to the Fund without compensation. When requested by the NAACP, the Defense Fund provides assistance in the form of legal research and counsel.

---

**NAACP v. Button,** 3 71 U.S. 415 (1963) 6–3

*editor's note.*

*Opinion authors are in bold; () indicates the party of appointing president. If the party of the justice differs from that of appointing president, the justice is listed second after the slash.*

| MAJORITY | CONCURRING | DISSENTING |
|---|---|---|
| **Brennan** (r/d) | **White** (d) [concurring in part and dissenting in part] | **Harlan** (r) |
| Warren (r) | | Clark (d) |
| Black (d) | | Stewart (r) |
| Goldberg (d) | | |
| Douglas (d) | | |

# INTEREST GROUPS AND SUPREME COURT DECISION-MAKING: AN OUTLINE

### Susan E. Lawrence

Below is some basic information about interest group participation in Supreme Court decision-making. As you study this information, as you read about interest groups litigation in the assigned course material, and as we discuss interest group litigation in lecture and section meeting, I would like you to keep a few basic questions in mind.

- How does interest group litigation affect/change who is able to participate in Supreme Court agenda setting and decision-making? How does this affect the Court's role in the national policy-making and implementation process?

- If we think of Supreme Court litigation as a method of participating in political/governmental decision making, what are the implications of interest group litigation for an assessment of who can, in practice, participate in the national policy-making process? (Is it helpful to think of political participation as something broader than voting and other efforts to affect electoral outcomes? Is majority rule the only way to think about citizen participation in government decision making, i.e., self-government?)

- What does an examination of interest group litigation reveal about the relationship between law and politics in Supreme Court decision-making?

- What does the study of interest group litigation suggest about the relationship between liberty, constitutionalism, and democracy in the American system?

## WHY DO INTEREST GROUPS PARTICIPATE IN LITIGATION?

1. To promote their policy goals

   *Why turn to courts rather than to legislatures? Why turn to courts in addition to legislatures?*

   A. Groups may represent constituencies who *lack political power* in legislatures.

      They may lack the power/influence to (a) get on the agenda, (b) win, once the issue is on the agenda.

   B. The group may have already lost (or won) in the legislature and *the political battle* may simply *shift venues*.

      Groups turn to litigation because they have already lost in the legislative process; or, groups may turn to litigation to *defend* a legislative victory that someone else is challenging in the courts.

In other words, the political battles that are fought in the legislative process may not end with the passage (or defeat) of a piece of legislation; rather, after legislative action, the battle may simply move to the courts.

C. Pursuing a policy goal through litigation may be *cheaper and faster* than pursuing it through legislative action.

While litigation campaigns can be quite expensive and slow, they may still be cheaper and faster than grass-roots lobbying, making campaign contribution to get supportive candidates elected, etc. While legislatures can always "duck" issues by failing to place them on the agenda, sending them off to committee for investigation, etc., courts (below the Supreme Court) *have* to decide all cases properly brought before them.

D. Often *lawyers are in leadership positions within interest groups* and, by training, they are accustomed to going to courts.

Indeed, lawyers' belief in the efficacy of judicial decisions may lead them to neglect the politics that can support or defeat effective implementation of a court decision.

E. *Policy issues of concern to the group may already be on the courts' agendas.*

Someone else may have initiated litigation in the policy area, and the group may believe that it needs to have a voice in the courts' decisions. Also, once a policy issues of concern to a specific group is on a court's agenda, groups may need to participate in the decision so as to demonstrate to the group's funding sources that it is 'leaving no stone unturned' in pursuing the group's policy goals.

F. Groups may be seeking to influence the interpretation and implementation of policies already passed by legislatures (or issued by administrative agencies).

Litigation is a major tool for *enforcing* government-made policies

G. Groups may be seeking a judicial declaration of a *"right"* because of the symbolic and rhetorical value of being able to cast their policy goals as "rights".

Groups may find "rights language" useful in:

   (1) Stimulating a grassroots movement in support of their policy goal—use to convince potential beneficiaries of policy change that they have a "right" to that policy change/benefit.

   (2) Pressuring government officials and/or relevant private actors to change their policies to the benefit of the group, i.e., to recognize the "right."

2. The *organization* itself may be a party to the *litigation*.

The group may be a defendant in a case, as in *NAACP* v. *Button*. Or, the group may be the plaintiff in a case; for example, the Sierra Club might file suit to prevent the human destruction of natural areas because the Club, itself, has a specific recreational and philosophic/moral interest in the preservation of natural spaces.

3. *The group's members may be a party to the litigation* and the group may provide legal representation to a member-litigant as a membership service, or to meet an overwhelming need, even when the specific case is not related to the specific policy-oriented litigation of the group. Example: the NAACP's representation of defendants in the sit-in cases; and, some of the Jehovah's Witnesses cases.

4. To gain *publicity*.

   A. For the policy issue: even unsuccessful litigation can be used as a way to gain publicity for a policy issue and perhaps spur legislative action and/or increased grass-roots activism.

   B. For the group: participation in litigation can be useful in demonstrating to funding sources (usually foundations, but sometimes individual members) that the group is really doing something to promote the stated policy goals.

The general rule is that interest groups only participate in cases when they believe that to do so will directly, or indirectly, further the group's policy goals. Interest groups and public interest law firms are not in the business of providing free counsel to any and every person unable to pay a private attorney; they select who they will represent based on the congruence between the litigant's case and the group's policy goals.

## WAYS INTEREST GROUPS USE LITIGATION TO PROMOTE THEIR POLICY GOALS:

A. **Sponsoring Litigation**: i.e. providing counsel—providing the litigant with legal representation and handling all aspects of the case—performing all the "lawyering tasks" that private, paid, attorneys do.

Bringing *"test cases"* challenging specific policies that the group wants to change or enforce. Groups often seek out clients with cases that have fact-patterns that will allow the interest groups to make its strategic legal/policy argument. At times, a group will create or stage its own test case by publicly violating a law that it wants to challenge. Basically, it is quite unusual for a group to agree to represent a litigant *if* that litigant's case does not fit the group's litigation strategy for achieving policy change.

Groups develop *"litigation strategies"*—long term strategies involving the bringing of a series of cases to the courts asking for small changes and creating new precedents so that, ultimately, broad new legal principles are established. The model example of a "litigation strategy" is the NAACP's campaign to overturn the *Plessy* doctrine of "separate but equal" by first challenging the principle in various graduate educational facilities and ultimately challenging it in segregated elementary schools that were equal in tangible resources in *Brown* v. *Board of Education.*

At times, there may be a tension between the group's desire to promote its policy goals and the attorney's professional obligation to serve the best interests of the specific client in the case.

Litigation strategies can be a chancy process.

- A group can work hard on a case in the trial court, but then the client can back-out when the case gets to the appellate court or the U.S. Supreme Court.
- The group can win, and the other side can decide not to appeal, so that the case never reaches the appellate courts or the U.S. Supreme Court.
- The U.S. Supreme Court can decide not to hear the strategic case.
- The U.S. Supreme Court can decide the 'wrong' way.
- Someone else can bring a case making the strategic argument before the group gets to the Court with it, handle it badly, lose, and kill the group's opportunity for a victory.
- If a group is pursuing a long term strategy running over 10, 20, 30 years (such as the NAACP's challenge to the *Plessy* doctrine), the personnel of the Supreme Court, and the political climate of the nation may change so much that the group cannot win its ultimate goal.

2. **Filing Amicus Curiae Briefs**: this is a safer way for groups to participate in Supreme Court decision-making, but it gives the group much less control, and probably, much less influence.

*Amicus Curiae* ("friend of the court") briefs are filed by groups or people that are not directly parties to a case. They are generally filed in support of one side or the other—in support of the petitioner or the respondent. Technically, those who want to file an amicus curiae brief have to get the consent of the party they are filing in support of, or of the Court. In practice, the Supreme Court grants permission to file 98% of the time; so functionally, anybody who wants to can file an amicus curiae brief.[1]

Amicus curiae briefs supplement the primary briefs submitted by the parties in the case. Amicus briefs present different and/or additional legal arguments; and/or different social background facts regarding the effect of the law and the likely effect of a change in the law.

Amicus Curiae briefs serve several *functions for the court*

1. Provide the court with more factual information

   Ex: It may report on the situation in other states.

2. Provide the court with information about the broader interests involved in the issue—show the clash of interests and who thinks they will be affected by the decision, and how.

3. Allow the court to identify potential supporters and opponents of a particular decision, which can be very important at the implementation and compliance stage.

There is evidence that amicus curiae briefs really do have an effect on the outcome of cases. There is evidence that the Supreme Court does read and use amicus briefs. One study that looked at the period between 1969–1981 found that amicus briefs were actually cited in the majority, a concurring, or dissenting opinion in about *one-fifth* (18%) of the cases in which they were filed. And, amicus briefs may exert an influence on the Court even when they are not cited in an opinion.

There has been a dramatic *growth* in the number of amicus curiae briefs filed by interest groups in U.S. Supreme Court cases. In the 1950s, amicus briefs were filed in only about 25% of all Supreme Court cases. By the late 1980s, amicus briefs were being filed in *over 80%* of all Supreme Court cases decided on the merits.

Some cases attract a phenomenal number of amicus briefs. There were 57 amicus briefs filed in *Regents of the University of California* v. *Bakke* (1973) [see pp. 136–137 of this book for a listing of the amicus briefs filed in *Bakke*], and there were 78 amicus briefs, signed by over 400 groups, filed in *Webster* v. *Reproductive Health Services* (1989).

## FACTORS SEEN AS CONTRIBUTING TO LITIGATION SUCCESS OF INTEREST GROUPS:

(Note: Litigation success, or a court victory, may not translate to policy success in the sense of automatically bringing about a change in the challenged practice. For example, consider the length of the interval between the Court's *Brown* v. *Board of Education* decision and the actual desegregation of schools.)

1. The *money* to litigate properly. Litigation-oriented interest groups generally receive the bulk of their funding from foundations or individual benefactors; some groups also receive a substantial portion of their funding from their membership.

2. *Longevity.* It takes a long time to bring a series of cases chipping away at a significant precedent, and it may take a long time for a group to develop a positive reputation with the Court.

> The NAACP has developed this type of positive reputation with the Court such that it is now extremely difficult to win a racial discrimination case without the NAACP's support.

3. *Expert legal staff and coordination between local attorneys* screening clients and handling cases at the trial court level and the group's national staff.

4. *Ability to generate extra-legal publicity*—law review articles; public spectacles, etc. Directly picketing the Supreme Court building is generally not a successful strategy, and it often serves merely to annoy the Justices, but other public demonstrations that create a supportive legal and political climate may have an indirect effect on the Court's decision-making.

5. *Cooperation with like-minded groups,* so that they don't bring the strategic case first and so that amicus briefs can be coordinated.

6. *Support of the federal government* in the form of support from the Solicitor General, especially as demonstrated through the S.G. filing a supportive amicus curiae brief. The S.G. wins over two-thirds of the time, so if a group can convince the S.G. to file on its side, it dramatically increases its chances of winning.

## HOW SUCCESSFUL ARE INTEREST GROUPS IN WINNING CASES?

Before the U.S. Supreme Court, generally, the MOST successful groups, get about half of their cases *accepted for review* by the Court. Once their cases are accepted for review, they *win* between *a half and two-thirds of them on the merits.*

> Examples of the most successful groups: The NAACP enjoyed a 56% review rate between 1947 and 1957; and an 88% success rate on-the-merits in cases that it sponsored between 1930 and 1956. Organized church-state groups enjoyed a 47% review rate and a 60% win rate on-the-merits in cases that they sponsored or filed amicus curiae briefs between 1951 and 1971. Between 1969 and 1980, women's rights groups were successful in 63% of the cases they sponsored or filed amicus briefs.

### Notes

1. Amicus can only be filed in appellate courts; they are never filed in trial courts. Some Court of Appeals cases will attract amicus curiae activity, but most amicus briefs are filed once a case reaches the U.S. Supreme Court. One can file an amicus curiae brief supporting a grant or denial of certiorari and/or on-the-merits after cert. is granted. Today, amicus curiae briefs are filed in over 80% of all U.S. Supreme Court cases decided on-the-merits.

# 8

# *Staffing the Federal Courts: The Politics of Judicial Selection*

$\mathcal{T}$he federal courts are institutions in which law and politics mix. The nature of legal reasoning structures judges' decision-making processes, but it does not provide them with formulas for determining what the one "right" decision is in any given case. The values, ideologies, and backgrounds of judges sometimes influence how they decide cases. This chapter focuses on the considerations that influence the Presidential nomination and the Senate confirmation processes and the characteristics of the federal bench that these processes produce. The politics of the judicial appointment process can have a profound effect on the law that emanates from our courts.

In the first article in this section, Senator Paul Simon, a long-standing member of the Senate judiciary committee, provides some reflections on what he thinks the Senate's role should be in the selection process. In the second article, Sheldon Goldman chronicles President Bush's judicial selection process, revealing the multiple ways in which politics influences the staffing of the federal courts. Goldman's article also presents an impressive array of data on the judges selected to sit on the federal bench over the last 40 years. Implicitly, these data raise political questions about what we think the federal bench should look like. Should it be ideologically and politically diverse or does the appointing president have free-reign to place only like-minded judges on the bench? Should the federal bench be representative of America? in terms of immutable physical characteristics such as race and gender? in terms of socio-economic status? in terms of diversity of educational background? Does it make any difference who is making the appointments to the federal courts? As Ronald Stidham,

Robert Carp, and Donald R. Songer's research shows us, the proof is in the proverbial pudding. They compare the voting records of the federal court appointees of our last six presidents in terms of their ideological direction. Using the empirical statistical analysis that has become common in political scientists' study of courts since C. Herman Pritchett pioneered the approach in the 1940s,[1] Stidham, Carp, and Songer find that the voting records of Clinton's appointees are closer to those of Carter's appointees than to those of the appointees of any Republican president. In short, the political party (of the appointing president) seems to influence how federal judges resolve questions of law in our system of liberal, constitutional, democracy. Hence, when we vote for president, we cast a ballot on the ideological direction the federal courts will take.

## Notes

1.  C. Herman Pritchett, *The Roosevelt Court* (New York: Macmillan, 1948).

# THE EXERCISE OF ADVICE AND CONSENT

## Paul Simon

Precisely what did those who wrote the Constitution mean by "advice and consent"? Like many political compromises, it offered less than complete clarity. Complicating matters, some delegates viewed the Senate as a sort of informal advisory council to the president, in addition to being the second legislative body of Congress. In one of his Federalist Papers, Alexander Hamilton—who favored a strong executive—wrote that the provision requires cooperation between the president and the Senate. But what does "cooperation" mean? Hamilton explained only that the advice and consent provision "would be an excellent check upon a spirit of favoritism in the President. . . . It would be an efficacious source of stability."[1] One of this century's major political scientists has written:

> It is reasonable to suppose that if the framers had intended to limit the Senate to something less than full participation in the political process of choosing men for public office, they would have put language in the Constitution to make that intention clear. If they had wanted such a procedure they might, for instance, have provided that the President should submit to the Senate the name of the person whom he preferred . . . and that the Senate should approve or reject the nomination by formal vote.[2]

"The Exercise of Advice and Consent" by Paul Simon. From JUDICATURE 76 (Dec.–Jan. 1993), pp. 189–191. Copyright ©1993 by the American Judicature Society. Reprinted by permission.

That is a reasonable conclusion. Clearly the delegates wanted to avoid the government they had as colonists in which the executive could dominate the judiciary. The delegates wanted the Senate to have a significant role in the process, but as in many other matters, they did not spell it out with precision.

Certainly, they had not the remotest idea of how important the Supreme Court would become, or what great controversies would be stirred through the simple "advice and consent" language of the Constitution.

## HISTORY LESSONS FOR THE SENATE

There is an old high-school debate question: "Can we learn from history, or are we destined to repeat our mistakes endlessly?" We can, of course, learn, and sometimes we do.

The Senate should keep in mind these lessons from history:

1. While the Senate has turned down a few good nominees for the Court it should have approved, by far the greater sin over two centuries has been in approving nominees who were mediocre or worse, often by voice vote.
2. Senators should not commit themselves too early on a nominee.
3. The Senate must be careful that our process does not encourage appointment of nominees with virtually no public record—who are mindless, voiceless ciphers—or that our process encourages evasion of the truth. We should not expect nominees to tell us with precision their stands on too many issues, but the process should produce candor, rather than evasion. We are now producing evasion. It is a fine line for the Senate and the nominee between stating how he or she would rule on an issue or case, which no nominee should provide, and expressing frankly his or her philosophical moorings, which the nominee should provide.
4. The Senate not only can examine a nominee's philosophical base, but it has the obligation to do so.

That is the conclusion of virtually all who have examined this question seriously, including Chief Justice William Rehnquist. It has been part of our history and should continue to be practiced. Upon reflection, most people will recognize that examination of the base from which justices emerge is essential because of the Court's immeasurable impact on the future of the nation. To use an extreme example, if the president were to nominate a Communist for the Court, would any one seriously question the right of senators to question his or her philosophy? The historic path that includes examination of the views of the nominee is a path the Senate has followed for 200 years and should continue to follow.

## PRESIDENTIAL ADVICE

A brief glance through history would be helpful to a president and to the chief adviser to the president on Supreme Court nominations, usually the attorney general. Such a study would tell us:

**The president should take seriously the "advice" part of advice and consent that the Constitution mandates**. The entire Clarence Thomas flap could have been avoided if the mandate of the Constitution had been followed. It wasn't. The Senate should not dominate the process, as it did for some years in the previous century. But the president would do well to follow the examples of several of our finest presidents.

The president should ask senators and others for suggestions and list several names as possibilities in conversations with senators. It would not take a president long to determine which potential nominees would face difficulty with confirmation if that is done. It is not asking too much to require that the president follow the Constitution. The effort of those who wrote the Constitution to avoid excessive power in the hands of the executive is critically important for the Supreme Court. And giving *advice* suggests doing it *before* a nomination, not afterward. The Bush handling of the Thomas nomination is a classic example of how a president should not proceed.

There may be rare times when a president believes a nominee is so outstanding that a battle with the Senate is calculated and necessary. Woodrow Wilson's appointment of Louis Brandeis would be such an example. Wilson consulted with only one senator, Robert La Follette, and knew that the nomination would cause a furor. He correctly calculated Brandeis's presence on the Court to be worth it. But the Brandeis-type appointment is the rare exception. The common sense procedure for the president is to follow the Constitution; then he or she will serve the administration, the nation, and the Court well.

**The president should not rush into a decision**. There are exceptions, but generally presidents have served the nation best by taking time to look over the legal landscape carefully. Because of the enormity of the importance of the nomination, it is good for the legal community and the public to know that the president is looking at this carefully and thoughtfully.

It is also to the advantage of the president, who inevitably will receive some good suggestions that would not occur to either the president or the attorney general. Abraham Lincoln waited almost a year in making three Supreme Court nominations. Even Andrew Jackson, not noted for his patience, waited months before nominating Roger Taney as chief justice. Theodore Roosevelt used great care in selecting nominees, inquiring of many people, taking time but using it wisely. The result: auspicious nominations.

**The president should have some criteria in mind as the selection is made.** Integrity should be the base on which the other qualities build. The other criteria the president might seek include:

**OUTSTANDING LEGAL ABILITY.** It is astonishing how rarely this has been a significant consideration for presidents. Yet when it has been made a priority, the service of the Court has been elevated. The president might ask 20 leaders whose judgment he or she trusts to list the 10 people in the nation who, based solely on legal ability, would make the best justices of the Court. Selecting one of the finest is something Theodore Roosevelt did when he selected Oliver Wendell Holmes Jr.; Woodrow Wilson did when he picked Louis Brandeis; Calvin Coolidge did when he named Harlan Stone; and Herbert Hoover did when he nominated Benjamin Cardozo and Charles Evans Hughes.

**DIVERSITY.** George Washington sought geographical diversity, as did most presidents until Theodore Roosevelt. Ronald Reagan named a woman to the Court, Lyndon Johnson an African-American, Woodrow Wilson a Jew. It is important that people look to the Court as a symbol of justice, and diversity is helpful. We can achieve diversity without sacrificing quality.

**BALANCE.** Too much attention has been paid to "fashioning" the Court in the mold of a president's philosophy. It is natural that the majority of nominations a president makes to the Court will at least partially fit that description, simply because a president wants to feel comfortable about the person named. But campaign promises to follow a certain philosophy are better not made. The law should not be a pendulum, swinging back and forth, depending on the political philosophy of the president making the appointments. This is more important today than a century ago, because there is much more litigation now and more of a role by the Court in determining the law. There is, as one writer puts it, a "fiction that the Court will somehow rise above politics if only the Senate does not focus on ideology."[3] There should be greater removal from partisan politics and a way found of achieving more philosophical balance on the Court. There should be fewer wide swings of the pendulum. Reaching a pre-nomination agreement with the Senate would foster both better relations and some assurance of greater balance on the Court. Attempts to "fashion" the Court in some special mold ultimately reduce the respect for, and the influence of, that body.

**COURAGE.** The Court, on occasion, must stand against public opinion, as it did not in 1942 in the *Korematsu* decision, as it did in the 1954 school desegregation case. Most Supreme Court decisions over two centuries on questions of separation of church and state have not been popular, but they have been good for both government and religious bodies. Freedom of religion has been preserved. The Court is the ultimate protector of our liberties, if the president and Congress falter. The Court should be composed of men and women with courage.

**BREADTH OF UNDERSTANDING BEYOND THE LAW**. Not everyone can be a Thomas Jefferson, but a good nominee should be one who knows a little about Plato and Beethoven, the Bible and the Koran, about Abraham Lincoln and Winston Churchill—one whose world is more than one-dimensional. The court system reflects life at its best and its worst. Some sense of perspective is needed by any good jurist, particularly one who sits on the highest court.

**SENSITIVITY TO CIVIL LIBERTIES**. Freedom is easier to give away than to preserve. The excuses for compromising our basic liberties are legion, and the reasons often seem good. But once given away, basic liberties are extremely difficult to recapture. The Court must be the defender of the unpopular, the minorities, those who sometimes appear not to deserve the freedom we give them.

**SENSITIVITY TO THE POWERLESS**. Many will not agree with this final quality I mention, but it is vital for the political health of the nation that justice is available not simply for those who can employ the finest lawyers. Court historian Henry Abraham observed with accuracy: "The Court is infinitely more qualified to protect minority rights than the far more easily pressured, more impulsive, and more emotion-charged legislative and executive branches."[4]

A president could easily follow these simple suggestions and elevate the quality of the Court and the quality of justice. In 1835, Horace Binney, a biographer of Chief Justice John Marshall, wrote: "The world has produced fewer instances of truly great judges than it has of great men in almost every other department of civilized life." That may be true. But it is not inevitable.

With leadership in the White House and the Senate working together, "advice and consent" can become more than a meaningless phrase and justice more than a distant dream.

## *Notes*

1. Hamilton, FEDERALIST PAPERS, Rossiter, (ed.), (New York: New American Library, 1961), Paper No. 76, p. 457.

2. Hyneman, BUREAUCRACY IN A DEMOCRACY 179 (New York: Harper and Brothers, 1950).

3. Mitzner, The Evolving Role of Judicial Nominations, *Journal of Law and Politics* (Winter 1989).

4. Abraham, JUSTICES AND PRESIDENTS 343 (New York: Oxford University Press, 1992), 3rd Edition.

# BUSH'S JUDICIAL LEGACY: THE FINAL IMPRINT

*Sheldon Goldman*

The Reagan-Bush era ended on November 3, 1992, with the election of Bill Clinton as president of the United States. Although the judiciary was not a major campaign issue, much concerning the third branch was at stake, including whether the historic transformation of the federal judiciary from the liberalism of the 1960s (reinforced by Carter appointments in the late 1970s) to the conservatism of the 1980s would continue. To the relief of liberals and dismay of conservatives, this transformation came to a halt with George Bush's defeat. Nevertheless, even with only one term in the White House, the Bush administration has left a judicial legacy that likely will have an impact into the next century.

The first section of this article reviews the major events concerning judicial selection during the last half of the Bush presidency,[1] followed by an examination of the Bush administration's judicial selection process. The next sections present profiles of Bush's appointees to the federal district and appellate courts confirmed in 1991 and 1992 during the 102nd Congress compared with those confirmed in 1989 and 1990 during the 101st Congress. The composite profile of Bush's appointees also is compared with the profiles of the appointees of Bush's five predecessors. The article concludes by assessing Bush's legacy and speculating on how this legacy may be affected by President Bill Clinton.

The tables contain data for those confirmed to lifetime appointments to the federal district and appeals courts of general jurisdiction. Sources include the questionnaires the judges completed for the Senate Judiciary Committee, confirmation hearings, personal interviews, biographical directories,[2] local newspaper stories, and responses from judges to questions posed in letters sent by the author.

## THE THOMAS FALLOUT

The 1990 congressional elections resulted in the Democrats retaining control of Congress and Senator Joseph Biden of Delaware continuing his leadership of the Senate Judiciary Committee. This would prove to be greatly significant for judicial selection during the last half of the Bush presidency.

The most important and far-reaching event involving the judiciary during this period was the nomination of Clarence Thomas to the U.S. Supreme Court and subsequent

---

"Bush's Judicial Legacy: The Final Imprint" by Sheldon Goldman. From JUDICATURE 76 (April-May 1993). Copyright @1993 by the American Judicature Society. Reprinted by permission.

Senate hearings. The confirmation battle in the Senate, particularly the Judiciary Committee hearings on the sexual harassment charges brought by Professor Anita Hill against Judge Thomas, riveted the nation.[3] Professor Hill's treatment before the all white male committee, particularly the assaults by some Republican senators on her character and veracity, created a national controversy. Sexual harassment of women in the workplace became a frontburner issue in American politics.

Nothing indicates that the Bush administration anticipated the level of controversy the Thomas nomination would bring. From the administration's standpoint, Thomas's background made him attractive. A man of accomplishment who rose from humble beginnings, Thomas was young, intelligent, judicially conservative, and thought to share the president's social policy agenda. He had administrative experience as chairman of the Equal Employment Opportunity Commission anti-judicial experience as a judge on the U.S. Court of Appeals for the District of Columbia Circuit. He had the active sponsorship of influential Republican Senator John Danforth of Missouri, Thomas's long-time mentor. And Thomas was an African American who would replace retiring justice Thurgood Marshall, the first African American to sit on the nation's highest court.

One can speculate about what would have occurred had the administration chosen instead the distinguished judge Amalya Kearse of the Second Circuit, an African American woman not identified with extremist views. At the very least, the women's movement would have been deprived of a potent issue with which to oppose President Bush. Arguably, the presidential election results might have been more favorable for Bush. Had Kearse been the nominee instead of Thomas, there likely would have been little controversy and quick confirmation. In addition, some individual senators would have been affected differently. For example, Republican Senator Arlen Specter of Pennsylvania, who vigorously attacked Hill's veracity in the Senate hearings, likely would not have had such a difficult reelection fight. Senator Alan Dixon of Illinois, who voted to confirm Thomas, might not have lost to Carol Moseley-Braun in the Democratic primary. Moseley-Braun went on to win the general election, becoming the first African American woman elected to the U.S. Senate.

Although Thomas was confirmed on October 15, 1991, by a narrow margin of 52–48, and the administration could claim victory, the immediate political consequences for Republicans were not beneficial. Women's groups mobilized, and women candidates, mostly Democrats, entered congressional races. The president's exercise of the power of judicial selection also became a campaign issue.

The Thomas nomination culminating in the Thomas-Hill hearings produced a bitterness and mutual suspicion between the Democrats on the Senate Judiciary Committee and the administration. Matters came to a head over committee access to FBI reports on judicial nominees. Angered because Hill's affidavit to the Judiciary Committee was leaked to the press, starting the publicity barrage that culminated in the televised Thomas-Hill hearings, President Bush concluded that Senate staff members should not have access to sensitive material in FBI reports and that senatorial access itself should be limited. In a speech to public employees on October 24, 1991, President Bush said:

> I have ordered that the FBI reports be carried directly to committee chairmen and any members designated by the chairmen. The members will read the reports immediately in the presence of the agent, and then return them. No FBI reports will stay on Capitol Hill. And furthermore, members only will have access to these reports.[4]

The Judiciary Committee received this new policy as a virtual declaration of war by the administration. Chairman Biden made it clear that in order for the committee to perform its constitutional duties, it would have to expand greatly its investigatory staff. This would require a budget increase of several millions of dollars annually to fund increased personnel costs and support to enable investigators to travel around the country duplicating the FBI's efforts.[5] Biden refused to move any nominations submitted under the new restrictions until the committee's new investigatory apparatus was functioning, meaning substantial delays in the confirmation process.

After Thomas's nomination was sent to the Senate on July 8, 1991, lower court nominations received lower priority as the Judiciary Committee's resources were devoted primarily to preparation for the Thomas hearings. Hill's allegations and the second round of hearings meant further delay with some lower-court nominations. When the president threw down the gauntlet over access to the FBI reports, the confirmation process for new appointees as well as for some on whom the committee already had FBI reports came to a standstill. Confirmation hearings that had been scheduled for November, however, proceeded on schedule, and these nominees were promptly confirmed.

The confrontation between the Senate Judiciary Committee and the administration lasted more than three months. Finally, the administration eased its position by restoring committee member and staff access, but with a stricter accounting of who would read the reports. The delay, however, would be fatal for the candidacies of a number of those who were nominated after President Bush restricted access to the FBI reports. Of the 65 individuals nominated to lifetime district judgeships on or before October 24, 1991, all but three were eventually confirmed, a rate of more than 95 percent.[6] But of the 19 subsequent nominations in 1991, only 14 were confirmed, a 74 percent confirmation rate. Of the 59 individuals nominated in 1992 for lifetime district judgeships, only 24, or 41 percent, were confirmed.[7]

## NOMINATIONS VS. CONFIRMATIONS

The delay caused by the administration's attempt to discipline the Judiciary Committee meant that when matters were resolved, the presidential election year was well underway. Traditionally, minimal confirmation activity occurs during presidential election years, especially when the Senate is controlled by one party and the White House by another. Partisan pressures on the Senate Judiciary Committee can be intense and no doubt were so in 1992, especially as President Bush appeared increasingly vulnerable in his reelection bid.[8]

Complicating judicial selection matters further was Attorney General Dick Thornburgh's resignation in August 1991 so that he could campaign in Pennsylvania's special election to fill the Senate vacancy created by the death of John Heinz. Thornburgh took with him his assistant, Murray Dickman, who had handled the political aspects of judicial selection. Barbara Drake, deputy assistant attorney general in the Justice Department's Civil Rights Division, had until then helped with judicial selection by evaluating the professional qualifications of candidates and dealing with the American Bar Association's Standing Committee on Federal Judiciary. With Dickman's departure, Drake assumed Dickman's responsibilities while carrying on her previous judicial selection work as well as working full time in the Civil Rights Division. The burden was undoubtedly great, particularly as the administration sought to fill the 85 new judgeships created in 1990. When the dust settled after the adjournment of the 102nd Congress in 1992, the administration had not submitted nominations for 42 district and five appeals court vacancies. And when it adjourned, the Senate had not acted on 42 district and 10 appeals court nominations. Thus the administration could reasonably justify its failure to send still more nominations. Nevertheless, some Republican senators were openly bitter about the long time it took for the administration to submit nominations,[9] and there was talk of missed opportunities. The issue of delay in the nomination and confirmation process during the Bush presidency certainly is complex and controversial.

In 1992 the Senate Judiciary Committee cleared a record number of nominations for a presidential election year, with 53 confirmations to lifetime district court positions and 10 to lifetime positions on appeals courts of general jurisdiction. But there was also a record number of nominations for which the committee took no action (42 district and 10 appeals court positions). In general, controversial nominees fell by the wayside, and others without strong backing from Democratic senators had rough going. On the other hand, nominees for district court positions in the states of the Republican members of the Senate Judiciary Committee were all confirmed. The same was true for district court nominees from Kansas, the home state of Senate Republican Minority Leader Robert Dole, and nominees from New Hampshire, backed by the popular

Republican Senator Warren Rudman, who was leaving the Senate at the end of the 102nd Congress.

Some indication exists that the Judiciary Committee considered the case load pressures on some district courts. For example, 9 of the 11 nominees to the district courts in Florida won confirmation. Because any one senator could hold up a nomination, the Judiciary Committee, during the presidential election year, was most likely to act on nominees for whom there was a strong consensus.[10]

## THE BUSH SELECTION PROCESS

As described in a previous article,[11] judicial selection in the Bush administration was centered in the office of the attorney general rather than the deputy attorney general. This resulted from the events surrounding Attorney General Dick Thornburgh's futile attempt to secure the appointment of Robert B. Fiske Jr. as deputy attorney general. Recall that Thornburgh had dismantled the Justice Department's Office of Legal Policy, which handled selection during the Reagan administration. Judicial selection was a shared endeavor with the White House, institutionalized by the White House-based President's Committee on Federal Judicial Selection, a Reagan administration innovation retained by the Bush administration. With the departure of Thornburgh and Dickman in August 1991, the weight of judicial selection decision making shifted even more to the White House.

The initial screening and processing of judicial candidates, however, continued as usual in the Justice Department. Barbara Drake, who had handled the professional screening of judicial candidates, also assumed the political and administrative responsibilities of selection while continuing her work in the Civil Rights Division. For her judicial selection activities, Drake had three full-time assistants and one secretary helping her. About 10 other Justice Department officials helped with the interviewing process, but Drake had the task of dealing with senators, the candidates themselves, other interested parties and interest groups, and the ABA Standing Committee on Federal Judiciary. In the last two years of the Bush administration, there were 142 district court nominations, 90 of which were made when Drake was in charge. Also during this time, there were 30 courts of appeals nominations to courts of general jurisdiction, 19 under Drake's management. Given the limited resources, this is an impressive accomplishment. The argument can be made that the Bush administration failed to invest sufficient resources in judicial selection.

The argument can be made, however, that the Bush administration failed to invest sufficient resources in judicial selection. The Reagan administration operated a separate Office of Legal Policy led by an assistant attorney general to handle judicial selection. In contrast, the Bush administration first employed an assistant to the attorney general and then a deputy assistant attorney general who worked fulltime in the Civil Rights Division to handle judicial selection. When the 102nd Congress adjourned in 1992, no nominations had been sent to the Senate for 42 district and five appeals court positions.

Delay in judicial selection cannot be attributed solely to the lack of sufficient resources devoted to the task in the Justice Department. For district court positions, the Justice Department awaited recommendations from Republican senators or (where there were no Republican senators) from state party leaders and Republican House members. The screening process, including extensive interviewing of the candidates, also took time. The White House counsel's office also screened candidates, but ordinarily did not personally interview them. Then when a prospective nominee was selected, the ABA Standing Committee on Federal Judiciary was given the name and asked for its rating. The ABA committee typically took two months and, on at least one occasion, even twice that for its evaluation. The Bush administration did not nominate anyone who received a not qualified rating. Thus, if a prospective nominee received the negative rating the administration dropped consideration and was back to square one. While the ABA conducted its evaluation, the FBI carried out its own investigation.

Despite all these sources of delay in the process, greater higher-level resources invested at the Justice Department level probably would have resulted in more candidates being considered for more positions at the same time. This is especially so for the 74 district and 11 appellate judgeships created by the Federal Judgeships Act of 1990, which became law on December 1, 1990. The administration knew well before this time which new judgeships were being created. Even so, from December 1, 1990, it took 15 months or more to select nominees to fill 12 of these new district judgeships. Furthermore, no nominations were made for 12 other new district judgeships including one each in Pennsylvania and Wyoming, states whose Republican senators were on the Senate Judiciary Committee, thus virtually ensuring committee processing and approval had nominations been submitted).[12] According to the Administrative Office of the U.S. Courts, in 1992 it took an average of 385 days from the day of the vacancy until a nomination was made by the administration. Added to this was the average of 139 days in 1992 for the Senate to confirm.[13]

## Table 1

U.S. District court appointees confirmed In 1989–1990 (Bush I)
compared with appointees confirmed in 1991–1992 (Bush II)

| | Bush I appointees<br>% (N) | Bush II appointees<br>% (N) |
|---|---|---|
| **Occupation** | | |
| Politics/government | 10.4% (5) | 11.0% (11) |
| Judiciary | 47.9% (23) | 39.0% (39) |
| Large law firm | | |
| 100 + members | 6.2% (3) | 13.0% (13) |
| 50–99 | 4.2% (2) | 9.0% (9) |
| 25–49 | 6.2% (3) | 8.0% (8) |
| Medium size firm | | |
| 10–24 members | 10.4% (5) | 8.0% (8) |
| 5–9 | 8.3% (4) | 5.0% (5) |
| Small firm | | |
| 2–4 members | 4.2% (2) | 3.0% (3) |
| solo | — | 2.0% (2) |
| Professor of law | 2.1% (1) | — |
| Other | — | 2.0% (2) |
| **Experience** | | |
| Judicial | 50.0% (24) | 45.0% (45) |
| Prosecutorial | 37.5% (18) | 40.0% (40) |
| Neither one | 27.1% (13) | 34.0% (34) |
| **Undergraduate education** | | |
| Public | 41.7% (20) | 46.0% (46) |
| Private | 50.0% (24) | 37.0% (37) |
| Ivy League | 8.3% (4) | 17.0% (17) |
| **Law school education** | | |
| Public | 47.9% (23) | 55.0% (55) |
| Private | 37.5% (18) | 31.0% (31) |
| Ivy League | 14.6% (7) | 14.0% (14) |
| **Gender** | | |
| Male | 89.6% (43) | 76.0% (76) |
| Female | 10.4% (5) | 24.0% (24) |
| **Ethnicity/race** | | |
| White | 95.8% (46) | 86.0% (86) |
| African American | 2.1% (1) | 9.0% (9) |
| Hispanic | 2.1% (1) | 5.0% (5) |
| Asian | — | — |
| **Percent white male** | 85.4% (41) | 67.0% (67) |

| | Bush I appointees<br>% (N) | Bush II appointees<br>% (N) |
|---|---|---|
| **ABA rating** | | |
| Well qualified | 58.3% (28) | 57.0% (57) |
| Qualified | 41.7% (20) | 43.0% (43) |
| **Political Identification** | | |
| Democrat | 4.2% (2) | 6.0% (6) |
| Republican | 93.8% (45) | 86.0% (86) |
| Independent | 2.1% (1) | 8.0% (8) |
| **Past party activism** | 62.5% (30) | 60.0% (60) |
| **Religious origin/afflliation** | | |
| Protestant | 64.6% (31) | 64.0% (64) |
| Catholic | 22.9% (11) | 31.0% (31) |
| Jewish | 12.5% (6) | 5.0% (5) |
| **Net worth** | | |
| Under $200,000 | 6.2% (3) | 12.0% (12) |
| $200,000–499.999 | 29.2% (14) | 32.0% (32) |
| $500.000–999.999 | 31.2% (15) | 24.0% (24) |
| $1 + million | 33.3% (16) | 32.0% (32) |
| **Average age at nomination** | 49.6 | 47.4 |
| **Total number of appointees** | 48 | 100 |

Sometimes delay occurred because Republican senators recommended people who were unsatisfactory to the administration. A senator's charge of delay in such a situation could well have been an expression of irritation at the administration for not rubberstamping the senator's choice. Evidence suggests the administration moved deliberately in its screening process and had to be reasonably satisfied that the nominee was not only professionally qualified but also shared the president's judicial philosophy.

The White House Counsel's office was a center for the philosophical screening of candidates, particularly for positions on the courts of appeals. White House Counsel C. Boyden Gray publicly acknowledged that the administration was very careful in its judicial appointments and took time to scrutinize the philosophy of judicial candidates.[14] Associate White House Counsel Lee Liberman did much of the screening, including reading and evaluating the judicial opinions of candidates who had judicial records. She also sought out candidates appropriate for various appeals court vacancies. There appeared to be close cooperation and an absence of rivalry between the White House counsel's office and the Justice Department over judicial selection. In part this may be attributable to the personalities involved and in part to the institutional arrangements in place, particularly the President's Committee on Federal Judicial

Selection, chaired by the White House counsel, that ensured a principal role for the White House in selection.

Another notable feature of judicial selection during the Bush administration was that for the first time in American history, women had major roles in the judicial selection process. Lee Liberman's and Barbara Drake's positions in the White House and Justice Department ensured that women judicial candidates would suffer no disadvantage in the selection process at the administration level. Furthermore, President Bush had explicitly urged Republican senators to seek out qualified women and minorities. Republican senators themselves were under some pressure as a result of the Anita Hill-Clarence Thomas hearings to demonstrate their sensitivity to women's rights. All these factors likely contributed to the Bush administrator's record proportion of women appointed to the judiciary.[15]

## DISTRICT COURT APPOINTEES

Table 1 contains various backgrounds and attributes of the 100 individuals selected by the Bush administration for lifetime district judgeships whom the Senate confirmed during the 102nd Congress. These judges are referred to here as Bush II judges. There were 42 additional district court nominees whose nominations lapsed because the Senate took no action on them by the end of the 102nd Congress on October 8, 1992. The 100 Bush II judges are compared with the 48 appointees confirmed during the 101st Congress. These appointees are referred to as Bush I judges.

Table 2 compares Bush's 148 confirmed lifetime district court appointments to those of Presidents Ronald Reagan, Jimmy Carter, Gerald Ford, Richard Nixon, and Lyndon Johnson.

OCCUPATION. Table 1 shows that 3 out of 10 Bush II appointees came from large law firms at the time of their nomination. This is close to twice the proportion of Bush I appointees. About one in eight Bush II judges came from so-called super firms, with 100 or more members.

The proportion of Bush II appointees who were members of the judiciary at the time of appointment fell somewhat compared with the Bush I judges. Of these 39 Bush II judges, 28 were serving on the state bench, 10 were U.S. magistrates, and 1 was a U.S. bankruptcy judge. This is the highest proportion of district judges drawn from the ranks of federal magistrates.[16] This development deserves watching, particularly as it comes within the long term trend shown in Table 2 of increasing proportions of district judges being drawn from the ranks of the judiciary. It will be interesting to see if the trend toward a career judiciary, including drawing upon federal magistrates, will continue under President Clinton.

# Table 2

### U.S. district court appointees compared by administration

| | Bush % (N) | Reagan % (N) | Carter % (N) | Ford % (N) | Nixon % (N) | Johnson % (N) |
|---|---|---|---|---|---|---|
| **Occupation** | | | | | | |
| Politics/ government | 10.8% (16) | 12.8% (37) | 4.4% (9) | 21.2% (11) | 10.6% (19) | 21.3% (26) |
| Judiciary | 41.9% (62) | 37.2% (108) | 44.6% (90) | 34.6% (18) | 28.5% (51) | 31.1% (38) |
| Large law firm | | | | | | |
| 100+ members | 10.8% (16) | 5.9% (17) | 2.0% (4) | 1.9% (1) | 0.6% (1) | 0.8% (1) |
| 50–99 | 7.49% (11) | 5.2% (15) | 6.0% (12) | 3.9% (2) | 0.6% (1) | 1.6% (2) |
| 25–49 | 7.4% (11) | 6.6% (19) | 6.0% (12) | 3.9% (2) | 10.1% (8) | — |
| Medium size firm | | | | | | |
| 10–24 members | 8.8% (13) | 10.3% (30) | 9.4% (19) | 7.7% (4) | 8.9% (16) | 12.3% (15) |
| 5–9 | 6.1% (9) | 9.0% (26) | 10.4% (21) | 17.3% (9) | 19.0% (34) | 6.6% (8) |
| Small firm | | | | | | |
| 2–4 members | 3.4% (5) | 7.6% (22) | 11.4% (23) | 7.7% (4) | 14.5% (26) | 11.5% (14) |
| solo | 1.4% (2) | 2.8% (8) | 2.5% (5) | 1.9% (1) | 4.5% (8) | 11.5% (14) |
| Professor of law | 0.7% (1) | 2.1% (6) | 3.0% (6) | — | 2.8% (5) | 3.3% (4) |
| Other | 1.4% (2) | 0.7% (2) | 0.5% (1) | — | — | — |
| **Experience** | | | | | | |
| Judicial | 46.6% (69) | 46.6% (135) | 54.5% (110) | 42.3% (22) | 35.2% (63) | 34.4% (42) |
| Prosecutorial | 39.2% (58) | 44.1% (128) | 38.6% (78) | 50.0% (26) | 41.9% (75) | 45.9% (56) |
| Neither | 31.8% (47) | 28.3% (82) | 28.2% (57) | 30.8% (16) | 36.3% (65) | 33.6% (41) |
| **Undergraduate education** | | | | | | |
| Public | 44.6% (66) | 35.5% (103) | 57.4% (116) | 48.1% (25) | 41.3% (74) | 38.5% (47) |
| Private | 41.2% (61) | 50.3% (146) | 32.7% (66) | 34.6% (18) | 38.5% (69) | 31.1% (36) |
| Ivy League | 14.2% (21) | 14.1% (41) | 9.9% (20) | 17.3% (9) | 19.6% (35) | 16.4% (20) |
| None indicated | — | — | — | — | 0.6% (1) | 13.9% (17) |
| **Law school education** | | | | | | |
| Public | 52.7% (78) | 42.4% (123) | 50.5% (102) | 44.2% (23) | 41.9% (75) | 40.2% (49) |
| Private | 33.1% (49) | 45.5% (132) | 32.2% (65) | 38.5% (20) | 36.9% (66) | 36.9% (46) |
| Ivy League | 14.2% (21) | 12.1% (35) | 17.3% (35) | 17.3% (9) | 21.2% (38) | 21.3% (26) |
| None indicated | — | — | — | — | — | 1.6% (2) |
| **Gender** | | | | | | |
| Male | 80.4% (119) | 91.7% (266) | 85.6% (173) | 98.1% (51) | 99.4% (178) | 98.4% (120) |
| Female | 19.6% (29) | 8.3% (24) | 14.4% (29) | 1.9% (1) | 0.6% (1) | 1.6% (2) |
| **Ethnicity/race** | | | | | | |
| White | 89.2% (132) | 92.4% (268) | 78.7% (159) | 88.5% (46) | 95.5% (171) | 93.4% (114) |
| African-American | 6.8% (10) | 2.1% (6) | 13.9% (28) | 5.8% (3) | 3.4% (6) | 4.1% (5) |

|  | Bush % (N) | Reagan % (N) | Carter % (N) | Ford % (N) | Nixon % (N) | Johnson % (N) |
|---|---|---|---|---|---|---|
| Hispanic | 4.0% (6) | 4.8% (14) | 6.9% (14) | 1.9% (1) | 1.1% (2) | 2.5% (3) |
| Asian | — | 0.7% (2) | 0.5% (1) | 3.9% (2) | — | — |
| **Percent white male** | 72.9% (108) | 84.8% (246) | 68.3% (138) | 86.5% (45) | 94.9% (170) | 92.6% (113) |
| **ABA rating** |  |  |  |  |  |  |
| Extremely well/ Well qualified | 57.4% (85) | 54.1% (157) | 50.9% (103) | 46.1% (24) | 45.3% (81) | 48.4% (69) |
| Qualified | 42.6% (63) | 45.9% (133) | 47.5% (96) | 53.8% (28) | 54.8% (98) | 49.2% (60) |
| Not qualified | — | — | 1.5% (3) | — | — | 2.5% (3) |
| Not qualified | — | — | 1.5% (3) | — | — | 2.5% (3) |
| **Political Identification** |  |  |  |  |  |  |
| Democrat | 5.4% (8) | 4.8% (14) | 92.6% (187) | 21.2% (11) | 7.3% (13) | 94.3% (115) |
| Republican | 88.5% (131) | 93.1% (270) | 4.4% (9) | 78.8% (41) | 92.7% (166) | 5.7% (7) |
| Independent | 6.1% (9) | 2.1% (6) | 2.9% (6) | — | — | — |
| **Past party activism** | 60.8% (90) | 58.6% (170) | 60.9% (123) | 50.0% (26) | 48.6% (87) | 49.2% (60) |
| **Religious origin/ affiliation** |  |  |  |  |  |  |
| Protestant | 64.2% (95) | 60.3% (175) | 60.4% (122) | 73.1% (38) | 73.2% (131) | 58.2% (71) |
| Catholic | 28.4% (42) | 30.0% (87) | 27.7% (56) | 17.3% (9) | 18.4% (33) | 31.1% (38) |
| Jewish | 7.4% (11) | 9.3% (27) | 11.9% (24) | 9.6% (5) | 8.4% (15) | 10.7% (13) |
| **Net worth** |  |  |  |  |  |  |
| Under $200,000 | 10.1% (15) | 17.6% (51) | 35.8% (53) | NA | NA | NA |
| $200,000– 499,999 | 31.1% (46) | 37.6% (109) | 41.2% (61) | NA | NA | NA |
| $500,000– 999,999 | 26.4% (39) | 21.7% (63) | 18.9% (28) | NA | NA | NA |
| $1 + million | 32.4% (48) | 23.1% (67) | 4.0% (6) | NA | NA | NA |
| **Average age at nomination** | 48.1 | 48.7 | 49.7 | 49.2 | 49.1 | 51.4 |
| **Total number of appointees** | 148 | 290 | 202 | 52 | 179 | 122 |

\* One Reagan district court appointee was self-classified as nondenominational.

\*\* These figures are for appointees confirmed by the 96th Congress. Professor Elliot Slotnick of Ohio State University generously provided the net worth figures for all but six Carter district court appointees (for whom no data were available).

Close to the same proportion of Bush I and Bush II judges were recruited from politics or government service. However, only 6 percent of the Bush I judges were serving in the U.S. attorney's office when nominated, whereas the figure for Bush II judges was 8 percent. During the Reagan administration, this figure was more than 10 percent.

Table 2 presents the composite figures for the Bush I and II judges compared to the judges appointed by Bush's five predecessors. The Bush appointees set a modern record with the highest proportion of judges recruited from large law firms. Changes in the practice of law during the past three decades are reflected by this finding, but it is also likely that highly qualified, wealthy, conservative Republican lawyers associated with these blue-chip firms had an advantage in the selection process and were considered by Republican senators and administration officials as highly desirable recruits to the federal bench.

The increasing proportion of district judges drawn from the judiciary, as shown in Table 2, suggests that recent administrations have found it desirable to select individuals whose judicial temperament and philosophy can be ascertained from their judicial track records.

The proportion of those drawn from law school faculties, never large to begin with, dwindled to almost nothing in the Bush administration. Only one of Bush's 148 confirmed nominees was a law professor when chosen for the district bench.

**EXPERIENCE.** Consistent with the occupation findings, Table I shows that a greater proportion of Bush appointees to the district bench had previous judicial experience than had prosecutorial experience. Table 2 suggests that this trend began with the Carter administration and continued with the Reagan and Bush administrations. The proportion of Bush and Reagan appointees with previous judicial experience was precisely the same. The proportion of Bush appointees with previous prosecutorial experience was lower than that of the Reagan appointees and was the second lowest of all six administrations. Slightly more, proportionately, of the Bush appointees than the Reagan, Carter, and Ford appointees had neither judicial nor prosecutorial experience.

The figures appear to show a continuation of the trend toward a career judiciary, although the American judiciary is far from approximating the European career judiciary. The American trend is dramatically exemplified in that all six most recent appointees to associate justice positions on the Supreme Court had been judges on lower courts.

**EDUCATION**. The educational profile of the Bush I and Bush II appointees is somewhat different. A larger proportion of Bush I judges than Bush II judges received their undergraduate education at private schools. Similarly a smaller proportion of

Bush I judges were educated at public-supported colleges and universities. Twice the proportion of Bush II than Bush I judges received an Ivy League undergraduate education.

If the socioeconomic differences between Democratic and Republican constituencies are reflected in the backgrounds of judicial appointees, undergraduate education is one background variable that can hint at such differences. Table 2 shows that the majority of appointees of Republican administrations received a relatively expensive private school (including Ivy League) education, while a minority of the appointees of Democratic administrations had such an undergraduate educational experience.

The law school education of the Bush appointees seen in Table 2 reveals that Bush's appointees had the largest proportion of district judges appointed by all six administrations who attended public-supported law schools. The proportion of Bush judges who attended Ivy League law schools is the second lowest of all six administrations. Given that Ivy League law schools are considered among the best and most prestigious law schools, the low proportion of Bush appointees with an Ivy League law school education might suggest a somewhat lower overall level of quality of appointees. But by the 1960s and 1970s, when most of the Bush appointees attended law school, a number of non-Ivy League law schools attained a prestige level comparable to the Ivy League schools. Thus, if we include prestigious non-Ivy League law schools such as Berkeley, Chicago, Duke, Georgetown, Michigan, Northwestern, Stanford, Texas, Vanderbilt, and Virginia, the proportion of Bush appointees with a prestige legal education rises to about 34 percent.

**AFFIRMATIVE ACTION.** As noted in the earlier study of Bush I judges,[17] President Bush made a commitment to open up judicial selection to appropriately qualified women and minorities. That commitment was kept in part for the Bush I judges: the proportion of women appointed exceeded Reagan's record and was the second best ever. The record for the Bush II appointees, as shown in Table 1, shows a much more dramatic increase in the proportion of women appointees. About one in four district court appointees were women, shattering the old record achieved by Carter. It is likely that in at least a few instances, Republican senators were convinced of the political importance of finding qualified women, particularly in light of the Clarence Thomas-Anita Hill hearings. But without the administration's commitment, it is unlikely that the record-breaking proportion of women appointees would have been achieved. The overall Bush record as revealed in Table 2 shows that one in five district court appointees were women,[18] compared with one in seven for Carter.

Table I illustrates a sharp increase in the proportion of Bush II judges who are African American or Hispanic. The Bush II proportion of African American judges was more than four times the proportion each of Bush I and overall Reagan appointees. The proportion of Bush's African American appointments overall exceeded every previous administration except Carter's; which was twice that of Bush.[19] The proportion of Hispanic district court appointees, however, fell below not only the Carter record, but also was less than Reagan's proportion.[20] And for the first time since the Nixon administration, no Asian American received a lifetime district judgeship.

The percentage of white male appointees dropped markedly from Bush I to Bush II. Two of three Bush II appointees were white males, a proportion slightly lower than Carter's historic record low. The proportion of white male appointees during Bush's entire term was somewhat larger than the proportion for the Carter judges, but was notably lower than that of all other administrations. Women had opportunities for recruitment to the federal bench, particularly during the second half of Bush's term that were clearly of historic importance.

**ABA RATINGS.** Starting with the Bush administration, the ABA Standing Committee on Federal judiciary dropped its *exceptionally well qualified* rating so that *well qualified* became the highest rating. Nominees who previously would have been rated *exceptionally well qualified* and nominees who would have been rated *well qualified* now received the same rating. In Table 2, the ABA ratings for Bush's appointees are compared with the ratings for the district court appointees of Bush's five predecessors. To facilitate comparisons, the *exceptionally well qualified* and *well qualified* categories are combined for all six administrations' appointees. If the ABA ratings represent quality, the Bush appointees were the best-qualified group of appointees of all six administrations.[21]

Although no Bush appointee received a *not qualified* rating, 30 percent of the Bush I judges who received a *qualified* rating did so by a non-unanimous vote of the ABA committee, with one or more dissenters voting *not qualified*. About 25 percent of the Bush II judges who received a *qualified* rating did so with such a split vote.[22] The overall proportion of Bush appointees with a *qualified* rating receiving such a split vote was about 27 percent. Of all Bush district court appointees, about 11 percent received the majority *qualified*/ minority *not qualified* rating.

When a majority of the ABA committee votes a qualified rating, the ABA's position is that the recipient of such a split rating is to be considered fully qualified for judicial office. Nevertheless, split ratings indicate that at least some members of the legal community have serious doubt about the individual's qualifications. In at least some instances, it is reasonable to infer that the person chosen, although presumptively qualified, was not the best choice. But an equally plausible explanation is that biases among some members of the legal community, or even one or more members of the ABA committee itself, may have been responsible for a split rating or even the tendency for women to have lower ratings than men.[23]

## Table 3
U.S. appeals court appointees confirmed In 1989–1990 (Bush I)
compared with appointees confirmed in 1991–1992 (Bush II)

| | Bush I appointees % (N) | Bush II appointees % (N) |
|---|---|---|
| **Occupation** | | |
| Politics/government | 11.1% (2) | 10.5% (2) |
| Judiciary | 55.6% (10) | 63.2% (12) |
| Large law firm | | |
| 100 members | 5.6% (1) | 10.5% (2) |
| 50–99 | 11.1% (2) | 5.3% (1) |
| 25–49 | — | — |
| Medium size firm | | |
| 10–24 members | 16.7% (3) | |
| 5–9 | — | 5.3% (1) |
| Small firm | | |
| 2–4 members | — | — |
| solo | — | — |
| Professor of law | — | 5.3% (1) |
| **Experience** | | |
| Judicial | 55.6% (10) | 68.4% (13) |
| Prosecutorial | 33.3% (6) | 26.3% (5) |
| Neither one | 38.9% (7) | 26.3% (5) |
| **Undergraduate education** | | |
| Public | 33.3% (6) | 26.3% (5) |
| Private | 50.0% (9) | 68.4% (13) |
| Ivy League | 16.7% (3) | 5.3% (1) |
| **Law school education** | | |
| Public | 22.2% (4) | 36.8% (7) |
| Private | 44.4% (8) | 36.8% (7) |
| Ivy League | 33.3% (6) | 26.3% (5) |
| **Gender** | | |
| Male | 88.9% (16) | 73.7% (14) |
| Female | 11.1% (2) | 26.3% (5) |
| **Ethnicity/race** | | |
| White | 88.9% (16) | 89.5% (17) |
| African American | 5.6% (1) | 5.3% (1) |
| Hispanic | 5.6% (1) | 5.3% (1) |
| Asian | — | — |
| **Percent white male** | 77.8% (14) | 63.2% (12) |
| **ABA rating** | | |
| Well qualified | 77.8% (14) | 52.6% (10) |

| | Bush I appointees<br>% (N) | Bush II appointees<br>% (N) |
|---|---|---|
| Qualified | 22.2% (4) | 47.4% (9) |
| **Political identification** | | |
| Democrat | — | 10.5% (2) |
| Republican | 94.4% (17) | 84.2% (16) |
| Independent | 5.6% (1) | 5.3% (1) |
| **Past party activism** | 66.7% (12) | 73.7% (14) |
| **Religious origin/affiliation** | | |
| Protestant | 55.6% (10) | 63.2% (12) |
| Catholic | 38.9% (7) | 10.5% (2) |
| Jewish | 5.6% (1) | 26.3% (5) |
| **Net worth** | | |
| Under $200,000 | 5.6% (1) | 5.3% (1) |
| $200,000–499,999 | 33.3% (6) | 26.3% (6) |
| $500,000–999,999 | 22.2% (4) | 21.0% (4) |
| $1 + million | 38.9% (7) | 47.4% (9) |
| **Average age at nomination** | 48.5 | 48.8 |
| **Total number of appointees** | 18 | 19 |

**PARTY AFFILIATION.** Tables 1 and 2 offer the findings for political party affiliation or identification and the proportion of appointees with a known record of previous partisan activity. Table 1 suggests that the Bush II judges were less Republican than the Bush I judges. Overall, the Bush appointees contained the largest proportion of all six administrations of those who were independent, but that proportion, about 6 percent (or one in 17) is small. The proportion of Democrats chosen by Bush was slightly more than that of the Reagan administration. About three out of five appointees had a record of previous party activism, but not all political activity was at the presidential or even senatorial level. (See "The Bush appointees' political and legal credentials," page 208, for examples of the types of previous party activism of appointees). Thus, about 9 out of 10 Bush appointees had some ties to the Republican Party, but only three out of five had ever engaged in noteworthy political activity.

**RELIGION.** The religious origin or affiliation of the district court appointees is indicated in the tables.[24] Table 2 provides the overall religious profile of the Bush appointees, which shows that the proportion of those with a Protestant origin or affiliation was the largest since the Nixon and Ford administrations. The proportion of Jewish appointees was the lowest of all six administrations, and the proportion of Catholic appointees, although slightly lower than that of the Reagan administration, was slightly higher than that of the Carter appointees.

**WEALTH.** The net worth of the Bush I and II appointees is shown in Table 1, and Table 2 presents the findings for the net worth of the combined Bush appointees along with the Reagan and Carter appointees. There was an increase for the Bush II appointees in the proportion of those with a modest net worth (under $500,000). This comes after the judicial pay increases authorized in 1989 legislation that took effect at the beginning of 1991. A previous analysis of judicial appointments in 1989 noted, "Without a more competitive pay scale, we can expect an increase in the number of wealthy individuals who become judges as some non-wealthy highly-qualified lawyers will not be able to afford a pay cut to go on the bench."[25] This in fact occurred, as during the first half of Bush's administration, there was a dramatic increase in the proportion of millionaires appointed, to about one in three. However, the proportion of millionaires did not increase for the Bush II appointees. This, combined with the fact of a higher proportion of judges in the under $500,000 net worth range, suggests that the increase in judicial salaries may be making a federal judicial career affordable for high-quality lawyers. However, it is premature to gauge the effect of the salary increases.[26]

**AGE.** One of the most dramatic differences between the Bush I and Bush II appointees is the average age at nomination. The Bush II judges, on average, were more than two years younger than the Bush I judges. As Table 2 shows, the average age for all Bush's district court appointees is 48.1 years, the youngest average age of all six administrations and, in all likelihood, the youngest this century. The proportion of Bush I judges *under* 45 when nominated was 44 percent. This compares with the Reagan first-term appointees, whose proportion was 26 percent, and his second-term appointees, whose proportion was 37 percent. If the Reagan administration sought to extend Reagan's legacy by appointing younger judges, this was also the case with the Bush administration, particularly with the Bush II appointments.

## APPEALS COURT APPOINTEES

Appointments to the district courts reflect the interplay of senatorial politics, local and state politics, bar and other interest-group politics, and the extent to which an administration has a policy agenda it wishes to pursue through judicial appointments. Appointments to the appeals court, while containing elements of these various types of politics, tend to emphasize an administration's priorities. An administration usually has greater leeway with appeals court appointments than with district court appointments. For an administration concerned with furthering its policy agenda through the courts, appeals court appointments offer an opportunity second only to Supreme Court appointments.

## Table 4
### U.S. appeals court appointees compared by administration

| | Bush %(N) | Reagan % (N) | Carter % (N) | Ford % (N) | Nixon % (N) | Johnson % (N) |
|---|---|---|---|---|---|---|
| **Occupation** | | | | | | |
| Politics/ government | 10.8% (4) | 6.4% (5) | 5.4% (3) | 8.3% (1) | 4.4% (2) | 10.0% (4) |
| Judiciary | 59.5% (22) | 55.1% (43) | 46.4% (26) | 75.0% (9) | 53.3% (24) | 57.5% (23) |
| Large law firm | | | | | | |
|   100+ members | 8.1% (3) | 3.9% (3) | 1.8% (1) | — | — | — |
|   50–99 | 8.1% (3) | 2.6% (2) | 5.4% (3) | 8.3% (1) | 2.2% (1) | 2.5% (1) |
|   25–49 | — | 6.4% (5) | 3.6% (2) | — | 2.2% (1) | 2.5% (1) |
| Medium size firm | | | | | | |
|   10–24 members | 8.1% (3) | 3.9% (3) | 14.3% (8) | — | 1.1% (5) | 7.5% (3) |
|   5–9 | 2.7% (1) | 6.4% (5) | 1.8% (1) | 8.3% (1) | 11.1% (5) | 10.0% (4) |
| Small firm | | | | | | |
|   2–4 members | — | 1.3% (1) | 3.6% (2) | — | 6.7% (3) | 2.5% (1) |
|   solo | — | — | 1.8% (1) | — | — | 5.0% (2) |
| Professor of law | 2.7% (1) | 12.8% (10) | 14.3% (8) | — | 2.2% (1) | 2.5% (1) |
| Other | — | 1.3% (1) | 1.8% (1) | — | 6.7% (3) | — |
| **Experience** | | | | | | |
| Judicial | 62.2% (23) | 60.3% (47) | 53.6% (30) | 75.0% (9) | 57.8% (26) | 65.0% (26) |
| Prosecutorial | 29.7% (11) | 28.2% (22) | 32.1% (18) | 25.0% (3) | 46.7% (21) | 47.5% (19) |
| Neither one | 32.4% (12) | 34.6% (27) | 37.5% (21) | 25.0% (3) | 17.8% (8) | 20.0% (8) |
| **Undergraduate education** | | | | | | |
| Public | 29.7% (11) | 24.4% (19) | 30.4% (17) | 50.0% (6) | 40.0% (18) | 32.5% (13) |
| Private | 59.5% (22) | 51.3% (40) | 50.0% (28) | 41.7% (5) | 35.6% (16) | 40.0% (16) |
| Ivy League | 10.8% (4) | 24.4% (19) | 19.6% (11) | 8.3% (1) | 20.0% (9) | 17.5% (7) |
| None indicated | — | — | — | — | 4.4% (2) | 10.0% (4) |
| **Law school education** | | | | | | |
| Public | 29.7% (11) | 39.7% (31) | 39.3% (22) | 50.0% (6) | 37.8% (17) | 40.0% (16) |
| Private | 40.5% (15) | 37.2% (29) | 19.6% (11) | 25.0% (3) | 26.7% (12) | 32.5% (13) |
| Ivy League | 29.7% (11) | 23.1% (18) | 41.1% (23) | 25.0% (3) | 35.6% (16) | 27.5% (11) |
| **Gender** | | | | | | |
| Male | 81.1% (30) | 94.9% (74) | 80.4% (45) | 100.0% (12) | 100.0% (45) | 97.5% (39) |
| Female | 18.9% (7) | 5.1% (4) | 19.6% (11) | — | — | 2.5% (1) |
| **Ethnicity/race** | | | | | | |
| White | 89.2% (33) | 97.4% (76) | 78.6% (44) | 100.0% (12) | 97.8% (44) | 95.0% (38) |

| | Bush %(N) | Reagan % (N) | Carter % (N) | Ford % (N) | Nixon % (N) | Johnson % (N) |
|---|---|---|---|---|---|---|
| African American | 5.4% (2) | 1.3% (1) | 16.1% (9) | .— | .— | 5.0% (2) |
| Hispanic | 5.4% (2) | 1.3% (1) | 3.6% (2) | — | — | — |
| Asian | — | — | 1.8% (1) | — | 2.2% (1) | — |
| **Percent white male** | 70.3% (26) | 92.3% (72) | 60.7% (34) | 100.0% (12) | 97.8% (44) | 92.5% (37) |
| **ABA rating** | | | | | | |
| Extremely well/ well qualified | 64.9% (24) | 59.0% (46) | 75.0% (42) | 58.3% (7) | 73.3% (33) | 75.0% (30)* |
| Qualified | 35.1% (13) | 41.0% (32) | 25.0% (14) | 33.3% (4) | 26.7% (12) | 20.0% (8) |
| Not qualified | — | — | — | 8.3% (1) | — | 2.5% (1) |
| **Political Identification** | | | | | | |
| Democrat | 5.4% (2) | — | 82.1% (46) | 8.3% (1) | 6.7% (3) | 95.0% (38) |
| Republican | 89.2% (33) | 97.4% (76) | 7.1% (4) | 91.7% (11) | 93.3% (42) | 5.0% (2) |
| Independent | 5.4% (2) | 1.3% (1) | 10.7% (6) | — | — | — |
| Other | — | 1.3% (1) | — | — | — | — |
| **Past party activism** | 70.3% (26) | 69.2% (54) | 73.2% (41) | 58.3% (7) | 60.0% (27) | 57.5% (23) |
| **Religious origin/ affillation** | | | | | | |
| Protestant | 59.4% (22) | 55.1% (43) | 60.7% (34) | 58.3% (7) | 75.6% (34) | 60.0% (24) |
| Catholic | 24.3% (9) | 30.8% (24) | 23.2% (13) | 33.3% (4) | 15.6% (7) | 25.0% (10) |
| Jewish | 16.3% (6) | 14.1% (11) | 16.1% (9) | 8.3% (1) | 8.9% (4) | 15.0% (6) |
| **Net worth** | | | | | | |
| Under $200,000 | 5.4% (2) | 15.6% (12)** | 33.3% (13)*** | NA | NA | NA |
| 200,000–499.999 | 29.7% (11) | 32.5% (25) | 38.5% (15) | NA | NA | NA |
| 500,000–999,999 | 21.6% (8) | 33.8% (26) | 17.9% (7) | NA | NA | NA |
| $1 + million | 43.2% (16) | 18.2% (14) | 10.3% (4) | NA | NA | NA |
| **Average age at nomination** | 48.7 | 50.0 | 51.9 | 62.1 | 53.8 | 52.2 |
| **Total number of appointees** | 37 | 78 | 56 | 12 | 45 | 40 |

\* No ABA rating was requested for one Johnson appointee.

\*\* Net worth was unavailable for one Reagan appointment.

\*\*\* Net worth only for Carter appointees confirmed by the 96th Congress with the exception of five appointees for whom net worth was unavailable.

The appeals courts, as is often noted, are the nation's mini supreme courts. For most litigation, they are the end of the line. Thus it is of special interest to examine the backgrounds and attributes of President Bush's appointees to the 11 numbered circuits and the U.S. Court of Appeals for the District of Columbia Court. These courts of general jurisdiction handle matters of constitutional and statutory law that span controversial issues concerning civil and economic rights and liberties.

Table 3 contains findings on the 19 confirmed Bush II appeals court appointees compared with the 18 confirmed Bush I appointees. Ten appeals court nominations had not been confirmed by the end of the 102nd Congress. Table 4 compares all of Bush's 37 confirmed appeals court appointees with those made by his five predecessors.[27]

Occupation and experience. Bush II appointees to the circuit courts were drawn somewhat more heavily from the sitting judiciary than Bush I judges, as Table 3 illustrates. All 12 Bush II appeals judges recruited from the judiciary were elevations from the federal district bench. Eight had been appointed to the district bench by Reagan, two by Bush, and one each by Ford and Carter. The Bush appointees overall were drawn more heavily from the judiciary than the Reagan, Carter, Nixon, and Johnson appointees, as Table 4 shows. They were also more heavily drawn from large law firms than previous administrations. Only one appointment went to a law professor, which was a throwback to the low Nixon, Ford, and Johnson levels.[28] This did not necessarily reflect a lack of interest in appointing law professors with a known and developed conservative judicial philosophy. Rather, the sort of law professor the Bush administration would have liked to appoint was likely to have a publication record espousing controversial conservative legal positions that undoubtedly would have made the confirmation process difficult.

More than three out of five Bush appointees had previous judicial experience, but less than a third of the appointees had prior prosecutorial experience. About one-third had neither judicial nor prosecutorial experience, which was close to the proportion of the Reagan appointees.

**EDUCATION.** Table 3 presents the undergraduate education of the Bush I and II appeals court appointees. Compared with the Bush I judges, the Bush II judges had a lower proportion educated at public-supported and Ivy League institutions. Overall, as Table 4 illustrates, the Bush appointees had the highest proportion of all six administrations of appointees attending private non-ivy League undergraduate institutions. Typically about one in five appointees of other administrations went to an Ivy League college, but for the Bush appointees it was 1 in 10.

A higher proportion of Bush II than Bush I appointees attended public supported law schools, and a lower proportion attended private law schools. Interestingly, all five of the Bush II appointees with an Ivy League law school education graduated from Harvard Law School. Three of the six Bush I appointees with an Ivy League legal education graduated from Yale Law School, two from Harvard, and one from the University of Pennsylvania. Compared with the appointees of the five previous administrations, Bush's appeals court appointees had the lowest proportion of those with a public-supported law school education and the highest proportion of those trained in a private non-Ivy League law school. If we consider prestige non-Ivy League law schools, including Michigan, New York University, Stanford, Texas, and Virginia, the proportion of Bush appointees with a prestige legal education rises to about 45 percent, the proportion of the Reagan appointees.

**AFFIRMATIVE ACTION.** Just as with appointments to the district bench, there was a marked increase in the proportion of women among the Bush II appeals court appointees. That proportion was about one in four appointees, a rate superior to the Carter administrations.[29] However, the proportion of African Americans and Hispanics did not change from the Bush I to the Bush II appointees.[30]

Table 4 shows that the overall rate of women appointees by the Bush administration was close to one in five, the rate shown for the Carter appointees. The proportion of African Americans was one-third that of the Carter appointees and about the level of the Johnson administration. The proportion of Hispanics, however, exceeded that of the Carter administration. Bush appointed no Asian Americans. In total, the proportion of white male appointees was about 7 in 10. The only lower proportion was the 6 in 10 rate of the Carter administration. The Bush administration made a commitment to achieve gender and racial diversity in its judicial appointments; for women it clearly was successful.

**ABA RATINGS.** There was a dramatic change in ABA ratings between the Bush I and Bush II appointees. Slightly more than half the Bush II appointees received the highest ABA rating, whereas more than three-fourths of the Bush I appointees received such a rating. Overall, a larger proportion of Bush appointees than Reagan appointees received the highest ABA ratings, but the proportion of Bush appointees was lower than that for the Carter, Nixon, and Johnson appointees. A total of three Bush appointees received a *qualified* rating with a minority of the ABA committee voting *not qualified*. Two of these split ratings were given to sitting district court judges. On balance, however, if the ABA ratings are considered a measure of quality, the large majority of the Bush appointees to the appeals courts were of high quality.

Staffing the Federal Courts

## Table 5

Proportion of presidents' appointees serving on federal bench,
November 3, 1992

| | Years after leaving office | District active % (N) | District senior % (N) | District total+ % (N) | Appeals active % (N) | Appeals senior % (N) | Appeals total % (N) | Supreme Court active % (N) |
|---|---|---|---|---|---|---|---|---|
| George Bush | — | 97.3% (144) | — | 97.3% (144) | 94.6% (35) | — | 94.6% (35) | 100% (2) |
| Ronald Reagan | 4 | 84.5% (245) | 1.0% (3) | 85.5% (248) | 85.9% (67) | 7.7% (6) | 93.6% (73) | 100% (4)* |
| Jimmy Carter | 12 | 62.9% (127) | 24.8% (50) | 87.6% (177) | 73.2% (41) | 23.2% (13) | 96.4% (54) | — |
| Gerald Ford | 16 | 25.0% (13) | 48.1% (25) | 73.1% (38) | 33.3% (4) | 33.3% (4) | 66.7% (8) | 100% (1) |
| Richard Nixon | 18 | 11.7% (21) | 40.8% (73) | 52.5% (94) | 6.7% (3) | 40.0% (18) | 46.7% (21) | 50% (2)* |
| Lyndon Johnson | 24 | 4.9% (6) | 45.9% (56) | 50.8% (62) | 2.5% (1) | 47.5% (19) | 50.0% (20) | — |
| John Kennedy | 29 | 2.9% (3) | 25.2% (26) | 28.2% (29) | 4.8% (1) | 9.5% (2) | 14.3% (3) | 50% (1) |
| Dwight Eisenhower | 32 | — | 11.2% (14) | 11.2% (14) | — | 20.0% (9) | 20.0% (9) | — |
| Harry Truman | 40 | 1.0% (1) | 5.2% (5) | 6.2% (6) | — | — | — | — |

Figures are for lifetime appointments to courts of general jurisdiction only.
* William Rehnquist is counted as an associate justice appointment of Nixon and as a chief justice appointment of Reagan.

**PARTY AFFILIATION**.  Although no Democrats were among the Bush I appointees to the circuit bench, two Democrats were among those in the Bush II group. About three in four Bush II appointees had some prior party activity, a rate larger than that for the Bush I appointees. Overall, just about 9 out of 10 Bush appointees were Republicans, and the overall proportion was the lowest of all three previous Republican administrations included in this study. Only Carter appointed a smaller proportion of individuals from his own political party. On the other hand, the proportion of Carter appointees was the highest with previous partisan activity, with the Bush appointees occupying second place. (See "The Bush appointees political and legal credentials," page 208.)

**RELIGION**.  The findings for religious origin or affiliation presented in Tables 3 and 4 suggest an absence of bias in any direction. For example, almost 4 in 10 of the Bush I appointees had some ties to Catholicism, but only about 1 in 10 Bush II judges had such links.[31] About 1 in 20 Bush I appointees was Jewish, whereas 1 in 4 Bush II appointees was Jewish. The proportions for the Bush appointees overall are similar to those of the Reagan administration, although the Reagan administration did have a higher proportion of Catholics and slightly lower proportion of Jewish and Protestant appointees. The proportions for the Bush appointees were almost identical to those for the Carter appointees.

**WEALTH**.  The net worth of the Bush appointees as presented in Tables 3 and 4 is startling. Close to half the Bush II appointees were millionaires.[32] The overall figures for the Bush appointees show that the proportion of millionaires was more than double that of the Reagan administration and was four times that of the Carter administration. Of course, whether one is a millionaire should not be relevant to the selection process. But these figures do suggest that those with less wealth are not being appointed to the appeals bench to the extent they once were. This may be in part because, until recently, judicial salaries were far behind what first-class lawyers could command in private practice, and the majority of appeals judges were drawn from a district bench that already had a disproportionate number of millionaires. It is possible that with the salary increases that went into effect in 1991, the proportion of millionaires may drop, particularly if President Clinton elevates non-millionaire Carter-appointed district judges.

**AGE**.  The average age of the Bush II appointees was slightly older than the Bush I judges, but even so was younger than the average age of all five previous administrations. Indeed, the Bush appointees to the courts of appeals were, on average, the youngest, with the exception of Reagan's second term appointments, since the first appointments to the courts of appeals in 1891.[33] An administration concerned with its judicial legacy can be expected to appoint younger judges.

## Table 6

Makeup of federal bench by appointing president, November 3, 1992

| | District courts | | Courts of appeals | |
| --- | --- | --- | --- | --- |
| | Active % (N) | Senior % (N) | Active % (N) | Senior % (N) |
| Bush | 22.3% (144) | — | 21.0% (35) | — |
| Reagan | 37.9% (245) | 1.2% (3) | 40.1% (67) | 8.4% (6) |
| Carter | 19.7% (127) | 19.8% (50) | 24.6% (41) | 18.3% (13) |
| Ford | 2.0% (13) | 9.9% (25) | 2.4% (4) | 5.6% (4) |
| Nixon | 3.3% (21) | 29.0% (73) | 1.8% (3) | 25.4% (18) |
| Johnson | 0.9% (6) | 22.2% (56) | 0.6% (1) | 26.8% (19) |
| Kennedy | 0.5% (3) | 10.3% (26) | 0.6% (1) | 2.8% (2) |
| Eisenhower | — | 5.6% (14) | — | 12.7% (9) |
| Truman | 0.2% (1) | 2.0% (5) | — | — |
| Vacancies | 13.2% (85) | — | 8.9% (15) | — |
| Totals | 100.0% (645) | 100% (252) | 100.0% (167) | 100.0% (71) |

Figures are for lifetime appointments to courts of general jurisdiction only.

## BUSH'S LEGACY

George Bush, in just one term, has left a judicial legacy that will last well into the next century. (See "How long the legacy?" page 214.) To the federal courts of general jurisdiction Bush made 187 lifetime appointments (two Supreme Court justices, 37 appeals court judges, and 148 district court judges). When Bush left office, 181 of his appointees remained on the bench (two Supreme Court justices, 35 appeals court judges, and 144 district court judges). President Bush himself made a commitment to gender and ethnic diversity on the bench that was realized by the historic proportion of women appointed to the lower federal courts and the appointment of an African American to the Supreme Court. Furthermore, for the first time, women at the White House and Justice Department levels played key roles in judicial selection. This is a legacy and standard, built upon Jimmy Carter's, that President Bill Clinton will be challenged to exceed.

Another legacy of the Bush administration is the shift in the locus of judicial selection decision making from the Justice Department to the White House counsel's office. This shift began with the Reagan administration and its creation of the President's Committee on Federal Judicial Selection, chaired by the White House counsel. This institutional innovation meant that the White House was systematically involved in the filling of judgeships. The White House counsel's office then shared decision making with the Justice Department's Office of Legal Policy.

But during the Bush presidency, the Office of Legal Policy was dismantled, the president's close friend C. Boyden Gray became White House counsel, and the chain of command was from the president to the White House counsel to the attorney general. Lee Liberman, associate White House counsel, took responsibility for major screening of judicial candidates, particularly those for positions on the appeals courts. Personal interviewing of all candidates for all but Supreme Court judgeships, however, was centered at the Justice Department, which continued its historic role of processing judicial nominations. The available evidence suggests that relations between the Justice Department officials concerned with judicial selection and the White House counsel's office were harmonious, with no major disagreements over nominations. Furthermore, after Attorney General Dick Thornburgh resigned, he was replaced by William Barr, who was as deeply conservative as his friend and mentor C. Boyden Gray.[34] Barr did not, as far as can be determined, challenge the role of the White House counsel's office in judicial selection.

The Bush administration, building upon the Reagan legacy, particularly with Supreme Court and appeals court appointments, but also to some extent with district court appointments, sought to transform the federal judiciary. Liberal activists in the tradition of Earl Warren, William Brennan, and Thurgood Marshall were not welcome. Although the evidence concerning the Bush appointees' decisional impact is slim, there is a body of literature that suggests that the Reagan judges on the whole have had a decisional impact that has made the federal bench far more conservative than when Reagan took office.[35] It is reasonable to expect that on the whole (undoubtedly with some exceptions) the Bush appointees will have a similar effect.

Another legacy from the Bush administration is the lesson that it is costly for a president to take on the Senate Judiciary Committee. The president's attempt to restrict access to the FBI reports likely cost the administration perhaps as many as two dozen confirmations. Controversial nominations, although fewer than during the Reagan administration, nevertheless took their toll in delaying the confirmation process for some non-controversial nominees. (See "Controversial nominations," page 291.)

George Bush left office having placed David Souter and Clarence Thomas on the Supreme Court and numerous well qualified men and women on the lower federal courts. Many, perhaps most, of the Bush appointees actively share Bush's judicial philosophy and conservative views. This surely is a legacy to be reckoned with.

## CLINTON AND THE BUSH LEGACY

On the day that Bill Clinton was elected president, the federal bench consisted of about one in five district judges in active service and one in four appeals judges in active service who were appointees of Democratic presidents. Most of these judges were moderate to liberal Democrats. Republican presidential appointees outnumbered Democrats by more than three to one. Not since Election Day 1952, after 20 years of Roosevelt and Truman appointees, was the federal bench so imbalanced politically and philosophically. Yet because 85 district court and 15 appeals court positions were vacant on the day Clinton was elected, the potential exists for the new president to redress the imbalance.

During the campaign, candidate Clinton addressed judicial selection. In a *National Law Journal* opinion piece, Clinton, without the benefit of the latest findings, asserted that President Bush's appointments showed a "sharp decline in the selection of women and minority judges, at the very time when more and more qualified women and minority candidates were reaching the time of their lives when they could serve as judges."[36] Clearly, President Clinton has signalled his intention of using judicial appointments to bring an even greater proportion than Bush's of women and minorities on the bench. It is reasonable to expect that the proportion of women and minorities appointed by Clinton will be substantially higher than the 33 percent level achieved by the Carter administration or the 28 percent level achieved by the Bush administration. It will not be surprising if the Clinton proportion is larger than 40 percent and even approaches the 50 percent level. Having women and minorities in key judicial selection roles in the administration will ensure that well qualified women and minorities are actively recruited for the bench.[37]

Clinton also pledged to appoint "men and women of unquestioned intellect, judicial temperament, broad experience and a demonstrated concern for, and commitment to, the individual rights protected by our Constitution, including the right to privacy."[38] This signals a change in philosophy of those to be recruited for the judiciary. How the Clinton administration designs its judicial selection process and the extent of active involvement of Clinton himself, who once was a law professor, will be of continuing interest.

The Reagan-Bush judicial legacy is most prominent at the Supreme Court level, and here we can expect the Clinton administration to make the most of his opportunity to replace Justice Byron White and to fill other vacancies if they occur. The distinguished judge Amalya Kearse of the U.S. Court of Appeals for the Second Circuit is likely to be high on the Clinton administration's list of candidates for the Supreme Court.[39] Other prominently mentioned names include federal district judge Jose Cabranes and Harvard Law School Professor Laurence Tribe. The extent to which President Clinton can undermine the Reagan-Bush legacy on the Supreme Court depends on which justice is being replaced and the number of seats Clinton will have an opportunity to fill. The replacement of conservative justice White with a more liberal Clinton appointee is a major step towards shifting the ideological balance on the Court.

In the cycle of American politics, the 1992 election of Bill Clinton as president may stand out as the start of a new political era, or it may turn out to have been a temporary aberration, like Carter's presidency, within the context of a Republican presidential era. Whatever significance the election has in the broader political sense, its significance and impact is sure to be felt with Clinton appointments to the federal bench. The precedents and doctrines that have been developed by conservative Republican judges during the past several decades will be more vulnerable with a new wave of more liberal judges coming to the bench joining the remaining liberal Democratic appointees (although liberals on the bench will remain in the minority throughout Clinton's first term). Whether constitutional and statutory guarantees of civil rights and civil liberties should be liberally construed and whether judges should read the Constitution in ways that enable them to participate actively in public policy making are broader issues that will continue to concern the nation's courts. The Bush judicial legacy in tandem with the Reagan legacy ensures that the debate will be a vigorous one.

## *Notes*

1.  Events from the first half of the Bush administration are discussed in Goldman, *The Bush Imprint on the Judiciary: Carrying on a Tradition*, 74 JUDICATURE 294 (1991).

2.  Among those consulted were THE AMERICAN BENCH (6th edition), MARTINDALE-HUBBELL LAW DIRECTORY, WHO'S WHO (national and regional editions), and THE JUDICIAL STAFF DIRECTORY (1992 edition).

3.  Books that describe and comment on the Thomas nomination and the Thomas-Hill hearings include Phelps and Winternitz, CAPITOL GAMES (New York: Hyperion, 1992); Simon, ADVICE & CONSENT (Washington: National Press Books 1992); Morrison, (ed.), RACING JUSTICE, EN-GENDERING POWER (New York: Pantheon, 1992); and Chrisman and Allen, (eds.), COURT OF APPEAL: THE BLACK COMMUNITY SPEAKS OUT ON THE RACIAL AND SEXUAL POLITICS OF CLARENCE THOMAS VS. ANITA HILL (New York: Ballentine, 1992).

4.  1 THE DOJ ALERT 15 (November, 1991).

5.  *Id. Also see* Johnston, *New Rules Stall U.S. Confirmations*, NEW YORK TIMES, January 20, 1992, at A–12.

6.  The three who were not confirmed were James R. McGregor (whose nomination was returned to the White House on August 2, 1991), Michael Kavanagh, and Thomas E. Sholts. Some degree of controversy surrounded each of these nominations.

7.  There were 14 nominations to the U.S. court of appeals (excluding the U.S. Court of Appeals for the Federal Circuit) before October 24, 1991. Nine were confirmed, a confirmation rate of 64 percent. There were three subsequent nominations in 1991, of which two were eventually confirmed, a two-thirds confirmation rate. In 1992 there were 13 nominations and nine confirmations, a confirmation rate of 69 percent. Several courts of appeals nominees were controversial because of their ideological positions and the importance of the circuits to which they were nominated. Interestingly, administration officials under-

stood that the committee would process 60 nominations to the lower courts in 1992, and they believed the issue of access to the FBI report was irrelevant to the number of confirmations.

8. *See* Lewis, *Waiting for Clinton, Democrats Hold Up Court Confirmations*, NEW YORK TIMES, September 1, 1992, at A–1, B–6.

9. *See, e.g.*, the remarks of Senator John Danforth, United States Senate, Committee on the Judiciary, *Judicial Nominations, Hearings July 29, 1992*, pp. 11–12 (transcript of proceedings). At that same hearing Senator John Seymour explicitly blamed "the previous attorney general's office and their staff" for delays in processing nominations, and he attacked the "bureaucracy and red tape and petty politics standing in the way of filling badly needed vacancies with caseloads piling up. . . ." (page 22. transcript of proceedings).

10. There are hints in the data that the particular Republican senator who was involved might also have been a variable in the process. Republican Senator John Danforth of Missouri, who strongly backed Clarence Thomas and personally vouched for him to his senatorial colleagues, perhaps suffered some fallout with the Senate Judiciary Committee—only three of the seven Missouri district court nominees were confirmed. Republican Senator Alfonse D'Amato of New York, considered vulnerable in his reelection bid, saw only five of the 12 New York district court nominees confirmed, although one of the unsuccessful nominees, a Democrat backed by Senator Patrick Moynihan, could well have been sabotaged by D'Amato with the assistance of Senator Strom Thurmond on the committee in retaliation for the delay on the other nominees. Senator Phil Gramm of Texas, who led the effort to defeat Democratic senators up for reelection, saw only six of the 11 Texas district court nominees win confirmation.

11. *Supra* n. 1, at 296-298.

12. In fairness to the administration, it appears that senatorial politics were responsible for many of the delays including those for the Wyoming and Pennsylvania positions. Strong leadership from the highest levels of the Justice Department, however, might have been able to break the logjam on the district courts. Note that only one of the new appeals court positions took 15 months or more to fill, and only one new appeals court position had no nominee.

13. 24 THE THIRD BRANCH 5 (Nov. 1992).

14. Interview with Carl Stern, NBC Nightly News, Oct. 5, 1992. An account of an interview with Gray noted that "the President is looking for judges who are not activists. Mr. Gray also said that if Mr. Bush is reelected, he would continue to name judges with a conservative philosophy." Lewis, *Biden Warns Bush on Supreme Court Nominations*, NEW YORK TIMES, June 26, 1992, p. B–8.

15. Where there were no Republican senators, the proportion of women selected by the Bush administration during 1991 and 1992 for the district bench was slightly more than 20 percent. Where there were Republican senators, the proportion of women selected for the district bench was slightly more than 18 percent.

16. *See* Smith, *Former U.S. Magistrates as District Judges: The Possibilities and Consequences of Promotion within the Federal Judiciary,* 73 JUDICATURE 268 (1990).

17. *Supra* n. 1, at 297.

18. Of the 42 district court nominees who did not win confirmation by the end of the 102nd Congress, three were women. Had all 42 nominees been confirmed, the proportion of women appointees among the Bush II judges would have dropped to 19 percent, which still would have been unprecedented. Similarly the combined Bush I and II proportion would have been about 17 percent, also the highest proportion of any administration.

19. Of the 42 nominees unconfirmed by the end of the 102nd Congress, three were black. Had they and their colleagues been confirmed, the Bush II proportion of African American appointees would have been about 8 percent, but the overall Bush record would have remained about the same.

20. Of the 42 unconfirmed district court nominees, two were Hispanic. Had all been confirmed the Hispanic proportion of Bush II judges and the Bush administration overall would have remained the same.

21. If the 42 unconfirmed Bush nominees had been confirmed, the proportion of *well qualified* appointees reported in Table 2 would have dropped to 54.7 percent, still the highest of all six administrations, but only slightly higher than that for the Reagan appointees.

22. Of the 42 unconfirmed Bush district court nominees, 23 received a *qualified* rating and, of these, 10 received a majority *qualified*/minority *not qualified* rating, a proportion in excess of 43 percent.

23. White males tended to receive the highest ratings. For example, about two-thirds of the white male Bush II appointees to the district courts received the highest ABA rating, but only a little more than one-third of the women received the highest rating. About three-fifths of the black males received the highest rating. For a study of an earlier era of the disparities in ABA ratings between traditional (i.e., white male) candidates and non-traditional candidates, see Slotnick, *The ABA Standing Committee on Federal Judiciary; A Contemporary Assessment.* 66 JUDICATURE 348, 385 (1983).

24. Some judges do not reveal their religious origins and are unaffiliated at the time of appointment. Others do not list their religious affiliations in biographical directories. Therefore, classification of these judges presents a challenge. *See* Goldman, *Reagan's Second term Judicial Appointments,* 70 JUDICATURE 324 at 330 (1987). The author is grateful to the many Bush appointees who responded to queries concerning religious origin or affiliation.

25. Goldman, *Reagan's Judicial Legacy,* 72 JUDICATURE 318 at 323 (1989).

26. But *see* the contradictory findings for appeals court appointees reported later in this article.

27. These figures do not include appointees to the U.S. Court of Appeals for the Federal Circuit, because this court is a court of specialized jurisdiction that does not consider the major civil liberties and economic issues likely to be relevant for a president's policy agenda.

28. Of the 10 appeals court nominations that lapsed at the end of the 102nd Congress, only one was to a law professor. Thus, even if this nominee, Lillian Riemer BeVier, and the nine

others had been confirmed, the Bush proportion of law professor appointees would still have been considerably less than the Reagan and Carter proportions.

29. When the 10 appeals court nominations that were not confirmed by the end of the 102nd Congress are included, the proportion of women falls to about 21 percent, or approximately the rate achieved by the Carter administration.

30. One of the 10 unconfirmed Bush II nominees was Hispanic. Had he and his nine colleagues been confirmed, the Bush II rate for Latinos would have been about 7 percent.

31. Note, however, that had the 10 appeals court nominations that died at the end of the 102nd Congress been confirmed, the proportion of Catholic Bush II appointees would have doubled to about 21 percent, which also would have been the proportion of Jewish Bush II appointees.

32. If the 10 unconfirmed nominees had been confirmed, the proportion of millionaires would have fallen to about the same proportion as the Bush I judges.

33. Goldman, *The Age of Judges*, 73 ABA JOURNAL 94 at 96 (1987). If all Reagan appointees to the courts of appeals are included, the proportion of Reagan appointees under the age of 45 was slightly lower (23.1 percent) than the proportion of Bush appointees (24.3 percent). The proportion of second-term Reagan appointees under the age of 45 was 27.6 percent; the proportion of Bush II appointees was 26.3 percent.

34. *See* Johnston, *New Attorney General Shifts Department's Focus*, NEW YORK TIMES, March 3, 1992, at A–17.

35. See the studies cited in *supra* n. 24, at 335–338 and *supra* n. I at 306. *Also see* Kovacic, *Reagan's Judicial Appointees and Antitrust in the 1990s*, 60 FORDHAM L. REV. 49 (1991); Kovacic, *The Reagan Judiciary and Environmental Policy: The Impact of Appointments to the Federal Courts of Appeals*, 18 ENVIRONMENTAL AFFAIRS 669 (1991); Rowland and Todd, *Where You Stand Depends on Who Sits: Platform Promises and Judicial Gatekeeping in the Federal District Courts*, 53 J. POL. 175 (1991). Evidence concerning the Bush appointees can be found in Carp, Songer, Rowland, Stidham and Richey-Tracy, *The Voting Behavior of Judges Appointed by President Bush*, 76 JUDICATURE 298 (1993).

36. Clinton, *Judiciary Suffers Racial, Sexual Lack of Balance*, NATIONAL L.J., November 2, 1992, at 15.

37. News accounts report that the Office of Legal Policy is being revived and will be run by a woman. *See* Johnston, *Executive Brief: The Justice Department*, NEW YORK TIMES, March 22, 1999, at A–15. The nation's first female attorney general, Janet Reno, can also be expected to be actively involved in broadening the gender and ethnic profile of the federal judiciary.

38. *Supra* n. 36, at 15, 16.

39. Her colleague on the second circuit, Judge Jon O. Newman, has written of Judge Kearse: "Most knowledgeable observers agree Judge Kearse is among the four or five persons most qualified for the High Court." She "has served with extraordinary distinction" on the Second Circuit. Newman, *A Replacement for Thomas*, NEW YORK TIMES, Oct. 10, 1991, at A-27.

# THE VOTING BEHAVIOR OF PRESIDENT CLINTON'S JUDICIAL APPOINTEES

*Ronald Stidham, Robert A. Carp, and Donald R. Songer*

Until now, information about the voting behavior of U.S. district and circuit judges appointed by President Bill Clinton has been largely anecdotal. A significant reason for this is the substantial time between a president's election and when his judicial appointees' decisions begin appearing in print in sufficient numbers to be subject to empirical analysis.

Even near the end of Clinton's four-year-term, the number of his appointees' published decisions is rather modest. Still, it is sufficiently large to begin making meaningful generalizations about the decisional patterns of the women and men Clinton has placed on the U.S. district courts and courts of appeals. We can also speculate about the impact of Clinton's appointees on the ideological content and direction of the U.S. judiciary as a whole.

The data on trial court decisions during the 1992–96 period were drawn from a larger study of 55,000 opinions published in the Federal Supplement by more than 1,500 judges from 1993 to 1996.[1] Only those cases that fit easily into one of 27 case types and contained a clear underlying liberal-conservative dimension were used. They included cases such as state and federal habeas corpus pleas, labor-management disputes, questions involving the right to privacy, and environmental protection cases, among others. Excluded were cases involving patents, admiralty disputes, and land condemnation hearings. The number of cases not selected was about the same as the number included.

The data on the voting patterns of circuit court judges appointed by Presidents Nixon through Clinton are from a random sample of 1,000 decisions drawn from the *Federal Reporter* from 1994 and 1995. Different time frames for the district and circuit court analyses were used because there is not a large enough body of votes by Clinton circuit court appointees prior to 1994 to make a meaningful analysis worthwhile.

Not included in the data were the votes of district court judges sitting on appellate panels. Only one case involved an en banc panel. The coding scheme used for the votes of circuit court judges followed the model for content and liberal-conservative direction of district court decisions.

From *Judicature*, Vol. 80, no. 1 July/August 1996 by Ronald Stidham, Robert A. Carp and Donald R. Songer, Copyright © 1996 by American Judicature Society. Reprinted by permission.

## EXPECTATIONS

There are four general criteria by which one might evaluate or predict a president's success in securing a judicial cohort whose decisions mirror his ideological and policy values.[2] They are:

1. the level of the president's commitment to making ideologically based appointments;
2. the number of vacancies he is able to fill;
3. the extent of the president's political clout; and
4. the judicial climate into which the new judges enter.

In order to have a significant impact on the orientation of the federal courts, a president must have a strong and consistent policy of nominating judges who reflect his ideological values. Not all presidents have ranked ideology that highly in their judicial selection criteria. For instance, President Harry Truman's primary concern when appointing judges was to select individuals who were loyal to him in the 1948 presidential campaign. Truman had been deserted by the Dixiecrats who supported Strom Thurmond and by the Progressive Party supporters who backed Henry Wallace. Truman, therefore, was much more concerned with loyalty than with ideology when it came time to fill seats on the federal bench. An examination of Truman's judicial cohort reveals a mixed bag of liberals and conservatives.

Dwight Eisenhower provides another interesting example. An almost apolitical man for whom ideology counted little, experience and solid common sense ranked high on Eisenhower's selection requirements. As a consequence, his judicial cohort, like Truman's, lacked a clear-cut ideological bent.

Clinton's ideological orientation and commitment are clearly not as liberal as those of many of his predecessors, and on several occasions he has stated that he will probably go down in history as the most conservative Democrat to occupy the White House this century. He has frequently referred to himself as a "new Democrat" and has tried to distance himself from the more liberal image that characterized the Democratic party for many years. It is fair to say, then, that Clinton's general ideological orientation is one of more moderate liberalism.

During the 1992 presidential campaign, Clinton pledged to appoint to the bench "men and women of unquestioned intellect, judicial temperament, broad experience and a demonstrated concern for, and commitment to, the individual rights protected by our Constitution, including the right to privacy."[3] He also criticized George Bush for appointing insufficient numbers of women and minority judges. All this suggests that Clinton has had a commitment to appointing judges who are more reflective of the racial and gender composition of American society and who are ideologically moderate to modestly liberal. One veteran court observer noted that "Clinton's Supreme Court choices, Ruth Bader Ginsburg and Stephen Breyer, are moderates, and so are most of his lower court appointees."[4] Assistant Attorney General Eleanor Dean Acheson, who oversees judicial selection in the Clinton administration, says that "the administration rejects candidates with ideological agendas and stresses diversity without sacrificing quality."[5] Indeed, Clinton has appointed a higher percentage of women and racial minorities to the bench than any of his predecessors.[6]

Clinton began his presidency with some 100 vacancies left over from the Bush administration. In addition to leftover vacancies a president can generally expect about 50 judgeships to open up annually as a result of deaths, retirements, and moves to senior status. Some presidents, such as Jimmy Carter, may also benefit from the creation of new judgeships by Congress.

A key factor to be considered in assessing Clinton's impact on the federal judiciary is whether he will be reelected to a second term. If that happens, his appointees will dominate the federal courts. According to a recent account, given that 50 district judges are eligible for senior status, and another 132 are slated to become eligible for such status in the next five years, a re-elected Clinton "could wind up naming well more than 300 of the 649 district judges, perhaps even a majority."[7]

A third criterion to be considered regarding a president's capacity to make an imprint on the federal judiciary is whether he possesses the political influence to obtain Senate confirmation of his ideologically based appointments. Clinton's clout has waxed and waned during his years in the White House, but for most of his term he was very successful in securing judicial confirmations. Not only did Clinton work with a Democratic-controlled Senate during the first half of his term, he earned a reputation for avoiding confirmation battles.[8] Assistant Attorney General Acheson recently said, "We've steered clear of a few people who might have been fabulous judges but who would have provoked a fight that we were likely to lose."[9]

The final criterion affecting the president's potential to make a major impact on the judiciary is the environment into which appointees to the bench enter. When Clinton began his presidency, three-fourths of the bench consisted of conservative judges appointed by his Republican predecessors. As one observer put it, "Not since election day 1952, after 20 years of Roosevelt and Truman appointees, was the federal bench so imbalanced politically and philosophically."[10] This means that the Clinton appointees must feel their way slowly and articulate their moderately liberal values only in those relatively close cases where their decisions do not risk being overturned by conservative appellate panels.

## VOTING BEHAVIOR

We now turn to the empirical data on judicial decisions at both the district and circuit court levels. First, the Clinton judges' decisions overall are compared with those of other presidential appointees at the trial and appellate levels. Then, the same comparison is made by focusing more precisely on cases involving criminal justice, civil rights and liberties, and labor and economic regulation.

Table 1 updates our continuing research that has mapped the effect of appointing presidents on the decisions of the district judges they appoint.[11] Across time the raw numbers continue to show something meaningful about the centers of gravity of the two major parties. For example, when the liberalism scores of Democratic appointees in recent decades are compared with those of Republican appointees, it is clear that the president's party makes a difference in the way decisions are made by the judges they appoint. The appointees of Democratic presidents have clearly been more liberal in their decision making than judges chosen by Republicans.

Yet there are problems associated with placing too much emphasis on these precise numbers. For one thing, the case mixture has varied greatly over time as the precise types of cases finding their way into the courts has changed. Also, definitions of "liberalism" and "conservatism" have varied to some degree over the years. Still, the indices do provide some insight into differences in the impact of the appointing president.

The data in Table 1, examining the appointees of Presidents Nixon through Clinton, indicate that Carter's judicial cohort is clearly the most liberal. Reagan's appointees are the most conservative. As one might expect, Clinton's district court appointees overall are less liberal than Carter's, but more liberal than judges appointed by any of the Republican presidents.

## Table I
### Liberal U.S. district court decisions overall, 1992–96

| Appointing president | % | N |
|----------------------|-----|-------|
| Richard Nixon | 39 | 8,680 |
| Gerald Ford | 44 | 2,069 |
| Jimmy Ford | 53 | 8,860 |
| Ronald Reagan | 36 | 7,047 |
| Geroge Bush | 37 | 639 |
| Bill Clinton | 48 | 332 |

## Table 2

Liberal district court decisions for three categories of cases, 1992–1996

| Appointing president | Criminal justice | | Civil rights and liberties | | Labor and economic regulation | |
|---|---|---|---|---|---|---|
| | % | N | % | N | % | N |
| Richard Nixon | 30 | 227 | 37 | 293 | 48 | 215 |
| Gerald Ford | 32 | 76 | 39 | 133 | 55 | 136 |
| Jimmy Carter | 38 | 656 | 52 | 1,224 | 62 | 965 |
| Ronald Reagan | 23 | 1,143 | 33 | 1,841 | 49 | 1,435 |
| George Bush | 29 | 101 | 33 | 162 | 51 | 142 |
| Bill Clinton | 34 | 47 | 39 | 174 | 62 | 111 |

Table 2 shows much more precisely where the Clinton cohort parts company with that of other recent presidents. On matters of criminal justice the Clinton judges are the second most liberal group, behind only Carter's appointees. Not unexpectedly, the Reagan, Bush, and Nixon cohorts are the most conservative on matters of criminal justice.

In civil rights and civil liberties cases the Carter jurists, with a liberal score of 52 percent, far outdistance all the other cohorts. The Clinton cohort's liberal score of 39 percent is identical with that of the Ford appointees and six points higher than the Reagan and Bush judges, who have identical liberal scores of 33 percent.

In cases involving labor and economic regulation the Clinton and Carter judicial appointees are most liberal with identical scores of 62 percent. However, Table 2 reveals that the liberalism scores of all the cohorts are rather high in this case category. Even the Reagan and Bush judges are at the 50 percent mark in labor and economic regulation cases.

A possible explanation for the high percentage of liberal decisions in this case category is that increasing numbers of women have been appointed to the bench in recent years. Limited research has found that on some narrow but key issues women on the bench decide cases differently from their male colleagues. One recent study of the voting behavior of judges on the U.S. courts of appeals, for instance, found no significant differences between male and female judges in obscenity or search and seizure cases, but did find that female jurists were significantly more liberal than their male counterparts in employment discrimination cases.[12] This may be at play in the district courts as well, since more than half of the labor and economic regulation cases deal with some type of worker, and underdog, who is claiming denial of a critical benefit, often his or her job.

## Table 3
### Liberal circuit court decisions overall, 1994–95

| Appointing president | % | N |
|---|---|---|
| Richard Nixon | 30 | 125 |
| Gerald Ford | 29 | 95 |
| Jimmy Carter | 43 | 502 |
| Ronald Reagan | 32 | 982 |
| Geroge Bush | 30 | 510 |
| Bill Clinton | 36 | 113 |

At the circuit court level, according to Table 3, the votes cast by judges overall reveals almost the same pattern as district court cases. The liberalism scores of the Clinton appointees are second only to those of Carter's, while the appointees of Republican presidents are more conservative. Table 4 presents a breakdown by the three broad case categories. An analysis of votes cast by judges on appellate court panels in criminal justice cases again reveals the same pattern.

In cases involving civil rights and liberties issues the votes of Clinton and Carter appointees are almost identical in terms of liberalism, with scores of 41 and 42 percent respectively. A comparison of Tables 2 and 4 reveals that Clinton's circuit court appointees are a bit more liberal in civil rights and liberties cases than his district court appointees. However, we caution against hasty conclusions since we are only talking about 32 votes by Clinton judges at the appellate court level.

## Table 4
### Liberal circuit court decisions for three categories of cases, 1994–1995

| Appointing president | Criminal justice | | Civil rights and liberties | | Labor and economic regulation | |
|---|---|---|---|---|---|---|
| | % | N | % | N | % | N |
| Richard Nixon | 26 | 66 | 29 | 34 | 44 | 25 |
| Gerald Ford | 20 | 55 | 35 | 20 | 50 | 20 |
| Jimmy Carter | 40 | 278 | 42 | 111 | 54 | 113 |
| Ronald Reagan | 26 | 533 | 32 | 238 | 50 | 211 |
| George Bush | 22 | 267 | 33 | 129 | 47 | 114 |
| Bill Clinton | 31 | 65 | 41 | 32 | 50 | 16 |

In labor and economic regulation cases there is once again the problem of a small number of votes by the Clinton appeals court judges. The data include only 16 votes by the Clinton cohort. The 50 percent liberalism score of his appointees ties them for second place with the Ford and Reagan cohorts. Once again, the Carter appointees lead the way with a liberalism score of 54 percent. There is a large difference between the Clinton appointees at the district and circuit court levels, a finding that might be explored in future studies.

This is the first study of what the data indicate about the degree of liberal or conservative ideology of the decisional behavior of Clinton's appointees to the lower federal courts. While studies have focused on Clinton's accomplishments in diversifying the federal bench and the decisional behavior of his two Supreme Court appointees, there has been little study of the Clinton appointees at the trial and intermediate appellate levels.

The basic conclusion to be drawn from this exploratory study is that the Clinton appointees, at this point, exhibit moderate decisional tendencies. This comes as no surprise, given the earlier-discussed model for assessing a president's chances for success in affecting judicial decision making. At any rate, the 1996 presidential election will be an important one not only for Bill Clinton, but for the federal judiciary as well.

## *Notes*

1. For a discussion of what types of cases are and are not published in the SUPPLEMENT, and also for a discussion of the methodological merits for using it as a basis for studying federal district court opinions, see Carp et. al. *The Voting Behavior of Judges Appointed by President Bush*, 76 JUDICATURE 298, 299 (1993).

2. Stidham, Carp, and Rowland, *Patterns of Presidential Influence on the Federal District Courts: An Analysis of the Appointment Process*, 14 PRESIDENTIAL STUDIES Q. 548–560 (1984).

3. Clinton, *Judiciary Suffers Racial, Sexual Lack of Balance*, Nat'l L.J., Nov. 2, 1992, at 15.

4. Gest, *Disorder in the Courts?*, U.S. NEWS AND WORLD REPORT, February 12, 1996, at 40.

5. Quoted in *id*.

6. Goldman, *Judicial Selection under Clinton: A Midterm Examination*, 78 JUDICATURE 276, (1995).

7. Eastland, *If Clinton Wins, Here's What the Courts Will Look Like*, Wall Street Journal, Feb. 28, 1996, at A-21.

8. *See e.g.*, Eastland, *id.*: Gest, *supra* n. 4.

9. Quoted in Gest, *supra*, n. 4.

10. Goldman, *Bush's Judicial Legacy: The Final Imprint*, 76 JUDICATURE 282 (1993).

11. *See, e.g.* , Carp and Rowland, POLICYMAKING AND POLITICS IN THE FEDERAL DISTRICT COURTS (Knoxville, University of Tennessee Press, 1983); Carp and Stidham, JUDICIAL PROCESS IN AMERICA 3rd ed. (Washington, D.C.; Congressional Quarterly Press, 1996).

12. Davis, Haire, and Songer, *Voting Behavior and Gender on the U.S. Courts of Appeals*, 77 JUDICATURE 276 (1995).

# *What Do Justices Do?*

## *Exercises in Judicial Activism and Judicial Restraint: Balancing Democracy, Constitutionalism, and Liberty*

To understand what Supreme Court justices do, and how they reach decisions, one has to look beyond the legal reasoning process and consider the institutional and political context in which the Supreme Court does its work. What justices do, and what they should do, is often the subject of heated political battles. Arguments about the desirability of the specific results of particular Supreme Court decisions, or doctrinal trends, are often cloaked as arguments about the proper role of the Supreme Court in the American system of liberal, constitutional, democracy. But, the justices also take debates about the proper institutional role of the Court quite seriously as an issue of balancing the American commitments to democracy, constitutionalism, and liberty. Hence, as students of law and politics, we must take these arguments seriously as questions of normative theory, while also recognizing that these arguments are often invoked for political purposes.

One of the greatest challenges for the U.S. Supreme Court has been the need to define, and enforce, the word "liberty" in the Fifth and Fourteenth Amendments' due process clauses. This struggle to define "liberty" as a restraint on legitimate government action, reveals the competing positions on the proper judicial role in our system of liberal, constitutional, democracy. At the same time, this struggle to define the limits on government action imposed by the word "liberty" has been emersed in some of the central political disputes of the 20th century. And, it led to the single most notorious effort of the political branches to curb the Supreme Court: Franklin Delano Roosevelt's (FDR) 1937 Court-Packing Plan.

The debate over the proper role of the Supreme Court in the American system of liberal, constitutional, democracy is often cast as a debate between *judicial activism* and *judicial restraint*. Judicial activism refers to a willingness on the part of judges/justices to make significant changes in the public policies established by the electorally-accountable branches. Judicial restraint, on the other hand, refers to an *un*willingness on the part of judges/justices to make significant changes in the public policies established by the electorally-accountable branches. Both advocates of judicial activism and advocates of judicial restraint acknowledge that judicial review is "undemocratic," since neither federal judges nor Supreme Court justices are electorally-accountable. However, while judicial restraint advocates see this as a problem, judicial activists see it as an advantage. Advocates of judicial activism point out that: (1) the constitution creates a government of limited powers and it is the courts' duty to enforce it; (2) it is the courts' duty to protect minorities (even minorities of one) from tyranny of the majority; (3) courts have the capacity to engage in reasoned deliberation shielded from the temporary "ill-humors," as Hamilton called them, that sweep through the populace; and (4) it is the courts' duty to protect fundamental values, such as liberty, which may be ignored elsewhere. Advocates of judicial restraint counter with: (1) the 'democratic' branches should govern; (2) judges and justices should not be able to replace the majority's preferences with their own; (3) courts lack the institutional capacity to make wise public policy; and (4) activism makes the courts subject to political attacks. In short, the two sides balance the demands of democracy, of constitutionalism, and of liberty differently.[1]

As the readings in this chapter demonstrate, the policy implications of activism and restraint depend upon the policy direction of the political branches at the time. More specifically, judicial activism produces conservative results when the legislation being reviewed is itself liberal, as in *Lochner* v. *New York* (1905); *Adkins* v. *Children's Hospital* (1923); and *Morehead* v. *N.Y. ex. rel. Tipaldo* (1936). And, judicial restraint produces liberal results when the legislation being reviewed is itself liberal, as in *West Coast Hotel* v. *Parish* (1937) and *U.S.* v. *Carolene Products* (1938). Hence, as one sees in the history of the Court-Packing Plan recounted in the selection by William H. Rehnquist, our great liberal president, FDR, was a proponent of judicial restraint! Conversely, judicial activism produces liberal results when the legislation being reviewed is itself conservative, as in *Griswold* v. *Connecticut* (1965). And, judicial restraint produces conservative results when the legislation being reviewed is itself conservative, as in *Palko* v. *Connecticut* (1965). Hence, the intersections between views of the proper role for the courts, and political policy preferences are dynamic and complex.

Substantively, all these cases share a concern with how the word "liberty" is to be interpreted, or defined. The chapter begins with the "liberty to contract" cases in which the Court sought to protect a formal equality of liberty rights between employers and employees in the face of very real disparities in ability to exercise those liberty rights.

In the early years of the 20th century, employers held all the bargaining chips, and the Supreme Court blocked legislative efforts taking some issues of health and wages off the table. In the wake of the Court-packing plan, the Supreme Court retreated from the active protection of such economic liberties, and turned to what we now think of as "civil liberties." The famous footnote four in *U.S.* v. *Carolene Products* (1938) signals this shift. One of the central doctrinal features of this shift was the emerging willingness to define "liberty" in the 14th Amendment by referring back to those liberties protected by the Bill of Rights: incorporation of the bill of Rights.

The Bill of Rights begins: "Congress shall make no law . . . ." In 1833, in a case called *Barron* v. *Baltimore*, 7 Pet. (32 U.S.) 243, the Supreme Court held that "Congress" means "Congress and the national government only." In short, the Court held that the first eight amendments to the constitution were a limit on the *national* government's power, but *not on state* government's power. One could not challenge a state law as violating the Bill of Rights. In a completely unrelated development, the nation adopted the Fourteenth Amendment in 1868. The Fourteenth Amendment was specifically designed to limit *state* government power. It reads, in part, "nor shall any State deprive any person of life, liberty, or property, without due process of law . . .". The Supreme Court, having gotten itself in considerable political hot water with its attempt to define "liberty" as "liberty to contract," sought a way to define the word "liberty" in the due process clause of the Fourteenth Amendment. What was needed was a definition that would place real limits on the power of state governments, while at the same time limiting the discretion of the justices to pick and choose among various liberty rights claims. Where could the justices turn for a definition of "liberty" grounded in law, rather than in their own personal policy preferences? Beginning in *Gitlow* v. *New York* (1925), the Court began to turn to the Bill of Rights as an authoritative list of those liberty rights which should limit government power, national *and state*.

Hence, the Court began to enforce the Bill of Rights as a limit on *state* government power by "incorporating" or "absorbing" the Bill of Rights into the word "liberty" in the Fourteenth Amendment due process clause which limits *state* government action. Since, 1925 the Court has embarked on process of "selective incorporation" meaning that the Court has "incorporated" specific Bill of Rights provisions on a case-by-case basis, as specific challenges reached the Court. In *Palko* v. *Connecticut* (1937), Justice Cardozo articulates a standard for "incorporation" or "absorption" that sets the terms of the debate for the rest of the century. He argues that only those Bill of Rights guarantees that are "of the very essence of [fundamental to] a scheme of ordered liberty" are "absorbed" into the meaning of the word "liberty" in the Fourteenth Amendment. In particular, the Court held that the Fifth Amendment prohibition on double jeopardy was not one of those "fundamental principles of liberty and justice which lie at the base of all our civil and political institutions."

This process of "selective incorporation" provoked some of the most intense divisions on the Court about the proper institutional role of the Supreme Court and the need for constraints on the justices' discretion to 'read their own policy preferences' into the meaning of the constitution. Today, almost all of the Bill of Rights guarantees have been "incorporated," including the double jeopardy provision of the Fifth Amendment that Cardozo had found not to be "fundamental" in 1937.[2] And, some justices have been willing to go beyond the Bill of Rights, arguing that the word "liberty" in the Fourteenth Amendment means all the provisions of the Bill of Rights plus any other claimed liberty rights that the justices agree are "fundamental to an ordered scheme of liberty." *Griswold* v. *Connecticut* (1965) provides a example of "incorporation plus."

What do justices do? The materials contained in this chapter offer a rich set of answers: they debate the proper role institutional of the Court within our system of liberal, constitutional, democracy; they take cognizance of the politically charged atmospheres in which they must decide; they consider the policy effects of their decisions, and they may pursue policy agendas; they engage in legal reasoning and construct arguments and word definitions that limit, or expand, government power; and they do all these things simultaneously. The fun and the frustration of these cases is that each can be read as a chapter in several different stories. Each of them has much to tell us.

## Notes

1.    Refer back to the interchanges between Justice Frankfurter and Justice Stone in *Minersville School District* v. *Gobitis*, 310 U.S. 586 (1940) and between Justice Jackson and Justice Frankfurter in *West Virginia Board of Education* v. *Barnette*, 319 U.S. 624 (1943) about the proper role of the Court in a liberal, constitutional, democracy. (See Chapter Three.)

2.    *Benton* v. *Maryland* 395 U.S. 784 (1969). To date, only the Second Amendment, Third Amendment, the Fifth Amendment's right to indictment by a grand jury; the Seventh Amendment, and the Eighth Amendment's rights against excessive bail and fines have not been incorporated.

# Lochner v. New York

198 U.S. 45 (1905)

## Error to the County Court of Oneida County, State of New York

No. 293. Argued February 23, 24, 1905. —Decided April 17, 1905.

## STATEMENT OF CASE

This is a writ of error to the County Court of Oneida County, in the State of New York (to which court the record had been remitted), to review the judgment of the Court of Appeals of that State, affirming the judgment of the Supreme Court, which itself affirmed the judgment of the County Court, convicting the defendant of a misdemeanor on an indictment under a statute of that State, known, by its short title, as the labor law. The section of the statute under which the indictment was found in section 110, and is reproduced in the margin,[1] (together with the other sections of the labor law upon the subject of bakeries, being sections 111 to 115, both inclusive).

The indictment averred that the defendant "wrongfully and unlawfully required and permitted an employee working for him in his biscuit, bread and cake bakery and confectionery establishment, at the city of Utica, in this county, to work more than sixty hours in one week, . . . he was convicted of misdemeanor, second offense, as indicted and sentenced to pay a fine of $50 and to stand committed until paid, not to exceed fifty days in the Oneida County jail. A certificate of reasonable doubt was granted by the county judge of Oneida County, whereon an appeal was taken to the Appellate Division of the Supreme Court, Fourth Department, where the judgment of conviction was affirmed. 73 App. Div. N.Y. 120. A further appeal was then taken to the Court of Appeals, where the judgment of conviction was again affirmed. 177 N.Y. 145.

*Mr. Frank Harvey Field* and *Mr. Henry Weissmann* for plaintiff in error: . . .

*Mr. Julius M. Mayer*, Attorney General of the State of New York, for defendant in error:

Mr. Justice Peckham, after making the foregoing statement of the facts, delivered the opinion of the court.

The indictment, it will be seen, charges that the plaintiff . . . violated the one hundred and tenth section of article 8, chapter 415, of the Laws of 1897, known as the labor law of the State of New York, in that he wrongfully and unlawfully required and permitted an employé working for him to work more than sixty hours in one week. There is nothing in any of the opinions delivered in this case, either in the Supreme Court or the Court of Appeals of the State, which construes the section, in using the word "required," as referring to any physical force being used to obtain the labor of an employé. It is assumed that the word means nothing more than the requirement arising from voluntary contract for such labor in excess of the number of hours specified in the statute. There is no pretense in any of the opinions that the statute was intended to meet a case of involuntary labor in any form. All the opinions assume that there is no real distinction, so far as this question is concerned, between the words "required" and "permitted." The mandate of the statute that "no employé shall be required or permitted to work," is the substantial equivalent of an enactment that "no employé shall contract or agree to work," more than ten hours per day, and as there is no provision for special emergencies the statute is mandatory in all cases. It is not an act merely fixing the number of hours which shall constitute a legal day's work, but an absolute prohibition upon the employer, permitting, under any circumstances, more than ten hours work to be done in his establishment. The employé may desire to earn the extra money, which would arise from his working more than the pre-scribed time, but this statute forbids the employer from permitting the employé to earn it.

The statute necessarily interferes with the right of contract between the employer and employés, concerning the number of hours in which the latter may labor in the bakery of the employer. The general right to make a contract in relation to his business is part of the liberty of the individual protected by the Fourteenth Amendment of the Federal Constitution. *Allgeyer* v. *Louisiana*, 165 U.S. 578. Under that provision no State can deprive any person of life, liberty or property without due process of law. The right to purchase or to sell labor is part of the liberty protected by this amendment, unless there are circumstances which exclude the right. There are, however, certain powers, existing in the sovereignty of each State in the Union, somewhat vaguely termed police powers, the exact description and limitation of which have not been attempted by the courts. Those powers, broadly stated and without, at present, any attempt at a more specific limitation, relate to the safety, health, morals and general welfare of the public. Both property and liberty are held on such reasonable conditions as may be imposed by the governing power of the State in the exercise of those powers, and with such conditions as may be imposed by the governing power of the State in the exercise of those powers, and with such conditions the Fourteenth Amendment was not designed to interfere. *Mugler* v. *Kansas*, 123 U.S. 623; *In re Kemmler*, 136 U.S. 436; *Crowley* v. *Christensen*, 137 U.S. 86; *In re Converse*, 137 U.S. 624.

The State, therefore, has power to prevent the individual from making certain kinds of contracts, . . . If the contract be one which the State, in the legitimate exercise of its police power, has the right to prohibit, it is not prevented from prohibiting it by the Fourteenth Amendment. . . . Therefore, when the State, by its legislature, in the assumed exercise of its police powers, has passed an act which seriously limits the right to labor or the right of contract in regard to their means of livelihood between persons who are *sui juris* (both employer and employé), it becomes of great importance to determine which shall prevail—the right of the individual to labor for such time as he may choose, or the right of the State to prevent the individual from laboring or from entering into any contract to labor, beyond a certain time prescribed by the State. . . .

It must, of course, be conceded that there is a limit to the valid exercise of the police power by the State. . . . In every case that comes before this court, therefore, where legislation of this character is concerned and where the protection of the Federal Constitution is sought, the question necessarily arises: Is this a fair, reasonable and appropriate exercise of the police power of the State, or is it an unreasonable, unnecessary and arbitrary interference with the right of the individual to his personal liberty or to enter into those contracts in relation to labor which may seem to him appropriate or necessary for the support of himself and his family? Of course the liberty of contract relating to labor includes both parties to it. The one has as much right to purchase as the other to sell labor.

This is not a question of substituting the judgment of the court for that of the legislature. If the act be within the power of the State it is valid, although the judgment of the court might be totally opposed to the enactment of such a law. But the question would still remain: Is it within the police power of the State? and that question must be answered by the court.

The question whether this act is valid as a labor law, pure and simple, may be dismissed in a few words. There is no reasonable ground for interfering with the liberty of person or the right of free contract, by determining the hours of labor, in the occupation of a baker. There is no contention that bakers as a class are not equal in intelligence and capacity to men in other trades or manual occupations, or that they are not able to assert their rights and care for themselves without the protecting arm of the State, interfering with their independence of judgment and of action. They are in no sense wards of the State. Viewed in the light of a purely labor law, with no reference whatever to the question of health, we think that a law like the one before us involves neither the safety, the morals nor the welfare of the public, and that the interest of the public is not in the slightest degree affected by such an act. The law must be upheld, if at all, as a law pertaining to the health of the individual engaged in the occupation of a baker. It does not affect any other portion of the public than those who are engaged in the occupation. Clean and wholesome bread does not depend upon whether the baker works but ten hours per day or only sixty hours a week. The limitation of the hours of labor does not come within the police power on that ground.

It is a question of two powers or rights shall prevail—the power of the State to legislate or the right of the individual to liberty of person and freedom of contract. The mere assertion that the subject relates though but in a remote degree to the public health does not necessarily render the enactment valid. The act must have a more direct relation, as a means to an end, and the end itself must be appropriate and legitimate, before an act can be held to be valid which interferes with the general right of an individual to be free in his person and in his power to contract in relation to his own labor. . . .

We think the limit of the police power has been reached and passed in this case. There is, in our judgment, no reasonable foundation for holding this to be necessary or appropriate as a health law to safeguard the public health or the health of the individuals who are following the trade of a baker. If this statute be valid, and if, therefore, a proper case is made out in which to deny the right of an individual, *sui juris*, as employer or employé, to make contracts for the labor of the latter under the protection of the provisions of the Federal Constitution, there would seem to be no length to which legislation of this nature might not go.

We think that there can be no fair doubt that the trade of a baker, in and of itself, is not an unhealthy one to that degree which would authorize the legislature to interfere with the right to labor, and with the right of free contract on the part of the individual, either as employer or employé. In looking through statistics regarding all trades and occupations, it may be true that the trade of a baker does not appear to be as healthy as some other trades, and is also vastly more healthy than still others. To the common understanding the trade of a baker has never been regarded as an unhealthy one. Very likely physicians would not recommend the exercise of that or of any other trade as a remedy for ill health. Some occupations are more healthy than others, but we think there are none which might not come under the power of the legislature to supervise and control the hours of working therein, if the mere fact that the occupation is not absolutely and perfectly healthy is to confer that right upon the legislative department of the Government. It might be safely affirmed that almost all occupations more or less affect the health. There must be more than the mere fact of the possible existence of small amount of unhealthiness to warrant legislative interference with liberty. It is unfortunately true that labor, even in any department, may possibly carry with it the seeds of unhealthiness. But are we all, on that account, at the mercy of legislative majorities? A printer, a tinsmith, a locksmith, a carpenter, a cabinetmaker, a dry goods clerk, a bank's, a lawyer's or a physician's clerk, or a clerk in almost any kind of business, would all come under the power of the legislature, on this assumption. No trade, no occupation, no mode of earning one's living, could escape this all-pervading power, and the acts of the legislature in limiting the hours of labor in all employments would be valid, although such limitation might seriously cripple the ability of the laborer to support himself and his family. In our large cities there are many buildings into which the sun penetrates for but a short time in each day, and these buildings are occupied by people carrying on the business of bankers, brokers, lawyers, real estate, and many other kinds of business, aided by many clerks, messengers, and other employés. Upon the assumption of the validity of this act under review, it is not possible to say that an act, prohibiting lawyers' or bank clerks, or others, from contracting to labor for their employers more than eight hours a day, would be invalid. It might be said that it is unhealthy to work more than that number of hours in an apartment lighted by artificial light during the working hours of the day; that the occupation of the bank clerk, the lawyer's clerk, the real estate clerk, or the broker's clerk in such offices is therefore unhealthy, and the legislature in its paternal wisdom must, therefore, have the right to legislate on the subject of and to limit the hours for such labor, and if it exercises that power and its validity be questioned, it is sufficient to say, it has reference to the public health; it has reference to the health of the employés condemned to labor day after day in buildings where the sun never shines; it is a health law, and therefore it is valid, and cannot be questioned by the courts.

It is also urged, pursuing the same line of argument, that it is to the interest of the State that its population should be strong and robust, and therefore any legislation which may be said to tend to make people healthy must be valid as health laws, enacted under the police power. If this be a valid argument and a justification for this kind of legislation, it follows that the protection of the Federal Constitution from undue interference with liberty of person and freedom of contract is visionary, wherever the law is sought to be justified as a valid exercise of the police power. Scarcely any law but might find shelter under such assumptions, and conduct, properly so called, as well as contract, would come under the restrictive sway of the legislature. Not only the hours of employés, but the hours of employers, could be regulated, and doctors, lawyers, scientists, all professional men, as well as athletes and artisans, could be forbidden to fatigue their brains and bodies by prolonged hours of exercise, lest the fighting strength of the State be impaired. We mention these extreme cases because the contention is extreme. We do not believe in the soundness of the views which uphold this law. On the contrary, we think that such a law as this, although passed in the assumed exercise of the police power, and as relating to the public health, or the health of the employés named, is not within that power, and is invalid. The act is not, within any fair meaning of the term, a health law, but is an illegal interference with the rights of individuals, both employers and employés, to make contracts regarding labor upon such terms as they may think best, or which they may agree upon with the other parties to such contracts. Statutes of the nature of that under review, limiting the hours in which grown and intelligent men may labor to earn their living, are mere meddlesome interferences with the rights of the individual, and they are not saved from condemnation by the claim that they are passed in the exercise of the police power and upon the subject of the health of the individual whose rights are interfered with, unless there be some fair ground, reasonable in and of itself, to say that there is material danger to the public health, or the health of the employés, if the hours of labor are not curtailed. . . .

. . . the legislature of the State has no power to limit their right as proposed in this statute. All that it could properly do has been done by it with regard to the conduct of bakeries, as provided for in the other sections of the act, above set forth. These several sections provide for the inspection of the premises where the bakery is carried on, with regard to furnishing proper wash-rooms and water-closets, apart from the bake-room, also with regard to providing proper drainage, plumbing and painting; the sections, in addition, provide for the height of the ceiling, the cementing or tiling of floors, where necessary in the opinion of the factory inspector, and for other things of that nature; alterations are also provided for and are to be made where necessary in the opinion of the inspector, in order to comply with the provisions of the statute. These various sections may be wise and valid regulations, and they certainly go to the full extent of providing for the cleanliness and the healthiness, so far as possible, of the quarters in which bakeries are to be conducted. Adding to all these requirements, a prohibition to enter into any contract of labor in a bakery for more than a certain number of hours a week, is, in our judgment, so wholly beside the matter of a proper, reasonable and fair provision, as to run counter to that liberty of person and of free contract provided for in the Federal Constitution.

It was further urged on the argument that restricting the hours of labor in the case of bakers was valid because it tended to cleanliness on the part of the workers, as a man was more apt to be cleanly when not overworked, and if cleanly then his "output" was also more likely to be so. What has already been said applies with equal force to this contention. We do not admit the reasoning to be sufficient to justify the claimed right of such interference. The State in that case would assume the position of a supervisor, or *pater familieas*, over every act of the individual and its right of governmental interference with his hours of labor, his hours of exercise, the character thereof, and the extent to which it shall be carried would be recognized and upheld. In our judgment it is not possible in fact to discover the connection between the number of hours a baker may work in the bakery and the healthful quality of the bread made by the workman. The connection, if any exists, is too shadowy and thin to build any argument for the interference of the legislature. If the man works ten hours a day it is all right, but if ten and a half or eleven his health is in danger and his bread may be unhealthful, and, therefore, he shall not be permitted to do it. This, we think, is unreasonable and entirely arbitrary. When assertions such as we have adverted to become necessary in order to give, if possible, a plausible foundation for the contention that the law is a "health law," it gives rise to at least a suspicion that there was some other motive dominating the legislature than the purpose to subserve the public health or welfare. . . .

It is impossible for us to shut our eyes to the fact that many of the laws of this character, while passed under what is claimed to be the police power for the purpose of protecting the public health or welfare, are, in reality, passed from other motives. We are justified in saying so when, from the character of the law and the subject upon which it legislates, it is apparent that the public health or welfare bears but the most remote relation to the law. The purpose of a statute must be determined from the natural and legal effect of the language employed; and whether it is or is not repugnant to the Constitution of the United States must be determined from the natural effect of such statutes when put into operation, and not from their proclaimed purpose. *Minnesota* v. *Barber*, 136 U.S. 313; *Brimmer* v. *Rebman*, 138 U.S. 78. The court looks beyond the mere letter of the law in such cases. *Yick Wo* v. *Hopkins*, 118 U.S. 356.

It is manifest to us that the limitation of the hours of labor as provided for in this section of the statute under which the indictment was found, and the plaintiff in error convicted, has no such direct relation to and no such substantial effect upon the health of the employé, as to justify us in regarding the section as really a health law. It seems to us that the real object and purpose were simply to regulate the hours of labor between the master and his employés (all being men, *sui juris*), in a private business, not dangerous in any degree to morals or in any real and substantial degree, to the health of the employés. Under such circumstances the freedom of master and employé to contact with each other in relation to their employment, and in defining the same, cannot be prohibited or interfered with, without violating the Federal Constitution.

The judgment of the Court of Appeals of New York as well as that of the Supreme Court and of the County Court of Oneida County must be reversed and the case remanded to the County Court for further proceedings not inconsistent with this opinion.

*Reversed.*

MR. JUSTICE HARLAN, with whom MR. JUSTICE WHITE and MR. JUSTICE DAY concurred, dissenting.

While this court has not attempted to mark the precise boundaries of what is called the police power of the State, the existence of the power has been uniformly recognized, both by the Federal and state courts.

All the cases agree that this power extends at least to the protection of the lives, the health and the safety of the public against the injurious exercise by any citizen of his own rights.

. . . Speaking generally, the State in the exercise of its powers may not unduly interfere with the right of the citizen to enter into contracts that may be necessary and essential in the enjoyment of the inherent rights belonging to every one, among which rights is the right "to be free in the enjoyment of all his faculties; to be free to use them in all lawful ways; to live and work where he will; to earn his livelihood by any lawful calling; to pursue any livelihood or avocation." This was declared in *Allgeyer* v. *Louisiana*, 165 U.S. 578, 589. But in the same case it was conceded that the right to contract in relation to persons and property or to do business, within a State, may be "regulated and sometimes prohibited, when the contracts or business conflict with the policy of the State as contained in its statutes." (p. 591).

So, as said in *Holden* v. *Hardy*, 169 U.S. 366, 391: "This right of contract, however, is itself subject to certain limitations which the State may lawfully impose in the exercise of its police powers. While this power is inherent in all governments, it has doubtless been greatly expanded in its application during the past century, owing to an enormous increase in the number of occupations which are dangerous, or so far detrimental to the health of the employés as to demand special precautions for their well-being and protection, or the safety of adjacent property. . . .

The authorities on the same line are so numerous that further citations are unnecessary.

I take it to be firmly established that what is called the liberty of contract may, within certain limits, be subjected to regulations designed and calculated to promote the general welfare or to guard the public health, the public morals or the public safety. "The liberty secured by the Constitution of the United States to every person within its jurisdiction does not import," this court has recently said, "an absolute right in each person to be, at all times and in all circumstances, wholly freed from restraint. There are manifold restraints to which every person is necessarily subject for the common good." *Jacobson* v. *Massachusetts*, 197 U.S. 11.

Granting then that there is a liberty of contract which cannot be violated even under the sanction of direct legislative enactment, but assuming, as according to settled law we may assume, that such liberty of contract is subject to such regulations as the State may reasonably prescribe for the common good and the well-being of society, what are the conditions under which the judiciary may declare such regulations to be in excess of legislative authority and void? Upon this point there is no room for dispute; for, the rule is universal that a legislative enactment, Federal or state, is never to be disregarded or held invalid unless it be, beyond question, plainly and palpably in excess of legislative power. In *Jacobson v. Massachusetts, supra,* we said that the power of the courts to review legislative action in respect of a matter affecting the general welfare exists *only* "when that which the legislature has done comes within the rule that if a statute purporting to have been enacted to protect the public health, the public morals or the public safety, has no real or substantial relation to those objects, or is, beyond all question, a plain, palpable invasion of rights secured by the fundamental law"—citing *Mugler v. Kansas,* 123 U.S. 623, 661; *Minnesota v. Barber,* 136 U.S. 313, 320: *Atkin v. Kansas,* 191 U.S. 207, 223. If there be doubt as to the validity of the statute, that doubt must therefore be resolved in favor of its validity, and the courts must keep their hands off, leaving the legislature to meet the responsibility for unwise legislation. If the end which the legislature seeks to accomplish be one to which its power extends, and if the means employed to that end, although not the wisest or best, are yet not plainly and palpably unauthorized by law, then the court cannot interfere. In other words,, when the validity of a statute is questioned, the burden of proof, so to speak, is upon those who assert it be unconstitutional. *McCulloch v. Maryland,* 4 Wheat. 316, 421.

Let these principles be applied to the present case. . . .

It is plain that this statute was enacted in order to protect the physical well-being of those who work in bakery and confectionery establishments. It may be that the statute had its origin, in part, in the belief that employers and employés in such establishments were not upon an equal footing, and that the necessities of the latter often compelled them to submit to such exactions as unduly taxed their strength. Be this as it may, the statute must be taken as expressing the belief of the people of New York that, as a general rule, and in the case of the average man, labor in excess of sixty hours during a week in such establishments may endanger the health of those who thus labor. Whether or not this be wise legislation it is not the province of the court to inquire. Under our systems of government the courts are not concerned with the wisdom or policy of legislation. So that in determining the question of power to interfere with liberty of contract, the court may inquire whether the means devised by the State are germane to an end which may be lawfully accomplished and have a real or substantial relation to the protection of health, as involved in the daily work of the persons, male and female, engaged in bakery and confectionery establishments. But when this inquiry is entered upon I find it impossible, in view of common experience, to say that there is here no real or substantial relation between the means employed by the State and the end sought to be accomplished by its legislation. *Mugler v. Kansas, supra.* Nor can I say that the statute has no appropriate or direct connection with that protection to health which each State owes to her citizens, *Patterson v. Kentucky, supra;* or that it is not promotive of the health of the employés in question, *Holden v. Hardy, Lawton v. Steele, supra;* or that the regulation prescribed by the State is utterly unreasonable and extravagant or wholly arbitrary, *Gundling v. Chicago, supra.* Still less can I say that the statute is, beyond question, a plain, palpable invasion of rights secured by the fundamental law. *Jacobson* v. *Massachusetts, supra.* Therefore I submit that this court will transcend its functions if it assumes to annul the statute of New York. It must be remembered that this statute does not apply to all kinds of business. It applies only to work in bakery and confectionery establishments, in which, as all know, the air constantly breathed by workmen is not as pure and healthful as that to be found in some other establishments or out of doors.

Professor Hirt in his treatise on the "Diseases of the Workers" has said: "The labor of the bakers is among the hardest and most laborious imaginable, because it has to be performed under conditions injurious to the health of those engaged in it. It is hard, very hard work, not only because it requires a great deal of physical exertion in an overheated workshop and during unreasonably long hours, but more so because of the erratic demands of the public, compelling the baker to perform the greater part of his work at night, thus depriving him of an opportunity to enjoy the necessary rest and sleep, in fact which is highly injurious to his health." Another writer says, "The constant inhaling of flour dust causes inflammation of the lungs and of the bronchial tubes. The eyes also suffer through this dust, which is responsible for the many cases of running eyes among the bakers. The long hours of toil to which all bakers are subjected produce rheumatism, cramps and swollen legs. The intense heat in the workshops induces the workers to resort to cooling drinks, which together with their habit of exposing the greater part of their bodies to the change in the atmosphere, is another source of a number of diseases of various organs. Nearly all bakers are pale-faced and of more delicate health than the workers of other crafts, which is chiefly due to their hard work and their irregular and unnatural mode of living, whereby the power of resistance against diseases is greatly diminished. The average age of a baker is below that of other workmen; they seldom live over their fiftieth year, most of them dying between the ages of forty and fifty. During periods of epidemic diseases the bakers are generally the first to succumb to the disease, and the number swept away during such periods far exceeds the number of other crafts in comparison to the men employed in the respective industries. When, in 1720, the plague visited the city of Marseilles, France, every baker in the city succumbed to the epidemic, which caused considerable excitement in the neighboring cities and resulted in measures for the sanitary protection of the bakers."

In the Eighteenth Annual Report by the New York Bureau of Statistics of Labor it is stated that among the occupations involving exposure to conditions that interfere with nutrition is that of a baker (p. 52). In that Report it is also stated that "from a social point of view, production will be increased by any change in industrial organization which diminishes the number of idlers, paupers and criminals. Shorter hours of work, by allowing higher standards of comfort and purer family life, promise to enhance the industrial efficiency of the wage-working class—improved health, longer life, more content and greater intelligence and inventiveness" (p. 82).

Statistics show that the average daily working time among workingmen in different countries is, in Australia, 8 hours; in Great Britain, 9; in the United States, 9-3/4; in Denmark, 9-3/4; in Norway, 10; Sweden, France and Switzerland, 10-1/2; Germany, 10-1/4; Belgium, Italy and Austria, 11; and in Russia, 12 hours.

We judicially know that the question of the number of hours during which a workman should continuously labor has been, for a long period, and is yet, a subject of serious consideration among civilized peoples, and by those having special knowledge of the laws of health. Suppose the statute prohibited labor in bakery and confectionery establishments in excess of eighteen hours each day. No one, I take it, could dispute the power of the State to enact such a statute. But the statute before us does not embrace extreme or exceptional cases. It may be said to occupy a middle ground for the State to take between legitimate protection, by legislation, of the public health and liberty of contract is not a question easily solved, nor one in respect of which there is or can be absolute certainty. . . .

We also judicially know that the number of hours that should constitute a day's labor in particular occupations involving the physical strength and safety of workmen has been the subject of enactments by Congress and by nearly all of the States. Many, if not most, of those enactments fix eight hours as the proper basis of a day's labor.

I do not stop to consider whether any particular view of this economic question presents the sounder theory. What the precise facts are it may be difficult to say. It is enough for the determination of this case, and it is enough for this court to know, that the question is one about which there is room for debate and for an honest difference of opinion. There are many reasons of a weighty, substantial character, based upon the experience of mankind, in support of the theory that, all things considered, more than ten hours' steady work each day, from week to week, in a bakery or confectionery establishment, may endanger the health, and shorten the lives of the workmen, thereby diminishing their physical and mental capacity to serve the State, and to provide for those dependent upon them.

If such reasons exist that ought to be the end of this case, for the State is not amenable to the judiciary, in respect of its legislative enactments, unless such enactments are plainly, palpably, beyond all question, inconsistent with the Constitution of the United States. We are not to presume that the State of New York has acted in bad faith. Nor can we assume that its legislature acted without due deliberation, or that it did not determine this question upon the fullest attainable information, and for the common good. We cannot say that the State has acted without reason nor ought we to proceed upon the theory that its action is a mere sham. Our duty, I submit, is to sustain the statute as not being in conflict with the Federal Constitution, for the reason—and such is an all-sufficient reason—it is not shown to be plainly and palpably inconsistent with that instrument. Let the State alone in the management of its purely domestic affairs, so long as it does not appear beyond all question that it has violated the Federal Constitution. This view necessarily results from the principle that the health and safety of the people of a State are primarily for the State to guard and protect. . . .

A decision that the New York statute is void under the Fourteenth Amendment will, in my opinion, involve consequences of a far-reaching and mischievous character; for such a decision would seriously cripple the inherent power of the States to care for the lives, health and well-being of their citizens. Those are matters which can be best controlled by the States. The preservation of the just powers of the State is quite as vital as the preservation of the powers of the General Government. . . . We are reminded by counsel that it is the solemn duty of the courts in cases before them to guard the constitutional rights of the citizen against merely arbitrary power. That is unquestionably true. But it is equally true—indeed, the public interests imperatively demand—that legislative enactments should be recognized and enforced by the courts as embodying the will of the people, unless they are plainly and palpably, beyond all question, in violation of the fundamental law of the Constitution. *Atkin* v. *Kansas*, 191 U.S. 207, 223.

The judgment in my opinion should be affirmed.

MR. JUSTICE HOLMES dissenting.

I regret sincerely that I am unable to agree with the judgment in this case, and that I think it my duty to express my dissent.

This case is decided upon an economic theory which a large part of the country does not entertain. If it were a question whether I agreed with that theory, I should desire to study it further and long before making up my mind. But I do not conceive that to be my duty, because I strongly believe that my agreement or disagreement has nothing to do with the right of a majority to embody their opinions in law. It is settled by various decisions of this court that state constitutions and state laws may regulate life in many ways which we as legislators might think as injudicious or if you like as tyrannical as this, and which equally with this interfere with the liberty to contract. Sunday laws and usury laws are ancient examples. A more modern one is the prohibition of lotteries. The liberty of the citizen to do as he likes so long as he does not interfere with the liberty of others to do the same, which has been a shibboleth for some well-known writers, is interfered with by school laws, by the Post Office, by every state or municipal institution which takes his money for purposes thought desirable, whether he likes it or not. The Fourteenth Amendment does not enact Mr. Herbert Spencer's Social Statics. . . . a constitution is not intended to embody a particular economic theory, whether of paternalism and the organic relation of the citizen to the State or of *laissez faire*. It is made for people of fundamentally differing views, and the accident of our finding certain opinions natural and familiar or novel and even shocking ought not to conclude our judgment upon the question whether statutes embodying them conflict with the Constitution of the United States.

General propositions do not decide concrete cases. The decision will depend on a judgment or intuition more subtle than any articulate major premise. But I think that the proposition just stated, if it is accepted, will carry us far toward the end. Every opinion tends to become a law. I think that the word liberty in the Fourteenth Amendment is perverted when it is held to prevent the natural outcome of a dominant opinion, unless it can be said that a rational and fair man necessarily would admit that the statute proposed would infringe fundamental principles as they have been understood by the traditions of our people and our law. It does not need research to show that no such sweeping condemnation can be passed upon the statute before us. A reasonable man might think it a proper measure on the score of health. Men whom I certainly could not pronounce unreasonable would uphold it as a first installment of a general regulation of the hours of work. Whether in the latter aspect it would be open to the charge of inequality I think it unnecessary to discuss.

## *Notes*

1. "§ 110. *Hours of labor in bakeries and confectionery establishments.*—No employé shall be required or permitted to work in a biscuit, bread or cake bakery or confectionery establishment more than sixty hours in any one week, or more than ten hours in any one day, unless for the purpose of making a shorter work day on the last day of the week; nor more hours in any one week than will make an average of ten hours per day for the number of days during such week in which such employé shall work.

   "§ 111. *Drainage and plumbing of buildings and rooms occupied by bakeries,*—All buildings or rooms occupied as biscuit, bread, pie or cake bakeries, shall be drained and plumbed in a manner conducive to the proper and healthful sanitary condition thereof, and shall be constructed with air shafts, windows or ventilating pipes, sufficient to insure ventilation. The factory inspector may direct the proper drainage, plumbing and ventilation of such rooms or buildings. No cellar or basement, not now used for a bakery shall hereafter be so occupied or used, unless the proprietor shall comply with the sanitary provisions of this article.

   "§ 112. *Requirements as to rooms, furniture, utensils and manufactured products.*—Every room used for the manufacture of flour or meal food products shall be at least eight feet in height and shall have, if deemed necessary by the factory inspector, an impermeable floor constructed of cement, or of tiles laid in cement, or an additional flooring of wood properly saturated with linseed oil. The side walls of such rooms shall be plastered or wainscoted. The factory inspector may require the side walls and ceiling to be whitewashed, at least once in three months. He may also require the wood work of such walls to be painted. The furniture and utensils shall be so arranged as to be readily cleansed and not prevent the proper cleaning of any part of a room. The manufactured flour or meal food products shall be kept in dry and airy rooms, so arranged that the floors, shelves and all other facilities for storing the same can be properly cleaned. No domestic animals, except cats, shall be allowed to remain in a room used as a biscuit, bread, pie, or cake bakery, or any room in such bakery where flour or meal products are stored.

"§ 113. *Wash-rooms and closets; sleeping places.*—Every such bakery shall be provided with a proper wash-room and water-closet or water-closets apart from the bake-room, or rooms where the manufacture of such food product is conducted, and no water-closet, earth-closet, privy or ash-pit shall be within or connected directly with the bake-room of any bakery, hotel or public restaurant.

"No person shall sleep in a room occupied as a bake-room. Sleeping places for the persons employed in the bakery shall be separate from the rooms where flour or meal food products are manufactured or stored. If the sleeping places are on the same floor where such products are manufactured, stored or sold, the factory inspector may inspect and order them put in a proper sanitary condition.

"§ 114. *Inspection of bakeries.*—The factory inspector shall cause all bakeries to be inspected. If it be found upon such inspection that the bakeries so inspected are constructed and conducted in compliance with the provisions of this chapter, the factory inspector shall issue a certificate to the persons owning or conducting such bakeries.

"§ 115. *Notice requiring alterations.*—If, in the opinion of the factory inspector, alterations are required in or upon premises occupied and used as bakeries, in order to comply with the provisions of this article, a written notice shall be served by him upon the owner, agent or lessee of such premises, either personally or by mail, requiring such alterations to be made within sixty days after such service, and such alterations shall be made accordingly."

---

**Lochner v. New York**, 198 U.S. 45 (1905) 5–4
*editor's note:*
*Opinion authors are in bold: () indicates the party of appointing president. If the party of the justice differs from that of appointment president, then the party of the justice is listed after the slash.*

| MAJORITY | CONCURRING | DISSENTING |
| --- | --- | --- |
| **Peckham** (d) | | **Harlan** (r) |
| Fuller (d) | | White, E. (d) |
| Brown (r) | | Day (r) |
| Brewer (r) | | **Holmes** (r) |
| McKenna (r) | | |

# Adkins et al., Constituting the Minimum Wage Board of the District of Columbia, v. Children's Hospital of the District of Columbia.

## 261 U.S. 525

## Appeals from the Court of Appeals of the District of Columbia

### Nos. 795, 796. Argued March 14, 1923.—Decided April 9, 1923.

... APPEALS from decrees of the Court of Appeals of the District of Columbia, affirming two decrees, entered, on mandate from that court, by the Supreme Court of the District, permanently enjoining the appellants from enforcing orders fixing minimum wages under the District of Columbia Minimum Wage Act.

... *Mr. Felix Frankfurter*, with whom *Mr. Francis H. Stephens* was on the brief, for appellants.

... *Mr. Wade H. Ellis* and *Mr. Challen B. Ellis*, with whom *Mr. Joseph W. Folk* was on the brief, for appellees. . .

*Mr. William L. Brewster*, by leave of court, on behalf of the States of Oregon, New York, California, Kansas, Wisconsin and Washington, as *amicus curiae*.

By leave of court, briefs were filed by counsel, appearing as *amici curiae*, as follows: *Mr. Isaac H. Van Winkle*, Attorney General of the State of Oregon, *Mr. Joseph N. Teal* and *Mr. William L. Brewster*, on behalf of the Industrial Welfare Commission of Oregon. *Mr. Carl Sherman*, Attorney General of the State of New York, and *Mr. Edward G. Griffin*, Deputy Attorney General, on behalf of that State. *Mr. Hiram Johnson* and *Mr. Jesse Steinhart*, on behalf of the Industrial Welfare Commission of California. *Mr. John G. Egan*, Assistant Attorney General of the State of Kansas, on behalf of that State. *Mr. Herman L. Ekern*, Attorney General of the State of Wisconsin, *Mr. J. E. Messerschmidt*, Assistant Attorney General and *Mr. Fred M. Wilcox*, on behalf of that State. *Mr. Edward Clifford* and *Mr. Kenneth Durham* on behalf of the Minimum Wage Committee of the State of Washington.

MR. JUSTICE SUTHERLAND delivered the opinion of the Court.

The question presented for determination by these appeals is the constitutionality of the Act of September 19, 1918, providing for the fixing of minimum wages for women and children in the District of Columbia. 40 Stat. 960, c. 174. . . .

Any violation of the act (§ 18) by an employer or his agent or by corporate agents is declared to be a misdemeanor, punishable by fine and imprisonment.

Finally, . . . it is declared (§ 23) that the purposes of the act are "to protect the women and minors of the District from conditions detrimental to their health and morals, resulting from wages which are inadequate to maintain decent standards of living; and the Act in each of its provisions and in its entirety shall be interpreted to effectuate these purposes."

The appellee in the first case is a corporation maintaining a hospital for children in the District. It employs a large number of women in various capacities, with whom it had agreed upon rates of wages and compensation satisfactory to such employees, but which in some instances were less than the minimum wage fixed by an order of the board made in pursuance of the act. The women with whom appellee had so contracted were all of full age and under no legal disability. The instant suit was brought by the appellee in the Supreme Court of the District to restrain the board from enforcing or attempting to enforce its order on the ground that the same was in contravention of the Constitution, and particularly the due process clause of the Fifth Amendment.

In the second case the appellee, a woman twenty-one years, was employed by the Congress Hall Hotel Company as an elevator operator, at a salary of $35.50 a month and two meals a day. She alleges that the work was light and healthful, the hours short, with surroundings clean and moral, and that she was anxious to continue it for the compensation she was receiving and that she did not earn more. Her services were satisfactory to the Hotel Company and it would have been glad to retain her but was obliged to dispense with her services by reason of the order of the board and on account of the penalties prescribed by the act. The wages received by this appellee were the best she was able to obtain for any work she was capable of performing and the enforcement of the order, she alleges, deprived her of such employment and wages. She further averred that she could not secure any other position at which she could make a living, with as good physical and moral surroundings, and earn as good wages, and that she was desirous of continuing and would continue the employment but for the order of the board. An injunction was prayed as in the other case. . . .

The trial court entered decrees in pursuance of the mandate, declaring the act in question to be unconstitutional and granting permanent injunctions. Appeals to the Court of Appeals followed and the decrees of the trial court were affirmed. It is from these final decrees that the cases come here.

The judicial duty of passing upon the constitutionality of an act of Congress is one of great gravity and delicacy. The statute here in question has successfully borne the scrutiny of the legislative branch of the government, which, by enacting it, has affirmed its validity; and that determination must be given great weight. This Court, by an unbroken line of decisions from Chief Justice Marshall to the present day, has steadily adhered to the rule that every possible presumption is in favor of the validity of an act of Congress until overcome beyond rational doubt. But if by clear and indubitable demonstration a statute be opposed to the Constitution we have no choice but to say so. The Constitution, by its own terms, is the supreme law of the land, emanating from the people, the repository of ultimate sovereignty under our form of government. A congressional statute, on the other hand, is the act of an agency of this sovereign authority and if it conflict with the Constitution must fall; for that which is not supreme must yield to that which is. To hold it invalid (if it be invalid) is a plain exercise of the judicial power—that power vested in courts to enable them to administer justice according to law. From the authority to ascertain and determine the law in a given case, there necessarily results, in case of conflict, the duty to declare and enforce the rule of the supreme law and reject that of an inferior act of legislation which, transcending the Constitution, is of no effect and binding on no one. This is not the exercise of a substantive power to review and nullify acts of Congress, for no such substantive power exists. It is simply a necessary concomitant of the power to hear and dispose of a case or controversy properly before the court, to the determination of which must be brought the test and measure of the law.

The statute now under consideration is attacked upon the ground that it authorizes an unconstitutional interference with the freedom of contract included within the guaranties of the due process clause of the Fifth Amendment. That the right to contract about one's affairs is a part of the liberty of the individual protected by this clause, is settled by the decisions of this Court and is no longer open to question. . . .

Within this liberty are contracts of employment of labor. In making such contracts, generally speaking, the parties have an equal right to obtain from each other the best terms they can as the result of private bargaining.

In *Adair* v. *United States, supra*, Mr. Justice Harlan (pp. 174, 175), speaking for the Court, said:

> "The right of a person to sell his labor upon, such terms as he deems proper is, in its essence, the same as the right of the purchaser of labor to prescribe the conditions upon which he will accept such labor from the person offering, to sell. . . . In all such particulars the employer and employees have equality of right, and any legislation that disturbs that equality is an arbitrary interference with the liberty of contract which no government can legally justify in a free land."

In *Coppage* v. *Kansas, supra (p. 14)*, this Court, speaking through Mr. Justice Pitney, said:

"Included in the right of personal liberty and the right of private property—partaking of the nature of each—is the right to make contracts for the acquisition of property. Chief among such contracts is that of personal employment, by which labor and other services are exchanged for money or other forms of property. If this right be struck down or arbitrarily interfered with, there is a substantial impairment of liberty in the long-established constitutional sense. The right is as essential to the laborer as to the capitalist, to the poor as to the rich; for the vast majority of persons have no other honest way to begin to acquire property, save by working for money. . . .

There is, of course, no such thing as absolute freedom of contract. It is subject to a great variety of restraints. But freedom of contract is, nevertheless, the general rule and restraint the exception; and the exercise of legislative authority to abridge it can be justified only by the existence of exceptional circumstances. Whether these circumstances exist in the present case constitutes the question to be answered. . . .

The essential characteristics of the statute now under consideration, which differentiate it from the laws fixing hours of labor, will be made to appear as we proceed. It is sufficient now to point out that the latter as well as the statutes mentioned under paragraph (3), deal with incidents of the employment having no necessary effect upon the heart of the contract, that is, the amount of wages to be paid and received. A law forbidding work to continue beyond a given number of hours leaves the parties free to contract about wages and thereby equalize whatever additional burdens may be imposed upon the employer as a result of the restrictions as to hours, by an adjustment in respect of the amount of wages. Enough has been said to show that the authority to fix hours of labor cannot be exercised except in respect of those occupations where work of long continued duration is detrimental to health. This Court has been careful in every case where the question has been raised, to place its decision upon this limited authority of the legislature to regulate hours of labor and to disclaim any purpose to uphold the legislation as fixing wages, thus recognizing an essential difference between the two. It seems plain that these decisions afford no real support for any form of law establishing minimum wages. . . .

It forbids two parties having lawful capacity—under penalties as to the employer—to freely contract with one another in respect of the price for which one shall render service to the other in a purely private employment where both are willing, perhaps anxious, to agree, even though the consequence may be to oblige one to surrender a desirable engagement and the other to dispense with the services of a desirable employee. The price fixed by the board need have no relation to the capacity or earning power of the employee, the number of hours which may happen to constitute the day's work, the character of the place where the work is to be done, or the circumstances or surroundings of the employment; and, while it has no other basis to support its validity than the assumed necessities of the employee, it takes no account of any independent resources she may have. It is based wholly on the opinions of the members of the board and their advisers—perhaps an average of their opinions, if they do not precisely agree as to what will be necessary to provide a living for a woman, keep her in health and preserve her morals. It applies to any and every occupation in the District, without regard to its nature or the character of the work.

The standard furnished by the statute for the guidance of the board is so vague as to be impossible of practical application with any reasonable degree of accuracy. . . .

This uncertainty of the statutory standard is demonstrated by a consideration of certain orders of the board already made. These orders fix the sum to be paid to a woman employed in a place where food is served or in a mercantile establishment, at $16.50 per week; in a printing establishment, at $15.50 per week; and in a laundry, at $15 per week, with a provision reducing this to $9 in the case of a beginner. If a woman employed to serve food requires a minimum of $16.50 per week, it is hard to understand how the same woman working in a printing establishment or in a laundry is to get on with an income lessened by from $1 to $7.50 per week. The board probably found it impossible to follow the indefinite standard of the statute, and brought other and different factors into the problem; and this goes far in the direction of demonstrating the fatal uncertainty of the act, an infirmity which, in our opinion, plainly exists.

The law takes account of the necessities of only one party to the contract. It ignores the necessities of the employer by compelling him to pay not less than a certain sum, not only whether the employee is capable of earning it, but irrespective of the ability of his business to sustain the burden, generously leaving him, of course, the privilege of abandoning his business as an alternative for going on at a loss. Within the limits of the minimum sum, he is precluded, under penalty of fine and imprisonment, from adjusting compensation to the differing merits of his employees. It compels him to pay at least the sum fixed in any event, because the employee needs it, but requires no service of equivalent value from the employee. It therefore undertakes to solve but one-half of the problem. The other half is the establishment of a corresponding standard of efficiency, and this forms no part of the policy of the legislation, although in practice the former half without the latter must lead to ultimate failure, in accordance with the inexorable law that no one can continue indefinitely to take out more than he puts in without ultimately exhausting the supply. The law is not confined to the great and powerful employers but embraces those whose bargaining power may be as weak as that of the employee. It takes no account of periods of stress and business depression, of crippling losses, which may leave the employer himself without adequate means of livelihood. To the extent that the sum fixed the fair value of the services rendered, it amounts to a compulsory exaction from the employer for the support of a partially indigent person, for whose condition there rests upon him no peculiar responsibility, and therefore, in effect, arbitrarily shifts to his shoulders a burden which, if it belongs to anybody, belongs to society as a whole.

The feature of this statute which, perhaps more than any other, puts upon it the stamp of invalidity is that it exacts from the employer an arbitrary payment for a purpose and upon a basis having no causal connection with his business, or the contract or the work the employee engages to do. The declared basis, as already pointed out, is not the value of the service rendered, but the extraneous circumstance that the employee needs to get a prescribed sum of money to insure her subsistence, health and morals. The ethical right of every worker, man or woman, to a living wage may be conceded. One of the declared and important purposes of trade organizations is to secure it. And with that principle and with every legitimate effort to realize it in fact, no one can quarrel; but the fallacy of the proposed method of attaining it is that it assumes that every employer is bound at all events to furnish it. The moral requirement implicit in every contract of employment, viz, that the amount to be paid and the service to be rendered shall bear to each other some relation of just equivalence, is completely ignored. The necessities of the employee are alone considered and these arise outside of the employment, are the same when there is no employment and as great in one occupation as in another. Certainly the employer by paying a fair equivalent for the service rendered, though not sufficient to support the employee, has neither caused nor contributed to her poverty. On the contrary, to the extent of what he pays he has relieved it. In principle, there can be no difference between the case of selling labor and the case of selling goods. If one goes to the butcher, the baker or grocer to buy food, he is morally entitled to obtain the worth of his money but he is not entitled to more. If what he gets is worth what he pays he is not justified in demanding more simply because he needs more; and the shopkeeper, having dealt fairly and honestly in that transaction, is not concerned in any peculiar sense with the question of his customer's necessities. Should a statute undertake to vest in a commission power to determine the quantity of food necessary for individual support and require the shopkeeper, if he sell to the individual at all, to furnish that quantity at not more than a fixed maximum, it would undoubtedly fall before the constitutional test. The fallacy of any argument in support of the validity of such a statute would be quickly exposed. The argument in support of that now being considered is equally fallacious, though the weakness of it may not be so plain. A statute requiring an employer to pay in money, to pay at prescribed and regular intervals, to pay the value of the services rendered, even today with fair relation to the extent of the benefit obtained from the service, would be understandable. But a statute which prescribes payment without regard to any of these things and solely with relation to circumstances apart from the contract of employment, the business affected by it and the work done under it, is so clearly the product of a naked, arbitrary exercise of power that it cannot be allowed to stand under the Constitution of the United States.

We are asked, upon the one hand, to consider the fact that several States have adopted similar statutes, and we are invited, upon the other hand, to give weight to the fact that three times as many States, presumably as well informed and as anxious to promote the health and morals of their people, have refrained from enacting such legislation. We have also been furnished with a large number of printed opinions approving the policy of the minimum wage, and our own reading has disclosed a large number to the contrary. These are all proper enough for the consideration of the lawmaking bodies, since their tendency is to establish the desirability or undesirability of the legislation; but they reflect no legitimate light upon the question of its validity, and that is what we are called upon to decide. The elucidation of that question cannot be aided by counting heads. . . .

Finally, it may be said that if, in the interest of the public welfare, the police power may be invoked to justify the fixing of a minimum wage, it may, when public welfare is thought to require it, be invoked to justify a maximum wage. The power to fix high wages connotes by like course of reasoning, the power to fix low wages. If, in the face of the guaranties of the Fifth Amendment, this form of legislation shall be legally justified, the field for the operation of the police power will have been widened to a great and dangerous degree. If, for example, in the opinion of future lawmakers, wages in the building trades shall become so high as to preclude people of ordinary means from building and owning homes, an authority which sustains the minimum wage will be invoked to support a maximum wage for building laborers and artisans, and the same argument which has been here urged to strip the employer of his constitutional liberty of contract in one direction will be utilized to strip the employee of his constitutional liberty of contract in the opposite direction. A wrong decision does not end with itself: it is a precedent, and, with the swing of sentiment, its bad influence may run from one extremity of the arc to the other. . . .

It follows from what has been said that the act in question passes the limit prescribed by the Constitution, and, accordingly, the decrees of the court below are

*Affirmed.*

Mr. Justice Brandeis took no part in the consideration or decision of these cases.

Mr. Chief Justice Taft, dissenting.

I regret much to differ from the Court in these cases.

The boundary of the police power beyond which its exercise becomes an invasion of the guaranty of liberty under the Fifth and Fourteenth Amendments to the Constitution is not easy to mark. . . .

Legislatures in limiting freedom of contract between employee and employer by a minimum wage proceed on the assumption that employees, in the class receiving least pay, are not upon a full level of equality of choice with their employer and in their necessitous circumstances are prone to accept pretty much anything that is offered. They are peculiarly subject to the overreaching of the harsh and greedy employer. The evils of the sweating system and of the long hours and low wages which are characteristic of it are well known. Now, I agree that it is a disputable question in the field of political economy how far a statutory requirement of maximum hours or minimum wages may be a useful remedy for these evils and whether it may not make the case of the oppressed employee worse than it was before. But it is not the function of this Court to hold congressional acts invalid simply because they are passed to carry out economic views which the Court believes to be unwise or unsound.

Legislatures which adopt a requirement of maximum hours or minimum wages may be presumed to believe that when sweating employers are prevented from paying unduly low wages by positive law they will continue their business, abating that part of their profits, which were wrung from the necessities of their employees, and will concede the better terms required by the law; and that while in individual cases hardship may result, the restriction will enure to the benefit of the general class of employees in whose interest the law is passed and so to that of the community at large. . . .

With deference to the very able opinion of the Court and my brethren who concur in it, it appears to me to exaggerate the importance of the wage term of the contract of employment as more inviolate than its other terms. Its conclusion seems influenced by the fear that the concession of the power to impose a minimum wage must carry with it a concession of the power to fix a maximum wage. This, I submit, is a *non sequitur*. A line of distinction like the one under discussion in this case is, as the opinion elsewhere admits, a matter of degree and practical experience and not of pure logic. Certainly the wide difference between prescribing a minimum wage and a maximum wage could as a matter of degree and experience be easily affirmed. . . .

Without, however, expressing an opinion that a minimum wage limitation can be enacted for adult men, it is enough to say that the case before us involves only the application of the minimum wage to women. If I am right in thinking that the legislature can find as much support in experience for the view that a sweating wage has as great and as direct a tendency to bring about an injury to the health and morals of workers, as for the view that long hours injure their health, then I respectfully submit that *Muller* v. *Oregon*, 208 U.S. 412, controls this case. The law which was there sustained forbade the employment of any female in any mechanical establishment or factory or laundry for more than ten hours. This covered a pretty wide field in women's work and it would not seem that any sound distinction between that case and this can be built up on the fact that the law before us applies to all occupations of women with power in the board to make certain exceptions. Mr. Justice Brewer, who spoke for the Court in *Muller* v. *Oregon,* based its conclusion on the natural limit to women's physical strength and the likelihood that long hours would therefore injure her health, and we have had since a series of cases which may be said to have established a rule of decision.

I am not sure from a reading of the opinion whether the Court thinks the authority of *Muller* v. *Oregon* is shaken by the adoption of the Nineteenth Amendment. The Nineteenth Amendment did not change the physical strength or limitations of women upon which the decision in *Muller* v. *Oregon* rests. The Amendment did give women political power and makes more certain that legislative provisions for their protection will be in accord with their interests as they see them. But I don't think we are warranted in varying constitutional construction based on physical differences be-tween men and women, because of the Amendment.

But for my inability to agree with some general observations in the forcible opinion of MR. JUSTICE HOLMES who follows me, I should be silent and merely record my concurrence in what he says. It is perhaps wiser for me, however, in a case of this importance, separately to give my reasons for dissenting.

I am authorized to say that MR. JUSTICE SANFORD concurs in this opinion.

MR. JUSTICE HOLMES, dissenting.

The question in this case is the broad one, Whether Congress can establish minimum rates of wages for women in the District of Columbia with due provision for special circumstances, or whether we must say that Congress has no power to meddle with the matter at all. To me, notwithstanding the deference due to the prevailing judgment of the Court, the power of Congress seems absolutely free from doubt. The end, to remove conditions leading to ill health, immorality and the deterioration of the race, no one would deny to be within the scope of constitutional legislation. The means are means that have the approval of Congress, of many States, and of those governments from which we have learned our greatest lessons. When so many intelligent persons, who have studied the matter more than any of us can, have thought that the means are effective and are worth the price, it seems to me impossible to deny that the belief reasonably may be held by reasonable men. . . .

The earlier decisions upon the same words in the Fourteenth Amendment began within our memory and went no farther than an unpretentious assertion of the liberty to follow the ordinary callings. Later that innocuous generality was expanded into the dogma, Liberty of Contract. Contract is not specially mentioned in the text that we have to construe. It is merely an example of doing what you want to do, embodied in the word liberty. But pretty much all law consists in forbidding men to do some things that they want to do, and contract is no more exempt from law than other acts. . . .

This statute does not compel anybody to pay anything. It simply forbids employment at rates below those fixed as the minimum requirement of health and right living. It is safe to assume that women will not be employed at even the lowest wages allowed unless they earn them, or unless the employer's business can sustain the burden. . . .

The criterion of constitutionality is not whether we believe the law to be for the public good.

I am of opinion that the statute is valid and that the decree should be reversed.

---

**Adkins v. Children's Hospital**, 261 U.S. 525 (1923) 5–3*
*editor's note:*
*Opinion authors are in bold: () indicates the party of appointing president. If the party of the justice differs from that of appointing president, then the party of the justice is listed second after the slash.*

| MAJORITY | CONCURRING | DISSENTING |
|---|---|---|
| **Sutherland** (r) | | **Taft** (r) |
| McKenna (r) | | Sanford (r) |
| Van Devanter (r) | | Holmes (r) |
| McReynolds (d) | | |
| Butler (r/d) | | |

*Brandeis (d) did not participate.

# Morehead, Warden, v. New York ex. rel. Tipaldo.

298 U.S. 587

## Certiorari to the Supreme Court of New York.

No. 838. Argued April 28, 29, 1936.—Decided June 1, 1936.

... CERTIORARI, 297 U. S. 702, to review a judgment of the Supreme Court of New York, entered on remittitur from the Court of Appeals. Tipaldo had been placed in custody on a charge of disobeying an administrative order prescribing minimum wages for women employees. The trial court's dismissal of a writ of habeas corpus was reversed by the decision under review.

*Mr. Henry Epstein,* Solicitor General of New York, with whom *Mr. John J. Bennett, Jr.,* Attorney General, and *Mr. John F. X. McGohey,* Assistant Attorney General, were on the brief, for petitioner. . . .

*Messrs. Arthur Levitt* and *Nathan L. Miller,* with whom *Messrs. Harold Allen Gates* and *Challen B. Ellis* were on the brief, for Tipaldo. . . .

By leave of Court, *Mr. Dean G. Acheson* argued the case on behalf of the States of Connecticut, Illinois, Massachusetts, New Hampshire, New Jersey, and Rhode Island, as *amici curiae,* in support of the statute. With him on the brief were *Mr. Edward J. Daly,* Attorney General of Connecticut; *Mr. Otto Kerner,* Attorney General of Illinois; *Mr. Paul A. Dever,* Attorney General of Massachusetts; *Mr. David T. Wilentz,* Attorney General of New Jersey; *Mr. Francis U. Johnston,* Attorney General of New Hampshire; and *Mr. John P. Hartigan,* Attorney General of Rhode Island.

By leave of Court, briefs of *amici curiae* were filed as follows:

*Mr. John W. Bricker,* Attorney General, *Messrs. Isadore Topper* and *John K. Evans,* Assistant Attorneys General, and *Messrs. William S. Evatt* and *Marvin C. Harrison,* on behalf of the State of Ohio; and *Messrs. Paul Windels, Paxton Blair,* and *Paul J. Kern,* on behalf of the City of New York, supporting the statute.

*Mr. Charles J. Campbell,* on behalf of the New York State Hotel Assn.; and *Burnita Shelton Matthews* and *Rebekah Scandrett Greathouse,* on behalf of the National Women's Party et al., challenging the statute.

MR. JUSTICE BUTLER delivered the opinion of the Court.

This is a habeas corpus case originating in the supreme court of New York. Relator was indicted in the county court of Kings county and sent to jail to await trial upon the charge that as manager of a laundry he failed to obey the mandatory order of the state industrial commissioner prescribing minimum wages for women employees. . . .

The Act extends to women and minors in any "occupation" which "shall mean an industry, trade or business or branch thereof or class of work therein in which women or minors are gainfully employed, but shall not include domestic service in the home of the employer or labor on a farm." § 551 (6). It is not an emergency law. It does not regulate hours or any conditions affecting safety or protection of employees. It relates only to wages of adult women and minors. . . .

The *Adkins* case, unless distinguishable, requires affirmance of the judgment below. The petition for the writ sought review upon the ground that this case is distinguishable from that one. No application has been made for reconsideration of the constitutional question there decided.[1] The validity of the principles upon which that decision rests is not challenged. This court confines itself to the ground upon which the writ was asked or granted. *Alice State Bank* v. *Houston Pasture Co.*, 247 U. S. 240, 242. *Clark* v. *Williard*, 294 U. S. 211, 216. Here the review granted was no broader than that sought by the petitioner. *Johnson* v. *Manhattan Ry. Co.*, 289 U.S. 479, 494. He is not entitled and does not ask to be heard upon the question whether the *Adkins* case should be overruled. He maintains that it may, be distinguished on the ground that the statutes are vitally dissimilar.

The District of Columbia Act provided for a board to ascertain and declare "standards of minimum wages" for women in any occupation and what wages were "inadequate to supply the necessary cost of living to any such women workers to maintain them in good health and to protect their morals." § 9. Violations were punishable by fine and imprisonment. § 18. The declared purposes were to protect women from conditions detrimental to their health and morals, resulting from wages inadequate to maintain decent standards of living. § 23.

The New York Act declares it to be against public policy for any employer to employ any woman at an oppressive and unreasonable wage (§ 552) defined as one which is "both less than the fair and reasonable value of the services rendered and less than sufficient to meet the minimum cost of living necessary for health." § 551 (7). "A fair wage" is one "fairly and reasonably commensurate with the value of the service or class of service rendered." § 551 (8). If the commissioner is of opinion that any substantial number of women in any occupation are receiving oppressive and unreasonable wages he shall appoint a wage board to report upon the establishment of minimum fair wage rates. § 554. After investigation, the board shall submit a report including its recommendations as to minimum fair wage standards. § 555. . . .

The state court rightly held that the *Adkins* case controls this one and requires that relator be discharged upon the ground that the legislation under which he was indicted and imprisoned is repugnant to the due process clause of the Fourteenth Amendment.

The general statement in the New York Act of the fields of labor it includes, taken in connection with the work not covered, indicates legislative intention to reach nearly all private employers of women. The Act does not extend to men. It does extend to boys and girls under the age of 21 years but there is here involved no question as to its validity in respect of wages to be prescribed for them. Relator's petition for the writ shows that the charge against him is that as manager of a laundry he "disobeyed a mandatory order prescribing certain minimum wages for certain adult women employees of the said laundry." The rights of no other class of workers are here involved.

Upon the face of the act the question arises whether the State may impose upon the employers state-made minimum wage rates for all competent experienced women workers whom they may have in their service. That question involves another one. It is: Whether the State has power similarly to subject to state-made wages all adult women employed in trade, industry or business, other than house and farm work. These were the questions decided in the *Adkins* case. So far at least as concerns the validity of the enactment under consideration, the restraint imposed by the due process clause of the Fourteenth Amendment upon legislative power of the State is the same as that imposed by the corresponding provision of the Fifth Amendment upon the legislative power of the United States.

This court's opinion shows (pp. 545, 546): The right to make contracts about one's affairs is a part of the liberty protected by the due process clause. Within this liberty are provisions of contracts between employer and employee fixing the wages to be paid. In making contracts of employment, generally speaking, the parties have equal right to obtain from each other the best terms they can by private bargaining. Legislative abridgement of that freedom can only be justified by the existence of exceptional circumstances. Freedom of contract is the general rule and restraint the exception. This court has found not repugnant to the due process clause statutes fixing rates and charges to be exacted by businesses impressed with a public interest, relating to contracts for the performance of public work, prescribing the character, methods and time of payment of wages, fixing hours of labor. Physical differences between men and women must be recognized in proper cases and legislation fixing hours or conditions of work may properly take them into account, but (p. 553) "we cannot accept the doctrine that women of mature age, *sui juris*, require or may be subjected to restrictions upon their liberty of contract which could not lawfully be imposed in the case of men under similar circumstances. To do so would be to ignore all the implications to be drawn from the present day trend of legislation, as well as that of common thought and usage, by which woman is accorded emancipation from the old doctrine that she must be given special protection or be subjected to special restraint in her contractual and civil relationships. . . . [p. 554] Enough has been said to show that the authority to fix hours of labor cannot be exercised except in respect of those occupations where work of long continued duration is detrimental to health. This Court has been careful in every case where the question has been raised, to place its decision upon this limited authority of the legislature to regulate hours of labor and to disclaim any purpose to uphold the legislation as fixing wages, thus recognizing an essential difference between the two. It seems plain that these decisions afford no real support for any form of law establishing minimum wages."

The decision and the reasoning upon which it rests clearly show that the State is without power by any form of legislation to prohibit, change or nullify contracts between employers and adult women workers as to the amount of wages to be paid. . . .

To distinguish this from the *Adkins* case, petitioner refers to changes in conditions that have come since that decision, cites great increase during recent years in the number of women wage earners and invokes the first section of the Act, called "Factual background."

The Act is not to meet an emergency; it discloses a permanent policy; the increasing number of women workers suggests that more and more they are getting and holding jobs that otherwise would belong to men. . . .

These legislative declarations, in form of findings or recitals of fact, serve well to illustrate why any measure that deprives employers and adult women of freedom to agree upon wages, leaving employers and men employees free so to do, is necessarily arbitrary. Much, if not all, that in them is said in justification of the regulations that the Act imposes in respect of women's wages applies with equal force in support of the same regulation of men's wages. While men are left free to fix their wages by agreement with employers, it would be fanciful to suppose that the regulation of women's wages would be useful to prevent or lessen the evils listed in the first section of the Act. Men in need of work are as likely as women to accept the low wages offered by unscrupulous employers. Men in greater number than women support themselves and dependents and because of need will work for whatever wages they can get and that without regard to the value of the service and even though the pay is less than minima prescribed in accordance with this Act. It is plain that, under circumstances such as those portrayed in the "Factual background," prescribing of minimum wages for women alone would unreasonably restrain them in competition with men and tend arbitrarily to deprive them of employment and a fair chance to find work.

This court, on the authority of the *Adkins* case and with the acquiescence of all the justices who dissented from the decision, held repugnant to the due process clause of the Fourteenth Amendment statutes of Arizona and Arkansas, respectively, fixing minimum wages for women. . . . States having similar enactments have construed it to prevent the fixing of wages for adult women.

The New York court's decision conforms to ours in the *Adkins* case, and the later rulings that we have made on the authority of that case. That decision was deliberately made upon careful consideration of the oral arguments and briefs of the respective parties and also of briefs submitted on behalf of States and others as amici curiae. In the Arizona case the attorney general sought to distinguish the District of Columbia Act from the legislation then before us and insisted that the latter was a valid exertion of the police power of the State. Counsel for the California commission submitted a brief amicus curiae in which he elaborately argued that our decision in the *Adkins* case was erroneous and ought to be overruled. In the Arkansas case the state officers, appellants there, by painstaking and thorough brief presented arguments in favor of the same contention. But this court, after thoughtful attention to all that was suggested against that decision, adhered to it as sound. And in each case, being clearly of opinion that no discussion was required to show that, having regard to the principles applied in the *Adkins* case, the state legislation fixing wages for women was repugnant to the due process clause of the Fourteenth Amendment, we so held and upon the authority of that case affirmed per curiam the decree enjoining its enforcement. It is equally plain that the judgment in the case now before us must also be

*Affirmed.*

MR. CHIEF JUSTICE HUGHES, dissenting.

I am unable to concur in the opinion in this case. In view of the difference between the statutes involved, I cannot agree that the case should be regarded as controlled by *Adkins* v. *Children's Hospital*, 261 U.S. 525. And I can find nothing in the Federal Constitution which denies to the State the power to protect women from being exploited by overreaching employers through the refusal of a fair wage as defined in the New York statute and ascertained in a reasonable manner by competent authority. . . .

That the difference is a material one, I think is shown by the opinion in the *Adkins* case. That opinion contained a broad discussion of state power, but it singled out as an adequate ground for the finding of invalidity that the statute gave no regard to the situation of the employer and to the reasonable value of the service for which the wage was paid. . . .

We have here a question of constitutional law of grave importance, applying to the statutes of several States in a matter of profound public interest. I think that we should deal with that question upon its merits, without feeling that we are bound by a decision which on its facts is not strictly in point. [Adkins]

The validity of the New York act must be considered in the light of the conditions to which the exercise of the protective power of the State was addressed.

The Legislature finds that the employment of women and minors in trade and industry in the state of New York at wages unreasonably low and not fairly commensurate with the value of the services rendered is a matter of vital public concern; that many women and minors are not as a class upon a level of equality in bargaining with their employers in regard to minimum fair wage standards, and that 'freedom of contract' as applied to their relations with employers is illusory; that, by reason of the necessity of seeking support for themselves and their dependents, they are forced to accept whatever wages are offered; and that judged by any reasonable standard, wages in many instances are fixed by chance and caprice and the wages accepted are often found to bear no relation to the fair value of the service. The Legislature further states that women and minors are peculiarly subject "to the overreaching of inefficient, harsh or ignorant employers," and that, in the absence of effective minimum fair wage rates, the constant lowering of wages by unscrupulous employers, constitutes a serious form of unfair competition against other employers, reduces the purchasing power of the workers and threatens the stability of industry. The Legislature deemed it essential to seek the correction of these evils by the exercise of the police power "for the protection of industry and of the women and minors employed therein and of the interest of the community at large in their health and well-being and in the prevention of the deterioration of the race." § 550.

In the factual brief, statistics are presented showing the increasing number of wage earning women, and that women are in industry and in other fields of employment because they must support themselves and their dependents. Data are submitted, from reports of the Women's Bureau of the United States Department of Labor, showing such discrepancies and variations in wages paid for identical work as to indicate that no relationship exists between the value of the services rendered and the wages paid. It also appears that working women are largely unorganized and that their bargaining power is relatively weak. The seriousness of the social problem is presented. Inquiries by the New York State Department of Labor in cooperation with the Emergency Relief Bureau of New York City disclosed the large number of women employed in industry whose wages were insufficient for the support of themselves and those dependent upon them. For that reason they had been accepted for relief and their wages were being supplemented by payments from the Emergency Relief Bureau. Thus the failure of overreaching employers to pay to women the wages commensurate with the value of services rendered has imposed a direct and heavy burden upon the taxpayers. The weight of this burden and the necessity for taking reasonable measures to reduce it, in the light of the enormous annual budgetary appropriation for the Department of Public Welfare of New York City, is strikingly exhibited in the brief filed by the Corporation Counsel of the City as an *amicus curiae*.

We are not at liberty to disregard these facts. We must assume that they exist and examine respondent's argument from that standpoint. That argument is addressed to the fundamental postulate of liberty of contract. I think that the argument fails to take account of established principles and ignores the historic relation of the State to the protection of women.

We have had frequent occasion to consider the limitations of liberty of contract. While it is highly important to preserve that liberty from arbitrary and capricious interference, it is also necessary to prevent its abuse, as otherwise it could be used to override all public interests and thus in the end destroy the very freedom of opportunity which it is designed to safeguard.

We have repeatedly said that liberty of contract is a qualified and not an absolute right. "There is no absolute freedom to do as one wills or to contract as one chooses. . . . Liberty implies the absence of arbitrary restraint, not immunity from reasonable regulations and prohibitions imposed in the interests of the community." . . .

The test of validity is not artificial. It is whether the limitation upon the freedom of contract is arbitrary and capricious or one reasonably required in order appropriately to serve the public interest in the light of the particular conditions to which the power is addressed.

When there are conditions which specially touch the health and well-being of women, the State may exert its power in a reasonable manner for their protection, whether or not a similar regulation is, or could be, applied to men. The distinctive nature and function of women—their particular relation to the social welfare—has put them in a separate class. This separation and corresponding distinctions in legislation is one of the outstanding traditions of legal history. The Fourteenth Amendment found the States with that protective power and did not take it away or remove the reasons for its exercise. Changes have been effected within the domain of state policy and upon an appraisal of state interests. We have not yet arrived at a time when we are at liberty to override the judgment of the State and decide that women are not the special subject of exploitation because they are women and as such are not in a relatively defenceless position. . . . We called attention to the ample precedents in regulatory provisions for a classification on the basis of sex. We said—"It has been recognized with regard to hours of work. . . . It is recognized in the respective rights of husband and wife in land during life, in the inheritance after the death of the spouse. Often it is expressed in the time fixed for coming of age. . . . The particular points at which that difference shall be emphasized by legislation are largely in the power of the State." *Id.* Not long before the decision in the *Quong Wing* case, the question had received elaborate consideration in *Muller* v. *Oregon*, 208 U.S. 412, where a regulation of the working hours of women was sustained. We thought that the disadvantage at which woman was placed in the struggle for subsistence was obvious and we emphasized the point that she "becomes an object of public interest and care in order to preserve the strength and vigor of the race." We added that "though limitations upon person and contractual rights may be removed by legislation," woman will still be in a situation "where some legislation to protect her seems necessary to secure a real equality of right." She therefore still may be "properly placed in a class by herself, and legislation designed for her protection may be sustained, even when like legislation is not necessary for men and could not be sustained." *Muller* v. *Oregon, supra*, pp. 421, 422. . . .

Here, the special conditions calling for the protection of women, and for the protection of society itself, are abundantly shown. The legislation is not less in the interest of the community as a whole than in the interest of the women employees who are paid less than the value of their services. That lack must be made good out of the public purse. Granted that the burden of the support of women who do not receive a living wage cannot be transferred to employers who pay the equivalent of the service they obtain, there is no reason why the burden caused by the failure to pay that equivalent should not be placed upon those who create it. The fact that the State cannot secure the benefit to society of a living wage for women employees by any enactment which bears unreasonably upon employers does not preclude the State from seeking its objective by means entirely fair both to employers and the women employed.

In the statute before us, no unreasonableness appears. The end is legitimate and the means appropriate. I think that the act should be upheld.

I am authorized to state that MR. JUSTICE BRANDEIS, MR. JUSTICE STONE and MR. JUSTICE CARDOZO join in this opinion.

MR. JUSTICE STONE, dissenting.

While I agree with all that the CHIEF JUSTICE has said, I would not make the differences between the present statute and that involved in the *Adkins* case the sole basis of decision. I attach little importance to the fact that the earlier statute was aimed only at a starvation wage and that the present one does not prohibit such a wage unless it is also less than the reasonable value of the service. Since neither statute compels employment at any wage, I do not assume that employers in one case, more than in the other, would pay the minimum wage if the service were worth less.

The vague and general pronouncement of the Fourteenth Amendment against deprivation of liberty without due process of law is a limitation of legislative power, not a formula for its exercise. It does not purport to say in what particular manner that power shall be exerted. It makes no fine-spun distinctions between methods which the legislature may and which it may not choose to solve a pressing problem of government. It is plain too, that, unless the language of the amendment and the decisions of this Court are to be ignored, the liberty which the amendment protects is not freedom from restraint of all law or of any law which reasonable men may think an appropriate means for dealing with any of those matters of public concern with which it is the business of government to deal. There is grim irony in speaking of the freedom of contract of those who, because of their economic necessities, give their services for less than is needful to keep body and soul together. But if this is freedom of contract no one has ever denied that it is freedom which may be restrained, notwithstanding the Fourteenth Amendment, by a statute passed in the public interest.

In many cases this Court has sustained the power of legislatures to prohibit or restrict the terms of a contract, including the price term, in order to accomplish what the legislative body may reasonably consider a public purpose. They include cases, which have neither been overruled nor discredited, in which the sole basis of regulation was the fact that circumstances, beyond the control of the parties, had so seriously curtailed the regulative power of competition as to place buyers or sellers at a disadvantage in the bargaining struggle, such that a legislature might reasonably have contemplated serious consequences to the community as a whole and have sought to avoid them by regulation of the terms of the contract. . . .

No one doubts that the presence in the community of a large number of those compelled by economic necessity to accept a wage less than is needful for subsistence is a matter of grave public concern, the more so when, as has been demonstrated here, it tends to produce ill health, immorality and deterioration of the race. The fact that at one time or another Congress and the legislatures of seventeen states, and the legislative bodies of twenty-one foreign countries, including Great Britain and its four commonwealths, have found that wage regulation is an appropriate corrective for serious social and economic maladjustments growing out of inequality in bargaining power, precludes, for me, any assumption that it is a remedy beyond the bounds of reason. It is difficult to imagine any grounds, other than our own personal economic predilections, for saying that the contract of employment is any the less an appropriate subject of legislation than are scores of others, in dealing with which this Court has held that legislatures may curtail individual freedom in the public interest.

"So far as the requirement of due process is concerned, and in the absence of other constitutional restriction, a state is free to adopt whatever economic policy may reasonably be deemed to promote public welfare, and to enforce that policy by legislation adapted to its purpose. The courts are without authority either to declare such policy, or, when it is declared by the legislature, to override it. If the laws passed are seen to have a reasonable relation to a proper legislative purpose, and are neither arbitrary nor discriminatory, the requirements of due process are satisfied, and judicial determination to that effect renders a court *functus officio.*"

That declaration and decision should control the present case. They are irreconcilable with the decision and most that was said in the *Adkins* case. They have left the Court free of its restriction as a precedent, and free to declare that the choice of the particular form of regulation by which grave economic maladjustments are to be remedied is for legislatures and not the courts.

In the years which have intervened since the *Adkins* case we have had opportunity to learn that a wage is not always the resultant of free bargaining between employees and employees; that it may be one forced upon employees by their economic necessities and upon employers by the most ruthless of their competitors. We have had opportunity to perceive more clearly that a wage insufficient to support the worker does not visit its consequences upon him alone; that it may affect profoundly the entire economic structure of society and, in any case, that it casts on every taxpayer, and on government itself, the burden of solving the problems of poverty, subsistence, health and morals of large numbers in the community. Because of their nature and extent these are public problems. A generation ago they were for the individual to solve; today they are the burden of the nation. I can perceive no more objection, on constitutional grounds, to their solution by requiring an industry to bear the subsistence cost of the labor which it employs, than to the imposition upon it of the cost of its industrial accidents. See *New York Central R. Co.* v. *White, supra; Mountain Timber Co.* v. *Washington,* 243 U.S. 219.

It is not for the courts to resolve doubts whether the remedy by wage regulation is as efficacious as many believe, or is better than some other, or is better even than the blind operation of uncontrolled economic forces. The legislature must be free to choose unless government is to be rendered impotent. The Fourteenth Amendment has no more embedded in the Constitution our preference for some particular economic beliefs than it has adopted, in the name of liberty, the system of theology which we may happen to approve. . . .

The judgment should be reversed.

MR. JUSTICE BRANDEIS and MR. JUSTICE CARDOZO join in this opinion.

# Notes

1. Briefs of amici curiae in support of the application were filed by the City of New York and the State of Illinois. Briefs on the merits supporting the New York Act, were filed by the State of Ohio, and by the States of Connecticut, Illinois, Massachusetts, New Hampshire, New Jersey and Rhode Island. Briefs for affirmance were filed by the New York State Hotel Association, National Woman's Party, National Association of Women Lawyers, et al.

---

**Morehead v. N.Y. ex. rel. Tipaldo**, 298 U.S. 587 (1936) 5–4

*editor's note:*
*Opinion authors are in bold: () indicates the party of appointing president. If the party of the justice differs from that of appointing president, then the party of the justice is listed second after the slash.*

| MAJORITY | CONCURRING | DISSENTING |
|---|---|---|
| **Butler** (r/d) | | **Hughes** (r) |
| Van Devanter (r) | | Brandeis (d) |
| McReynolds (d) | | **Stone** (r) |
| Sutherland (r) | | Cardozo (r/d) |
| Roberts (r) | | |

---

# Remarks of William E. Rehnquist

## University of Wyoming

### Friday, October 25, 1985

---

The American system of government contains more than one paradox, but surely one of the most interesting is the contrast between the legal relationship of the Judicial Branch of the federal government to the other two co-equal branches, and the political relationship between these branches. Legally the federal judiciary, with the Supreme

---

A Speech, October 25, 1985 by William H. Rehnquist. Copyright © 1985 by William H. Rehnquist, Chief Supreme Court Justice. Reprinted by permission.

Court of the United States at its apex, is the final arbiter of questions arising under the United States Constitution, and its judgments bind Congress and the President. But politically any vacancy in the federal judiciary, including of course the Supreme Court, is filled by Presidential nomination subject to Senate confirmation. Thus the political branches of the federal government do have something to say as to who shall judge the constitutionality of their actions. It would be difficult to find a morality play better illustrating this paradox than the effort of President Franklin D. Roosevelt to pack the Supreme Court shortly after he was reelected for a second term in office by a landslide vote in November 1936. And since the story contains bit parts played by a Senator from my home state of Arizona, and a Supreme Court Justice from Wyoming, I propose to tell it tonight.

Franklin Roosevelt took his first of four oaths of office as President of the United States in March 1933, at a time when mass unemployment, agricultural depression, and bank failures gave a note of desperation to the usually optimistic American scene. He told the American people that "the only thing we have to fear is fear itself," and during the next four years he was able to get from Congress, both Houses of which were controlled by his Democratic party, virtually every law which he requested. All seemed to be smooth sailing for Roosevelt's "New Deal" during the first couple of years of his Presidency, with Congress working in harmony with, if not in subordination to, the President.

But the third branch—the Judiciary, had not yet been heard from. It was not controlled by Democrats, and its members were more and more frequently being called "The Nine Old Men" by those who disagreed with the Court's judgments. Charles Evans Hughes, the Chief Justice, had been appointed by President Hoover in 1930; the most senior Associate Justice, Willis Van Devanter from Wyoming, had been appointed by President Taft in 1911. The most junior Associate Justice, Owen Roberts, had been appointed by President Hoover in 1932. Seven members of the Court had been appointed by Republican Presidents, and only two by a Democratic President.

Because it usually takes at least a year, and often two years, from the time a lawsuit is begun in the court where it is filed until the time that a ruling of the Supreme Court may be had on the case, no questions involving New Deal legislation came before the Court in the first two years of Roosevelt's Presidency. But in 1935, the Court began to deal with these questions, giving the administration a victory in one important series of cases and a defeat in two others. But if there was any doubt as to which way the judicial wind was blowing, that doubt was resolved on a day in May 1935 which was later known to New Dealers as "Black Monday." In one case the Court held unanimously that a provision of the Frazier Lemke Act designed to assist farmers in danger of having their farms foreclosed violated the provision of the Fifth Amendment to the Constitution which provides that "private property shall not be taken for public use without payment of just compensation." In a second case, which carried a bit of personal affront to President Roosevelt, the Court held by a vote of eight to one that he was not empowered to remove a member of the Federal Trade Commission with whose philosophical outlook he disagreed. Perhaps these two decisions, by unanimous or nearly unanimous Courts, could have been borne, but the third decision rendered on that day—in the so-called "Sick Chicken Case"—declared unconstitutional the National Industrial Recovery Act. Here, too, the Court was unanimous, but the stakes for the New Deal program were a good deal greater.

This trio of decisions was enough to bring the President himself into action. At an off-the-record press conference later in that week, Roosevelt criticized the decision in the "sick chicken" case, and was quoted as saying:

> "The issue is going to be whether we go one way or the other. Don't call it right or left; that is just first-year high school language, just about. It is not right or left—it is a question for national decision on a very important problem of government. We are the only nation in the world that has not solved that problem. We thought we were solving it, and now it has been thrown straight in our faces and we have been relegated to the horse-and-buggy definition of interstate commerce."

Administration officials continued to criticize the Court, and the Court continued to invalidate New Deal legislation. In January 1936, it held the Agricultural Act—the New Deal's principal piece of farm legislation—unconstitutional. Here, however, the decision was by a divided vote of six to three, and Justice Stone in a biting dissent made the comment that "[c]ourts are not the only agency of government that must be assumed to have capacity to govern."

In the Presidential election of November 1936, Franklin Roosevelt was reelected President by an overwhelming majority. Alfred M. Landon, a Republican candidate, received the electoral votes of only Maine and Vermont, and received a popular vote of roughly nine million as compared to Roosevelt's sixteen million. The Republicans in that year used as one of their arguments for opposing Roosevelt the fact that if he were elected he would undoubtedly be able to fill forthcoming vacancies on the Supreme Court, which was the only branch of the federal government not totally subservient to the New Deal. The Democrats make little of the Court in their campaign, but only a few days after he was inaugurated for a second term Franklin Roosevelt proclaimed to the country that he was not going to wait for vacancies on the Court to occur before he sought to remold it to his own image.

On Friday, February 5, 1937, members of the President's cabinet, the Democratic leadership of both Houses of Congress, and the chairmen of the House and Senate Judiciary Committee were summoned to meet with the President in the Cabinet Room of the White House. When Roosevelt entered the Cabinet Room from the Oval Office, he was followed by a secretary who placed a pile of papers at each seat around the table. The papers contained a message to Congress from the President, recommending that the Judicial Branch of the Government be "reorganized." The President explained to the assembled dignitaries that the present Supreme Court had declared unconstitutional one New Deal measure after another, and that it in effect stood as a road block to the progressive reforms which the country had overwhelmingly indicated in the November election that it had wanted. He then spent over an hour reading the message to the cabinet members and congressional leaders.

The reorganization was to be accompanied by a draft bill providing that for each member of the Supreme Court who was over seventy years of age, and did not elect to retire, the President would be empowered to appoint an additional Justice to the Court and thereby enlarge the Court's membership up to a total of fifteen. Since six of the nine members of the Court were then over seventy years of age, if none of them chose to retire upon the enactment of the bill the President would immediately be authorized to appoint six additional Justices to the Court. The President based his case on the argument that the older judges were unable to carry a full share of the Court's workload. The bill also contained other provisions dealing with the lower federal courts, but these were soon lost in the furor resulting from the provision dealing with the enlargement of the Supreme Court.

The measure stunned not only the country, but the Democratic leadership in Congress as well. None of them had been privy to the drafting of the plan which had been a well-kept secret between Roosevelt, his Attorney General Homer Cummings, and one or two trusted assistants of the latter in the Justice Department. Because of the lukewarm attitude of key members of the House Judiciary Committee, the administration decided that issue must first be joined in the Senate. And so it was, from the first part of February until the last part of July.

The President himself would be the chief strategist for the administration forces. But while the President kept the reins of leadership to himself and a small coterie of associates in the White House, there must necessarily be leadership in favor of the plan in the Senate. This mantle fell in the first instance on Senator Joe Robinson from Arkansas, the Democratic Majority Leader, and secondarily on the uncertain shoulders of Henry F. Ashurst of Arizona, the Chairman of the Senate Judiciary Committee.

Robinson had worked his way up the political ladder in his home state of Arkansas, serving as a member of the House of Representatives and briefly as Governor before being elected to the Senate in 1912. Now sixty-five years of age, he had been Majority Leader in the Senate since 1923 by reason of the almost unvarying adherence of the "solid south" to the Democratic ticket in Senatorial elections. He was a big, heavy-set man with small eyes and a jutting jaw. He had been a faithful Democratic wheelhorse in the Senate for twenty-three years, and he was not going to stop now, whatever personal reservations he might have about the President's plan. And above all, he had for years nurtured an ambition for a seat on the Supreme Court—an ambition which, he felt, would surely be realized if the President's plan became law.

Arizona's Henry F. Ashurst was a far more uncertain ally in the forthcoming struggle. He was now sixty-two years old, and like Robinson had risen to the powerful position he occupied as Chairman of the Senate Judiciary Committee by the simple device of having been reelected to the Senate time and again. His middle name was "Fountain," and he had a passion for oratory in the old style. "I am a fountain," he said, referring to himself "not a cistern." he had grown up on the Arizona frontier, but now in Washington he affected the cutaway-coat garb of a Southern statesman. Ashurst announced in favor of the President's Court plan, but he would prove to be a weak and unreliable reed for the administration to lean on in the forthcoming hearings.

One year earlier, Roosevelt had discussed with Ashurst the possibility of removing some of the older Justices from the Court, and Ashurst had urged him to be patient. Ashurst wrote the President in his florid style "It will fall to your lot to nominate more Justices of the Supreme Court than any other President since General Washington. You will nominate four, possibly five, Supreme Court Justices. Father Time, with his scythe, is on your side. Anno Domini is your invincible ally."

Meanwhile, back at the White House, Roosevelt intimates such as Thomas F. Corcoran and Robert H. Jackson were urging the President to switch from the justification for the plan which he stated in his message to Congress to the real justification. The message drafted by Attorney General Cummings put the need for "Court reorganization" entirely on the basis of the age of the incumbent judges. Nothing was said about the present Court's perceived role as a roadblock to the accomplishment of New Deal reforms. Proponents were troubled by the fact that the oldest Justice on the Court, Louis D. Brandeis, was regarded as a sort of spiritual Godfather of the New Deal, and had taken a much broader view of the Congressional power to regulate business than had some of his younger colleagues. Corcoran and Jackson had picked a good time to importune the President. Homer Cummings, smug in his knowledge that he alone of major Presidential advisors had played a role in the drafting of the plan, had packed his bags and left for a Florida vacation. In his absence, the President was persuaded that the justification based on age appeared disingenuous to the public, and created a suspicion of the President's motives in proposing it. Roosevelt seized the opportunity of a Democratic victory dinner held at the Mayflower Hotel in Washington on March 4th to shift from the basis of age to the basis of constitutional obstructionism in his attack on the Supreme Court. He delivered a rip-snorting oration outlining the New Deal efforts to meet the critical problems of farmers, laborers, and the common man in general, and then told of how the Supreme Court had declared these plans unconstitutional. Cheered to a fare-thee-well by the thirteen hundred diners at the

Mayflower, he urged upon his audience and upon the nation his message that "We must act—now!" Five days later, the night before the Senate Judiciary Committee hearings on the bill were scheduled to open, he followed up his Mayflower speech with one of his famous "fireside chats" urging the need for the Court plan and assuring his nationwide audience that he had no desire to be a dictator.

Most of the men who occupied the nine seats on the Supreme Court at this time seemed shadowy and two-dimensional compared to Franklin D. Roosevelt. But not Charles Evans Hughes, the Chief Justice. Now seventy-seven years old, he had been both a Reform Republican Governor of New York, and an Associate Justice of the Supreme Court of the United States from 1910 until 1916. In the latter year he resigned from that position to accept the Republican nomination for the Presidency, but was narrowly defeated by Woodrow Wilson. He returned to New York City and a very successful law practice, from which he was lured by President Harding in 1921 to become Secretary of State. Upon Harding's death he had again returned to a successful law practice in New York, including many arguments in the Supreme Court; President Hoover had appointed him Chief Justice in 1930. Charles Evans Hughes was something above medium height with gray hair and a beard best described as Jovian. Central casting could not have produced a better image of a Chief Justice, and his presence matched his appearance. Felix Frankfurter, who knew them both well, said that in any group which included Franklin Roosevelt and Charles Evans Hughes they were the two dominant figures.

The eight Associate Justices who sat with Hughes were a varied lot. The four whose legal philosophy was least sympathetic to sustaining New Deal measures were dubbed the "four horsemen": Willis Van Devanter, James C. McReynolds, appointed by Wilson in 1914, George C. Sutherland, appointed by Harding in 1922, and Pierce Butler, appointed by Harding in 1923. All were over seventy years of age, and therefore if the President's Court plan was approved, for each one of them who failed to retire the President could appoint a new Associate Justice.

On the other side of the bench, jurisprudentially, were three Justices regarded as "liberals": Louis D. Brandeis, Harlan F. Stone, appointed by President Coolidge in 1924, and Benjamin Cardozo, appointed by President Hoover in 1932. Of these three only Brandeis was over seventy years of age, and he was seventy-nine. The remaining Justice, Owen Roberts, was, along with Chief Justice Hughes regarded as a "swing man" in the Court's ideological spectrum. He had been appointed by President Hoover in 1930, and was sixty-two years of age.

As national debate over the President's plan mushroomed in the first few weeks after its proposal, members of the Court were urged by radio networks to speak about it, but all refused. While the Justices could, safe within the walls of their marble palace, safely and properly do this, the members of the Senate where the battle was to be fought could not.

President Roosevelt had not merely been himself reelected in 1936, but had carried with him overwhelming majorities in both Houses of Congress. In the Senate the Democrats outnumbered the Republicans seventy-five to eighteen, with an independent and two farmer labor members rounding out the complement of ninety-six. The Republicans to a man were against the President's plan, but their elected minority leader, Charles McNary of Oregon, and senior members such as Arthur Vandenberg of Michigan and William E. Borah of Idaho saw that if the fight over the Court packing bill were seen as a battle between Republicans and Democrats, the issue would in all probability turn out just as it had in the Presidential election a few months earlier. They therefore imposed upon themselves and urged upon their colleagues and other figures in the Republican party a policy of silence. There can be no doubt that the silence on behalf of the Republicans immeasurably strengthened the Democratic opponents of the President's plan.

The leader of the Democratic opposition in the Senate by common consent was Burton K. Wheeler of Montana. Wheeler's credentials for this role were impeccable. Born in Massachusetts, he attended law school at the University of Michigan and then settled in Butte, Montana. He had been elected to the United States Senate in 1922, and reelected in 1928 and 1934. He had been the Vice-Presidential running mate on Robert M. La Follette Sr.'s Progressive Presidential ticket in 1924, and had been a strong supporter of Roosevelt's campaign for the Presidential nomination in 1932 before the Chicago convention. He had been an ardent supporter of Roosevelt's policies during the latter's first term, and had actively campaigned for his reelection in 1936.

What, then, caused Wheeler to break with the administration now? Genuine distaste for the plan was undoubtedly the principle factor; dissatisfaction with the way Democratic patronage in Montana had been handled may also have been a contributing cause. But once enlisted, Wheeler proved to be a formidable opponent.

Because he was not only Democrat but had been a strong supporter of many of Roosevelt's policies, he could appeal to a broad spectrum of Democrats in the Senate. Senator Millard Tydings of Maryland invited Wheeler and a dozen and a half southern Democrats in the Senate who were likewise opposed to the President's plan to his home for dinner. There they later agreed to follow Wheeler's leadership in the fight. Just as the maximum effect could not have been obtained under the banner of a Republican leader, so it could not have been obtained by a southern Democrat.

Adverse editorial criticism of his programs was nothing new to President Roosevelt, since the great majority of daily newspapers in the United States were controlled by people whom he dubbed "economic loyalists." But soon the news columns of these papers were reporting opposition from sources which did not normally voice opposition to New Deal programs, and similar messages were conveyed personally to the President and his strategists.

The day after the President's "fireside chat" urging the need for the Court plan, the Senate Judiciary Committee, headed by Senator Ashurst, filed into the huge, ornate caucus room of the Senate to begin the hearings on the President's bill. The hearing room was packed with hundreds of spectators, reporters, and important administration officials. The first administration witness was Homer Cummings, who in the tradition of administration witnesses both before and since read to the assembled multitude a five thousand word statement. The next witness was Assistant Attorney General Robert H. Jackson, who made a spirited and articulate defense of the bill on the basis advanced by it for the President in his Mayflower speech—that the Court by unreasonably grudging interpretation of the Constitution was denying the people the right to govern themselves. Succeeding administration witnesses occupied the Committee for about two weeks.

Proponents and opponents of the bill viewed the Committee hearings differently. To the proponents they were an obstacle to be overcome; thus the administration strategists sought to convince Ashurst, and the opposition as well, that an arrangement should be worked out whereby each side would agree to confine its presentation of witnesses to two weeks. But to the opposition, the hearings were a method of delaying the ultimately crucial vote on the bill in the Senate until public opinion, which they felt was on their side, would have a chance to build up. Washington was rife with speculation at the time as to how the Judiciary Committee members themselves stood on the bill; the consensus was that of its eighteen members, eight favored the bill, eight were opposed to it, and two were undecided. As the administration witnesses wound up the second week of the hearings, Senator Wheeler looked about for a way to put some punch and drama into his testimony as the first opposition witness the following week.

Late in the week Wheeler went to his old friend, Justice Louis D. Brandeis, and sought help in obtaining testimony from some member of the Court. Brandeis had already discussed the matter with Chief Justice Hughes, and said to Wheeler: "You call the Chief Justice. He'll give you a letter." But Wheeler was extremely reluctant to call Hughes, because in 1930 Wheeler had been one of the most vigorous opponents of Hughes' confirmation as Chief Justice; Brandeis, however, not wanting to see the opportunity lost, insisted on telephoning Hughes himself and then handing the telephone to Wheeler. Hughes invited Wheeler to his home, where Wheeler explained to him late that Saturday afternoon that he needed a letter explaining how the Court was current in its docket by the following Monday morning. The letter would be addressed only to the President's original arguments for the Court plan—that the septuagenarian Justices were unable to keep abreast of their docket and had fallen badly behind in their work. Hughes was unwilling to address himself to the other arguments in favor of the plan offered by Roosevelt in his March speeches.

Hughes had the letter ready on Sunday, and showed it to Justices Brandeis and Van Devanter, who expressed agreement with its contents and signed it with him. He did not seek approval of the other six Justices for the letter. When Wheeler came to the Hughes home Sunday afternoon to pick up the letter, Hughes handed it to him and said: "The baby is born."

Wheeler commenced his testimony as lead-off opposition witness before the Judiciary Committee the next morning, and said that after the Attorney General had testified as to the inability of the Supreme Court to keep abreast of its docket, he, Wheeler, had gone "to the only source in this country that could know exactly what the facts were. . . ." As he paused, a hush fell over the Caucus Room, in anticipation of a surprise. Wheeler continued: "And I have here now a letter by the Chief Justice of the Supreme Court, Mr. Charles Evans Hughes, dated March 21, 1937, written by him and approved by Mr. Justice Brandeis and Mr. Justice Van Devanter. Let us see what these gentlemen say about it." Wheeler then read the letter, addressed to him. The letter was couched in factual terms:

"The Supreme Court is fully abreast of its work. When we rose on March 15th (for the present recess) we had heard argument in cases in which certiorari had been granted only four weeks before—February 15th. . . there is no congestion of cases upon our calendar. This gratifying condition has obtained for several years. We have been able for several Terms to adjourn after disposing of all cases which are ready to be heard."

Hughes' letter also contained this observation:

"An increase in the number of Justices of the Supreme Court, apart from any question of policy, which I do not discuss, would not promote the efficiency of the Court. . . . There would be more judges to hear, more judges to confer, more judges to discuss, more judges to be convinced to decide. The present number of Justices is thought to be large enough so far as the prompt, adequate, and efficient conduct of the work of the court is concerned. . . ." [Baker-Pusey].

There seems to be little doubt among contemporary observers that the Hughes letter had the effect of a bombshell in the debate over the Court packing plan. Robert Jackson later said that the Hughes letter was the most significant factor in the defeat of the Court plan. It dealt only with the original arguments made in the Presidential message in favor of the plan, but it virtually demolished those arguments. While the arguments later adduced by Roosevelt in his Mayflower speech and fireside chat were not addressed by the Hughes letter, the now exposed baselessness of the first set of arguments necessarily made the public suspicious of the second set of arguments.

From now on, it was all downhill for the Court packing plan. Late in March the Supreme Court handed down opinions upholding the constitutionality of the National Labor Relation Act and the constitutionality of the minimum wage law enacted by the state of Washington. Although both of these decisions were by five to four votes, they seemed to signal a change in the high Court's constitutional jurisprudence in these areas. The result of these decisions was that several wavering members of the Senate came to the conclusion that the President's plan, dubious to begin with, was no longer necessary to the accomplishment of the goals of the New Deal, and they privately told Majority Leader Joe Robinson to count them as "no" votes.

President Roosevelt, irked by the length of the judiciary committee hearings, summoned Ashurst to the White House and chided him for trying to kill the Court plan by delay. Henry Ashurst's public posture during this time had been a study in ambiguity. All of his public statements were in favor of the Court plan, but as Chairman of the Senate Judiciary Committee he permitted and even encouraged the hearings before that Committee to be drawn out by the opponents of the bill. The Senate opposition did not have the votes to kill the President's plan outright, but they did have the necessary strength to filibuster and thereby prevent the proposal from ever coming to a vote. During the March hearings before his Committee, Ashurst blithely told the press that "I could win easily in June, more easily in July, quite easily in August, and by September it would be no fight at all. Time is my invincible ally because, when the people understand it, there will be a tremendous feeling throughout the country that the reform is needed. . . . This bill is wholesome, a good reform. I am not afraid to have the searchlights played on it for weeks. I court searchlights."

Of course, the "searchlights" which were playing on the bill were having exactly the opposite effect from that publicly envisioned by Ashurst. Newspaper editorial comment was almost entirely hostile, and many normal supporters of New Deal measures could not swallow this one. Time appeared to be the ally, not of the President's forces, but of the opposition.

Now enter Wyoming's Willis Van Devanter, the senior Associate Justice of the Supreme Court, on the stage of the Court packing drama. Van Devanter had emigrated to Wyoming from Indiana as a young man, and had become an ally of Republican Governor and Senator Francis E. Warren. He served successively as Chief Justice of the Supreme Court of Wyoming, Assistant Secretary of the Interior, and as a judge of the United States Court of Appeals for the Eighth Circuit at a time when that circuit included the state of Wyoming within its jurisdiction. President William Howard Taft appointed him to the Supreme Court of United States in 1911 when he was fifty-one years old. Now, twenty-six years later, he had served on the Court longer than any of its other members. Justice Van Devanter had been considering retirement for some time, and he was a good friend of his fellow westerner in the Senate, William E. Borah of Idaho. Borah suggested to Van Devanter that if he were going to retire, he might as well do it at a time which would help to defeat the Court bill. Van Devanter accordingly picked the morning of May 18, 1937 to call in a wire service reporter covering the Supreme Court and announce that he had moments earlier sent by messenger a letter of resignation to the President. Coincidentally, May 18th was the day on which the Judiciary Committee was to meet and vote on the President's plan, and as the Committee convened Senator Wheeler made sure that each member was aware of the news of the Van Devanter resignation which had just gone out on the ticker tape. The Committee, meeting in closed door session, quickly voted on six variations of the same proposal, designed to save some part of the President's original plan. Each proposal failed, and the Committee then by a vote of ten to eight adopted a recommendation that the bill "do not pass" and approved a report to that effect prepared by its staff. The report concluded that the bill was

> "A measure which should be so emphatically rejected that its parallel will never again be presented to the free representatives of the free people of America."

It was now apparent to the administration leaders in the Senate that the votes were simply not there to pass the Court packing plan as originally devised, but that the votes probably were there to pass a modified version which would allow the President to appoint only one additional Justice per year for each Justice over seventy who did not retire. The opponents, realizing they did not have the votes to defeat the scaled down plan outright, proposed to filibuster. The compromised version was introduced in the Senate in early July 1937, and Senator Robinson led off the debate for the administration. During that part of July a heat wave engulfed the eastern United States; in Washington the temperature hovered about ninety-five degrees each afternoon, and the nationwide death toll from the heat wave was one-hundred and fifty. Robinson, sixty-four, overweight, and suffering from a heart condition, seemed to his colleagues to be noticeably bothered by the heat. In the second week of the debate on the bill, Robinson was found dead in his apartment on Capitol Hill by a maid who had come in to fix breakfast for him.

A special funeral train left Washington for Little Rock on Saturday, July 17th, carrying thirty-eight members of the Senate, Post Master General Jim Farley and Vice-President John Nance Garner. On the return trip from Little Rock, Garner held court on the train with bourbon and branch water and talked to nearly every one of the thirty-eight Senators. He was convinced that sentiment was shifting against even the President's compromise plan.

When Garner returned to Washington he visited with the President, and was asked how he had found the Court situation. In a famous conversation he replied:

> "Do you want it with the bark on or off, Cap'n?" Roosevelt replied: "The rough way."
> "Alright," answered Cactus Jack. "You are beat, you haven't got the votes."

At this point Roosevelt finally capitulated, and instructed Garner to make the best deal he could to save face for the administration. This proved in retrospect to be virtually no deal at all. A parliamentary plan was worked out designed to mask the fact that the Court packing plan was being killed: a motion to recommit the bill would be made in the Senate, a motion which would not expressly refer to the deletion of the provisions with respect to the Supreme Court. But it was understood that when the committee received the bill back it would eliminate those provisions. On Thursday, July 22nd, Senator Marvel Logan of Kentucky rose in the Senate and moved to recommit the President's bill. But before a vote could be taken on the measure, Senator Hiram Johnson of California, a Republican who opposed the President's plan, asked whether the new version which the committee was to prepare would include the Supreme Court. Logan tried to replay by indirection, but he elderly California Senator would not accept this.

"The Supreme Court is out of the way?" Inquired Senator Johnson. "The Supreme Court is out of the way," acknowledged Senator Logan. Hiram Johnson then explained "Glory be to God!" and sat down. After a momentary pause, as if by prearranged signal the spectator's galleries broke into applause. The President's plan was dead.

The President's supporters spoke of having "lost the battle, but won the war." If they meant to suggest that the threat of packing the Court caused that body to decide the National Labor Relations Board case and the State of Washington minimum wage case the way it did in March, 1937, the evidence seems to be to the contrary; those cases were apparently voted on in Conference before the Court packing plan was ever announced. If by "winning the war" they meant that the Court had now permanently shifted its view as to the constitutional doctrine previously used to invalidate New Deal legislation, there was some truth to the statement. When within a month after his Court packing plan was buried in the Senate President Roosevelt appointed one of its principal supporters in that body, Senator Hugo L. Black from Alabama, to succeed Willis Van Devanter as an Associate Justice of the Supreme Court, the lasting nature of the shift in the Court's constitutional jurisprudence became all but foreordained.

But in retrospect it seems quite unnecessary to have fought the Court packing "battle" to win the jurisprudential "war." Had Franklin Roosevelt but heeded the advice of Senator Henry Ashurst before the Court packing plan was ever devised—that "Father Time, with his scythe, is on your side. Anno Domini is your invisible ally," he would have in the normal course of events been able to largely remake the Supreme Court. For the people of the United States were not about to deny to Franklin Roosevelt the same authority that other strong Presidents before him—Abraham Lincoln and Theodore Roosevelt, for example—had exercised in an attempt to remold the Court to a judicial philosophy more congenial to their own by the process of filling vacancies. During Franklin Roosevelt's second term, he nominated not only Hugo Black, but Stanley Reed, Felix Frankfurter, William O. Douglas, Frank Murphy, and Robert H. Jackson to the Supreme Court. These men were most assuredly not peas in a pod, but on the major constitutional question which concerned Franklin Roosevelt—the constitutionality of New Deal economic legislation—they were of pretty much one mind. Only four years after the President was defeated on the floor of the Senate in his effort to pack the Court, he had appointed six out of the nine Justices of the Court. The doctrines of the "Old Court" that had been used to invalidate New Deal legislation before 1937 were sunk without a trace, not by some novel scheme to enlarge the membership of the Court, but by an inevitable process of attrition.

In short, it was never necessary to fight the Court packing "battle" in order to win the constitutional "war." The American constitutional system provides for popular input into the deliberations of the Judicial Branch by allowing the President with the consent of the Senate to fill vacancies occurring on the federal courts. But Franklin Roosevelt, flushed with his landslide victory in 1936, was too impatient to wait for vacancies to occur. As a result, he was taught the valuable lesson that the American people, and their representatives in the United States Senate, were unwilling to allow even a very popular President to tinker with the basic structure of the Supreme Court in order to subordinate that body to his will. The American public did not object to Franklin Roosevelt's attempting to influence the decisions of the Supreme Court by appointments made in the normal course of filling vacancies, but they rose up in righteous wrath at the spectacle of a President so determined to have his way that he was unwilling to wait for vacancies to occur.

And what of the players in this constitutional morality play? Franklin Roosevelt, of course, was reelected not merely to a third term in 1940, but to a fourth term in 1944; one month after his inauguration for a fourth term, he died suddenly and was succeeded by Harry S. Truman. Charles Evans Hughes retired from the Supreme Court in June 1941, and died seven years later at the age of eighty-eight. Burton Wheeler lived into his nineties, practicing law in Washington. Willis Van Devanter lived several years, happily, one hopes, after his retirement on a farm in northeastern Maryland.

Henry F. Ashurst, the florid Arizonan, was defeated in the 1940 Democratic primary in that state by a politically unknown trial judge from one of the cow counties—Ernest McFarland, who later worked his way up to be Democratic majority Leader in the Senate. Upon learning of his defeat, Senator Ashurst took the floor of the Senate and proclaimed that he welcomed the opportunity to return to his native Arizona, and to stand by the Hassayampa River in Wickenburg, Arizona, and enjoy the starry nights. Some fifteen years later, he died at the Wardman Park Hotel in Washington, where he had lived ever since his retirement.

## SUPREME COURT REVIEW OF ECONOMIC LEGISLATION, THE NEW DEAL, AND FDR'S COURT PACKING PLAN—AN OUTLINE

### Susan E. Lawrence

**October 29, 1929**—The stock market crashed, precipitating (or signaling) a major economic depression.

**1932**—FDR elected to his first term as President.

Court Membership:

"Four Horsemen"—pro-laissez faire economics

Van Devanter (78)
Sutherland (75)
McReynolds (75)
Butler (71)

Swing Votes—conservative professional relationships. Republicans. But, Hughes had a liberal record as governor of NY and Roberts wrote a liberal opinion in *Nebbia*.

Hughes (75)
Roberts

Judicial Restraint—"ers." Saw Court as having a limited role in supervising the legislature's policy choices. Usually allowed government regulation of the economy.

Brandeis (81)
Stone
Cardozo

**1935:**

*Panama Refining Co.* v. *Ryan*—first ruling on a piece of New Deal legislation. Struck down portions of the NIRA on grounds of excessive delegation.

*Railroad Retirement Board* v. *Alton RR Co.*—5–4 (with Roberts in the majority), first commerce clause ruling on New Deal legislation. Struck down the Railroad Retirement Act of 1934.

## BLACK MONDAY—May 27, 1935

*Schecter Corp.* v. *U.S.*—unanimously overturned the NIRA.

*Louisville Bank* v. *Radford*—unanimously overturned the Fraizer-Lemke Act which provided relief for farm mortgagors.

*Humphrey's Executor* v. *U.S.*—unanimously declared that the president could not remove members of the FTC without Congressional authorization.

## 1936:

*Carter* v. *Carter Coal*

*U.S.* v. *Butler*—invalidated the Agricultural Adjustment Act.

FDR was reelected in a Landslide election.

**Feb. 5, 1937:** FDR submitted the Court Packing Plan to Congress. Marketed the plan as a judicial reform needed to keep the federal courts abreast of their workload.

Provisions:
1. when a judge of a federal court who had served 10 years did not resign or retire within 6 months after his 70th birthday, the President could name another judge as co-adjudicator.
2. the Supreme Court should not have more than six added Justices; nor any lower court bench more than 2; nor the total federal judiciary more than 50.
3. lower court judges might be assigned to exceptionally busy courts.
4. the lower courts should be supervised by the Supreme Court through a proctor.

## WHITE MONDAY—March 29, 1937

*West Coast Hotel Co.* v. *Parrish*—5-4, upheld Washington state statute providing for establishment of minimum wages for women in certain industries—overruled *Adkins* v. *Children's Hospital* (1923) and ran counter to *Morehead* v. *NY ex. rel. Tipaldo* (1936). JUSTICE ROBERTS VOTE HAD SWITCHED.

*Virginian RR* v. *Federation*—unanimously upheld amended Railway Labor Act.

*Wright* v. *Vinton Branch*—upheld amended Frazier-Lemke Act.

## April 12, 1937

*NLRB* v. *Jones and Laughlin Steel*—upheld the Wagner Labor Relations Act.

**1937:** Court also upheld other New Deal legislation—particularly the Social Security Act in *Stewart Machine Co.* v. *Davis* and *Helverin* v. *Davis*.

## "SWITCH IN TIME THAT SERVES (SAVES) NINE"?

Refers to Roberts' vote in *Parrish*, which ran contrary to this vote in *Tipaldo*. Both were 5-4 decisions, and Roberts' "switch" meant that the Court basically overruled its *Tipaldo* decision in *Parrish*.

It is unlikely that Roberts' switch was precipitated directly by FDR's Court-packing scheme. The Plan was shrouded in secrecy up until Feb. 5, 1937. In October 1936, Roberts had already voted to grant cert. in *Parrish*, much to his colleagues' surprise. December 19, 1936, Roberts voted to uphold the statute in *Parrish*, however, the final vote in the case and announcement of the Court's decision was delayed several months because of Stone's absence from the Court caused by his severe attack of dysentery.

Roberts may have simply joined the conservative majority in *Tipaldo* because, at the time, there was talk of his becoming the Republican Presidential candidate in 1936. Roberts, himself, claimed that NY did not present an adequate argument to uphold the law in *Tipaldo*. Nonetheless, there had been general anticipation of the FDR move against the Court between June and December of 1936.

**May 1937:** Van Devanter retired; replaced by Hugo Black.

**June 14, 1937:** Senate Judiciary Committee submitted an adverse report on the Court packing plan.

IN CONCLUSION: FDR's Court-packing plan never commanded a majority in the Senate and probably would have failed in the face of a filibuster. Members of the Court unanimously opposed the plan. Chief Justice Hughes submitted data showing that the Court was not at all behind in its work (the lower courts did have case load problems though). Although there was widespread public opposition to the Court's Anti-New Deal decisions, the unveiling of the Plan met with extensive public criticism and called forth the popular reverence for the Court. Part of the problem, according to some historians, is that the plan was too clever. Packaged as a judicial efficiency measure, it was an evasive, disingenuous way of meeting a clear-cut problem. The secrecy surrounding its development and the method of presentation FDR used alienated some potential supporters and prevented the building of a coalition around the plan.

**By 1941,** FDR had put Black, Reed, Frankfurter, Douglas, and Murphy on the Court.

# West Coast Hotel Co. v. Parrish et al.

## 300 U.S. 379

## Appeal from the Supreme Court of Washington.

### No. 293. Argued December 16, 17, 1936.—Decided March 29, 1937.

. . . This was an appeal from a judgment for money directed by the Supreme Court of Washington, reversing the trial court, in an action by a chambermaid against a hotel company to recover the difference between the amount of wages paid or tendered to her as per contract, and a larger amount computed on the minimum wage fixed by a state board or commission.

*Mr. E. L. Skeel*, with whom *Mr. John W. Roberts* was on the brief, for appellant.

*Messrs. C. B. Conner* and *Sam M. Driver* filed a brief on behalf of appellees.

*Mr. W. A. Toner*, Assistant Attorney General of Washington, with whom *Mr. G. W. Hamilton*, Attorney General, and *Mr. George G. Hannan*, Assistant Attorney General, were on the brief, by special leave of Court, on behalf of the State of Washington, as *amicus curiae*.

MR. CHIEF JUSTICE HUGHES delivered the opinion of the Court.

This case presents the question of the constitutional validity of the minimum wage law of the State of Washington.

The Act, entitled "Minimum Wages for Women," authorizes the fixing of minimum wages for women and minors. Laws of 1913 (Washington) chap. 174; Remington's Rev. Stat. (1932), §§ 7623 *et seq.* It provides:

"SECTION 1. The welfare of the State of Washington demands that women and minors be protected from conditions of labor which have a pernicious effect on their health and morals. The State of Washington, therefore exercising herein its police and sovereign power declares that inadequate wages and unsanitary condition of labor exert such pernicious effect.

"SEC. 2. It shall be unlawful to employ women or minors in any industry or occupation within the State of Washington under conditions of labor detrimental to their health or morals; and it shall be unlawful to employ women workers in any industry within the State of Washington at wages which are not adequate for their maintenance. . . .

The appellant conducts a hotel. The appellee Elsie Parrish was employed as a chambermaid and (with her husband) brought this suit to recover the difference between the wages paid her and the minimum wage fixed pursuant to the state law. The minimum wage was $14.50 per week of 48 hours. The appellant challenged the act as repugnant to the due process clause of the Fourteenth Amendment of the Constitution of the United States. The Supreme Court of the State, reversing the trial court, sustained the statute and directed judgment for the plaintiffs. *Parrish* v. *West Coast Hotel Co.*, 185 Wash. 581; 55 P. (2d) 1083. The case is here on appeal.

The appellant relies upon the decision of this Court in *Adkins* v. *Children's Hospital*, 261 U.S. 525, which held invalid the District of Columbia Minimum Wage Act, which was attacked under the due process clause of the Fifth Amendment. On the argument at bar, counsel for the appellees attempted to distinguish the *Adkins* case upon the ground that the appellee was employed in a hotel and that the business of an innkeeper was affected with a public interest. That effort at distinction is obviously futile, as it appears that in one of the cases ruled by the *Adkins* opinion the employee was a woman employed as an elevator operator in a hotel. *Adkins* v. *Lyons*, 261 U.S. 525, at p. 542.

The recent case of *Morehead* v. *New York ex rel. Tipaldo*, 298 U.S. 587, came here on certiorari to the New York court, which had held the New York minimum wage act for women to be invalid. A minority of this Court thought that the New York statute was distinguishable in a material feature from that involved in the *Adkins* case, and that for that and other reasons the New York statute should be sustained. . . .

We think that the question which was not deemed to be open in the *Morehead* case is open and is necessarily presented here. The Supreme Court of Washington has upheld the minimum wage statute of that State. It has decided that the statute is a reasonable exercise of the police power of the State. In reaching that conclusion the state court has invoked principles long established by this Court in the application of the Fourteenth Amendment. The state court has refused to regard the decision in the *Adkins* case as determinative and has pointed to our decisions both before and since that case as justifying its position. We are of the opinion that this ruling of the state court demands on our part a reexamination of the *Adkins* case. The importance of the question, in which many States having similar laws are concerned, the close division by which the decision in the *Adkins* case was reached, and the economic conditions which have supervened, and in the light of which the reasonableness of the exercise of the protective power of the State must be considered, make it not only appropriate, but we think imperative, that in deciding the present case the subject should receive fresh consideration.

The history of the litigation of this question may be briefly stated. The minimum wage statute of Washington was enacted over twenty-three years ago. Prior to the decision in the instant case it had twice been held valid by the Supreme Court of the State. *Larsen v. Rice*, 100 Wash. 642; 171 Pac. 1037; *Spokane Hotel Co. v. Younger*, 113 Wash. 359; 194 Pac. 595. The Washington statute is essentially the same as that enacted in Oregon in the same year. Laws of 1913 (Oregon) chap. 62. The validity of the latter act was sustained by the Supreme Court of Oregon in *Stettler v. O'Hara*, 69 Ore. 519; 139 Pac. 743, and *Simpson v. O'Hara*, 70 Ore. 261; 141 Pac. 158. These cases, after reargument, were affirmed here by an equally divided court, in 1917. 243 U.S. 629. The law of Oregon thus continued in effect. The District of Columbia Minimum Wage Law (40 Stat. 960) was enacted in 1918. The statute was sustained by the Supreme Court of the District in the *Adkins* case. Upon appeal the Court of Appeals of the District first affirmed that ruling but on rehearing reversed it and the case came before this Court in 1923. The judgment of the Court of Appeals holding the Act invalid was affirmed, but with Chief Justice Taft, Mr. Justice Holmes and Mr. Justice Sanford dissenting, and Mr. Justice Brandeis taking no part. The dissenting opinions took the ground that the decision was at variance with the principles which this Court had frequently announced and applied. In 1925 and 1927, the similar minimum wage statutes of Arizona and Arkansas were held invalid upon the authority of the *Adkins* case. The Justices who had dissented in that case bowed to the ruling and Mr. Justice Brandeis dissented. *Murphy v. Sardell*, 269 U.S. 530; *Donham v. West-Nelson Co.*, 273 U.S. 657. The question did not come before us again until the last term in the *Morehead* case, as already noted. In that case, briefs supporting the New York statute were submitted by the States of Ohio, Connecticut, Illinois, Massachusetts, New Hampshire, New Jersey and Rhode Island. 298 U. S., p. 604, note. Throughout this entire period the Washington statute now under consideration has been in force.

The principle which must control our decision is not in doubt. The constitutional provision invoked is the due process clause of the Fourteenth Amendment governing the States, as the due process clause invoked in the *Adkins* case governed Congress. In each case the violation alleged by those attacking minimum wage regulation for women is deprivation of freedom of contract. What is this freedom? The Constitution does not speak of freedom of contract. It speaks of liberty and prohibits the deprivation of liberty without due process of law. In prohibiting that deprivation the Constitution does not recognize an absolute and uncontrollable liberty. Liberty in each of its phases has its history and connotation. But the liberty safeguarded is liberty in a social organization which requires the protection of law against the evils which menace the health, safety, morals and welfare of the people. Liberty under the Constitution is thus necessarily subject to the restraints of due process and regulation which is reasonable in relation to its subject and is adopted in the interests of the community is due process.

This essential limitation of liberty in general governs freedom of contract in particular. More than twenty-five years ago we set forth the applicable principle in these words, after referring to the cases where the liberty guaranteed by the Fourteenth Amendment had been broadly described:

"But it was recognized in the cases cited, as in many others, that freedom of contract is a qualified and not an absolute right. There is no absolute freedom to do as one wills or to contract as one chooses. The guaranty of liberty does not withdraw from legislative supervision that wide department of activity which consists of the making of contracts, or deny to government the power to provide restrictive safeguards. Liberty implies the absence of arbitrary restraint, not immunity from reasonable regulations and prohibitions imposed in the interests of the community." *Chicago, B. & Q. R. Co.* v. *McGuire,* 219 U.S. 549, 567.

This power under the Constitution to restrict freedom of contract has had many illustrations. That it may be exercised in the public interest with respect to contracts between employer and employee is undeniable. . . .

In dealing with the relation of employer and employed, the legislature has necessarily a wide field of discretion in order that there may be suitable protection of health and safety, and that peace and good order may be promoted through regulations designed to insure wholesome conditions of work and freedom from oppression. *Chicago, B. & Q. R. Co.* v. *McGuire, supra,* p. 570.

The point that has been strongly stressed that adult employees should be deemed competent to make their own contracts was decisively met nearly forty years ago in *Holden* v. *Hardy, supra,* where we pointed out the inequality in the footing of the parties. We said *(Id.,* 397):

"The legislature has also recognized the fact, which the experience of legislators in many States has corroborated, that the proprietors of these establishments and their operatives do not stand upon an equality, and that their interests are, to a certain extent, conflicting. The former naturally desire to obtain as much labor as possible from their employees, while the latter are often induced by the fear of discharge to conform to regulations which their judgment, fairly exercised, would pronounce to be detrimental to their health or strength. In other words, the proprietors lay down the rules and the laborers are practically constrained to obey them. In such cases self-interest is often an unsafe guide, and the legislature may properly interpose its authority."

And we added that the fact "that both parties are of full age and competent to contract does not necessarily deprive the State of the power to interfere where the parties do not stand upon an equality, or where the public health demands that one party to the contract shall be protected against himself." "The State still retains an interest in his welfare, however reckless he may be. The whole is no greater than the sum of all the parts, and when the individual health, safety and welfare are sacrificed or neglected, the State must suffer."

It is manifest that this established principle is peculiarly applicable in relation to the employment of women in whose protection the State has a special interest. That phase of the subject received elaborate consideration in *Muller* v. *Oregon* (1908), 208 U.S. 412, where the constitutional authority of the State to limit the working hours of women was sustained. We emphasized the consideration that "woman's physical structure and the performance of maternal functions place her at a disadvantage in the struggle for subsistence" and that her physical well being "becomes an object of public interest and care in order to preserve the strength and vigor of the race." We emphasized the need of protecting women against oppression despite her possession of contractual rights. We said that "though limitations upon personal and contractual rights may be removed by legislation, there is that in her disposition and habits of life which will operate against a full assertion of those rights. She will still be where some legislation to protect her seems necessary to secure a real equality of right." Hence she was "properly placed in a class by herself, and legislation designed for her protection may be sustained even when like legislation is not necessary for men and could not be sustained." We concluded that the limitations which the statute there in question "placed upon her contractual powers, upon her right to agree with her employer as to the time she shall labor" were "not imposed solely for her benefit, but also largely for the benefit of all.". . .

This array of precedents and the principles they applied were thought by the dissenting Justices in the Adkins case to demand that the minimum wage statute be sustained. . . .

The minimum wage to be paid under the Washington statute is fixed after full consideration by representatives of employers, employees and the public. It may be assumed that the minimum wage is fixed in consideration of the services that are performed in the particular occupations under normal conditions. Provision is made for special licenses at less wages in the case of women who are incapable of full service. . . .

We think . . . that the decision in the *Adkins* case was a departure from the true application of the principles governing the regulation by the State of the relation of employer and employed. . . .

With full recognition of the earnestness and vigor which characterize the prevailing opinion in the *Adkins* case, we find it impossible to reconcile that ruling with these well considered declarations. (What can be closer to the public interest than the health of women and their protection from unscrupulous and overreaching employers?) And if the protection of women is a legitimate end of the exercise of state power, how can it be said that the requirement of the payment of a minimum wage fairly fixed in order to meet the very necessities of existence is not an admissible means to that end? The legislature of the State was clearly entitled to consider the situation of women in employment, the fact that they are in the class receiving the least pay, that their bargaining power is relatively weak and that they are the ready victims of those who would take advantage of their necessitous circumstances. The legislature was entitled to adopt measures to reduce the evils of the "sweating system," the exploiting of workers at wages so low as to lie insufficient to meet the bare cost of living, thus making their very helplessness the occasion of a most injurious competition. The legislature had the right to consider that its minimum wage requirements would be an important aid in carrying out its policy of protection. The adoption of similar requirements by many States evidences a deep-seated conviction both as to the presence of the evil and as to the means adapted to check it. Legislative response to that conviction cannot be regarded as arbitrary or capricious, and that is all we have to decide. Even if the wisdom of the policy be regarded as debatable and its effects uncertain, still the legislature is entitled to its judgment.

There is an additional and compelling consideration which recent economic experience has brought into a strong light. The exploitation of a class of workers who are in an unequal position with respect to bargaining power and are thus relatively defenceless against the denial of a living wage is not only detrimental to their health and well being but casts a direct burden for their support upon the community. What these workers lose in wages the taxpayers are called upon to pay. The bare cost of living must be met. We may take judicial notice of the unparalleled demands for relief which arose during the recent period of depression and still continue to an alarming extent despite the degree of economic recovery which has been achieved. . . .

The community may direct its law-making power to correct the abuse which springs from their selfish disregard of the public interest. The argument that the legislation in question constitutes an arbitrary discrimination, because it does not extend to men, is unavailing. This Court has frequently held that the legislative authority, acting within its proper field, is not bound to extend its regulation to all cases which it might possibly reach. The legislature "is free to recognize degrees of harm and it may confine its restrictions to those classes of cases where the need is deemed to be clearest." If "the law presumably hits the evil where it is most felt, it is not to be overthrown because there are other instances to which it might have been applied." There is no "doctrinaire requirement" that the legislation should be couched in all embracing terms. . . .

This familiar principle has repeatedly been applied to legislation which singles out women, and particular classes of women, in the exercise of the State's protective power. . . .

Their relative need in the presence of the evil, no less than the existence of the evil itself, is a matter for the legislative judgment.

Our conclusion is that the case of *Adkins* v. *Children's Hospital, supra,* should be, and it is, overruled. The judgment of the Supreme Court of the State of Washington is

*Affirmed*

MR. JUSTICE SUTHERLAND, dissenting:

MR. JUSTICE VAN DEVANTER, MR. JUSTICE MCREYNOLDS, MR. JUSTICE BUTLER and I think the judgment of the court below should be reversed.

The principles and authorities relied upon to sustain the judgment, were considered in *Adkins* v. *Children's Hospital,* 261 U.S. 525, and *Morehead* v. *New York ex rel. Tipaldo,* 298 U.S. 587; and their lack of application to cases like the one in hand was pointed out. A sufficient answer to all that is now said will be found in the opinions of the court in those cases. Nevertheless, in the circumstances, it seems well to restate our reasons and conclusions.

Under our form of government, where the written Constitution, by its own terms, is the supreme law, some agency, of necessity, must have the power to say the final word as to the validity of a statute assailed as unconstitutional. The Constitution makes it clear that the power has been intrusted to this court when the question arises in a controversy within its jurisdiction; and so long as the power remains there, its exercise cannot be avoided without betrayal of the trust.

It has been pointed out many times, as in the *Adkins* case, that this judicial duty is one of gravity and delicacy; and that rational doubts must be resolved in favor of the constitutionality of the statute. But whose doubts, and by whom resolved? Undoubtedly it is the duty of a member of the court, in the process of reaching a right conclusion, to give due weight to the opposing views of his associates; but in the end, the question which he must answer is not whether such views seem sound to those who entertain them, but whether they convince him that the statute is constitutional or engender in his mind a rational doubt upon that issue. The oath which he takes as a judge is not a composite oath, but an individual one. And in passing upon the validity of a statute, he discharges a duty imposed upon *him,* which cannot be consummated justly by an automatic acceptance of the views of others which have neither convinced, nor created a reasonable doubt in, his mind. If upon a question so important he thus surrender his deliberate judgment, he stands forsworn. He cannot subordinate his convictions to that extent and keep faith with his oath or retain his judicial and moral independence.

The suggestion that the only check upon the exercise of the judicial power, when properly invoked, to declare a constitutional right superior to an unconstitutional statute is the judge's own faculty of self-restraint, is both ill considered and mischievous. Self-restraint belongs in the domain of will and not of judgment. The check upon the judge is that imposed by his oath of office, by the Constitution and by his own conscientious and informed convictions; and since he has the duty to make up his own mind and adjudge accordingly, it is hard to see how there could be any other restraint. This court acts as a unit. It cannot act in any other way; and the majority (whether a bare majority or a majority of all but one of its members), therefore, establishes the controlling rule as the decision of the court, binding, so long as it remains unchanged, equally upon those who disagree and upon those who subscribe to it. Otherwise, orderly administration of justice would cease. But it is the right of those in the minority to disagree, and sometimes, in matters of grave importance, their imperative duty to voice their disagreement at such length as the occasion demands—always, of course, in terms which, however forceful, do not offend the proprieties or impugn the good faith of those who think otherwise.

It is urged that the question involved should now receive fresh consideration, among other reasons, because of "the economic conditions which have supervened"; but the meaning of the Constitution does not change with the ebb and flow of economic events. We frequently are told in more general words that the Constitution must be construed in the light of the present. If by that it is meant that the Constitution is made up of living words that apply to every new condition which they include, the statement is quite true. But to say, if that be intended, that the words of the Constitution mean today what they did not mean when written—that is, that they do not apply to a situation now to which they would have applied then—is to rob that instrument of the essential element which continues it in force as the people have made it until they, and not their official agents, have made it otherwise.

The words of Judge Campbell in *Twitchell* v. *Blodgett*, 13 Mich. 127, 139–140, apply with peculiar force. "But it may easily happen, he said, "that specific provisions may, in unforeseen emergencies, turn out to have been inexpedient. This does not make these provisions any less binding. Constitutions can not be changed by events alone. They remain binding as the acts of the people in their sovereign capacity, as the framers of Government, until they are amended or abrogated by the action prescribed by the authority which created them. It is not competent for any department of the Government to change a constitution, or declare it changed, simply because it appears ill adapted to a new state of things.

The judicial function is that of interpretation; it does not include the power of amendment under the guise of interpretation. To miss the point of difference between the two is to miss all that the phrase "supreme law of the land" stands for and to convert what was intended as inescapable and enduring mandates into mere moral reflections.

If the Constitution, intelligently and reasonably construed in the light of these principles, stands in the way of desirable legislation, the blame must rest upon that instrument, and not upon the court for enforcing it according to its terms. The remedy in that situation—and the only true remedy is to amend the Constitution.

. . . much of the benefit expected from written constitutions would be lost if their provisions were to be bent to circumstances or modified by public opinion. . . .

What a court is to do, therefore, is *to declare the law as written*, leaving it to the people themselves to make such changes as new circumstances may require. The meaning of the constitution is fixed when it is adopted, and it is not different at any subsequent time when a court has occasion to pass upon it."

The *Adkins* case dealt with an act of Congress which had passed the scrutiny both of the legislative and executive branches of the government. We recognized that thereby these departments had affirmed the validity of the statute, and properly declared that their determination must be given great weight, but we then concluded, after thorough consideration, that their view would not be sustained. We think it not inappropriate now to add a word on that subject before coming to the question immediately under review.

The people by their Constitution created three separate, distinct, independent and coequal departments of government. The governmental structure rests, and was intended to rest, not upon any one or upon any two, but upon all three of these fundamental pillars. It seems unnecessary to repeat, what so often has been said, that the powers of these departments are different and are to be exercised independently. The differences clearly and definitely appear in the Constitution. Each of the departments is an agent of its creator; and one department is not and cannot be the agent of another. Each is answerable to its creator for what it does, and not to another agent. The view, therefore, of the Executive and of Congress that an act is constitutional is persuasive in a high degree; but it is not controlling.

Coming, then, to a consideration of the Washington statute, it first is to be observed that it is in every substantial respect identical with the statute involved in the *Adkins* case. Such vices as existed in the latter are present in the former. And if the *Adkins* case was properly decided, as we who join in this opinion think it was, it necessarily follows that the Washington statute is invalid.

In support of minimum-wage legislation it has been urged, on the one hand, that great benefits will result in favor of underpaid labor, and, on the other hand, that the danger of such legislation is that the minimum will tend to become the maximum and thus bring down the earnings of the more efficient toward the level of the less-efficient employees. But with these speculations we have nothing to do. We are concerned only with the question of constitutionality.

That the clause of the Fourteenth Amendment which forbids a state to deprive any person of life, liberty or property without due process of law includes freedom of contract is so well settled as to be no longer open to question. Nor reasonably can it be disputed that contracts of employment of labor are included in the rule.

Two cases were involved in the *Adkins* decision. In one of them it appeared that a woman 21 years of age, who brought the suit, was employed as an elevator operator at a fixed salary. Her services were satisfactory, and she was anxious to retain her position, and her employer, while willing to retain her, was obliged to dispense with her services on account of the penalties prescribed by the act. The wages received by her were the best she was able to obtain for any work she was capable of performing; and the enforcement of the order deprived her, as she alleged, not only of that employment, but left her unable to secure any position at which she could make a living with as good physical and moral surroundings and as good wages as she was receiving and was willing to take. The Washington statute, of course, admits of the same situation and result, and, for aught that appears to the contrary, the situation in the present case may have been the same as that just described. Certainly, to the extent that the statute applies to such cases, it cannot be justified as a reasonable restraint upon the freedom of contract. On the contrary, it is essentially arbitrary.

Neither the statute involved in the *Adkins* case nor the Washington statute, so far as it is involved here, has the slightest relation to the capacity or earning power of the employee, to the number of hours which constitute the day's work, the character of the place where the work is to be done, or the circumstances or surroundings of the employment. The sole basis upon which the question of validity rests is the assumption that the employee is entitled to receive a sum of money sufficient to provide a living for her, keep her in health and preserve her morals. And, as we pointed out at some length in that case (pp. 555–557), the question thus presented for the determination of the board can not be solved by any general formula prescribed by a statutory bureau, since it is not a composite but an individual question to be answered for each individual, considered by herself.

. . . The Washington statute, like the one for the District of Columbia, fixes minimum wages for adult women. Adult men and their employers are left free to bargain as they please; and it is a significant and an important fact that all state statutes to which our attention has been called are of like character. The common-law rules restricting the power of women to make contracts have, under our system, long since practically disappeared. Women today stand upon a legal and political equality with men. There is no longer any reason why they should be put in different classes in respect of their legal right to make contracts; nor should they be denied, in effect, the right to compete with men for work paying lower wages which men may be willing to accept. And it is an arbitrary exercise of the legislative power to do so.

. . . An appeal to the principle that the legislature is free to recognize degrees of harm and confine its restrictions accordingly, is but to beg the question, which is—since the contractual rights of men and women are the same, does the legislation here involved, by restricting only the rights of women to make contracts as to wages, create an arbitrary discrimination? We think it does. Difference of sex affords no reasonable ground for making a restriction applicable to the wage contracts of all working women from which like contracts of all working men are left free. Certainly a suggestion that the bargaining ability of the average woman is not equal to that of the average man would lack substance. The ability to make a fair bargain, as everyone knows, does not depend upon sex.

If, in the light of the facts, the state legislation, without reason or for reasons of mere expediency, excluded men from the provisions of the legislation, the power was exercised arbitrarily. On the other hand, if such legislation in respect of men was properly omitted on the ground that it would be unconstitutional, the same conclusion of unconstitutionality is inescapable in respect of similar legislative restraint in the case of women, 261 U.S. 553. . . .

A more complete discussion may be found in the *Adkins* and *Tipaldo* cases cited supra.

---

**West Coat Hotel v. Parrish**, 300 U.S. 379 (1937) 5–4
*editor's note.*
*Opinion authors are in bold; () indicates the party of appointing president. If the party of the justice differs from that of appointing president, then the party of the justice is listed second after the slash.*

| MAJORITY | CONCURRING | DISSENTING |
| --- | --- | --- |
| **Hughes** (r) | | **Sutherland** (r) |
| Brandeis (d) | | Van Devanter (r) |
| Stone (r) | | McReynolds (d) |
| Roberts (r) | | Butler (r/d) |
| Cardozo (r/d) | | |

# United States v. Carolene Products Co.

## 304 U.S. 144

## Appeal from the District Court of the United States for the Southern District of Illinois

## No. 640. Argued April 6, 1938.—Decided April 25, 1938.

. . . *Assistant Attorney General McMahon,* with whom *Acting Solicitor General Bell,* and *Messrs. William W. Barron* and *Paul A. Freund* were on the brief, for the United States.

*Mr. Geo. N. Murdock* for appellee.

MR. JUSTICE STONE delivered the opinion of the Court.

The question for decision is whether the "Filled Milk Act" of Congress of March 4, 1923 (c. 262, 42 Stat. 1486. 21 U.S. C. §§ 61–63), which prohibits the shipment in interstate commerce of skimmed milk compounded with any fat or oil other than milk fat, so as to resemble milk or cream, transcends the power of Congress to regulate interstate commerce or infringes the Fifth Amendment.

Appellee was indicted in the district court for southern Illinois for violation of the Act by the shipment in interstate commerce of certain packages of "Milnut," a compound of condensed skimmed milk and coconut oil made in imitation or semblance of condensed milk or cream. The indictment states, in the words of the statute, that Milnut "is an adulterated article of food, injurious to the public health," and that it is not a prepared food product of the type excepted from the prohibition of the Act.

. . . Appellee assails the statute as beyond the power of Congress over interstate commerce, and hence an invasion of a field of action said to be reserved to the states by the Tenth Amendment. "Appellee also complains that the statute denies to it equal protection of the laws and, in violation of the Fifth Amendment, deprives it of its property without due process of law, particularly in that the statute purports to make binding and conclusive upon appellee the legislative declaration that appellee's product "is an adulterated article of food injurious to the public health and its sale constitutes a fraud on the public."

**FIRST**.  The power to regulate commerce is the power "to prescribe the rule by which commerce is to be governed." *Gibbons* v. *Ogden*, 9 Wheat, 1, 196, and extends to the prohibition of shipments in such commerce. . . .

Hence Congress is free to exclude from interstate commerce articles whose use in the states for which they are destined it may reasonably conceive to be injurious to the public health, morals or welfare . . . prohibition of the shipment of filled milk in interstate commerce is a permissible regulation of commerce, subject only to the restrictions of the Fifth Amendment.

**SECOND**.  The prohibition of shipment of appellee's product in interstate commerce does not infringe the Fifth Amendment. Twenty years ago this Court, in *Hebe Co.* v. *Shaw*, 248 U.S. 297, held that a state law which forbids the manufacture and sale of a product assumed to be wholesome and nutritive, made of condensed skimmed milk, compounded with coconut oil, is not forbidden by the Fourteenth Amendment. The power of the legislature to secure a minimum of particular nutritive elements in a widely used article of food and to protect the public from fraudulent substitutions, was not doubted; and the Court thought that there was ample scope for the legislative judgment that prohibition of the offending article was an appropriate means of preventing injury to the public.

We see no persuasive reason for departing from that ruling, here, where the Fifth Amendment is concerned; and since none is suggested, we might rest decision wholly on the presumption of constitutionality. But affirmative evidence also sustains the statute. In twenty years evidence has steadily accumulated of the danger to the public health from the general consumption of foods which have been stripped of elements essential to the maintenance of health. The Filled Milk Act was adopted by Congress after committee hearings, in the course of which eminent scientists and health experts testified. An extensive investigation was made of the commerce in milk compounds in which vegetable oils have been substituted for natural milk fat, and of the effect upon the public health of the use of such compounds as a food substitute for milk. The conclusions drawn from evidence presented at the hearings were embodied in reports of the House Committee on Agriculture, H. R. No. 365, 67th Cong., 1st Sess., and the Senate Committee on Agriculture and Forestry, Sen. Rep. No. 987, 67th Cong., 4th Sess. Both committees concluded, as the statute itself declares, that the use of filled milk as a substitute for pure milk is generally injurious to health and facilitates fraud on the public.[1]

There is nothing in the Constitution which compels a legislature, either national or state, to ignore such evidence, nor need it disregard the other evidence which amply supports the conclusions of the Congressional committees that the danger is greatly enhanced where an inferior product, like appellee's is indistinguishable from a valuable food of almost universal use, thus making fraudulent distribution easy and protection of the consumer difficult.[2]

Here the prohibition of the statute is inoperative unless the product is "in imitation or semblance of milk, cream, or skimmed milk, whether or not condensed." Whether in such circumstances the public would be adequately protected by the prohibition of false labels and false branding imposed by the Pure Food and Drugs Act, or whether it was necessary to go farther and prohibit a substitute food product thought to be injurious to health if used as a substitute when the two are not distinguishable, was a matter for the legislative judgment and not that of courts. . . .[3, omitted]

**THIRD.** We may assume for present purposes that no pronouncement of a legislature can forestall attack upon the constitutionality of the prohibition which it enacts by applying opprobrious epithets to the prohibited act, and that a statute would deny due process which precluded the disproof in judicial proceedings of all facts which would show or tend to show that a statute depriving the suitor of life, liberty or property had a rational basis.

But such we think is not the purpose or construction of the statutory characterization of filled milk as injurious to health and as a fraud upon the public. There is no need to consider it here as more than a declaration of the legislative findings deemed to support and justify the action taken as a constitutional exertion of the legislative power, aiding informed judicial review, as do the reports of legislative committees, by revealing the rationale of the legislation. Even in the absence of such aids the existence of facts supporting the legislative judgment is to be presumed, for regulatory legislation affecting ordinary commercial transactions is not to be pronounced unconstitutional unless in the light of the facts made known or generally assumed it is of such a character as to preclude the assumption that it rests upon some rational basis within the knowledge and experience of the legislators.[4] See *Metropolitan Casualty Ins. Co.* v. *Brownell*, 294 U. S. 580, 584, and cases cited. The present statutory findings affect appellee no more than the reports of the Congressional committees; and since in the absence of the statutory findings they would be presumed, their incorporation in the statute is no more prejudicial than surplusage. . . . But by their very nature such inquiries, where the legislative judgment is drawn in question, must be restricted to the issue whether any state of facts either known or which could reasonably be assumed affords support for it. Here the demurrer challenges the validity of the statute on its face and it is evident from all the considerations presented to Congress, and those of which we may take judicial notice, that the question is at least debatable whether commerce in filled milk should be left unregulated, or in some measure restricted, or wholly prohibited. As that decision was for Congress, neither the finding of a court arrived at by weighing the evidence, nor the verdict of a jury can be substituted for it. . . .

The prohibition of shipment in interstate commerce of appellee's product, as described in the indictment, is a constitutional exercise of the power to regulate interstate commerce. As the statute is not unconstitutional on its face the demurrer should have been overruled and the judgment will be

*Reversed.*

MR. JUSTICE BLACK concurs in the result and in all of the opinion except the part marked *"Third."*

MR. JUSTICE MCREYNOLDS thinks that the judgment should be affirmed.

MR. JUSTICE CARDOZO and MR. JUSTICE REED took no part in the consideration or decision of this case.

## Notes

1.  The reports may be summarized as follows: There is an extensive commerce in milk compounds made of condensed milk from which the butter fat has been extracted and an equivalent amount of vegetable oil, usually coconut oil, substituted. These compounds resemble milk in taste and appearance and are distributed in packages resembling those in which pure condensed milk is distributed. By reason of the extraction of the natural milk fat the compounded product can be manufactured and sold at a lower cost than pure milk. Butter fat, which constitutes an important part of the food value of pure milk, is rich in vitamins, food elements which are essential to proper nutrition and are wanting in vegetable oils. The use of filled milk as a dietary substitute for pure milk results, especially in the case of children, in undernourishment, and induces diseases which attend malnutrition. Despite compliance with the branding and labeling requirements of the Pure Food and Drugs Act, there is widespread use of filled milk as a food substitute for pure milk. This is aided by their identical taste and appearance, by the similarity of the containers in which they are sold, by the practice of dealers in offering the inferior product to customers in being as good as or better than pure condensed milk sold at a higher price, by customers' ignorance of the respective food values of the two products, and in many sections of the country by their inability to read the labels placed on the containers. Large amounts of filled milk, much of it shipped and sold in bulk, are purchased by hotels and boarding houses, and by manufacturers of food products, such as ice cream, to whose customers labeling restrictions afford no protection.

2.  There is now an extensive literature indicating wide recognition by scientists and dietitians of the great importance to the public health of butter fat and whole milk as the prime source of vitamins, which are essential growth producing and disease preventing elements in the diet....

    When the Filled Milk Act was passed, eleven states had rigidly controlled the exploitation of filled milk, or forbidden it altogether. H. R. 365, 67th Cong., 1st Sess. Some thirty-five states have now adopted laws which in terms, or by their operation, prohibit the sale of filled milk. . . .

3.  Text for footnote 3 of the original material was omitted from this book.

4.  There may be narrower scope for operation of the presumption of constitutionality when legislation appears on its face to be within a specific prohibition of the Constitution, such as those of the first ten amendments, which are deemed equally specific when held to be embraced within the Fourteenth. See *Stromberg* v. *California*, 283 U.S. 359, 369–370; *Lovell* v. *Griffin*, 303 U.S. 444, 452.

It is unnecessary to consider now whether legislation which restricts those political processes which can ordinarily be expected to bring about repeal of undesirable legislation, is to be subjected to more exacting judicial scrutiny under the general prohibitions of the Fourteenth Amendment than are most other types of legislation. On restrictions upon the right to vote, see *Nixon* v. *Herndon*, 273 U.S. 536; *Nixon* v. *Condon*, 286 U.S. 73; on restraints upon the dissemination of information, see *Near* v. *Minnesota ex rel. Olson*, 283 U.S. 697, 713–714, 718–720, 722; *Grosjean* v. *American Press Co.*, 297 U.S. 233; *Lovell* v. *Griffin*, supra; on interferences with political organizations, see *Stromberg* v. *California, supra,* 369; *Fiske* v. *Kansas*, 273 U.S. 380; *Whitney* v. *California*, 274 U.S. 357, 373–378; *Herndon* v. *Lowry*, 301 U.S. 242; and see Holmes, J., in *Gitlow* v. *New York*, 268 U.S. 652, 673; as to prohibition of peaceable assembly, see *De Jonge* v. *Oregon*, 299 U.S. 353, 365.

Nor need we enquire whether similar considerations enter into the review of statute directed at particular religious, *Pierce* v. *Society of Sisters*, 268 U.S. 510, or national, *Meyer* v. *Nebraska*, 262 U.S. 390; *Bartels* v. *Iowa*, 262 U.S. 404; *Farrington* v. *Tokushige*, 273 U.S. 484, or racial minorities, *Nixon* v. *Herndon, supra; Nixon* v. *Condon, supra:* whether prejudice against discrete and insular minorities may be a special condition, which tends seriously to curtail the operation of those political processes ordinarily to be relied upon to protect minorities, and which may call for a correspondingly more searching judicial inquiry. Compare *McCulloch* v. *Maryland*, 4 Wheat 316, 428; *South Carolina* v. *Barnwell Bros.*, 303 U.S. 177, 184, n. 2, and cases cited.

---

**U.S. v. Carolene Products**, 304 U.S. 144 (1938) 6–1*

*editor's note.*

*Opinion authors are in bold; () indicates the party of appointing president. If the party of the justice differs from that of appointing president, then the party of the justice is listed second after the slash.*

| MAJORITY | CONCURRING | DISSENTING |
|---|---|---|
| **Stone** (r) | Black (d) | McReynolds (d) |
| Hughes (r) | | |
| Brandeis (d) | | |
| Roberts (r) | | |
| Butler (r/d) | | |

*Cardozo (r/d) and Reed (d) did not participate.

---

# Gitlow v. People of New York

## 268 U.S. 652 (1925)

## Error to the Supreme Court of the State of New York

### No. 19. Argued April 12, 1923; reargued November 23, 1923.— Decided June 8, 1925.

---

*Messrs. Walter Nelles* and *Walter H. Pollack*, with whom *Messrs. Albert De Silver* and *Charles S. Ascher* were on the brief, for plaintiff in error.

*Messrs W. J. Weatherbee*, Deputy Attorney General of New York, and *John Caldwell Myers*, Assistant District Attorney of New York County, with whom *Messrs. Carl Sherman*, Attorney General of New York, *Claude T. Dawes*, Deputy Attorney General of New York, *Joab H. Banton*, District Attorney of New York County, and *John F. O'Neil*, Assistant District Attorney of New York County, were on the briefs, for defendant in error.

MR. JUSTICE SANFORD delivered the opinion of the Court.

Benjamin Gitlow was indicted in the Supreme Court of New York, with three others, for the statutory crime of criminal anarchy. New York Penal Laws, § 160, 161.1 He was separately tired, convicted, and sentenced to imprisonment. The judgment was affirmed by the Appellate Division and by the Court of Appeals. 195 App. Div. 773; 234 N. Y. 132 and 539. The case is here on writ of error to the Supreme Court, to which the record was remitted. 260 U.S. 703.

The contention here is that the statute, by its terms and as applied in this case, is repugnant to the due process clause of the Fourteenth Amendment. Its material provisions are:

"§ 160. *Criminal anarchy defined.* Criminal anarchy is the doctrine that organized government should be overthrown by force or violence, or by assassination of the executive head or of any of the executive officials of government, or by any unlawful means. The advocacy of such doctrine either by word of mouth or writing is a felony.

"§ 161. *Advocacy of criminal anarchy.* Any person who:

"1. By word of mouth or writing advocates, advises or teaches the duty, necessity or propriety of overthrowing or overturning organized government by force or violence, or by assassination of the executive officials of government, or by any unlawful means; or,

"2. Prints, publishes, edits, issues or knowingly circulates, sells, distributes or publicly displays any book, paper, document, or written or printed matter in any form, containing or advocating, advising or teaching the doctrine that organized government should be overthrown by force, violence or any unlawful means. . . ,

"Is guilty of a felony and punishable" by imprisonment or fine, or both.

The indictment was in two counts. The first charged that the defendant had advocated, advised and taught the duty, necessity and propriety of overthrowing and overturning organized government by force, violence and unlawful means, by certain writings therein set forth entitled "The Left Wing Manifesto"; the second that he had printed, published and knowingly circulated and distributed a certain paper called "The Revolutionary Age," containing the writings set forth in the first count advocating, advising and teaching the doctrine that organized government should be overthrown by force, violence and unlawful means.

The following facts were established on the trial by undisputed evidence and admissions: The defendant is a member of the Left Wing Section of the Socialist Party, a dissenting branch or faction of that party formed in opposition to its dominant policy of "moderate Socialism." Membership in both is open to aliens as well as citizens. The Left Wing Section was organized nationally at a conference in New York City in June, 1919, attended by ninety delegates from twenty different States. The conference elected a National Council, of which the defendant was a member, and left to it the adoption of a "Manifesto." This was published in The Revolutionary Age, the official organ of the Left Wing. The defendant was on the board of managers of the paper and was its business manager. He arranged for the printing of the paper and took to the printer the manuscript of the first issue which contained the Left Wing Manifesto, and also a Communist Program and a Program of the Left Wing that had been adopted by the conference. Sixteen thousand copies were printed, which were delivered at the premises in New York City used as the office of the Revolutionary Age and the headquarters of the Left Wing, and occupied by the defendant and other officials. These copies were paid for by the defendant, as business manager of the paper. Employees at this office wrapped and mailed out copies of the paper under the defendant's direction; and copies were sold from this office. It was admitted that the defendant signed a card subscribing to the Manifesto and Program of the Left Wing, which all applicants were required to sign before being admitted to membership; that he went to different parts of the State to speak to branches of the Socialist Party about the principles of the Left Wing and advocated their adoption; and that he was responsible for the Manifesto as it appeared, that "he knew of the publication, in general way and he knew of its publication afterwards, and is responsible for its circulation."

There was no evidence of any effect resulting from the publication and circulation of the Manifesto.

No witnesses were offered in behalf of the defendant.

Extracts from the Manifesto are set forth in the margin. Coupled with a review of the rise of Socialism, it condemned the dominant "moderate Socialism" for its recognition of the necessity of the democratic parliamentary state; repudiated its policy of introducing Socialism by legislative measures; and advocated, in plain and unequivocal language, the necessity of accomplishing the "Communist Revolution" by a militant and "revolutionary Socialism," based on "the class struggle" and mobilizing the "power of the proletariat in action," through mass industrial revolts developing into mass political strikes and "revolutionary mass action," for the purpose of conquering and destroying the parliamentary state and establishing in its place, through a "revolutionary dictatorship of the proletariat," the system of Communist Socialism. The then recent strikes in Seattle and Winnipeg were cited as instances of a development already verging on revolutionary action and suggestive of proletarian dictatorship, in which the strike-workers were "trying to usurp the functions of municipal government"; and revolutionary Socialism, it was urged, must use these mass industrial revolts to broaden the strike, make it general and militant, and develop it into mass political strikes and revolutionary mass action for the annihilation of the parliamentary state. . . .

The Court of Appeals held that the Manifesto "advocated the overthrow of this government by violence, or by unlawful means." . . .

And both the Appellate Division and the Court of Appeals held the statute constitutional. . . . The sole contention [of Gitlow] here is, essentially, that as there was no evidence of any concrete result flowing from the publication of the Manifesto or of circumstances showing the likelihood of such result, the statute as construed and applied by the trial court penalizes the mere utterance, as such, of "doctrine" having no quality of incitement, without regard either to the circumstances of its utterance or to the likelihood of unlawful sequences; and that, as the exercise of the right of free expression with relation to government is only punishable "in circumstances involving likelihood of substantive evil," the statute contravenes the due process clause of the Fourteenth Amendment. The argument in support of this contention rests primarily upon the following propositions: 1st, That the "liberty" protected by the Fourteenth Amendment includes the liberty of speech and of the press; and 2nd, That while liberty of expression "is not absolute," it may be restrained "only in circumstances where its exercise bears a causal relation with some substantive evil, consummated, attempted or likely," and as the statute "takes no account of circumstances," it unduly restrains this liberty and is therefore unconstitutional.

The precise question presented, and the only question which we can consider under this writ of error, then is, whether the statute, as construed and applied in this case by the state courts, deprived the defendant of his liberty of expression in violation of the due process clause of the Fourteenth Amendment.

The statute does not penalize the utterance or publication of abstract "doctrine" or academic discussion having no quality of incitement to any concrete action. It is not aimed against mere historical or philosophical essays. It does not restrain the advocacy of changes in the form of government by constitutional and lawful means. What it prohibits is language advocating, advising or teaching the overthrow of organized government by unlawful means. These words imply urging to action. Advocacy is defined in the Century Dictionary as: "1. The act of pleading for, supporting, or recommending; active espousal." It is not the abstract "doctrine" of overthrowing organized government by unlawful means which is denounced by the statute, but the advocacy of action for the accomplishment of that purpose. . . .

The Manifesto, . . . concludes with a call to action in these words: "the proletariat revolution and the Communist reconstruction of society—*the struggle for these*—is now indispensable. . . . The Communist International calls the proletariat of the world to the final struggle!" This is not the expression of philosophical abstraction, the mere prediction of future events; it is the language of direct incitement.

The means advocated for bringing about the destruction of organized parliamentary government, namely, mass industrial revolts usurping the functions of municipal government, political mass strikes directed against the parliamentary state, and revolutionary mass action for its final destruction, necessarily imply the use of force and violence, and in their essential nature are inherently unlawful in a constitutional government of law and order. . . .

For present purposes we may and do assume that freedom of speech and of the press—which are protected by the First Amendment from abridgment by Congress—are among the fundamental personal rights and "liberties" protected by the due process clause of the Fourteenth Amendment from impairment by the States. . . .

It is a fundamental principle, long established, that the freedom of speech and of the press which is secured by the Constitution, does not confer an absolute right to speak or publish, without responsibility, whatever one may choose, or an unrestricted and unbridled license that gives immunity for every possible use of language and prevents the punishment of those who abuse this freedom. . . . *Robinson v. Baldwin*, 165 U.S. 275, 281; *Patterson v. Colorado*, 205 U.S. 454, 462; *Fox v. Washington*, 236 U.S. 273, 276; *Schenck v. United States*, 249 U.S. 47, 52; *Frohwerk v. United States*, 249 U.S. 204, 206; *Debs v. United States*, 249 U.S. 211, 213; *Schaefer v. United States*, 251 U.S. 466, 474; *Gilbert v. Minnesota*, 254 U.S. 325, 332; . . .

That a State in the exercise of its political power may punish those who abuse this freedom by utterances inimical to the public welfare, tending to corrupt public morals, incite to crime, or disturb the public peace, is not open to question. *Robertson v. Baldwin, supra*, p. 281; *Patterson v. Colorado, supra*, p. 462; *Fox v. Washington, supra*, p. 277; *Gilbert v. Minnesota, supra*, p. 339; *People v. Most*, 171 N. Y. 423, 431; *State v. Holm*, 139 Minn. 267, 275; *State v. Hennessy*, 114 Wash. 351, 359; *State v. Boyd*, 86 N. J. L. 75, 79; *State v. McKee*, 73 Conn. 18, 27. Thus it was held by this Court in the *Fox Case*, that a State may punish publications advocating and encouraging a breach of its criminal laws; and, in the *Gilbert Case*, that a State may punish utterances teaching or advocating that its citizens should not assist the United States in prosecuting or carrying on war with its public enemies.

And, for yet more imperative reasons, a State may punish utterances endangering the foundations of organized government and threatening its overthrow by unlawful means. These imperil its own existence as a constitutional State. Freedom of speech and press, does not protect disturbances to the public peace or the attempt to subvert the government. It does not protect publications or teachings which tend to subvert or imperil the government or to impede or hinder it in the performance of its governmental duties. It does not protect publications prompting the overthrow of government by force; the punishment of those who publish articles which tend to destroy organized society being essential to the security of freedom and the stability of the State. And a State may penalize utterances which openly advocate the overthrow of the representative and constitutional form of government of the United States and the several States, by violence or other unlawful means. In short this freedom does not deprive a State of the primary and essential right of self preservation; which so long as human governments endure, they cannot be denied. In *Toledo Newspaper Co.* v. *United States*, 247 U.S. 402, 419, it was said: "The safeguarding and fructification of free and constitutional institutions is the very basis and mainstay upon which the freedom of the press rests, and that freedom, therefore, does not and cannot be held to include the right virtually to destroy such institutions."

By enacting the present statute the State has determined, through its legislative body, that utterances advocating the overthrow of organized government by force, violence and unlawful means, are so inimical to the general welfare and involve such danger of substantive evil that they may be penalized in the exercise of its police power. That determination must be given great weight. Every presumption is to be indulged in favor of the validity of the statute. *Mugler* v. *Kansas*, 123 U.S. 623, 661. And the case is to be considered "in the light of the principle that the State is primarily the judge of regulations required in the interest of public safety and welfare;" and that its police "statutes may only be declared unconstitutional where they are arbitrary or unreasonable attempts to exercise authority vested in the State in the public interest." That utterances inciting to the overthrow of organized government by unlawful means, present a sufficient danger of substantive evil to bring their punishment within the range of legislative discretion, is clear. Such utterances, by their very nature, involve danger to the public peace and to the security of the State. They threaten breaches of the peace and ultimate revolution. And the immediate danger is none the less real and substantial, because the effect of a given utterance cannot be accurately foreseen. The State cannot reasonably be required to measure the danger from every such utterance in the nice balance of a jeweler's scale. A single revolutionary spark may kindle a fire that, smouldering for a time, may burst into a sweeping and destructive conflagration. It cannot be said that the State is acting arbitrarily or unreasonably when in the exercise of its judgment as to the measure necessary to protect the public peace and safety, it seeks to extinguish the spark without waiting until it has enkindled the flame or blazed into the conflagration. It cannot reasonably be required to defer the adoption of measures for its own peace and safety until the revolutionary utterances lead to actual disturbances of the public peace or imminent and immediate danger of its own destruction; but it may, in the exercise of its judgment, suppress the threatened danger in its incipiency. . . .

We cannot hold that the present statute is an arbitrary or unreasonable exercise of the police power of the State unwarrantably infringing the freedom of speech or press; and we must and do sustain its constitutionality.

It is clear that the question in such cases is entirely different from that involved in those cases where the statute merely prohibits certain acts involving the danger of substantive evil, without any reference to language itself, and it is sought to apply its provisions to language used by the defendant for the purpose of bringing about the prohibited results. . . . And the general statement in the *Schenck Case* (p.52) that the "question in every case is whether the words are used in such circumstances and are of such a nature as to create a clear and present danger that they will bring about the substantive evils,"—upon which great reliance is placed in the defendant's argument—was manifestly intended, as shown by the context, to apply only in cases of this class, and has no application to those like the present, where the legislative body itself has previously determined the danger of substantive evil arising from utterances of a specified character. . . . It was not necessary, within the meaning of the statute, that the defendant should have advocated "some definite or immediate act or acts" of force, violence or unlawfulness. It was sufficient if such acts were advocated in general terms; and it was not essential that their immediate execution should have been advocated. . . . The advocacy need not be addressed to specific persons. . . .

And finding, for the reasons stated, that the statute is not in itself unconstitutional, and that it has not been applied in the present case in derogation of any constitutional right, the judgment of the Court of Appeals is

*Affirmed.*

MR. JUSTICE HOLMES, dissenting. [with Justice Brandeis]

MR. JUSTICE BRANDEIS and I are of opinion that this judgment should be reversed. The general principle of free speech, it seems to me, must be taken to be included in the Fourteenth Amendment, in view of the scope that has been given to the word 'liberty' as there used, although perhaps it may be accepted with a somewhat larger latitude of interpretation than is allowed to Congress by the sweeping language that governs or ought to govern the laws of the United States. If I am right, then I think that the criterion sanctioned by the full Court in *Schenck* v. *United States*, 249 U.S. 47, 52, applies. "The question in every case is whether the words used are used in such circumstances and are of such a nature as to create a clear and present danger that they will bring about the substantive evils that [the State] has a right to prevent." . . . If what I think the correct test is applied, it is manifest that there was no present danger of an attempt to overthrow the government by force on the part of the admittedly small minority who shared the defendant's views. It is said that this manifesto was more than a theory, that it was an incitement. Every idea is an incitement. It offers itself for belief and if believed it is acted on unless some other belief outweighs it or some failure of energy stifles the movement at its birth. The only difference between the expression of an opinion and an incitement in the narrower sense is the speaker's enthusiasm for the result. Eloquence may set fire to reason. But whatever may be thought of the redundant discourse before us it had no chance of starting a present conflagration. If in the long run the beliefs expressed in proletarian dictatorship are destined to be accepted by the dominant forces of the community, the only meaning of free speech is that they should be given their chance and have their way.

If the publication of this document had been laid as an attempt to induce an uprising against government at once and not at some indefinite time in the future it would have presented a different question. The object would have been one with which the law might deal, subject to the doubt whether there was any danger that the publication could produce any result, or in other words, whether it was not futile and too remote from possible consequences. But the indictment alleges the publication and nothing more.

## *Notes*

1. Laws of 1909, ch. 88; Consol. Laws, 1909, ch. 40. This statute was originally enacted in 1902. Laws of 1902, ch. 371.

---

**Gitlow v. New York**, 268 U.S. 652 (1925) 7–2
*editor's note.*
*Opinion authors are in bold; () indicates the party of appointing president. If the party of the justice differs from that of appointing president, then the party of the justice is listed second after the slash.*

| MAJORITY | CONCURRING | DISSENTING |
|---|---|---|
| **Sanford** (r) | | **Holmes** (r) |
| Taft (r) | | Brandeis (d) |
| Van Devanter (r) | | |
| McReyonlds (d) | | |
| Butler (r/d) | | |
| Sutherland (r) | | |
| Stone (r) | | |

# Palko v. Connecticut

## 302 U.S. 310 (1937)

## Appeal from the Supreme Court of Errors of Connecticut.

### No. 135. Argued November 12, 1937.—Decided December 6, 1937.

Appeal from a judgment sustaining a sentence of death upon a verdict of guilty of murder in the first degree. The defendant had previously been convicted upon the same indictment of murder in the second degree; whereupon the State appealed a new trial was ordered.

*Messrs. David Goldstein* and *George A. Saden* for appellant.

*Mr. Wm. H. Comley*, with whom *Mr. Lorin W. Willis*, State's Attorney, was on the brief, for Connecticut.

MR. JUSTICE CARDOZO delivered the opinion of the Court.

A statute of Connecticut permitting appeals in criminal cases to be taken by the state is challenged by appellant as an infringement of the Fourteenth Amendment of the Constitution of the United States. Whether the challenge should be upheld is now to be determined.

Appellant was indicted in Fairfield County, Connecticut, for the crime of murder in the first degree. A jury found him guilty of murder in the second degree, and he was sentenced to confinement in the state prison for life. Thereafter the State of Connecticut, with the permission of the judge presiding at the trial, gave notice of appeal to the Supreme Court of Errors. This it did pursuant to an act adopted in 1886 which is printed in the margin.[1] Public Acts, 1886, p. 560; now § 6494 of the General Statutes. Upon such appeal, the Supreme Court of Errors reversed the judgment and ordered a new trial. *State* v. *Palko*, 121 Conn. 669; 186 Atl. 657. It found that there had been error of law to the prejudice of the state (1) in excluding testimony as to a confession by defendant; (2) in excluding testimony upon cross-examination of defendant to impeach his credibility, and (3) in the instructions to the jury as to the difference between first and second degree murder.

Pursuant to the mandate of the Supreme Court of Errors, defendant was brought to trial again. Before a jury was impaneled and also at later stages of the case he made the objection that the effect of the new trial was to place him twice in jeopardy for the same offense, and in so doing to violate the Fourteenth Amendment of the Constitution of the United States. Upon the overruling of the objection the trial proceeded. The jury returned a verdict of murder in the first degree, and the court sentenced the defendant to the punishment of death. The Supreme Court of Errors affirmed the judgment of conviction, . . .

The case is here upon appeal.

1. The execution of the sentence will not deprive appellant of his life without the process of law assured to him by the Fourteenth Amendment of the Federal Constitution.

The argument for appellant is that whatever is forbidden by the Fifth Amendment is forbidden by the Fourteenth also. The Fifth Amendment, which is not directed to the states, but solely to the federal government, creates immunity from double jeopardy. No person shall be "subject for the same offense to be twice put in jeopardy of life or limb." The Fourteenth Amendment ordains, "nor shall any State deprive any person of life, liberty, or property, without due process of law." To retry a defendant, though under one indictment and only one, subjects him, it is said, to double jeopardy in violation of the Fifth Amendment, if the prosecution is one on behalf of the United States. From this the consequence is said to follow that there is a denial of life or liberty without due process of law, if the prosecution is one on behalf of the People of a State.

The tyranny of labels, *Snyder* v. *Massachusetts*, 291 U.S. 97, 114, must not lead us to leap to a conclusion that a word which in one set of facts may stand for oppression or enormity is of like effect in every other.

We have said that in appellant's view the Fourteenth Amendment is to be taken as embodying the prohibitions of the Fifth. His thesis is even broader. Whatever would be a violation of the original bill of rights (Amendments I to VIII) if done by the federal government is now equally unlawful by force of the Fourteenth Amendment if done by a state. There is no such general rule.

The Fifth Amendment provides, among other things, that no person shall be held to answer for a capital or otherwise infamous crime unless on presentment or indictment of a grand jury. This court has held that, in prosecutions by a state, presentment or indictment by a grand jury may give way to informations at the instance of a public officer. *Hurtado* v. *California*, 110 U.S. 516; *Gaines* v. *Washington*, 277 U.S. 81, 86. The Fifth Amendment provides also that no person shall be compelled in any criminal case to be a witness against himself. This court has said that, in prosecutions by a state, the exemption will fail if the state elects to end it. *Twining v. New Jersey*, 211 U.S. 78, 106, 111, 112. Cf. *Snyder v. Massachusetts, supra*, p. 105; *Brown v. Mississippi*, 297 U.S. 278, 285. The Sixth Amendment calls for a jury trial in criminal cases and the Seventh for a jury trial in civil cases at common law where the value in controversy shall exceed twenty dollars. This court has ruled that consistently with those amendments trial by jury may be modified by a state or abolished altogether. *Walker v. Sauvinet*, 92 U.S. 90; *Maxwell v. Dow*, 176 U.S. 581; *New York Central R. Co. v. White*; 243 U.S. 188, 208; *Wagner Electric Mfg. Co. v. Lyndon*, 262 U.S. 226, 232. As to the Fourth Amendment, one should refer to *Weeks v. United States*, 232 U.S. 383, 398, and as to other provisions of the Sixth, to *West v. Louisiana*, 194 U.S. 258.

On the other hand, the due process clause of the Fourteenth Amendment may make it unlawful for a state to abridge by its statutes the freedom of speech which the First Amendment safeguards against encroachment by the Congress, *De Jonge v. Oregon*, 299 U.S. 353, 364; *Herndon v. Lowry*, 301 U.S. 242, 259; or the like freedom of the press, *Grosjean v. American Press Co.*, 297 U.S. 233; *Near v. Minnesota ex rel. Olson*, 283 U.S. 697, 707; or the free exercise of religion, *Hamilton v. Regents*, 293 U.S. 245, 262; cf. *Grosjean v. American Press Co., supra*; *Pierce v. Society of Sisters*, 268 U.S. 510; or the right of peaceable assembly, without which speech would be unduly trammeled, *De Jonge v. Oregon, supra*; *Herndon v. Lowry, supra*; or the right of one accused of crime to the benefit of counsel, *Powell v. Alabama*, 287 U.S. 45. In these and other situations immunities that are valid as against the federal government by force of the specific pledges of particular amendments have been found to be implicit in the concept of ordered liberty, and thus, through the Fourteenth Amendment, become valid as against the states.

The line of division may seem to be wavering and broken if there is a hasty catalogue of the cases on the one side and the other. Reflection and analysis will induce a different view. There emerges the perception of a rationalizing principle which gives to discrete instances a proper order and coherence. The right to trial by jury and the immunity from prosecution except as the result of an indictment may have value and importance. Even so, they are not of the very essence of a scheme of ordered liberty. To abolish them is not to violate a "principle of justice so rooted in the traditions and conscience of our people as to be ranked as fundamental." *Snyder v. Massachusetts, supra*, p. 105; *Brown v. Mississippi, supra*, p. 285; *Herbert v. Louisiana*, 272 U.S. 312, 316. Few would be so narrow or provincial as to maintain that a fair and enlightened system of justice would be impossible without them. What is true of jury trials and indictments is true also, as the cases show, of the immunity from compulsory self-incrimination. *Twining v. New Jersey, supra*. This too might be lost, and justice still be done. . . . The exclusion of these immunities and privileges from the privileges and immunities protected against the action of the states has not been arbitrary or casual. It has been dictated by a study and appreciation of the meaning, the essential implications, of liberty itself.

We reach a different plane of social and moral values when we pass to the privileges and immunities that have been taken over from the earlier articles of the federal bill of rights and brought within the Fourteenth Amendment by a process of absorption. These in their origin were effective against the federal government alone. If the Fourteenth Amendment has absorbed them, the process of absorption has had its source in the belief that neither liberty nor justice would exist if they were sacrificed. This is true, for illustration, of freedom of thought, and speech. Of that freedom one may say that it is the matrix, the indispensable condition, of nearly every other form of freedom. With rare aberrations a pervasive recognition of that truth can be traced in our history, political and legal. So it has come about that the domain of liberty, withdrawn by the Fourteenth Amendment from encroachment by the states, has been enlarged by latter-day judgments to include liberty of the mind as well as liberty of action. . . . Fundamental too in the concept of due process, and so in that of liberty, is the thought that condemnation shall be rendered only after trial. *Scott* v. *NcNeal*, 154 U.S. 34; *Blackmer* v. *United States*, 284 U.S. 421. The hearing, moreover, must be a real one, not a sham or a pretense. *Moore* v. *Dempsey*, 261 U.S. 86; *Mooney* v. *Holohan*, 294 U.S. 103. For that reason, ignorant defendants in a capital case were held to have been condemned unlawfully when in truth, though not in form, they were refused the aid of counsel. *Powell* v. *Alabama, supra*, pp. 67, 68. The decision did not turn upon the fact that the benefit of counsel would have been guaranteed to the defendants by the provisions of the Sixth Amendment if they had been prosecuted in a federal court. The decision turned upon the fact that in the particular situation laid before us in the evidence the benefit of counsel was essential to the substance of a hearing.

Our survey of the cases serves, we think, to justify the statement that the dividing line between them, if not unfaltering throughout its course, has been true for the most part to a unifying principle. On which side of the line the case made out by the appellant has appropriate location must be the next inquiry and the final one. Is that kind of double jeopardy to which the statute has subjected him a hardship so acute and shocking that our polity will not endure it? Does it violate those "fundamental principles of liberty and justice which lie at the base of all our civil and political institutions"? *Hebert* v. *Louisiana, supra*. The answer surely must be "no." What the answer would have to be if the state were permitted after a trial free from error to try the accused over again or to bring another case against him, we have no occasion to consider. We deal with the statute before us and no other. The state is not attempting to wear the accused out by a multitude of cases with accumulated trials. It asks no more than this, that the case against him shall go on until there shall be a trial free from the corrosion of substantial legal error. *State* v. *Felch*, 92 Vt. 477; 105 Atl. 23; *State* v. *Lee, supra*. This is not cruelty at all, nor even vexation in any immoderate degree. If the trial had been infected with error adverse to the accused, there might have been review at his instance, and as often as necessary to purge the vicious taint. A reciprocal privilege, subject at all times to the discretion of the presiding judge, *State* v. *Carabetta*, 106 Conn.

114; 127 Atl. 394, has now been granted to the state. There is here no seismic innovation. The edifice of justice stands, its symmetry, to many, greater than before.

2. The conviction of appellant is not in derogation of any privileges or immunities that belong to him as a citizen of the United States. . . .

*Maxwell* v. *Dow.* . .

The judgment is

*Affirmed.*

Mr. Justice Butler dissents.

---

**Palko v. Connecticut**, 302 U.S. 319 (1937) 8–1
*editor's note.*
*Opinion authors are in bold; () indicates the party of appointing president. If the party of the justice differs from that of appointing president, then the party of the justice is listed second after the slash.*

| MAJORITY | CONCURRING | DISSENTING |
|----------|------------|------------|
| **Cardozo** (r/d) | | Butler (r/d) |
| Hughes (r) | | |
| Black (d) | | |
| McReynolds (d) | | |
| Brandeis (d) | | |
| Sutherland (r) | | |
| Roberts (r) | | |
| Stone (r) | | |

# Griswold et al. v. Connecticut

## 381 U.S. 479

## Appeal from the Supreme Court of Errors of Connecticut

### No. 496. Argued March 29–30, 1965.—Decided June 7, 1965

Appellants, the Executive Director of the Planned Parenthood League of Connecticut, and its medical director, a licensed physician, were convicted as accessories for giving married persons information and medical advice on how to prevent conception and, following examination, prescribing a contraceptive device or material for the wife's use. A Connecticut statute makes it a crime for any person to use any drug or article to prevent conception. Appellants claimed that the accessory statute as applied violated the Fourteenth Amendment. An intermediate appellate court and the State's highest court affirmed the judgment. *Held:*

1. Appellants have standing to assert the constitutional rights of the married people. *Tileston* v. *Ullman,* 318 U. S. 44, distinguished. p. 481.

2. The Connecticut statute forbidding use of contraceptives violates the right of marital privacy which is within the penumbra of specific guarantees of the Bill of Rights. Pp. 481–486.

151 Conn. 544, 200 A. 2d 479, reversed.

*Thomas I. Emerson* argued the cause for appellants. With him on the briefs was *Catherine G. Roraback.*

*Joseph B. Clark* argued the cause for appellee. With him on the brief was *Julius Maretz.*

Briefs of *amici curiae,* urging reversal, were filed by *Whitney North Seymour* and *Eleanor M. Fox* for Dr. John M. Adams et al.; by *Morris L. Ernst, Harriet F. Pilpel* and *Nancy P. Wechsler* for the Planned Parenthood Federation of America, Inc.; by *Alfred L. Scanlon* for the Catholic Council on Civil Liberties, and by *Rhoda H. Karpatkin, Melvin L. Wulf* and *Jerome E. Caplan* for the American Civil Liberties Union et al.

MR. JUSTICE DOUGLAS delivered the opinion of the Court.

Appellant Griswold is Executive Director of the Planned Parenthood League of Connecticut. Appellant Buxton is a licensed physician and a professor at the Yale Medical School who served as Medical Director for the League at its Center in New Haven—a center open and operating from November 1 to November 10, 1961, when appellants were arrested.

They gave information, instruction, and medical advice to *married persons* as to the means of preventing conception. They examined the wife and prescribed the best contraceptive device or material for her use. Fees were usually charged, although some couples were serviced free.

The statutes whose constitutionality is involved in this appeal are §§ 53–32 and 54–196 of the General Statutes of Connecticut (1958 rev.). The former provides:

> "Any person who uses any drug, medicinal article or instrument for the purpose of preventing conception shall be fined not less than fifty dollars or imprisoned not less than sixty days nor more than one year or be both fined and imprisoned."

Section 54–196 provides:

> "Any person who assists, abets, counsels, causes, hires or commands another to commit any offense may be prosecuted and punished as if he were the principal offender."

The appellants were found guilty as accessories and fined $100 each, against the claim that the accessory statute as so applied violated the Fourteenth Amendment. The Appellate Division of the Circuit Court affirmed. The Supreme Court of Errors affirmed that judgment. 151 Conn. 544, 200 A. 2d 479. We noted probable jurisdiction. 379 U. S. 926. . . .

Coming to the merits, we are met with a wide range of questions that implicate the Due Process Clause of the Fourteenth Amendment. We do not sit as a super-legislature to determine the wisdom, need, and propriety of laws that touch economic problems, business affairs, or social controls. This law, however, operates directly on an intimate relation of husband and wife and their physician's role in one aspect of that relation.

The association of people is not mentioned in the Constitution nor in the Bill of Rights. The right to educate a child in a school of the parents' choice—whether public or private or parochial—is also not mentioned. Nor is the right to study any particular subject or any foreign language. Yet the First Amendment has been construed to include certain of those rights.

By *Pierce* v. *Society of Sisters, supra,* the right to educate one's children as one chooses is made applicable to the States by the force of the First and Fourteenth Amendments. By *Meyer* v. *Nebraska, supra,* the same dignity is given the right to study the German language in a private school. In other words, the State may not, consistently with the spirit of the First Amendment, contract the spectrum of available knowledge. The right of freedom of speech and press includes not only the right to utter or to print, but the right to distribute, the right to receive, the right to read (*Martin* v. *Struthers,* 319 U. S. 141, 143) and freedom of inquiry, freedom of thought, and freedom to teach (see *Wieman* v. *Updegraff,* 344 U. S. 183, 195)—indeed the freedom of the entire university community. *Sweezy* v. *New Hampshire,* 354 U. S. 234, 249–250, 261–263; *Barenblatt* v. *United States,* 360 U. S. 109, 112; *Baggett* v. *Bullitt,* 377 U. S. 360, 369. Without those peripheral rights the specific rights would be less secure. And so we reaffirm the principle of the *Pierce* and the *Meyer* cases.

In *NAACP* v. *Alabama,* 357 U. S. 449, 462, we protected the "freedom to associate and privacy in one's associations," noting that freedom of association was a peripheral First Amendment right. Disclosure of membership lists of a constitutionally valid association, we held was invalid "as entailing the likelihood of a substantial restraint upon the exercise by petitioner's members of their right to freedom of association." *Ibid.* In other words, the First Amendment has a penumbra where privacy is protected from governmental intrusion. In like context, we have protected forms of "association" that are not political in the customary sense but pertain to the social, legal, and economic benefit of the members. *NAACP* v. *Button,* 371 U. S. 415, 430–431. . . .

The foregoing cases suggest that specific guarantees in the Bill of Rights have penumbras, formed by emanations from those guarantees that help give them life and substance. See *Poe* v. *Ullman,* 367 U. S. 497, 516–522 (dissenting opinion). Various guarantees create zones of privacy. The right of association contained in the penumbra of the First Amendment is one, as we have seen. The Third Amendment in its prohibition against the quartering of soldiers "in any house" in time of peace without the consent of the owner is another facet of that privacy. The Fourth Amendment explicitly affirms the "right of the people to be secure in their persons, houses, papers, and effects, against unreasonable searches and seizures." The Fifth Amendment in its Self-Incrimination Clause enables the citizen to create a zone of privacy which government may not force him to surrender to his detriment. The Ninth Amendment provides: "The enumeration in the Constitution, of certain rights, shall not be construed to deny or disparage others retained by the people.". . .

The present case, then, concerns a relationship lying within the zone of privacy created by several fundamental constitutional guarantees. And it concerns a law which, in forbidding the use of contraceptives rather than regulating their manufacture or sale, seeks to achieve its goals by means having a maximum destructive impact upon that relationship. Such a law cannot stand in light of the familiar principle, so often applied by this Court, that a "governmental purpose to control or prevent activities constitutionally subject to state regulation may not be achieved by means which sweep unnecessarily broadly and thereby invade the area of protected freedoms." *NAACP* v. *Alabama,* 377 U. S. 288, 307. Would we allow the police to search the sacred precincts of marital bedrooms for telltale signs of the use of contraceptives? The very idea is repulsive to the notions of privacy surrounding the marriage relationship.

We deal with a right of privacy older than the Bill of Rights—older than our political parties, older than our school system. Marriage is a coming together for better or for worse, hopefully enduring, and intimate to the degree of being sacred. It is an association that promotes a way of life, not causes; a harmony in living, not political faiths; a bilateral loyalty, not commercial or social projects. Yet it is an association for as noble a purpose as any involved in our prior decisions.

*Reversed.*

MR. JUSTICE GOLDBERG, whom THE CHIEF JUSTICE and MR. JUSTICE BRENNAN join, concurring.

I agree with the Court that Connecticut's birth-control law unconstitutionally intrudes upon the right of marital privacy, and I join in its opinion and judgment. Although I have not accepted the view that "due process" as used in the Fourteenth Amendment incorporates all of the first eight Amendments (see my concurring opinion in *Pointer* v. *Texas,* 380 U. S. 400, 410, and the dissenting opinion of MR. JUSTICE BRENNAN in *Cohen* v. *Hurley,* 366 U. S. 117, 154), I do agree that the concept of liberty protects those personal rights that are fundamental, and is not confined to the specific terms of the Bill of Rights. My conclusion that the concept of liberty is not so restricted and that it embraces the right of marital privacy though that right is not mentioned explicitly in the Constitution is supported both by numerous decisions of this Court, referred to in the Court's opinion, and by the language and history of the Ninth Amendment. In reaching the conclusion that the right of marital privacy is protected, as being within the protected penumbra of specific guarantees of the Bill of Rights, the Court refers to the Ninth Amendment, *ante,* at 484. I add these words to emphasize the relevance of that Amendment to the Court's holding.

The Court stated many years ago that the Due Process Clause protects those liberties that are "so rooted in the traditions and conscience of our people as to be ranked as fundamental." *Snyder* v. *Massachusetts,* 291 U. S. 97, 105. In *Gitlow* v. *New York,* 268 U. S. 652, 666 [1925], the Court said:

"For present purposes we may and do assume that freedom of speech and of the press—which are protected by the First Amendment from abridgment by Congress are among the *fundamental* personal rights and 'liberties' protected by the due process clause of the Fourteenth Amendment from impairment by the States." (Emphasis added.) . . .

This Court, in a series of decisions, has held that the Fourteenth Amendment absorbs and applies to the States those specifics of the first eight amendments which express fundamental personal rights. The language and history of the Ninth Amendment reveal that the Framers of the Constitution believed that there are additional fundamental rights, protected from governmental infringement, which exist alongside those fundamental rights specifically mentioned in the first eight constitutional amendments.

The Ninth Amendment reads, "The enumeration in the Constitution, of certain rights, shall not be construed to deny or disparage others retained by the people." The Amendment is almost entirely the work of James Madison. It was introduced in Congress by him and passed the House and Senate with little or no debate and virtually no change in language. It was proffered to quiet expressed fears that a bill of specifically enumerated rights could not be sufficiently broad to cover all essential rights and that the specific mention of certain rights would be interpreted as a denial that others were protected.

In presenting the proposed Amendment, Madison said:

"It has been objected also against a bill of rights that, by enumerating particular exceptions to the grant of power, it would disparage those rights which were not placed in that enumeration; and it might follow by implication, that those rights which were not singled out, were intended to be assigned into the hands of the General Government, and were consequently insecure. This is one of the most plausible arguments I have ever heard urged against the admission of a bill of rights into this system; but, I conceive, that it may be guarded against. I have attempted it, as gentlemen may see by turning to the last clause of the fourth resolution [the Ninth Amendment]." I Annals of Congress 439 (Gales and Seaton ed. 1834). . . .

[The statement of Madison makes] clear that the Framers did not intend that the first eight amendments be construed to exhaust the basic and fundamental rights which the Constitution guaranteed to the people. While this Court has had little occasion to interpret the Ninth Amendment, "[i]t cannot be presumed that any clause in the constitution is intended to be without effect." *Marbury* v. *Madison*, 1 Cranch 137, 174. In interpreting the Constitution, "real effect should be given to all the words it uses." *Myers* v. *United States.* 272 U. S. 52, 151. The Ninth Amendment to the Constitution may be regarded by some as a recent discovery and may be forgotten by others, but since 1791 it has been a basic part of the Constitution which we are sworn to uphold. To hold that a right so basic and fundamental and so deep-rooted in our society as the right of privacy in marriage may be infringed because that right is not guaranteed in so many words by the first eight amendments to the Constitution is to ignore the Ninth Amendment and to give it no effect whatsoever. Moreover, a judicial construction that this fundamental right is not protected by the Constitution because it is not mentioned in explicit terms by one of the first eight amendments or elsewhere in the Constitution would violate the Ninth Amendment, which specifically states that "[t]he enumeration in the Constitution, of certain rights, shall not be *construed* to deny or disparage others retained by the people." (Emphasis added.)

A dissenting opinion suggests that my interpretation of the Ninth Amendment some-how "broaden[s] the powers of this Court." *Post,* at 520. With all due respect, I believe that it misses the import of what I am saying. I do not take the position of my Brother BLACK in his dissent in *Adamson* v. *California,* 332 U. S. 46, 68, that the entire Bill of Rights is incorporated in the Fourteenth Amendment, and I do not mean to imply that the Ninth Amendment is applied against the States by the Fourteenth. Nor do I mean to state that the Ninth Amendment constitutes an independent source of rights protected from infringement by either the States or the Federal Government. Rather, the Ninth Amendment shows a belief of the Constitution's authors that fundamental rights exist that are not expressly enumerated in the first eight amendments and an intent that the list of rights included there not be deemed exhaustive. As any student of this Court's opinions knows, this Court has held, often unanimously, that the Fifth and Fourteenth Amendments protect certain fundamental personal liberties from abridgment by the Federal Government or the States. See, *e. g., Bolling* v. *Sharpe,* 347 U. S. 497; *Aptheker* v. *Secretary of State,* 378 U. S. 500; *Kent* v. *Dulles,* 357 U. S. 116; *Cantwell* v. *Connecticut,* 310 U. S. 296; *NAACP* v. *Alabama,* 357 U. S. 449; *Gideon* v. *Wainwright,* 372 U. S. 335; *New York Times Co.* v. *Sullivan,* 376 U. S. 254. The Ninth Amendment simply shows the intent of the Constitution's authors that other fundamental personal rights should not be denied such protection or disparaged in any other way simply because they are not specifically listed in the first eight constitutional amendments. I do not see how this broadens the authority of the Court; rather it serves to support what this Court has been doing in protecting fundamental rights. . . .

In sum, the Ninth Amendment simply lends strong support to the view that the "liberty" protected by the Fifth and Fourteenth Amendments from infringement by the Federal Government or the States is not restricted to rights specifically mentioned in the first eight amendments. Cf. *United Public Workers* v. *Mitchell,* 330 U. S. 75, 94–95.

In determining which rights are fundamental, judges are not left at large to decide cases in light of their personal and private notions. Rather, they must look to the "traditions and [collective] conscience of our people" to determine whether a principle is "so rooted [there] . . . as to be ranked as fundamental." *Snyder* v. *Massachusetts*, 291 U. S. 97, 105. The inquiry is whether a right involved "is of such a character that it cannot be denied without violating those 'fundamental principles of liberty and justice which lie at the base of all our civil and political institutions'. . . ." *Powell* v. *Alabama*, 287 U. S. 45, 67. "Liberty" also "gains content from the emanations of . . . specific [constitutional] guarantees" and "from experience with the requirements of a free society." . . .

The Connecticut statutes here involved deal with a particularly important and sensitive area of privacy—that of the marital relation and the marital home. This Court recognized in *Meyer* v. *Nebraska, supra,* that the right "to marry, establish a home and bring up children" was an essential part of the liberty guaranteed by the Fourteenth Amendment. . . .

The entire fabric of the Constitution and the purposes that clearly underlie its specific guarantees demonstrate that the rights to marital privacy and to marry and raise a family are of similar order and magnitude as the fundamental rights specifically protected.

Although the Constitution does not speak in so many words of the right of privacy in marriage, I cannot believe that it offers these fundamental rights no protection. The fact that no particular provision of the Constitution explicitly forbids the state from disrupting the traditional relation of the family—a relation as old and as fundamental as our entire civilization—surely does not show that the Government was meant to have the power to do so. Rather, as the Ninth Amendment expressly recognizes, there are fundamental personal rights such as this one, which are protected from abridgment by the Government though not specifically mentioned in the Constitution. . . .

The logic of the dissents would sanction federal or state legislation that seems to me even more plainly unconstitutional than the statute before us. Surely the Government, absent a showing of a compelling subordinating state interest, could not decree that all husbands and wives must be sterilized after two children have been born to them. Yet by their reasoning such an invasion of marital privacy would not be subject to constitutional challenge because, while it might be "silly," no provision of the Constitution specifically prevents the Government from curtailing the marital right to bear children and raise a family. While it may shock some of my Brethren that the Court today holds that the Constitution protects the right of marital privacy, in my view it is far more shocking to believe that the personal liberty guaranteed by the Constitution does not include protection against such totalitarian limitation of family size, which is at complete variance with our constitutional concepts. Yet, if upon a showing of a slender basis of rationality, a law outlawing voluntary birth control by married persons is valid, then, by the same reasoning, a law requiring compulsory birth control also would seem to be valid. In my view, however, both types of law would unjustifiably intrude upon rights of marital privacy which are constitutionally protected. . . .

Although the Connecticut birth-control law obviously encroaches upon a fundamental personal liberty, the State does not show that the law serves any "subordinating [state] interest which is compelling" or that it is "necessary . . . to the accomplishment of a permissible state policy." The State, at most, argues that there is some rational relation between this statute and what is admittedly a legitimate subject of state concern—the discouraging of extramarital relations. It says that preventing the use of birth-control devices by married persons helps prevent the indulgence by some in such extramarital relations. The rationality of this justification is dubious, particularly in light of the admitted widespread availability to all persons in the State of Connecticut, unmarried as well as married, of birth control devices for the prevention of disease, as distinguished from the prevention of conception, see *Tileston* v. *Ullman,* 129 Conn. 84, 26 A. 2d 582. But, in any event, it is clear that the state interest in safeguarding marital fidelity can be served by a more discriminately tailored statute, which does not, like the present one, sweep unnecessarily broadly, reaching far beyond the evil sought to be dealt with and intruding upon the privacy of all married couples. . . . The State of Connecticut does have statutes, the constitutionality of which is beyond doubt, which prohibit adultery and fornication. See Conn. Gen. Stat. §§ 53–218, 53–219 *et seq.* These statutes demonstrate that means for achieving the same basic purpose of protecting marital fidelity are available to Connecticut without the need to "invade the area of protected freedoms." *NAACP* v. *Alabama, supra,* at 307. See *McLaughlin* v. *Florida, supra,* at 196.

Finally, it should be said of the Court's holding today that it in no way interferes with a State's proper regulation of sexual promiscuity or misconduct.

MR. JUSTICE HARLAN, concurring in the judgment.

I fully agree with the judgment of reversal, but find myself unable to join the Court's opinion. The reason is that it seems to me to evince an approach to this case very much like that taken by my Brothers BLACK and STEWART in dissent, namely: the Due Process Clause of the Fourteenth Amendment does not touch this Connecticut statute unless the enactment is found to violate some right assured by the letter or penumbra of the Bill of Rights.

In sum, I believe that the right of privacy in the marital relation is fundamental and basic—a personal right "retained by the people" within the meaning of the Ninth Amendment. Connecticut cannot constitutionally abridge the fundamental right, which is protected by the Fourteenth Amendment from infringement by the States. I agree with the Court that petitioners' convictions must therefore be reversed.

In other words, what I find implicit in the Court's opinion is that the "incorporation" doctrine may be used to *restrict* the reach of Fourteenth Amendment Due Process. For me this is just as unacceptable constitutional doctrine as is the use of the "incorporation" approach to *impose* upon the States all the requirements of the Bill of Rights as found in the provisions of the first eight amendments and in the decisions of this Court interpreting them. See, *e. g.,* my concurring opinions in *Pointer* v. *Texas,* 380 U. S. 400, 408, and *Griffin* v. *California,* 380 U. S. 609, 615, and my dissenting opinion in *Poe* v. *Ullman,* 367 U. S. 497, 522, at pp. 539–545.

In my view, the proper constitutional inquiry in this case is whether this Connecticut statute infringes the Due Process Clause of the Fourteenth Amendment because the enactment violates basic values "implicit in the concept of ordered liberty," *Palko* v. *Connecticut,* 302 U. S. 319, 325. For reasons stated at length in my dissenting opinion in *Poe* v. *Ullman, supra,* I believe that it does. While the relevant inquiry may be aided by resort to one or more of the provisions of the Bill of Rights, it is not dependent on them or any of their radiations. The Due Process Clause of the Fourteenth Amendment stands, in my opinion, on its own bottom.

A further observation seems in order respecting the justification of my Brothers BLACK and STEWART for their "incorporation" approach to this case. Their approach does not rest on historical reasons, which are of course wholly lacking (see Fairman, Does the Fourteenth Amendment Incorporate the Bill of Rights? The Original Understanding, 2 Stan. L. Rev. 5 (1949)), but on the thesis that by limiting the content of the Due Process Clause of the Fourteenth Amendment to the protection of rights which can be found elsewhere in the Constitution, in this instance in the Bill of Rights, judges will thus be confined to "interpretation" of specific constitutional provisions, and will thereby be restrained from introducing their own notions of constitutional right and wrong into the "vague contours of the Due Process Clause." *Rochin* v. *California,* 342 U. S. 165, 170.

While I could not more heartily agree that judicial "self restraint" is an indispensable ingredient of sound constitutional adjudication, I do submit that the formula suggested for achieving it is more hollow than real.

"Specific" provisions of the Constitution, no less than "due process," lend themselves as readily to "personal" interpretations by judges whose constitutional outlook is simply to keep the Constitution in supposed "tune with the times" (post, p. 522). Need one go further than to recall last Term's reapportionment cases, *Wesberry* v. *Sanders,* 376 U.S. 1, and *Reynolds* v. *Sims,* 377 U.S. 533, where a majority of the Court "interpreted" "by the People" (Art. 1, § 2) and "equal protection" (Amdt. 14) to command "one person, one vote," an interpretation that was made in the face of irrefutable and still unanswered history to the contrary? See my dissenting opinions in those cases, 376 U. S., at 20; 377 U.S., at 589.

Judicial self-restraint will not, I suggest, be brought about in the "due process" area by the historically unfounded incorporation formula long advanced by my Brother BLACK, and now in part espoused by my Brother STEWART. It will be achieved in this area, as in other constitutional areas, only by continual insistence upon respect for the teachings of history, solid recognition of the basic values that underlie our society, and wise appreciation of the great roles that the doctrines of federalism and separation of powers have played in establishing and preserving American freedoms. See *Adamson v. California*, 332 U.S. 46, 59 (Mr. Justice Frankfurter, concurring). Adherence to these principles will not, of course, obviate all constitutional differences of opinion among judges, nor should it. Their continued recognition will, however, go farther toward keeping most judges from roaming at large in the constitutional field than will the interpolation into the Constitution of an artificial and largely illusory restriction on the content of the Due Process Clause.

MR. JUSTICE WHITE, concurring in the judgment.

In my view this Connecticut law as applied to married couples deprives them of "liberty" without due process of law, as that concept is used in the Fourteenth Amendment. I therefore concur in the judgment of the Court reversing these convictions under Connecticut's aiding and abetting statute. . . .

As I read the opinions of the Connecticut courts and the argument of Connecticut in this Court, the State claims but one justification for its anti-use statute. Cf. *Allied Stores of Ohio* v. *Bowers*, 358 U.S. 522, 530; *Martin* v. *Walton*, 368 U.S. 25, 28 (DOUGLAS, J., dissenting). There is no serious contention that Connecticut thinks the use of artificial or external methods of contraception immoral or unwise in itself, or that the anti-use statute is founded upon any policy of promoting population expansion. Rather, the statute is said to serve the policy against all forms of promiscuity or illicit sexual relationships, be they premarital or extramarital, concededly a permissible and legitimate legislative goal.

Without taking issue with the premise that the fear of conception operates as a deterrent to such relationships in addition to the criminal proscriptions Connecticut has against such conduct, I wholly fail to see how the ban on the use of contraceptives by married couples in any way reinforces the State's ban on illicit sexual relationships. See *Schware* v. *Board of Bar Examiners*, 353 U. S. 232, 239. Connecticut does not bar the importation or possession of contraceptive devices; they are not considered contraband material under state law, *State* v. *Certain Contraceptive Materials*, 126 Conn. 428, 11 A. 2d 863, and their availability in that State is not seriously disputed. The only way Connecticut seeks to limit or control the availability of such devices is through its general aiding and abetting statute whose operation in this context has been quite obviously ineffective and whose most serious use has been against birth-control clinics rendering advice to married, rather than unmarried, persons. Cf. *Yick Wo* v. *Hopkins*, 118 U. S. 356. Indeed, after over 80 years of the State's proscription of use, the legality of the sale of such devices to prevent disease has never been expressly passed upon, although it appears that sales have long occurred and have only infrequently been challenged. This "undeviating policy . . . throughout all the long years . . . bespeaks more than prosecutorial paralysis." *Poe* v. *Ullman*, 367 U. S. 497, 502. Moreover, it would appear that the sale of contraceptives to prevent disease is plainly legal under Connecticut law.

In these circumstances one is rather hard pressed to explain how the ban on use by married persons in any way prevents use of such devices by persons engaging in illicit sexual relations and thereby contributes to the State's policy against such relationships. . . . I find nothing in this record justifying the sweeping scope of this statute, with its telling effect on the freedoms of married persons, and therefore conclude that it deprives such persons of liberty without due process of law.

MR. JUSTICE BLACK, with whom MR. JUSTICE STEWART joins, dissenting.

I agree with my Brother STEWART's dissenting opinion. And like him I do not to any extent whatever base my view that this Connecticut law is constitutional on a belief that the law is wise or that its policy is a good one. In order that there may be no room at all to doubt why I vote as I do, I feel constrained to add that the law is every bit as offensive to me as it is to my Brethren of the majority and my Brothers HARLAN, WHITE and GOLDBERG who, reciting reasons why it is offensive to them, hold it unconstitutional. There is no single one of the graphic and eloquent strictures and criticisms fired at the policy of this Connecticut law either by the Court's opinion or by those of my concurring Brethren to which I cannot subscribe—except their conclusion that the evil qualities they see in the law make it unconstitutional.

Had the doctor defendant here, or even the nondoctor defendant, been convicted for doing nothing more than expressing opinions to persons coming to the clinic that certain contraceptive devices, medicines or practices would do them good and would be desirable, or for telling people how devices could be used, I can think of no reason at this time why their expressions of views would not be protected by the First and Fourteenth Amendments, which guarantee freedom of speech . . . . But speech is one thing; conduct and physical activities are quite another . . . . The two defendants here were active participants in an organization which gave physical examinations to women, advised them what kind of contraceptive devices or medicines would most likely be satisfactory for them, and then supplied the devices themselves, all for a graduated scale of fees, based on the family income. Thus these defendants admittedly engaged with others in a planned course of conduct to help people violate the Connecticut law. Merely because some speech was used in carrying on that conduct—

just as in ordinary life some speech accompanies most kinds of conduct—we are not in my view justified in holding that the First Amendment forbids the State to punish their conduct. Strongly as I desire to protect all First Amendment freedoms, I am unable to stretch the Amendment so as to afford protection to the conduct of these defendants in violating the Connecticut law. What would be the constitutional fate of the law if hereafter applied to punish nothing but speech is, as I have said, quite another matter.

The Court talks about a constitutional "right of privacy" as though there is some constitutional provision or provisions forbidding any law ever to be passed which might abridge the "privacy" of individuals. But there is not. There are, of course, guarantees in certain specific constitutional provisions which are designed in part to protect privacy at certain times and places with respect to certain activities. Such, for example, is the Fourth Amendment's guarantee against "unreasonable searches and seizures." But I think it belittles that Amendment to talk about it as though it protects nothing but "privacy." To treat it that way is to give it a niggardly interpretation, not the kind of liberal reading I think any Bill of Rights provision should be given. The average man would very likely not have his feelings soothed any more by having his property seized openly than by having it seized privately and by stealth. He simply wants property left alone. And a person can be just as much, if not more, irritated, annoyed and injured by an unceremonious public arrest by a policeman as he is by a seizure in the privacy of his office or home.

One of the most effective ways of diluting or expanding a constitutionally guaranteed right is to substitute for the crucial word or words of a constitutional guarantee another word or words, more or less flexible and more or less restricted in meaning. This fact is well illustrated by the use of the term "right of privacy" as a comprehensive substitute for the Fourth Amendment's guarantee against "unreasonable searches and seizures." "Privacy" is a broad, abstract and ambiguous concept which can easily be shrunken in meaning but which can also, on the other hand, easily be interpreted as a constitutional ban against many things other than searches and seizures. I have expressed the view many times that First Amendment freedoms, for example, have suffered from a failure of the courts to stick to the simple language of the First Amendment in construing it, instead of invoking multitudes of words substituted for those the Framers used. See, *e. g., New York Times Co.* v. *Sullivan*, 376 U.S. 254, 293 (concurring opinion); cases collected in *City of El Paso* v. *Simmons*, 379 U. S. 497, 517, n. 1 (dissenting opinion); Black, The Bill of Rights, 35 N.Y.U.L. Rev. 865. For these reasons I get nowhere in this case by talk about a constitutional "right of privacy" as an emanation from one or more constitutional provisions. I like my privacy as well as the next one, but I am nevertheless compelled to admit that government has a right to invade it unless prohibited by some specific constitutional provision. For these reasons I cannot agree with the Court's judgment and the reasons it gives for holding this Connecticut law unconstitutional.

This brings me to the arguments made by my Brother HARLAN, WHITE and GOLDBERG for invalidating the Connecticut law. . . .

The due process argument which my Brothers HARLAN and WHITE adopt here is based, as their opinions indicate, on the premise that this Court is vested with power to invalidate all state laws that it considers to be arbitrary, capricious, unreasonable, or oppressive, or on this Court's belief that a particular state law under scrutiny has no "rational or justifying" purpose, or is offensive to a "sense of fairness and justice." If these formulas based on "natural justice," or others which mean the same thing, are to prevail, they require judges to determine what is or is not constitutional on the basis of their own appraisal of what laws are unwise or unnecessary. The power to make such decisions is of course that of a legislative body. Surely it has to be admitted that no provision of the Constitution specifically gives such blanket power to courts to exercise such a supervisory veto over the wisdom and value of legislative policies and to hold unconstitutional those laws which they believe unwise or dangerous. I readily admit that no legislative body, state or national, should pass laws that can justly be given any of the invidious labels invoked as constitutional excuses to strike down state laws. But perhaps it is not too much to say that no legislative body ever does pass laws without believing that they will accomplish a sane, rational, wise and justifiable purpose. While I completely subscribe to the holding of *Marbury* v. *Madison,* 1 Cranch 137, and subsequent cases, that our Court has constitutional power to strike down statutes, state or federal, that violate commands of the Federal Constitution, I do not believe that we are granted power by the Due Process Clause or any other constitutional provision or provision to measure constitutionality by our belief that legislation is arbitrary, capricious, or unreasonable, or accomplishes no justifiable purpose, or is offensive to our own notions of "civilized standards of conduct." Such an appraisal of the wisdom of legislation is an attribute of the power to make laws, not of the power to interpret them. The use by federal courts of such a formula or doctrine or whatnot to veto federal or state laws simply takes away from Congress and States the power to make laws based on their own judgment of fairness and wisdom and transfers that power to this Court for ultimate determination—a power which was specifically denied to federal courts by the convention that framed the Constitution.

Of the cases on which my Brothers WHITE and GOLDBERG rely so heavily, undoubtedly the reasoning of two of them supports their result here—as would that of a number of others which they do not bother to name. . . .

Without expressing an opinion as to whether either of those cases reached a correct result in light of our later decisions applying the First Amendment to the States through the Fourteenth, I merely point out that the reasoning stated in *Meyer* and *Pierce* was the same natural law due process philosophy which many later opinions repudiated, and which I cannot accept. . . .

. . . My Brother GOLDBERG has adopted the recent discovery that the Ninth Amendment as well as the Due Process Clause can be used by this Court as authority to strike down all state legislation which this Court thinks violates "fundamental principles of liberty and justice," or is contrary to the "traditions and [collective] conscience of our people." He also states, without proof satisfactory to me, that in making decisions on this basis judges will not consider "their personal and private notions." One may ask how they can avoid considering them. Our Court certainly has no machinery with which to take a Gallup Poll. And the scientific miracles of this age have not yet produced a gadget which the Court can use to determine what traditions are rooted in the [collective] conscience of our people." Moreover, one would certainly have to look far beyond the language of the Ninth Amendment to find that the Framers vested in this Court any such awesome veto powers over lawmaking, either by the States or by the Congress. Nor does anything in the history of the Amendment offer any support for such a shocking doctrine. The whole history of the adoption of the Constitution and Bill of Rights points the other way. . . . That Amendment was passed, not to broaden the powers of this Court or any other department of "the General Government," but, as every student of history knows, to assure the people that the Constitution in all its provisions was intended to limit the Federal Government to the powers granted expressly or by necessary implication. If any broad, unlimited power to hold laws unconstitutional because they offend what this Court conceives to be the "[collective] conscience of our people" is vested in this Court by the Ninth Amendment, the Fourteenth Amendment or any other provision of the Constitution, it was not given by the Framers, but rather has been bestowed on the Court by the Court.

. . . I repeat so as not to be misunderstood that this Court does have power, which it should exercise, to hold laws unconstitutional where they are forbidden by the Federal Constitution. My point is that there is no provision of the Constitution which either expressly or impliedly vest power in this Court to sit as a supervisory agency over acts of duly constituted legislative bodies and set aside their laws because of the Court's belief that the legislative policies adopted are unreasonable, unwise, arbitrary, capricious or irrational. The adoption of such a loose, flexible, uncontrolled standard for holding laws unconstitutional, if ever it is finally achieved, will amount to a great unconstitutional shift of power to the courts which I believe and am constrained to say will be bad for the courts and worse for the country. . . .

I realize that many good and able men have eloquently spoken and written, sometimes in rhapsodical strains, about the duty of this Court to keep the Constitution in tune with the times. The idea is that the Constitution must be changed from time to time and that this Court is charged with a duty to make those changes. For myself, I must with all deference reject that philosophy. The Constitution makers knew the need for change and provided for it. Amendments suggested by the people's elected representatives can be submitted to the people or their selected agents for ratification. That method of change was good for our Fathers, and being somewhat old-fashioned I must add it is good enough for me. And so, I cannot rely on the Due Process Clause or the Ninth Amendment or any mysterious and uncertain natural law concept as a reason for striking down this state law. The Due Process Clause with an "arbitrary and capricious" or "shocking to the conscience" formula was liberally used by this Court to strike down economic legislation in the early decades of this century, threatening, many people thought, the tranquillity and stability of the Nation. See, *e. g., Lochner* v. *New York*, 198 U.S. 45. That formula, based on subjective considerations of "natural justice," is no less dangerous when used to enforce this Court's views about personal rights than those about economic rights. . . .

So far as I am concerned, Connecticut's law as applied here is not forbidden by any provision of the Federal Constitution as that Constitution was written, and I would therefore affirm.

MR. JUSTICE STEWART, whom MR. JUSTICE BLACK joins, dissenting.

Since 1879 Connecticut has had on its books a law which forbids the use of contraceptives by anyone. I think this is an uncommonly silly law. As a practical matter, the law is obviously unenforceable, except in the oblique context of the present case. As a philosophical matter, I believe the use of contraceptives in the relationship of marriage should be left to personal and private choice, based upon each individual's moral, ethical, and religious beliefs. As a matter of social policy, I think professional counsel about methods of birth control should be available to all, so that each individual's choice can be meaningfully made. But we are not asked in this case to say whether we think this law is unwise, or even asinine. We are asked to hold that it violates the United States Constitution. And that I cannot do.

In the course of its opinion the Court refers to no less than six Amendments to the Constitution: the First, the Third, the Fourth, the Fifth, the Ninth, and the Fourteenth. But the Court does not say which of these Amendments, if any, it thinks is infringed by this Connecticut law. . . .

As to the First, Third, Fourth, and Fifth Amendments, I can find nothing in any of them to invalidate this Connecticut law, even assuming that all those Amendments are fully applicable against the States. . . .

The Court also quotes the Ninth Amendment, and my Brother GOLDBERG's concurring opinion relies heavily upon it. But to say that the Ninth Amendment has anything to do with this case is to turn somersaults with history. The Ninth Amendment, like its companion the Tenth, which this Court held "states but a truism that all is retained which has not been surrendered," *United States* v. *Darby*, 312 U. S. 100, 124, was framed by James Madison and adopted by the States simply to make clear that the adoption of the Bill of Rights did not alter the plan that the *Federal Government* was to be a government of express and limited powers, and that all rights and powers not delegated to it were retained by the people and the individual States. Until today no member of this Court has ever suggested that the Ninth Amendment meant anything else, and the idea that a federal court could ever use the Ninth Amendment to annul a law passed by the elected representatives of the people of the State of Connecticut would have caused James Madison no little wonder.

What provision of the Constitution, then, does make this state law invalid? The Court says it is the right of privacy "created by several fundamental constitutional guarantees." With all deference, I can find no such general right of privacy in the Bill of Rights, in any other part of the Constitution, or in any case ever before decided by this Court.

At the oral argument in this case we were told that the Connecticut law does not "conform to current community standards." But it is not the function of this Court to decide cases on the basis of community standards. We are here to decide cases "agreeably to the Constitution and laws of the United States." It is the essence of judicial duty to subordinate our own personal views, our own ideas of what legislation is wise and what is not. If, as I should surely hope, the law before us does not reflect the standards of the people of Connecticut, the people of Connecticut can freely exercise their true Ninth and Tenth Amendment rights to persuade their elected representatives to repeal it. That is the constitutional way to take this law off the books.

## Note

1.  Of course one cannot be oblivious to the fact that Mr. Gallup has already published the results of a poll which he says show that 40% of the people in this country believe schools should teach about birth control. Washington Post, May 21, 1965, p. 2, col. 1. I can hardly believe, however, that Brother GOLDBERG would view 46% of the persons polled as so overwhelming a proportion that this Court may now rely on it to declare that the Connecticut law infringed "fundamental" rights, and overrule the long standing view of the people of Connecticut expressed through their elected representatives.

**Griswold v. Connecticut**, 381 U.S. 479 (1965) 7–2
*editor's note:*
*Opinion authors are in bold: () indicates the party of appointing president. If the party of the justice differs from that of appointing president, then the party of the justice is listed second after the slash.*

| MAJORITY | CONCURRING | DISSENTING |
|---|---|---|
| **Douglas** (d) | **Goldberg** (d) | **Black** (d) |
| Clark (d) | Warren (r) | **Stewart** (r) |
| | Brennan (r/d) | |
| | **Harlan** (r) | |
| | **White** (d) | |

# Checks on Supreme Court Decision Making

## *Balancing Liberty, Constitutionalism, and Democracy*

*C*hecks and balances between the three branches of the national government is an integral part of the American system of liberal, constitutional, democracy. Indeed, it was through separation of powers at the national level, and division of power between a national government and state governments, that the framers sought to protect liberty from the excesses of majoritarian, republican democracy. We are accustomed to thinking of the Supreme Court as a "check" that protects liberty, however the other branches' "checks" on the Court may also serve to promote liberty. But, does the system of checks and balances provide any protection for democracy?

While many fear that the Supreme Court's power of judicial review makes it a "super-legislature" of electorally-unaccountable justices overturning the will of the other branches and handing down decisions that cannot be overturned or revised except through the cumbersome constitutional amendment process, in fact, there are a number of checks that the President and Congress have on the judicial branch. Most obviously, the President can check the Court through the appointment power. And, through the Solicitor General, the executive branch can play an influential role in setting the Court's agenda and shaping its decisions. The executive also holds important power over the implementation of Court decisions. Finally, as we saw in the previous chapter's chronicling of FDR's Court-packing Plan, the President, in concert with Congress, can attempt to change the policy direction of the Court by re-structuring, and re-staffing, the federal judiciary within the broad parameters set by Article III. One can certainly argue that the ultimate result of FDR's failed Court-packing Plan

493

was to restore republican democracy by persuading the Court to abandon its attempt to protect the economic rights of the powerful by overturning state and national legislation.

Congress is the most representative branch of the national government and has the closest link to the voters. Indeed, Congress may be seen as the institutional embodiment of our commitment to republican democracy. This chapter focuses on Congress' arsenal of powers to check the Supreme Court, including the Senate's power to withhold confirmation of Presidential nominees to the bench. Congress has various tools with which it can seek to shape the substantive policy results of Supreme Court decisions. And, it has a panoply of procedural tactics it can use to influence the Court's agenda and its decision-making on the merits in actual cases before the Court.

Perhaps Congress's single most powerful check on the Court is its Article Three authority to strip the Court of its jurisdiction to hear a case or category of cases. Congress's most successful use of this power came in *Ex parte McCardle* (1869), which opens this chapter. After the Civil War, Congress engaged in a massive policy of reconstruction in the South, maintaining military rule long after hostilities had ceased. Indeed, under the Reconstruction Act of 1867, Congress set up five military districts in the South and Northern troops were not withdrawn until 1877. McCardle was a Mississippi newspaper editor charged with publishing "incendiary and libelous" articles. The reconstruction troops placed McCardle in custody. Relying on a statute Congress passed in February 1867 which authorized the federal courts to grant habeas corpus to anyone restrained in violation of the Constitution and authorizing appeals to the Supreme Court, McCardle filed a petition for a writ of habeas corpus in federal courts. McCardle argued that since the Civil War had ended, only civil, not military, courts could rightfully try and imprison him. Congress became somewhat nervous when McCardle lost in the lower federal courts, appealed to the Supreme Court, and the Supreme Court announced that it would decide his case. Congress was concerned that the Court would use McCardle's case to declare Reconstruction unconstitutional, a position taken by the recently impeached, but not removed, President Andrew Johnson. To prevent such a Court decision, Congress passed a law in March 1868 withdrawing the Supreme Court's jurisdiction to hear appeals in habeas corpus cases. In the case excerpt that follows, the Court explains why it is bound by the second Congressional statute and cannot rule on the substance of McCardle's claim. Congress successfully checked the Supreme Court's power in this instance.

Of course, Congress has other checks on the Court that fall short of the dramatic withdrawal of jurisdiction which makes the *McCardle* case so important. "Congress and the Court" categorizes and outlines these checks. "Indicting the Courts: Congress's Feud with Judges," tells of the use of such tactics in recent political battles between Congress and the federal courts. Together, the Presidential and Congressional checks on the Court make certain that the Supreme Court rarely veers too far from democratic preferences as it balances them with liberty and constitutionalism. The institutional structure of our national government insures that politics are never far from the minds of the justices and that the Court remains but one voice among three, rather than sitting as a single super-legislature. Politics checks law, just as law checks politics.

# Ex Parte McCardle

## 7 Wall. (74 U.S.) 506 (1869)

. . . Appeal from the Circuit Court for the Southern District of Mississippi. . . .

The CHIEF JUSTICE CHASE delivered the opinion of the court.

The first question necessarily is that of jurisdiction; for, if the act of March, 1868, takes away the jurisdiction defined by the act of February, 1867, it is useless, if not improper, to enter into any discussion of other questions.

It is quite true, as was argued by the counsel for the petitioner, that the appellate jurisdiction of this court is not derived from acts of Congress. It is, strictly speaking, conferred by the Constitution. But it is conferred "with such exceptions and under such regulations as Congress shall make."

It is unnecessary to consider whether, if Congress had made no exceptions and no regulations, this court might not have exercised general appellate jurisdiction under rules prescribed by itself. For among the earliest acts of the first Congress, at its first session, was the act of September 24th, 1789, to establish the judicial courts of the United States. That act provided for the organization of this court, and prescribed regulations for the exercise of its jurisdiction.

The source of that jurisdiction, and the limitations of it by the Constitution and by statute, have been on several occasions subjects of consideration here. In the case of *Durousseau* v. *The United States*, particularly, the whole matter was carefully examined, and the court held, that while "the appellate powers of this court are not given by the judicial act, but are given by the Constitution," they are, nevertheless, "limited and regulated by that act, and by such other acts as have been passed on the subject." The court said, further, that the judicial act was an exercise of the power given by the Constitution to Congress "of making exceptions to the appellate jurisdiction of the Supreme Court." "They have described affirmatively," said the court, "its jurisdiction, and this affirmative description has been understood to imply a negation of the exercise of such appellate power as is not comprehended within it."

The principle that the affirmation of appellate jurisdiction implies the negation of all such jurisdiction not affirmed having been thus established, it was an almost necessary consequence that acts of Congress, providing for the exercise of jurisdiction, should come to be spoken of as acts granting jurisdiction, and not as acts making exceptions to the constitutional grant of it.

The exception to appellate jurisdiction in the case before us, however, is not an inference from the affirmation of other appellate jurisdiction. It is made in terms. The provision of the act of 1867, affirming the appellate jurisdiction of this court in cases of *habeas corpus is* expressly repealed. It is hardly possible to imagine a plainer instance of positive exception.

We are not at liberty to inquire into the motives of the legislature. We can only examine into its power under the Constitution; and the power to make exceptions to the appellate jurisdiction of this court is given by expressed words.

What, then, is the effect of the repealing act upon the case before us? We cannot doubt as to this. Without jurisdiction the court cannot proceed at all in any cause. Jurisdiction is power to declare the law, and when it ceases to exist, the only function remaining to the court is that of announcing the fact and dismissing the cause. And this is not less clear upon authority than upon principle.

Several cases were cited by the counsel for the petitioner in support of the position that jurisdiction of this case is not affected by the repealing act. But none of them, in our judgment, afford any support to it. They are all cases of the exercise of judicial power by the legislature, or of legislative interference with courts in the exercising of continuing jurisdiction.

On the other hand, the general rule, supported by the best elementary writers, is, that "when an act of the legislature is repealed, it must be considered, except as to transactions past and closed, as if it never existed." And the effect of repealing acts upon suits under acts repealed, has been determined by the adjudications of this court. The subject was fully considered in *Norris v. Crocker*, and more recently in *Insurance Company* v. *Ritchie*. In both of these cases it was held that no judgment could be rendered in a suit after the repeal of the act under which it was brought and prosecuted.

It is quite clear, therefore, that this court cannot proceed to pronounce judgment in this case, for it has no longer jurisdiction of the appeal; and judicial duty is not less fitly performed by declining ungranted jurisdiction than in exercising firmly that which the Constitution and the laws confer.

Counsel seem to have supposed, if effect be given to the repealing act in question, that the whole appellate power of the court, in cases of *habeas corpus,* is denied. But this is an error. The act of 1868 does not except from that jurisdiction any cases but appeals from Circuit Courts under the act of 1867. It does not affect the jurisdiction which was previously exercised.

The appeal of the petitioner in this case must be

*DISMISSED FOR WANT OF JURISDICTION.*

---

**Ex parte McCardle,** 7 Wall. (74 U.S.) 506 (1869) 8–0
*editor's note:*
*Opinion authors are in bold.() indicates the party of appointing president. If the party of the justice differs from that of appointing president, then the party of the justice is listed second after the slash.*

| MAJORITY | CONCURRING | DISSENTING |
| --- | --- | --- |
| **Chase** (r) | | |
| Nelson (whig/d) | | |
| Clifford (d) | | |
| Miller (r) | | |
| Grier (d) | | |
| Swayne (r) | | |
| Davis (r) | | |
| Field (r/d) | | |

# CONGRESS AND THE COURT: AGENDA SETTING AND DECISIONS ON THE MERITS: AN OUTLINE

*Susan E. Lawrence*

Congress has at its disposal a number of strategies for checking the Supreme Court. Congress can "check" and/or influence the **substantive policy results** of Supreme Court decisions in a number of ways. Some of them are listed here:

1.  Congress may propose constitutional amendments overturning Supreme Court decisions. Requires a 2/3rds vote in both houses of Congress and ratification by 3/4ths of the states.

    This strategy has only been successful four times: The 11th Amendment; the Civil War Amendments (13th, 14th, and 15th); the 16th Amendment; and the 26th Amendment.

    The two most famous examples of unsuccessful attempts to employ this strategy are (1) an amendment submitted to the states in 1926 which would give Congress the power to prohibit child labor (later Court decision's reinterpreted the commerce clause and granted Congress this power through constitutional reinterpretation of Article One, Sec. 8, para. 3); and (2) the **Equal Rights Amendment** submitted to the states in 1971 which would require the Court to treat sex (gender) as a "suspect class," analogous to race, in its equal protection decisions. Neither of these amendments has been ratified by 3/4ths of the states.

2.  Congress may pass statutes that limit the effect of a Supreme Court decision.

    For example, Congress has passed legislation cutting off Medicaid funding for abortions.

3.  Congress may rewrite statutes that are overturned to avoid the constitutional problem identified by the Court while still seeking the same policy objectives.

    For example, when the Court held that Congress could not prohibit child labor using its commerce clause power (Hammer v. Dagenhart, 1918); Congress then attempted to use its taxing power to prohibit child labor. The Court found this, too, to be an unconstitutional usurpation of power by Congress in *Bailey* v. *Drexel Furniture Co.* (1922).

    > OR, Congress may just chose to 'ignore' the Court's decision, and continue doing whatever it was the Court found to be unconstitutional—at least until it is challenged again in a Court case. For example, Congress seems to have largely ignored the Court's decision in *INS* v. *Chadda* (1983) holding the legislative veto unconstitutional.

4. Congress may rewrite a statute that it believes the Court has "misinterpreted." (Civil Rights Act of 1990, vetoed by Pres.)

5. **If Congress likes the Court's decision:**

   A. If the decision is directed to the federal government, Congress can use the Court's interpretation in its own future deliberations and/or provide funds for implementation of the decision.

   B. If the decision is directed at state and/or local governments, Congress can create financial incentives for compliance. For example, local compliance with *Brown* v. *Bd. of Education* (1954) increased dramatically once Congress made compliance with the decision a condition of receipt of federal education funds in the early 1960s.

In addition, there are a number of **procedural tactics** Congress can employ to influence the Supreme Court's agenda and decisions on the merits.

Here is a list of the ways that are discussed more fully below:

   I.   appointment
   II.  funding
   III. rules and procedures
   IV.  jurisdiction and statutory claims

I. We have already discussed the Senate's role in the judicial **appointment process.** The hearings can also be used to send the nominees, the President, and the current Court a message about Congress's views on the policy trends of the Court.

II. The federal judiciary is dependent on Congress for **funding:**
   Two themes : (a) procedurally—how do the courts get their money?
   and (b) how can Congress use this process to "control" the courts?

Procedurally:—the court funding process provides a very good example of the kinds of subtle interactions that go on between the federal courts and Congress—between our "legal" institutions and our "political" institutions.

In 1939, the federal courts became responsible for drawing up and presenting their own budget requests to Congress (they had previously been done by the executive branch)—Now, unlike any other government agency, the OMB is prohibited, by statute, from changing any of the budgetary requests submitted by the judiciary. Courts' budget covers things like overhead—building maintenance, heat, electricity etc., printing and photocopying, support staff—secretaries, law clerks, security staff, court reporters, jurors, etc., federal public defenders costs, basic operating costs.

These days, the federal courts' budget is less than one-tenth of one percent of the entire federal budget.

As you know, the federal budget process is a very political process. The courts are, strategically, in a bad position to try to get funding from Congress.

The prime motivation of Congressmen is reelection—the courts cannot provide Congressmen with any rewards or punishments related to reelection.

Often in recent decades, Congressmen have found it useful to campaign *against* the courts and their decisions—not to be able to point out to voters that they increased funding for the courts. (Even the anti-drug rhetoric, calls for law and order, etc. mostly relate to state, rather than federal courts; and the courts are often accused of being part of the problem, rather than part of a solution).

It is difficult for the judiciary to command the attention of the budget writers because the courts' budget is so small. Consequently, the judiciary has developed tactics to maximize credibility and support from appropriate committee members.

The budget is written and presented by the JUDICIAL CONFERENCE OF THE U.S., which is part of the Administrative Office of the Courts. The Judicial Conference consists of the U.S. Supreme Court Chief Justice (Chair); the Chief Judge of each circuit; and an elected district court judge from each circuit.

Lobbying Congress for the budget is done by a BUDGET COMMITTEE of the Judicial Conference. Members of this committee are selected by the Chief Justice and he tends to appoint judges from states or districts with Senators or Representatives on the appropriations committee. He tends to appoint judges that have experience in congressional or state legislative politics. The Chairmen of the budget committee have been judges with important Congressional connections. These strategies maximize the judiciary's influence with Congress, absent any ability "to play the re-election card."

The judiciary has also developed a reputation with Congress for sound fiscal management and of not over-estimating how much money it needs. The budget committee can point to the fact that over 40% of the judiciary's budget is uncontrollable—i.e., defense services for indigents; grand jurors; petit jurors; and judicial salaries, etc. And, a portion of the budget is tied to implementation of legislation already passed by Congress such as the Speedy Trial Act and other legislation that mandates certain pretrial services.

By and large, the judiciary has been very successful. During the period from 1969–85, the federal judiciary received a 16 percent increase per year—reflecting inflation and increases in the number of federal judicial positions created by Congress. FINAL APPROPRIATIONS TO THE FEDERAL COURTS AVERAGED 96% OF THEIR ORIGINAL REQUEST. This is any extremely high funding rate compared to other federal agencies.

**BUT**, sometimes, the federal courts' budget requests become embroiled in political controversy having nothing to do with actual budget concerns. Members of Congress use the budget process as a forum for **symbolic punitive actions** designed to send a message to their constituents and to the courts.

Examples: (from Johnson & Cannon, p. 148)

1980: Congress refused to appropriate money for an automobile to take Supreme Court justices to and from work or on other official business. Every other federal court judge was provided with such a car. One of the Southern Senators said in response to the Justices' request for such cars: "Couldn't we get a bus to bus the judges? I learned about busing from reading the *Swann* case." *Swann* v. *Charlotte-Mecklenburg Bd. of Ed.* (1970) is a Burger Court decision allowing court-ordered busing to achieve integration.

1964 pay raises: Congress raised the salaries of all federal judges except those on the Supreme Court by $7,000. Supreme Court Justices only received a $4500 raise (a $2500 difference). In debating the pay raises, several Congressmen made it clear that they were expressing dissatisfaction with the Supreme Court's decisions. Then Republican Representative Bob Dole (Kansas) said: "Whenever thinking of the Supreme Court I think of last June 15, 1964, and reapportionment decisions handed down in *Reynolds against Sims* [sic] and the related cases. It has been suggested that perhaps Section 2 of the Bill might be amended whereby the effective date of the pay increase if adopted by this House, would be the date the Supreme Court reverses the decision in *Reynolds against Sims* [sic]." In *Reynolds* the Court held that states must make a good faith effort to construct state legislative districts, in both houses of their legislatures, as nearly of equal population as is practicable.

## III. Attempts to change the Courts' **Rules and/or Procedures**

Article III only provides the barest outline of the federal courts, leaving much to Congress to work out through legislation.

> From the Constitution:
>
> > Article Three: "The judicial power of the United States, shall be vested in one Supreme Court, and in such inferior courts as the Congress may from time to time ordain and establish."
> >
> > Article Three: Congress sets salaries ". . . which shall not be diminished during their [the judges] Continuance in Office."
> >
> > Article Three: U.S. Supreme Court is given original jurisdiction in cases affecting ambassadors etc. and in which a state shall be a party. "in all other Cases . . . the Supreme Court shall have appellate Jurisdiction . . . with such exceptions, and under such Regulations as the Congress shall make."

And, then, of course, there is always the amendment process, which can be used to make structural changes as well as substantive policy changes. Indeed, in our history, the amendment process has been used much more frequently for the former than the later.

Congress can exercise these seemingly administrative, merely structural and organizational, powers for POLITICAL reasons—to pursue political goals. What may seem merely "legal," is, at times, motivated by "politics."

A. *Proposed constitutional amendments relating to the structure and power of the judicial branch:*

In the early 20th century, the Progressives were angered by the Court's negation of laws regulating labor practices. In the 1950s, there were strong negative reactions to the Warren Court's liberal rulings in the internal security (communist/freedom of speech) cases and in the criminal justice area. Both the Progressives and the opponents of the Warren Court's decisions proposed numerous constitutional amendments relating to the structure and power of the judicial branch. These proposals were motivated by substantive political conflicts rather than by abstract notions of the proper limits on judicial power and/or efficiency concerns. Some of these proposed amendments have again been surfaced by opponents of the Court's decisions on school prayer, reproductive choice, and race-related policies such as desegregation and affirmative action.

Proposed amendments:

1. require 2/3rds vote of Supreme Court justices (6 out of 9) to declare a federal law unconstitutional.

2. allow Congress to "override" a Supreme Court "veto"—holding of a law as unconstitutional—by a 2/3rds vote.

B. *Proposals to change the number of justices* (remember that the number of justices that sit on the Supreme Court is **not** specified in the Constitution.)

During the 19th century, Congress increased (and decreased when vacancies occurred) the number of justices several times for "policy reasons." SINCE 1869, THE NUMBER OF JUSTICES HAS REMAINED AT NINE.

Since 1869, there has been only one significant attempt to change the number *of* justices—and it was a very significant attempt. In 1937, President Franklin Delanor Roosevelt proposed what is commonly called **THE COURT-PACKING PLAN.** He sent a proposal to Congress that would have allowed the President to appoint a new/additional justice for each sitting justice over the age of 70. Had this proposal passed in Congress, FDR would have been able to make 6 new appointments to the Supreme Court. Roosevelt argued that this plan was merely an effort to improve the efficiency of the Supreme Court, and to make this argument more plausible he also included some provisions relating to the workload of the lower federal courts. *However,* it was commonly known that FDR was strongly opposed to many of the Court's decisions which he attributed to "the four horsemen"—four very old justices who seemed intent on interpreting the Constitution in a way that seemed quite out-dated and old-fashion to FDR. In particular, FDR was concerned that the Court kept striking down federal legislation that FDR had designed to bring the country out of the severe economic depression it experienced after the 1929 stock-market crash. The Court seemed to have a very narrow view of the scope of the national government's constitutional powers under Article One. For a variety of reasons, FDR's **COURT-PACKING PROPOSAL** failed to pass in Congress. *But,* at the same time, *the Supreme Court did change the policy direction of its decisions, switching from generally striking down state and national government power in the economic realm, to generally upholding state and national government legislation regulating economic enterprises.* While correlation does not always indicate causation, it seems that the Court "read the writing on the wall," and backed down in the face of a very real threat to its independence. This is referred to as ***the switch in time that saved nine.***[1]

*Query:* What interactions between "law" and "politics" are revealed by this episode in the Court's history?

C. *Proposals to change the criteria for selecting Justices:* Proposals have been offered to require 5 or 10 years of prior judicial service before someone could be appointed to the Supreme Court. This has been seen as a way to prevent the appointment of liberal, or activist, justices such as Wrn. Douglas, Hugo Black, and Earl Warren, none of whom had any significant prior judicial service. The weakness in this proposal is that prior judicial service does not seem to be a reliable predictor of ideology or judicial role orientation. For example, Wm. Brennan and Thurgood Marshall had five or more years of prior judicial experience AND their voting records are as liberal and/or activist as Douglas', Black's, and Warren's. Neither Rehnquist nor Bork had five years of prior judicial service at the time of their nominations, yet both were seen as conservative, and Rehnquist's voting record indicates a commitment to judicial restraint.

IV. **Changes in Jurisdiction**—closely related to changes in rules and procedures.

Congress controls the Supreme Court's appellate jurisdiction.

Article Three says that the Supreme Court shall have original jurisdiction in cases affecting ambassadors etc. and in which a state shall be a party. "In all other Cases . . . the Supreme Court shall have appellate Jurisdiction . . . with such exceptions, and under such Regulations as the Congress shall make."

## A. *Politically-motivated Reform*

Most famous, and successful, example of Congress's use of its power to control the Supreme Court's jurisdiction for political purposes occurred in relation to *Ex parte McCardle* (1869).

Civil War = 1861–65; Reconstruction = 1865–77; Reconstruction Act of 1867, set up 5 military districts in the South—Northern troops were not withdrawn until 1877.

McCardle was a Mississippi newspaper editor held in military custody. He had been charged with publishing "incendiary and libelous articles."

> Congress passed a statute in Feb. 1967 which authorized the federal courts to grant habeas corpus to anyone restrained "in violation of the Constitution" and authorized appeals to the Supreme Court.
>
>> Habeas corpus is used to release people from unlawful imprisonment. When you file for a writ of habeas corpus you get a hearing before a judge to see if you had "due process" before being deprived of your liberty or to see if the law under which you were imprisoned is constitutional.

McCardle filed a petition for a writ of habeas corpus in federal courts arguing that since the war had ended, only civil, not military courts, could try and imprison him. He lost in the lower courts and appealed to the Supreme Court.

Congress took note of this and it was scared that the Supreme Court would use McCardle's case to declare reconstruction and the military courts unconstitutional. So in March 1868, after the Court had announced that it would decide McCardle's case, Congress passed a law withdrawing (revoking) the Supreme Court's jurisdiction to hear appeals in habeas corpus cases.

The Court knew exactly why Congress had done that, but the Court read Article Three which said that Congress could regulate the Supreme Court's appellate jurisdiction and the Court read the March 1868 statute and found that Congress had plainly repealed its jurisdiction to hear McCardle's case—and the Court dismissed McCardle's case for "want of jurisdiction." The Supreme Court held that it had no power to hear McCardle's case.

The Court said:

> "We are not at liberty to inquire into the motives of the legislature. We can only examine into its power under the Constitution, and the power to make exceptions to the appellate jurisdiction of this court is given by express words." [in Article 3 of the Constitution]

So, Congress successfully prevented a judicial ruling on the constitutionality of its reconstruction policies.

In the 1950s and 1960s, as the Court's decisions began to take a liberal turn, opponents of the Warren Court's rulings often suggested limiting the Court's jurisdiction so as to prevent the Court from making decisions in areas where the opponents disagreed with the Court's policy trends.

> federal employees' security program
> state subversive legislation
> state bar admissions
> state criminal convictions based on voluntary confessions
> reapportionment
> school prayer
> busing
> abortion

All of these proposals were defeated.

In April 1979, Senator Helms introduced a statutory amendment which would have removed all federal court jurisdiction over suits challenging state-sanctioned voluntary school prayers (limiting the jurisdiction of both the lower federal courts and the U.S. Supreme Court). The Carter Administration lobbied against it and the Senate killed it. There have been numerous other attempts to limit the federal court's jurisdiction in busing and abortion cases.

Since *McCardle*, there have been other attempts to limit the Court's jurisdiction for political reasons; but none of them have been successful.

> Nonetheless, Congressional power to alter the federal courts' jurisdiction remains a way the political branches can check the courts. Congressional proposals to limit the courts' jurisdiction can be used to send a message that the Court is "skating on thin ice"—presumably, the threat keeps the Court from "going off the deep end."

B.  Non-politically Motivated Reform

Congress can expand what the Court will hear by passing statutes that create new legal claims—Civil Rights laws, environment laws, etc. Often, Congress will write into the legislation, who has a right to sue if the law is violated. Congress often gives individuals the right to sue instead of setting up a government enforcement agency.

**Judiciary Act of 1925**—gave the Supreme Court *discretionary jurisdiction* so that the Court could pick and choose what cases appealed to it would get a full review. This was a response to a real workload problem; in the early 1920s, the Supreme Court was facing a 4 or 5 year backlog of cases. The Judiciary Act of 1925 created the Supreme Court's **certiorari jurisdiction.** It gave the Justices more of a role in setting their own agenda. This trend was continued in 1988 when Congress passed legislation eliminating 3 of the 4 categories of *mandatory* **appeal jurisdiction** that the Judiciary Act of 1925 had left in place. The cases that fit these 3 abolished categories now come to the Court as petitions for writs of certiorari and there is no presumption that the Court has to accept them for review. The one remaining category consists of cases brought under Congressional statutes that specifically designate that trials will be conducted by three-judge district courts with a right of direct appeal to the Supreme Court, such as the 1964 Civil Rights Act, the 1965 Voting Rights Act, the 1974 Presidential Election Campaign Fund Act, and certain reapportionment statutes.

Today, the Supreme Court's jurisdiction is virtually all discretionary, so to understand agenda-setting in the Court, we need to examine the Court's case selection process.

## Notes

1.  This is a play on Ben Franklin's aphorism that "a stitch in time saves nine," meaning that if one mends one's garments as soon as they begin to ravel, one will save a great deal of work mending a much larger tear later. Obviously, this aphorism resonated better before J.Crew and the Gap figured out that they could make a fortune by selling clothes that are already half worn out. In the age of grunge, Franklin's witticism, and the play on it, seem anachronistic.

## INDICTING THE COURTS: CONGRESS' FEUD WITH JUDGES

### Dan Carney

The question is not altogether academic. Simpson says he has seen many would-be judges of today turned into "gargoyles" by a process that has gotten out of hand. One can almost imagine the press releases from whatever faction that would want to end his chances: "Al Simpson Coddles Criminals, Defends Weirdos!"

Simpson, who served from 1979–97, is one in a host of former lawmakers, judges and academics who are alarmed by what they see as an increasing hostility on the part of Congress toward the federal judiciary. Fierce attacks on judicial nominees, they argue, are but one front in an extraordinary, escalating war of wills between the legislative and judicial branches of government. This war is being driven in considerable part by politics and mistrust. But it shows more fundamental differences as well, over such matters as the proper balance in a democracy between the rule of law and the rule of popular sentiment, and the proper role and scope of government in general.

Three broad areas of confrontation are at the center of this conflict:

Republished with permission of *CQ Weekly*, by Dan Carney, June 20, 1998. Copyright © 1998. Permission conveyed through the Copyright Clearance Center, Inc.

## CONFIRMATIONS

The Senate has turned the process of confirming federal judges into a political side-show for the two parties to curry favor with their hard-core supporters. In some cases, this has meant distorting the nominees' records. In others, it has meant quietly holding up whole blocks of nominees for months or years at a time. Many Republicans trace this trend to the villainization of Robert H. Bork by Senate Democrats, when they defeated his Supreme Court nomination in 1987. Most Democrats argue that the atmosphere is much worse now that the tables have turned. There are 73 vacancies on the 845-member federal bench. The number passed 100 last year. It is not uncommon for nominees to wait two or three years for confirmation. *(Bork, 1987 Almanac, p. 271)*

## ATTACKS ON SITTING JUDGES

A number of judges, ranging from District Judge Harold Baer Jr. of New York to District Judge Thelton E. Henderson of California, have come under virulent criticism from members of Congress. House Majority Whip Tom DeLay, R-Texas, has called for widespread impeachments, and individual members have launched rhetorical broad-sides: "There is no doubt in my mind that there is a special place in hell for a number of federal court judges . . ." Rep. Jack Kingston, R-Ga., declared in a May 4 floor speech on school prayer.

## JURISDICTION

In the past several years, Congress has passed bills to prevent federal judges from hearing cases that could undermine policies advocated by conservative lawmakers. Specifically, they have prevented judges from hearing cases involving prison conditions or appeals from immigrants about to be deported. At the same time, it has forced the courts to participate in a cause very popular in Congress—prosecuting crime at the federal level. This intrusion into an area previously left to state courts has loaded the federal dockets, crowding out other important cases.

The courts' harshest critics argue they are merely preventing the worst judicial abuses. Simpson and his compatriots say such attacks on the judiciary threaten its very independence and ultimately could upset the system of checks and balances envisioned by the Founding Fathers.

"The erosion of the independence of the judiciary is not something absolutely dramatic," said Sheldon Goldman, a political scientist at the University of Massachusetts. "It's an incremental thing. It's a cancer on the American constitutional framework. Someday we may wake up to find a very different United States."

## A LONG TRADITION

Attacking the judiciary is an old tradition in American politics. The biggest actual threats to the courts came in the early years of the republic, the Civil War era, and during Franklin D. Roosevelt's New Deal, when he demanded the chance to pick six additional Supreme Court justices.

Sharp verbal criticism of the federal judiciary has been particularly popular among presidents and members of Congress with a populist bent. The notion of an unelected group of powerful jurists serving for life, and accountable to virtually no one, has been an irresistible target for politicians ranging from President Andrew Jackson to Wisconsin Sen. Robert M. LaFollette Jr. (1925–47), leader of the Progressive movement in the 1920s. A few Supreme Court rulings—most notably the landmark 1954 desegregation case *Brown* v. *Board of Education*—have produced an avalanche of hostility to the federal courts.

Today's generation of court critics is led by DeLay in the House and John Ashcroft, R-Mo., in the Senate. While the Democrats held up some Republican judges and passed legislation unpopular with the third branch, most legal scholars agree that the relationship between Congress and the courts has deteriorated since the GOP took control in 1995.

Many Republicans see some sitting judges as arrogant, unresponsive to the public and prone to "activist" rulings that overstep their constitutional role of applying, rather than creating the law.

"There is an activist judge behind each of most of the perverse failures of today's justice system," DeLay said in a floor speech April 23. "When judges legislate, they usurp the power of Congress. When judges stray beyond the Constitution, they usurp the power of the people."

One of the most often-cited examples is Missouri District Court Judge Russell Clark, who forced $1.8 billion in tax increases in Kansas City to fund court-ordered improvements to inner-city schools. (*Judges*, p. 1664)

Also cited are several judges who have struck down public referendums that won popular majorities, such as a California vote to limit affirmative action (Proposition 209) and a 1992 Colorado proposition to limit civil rights protections for homosexuals. Judges who are considered soft on crime are highly unpopular with conservatives, as are those who impose a rigid church-state separation.

Much of the criticism of the courts centers on their interpretation of the Constitution. For instance, when Rep. Ernest Istook, R-Okla., is asked why Republicans are so quick to propose amendments to the Constitution, he responds that the courts do it all the time. Istook, sponsor of a proposal (H J Res 78) that would expand rights of religious expression, argues that the Supreme Court has perverted the First Amendment through a series of church-state rulings in the past three decades.

DeLay argues that such rulings indicate the judicial branch has exceeded its authority. "The system of checks and balances so carefully crafted is in serious disrepair and has been for years," he said.

Others criticize the expansive role of government advocated by some judges. Judge Clark's rulings in Kansas City have been attacked not just for their activism but for their liberalism. The notion of transferring almost $2 billion to inner-city schools strikes many conservatives as an exercise in social engineering reminiscent of President Lyndon B. Johnson's Great Society or of the New Deal.

In essence, many Republicans see themselves using pressure on the courts to undo what Roosevelt may have done in part through pressure in his day. Even though Roosevelt's bid to "pack" the Supreme Court failed because Congress would not allow it, it apparently had an impact.

For reasons that are still being debated by legal scholars, the Supreme Court began a shift to the left not long after the episode in 1937. Initially, this appeared to be driven by a switch in positions by sitting members, though by 1941, the trend had been accelerated by a string of seven Roosevelt appointments in just four years.

This shift represented the beginning of a major expansion of the federal government's size and function. Subsequent courts championed integration, and later busing; created a limited constitutional right to abortion; took officially sanctioned prayer out of schools; and made other rulings opposed by conservatives.

Today's criticisms of the federal judiciary are not merely an inside-the-Beltway spat between two branches. They have broad resonance among religious conservatives, libertarians and populists.

Sitting judges are a regular target of conservative talk radio shows. Blocking pending nominees is also a popular topic. President Clinton has already appointed almost a third of the federal bench, and he will get more opportunities as judges retire.

Supporters of a more independent judiciary argue the judiciary is being dragged into a fight between the two other branches. Furthermore, they argue, it is Congress, not the courts, that is jeopardizing the balance of power envisioned by the Constitution.

## OUT OF BALANCE

The judicial branch "is beyond comparison the weakest of the three departments of power," Alexander Hamilton wrote in Federalist Paper Number 78. ". . . It can never attack with success the other two; and all possible care is requisite to enable it to defend itself against their attacks."

That the judiciary is the weakest branch is evident in Article III of the Constitution, which makes its very existence subject to the good will of the two other branches. The Senate could strangle it by refusing to confirm judges. The president could do the same by not nominating any. Congress could refuse to fund it, or even abolish all but the Supreme Court, which is created by the Constitution.

Last year, DeLay proposed widespread impeachments, naming three district court judges he thought were ready to be taken on immediately: Henderson, who blocked California's referendum limiting affirmative action; Baer, who dismissed key evidence in a drug case; and Fred Biery, in Texas, who refused to seat a Republican sheriff and county commissioner because of controversy over absentee ballots.

In Tennessee, the ouster of District Court Judge John T. Nixon has become a crusade of victims' rights advocates. His decisions blocking executions has enraged them to the point of bringing a judicial misconduct suit and persuading the state legislature to pass a resolution asking Congress to impeach him.

Baer's case may be the most illustrative because of the 1996 presidential campaign and its aftermath. GOP candidate Bob Dole made Baer, and his evidentiary ruling, the centerpiece of his criticism of Clinton appointees. Not wanting to be outflanked, Clinton joined the criticisms.

Under attack from both sides, Baer reversed his decision. Regardless of the merits of his original ruling, and his switch, champions of an independent judiciary are horrified by the possibility that a judge changed his opinion under political pressure.

"After taking a battering in the press for some days, he reviewed his decision and altered it," said former New York Democratic Gov. Mario M. Cuomo. "He altered it into a form that was acceptable to the people who were criticizing him. . . . And no one but God knows exactly why he did that."

Cuomo has joined with Simpson and a number of other former lawmakers and legal experts to form a group called "Citizens for Independent Courts." The group will argue that granting the courts considerable autonomy is in the nation's best interest.

The judiciary is designed to be the only branch of government that does not respond to political pressure. The Constitution gives judges lifetime tenure so they can make rulings based solely on the law, as informed by their legal education and experience. If parties in lawsuits believe that rulings are made on the basis of polls, popular sentiment or political pressure, it undermines judges' authority, said William S. Sessions, a former district judge and FBI director from 1987-93.

"Having judges rule on the basis of law is a tremendous advantage to society," Sessions said.

Another function of a strong and independent judiciary is to check the excesses of the other two branches. When Roosevelt attempted his court-packing scheme, he was, in essence, trying to take over all three branches of government. Thanks to huge Democratic majorities in both houses of Congress after the 1936 election, he had control of two but mused over a recalcitrant court that blocked many of his early legislative proposals. He looked at the three branches not as autonomous entities striving to check each other, but as a team of horses that should function together, with the president as driver.

"Two of the three horses are pulling in unison," he said in a radio address advocating his plan. "A third is not."

The courts routinely rule on congressional and presidential powers and prerogatives. The Supreme Court has recently struck down a number of public laws on the grounds that they represented an overstepping of congressional authority. A unanimous court in 1974 forced President Richard M. Nixon to release his White House tape recordings, precipitating the end of his presidency. And Judge Norma Holloway Johnson has ruled against President Clinton, who sought to shield his aides from having to testify in the ongoing investigation by Independent Counsel Kenneth W. Starr. *(Starr, p. 1686)*

Defenders of the courts say the judiciary needs its independence to serve as a counterweight to the other branches. Attacking it, they say, could come back to haunt conservatives.

"A true conservative would want to maintain the independence of the judiciary, because it is the last best break on a runaway executive," said Sen. Patrick J. Leahy, D-Vt.

## A NEW LEVEL

After being virtually shut down in 1996 and 1997, the pace of confirmations has picked up this year, partly because of some pointed complaints from Chief Justice William H. Rehnquist (who even took the unusual step of attending a Democrats-only luncheon in the Senate). Also Senate Judiciary Committee Chairman Orrin G. Hatch, R-Utah, has been willing to stand up to pressure from other committee members who want to block the nominees.

Certain courts have been hit harder than others by this slowdown. The San Francisco-based 9th Circuit Court of Appeals, which has a reputation for liberalism and a knack for being reversed by the Supreme Court, had 10 open slots out of 28 at the end of last year. This shortfall of judges has meant lengthy delays in trials, and considerable haste when they do come up, said Chief Judge Proctor Hug Jr. Struggling to keep up with his caseload, he has had to bring some judges out of semi-retirement and import others from other regions.

"We have made superhuman efforts," said Hug. "I have pleaded with our judges to take more than they otherwise would. I've noticed there is a real burnout level in the judges. There's a feeling we just need more time with these cases."

A debate rages over whether these types of holdups are merely Republicans retaliating for the Bork affair, or whether they are so widespread that they represent an entirely new level of partisan judicial politics.

Democrats tended to go after high court judges such as Bork and a select few lower court judges. Their strategy was to publicly attack them to build enough votes to defeat the nominations.

"Before my eyes, they turned [Bork] into a gargoyle—a sexist, racist, invader of the bedroom, violator of women," said Simpson. "That was repugnant to me."

Republican senators who were elected in 1994 have not had a crack at a Clinton nominee to the Supreme Court yet. But in lower court positions, their main strategy in the past three years has been to hold up scores of nominees, preventing them from even coming up for floor vote. Groups such as the Judicial Selection Monitoring Project, a division of the conservative Free Congress Research and Education Foundation, have mounted a full court press against Clinton nominees. *(Groups, p. 1663)*

"We want to make sure that the Senate does not underestimate how strongly the American people feel about standing up to judicial activism," said project director Thomas L. Jipping.

The Senate has responded to this pressure not so much by defeating nominees as delaying them. If and when nominations do reach the floor and are openly debated, they usually pass with relative ease. For instance, Margaret M. Morrow, a corporate lawyer from Los Angeles, saw her nomination to a district court judgeship held up for nearly two years amid intense criticism that she was an activist in waiting. When she finally got a vote Feb. 11, she was approved 67–28.

"You have extremely good people who are held in limbo for year after year," said Leahy. "If you are a woman or a minority, you are held longer. It may be coincidental but it's what happens. It's demeaning to the court, and it's demeaning to the Senate."

# ISSUES OF JURISDICTION

Starting when the Democrats controlled Capitol Hill, but picking up considerably under Republican rule, Congress has been keen to tell the courts what they can and cannot rule on.

The 1996 immigration bill (PL 104–208), for instance, contains a section saying certain deportation orders issued by the Justice Department are "not reviewable in a court of law." A similar provision, included in a portion of the 1996 omnibus spending bill, was designed to limit prison inmates' ability to file grievance cases in federal courts (PL 103–134). Another measure (PL 104–132) would significantly limit the ability of prisoners to use habeas corpus appeals to federal judges to question the constitutionality of their convictions. These appeals are often used by death row inmates to have their executions delayed or blocked entirely. (*Immigration, 1996 Almanac,* p. 5–3; *prison litigation,* p. 10–5; *anti-terrorism death penalty,* p. 5–18)

Not surprisingly, these types of limitations enrage civil rights groups, which say Congress is imposing its ideology on the courts by preventing them from ruling on certain issues.

"When Congress selectively removes particular issues, then it is in effect prescribing the outcome," said Nadine Strossen, national president of the American Civil Liberties Union.

Limiting the jurisdiction of federal judges was the purpose behind a bill (HR 1252) the House passed April 23. In its original form it would have prevented any judge from issuing an order that forced a local jurisdiction to raise taxes. It also would have allowed civil litigants to reject the first judge assigned to them. (*CQ Weekly,* p. 1074)

Although these two provisions were dropped, the measure still included jurisdictional limits and an overall tone expressing a lack of confidence in the courts. It would strengthen provisions in earlier laws limiting federal court involvement with prison crowding issues. And it would further limit habeas corpus appeals.

The bill would also attempt to protect public referendums from judges such as Henderson by stipulating that they could be struck down only by a three-judge panel. The measure would take a swipe at the judiciary's ability to police itself by requiring that judicial misconduct cases be automatically transferred to another part of the country. (The provision arose from the Nixon case in Tennessee, after judges there quickly dismissed a misconduct case against him.)

At the same time that Congress has limited federal court involvement in liberal causes, it has greatly increased its role in dealing with crime. As Congress has passed numerous bills creating new federal offenses, it has not only increased the workload for the Justice Department and the FBI but also for the federal courts that must now hear all these cases. Since criminal defendants have a constitutional right to a speedy trial, this onslaught of cases means important civil cases are often put on the back burner or not heard, because the litigants do not think it worth the wait.

This trend has not only come under attack from liberal groups, which see it as more evidence that Congress is attempting to legislate judicial output by dictating input. It has also been sternly criticized by Rehnquist.

In a May 11 speech, the chief justice complained bitterly about expanded federal authority in pending juvenile crime legislation (HR 3 S 10). Rather than focus the burden on the courts (which he has cited before), Rehnquist spoke in terms designed to capture the attention of congressional Republicans. He said the juvenile crime bills are hardly conservative, because they involve a vast expansion of the federal government's role in crime fighting. Indeed, he said, they represent a fundamental violation of federalist principles developed by some of the party's brightest lights—namely Abraham Lincoln and Dwight D. Eisenhower.

He suggested Congress was unwittingly erecting a government not unlike the highly centralized system in France.

"How much of the complex system of legal relationships in this country should be decided in Washington, and how much by state and local governments?" he asked. "Do we really want to move forward into the 21st century with the prospect that our system will look more and more like the French government?"

## A 'THREE BOWLER' ISSUE

Criticizing judges and nominees is fairly easy. And passing bills limiting their jurisdiction wins plaudits from conservative groups. In contrast, advocates of a more independent judiciary, such as Cuomo and Simpson, find themselves dealing with a very dry and complicated issue when they start talking.

Charles Geyh, a professor at Case Western Reserve University in Cleveland and a consultant to the American Judicature Society, an organization of legal professionals, calls it a "three bowler" issue. This means that even if he can get a newspaper writer to tackle the issue, it usually results in little more than a series of sleep-induced splashes.

"Your face falls into the cereal bowl three times before getting through the article," he said.

Be that as it may, defenders of an independent judiciary say it is vital that the issue be raised. Judges do not feel it appropriate to publicly defend themselves, their rulings or the institution they represent. Rehnquist's comments are considered by many to be extraordinary, even though they are couched in measured and legalistic terms.

Because judges usually steer clear of political debate, it is vital that someone speak up on behalf of the judiciary, said Sessions.

"We should be very concerned about this," he said. "It is very easy in this day and time to destroy a perfectly valid judge. Similarly, it is possible to attack the judiciary broadly and take away respect for the rule of law."

*Susan Benkelman*

# The Right to Privacy: Law and/or Politics?

$\mathcal{T}$he Court's privacy decisions have been among its most controversial decisions in recent decades. Apart from the widespread dispute over the substantive policy contained in decisions such as *Roe* v. *Wade* (1973), commentators have raised a number of questions about the nature of constitutional interpretation in these cases given that the Constitution and Bill of Rights do not explicitly acknowledge a "right to privacy." Some accuse the Court of legislating from the bench, making up limits on government power that reflect the justices' own policy preferences. Others reject such a narrow construction and argue that a "right to privacy" can be found in the Fifth and Fourteenth Amendment's due process clause guarantee of liberty, in the Ninth Amendment, or in the general intent or spirit of the Bill of Rights and a government of limited powers. Some see the right to privacy decisions as nothing more than politics from the bench; others see the right to privacy decisions as a triumph of the rule of law and as constitutionalism at the service of liberty. These conflicting views on the Court's work in the right to privacy decisions have played predominate roles in confirmation hearings, judicial decisions, constitutional commentary, and American electoral politics over the last several decades. They reveal the fundamental disputes that characterize the modern debate over the proper role of the Court in the American system of liberal, constitutional, democracy.

Right to privacy doctrine in the area of reproductive rights received its first major explication in *Griswold* v. *Connecticut* (1965), the concluding case in Chapter Nine's examination of the Court's attempt to define "liberty" as an example of "incorporation plus." Relying on the Bill of Rights and its "penumbra," the Court struck down an 1879 state law prohibiting the use of contraceptives by married persons in *Griswold*. Seven years later, in *Eisenstadt* v. *Baird* (1972), the Court extended its ruling, holding that under the equal protection clause, states could not prohibit the use of contraceptives by unmarried persons either.

After years of avoiding the issue through certiorari denials, the Court considered the constitutionality of state statutes prohibiting abortion in *Roe* v. *Wade* (1973). In the excerpt provided in this chapter, much of Justice Blackmun's recounting of the history of abortion regulation is included, along with his discussion of a right to privacy as a part of the concept embodied in the word "liberty" in the Fourteenth Amendment due process clause. Justice Blackmun writes:

> "This right of privacy, whether it be found in the Fourteenth Amendment's concept of personal liberty and restrictions on state action, as we feel it is, or, as the District Court determined, in the Ninth Amendment's reservation of rights to the people, is broad enough to encompass a woman's decision whether or not to terminate her pregnancy."

Over the last three decades *Roe* has generated a great deal of political controversy and the Court has been faced with a long series of follow-up cases testing the constitutionality of parental consent polices, restrictions on Medicaid funding of abortions, fetal protection policies, and various other statutory requirements placed on doctors and women seeking abortions.

In *Planned Parenthood* v. *Casey* (1992), five members of the Court voted to uphold the central holding of *Roe* v. *Wade* (1973) despite repeated challenges; but, the co-authored majority opinion announced a new "undue burden" test for determining the constitutionality of restrictive abortion legislation. The precise meaning of this test is unclear, insuring that this issue will continue to unfold on the Court's docket. For students of law and politics, one of the fascinating things about the *Casey* opinion is the degree to which the justices self-consciously and openly discuss the competing claims of legal reasoning norms [e.g. precedent and stare decision], intensely divisive political controversy, maintenance of the Court's legitimacy within the political system, and implicit differences in judicial policy preferences. Clearly, the justices know that Supreme Court decision-making inevitably and inescapably mixes law and politics.

The majority opinion co-authored by Justices O'Connor, Kennedy, and Souter firmly places the *Casey* decision in the context of the Court's long struggle over the scope of the limits on state action enforceable under the due process clause guarantee of liberty in the Fourteenth Amendment. The legal and political history they recount should sound quite familiar in light of the materials presented in Chapter Nine of this volume.

Indeed, the *Casey* decision provides an unusually good review of the themes of this volume and, despite its length—or perhaps because of its length—it should make clear how much as been learned through exploration of the materials in the previous chapters.

This chapter ends with *Washington* v. *Glucksberg* (1997) in which the Court considers the right to privacy, not in the area of reproductive rights, but in the context of physician-assisted suicide. *Glucksberg* serves to remind us that the right to privacy involves issues that reach far beyond reproductive rights and far beyond questions of sexuality. Fundamentally, the right to privacy debate is about the parameters of liberty and the Court's role in protecting that liberty in our liberal, constitutional, democracy. These cases, along with those in Chapter Nine, reveal the enormous complexity of defining the word "liberty" and thereby defining the boundary between the arenas of individual sovereignty and government power; and, the tremendous challenge posed by the necessity of balancing our, at times, competing commitments to liberty, constitutionalism, and democracy.

# Roe et al. v. Wade, District Attorney of Dallas County

## 410 U.S. 113

## Appeal from the United States District Court for the Northern District of Texas

### No. 70–18. Argued December 13, 1971—Reargued October 11, 1972—Decided January 22, 1973

A pregnant single woman (*Roe*) brought a class action challenging the constitutionality of the Texas criminal abortion laws, which proscribe procuring or attempting an abortion except on medical advice for the purpose of saving the mother's life. A licensed physician (Hallford), who had two state abortion prosecutions pending against him, was permitted to intervene. A childless married couple (the Does), the wife not being pregnant, separately attacked the laws, basing alleged injury on the future possibilities of contraceptive failure, pregnancy, unpreparedness for parenthood, and impairment of the wife's health. A three-judge District Court, which consolidated the actions, held that Roe and Hallford, and members of their classes, had standing to sue and presented justifiable controversies. Ruling that declaratory, though not injunctive, relief was warranted, the court declared the abortion statutes void as vague and overbroadly infringing those plaintiffs' Ninth and Fourteenth Amendment rights. The court ruled the Does' complaint not justifiable. Appellants directly appealed to this Court on the injunctive rulings, and the appellee cross-appealed from the District Court's grant of declaratory relief to Roe and Hallford. . . .

*Sarah Weddington* reargued the cause for appellants. With her on the briefs were *Roy Lucas, Fred Bruner, Roy L. Merrill, Jr.,* and *Norman Dorsen.*

*Robert C. Flowers,* Assistant Attorney General of Texas, argued the cause for appellee on the reargument. *Jay Floyd,* Assistant Attorney General, argued the cause for appellee on the original argument. With them on the brief were *Crawford C. Martin,* Attorney General, *Nola White,* First Assistant Attorney General, *Alfred Walker,* Executive Assistant Attorney General, *Henry Wade,* and *John B. Tolle.**

MR. JUSTICE BLACKMUN delivered the opinion of the Court.

This Texas federal appeal and its Georgia companion, *Doe* v. *Bolton, post,* p. 179, present constitutional challenges to state criminal abortion legislation. The Texas statutes under attack here are typical of those that have been in effect in many States for approximately a century. The Georgia statutes, in contrast, have a modern cast and are a legislative product that, to an extent at least, obviously reflects the influences of recent attitudinal change, of advancing medical knowledge and techniques, and of new thinking about an old issue.

We forthwith acknowledge our awareness of the sensitive and emotional nature of the abortion controversy, of the vigorous opposing views, even among physicians, and of the deep and seemingly absolute convictions that the subject inspires. One's philosophy, one's experiences, one's exposure to the raw edges of human existence, one's religious training, one's attitudes toward life and family and their values, and the moral standards one establishes and seeks to observe, are all likely to influence and to color one's thinking and conclusions about abortion.

In addition, population growth, pollution, poverty, and racial overtones tend to complicate and not to simplify the problem.

Our task, of course, is to resolve the issue by constitutional measurement, free of emotion and of predilection. We seek earnestly to do this, and, because we do, we have inquired into, and in this opinion place some emphasis upon, medical and medical-legal history and what that history reveals about man's attitudes toward the abortion procedure over the centuries. We bear in mind too, Mr. Justice Holmes' admonition in his now-vindicated dissent in *Lochner* v. *New York,* 198 U.S. 45, 76 (1905):

> "[The Constitution] is made for people of fundamentally differing views, and the accident of our finding certain opinions natural and familiar or novel and even shocking ought not to conclude our judgment upon the question whether statutes embodying them conflict with the Constitution of the United States."

The Texas statutes that concern us here are Arts. 1191–1194 and 1196 of the State's Penal Code.[1] These make it a crime to "procure an abortion," as therein defined, or to attempt one, except with respect to "an abortion procured or attempted by medical advice for the purpose of saving the life of the mother." Similar statutes are in existence in a majority of the States.[2]

Texas first enacted a criminal abortion statute in 1854. Texas Laws 1854, c. 49. § 1, set forth in 3 H. Gammel Laws of Texas 1502 (1898). This was soon modified into language that has remained substantially unchanged to the present time. See Texas Penal Code of 1857. c. 7. Arts. 531–536; G. Paschal, Laws of Texas. Arts. 2192–2197 (1866); Texas Rev. Stat., c. 8. Arts. 536–541 (1879); Texas Rev. Crim. Stat., Arts 1071–1076 (1911). The final article in each of these compilations provided the same exception, as does the present Article 1196, for an abortion by "medical advice for the purpose of saving the life of the mother."

Jane Roe, a single woman who was residing in Dallas County, Texas, instituted this federal action in March 1970 against the District Attorney of the county. She sought a declaratory judgment that the Texas criminal abortion statutes were unconstitutional on their face, and an injunction restraining the defendant from enforcing the statutes.

Roe alleged that she was unmarried and pregnant; that she wished to terminate her pregnancy by an abortion "performed by a competent, licensed physician, under safe, clinical conditions"; that she was unable to get a "legal" abortion in Texas because her life did not appear to be threatened by the continuation of her pregnancy; and that she could not afford to travel to another jurisdiction in order to secure a legal abortion under safe conditions. She claimed that the Texas statutes were unconstitutionally vague and that they abridged her right of personal privacy, protected by the First, Fourth, Fifth, Ninth, and Fourteenth Amendments. By an amendment to her complaint Roe purported to sue "on behalf of herself and all other women" similarly situated. . . .

The principal thrust of appellant's attack on the Texas statutes is that they improperly invade a right, said to be possessed by the pregnant woman, to choose to terminate her pregnancy. Appellant would discover this right in the concept of personal "liberty" embodied in the Fourteenth Amendment's Due Process Clause; or in the personal, marital, familial, and sexual privacy said to be protected by the Bill of Rights or its penumbras, see *Griswold* v. *Connecticut*, 381 U.S. 470 (1965); *Eisenstadt* v. *Baird*, 405 U.S. 438 (1972); *id.*, at 460 (WHITE, J., concurring in result); or among those rights reserved to the people by the Ninth Amendment, *Griswold* v. *Connecticut*, 381 U.S. 486 (Goldberg, J., concurring). Before addressing this claim, we feel it desirable briefly to survey, in several aspects, the history of abortion, for such insight as that history may afford us, and then to examine the state purposes and interests behind the criminal abortion laws.

## — VI —

It perhaps is not generally appreciated that the restrictive criminal abortion laws in effect in a majority of States today are of relatively recent vintage. Those laws, generally proscribing abortion or its attempt at any time during pregnancy except when necessary to preserve the pregnant woman's life, are not of ancient or even common-law origin. Instead, they derive from statutory changes effected, for the most part, in the latter half of the 19th century.

1. *Ancient attitudes.* These are not capable of precise determination. We are told that at the time of the Persian Empire abortifacients were known and that criminal abortions were severely punished. We are also told, however, that abortion was practiced in Greek times as well as in the Roman Era, and that "it was resorted to without scruple." The Ephesian, Soranos, often described as the greatest of the ancient gynecologists, appears to have been generally opposed to Rome's prevailing free-abortion practices. He found it necessary to think first of the life of the mother, and he resorted to abortion when, upon this standard, he felt the procedure advisable. Greek and Roman law afforded little protection to the unborn. If abortion was prosecuted in some places, it seems to have been based on a concept of a violation of the father's right to his offspring. Ancient religion did not bar abortion.

2. *The Hippocratic Oath.* What then of the famous Oath that has stood so long as the ethical guide of the medical profession and that bears the name of the great Greek (460(?)–377(?) B.C.), who has been described as the Father of Medicine, the "wisest and the greatest practitioner of his art," and the "most important and most complete medical personality of antiquity," who dominated the medical schools of his time, and who typified the sum of the medical knowledge of the past? The Oath varies somewhat according to the particular translation, but in any translation the content is clear: "I will give no deadly medicine to anyone if asked, nor suggest any such counsel; and in like manner I will not give to a woman a pessary to produce abortion," or "I will neither give a deadly drug to anybody if asked for it, nor will I make a suggestion to this effect. Similarly, I will not give to a woman an abortive remedy."

Although the Oath is not mentioned in any of the principal briefs in this case or in *Doe v. Bolton*, p. 179, it represents the apex of the development of strict ethical concepts in medicine, and its influence endures to this day. Why did not the authority of Hippocrates dissuade abortion practice in his time and that of Rome? The late Dr. Edelstein provides us with a theory: The Oath was not uncontested even in Hippocrates' day; only the Pythagorean school of philosophers frowned upon the related act of suicide. Most Greek thinkers, on the other hand, commended abortion, at least prior to viability. See Plato, Republic, V, 461; Aristotle, Politics, VII, 1335b 25. For the Pythagoreans, however, it was a matter of dogma. For them the embryo was animate from the moment of conception, and abortion meant destruction of a living being. The abortion clause of the Oath, therefore, "echoes Pythagorean doctrines," and "[i]n no other stratum of Greek opinion were such views held or proposed in the same spirit of uncompromising austerity."

Dr. Edelstein then concludes that the Oath originated in a group representing only a small segment of Greek ancient physicians. He points out that medical writings down to Galen (A.D. 130–200) "give evidence of the violation of almost every one of its injunctions." But with the end of antiquity a decided change took place. Resistance against suicide and against abortion became common. The Oath came to be popular. The emerging teachings of Christianity were in agreement with the Pythagorean ethic. The Oath "became the nucleus of all medical ethics" and "was applauded as the embodiment of truth." Thus, suggests Dr. Edelstein, it is "a Pythagorean manifesto and not the expression of an absolute standard of medical conduct."

This, is seems to us, is a satisfactory and acceptable explanation of the Hippocratic Oath's apparent rigidity. It enables us to understand, in historical context, a long-accepted and revered statement of medical ethics.

3. *The common law.* It is undisputed that at common law, abortion performed *before* "quickening"—the first recognizable movement of the fetus *in utero,* appearing usually from the 16th to the 18th week of pregnancy—was not an indictable offense. The absence of a common-law crime for pre-quickening abortion appears to have developed from a confluence of earlier philosophical, theological, and civil and canon law concepts of when life begins. These disciplines variously approached the question in terms of the point at which the embryo or fetus became "formed" or recognizably human, or in terms of when a "person" came into being, that is infused with a "soul" or "animated." A loose consensus evolved in early English law that these events occurred at some point between conception and live birth. This was "mediate animation." Although Christian theology and the canon law came to fix the point of animation at 40 days for a male and 80 days for a female, a view that persisted until the 19th century, there was otherwise little agreement about the precise time of formation or animation. There was agreement, however, that prior to this point the

fetus was to be regarded as part of the mother, and its destruction, therefore, was not homicide. Due to the continued uncertainty about the precise time when animation occurred, to the lack of any empirical basis for the 40–80-day view, and perhaps to Aquinas' definition of movement as one of the two first principles of life, Bracton focused upon quickening as the critical point. The significance of quickening was echoed by later common-law scholars and found its way into the received common law of this country.

Whether abortion of a *quick* fetus was a felony at common law, or even a lesser crime, is still disputed. Bracton, writing early in the 13th century, thought it homicide. But the later and predominant view, following the great common-law scholars, has been that it was, at most, a lesser offense. In a frequently cited passage, Coke took the position that abortion of a woman "quick with childe" is "a great misprision, and no murder." Blackstone followed, saying that while abortion after quickening had once been considered manslaughter (though not murder), "modern law" took a less severe view. A recent review of the common-law precedents argues, however, that those precedents contradict Coke and that even post-quickening abortion was never established as a common-law crime. This is of some importance because while most American courts ruled, in holding or dictum, that abortion of an unquickened fetus was not criminal under their received common laws, others followed Coke in stating that abortion of a quick fetus was a "misprision," a term they translated to mean "misdemeanor." That their reliance on Coke on this aspect of the law was uncritical and, apparently in all the reported cases, dictum (due probably to the paucity of common-law prosecutions for post-quickening abortion), makes it now appear a common-law crime even with respect to the destruction of a quick fetus.

4. *The English statutory law.* England's first criminal abortion statute, Lord Ellenborough's Act, 43 Geo. 3, c. 58, came in 1803. It made abortion of a quick fetus, § 1, a capital crime, but in § 2 it provided lesser penalties for the felony of abortion before quickening, and thus preserved the "quickening" distinction. This contrast was continued in the general revision of 1828, 9 Geo. 4, c. 31, § 13. It disappeared, however, together with the death penalty, in 1837, 7 Will. 4 & 1 Vict., c. 85. § 6, and did not reappear in the Offenses Against the Person Act of 1861, 24 & 25 Vict., c. 100, § 59, that formed the core of English anti-abortion law until the liberalizing reforms of 1967. In 1929, the Infant Life (Preservation) Act, 19 & 20 Geo. 5, c. 34, came into being. Its emphasis was upon the destruction of "the life of a child capable of being born alive." It made a willful act performed with the necessary intent a felony. It contained a proviso that one was not to be found guilty of the offense "unless it is proved that the act which caused the death of the child was not done in good faith for the purpose only of preserving the life of the mother."

A seemingly notable development in the English law was the case of *Rex* vs. *Bourne*, [1939] 1 K.B. 687. This case apparently answered in the affirmative the question whether an abortion necessary to preserve the life of the pregnant woman was excepted from the criminal penalties of the 1861 Act. In his instructions to the jury, Judge Macnaghten referred to the 1929 Act, and observed that the Act related to "the case where a child is killed by a willful act at the time when it is being delivered in the ordinary course of nature." *Id.,* at 691. He concluded that the 1861 Act's use of the word "unlawfully," imported the same meaning expressed by the specific proviso in the 1929 Act, even though there was no mention of preserving the mother's life in the 1861 Act. He then construed the phrase "preserving the life of the mother" broadly, that is, "in a reasonable sense," to include a serious and permanent threat to the mother's *health,* and instructed the jury to acquit Dr. Bourne if it found he had acted in a good-faith belief that the abortion was necessary for this purpose. *Id.,* at 693–694. The jury did acquit.

Recently, Parliament enacted a new abortion law. This is the Abortion Act of 1967, 15 & 16 Eliz. 2, c. 87. The Act permits a licensed physician to perform an abortion where two other licensed physicians agree (a) "that the continuance of the pregnancy would involve risk to the life of the pregnant woman, or of injury to the physical or mental health of the pregnant woman or any existing children of her family, greater than if the pregnancy were terminated," or (b) "that there is a substantial risk that if the child were born it would suffer from such physical or mental abnormalities as to be seriously handicapped." The Act also provides that, in making this determination, "account may be taken of the pregnant woman's actual or reasonably foreseeable environment." It also permits a physician, without the concurrence of others, to terminate a pregnancy where he is of the good-faith opinion that the abortion "is immediately necessary to save the life or to prevent grave permanent injury to the physical or mental health of the pregnant woman."

5. *The American law.* In this country, the law in effect in all but a few States until mid-19th century was the pre-existing English common law. Connecticut, the first State to enact abortion legislation, adopted in 1821 that part of Lord Ellenborough's Act that related to a woman "quick with child." The death penalty was not imposed. Abortion before quickening was made a crime in that State only in 1860. In 1828, New York enacted legislation that, in two respects, was to serve as a model for early anti-abortion statutes. First, while barring destruction of an unquickened fetus as well as a quick fetus, it made the former only a misdemeanor, but the latter second-degree manslaughter. Second, it incorporated a concept of therapeutic abortion by providing that an abortion was excused if it "shall have been necessary to preserve the life of such mother, or shall have been advised by two physicians to be necessary for such purpose." By 1840, when Texas had received the common law, only eight American States had statutes dealing with abortion. It was not until after the War Between the

States that legislation began generally to replace the common law. Most of these initial statutes dealt severely with abortion after quickening but were lenient with it before quickening. Most punished attempts equally with completed abortions. While many statutes included the exception for an abortion thought by one or more physicians to be necessary to save the mother's life, that provision soon disappeared and the typical law required that the procedure actually be necessary for that purpose.

Gradually, in the middle and late 19th century the quickening distinction disappeared from the statutory law of most States and the degree of the offense and the penalties were increased. By the end of the 1950s, a large majority of the jurisdictions banned abortion, however and whenever performed, unless done to save or preserve the life of the mother. The exceptions, Alabama and the District of Columbia, permitted abortion to preserve the mother's health. Three States permitted abortions that were not "unlawfully" performed or that were not "without lawful justification," leaving interpretation of those standards to the courts. In the past several years, however, a trend toward liberalization of abortion statutes has resulted in adoption, by about one-third of the States, of less stringent laws, most of them patterned after the ALI Model Penal Code, § 230.3.[3]

It is thus apparent that at common law, at the time of the adoption of our Constitution, and throughout the major portion of the 19th century, abortion was viewed with less disfavor than under most American statutes currently in effect. Phrasing it another way, a woman enjoyed a substantially broader right to terminate a pregnancy than she does in most States today. At least with respect to the early stage of pregnancy, and very possibly without such a limitation, the opportunity to make this choice was present in this country well into the 19th century. Even later, the law continued for some time to treat less punitively an abortion procured in early pregnancy.

6. *The position of the American Medical Association.* The anti-abortion mood prevalent in this country in the late 19th century was shared by the medical profession. Indeed, the attitude of the profession may have played a significant role in the enactment of stringent criminal abortion legislation during that period.

An AMA Committee on Criminal Abortion was appointed in May 1857. It presented its report, 12 Trans. of the Am. Med. Assn. 73–78 (1859), to the Twelfth Annual Meeting. That report observed that the Committee had been appointed to investigate criminal abortion "with a view to its general suppression." It deplored abortion and its frequency and it listed three causes of "this general demoralization":

> "The first of these causes is a widespread popular ignorance of the true character of the crime—a belief, even among mothers themselves, that the foetus is not alive till after the period of quickening.

"The second of the agents alluded to is the fact that the profession themselves are frequently supposed careless of foetal life. . . .

"The third reason of the frightful extent of this crime is found in the grave defects of our laws, both common and statute, as regards the independent and actual existence of the child before birth, as a living being. These errors, which are sufficient in most instances to prevent conviction, are based, and only based, upon mistaken and exploded medical dogmas. With strange inconsistency, the law fully acknowledges the foetus in utero and its inherent rights, for civil purposes; while personally and as criminally affected, it fails to recognize it, and to its life as yet denies all protection." *Id.*, at 75–76.

The Committee then offered, and the Association adopted, resolutions protesting "against such unwarrantable destruction of human life," calling upon state legislatures to revise their abortion laws, and requesting the cooperation of state medical societies "in pressing the subject." *Id.*, at 28, 78.

In 1871 a long and vivid report was submitted by the Committee on Criminal Abortion. It ended with the observation, "We had to deal with human life. In a matter of less importance we would entertain no compromise. An honest judge on the bench would call things by their proper names. We could do no less." 22 Trans. of the Am. Med. Assn. 258 (1871). It proffered resolutions, adopted by the Association, *id.*, at 38–39, recommending, among other things, that it "be unlawful and unprofessional for any physician to induce abortion or premature labor, without the concurrent opinion of at least one respectable consulting physician, and then always with a view to the safety of the child—if that be possible," and calling "the attention of the clergy of all denominations to the perverted views of morality entertained by a large class of females—aye, and men also, on this important question."

Except for periodic condemnation of the criminal abortionist, no further formal AMA action took place until 1967. In that year, the Committee on Human Reproduction urged the adoption of a stated policy of opposition to induced abortion, except when there is "documented medical evidence" of a threat to the health or life of the mother, or that the child "may be born with incapacitating physical deformity or mental deficiency," or that a pregnancy "resulting from legally established statutory or forcible rape or incest may constitute a threat to the mental or physical health of the patient," two other physicians "chosen because of their recognized professional competence have examined the patient and have concurred in writing," and the procedure "is performed in a hospital accredited by the joint Commission on Accreditation of Hospitals." The providing of medical information by physicians to state legislatures in their consideration of legislation regarding therapeutic abortion was "to be considered consistent with the principles of ethics of the American Medical Association." This recommendation was adopted by the House of Delegates. Proceedings of the AMA House of Delegates 40 51 (June 1967).

In 1970, after the introduction of a variety of proposed resolutions, and of a report from its Board of Trustees, a reference committee noted "polarization of the medical profession on this controversial issue": division among those who had testified; a difference of opinion among AMA councils and committees: "the remarkable shift in testimony" in six months, felt to be influenced "by the rapid changes in state laws and by the judicial decisions which tend to make abortion more freely available;" and a feeling "that this trend will continue." On June 25, 1970, the House of Delegates adopted preambles and most of the resolutions proposed by the reference committee. The preambles emphasized "the best interests of the patient," "sound clinical judgment," and "informed patient consent," in contrast to "mere acquiescence to the patient's demand." The resolutions asserted that abortion is a medical procedure that should be performed by a licensed physician in an accredited hospital only after consultation with two other physicians and in conformity with state law, and that no party to the procedure should be required to violate personally held moral principles. Proceedings of the AMA House of Delegates 220 (June 1970). The AMA Judicial Council rendered a complementary opinion.

7. *The position of the American Public Health Association.* In October 1970, the Executive Board of the AMA adopted Standards for Abortion Services. These were five in number:

    a.   Rapid and simple abortion referral must be readily available through state and local public health departments, medical societies, or other nonprofit organizations.

    b.   An important function of counseling should be to simplify and expedite the provision of abortion services; it should not delay the obtaining of these services.

    c.   Psychiatric consultation should not be mandatory. As in the case of other specialized medical services, psychiatric consultation should be sought for definite indications and not on a routine basis.

    d.   A wide range of individuals from appropriately trained, sympathetic volunteers to highly skilled physicians may qualify as abortion counselors.

    e.   Contraception and/or sterilization should be discussed with each abortion patient." Recommended Standards for Abortion Services, 61 Am. J. Pub. Health 396 (1971).

Among factors pertinent to life and health risks associated with abortion were three that "are recognized as important":

a.   the skill of the physician,

b.   the environment in which the abortion is performed, and above all

c.   the duration of pregnancy, as determined by uterine size and confirmed by menstrual history." *Id.,* at 397.

It was said that "a well-equipped hospital" offers more protection "to cope with unforeseen difficulties than an office or clinic without such resources. . . . The factor of gestational age is of overriding importance." Thus, it was recommended that abortions in the second trimester and early abortions in the presence of existing medical complications be performed in hospitals as inpatient procedures. For pregnancies in the first trimester, abortion in the hospital with or without overnight stay "is probably the safest practice." An abortion in an extramural facility, however, is an acceptable alternative "provided arrangements exist in advance to admit patients promptly if unforeseen complications develop." Standards for an abortion facility were listed. It was said that at present abortions should be performed by physicians or osteopaths who are licensed to practice and who have "adequate training." *Id.,* at 398.

8. *The position of the American Bar Association.* At its meeting in February 1972 the ABA House of Delegates approved, with 17 opposing votes, the Uniform Abortion Act that had been drafted and approved the preceding August by the Conference of Commissioners on Uniform State Laws. 58 A.B.A.J. 380 (1972). We set forth the Act in full in the margin. The Conference has appended an enlightening Prefatory Note.

— VII —

Three reasons have been advanced to explain historically the enactment of criminal abortion laws in the 19th century and to justify their continued existence.

It has been argued occasionally that these laws were the product of a Victorian social concern to discourage illicit sexual conduct. Texas, however, does not advance this justification in this present case, and it appears that no court or commentator has taken the argument seriously. The appellants and *amici* contend, moreover, that this is not a proper state purpose at all and suggest that, if it were, the Texas statutes are overbroad in protecting it since the law fails to distinguish between married and unwed mothers.

A second reason is concerned with abortion as a medical procedure. When most criminal abortion laws were first enacted, the procedure was a hazardous one for the woman. This was particularly true prior to the development of antisepsis. Antiseptic techniques, of course, were based on discoveries by Lister, Pasteur, and others first announced in 1867, but were not generally accepted and employed until about the turn of the century. Abortion mortality was high. Even after 1900, and perhaps until as late as the development of antibiotics in the 1940s, standard modern techniques such as dilation and curettage were not nearly so safe as they are today. Thus, it has been argued that a State's real concern in enacting a criminal abortion law was to protect the pregnant women, that is, to restrain her from submitting to a procedure that placed her life in serious jeopardy.

Modern medical techniques has altered this situation. Appellants and various *amici* refer to medical data indicating that abortion in early pregnancy, that is, prior to the end of the first trimester, although not without its risk, is now relatively safe. Mortality rates for women undergoing early abortions, where the procedure is legal, appear to be as low as or lower than the rates for normal childbirth. Consequently, any interest of the State in protecting the woman from an inherently hazardous procedure, except when it would be equally dangerous for her to forgo it, has largely disappeared. Of course, important state interests in the areas of health and medical standards do remain. The State has a legitimate interest in seeing to it that abortion, like any other medical procedure, is performed under circumstances that insure maximum safety for the patient. This interest obviously extends at least to the performing physician and his staff, to the facilities involved, to the availability of aftercare, and to adequate provision for any complication or emergency that might arise. The prevalence of high mortality rates in illegal "abortion mills" strengthens, rather than weakens, the State's interest in regulating the conditions under which abortions are performed. Moreover, the risk to the woman increases as her pregnancy continues. Thus, the State retains a definite interest in protecting the woman's own health and safety when an abortion is proposed at a late state of pregnancy.

The third reason is the State's interest—some phrase it in terms of duty—in protecting prenatal life. Some of the argument for this justification rests on the theory that a new human life is present from the moment of conception. The State's interest and general obligation to protect life then extends, it is argued, to prenatal life. Only when the life of the pregnant mother herself is at stake, balanced against the life she carries within her, should the interest of the embryo or fetus not prevail. Logically, of course, a legitimate state interest in this area need not stand or fall on acceptance of the belief that life begins at conception or at some other point prior to live birth. In assessing the State's interest, recognition may be given to the less rigid claim that as long as at least *potential* life is involved, the State may assert interests beyond the protection of the pregnant woman alone.

Parties challenging state abortion laws have sharply disputed in some courts the contention that a purpose of these laws, when enacted, was to protect prenatal life. Pointing to the absence of legislative history to support the contention, they claim that most state laws were designed solely to protect the woman. Because medical advances have lessened this concern, at least with respect to abortion in early pregnancy, they argue that with respect to such abortions the laws can no longer be justified by any state interest. There is some scholarly support for this view of original purpose. The few state courts called upon to interpret their laws in the late 19th and early 20th centuries did focus on the State's interest in protecting the woman's health rather than in preserving the embryo and fetus. Proponents of this view point out that in many States, including Texas, by statute or judicial interpretation, the pregnant woman herself could not be prosecuted for self-abortion or for cooperating in an abortion performed upon her by another. They claim that adoption of the "quickening" distinction through received common law and state statutes tacitly recognizes the greater health hazards inherent in late abortion and impliedly repudiates the theory that life begins at conception.

It is with these interests, and the weight to be attached to them, that this case is concerned.

## — VIII —

The Constitution does not explicitly mention any right of privacy. In a line of decisions, however, going back perhaps as far as *Union Pacific R. Co.* v. *Botsford*, 141 U.S. 250, 251 (1891), the Court has recognized that a right of personal privacy, or a guarantee of certain areas or zones of privacy, does exist, under the Constitution. In varying contexts, the Court or individual Justices have, indeed, found at least the roots of that right in the First Amendment, *Stanley* v. *Georgia*, 394 U.S. 557, 564 (1969); in the Fourth and Fifth Amendments, *Terry* v. *Ohio*, 392 U.S. 1, 8–9 (1968), *Katz* v. *United States*, 389 U.S. 347, 350 (1967), *Boyd* v. *United States*, 116 U.S. 616 (1886), see *Olmstead* v. *United States*, 277 U.S. 438, 478 (1928) (Brandeis, J., dissenting); in the penumbras of the Bill of Rights, *Griswold* v. *Connecticut*, 381 U.S. at 484–485; in the Ninth Amendment, *id.*, at 486 (Goldberg, J., concurring); or in the concept of liberty guaranteed by the first section of the Fourteenth Amendment, see *Meyer* v. *Nebraska*, 262 U.S. 390, 399 (1923). These decisions make it clear that only personal rights that can be deemed "fundamental" or "implicit in the concept of ordered liberty," *Palko* v. *Connecticut*, 302 U.S. 319, 325 (1937), are included in this guarantee of personal privacy. They also make it clear that the right has some extension to activities relating to marriage, *Loving* v. *Virginia*, 388 U.S. 1, 12 (1967); procreation, *Skinner* v. *Oklahoma*, 316 U.S. 535, 541–542 (1942); contraception, *Eisenstadt* v. *Baird*, 405 U.S., at 453–454; *Id.*, at 460, 463–465 (WHITE, J., concurring in result); family relationships, *Prince* v. *Massachusetts*, 321 U.S. 158, 166 (1944); and child rearing and education, *Pierce* v. *Society of Sisters*, 268 U.S. 510, 535 (1925), *Meyer* v. *Nebraska, supra.*

This right of privacy, whether it be founded in the Fourteenth Amendment's concept of personal liberty and restrictions upon state action, as we feel it is, or, as the District

Court determined, in the Ninth Amendment's reservation of rights to the people, is broad enough to encompass a woman's decision whether or not to terminate her pregnancy. The detriment that the State would impose upon the pregnant woman by denying this choice altogether is apparent. Specific and direct harm medically diagnosable even in early pregnancy may be involved. Maternity, or additional offspring may force upon the woman a distressful life and future. Psychological harm may be imminent. Mental and physical health may be taxed by child care. There is also the distress, for all concerned, associated with the unwanted child, and there is the problem of bringing a child into a family already unable, psychologically and otherwise, to care for it. In other cases, as in this one, the additional difficulties and continuing stigma of unwed motherhood may be involved. All these are factors the woman and her responsible physician necessarily will consider in consultation.

On the basis of elements such as these appellant and some *amici* argue that the woman's right is absolute and that she is entitled to terminate her pregnancy at whatever time, in whatever way, and for whatever reason she alone chooses. With this we do not agree. Appellant's arguments that Texas either has no valid interest at all in regulating the abortion decision, or no interest strong enough to support any limitation upon the woman's sole determination, are unpersuasive. The Court's decisions recognizing a right of privacy also acknowledge that some state regulation in areas protected by that right is appropriate. As noted above, a State may properly assert important interests in safeguarding health, in maintaining medical standards and in protecting potential life. At some point in pregnancy, these respective interests become sufficiently compelling to sustain regulation of the factors that govern the abortion decision. The privacy right involved, therefore, cannot be said to be absolute. In fact, it is not clear to us that the claim asserted by some *amici* that one has an unlimited right to do with one's body as one pleases bears close relationship to the right of privacy previously articulated in the Court's decisions. The Court has refused to recognize an unlimited right of this kind in the past. *Jacobsen* v. *Massachusetts*, 197 U.S. 11 (1905) (vaccination); *Buck* v. *Bell*, 274 U.S. 200 (1927) (sterilization).

We, therefore, conclude that the right of personal privacy includes the abortion decision, but that this right is not unqualified and must be considered against important state interests in regulation.

We note that those federal and state courts that have recently considered abortion law challenges have reached the same conclusion. A majority, in addition to the District Court in the present case, have held state laws unconstitutional, at least in part, because of vagueness or because of overbreadth and abridgment of rights.

Although the results are divided; most of these courts have agreed that the right of privacy, however based, is broad enough to cover the abortion decision; that the right, nonetheless, is not absolute and is subject to some limitations; and that at some point the state interests as to protection of health, medical standards, and prenatal life, become dominant. We agree with this approach.

Where certain "fundamental rights" are involved, the Court has held that regulation limiting these rights may be justified only by a "compelling state interest." *Kramer* v. *Union Free School District*, 395 U.S. 621, 627 (1969); *Shapiro* v. *Thompson*, 394 U.S. 618, 634 (1969), *Sherbert* v. *Verner*, 374 U.S. 398, 406 (1963), and that legislative enactments must be narrowly drawn to express only the legitimate state interests at stake. *Griswold* v. *Connecticut*, 381 U.S., at 485; *Aptheker* v. *Secretary of State*, 378 U.S. 500, 508 (1964); *Cantwell* v. *Connecticut*, 310 U.S. 296, 307–308 (1940); see *Eisenstadt* v. *Baird*, 405 U. S., at 460, 463–464 (WHITE, J., concurring in result).

In the recent abortion cases, cited above, courts have recognized these principles. Those striking down state laws have generally scrutinized the State's interests in protecting health and potential life, and have concluded that neither interest justified broad limitations on the reasons for which a physician and his pregnant patient might decide that she should have an abortion in the early stages of pregnancy. Courts sustaining state laws have held that the State's determinations to protect health or prenatal life are dominant and constitutionally justifiable.

## — IX —

The District Court held that the appellee failed to meet his burden of demonstrating that the Texas statute's infringement upon Roe's rights was necessary to support a compelling state interest, and that, although the appellee presented "several compelling justifications for state presence in the area of abortions," the statutes outstripped these justifications and swept "far beyond any areas of compelling state interest." 314 F. Supp., at 1222–1223. Appellant and appellee both contest that holding. Appellant, as has been indicated, claims an absolute right that bars any state imposition of criminal penalties in the area. Appellee argues that the State's determination to recognize and protect prenatal life from and after conception constitutes a compelling state interest. As noted above, we do not agree fully with either formulation.

A. The appellee and certain *amici* argue that the fetus is a "person" within the language and meaning of the Fourteenth Amendment. In support of this, they outline at length and in detail the well-known facts of fetal development. If this suggestion of personhood is established, the appellant's case, of course, collapses, for the fetus' right to life would then be guaranteed specifically by the Amendment. The appellant conceded as much on reargument. On the other hand, the appellee conceded on reargument that no case could be cited that holds that a fetus is a person within the meaning of the Fourteenth Amendment.

The Constitution does not define "person" in so many words. Section 1 of the Fourteenth Amendment contains three references to "person." The first, in defining "citizens," speaks of "persons born or naturalized in the United States." The word also appears both in the Due Process Clause and in the Equal Protection Clause. "Person" is used in other places in the Constitution: in the listing of qualifications for Representatives and Senators, Art. I, § 2, cl. 2, and § 3. cl. 3; in the Apportionment Clause, Art. 1, § 2, cl. 3; in the Migration and Importation provision, Art. I, § 9, cl. 1; in the Emolument Clause, Art. I, § 9, cl. 8; in the Electors provisions, Art. II, § 1, cl. 2. and the superseded cl. 3; in the provision outlining qualifications for the office of President, Art. II, § 1, cl. 5; in the Extradition provisions, Art. IV, § 2, cl. 2, and the superseded Fugitive Slave Clause 3; and in the Fifth, Twelfth, and Twenty-second Amendments, as well as in §§ 2 and 3 of the Fourteenth Amendment. But in nearly all these instances, the use of the word is such that it has application only postnatally. None indicates, with any assurance, that it has any possible pre-natal application.[4]

All this, together with our observation, *supra,* that throughout the major portion of the 19th century prevailing legal abortion practices were far freer than they are today, persuades us that the word "person" as used in the Fourteenth Amendment, does not include the unborn.[5] This is in accord with the results reached in those few cases where the issue has been squarely presented. . . .

Indeed, our decision in *United States* v. *Vuitch,* 402 U.S. 62 (1971), inferentially is to the same effect, for we there would not have indulged in statutory interpretation favorable to abortion in specified circumstances if the necessary consequence was the termination of life entitled to Fourteenth Amendment protection.

This conclusion, however, does not of itself fully answer the contentions raised by Texas, and we pass on to other considerations.

**B.** The pregnant woman cannot be isolated in her privacy. She carries an embryo and, later, a fetus, if one accepts the medical definitions of the developing young in the human uterus. See Dorland's Illustrated Medical Dictionary 478–479, 547 (24th ed. 1965). The situation therefore is inherently different from marital intimacy, or bedroom possession of obscene material, or marriage, or procreation, or education, with which *Eisenstadt* and *Griswold, Stanley, Loving, Skinner,* and *Pierce* and *Meyer* were respectively concerned. As we have intimated above, it is reasonable and appropriate for a State to decide that at some point in time another interest, that of health of the mother or that of potential human life becomes significantly involved. The woman's privacy is no longer sole and any right of privacy she possesses must be measured accordingly.

Texas urges that, apart from the Fourteenth Amendment, life begins at conception and is present throughout pregnancy, and that, therefore, the State has a compelling interest in protecting that life from and after conception. We need not resolve the difficult question of when life begins. When those trained in the respective disciplines of medicine, philosophy, and theology are unable to arrive at any consensus, the judiciary at this point in the development of man's knowledge, is not in a position to speculate as to the answer.

It should be sufficient to note briefly the wide divergence of thinking on this most sensitive and difficult question. There has always been strong support for the view that life does not begin until live birth. This was the belief of the Stoics. It appears to be the predominant, though not the unanimous, attitude of the Jewish faith. It may be taken to represent also the position of a large segment of the Protestant community insofar as that can be ascertained; organized groups that have taken a formal position on the abortion issue have generally regarded abortion as a matter for the conscience of the individual and her family. As we have noted, the common law found greater significance in quickening. Physicians and their scientific colleagues have regarded that event with less interest and have tended to focus either upon conception, upon live birth, or upon the interim point at which the fetus becomes "viable," that is, potentially able to live outside the mother's womb, albeit with artificial aid. Viability is usually placed at about seven months (28 weeks) but may occur earlier, even at 24 weeks. The Aristotelian theory of "mediate animation," that held sway throughout the Middle Ages and the Renaissance in Europe, continued to be official Roman Catholic dogma until the 19th century, despite opposition to this "ensoulment" theory from those in the Church who would recognize the existence of life from the moment of conception. The latter is now, of course, the official belief of the Catholic Church. As one brief *amicus* discloses, this is a view strongly held by many non-Catholics as well, and by many physicians. Substantial problems for precise definition of this view are posed, however, by new embryological data that purport to indicate that conception is a "process" over time, rather than an event, and by new medical techniques such as menstrual extraction, the "morning-after" pill, implantation of embryos, artificial insemination, and even artificial wombs.

In areas other than criminal abortion, the law has been reluctant to endorse any theory that life, as we recognize it, begins before live birth or to accord legal rights to the unborn except in narrowly defined situations and except when the rights are contingent upon live birth. For example, the traditional rule of tort law denied recovery for prenatal injuries even though the child was born alive. That rule has been changed in almost every jurisdiction. In most States, recovery is said to be permitted only if the fetus was viable, or at least quick, when the injuries were sustained, though few courts have squarely so held. In a recent development, generally opposed by the commentators, some States permit the parents of a stillborn child to maintain an action for wrongful death because of prenatal injuries. Such an action, however, would appear to be one to vindicate the parents' interest and is thus consistent with the view that the fetus, at most, represents only the potentiality of life. Similarly, unborn children have been recognized as acquiring rights or interests by way of inheritance or other devolution of property, and have been represented by guardians *ad litem*. Perfection of the interests involved, again, has generally been contingent upon live birth. In short, the unborn have never been recognized in the law as persons in the whole sense.

— X —

In view of all this, we do not agree that, by adopting one theory of life, Texas may override the rights of the pregnant woman that are at stake. We repeat, however, that the State does have an important and legitimate interest in preserving and protecting the health of the pregnant woman, whether she be a resident of the State or a nonresident who seeks medical consultation and treatment there, and that it has still *another* important and legitimate interest in protecting the potentiality of human life. These interests are separate and distinct. Each grows in substantiality as the woman approaches term and, at a point during pregnancy, each becomes "compelling."

With respect to the State's important and legitimate interest in the health of the mother, the "compelling" point, in the light of present medical knowledge, is at approximately the end of the first trimester. This is so because of the now-established medical fact, referred to above at 149, that until the end of the first trimester mortality in abortion may be less than mortality in normal childbirth. It follows that, from and after this point, a State may regulate the abortion procedure to the extent that the regulation reasonably relates to the preservation and protection of maternal health. Examples of permissible state regulation in this area are requirements as to the qualifications of the person who is to perform the abortion; as to the licensure of that person; as to the facility in which the procedure is to be performed, that is whether it must be a hospital or may be a clinic or some other place of less-than-hospital status; as to the licensing of the facility; and the like.

This means, on the other hand, that, for the period of pregnancy prior to this "compelling" point, the attending physician, in consultation with his patient, is free to determine, without regulation by the State, that, in his medical judgment, the patient's pregnancy should be terminated. If that decision is reached, the judgment may be effectuated by an abortion free of interference by the State.

With respect to the State's important and legitimate interest in potential life, the "compelling" point is at viability. This is so because the fetus then presumably has the capability of meaningful life outside the mother's womb. State regulation protective of fetal life after viability thus has both logical and biological justifications. If the State is interested in protecting fetal life after viability, it may go so far as to proscribe abortion during that period, except when it is necessary to preserve the life or health of the mother.

Measured against these standards, Art. 1196 of the Texas Penal Code, in restricting legal abortions to those "procured or attempted by medical advice for the purpose of saving the life of the mother," sweeps too broadly. The statute makes no distinction between abortions performed early in pregnancy and those performed later, and it limits to a single reason, "saving" the mother's life, the legal justification for the procedure. The statute, therefore, cannot survive the constitutional attack made upon it here.

This conclusion makes it unnecessary for us to consider the additional challenge to the Texas statute asserted on grounds of vagueness. See *United States* v. *Vuitch*, 402 U.S., at 67–72.

To summarize and to repeat:

1.  A state criminal abortion statute of the current Texas type, that excepts from criminality only a *lifesaving* procedure on behalf of the mother, without regard to pregnancy stage and without recognition of the other interests involved, is violative of the Due Process Clause of the Fourteenth Amendment.

    a.  For the stage prior to approximately the end of the first trimester, the abortion decision and its effectuation must be left to the medical judgment of the pregnant woman's attending physician.
    b.  For the stage subsequent to approximately the end of the first trimester, the State, in promoting its interest in the health of the mother, may, if it chooses, regulate the abortion procedure in ways that are reasonably related to maternal health.
    c.  For the stage subsequent to viability, the State in promoting its interest in the potentiality of human life may, if it chooses, regulate, and even proscribe, abortion except where it is necessary, in appropriate medical judgment, for the preservation of the life or health of the mother.

2.  The State may define the term "physician," as it has been employed in the preceding paragraphs of this Part XI of this opinion, to mean only a physician currently licensed by the State, and may proscribe any abortion by a person who is not a physician as so defined.

In *Doe* v. *Bolton*, post, p. 179, procedural requirements contained in one of the modern abortion statutes are considered. That opinion and this one, of course, are to be read together.

This holding, we feel, is consistent with the relative weights of the respective interests involved, with the lessons and examples of medical and legal history, with the lenity of the common law, and with the demands of the profound problems of the present day. The decision leaves the State free to place increasing restrictions on abortion as the period of pregnancy lengthens, so long as those restrictions are tailored to the recognized state interests. The decision vindicates the right of the physician to administer medical treatment according to his professional judgment up to the points where important state interests provide compelling justifications for intervention. Up to those points, the abortion decision in all its aspects is inherently, and primarily, a medical decision, and basic responsibility for it must rest with the physician. If an individual practitioner abuses the privilege of exercising proper medical judgment, the usual remedies, judicial and intraprofessional, are available.

## — XII —

Our conclusion that Art. 1196 is unconstitutional means, of course, that the Texas abortion statutes, as a unit, must fall. The exception of Art. 1196 cannot be struck down separately, for then the State would be left with a statute proscribing all abortion procedures no matter how medically urgent the case. . . .

We find it unnecessary to decide whether the District Court erred in withholding injunctive relief, for we assume the Texas prosecutorial authorities will give full credence to this decision that the present criminal abortion statutes of that State are unconstitutional.

The judgment of the District Court as to intervenor Hallford is reversed, and Dr. Hallford's complaint in intervention is dismissed. In all other respects, the judgment of the District Court is affirmed. Costs are allowed to the appellee.

*It is so ordered.*

MR. JUSTICE STEWART, concurring.

In 1963, this Court, in *Ferguson* v. *Skrupa*, 372 U.S. 726, purported to sound the death knell for the doctrine of substantive due process, a doctrine under which many state laws had in the past been held to violate the Fourteenth Amendment. As Mr. Justice Black's opinion for the Court in *Skrupa* put it: "We have returned to the original constitutional proposition that courts do not substitute their social and economic beliefs for the judgment of legislative bodies, who are elected to pass laws." *Id.*, at 730.

Barely two years later, in *Griswold* v. *Connecticut*, 381 U.S. 479, the Court held a Connecticut birth control law unconstitutional. In view of what had been so recently said in *Skrupa*, the Court's opinion in *Griswold* understandably did its best to avoid reliance on the Due Process Clause of the Fourteenth Amendment as the ground for decision. Yet, the Connecticut law did not violate any provision of the Bill of Rights, nor any other specific provision of the Constitution. So it was clear to me then, and it is equally clear to me now, that the *Griswold* decision can be rationally understood only as a holding that the Connecticut statute substantively invaded the "liberty" that is protected by the Due Process Clause of the Fourteenth Amendment. As so understood, *Griswold* stands as one in a long line of pre-*Skrupa* cases decided under the doctrine of substantive due process, and I now accept it as such.

"In a Constitution for a free people, there can be no doubt that the meaning of 'liberty' must be broad indeed." *Board of Regents* v. *Roth,* 408 U.S. 564, 572. The Constitution nowhere mentions a specific right of personal choice in matters of marriage and family life, but the "liberty" protected by the Due Process Clause of the Fourteenth Amendment covers more than those freedoms explicitly named in the Bill of Rights. . . .

Several decisions of this Court make clear that freedom of personal choice in matters of marriage and family life is one of the liberties protected by the Due Process Clause of the Fourteenth Amendment. *Loving* v. *Virginia,* 388 U.S. 1, 12; *Griswold* v. *Connecticut, supra; Pierce* v. *Society of Sisters, supra; Meyer* v. *Nebraska, supra.* See also *Prince* v. *Massachusetts,* 321 U.S. 158, 166; *Skinner* v. *Oklahoma,* 316 U.S. 535, 541. As recently as last Term, in *Eisenstadt* v. *Baird,* 405 U.S. 438, 453, we recognized "the right of the *individual,* married or single, to be free from unwarranted governmental intrusion into matters so fundamentally affecting a person as the decision whether to bear or beget a child." That right necessarily includes the right of a woman to decide whether or not to terminate her pregnancy. "Certainly the interests of a woman in giving of her physical and emotional self during pregnancy and the interests that will be affected throughout her life by the birth and raising of a child are of a far greater degree of significance and personal intimacy than the right to send a child to private school protected in *Pierce* v. *Society of Sisters,* 268 U.S. 510 (1925), or the right to teach a foreign language protected in *Meyer* v. *Nebraska,* 262, U.S. 390 (1923)." *Abele* v. *Markle,* 351 F. Supp. 224, 227 (Conn. 1972).

Clearly, therefore, the Court today is correct in holding that the right asserted by Jane Roe is embraced within the personal liberty protected by the Due Process Clause of the Fourteenth Amendment.

It is evident that the Texas abortion statute infringes that right directly. Indeed, it is difficult to imagine a more complete abridgment of a constitutional freedom than that worked by the inflexible criminal statute now in force in Texas. The question then becomes whether the state interests advanced to justify this abridgment can survive the "particularly careful scrutiny" that the Fourteenth Amendment here requires.

The asserted state interests are protection of the health and safety of the pregnant woman, and the protection of the potential future human life within her. These are legitimate objectives, amply sufficient to permit a State to regulate abortions as it does other surgical procedures, and perhaps sufficient to permit a State to regulate abortions more stringently or even to prohibit them in the last stages of pregnancy. But such legislation is not before us, and I think the Court today has thoroughly demonstrated that these state interests cannot constitutionally support the broad abridgment of personal liberty worked by the existing Texas law. Accordingly, I join the Court's opinion holding that that law is invalid under the Due Process Clause of the Fourteenth Amendment.

MR. CHIEF JUSTICE BURGER, concurring.
[This opinion applies also to *Doe* v. *Bolton*, 410 U.S. 179 (1973)]

I agree that, under the Fourteenth Amendment to the Constitution, the abortion statutes of Georgia and Texas impermissibly limit the performance of abortions necessary to protect the health of pregnant women, using the term health in its broadest medical context. . . .

I do not read the Court's holdings today as having the sweeping consequences attributed to them by the dissenting Justices; the dissenting views discount the reality that the vast majority of physicians observe the standards of their profession, and act only on the basis of carefully deliberated medical judgments relating to life and health. Plainly, the Court today rejects any claim that the Constitution requires abortions on demand.

MR. JUSTICE DOUGLAS, concurring.
[This opinion applies also to *Doe* v. *Bolton*, 410 U.S. 179 (1973)]

While I join the opinion of the Court, I add a few words.

## — I —

The Ninth Amendment obviously does not create federally enforceable rights. It merely says, "The enumeration in the Constitution, of certain rights, shall not be construed to deny or disparage others retained by the people." But a catalogue of these rights includes customary, traditional, and time-honored rights, amenities, privileges, and immunities that come within the sweep of "the Blessings of Liberty" mentioned in the preamble to the Constitution. Many of them, in my view, come within the meaning of the term "liberty" as used in the Fourteenth Amendment.

First is the autonomous control over the development and expression of one's intellect, interests, tastes, and personality.

These are rights protected by the First Amendment and, in my view, they are absolute, permitting of no exceptions. See *Terminiello* v. *Chicago*, 337 U.S. 1; *Roth* v. *United States*, 354 U.S. 476, 508 (dissent), *Kingsley Pictures Corp.* v. *Regents*, 60 U.S. 684, 697 (concurring); *New York Times Co.* v. *Sullivan* 376 U.S. 254, 293 (Black, J., concurring, in which I joined). The Free Exercise Clause of the First Amendment is one facet of this constitutional right. The right to remain silent as respects one's own beliefs, *Watkins* v. *United States*, 354 U.S. 178 196–199, is protected by the First and the Fifth. The First Amendment grants the privacy of first-class mail, *United States* v. *Van Leeuwen*, 397 U.S. 249, 253. All of these aspects of the right of privacy are rights "retained by the people" in the meaning of the Ninth Amendment.

Second is freedom of choice in the basic decisions of one's life respecting marriage, divorce, procreation, contraception, and the education and upbringing of children.

These rights, unlike those protected by the First Amendment, are subject to some control by the police power. Thus, the Fourth Amendment speaks only of "unreasonable searches and seizures" and of "probable cause." These rights are "fundamental," and we have held that in order to support legislative action the statute must be narrowly and precisely drawn and that a "compelling state interest" must be shown in support of the limitation. *E.g., Kramer* v. *Union Free School District*, 395 U.S. 621; *Shapiro* v. *Thompson*, 394 U.S. 618; [410 U.S. 179, 212] *Carrington* v. *Rash*, 380 U.S. 89; *Sherbert* v. *Verner*, 374 U.S. 398; *NAACP* v. *Alabama*, 357 U.S. 449.

The liberty to marry a person of one's own choosing, *Loving* v. *Virginia*, 388 U.S. 1; the right of procreation, *Skinner* v. *Oklahoma*, 316 U.S. 535: the liberty to direct the education of one's children, *Pierce* v. *Society of Sisters*, 268 U.S. 510, and the privacy of the marital relation, *Griswold* v. *Connecticut*. Only last Term in *Eisenstadt* v. *Baird*, 405 U.S. 438, another contraceptive case, we expanded the concept of *Griswold* by saying:

"It is true that in *Griswold* the right of privacy in question inhered in the marital relationship. Yet the marital couple is not an independent entity with a mind and heart of its own, but an association of two individuals each with a separate intellectual and emotional makeup. If the right of privacy means anything, it is the right of the individual, married or single, to be free from unwarranted governmental intrusion into matters so fundamentally affecting a person as the decision whether to bear or beget a child."

This right of privacy was called by Mr. Justice Brandeis the right "to be let alone." *Olmstead* v. *United States*, 277 U.S. 438, 478 (dissenting opinion). That right includes the privilege of an individual to plan his own affairs, for, "outside areas of plainly harmful conduct, every American is left to shape his own life as he thinks best, do what he pleases, go where he pleases." *Kent* v. *Dulles*, 357 U.S. 116, 126.

Third is the freedom to care for one's health and person, freedom from bodily restraint or compulsion, freedom to walk, stroll, or loaf.

These rights, though fundamental, are likewise subject to regulation on a showing of "compelling state interest." We stated in *Papachristou* v. *City of Jacksonville*, 405 U.S. 156, 164, that walking, strolling, and wandering "are historically part of the amenities of life as we have known them." As stated in *Jacobson* v. *Massachusetts*, 197 U.S. 11, 29:

"There is, of course, a sphere within which the individual may assert the supremacy of his own amd will rightfully dispute the authority of any human government, especially of any free government existing under a written constitution, to interfere with the exercise of that will."

In *Union Pacific R. Co.* v. *Botsford*, 141 U.S. 250, 252, the Court said, "The inviolability of the person is as much invaded by a compulsory stripping and exposure as by a blow."

In *Terry* v. *Ohio*, 392 U.S. 1, 8–9, the Court, in speaking of the Fourth Amendment stated, "This inestimable right of personal security belongs as much to the citizen on the streets of our cities as to the homeowner closeted in his study to dispose of his secret affairs."

*Katz* v. *United States*, 389 U.S. 347, 350, emphasizes that the Fourth Amendment "protects individual privacy against certain kinds of governmental intrusion."

In *Meyer* v. *Nebraska*, 262 U.S. 390, 399, the Court said:

"Without doubt, [liberty] denotes not merely freedom from bodily restraint but also the right of the individual to contract, to engage in any of the common occupations of life, to acquire useful knowledge, to marry, establish a home and bring up children, to worship God according to the dictates of his own conscience, and generally to enjoy those privileges long recognized at common law as essential to the orderly pursuit of happiness by free men."

. . . the clear message of these cases is that a woman is free to make the basic decision whether to bear an unwanted child.

## — II —

Such reasoning is, however, only the beginning of the problem. The State has interests to protect. Vaccinations to prevent epidemics are one example, as *Jacobson, supra,* holds. The Court held that compulsory sterilization of imbeciles afflicted with hereditary forms of insanity or imbecility is another.

*Buck* v. *Bell*, 274 U.S. 200. Abortion affects another. While childbirth endangers the lives of some women, voluntary abortion at any time and place regardless of medical standards would impinge on a rightful concern of society. The woman's health is part of that concern; as is the life of the fetus after quickening. These concerns justify the State in treating the procedure as a medical one.

MR. JUSTICE REHNQUIST, dissenting.

The Court's opinion brings to the decision of this troubling question both extensive historical fact and a wealth of legal scholarship. While the opinion thus commands my respect, I find myself nonetheless in fundamental disagreement with those parts of it that invalidate the Texas statute in question, and therefore dissent. I would reach a conclusion opposite to that reached by the Court. I have difficulty in concluding, as the Court does, that the right of "privacy" is involved in this case. Texas, by the statute here challenged, bars the performance of a medical abortion by a licensed physician on a plaintiff such as Roe. A transaction resulting in an operation such as this is not "private" in the ordinary usage of that word. Nor is the "privacy" that the Court finds here even a distant relative of the freedom from searches and seizures protected by the Fourth Amendment to the Constitution, which the Court has referred to as embodying a right to privacy. *Katz* v. *United States*, 389 U.S. 347 (1967).

If the Court means by the term "privacy" no more than that the claim of a person to be free from unwanted state regulation of consensual transactions may be a form of "liberty" protected by the Fourteenth Amendment, there is no doubt that similar claims have been upheld in our earlier decisions on the basis of that liberty. I agree with the statement of MR. JUSTICE STEWART in his concurring opinion that the "liberty," against deprivation of which without due process the Fourteenth Amendment protects, embraces more than the rights found in the Bill of Rights. But that liberty is not guaranteed absolutely against deprivation, only against deprivation without due process of law. The test traditionally applied in the area of social and economic legislation is whether or not a law such as that challenged has a rational relation to a valid state objective. *Williamson* v. *Lee Optical Co.*, 348 U.S. 483, 491 (1955). The Due Process Clause of the Fourteenth Amendment undoubtedly does place a limit, albeit a broad one, on legislative power to enact laws such as this. If the Texas statute were to prohibit an abortion even where the mother's life is in jeopardy, I have little doubt that such a statute would lack a rational relation to a valid state objective under the test stated in *Williamson, supra*. But the Court's sweeping invalidation of any restrictions on abortion during the first trimester is impossible to justify under that standard, and the conscious weighing of competing factors that the Court's opinion apparently substitutes for the established test is far more appropriate to a legislative judgment than to a judicial one.

The Court eschews the history of the Fourteenth Amendment in its reliance on the "compelling state interest" test. See *Weber* v. *Aetna Casualty & Surety Co.*, 406 U.S. 164, 179 (1972) (dissenting opinion). But the Court adds a new wrinkle to this test by transposing it from the legal considerations associated with the Equal Protection Clause of the Fourteenth Amendment to this case arising under the Due Process Clause of the Fourteenth Amendment. Unless I misapprehend the consequences of this transplanting of the "compelling state interest test," the Court's opinion will accomplish the seemingly impossible feat of leaving this area of the law more confused than it found it.

While the Court's opinion quotes from the dissent of Mr. Justice Holmes in *Lochner* v. *New York*, 198 U.S. 45, 74 (1905), the result it reaches is more closely attuned to the majority opinion of Mr. Justice Peckham in that case. As in *Lochner* and similar cases applying substantive due process standards to economic and social welfare legislation, the adoption of the compelling state interest standard will inevitably require this Court to examine the legislative policies and pass on the wisdom of these policies in the very process of deciding whether a particular state interest put forward may or may not be "compelling." The decision here to break pregnancy into three distinct terms and to outline the permissible restrictions the State may impose in each one, for example, partakes more of judicial legislation than it does of a determination of the intent of the drafters of the Fourteenth Amendment.

The fact that a majority of the States reflecting, after all, the majority sentiment in those States, have had restrictions on abortions for at least a century is a strong indication, it seems to me, that the asserted right to an abortion is not "so rooted in the traditions and conscience of our people as to be ranked as fundamental," *Snyder* v. *Massachusetts*, 291 U.S. 97, 105 (1934). Even today, when society's views on abortion are changing, the very existence of the debate is evidence that the "right" to an abortion is not so universally accepted as the appellant would have us believe.

To reach its result, the Court necessarily has had to find within the scope of the Fourteenth Amendment a right that was apparently completely unknown to the drafters of the Amendment. As early as 1821, the first state law dealing directly with abortion was enacted by the Connecticut Legislature. Conn. Stat., Tit. 22, §§ 14, 16. By the time of the adoption of the Fourteenth Amendment in 1868, there were at least 36 laws enacted by state or territorial legislatures limiting abortion. While many States have amended or updated their laws, 21 of the laws on the books in 1868 remain in effect today. Indeed, the Texas statute struck down today was, as the majority notes, first enacted in 1857 and "has remained substantially unchanged to the present time." *Ante,* at 119.

There apparently was no question concerning the validity of this provision or of the other state statutes when the Fourteenth Amendment was adopted. The only conclusion possible from this history is that the drafters did not intend to have the Fourteenth Amendment withdraw from the States the power to legislate with respect to this matter.

## — III —

Even if one were to agree that the case that the Court decides were here, and that the enunciation of the substantive constitutional law in the Court's opinion were proper, the actual disposition of the case by the Court is still difficult to justify. The Texas statute is struck down *in toto,* even though the Court apparently concedes that at later periods of pregnancy Texas might impose these selfsame statutory limitations on abortion. My understanding of past practice is that a statute found to be invalid as applied to a particular plaintiff, but not unconstitutional as a whole, is not simply "struck down" but is, instead, declared unconstitutional as applied to the fact situation before the Court. *Yick Wo* v. *Hopkins,* 118 U.S. 356 (1886); *Street* v. *New York,* 394 U.S. 576 (1969).

For all of the foregoing reasons, I respectfully dissent.

MR. JUSTICE WHITE, with whom MR. JUSTICE REHNQUIST joins, dissenting.
[This opinion applies also to *Doe* v. *Bolton,* 410 U.S. 179 (1973)]

At the heart of the controversy in these cases are those recurring pregnancies that pose no danger whatsoever to the life or health of the mother but are, nevertheless, unwanted for any one or more of a variety of reasons—convenience, family planning, economics, dislike of children, the embarrassment of illegitimacy, etc. The common claim before us is that for any one of such reasons, or for no reason at all, and without asserting or claiming any threat to life or health, any woman is entitled to an abortion at her request if she is able to find a medical advisor willing to undertake the procedure.

The Court for the most part sustains this position: During the period prior to the time the fetus becomes viable, the Constitution of the United States values the convenience, whim, or caprice of the putative mother more than the life or potential life of the fetus; the Constitution, therefore, guarantees the right to an abortion as against any state law or policy seeking to protect the fetus from an abortion not prompted by more compelling reasons of the mother.

With all due respect, I dissent. I find nothing in the language or history of the Constitution to support the Court's judgment. The Court simply fashions and announces a new constitutional right for pregnant mothers and, with scarcely any reason or authority for its action, invests that right with sufficient substance to override most existing state abortion statutes. The upshot is that the people and the legislatures of the 50 States are constitutionally disentitled to weigh the relative importance of the continued existence and development of the fetus, on the one hand, against a spectrum of possible impacts on the mother, on the other hand. As an exercise of raw judicial power, the Court perhaps has authority to do what it does today; but in my view its judgment is an improvident and extravagant exercise of the power of judicial review that the Constitution extends to this Court.

The Court apparently values the convenience of the pregnant mother more than the continued existence and development of the life or potential life that she carries. Whether or not I might agree with that marshaling of values, I can in no event join the Court's judgment because I find no constitutional warrant for imposing such an order of priorities on the people and legislatures of the States. In a sensitive area such as this, involving as it does issues over which reasonable men may easily and heatedly differ, I cannot accept the Court's exercise of its clear power of choice by interposing a constitutional barrier to state efforts to protect human life and by investing mothers and doctors with the constitutionally protected right to exterminate it. This issue, for the most part, should be left with the people and to the political processes the people have devised to govern their affairs.

It is my view, therefore, that the Texas statute is not constitutionally infirm.

## *Notes*

\*   Briefs of *amici curae* were filed by *Gary K. Nelson*, Attorney General of Arizona, *Robert K. Killian*, Attorney General of Connecticut, *Ed. W. Hancock*, Attorney General of Kentucky, *Clarence A. H. Meyer*, Attorney General of Nebraska, and *Vernon B. Romney*, Attorney General of Utah; by *Joseph P. Witherspoon, Jr.*, for the Association of Texas Diocesan Attorneys; by *Charles E. Rice* for Americans United for Life; by *Eugene J. McMahon* for Women for the Unborn et al.; by *Carol Ryan* for the American College of Obstetricians and Gynecologists et al.; by *Dennis J. Horan, Jerome A. Frazel, Jr., Thomas M. Crisham,* and *Dolores v. Horan* for Certain Physicians, Professors and Fellows of the American College of Obstetrics and Gynecology; by *Harriet F. Pilpel, Nancy F. Wechsler,* and *Frederic S. Nathan* for Planned Parenthood Federation of American, Inc., et al.; by *Alan F. Charles* for the National Legal Program on Health Problems of the Poor et al.; by *Marttie L. Thompson* for State Communities Aid Assn.; by *Alfred L. Scanlan, Martin J. Flynn,* and *Robert M. Byrn* for the National Right to Life Committee; by *Helen L. Buttenwieser* for the American Ethical Union et al.; by *Norma G. Zarky* for the American Association of University Women et al.; by *Nancy*

*Stearns* for New Women Lawyers et al.; by the California Committee to Legalize Abortion et al.; and by *Robert E. Dunne* for Robert L. Sassone.

1.  "Article 1191. Abortion
    "If any person shall designedly administer to a pregnant woman or knowingly procure to be administered with her consent any drug or medicine, or shall use towards her any violence or means whatever externally or internally applied, and thereby procure an abortion, he shall be confined in the penitentiary not less than two nor more than five years; if it be done without her consent, the punishment shall be doubled. By 'abortion' is meant that the life of the fetus or embryo shall be destroyed in the woman's womb or that a premature birth thereof be caused.

    " Art. 1192. Furnishing the means
    "Whoever furnishes the means for procuring an abortion knowing the purpose intended is guilty as an accomplice.

    "Art. 1193. Attempt at abortion
    "If the means used shall fail to produce an abortion, the offender is nevertheless guilty of an attempt to produce abortion, provided it be shown that such means were calculated to produce that result, and shall be fined not less than one hundred nor more than one thousand dollars.

    "Art. 1194. Murder in producing abortion
    "If the death of the mother is occasioned by an abortion so produced or by an attempt to effect the same it is murder."

    "Art. 1196. By medical advice
    "Nothing in this chapter applies to an abortion procured or attempted by medical advice for the purpose of saving the life of the mother."

    The foregoing Articles, together with Art. 1195, compose Chapter 9 of Title 15 of the Penal Code. Article 1195, not attacked here, reads:

    "Art. 1195. Destroying unborn child
    "Whoever shall during parturition of the mother destroy the vitality or life in a child in a state of being born and before actual birth, which child would otherwise have been born alive, shall be confined to the penitentiary for life or for not less than five years."

2.  Ariz. Rev. Stat. Ann. § 13–211 (1956); Conn. Pub. Act No. I (May 1972 special session) (in 4 Conn. Leg. Serv. 677 (1972)), and Conn. Gen. Stat. Rev. §§ 5329, 53–30 (1968) (or unborn child); Idaho Code § 18–601 (1948); Ill. Rev. Stat., c. 38, § 231 (1971); Ind. Code § 35–158–1 (1971); Iowa Code § 701.1 (1971); Ky. Rev. Stat. § 436.020 (1962); La. Rev. Stat. § 37:1285 (6) (1964) (loss of medical license) (but see § 14:87 (Supp. 1972) containing no exception for the life of the mother under the criminal statute); Me. Rev. Stat. Ann., Tit. 17, § 51 (1964); Mass. Gen. Laws Ann., c. 272, § 19 (1970) (using the term "unlawfully," construed to exclude an abortion to save the mother's life, *Kudish* v. *Bd. of Registration*, 356 Mass. 98, 248 N. E. 2d 264 (1969); Mich. Comp. Laws § 750.14 (1948); Minn. Stat. § 617.18 (1971); Mo. Rev. Stat. § 559.100 (1969); Mont. Rev. Codes Ann. § 94–401 (1969); Neb. Rev. Stat. § 28–405 (1964); Nev. Rev. Stat. § 200.220 (1967); N. H. Rev. Stat. Ann. § 585:13 (1955); N. J. Stat. Ann. § 2A:871 (1969) ("without lawful justification"); N. D. Cent. Code §§ 12–25–01, 12–25—02 (1960); Ohio Rev.

Code Ann. § 2901.16 (1953); Okla. Stat. Ann., Tit. 21, § 861 (1972–1973 Supp.); Pa. Stat. Ann., Tit. 18, §§ 4718, 4719 (1963) ("unlawful"); R. 1. Gen. Laws Ann. § 11–3–1 (1969); S. D. Comp. Laws Ann. § 22–17–1 (1967); Tenn. Code Ann. §§ 39–301, 39–302 (1956); Utah Code Ann. §§ 7–6–21, 7–6–22 (1953); Vt. Stat. Ann., Tit. 13, § 101 (1958); W. Va. Code Ann. § 6–1–28 (1966); Wis. Stat. § 940.04 (1969); Wyo. Stat. Ann. §§ 6–77, 6–78 (1957).

3.  Fourteen States have adopted some form of the ALI statute. See Ark. Stat. Ann. §§ 41–303 to 41–310 (Supp. 1971); Calif. Health & Safety Code §§ 25950–25955.5 (Supp. 1972); Colo. Rev. Stat. Ann. §§ 40–2–50 to 40–2–53 (Cum. Supp. 1967); Del. Code Ann., Tit. 24, §§ 1790–1793 (Supp 1972); Florida Law of Apr. 13, 1972, c. 72–196, 1972 Fla. Sess. Law Serv., pp. 380–382; Ga. Code §§ 26–1201 to 26–1203 (1972); Kan. Stat. Ann. § 21–3407 (Supp. 1971); Md. Ann. Code, Art. 43, §§ 137–139 (1971); Miss. Code Ann. § 2223 (Supp. 1972); N. W. Stat. Ann. §§ 40A–5–1 to 40A–5–3 (1972); N. C. Gen. Stat. § 14–45.1 (Supp. 1971); Ore. Rev. Stat. §§ 435.405 to 435.495 (1971); S. C. Code Ann. §§ 16–82 to 16–89 (1962 and Supp. 1971); Va. Code Ann. §§18.1–62 to 18.1–62.3 (Supp. 1972). Mr. Justice Clark described some of these States as having "led the way." Religion, Morality, and Abortion: A Constitutional Appraisal, 2 Loyola U. (L. A.) L. Rev. 1, 11 (1969).

    By the end of 1970, four other States had repealed criminal penalties for abortions performed in early pregnancy by a licensed physician, subject to stated procedural and health requirements. Alaska Stat. § 11.15.060 (1970); Haw. Rev. Stat. § 453–16 (Supp. 1971); N. Y. Penal Code § 125.05, subd. 3 (Supp. 1972–1973); Wash. Rev. Code §§ 9.02.060 to 9.02.080 (Supp. 1972). The precise status of criminal abortion laws in some States is made unclear by recent decisions in state and federal courts striking down existing state laws, in whole or in part.

4.  When Texas urges that a fetus is entitled to Fourteenth Amendment protection as a person, it faces a dilemma. Neither in Texas nor in any other State are all abortions prohibited. Despite broad proscription, an exception always exists. The exception contained in Art. 1196, for an abortion procured or attempted by medical advice for the purpose of saving the life of the mother, is typical. But if the fetus is a person who is not to be deprived of life without due process of law, and if the mother's condition is the sole determinant, does not the Texas exception appear to be out of line with the Amendment's command?

    There are other inconsistencies between Fourteenth Amendment status and the typical abortion statute. It has already been pointed out, n. 49, *supra*, that in Texas the woman is not a principal or an accomplice with respect to an abortion upon her. If the fetus is a person, why is the woman not a principal or an accomplice? Further, the penalty for criminal abortion specified by Art. 1195 is significantly less than the maximum penalty for murder prescribed by Art. 1257 of the Texas Penal Code. If the fetus is a person, may the penalties be different?

5.  Cf. the Wisconsin abortion statute, defining "unborn child" to mean "a human being from the time of conception until it is born alive," Wis. Stat. § 940.04 (6) (1969), and the new Connecticut statute, Pub. Act No. 1 (May 1972 special session), declaring it to be the public policy of the State and the legislative intent "to protect and preserve human life from the moment of conception."

**Roe v. Wade**, 410 U.S. 113 (1973) 7–2

*editor's note:*

*Opinion authors are in bold: () indicates the party of appointing president. If the party of the justice differs from that of appointing president, then the party of the justice is listed second after the slash.*

| MAJORITY | CONCURRING | DISSENTING |
|---|---|---|
| **Blackmun** (r) | **Stewart** (r) | **White** (d) |
| Brennan (r/d) | **Douglas** (d) | **Rehnquist** (r) |
| Marshall (d) | **Burger** (r) | |
| Powell (r/d) | | |

# Planned Parenthood of Southeastern Pennsylvania et al. v. Casey, Governor of Pennsylvania, et al.

## 505 U.S. 855 (1993)

## Certiorari to the United States Court of Appeals for The Third Circuit

### No. 91–744, Argued April 22, 1992—Decided June 29, 1992*

*Kathryn Kolbert* argued the cause for petitioners in No. 91–744 and respondents in No. 91–902. With her on the briefs were *Janet Benshoof, Lynn M. Paltrow, Rachael N. Pine, Steven R. Shapiro, John A. Powell, Linda J. Wharton,* and *Carol E. Tracy.*

*Ernest D. Preate, Jr.,* Attorney General of Pennsylvania, argued the cause for respondents in No. 91–744 and petitioners in No. 91–902. With him on the brief were *John G. Knorr III,* Chief Deputy Attorney General, and *Kate L. Mershimer,* Senior Deputy Attorney General.

*Solicitor General Starr* argued the cause for the United States as *amicus curiae* in support of respondents in No. 91–744 and petitioners in No. 91–902. With him on the brief were *Assistant Attorney General Gerson, Paul J. Larkin, Jr., Thomas G. Hungar,* and *Alfred R. Mollin.*[†]

JUSTICE O'CONNOR, JUSTICE KENNEDY, and JUSTICE SOUTER announced the judgment of the Court and delivered the opinion of the Court with respect to Parts I, II, III, V–A,

V–C, and VI, an opinion with respect to Part V–E, in which JUSTICE STEVENS joins, and an opinion with respect to Parts IV, V–B, and V–D.

— I —

Liberty finds no refuge in a jurisprudence of doubt. Yet 19 years after our holding that the Constitution protects a woman's right to terminate her pregnancy in its early stages, *Roe* v. *Wade,* 410 U.S. 113 (1973), that definition of liberty is still questioned. Joining the respondents as *amicus curiae,* the United States, as it has done in five other cases in the last decade, again asks us to overrule *Roe.* . . .

At issue in these cases are five provisions of the Pennsylvania Abortion Control Act of 1982, as amended in 1988 and 1989. 18 Pa. Cons. Stat. §§ 3203–3220 (1990). . . .The Act requires that a woman seeking an abortion give her informed consent prior to the abortion procedure and specifies that she be provided with certain information at least 24 hours before the abortion is performed. § 3205. For a minor to obtain an abortion, the Act requires the informed consent of one of her parents, but provides for a judicial bypass option if the minor does not wish to or cannot obtain a parent's consent. § 3206. Another provision of the Act requires that, unless certain exceptions apply, a married woman seeking an abortion must sign a statement indicating that she has notified her husband of her intended abortion. § 3209. The Act exempts compliance with these three requirements in the event of a "medical emergency," which is defined in § 3203 of the Act. See §§ 3203, 3205(a), 3206(a), 3209(c). In addition to the above provisions regulating the performance of abortions, the Act imposes certain reporting requirements on facilities that provide abortion services. §§ 3207(b), 3214(a), 3214(f).

Before any of these provisions took effect, the petitioners, who are five abortion clinics and one physician representing himself as well as a class of physicians who provide abortion services, brought this suit seeking declaratory and injunctive relief. Each provision was challenged as unconstitutional on its face. The District Court entered a preliminary injunction against the enforcement of the regulations, and, after a 3-day bench trial, held all the provisions at issue here unconstitutional, entering a permanent injunction against Pennsylvania's enforcement of them. 744 F. Supp. 1323 (ED Pa. 1990). The Court of Appeals for the Third Circuit affirmed in part and reversed in part, upholding all of the regulations except for the husband notification requirements. 947 F. 2d 682 (1991). We granted certiorari. 502 U.S. 1056 (1992). . . . we find it imperative to review once more the principles that define the rights of the woman and the legitimate authority of the State respecting the termination of pregnancies by abortion procedures.

After considering the fundamental constitutional questions resolved by *Roe*, principles of institutional integrity, and the rule of *stare decisis*, we are led to conclude this: the essential holding of *Roe* v. *Wade* should be retained and once again reaffirmed.

It must be stated at the outset and with clarity that *Roe's* essential holding, the holding we reaffirm, has three parts. First is a recognition of the right of the woman to choose to have an abortion before viability and to obtain it without undue interferences from the State. Before viability, the State's interests are not strong enough to support a prohibition of abortion or the imposition of a substantial obstacle to the woman's effective right to elect the procedure. Second is a confirmation of the State's power to restrict abortions after fetal viability, if the law contains exceptions for pregnancies which endanger the woman's life or health. And third is the principle that the State has legitimate interests from the outset of the pregnancy in protecting the health of the woman and the life of the fetus that may become a child. These principles do not contradict one another, and we adhere to each.

## — II —

Constitutional protection of the woman's decision to terminate her pregnancy derives from the Due Process Clause of the Fourteenth Amendment. It declares that no State shall "deprive any person of life, liberty, or property, without due process of law." The controlling word in the cases before us is "liberty." Although a literal reading of the Clause might suggest that it governs only the procedures by which a State may deprive persons of liberty, for at least 105 years, since *Mugler* v. *Kansas*, 123 U.S 623, 660–661 (1887), the Clause has been understood to contain a substantive component as well, one "barring certain government actions regardless of the fairness of the procedures used to implement them." *Daniels* v. *Williams*, 474 U.S. 327, 331 (1986). . . .

The most familiar of the substantive liberties protected by the Fourteenth Amendment are those recognized by the Bill of Rights. We have held that the Due Process Clause of the Fourteenth Amendment incorporates most of the Bill of Rights against the States. See, *e.g., Duncan* v. *Louisiana*, 391 U.S. 145, 147–148 (1968). It is tempting as a means of curbing the discretion of federal judges, to suppose that liberty encompasses no more than those rights already guaranteed to the individual against federal interference by the express provisions of the first eight Amendments to the Constitution. See *Adamson*

v. *California*, 332 U.S. 46, 68–92 (1947) (Black, J., dissenting). But of course this Court has never accepted that view.

It is also tempting, for the same reason, to suppose that the Due Process Clause protects only those practices, defined at the most specific level, that were protected against government interference by other rules of law when the Fourteenth Amendment was ratified. See *Michael H. v. Gerald D.*, 491 U.S. 110, 127–128, n. 6 (1989) (opinion of SCALIA, J.). But such a view would be inconsistent with our law. It is a promise of the Constitution that there is a realm of personal liberty which the government may not enter. . . .

Neither the Bill of Rights nor the specific practices of States at the time of the adoption of the Fourteenth Amendment marks the outer limits of the substantive sphere of liberty which the Fourteenth Amendment protects. . . . In *Griswold*, we held that the Constitution does not permit a State to forbid a married couple to use contraceptives. That same freedom was later guaranteed, under the Equal Protection Clause, for unmarried couples. See *Eisenstadt v. Baird*, 405 U.S. 438 (1972). Constitutional protection was extended to the sale and distribution of contraceptives in *Carey v. Population Services International, supra*. It is settled now, as it was when the Court heard arguments in *Roe v. Wade*, that the Constitution places limits on a State's right to interfere with a person's most basic decisions about family and parenthood, see *Carey v. Population Services International, supra; Moore v. East Cleveland*, 431 U.S. 494 (1977); *Eisenstadt v. Baird, supra; Loving v. Virginia, supra; Griswold v. Connecticut, supra; Skinner v. Oklahoma ex rel Williamson*, 316 U.S. 535 (1942); *Pierce v. Society of Sisters, supra; Meyer v. Nebraska, supra*, as well as bodily integrity, see, *e.g., Washington v. Harper*, 494 U.S. 210, 221–222 (1990); *Winston v. Lee*, 470 U.S. 753 (1985); *Rochin v. California*, 342 U.S. 165 (1952).

The inescapable fact is that adjudication of substantive due process claims may call upon the Court in interpreting the Constitution to exercise that same capacity which by tradition courts always have exercised: reasoned judgment. Its boundaries are not susceptible of expression as a simple rule. That does not mean we are free to invalidate state policy choices with which we disagree; yet neither does it permit us to shrink from the duties of our office. . . .

Men and women of good conscience can disagree, and we suppose some always shall disagree, about the profound moral and spiritual implications of terminating a pregnancy, even in its earliest stage. Some of us as individuals find abortion offensive to our most basic principles of morality, but that cannot control our decision. Our obligation is to define the liberty of all, not to mandate our own moral code. The underlying constitutional issue is whether the State can resolve these philosophic questions in such a definitive way that a woman lacks all choice in the matter, except perhaps in those rare circumstances in which the pregnancy is itself a danger to her own life or health, or is the result of rape or incest.

It is conventional constitutional doctrine that where reasonable people disagree the government can adopt one position or the other. . . . That theorem, however, assumes a state of affairs in which the choice does not intrude upon a protected liberty. Thus, while some people might disagree about whether or not the flag should be saluted, or disagree about the proposition that it may not be defiled, we have ruled that a State may not compel or enforce one view or the other. See *West Virginia Bd. of Ed.* v. *Barnette*, 319 U.S. 624 (1943); *Texas* v. *Johnson*, 491 U.S. 397 (1989).

Our law affords constitutional protection to personal decisions relating to marriage, procreation, contraception, family relationships, child rearing, and education. *Carey* v. *Population Services International*, 431 U.S., at 685. Our cases recognize "the right of the *individual*, married or single, to be free from unwarranted governmental intrusion into matters so fundamentally affecting a person as the decision whether to bear or beget a child." *Eisenstadt* v. *Baird, supra*, at 453 (emphasis in original). Our precedents "have respected the private realm of family life which the state cannot enter." *Prince* v. *Massachusetts*, 321 U.S. 158, 166 (1944). These matters, involving the most intimate and personal choices a person may make in a lifetime, choices central to personal dignity and autonomy, are central to the liberty protected by the Fourteenth Amendment. At the heart of liberty is the right to define one's own concept of existence, of meaning, of the universe, and of the mystery of human life. Beliefs about these matters could not define the attributes of personhood were they formed under compulsion of the State.

These considerations begin our analysis of the woman's interest in terminating her pregnancy but cannot end it, for this reason: though the abortion decision may originate within the zone of conscience and belief, it is more than a philosophic exercise. Abortion is a unique act. It is an act fraught with consequences for others: for the woman who must live with the implications of her decision; for the persons who perform and assist in the procedure; for the spouse, family, and society which must confront the knowledge that these procedures exist, procedures some deem nothing short of an act of violence against innocent human life; and, depending on one's beliefs, for the life or potential life that is aborted. Though abortion is conduct, it does not follow that the State is entitled to proscribe it in all instances. That is because the liberty of the woman is at stake in a sense unique to the human condition and so unique to the law. The mother who carries a child to full term is subject to anxieties, to physical constraints, to pain that only she must bear. That these sacrifices have from the beginning of the human race been endured by woman with a pride that ennobles her in the eyes of others and gives to the infant a bond of love cannot alone be grounds for the State to insist she make the sacrifice. Her suffering is too intimate and personal for the State to insist, without more, upon its own vision of the woman's role, however, dominant that vision has been in the course of our history and our culture. The destiny of the woman must be shaped to a large extent on her own conception of her spiritual imperatives and her place in society.

It should be recognized, moreover, that in some critical respects the abortion decision is of the same character as the decision to use contraception, to which *Griswold* v. *Connecticut, Eisenstadt* v. *Baird,* and *Carey* v. *Population Services International* afford constitutional protection. We have no doubt as to the correctness of those decisions. They support the reasoning in *Roe* relating to the woman's liberty because they involve personal decisions concerning not only the meaning of procreation but also human responsibility and respect for it. As with abortion, reasonable people will have differences of opinion about these matters. One view is based on such reverence for the wonder of creation that any pregnancy ought to be welcomed and carried to full term no matter how difficult it will be to provide for the child and ensure its well-being. Another is that the inability to provide for the nurture and care of the infant is a cruelty to the child and an anguish to the parent. These are intimate views with infinite variations, and their deep, personal character underlay our decisions in *Griswold, Eisenstadt,* and *Carey.* The same concerns are present when the woman confronts the reality that, perhaps despite her attempts to avoid it, she has become pregnant.

It was this dimension of personal liberty that *Roe* sought to protect, and its holding invoked the reasoning and tradition of the precedents we have discussed, granting protection to substantive liberties of the person. *Roe* was, of course, an extension of those cases and, as the decision itself indicated, the separate States could act in some degree to further their own legitimate interests in protecting prenatal life. The extent to which the legislatures of the States might act to outweigh the interests of the woman in choosing to terminate her pregnancy was a subject of debate both in *Roe* itself and in decisions following it.

While we appreciate the weight of the arguments made on behalf of the State in the cases before us, arguments which in their ultimate formulation conclude that *Roe* should be overruled, the reservations any of us may have in reaffirming the central holding of *Roe* are outweighed by the explication of individual liberty we have given combined with the force of *stare decisis.* We turn now to that doctrine.

— III —

A

The obligation to follow precedent begins with necessity, and a contrary necessity marks its outer limit. With Cardozo, we recognize that no judicial system could do society's work if it eyed each issue afresh in every case that raised it. See B. Cardozo, The Nature of the Judicial Process 149 (1921). Indeed, the very concept of the rule of law underlying our own Constitution requires such continuity over time that a respect for precedent is, by definition, indispensable. See Powell, Stare Decisis and Judicial

Restraint, 1991 Journal of Supreme Court History 13, 16. At the other extreme, a different necessity would make itself felt if a prior judicial ruling should come to be seen so clearly as error that its enforcement was for that every reason doomed.

Even when the decision to overrule a prior case is not, as in the rare, latter instance, virtually foreordained, it is common wisdom that the rule of *stare decisis* is not an "inexorable command," and certainly it is not such in every constitutional case. . . . Rather, when this Court reexamines a prior holding, its judgment is customarily informed by a series of prudential and pragmatic considerations designed to test the consistency of overruling a prior decision with the ideal of the rule of law, and to gauge the respective costs of reaffirming and overruling a prior case. Thus, for example, we may ask whether the rule has proven to be intolerable simply in defying practical workability, *Swift & Co.* v. *Wickham*, 382 U.S. 111, 116 (1965); whether the rule is subject to a kind of reliance that would lend a special hardship to the consequences of overruling and add inequity to the cost of repudiation, *e.g.*, *United States* v. *Title Ins. & Trust Co.*, 265 U.S. 472, 486 (1924); whether related principles of law have so far developed as to have left the old rule no more than a remnant of abandoned doctrine, see *Patterson* v. *McLean Credit Union*, 491 U.S. 164, 173–174 (1989); or whether facts have so changed, or come to be seen so differently, as to have robbed the old rule of significant application or justification, *e.g.*, *Burnet, supra,* at 412 (Brandeis, J., dissenting). . . .

Although *Roe* has engendered opposition, it has in no sense proven "unworkable," see *Garcia* v. *San Antonio Metropolitan Transit Authority*, 469 U.S. 528, 546 (1985), representing as it does a simple limitation beyond which a state law is unenforceable. While *Roe* has, of course, required judicial assessment of state laws affecting the exercise of the choice guaranteed against government infringement, and although the need for such review will remain as a consequence of today's decision, the required determinations fall within judicial competence.

## 2

The inquiry into reliance counts the cost of a rule's repudiation as it would fall on those who have relied reasonably on the rule's continued application. . . .

For two decades of economic and social developments, people have organized intimate relationships and made choices that define their views of themselves and their places in society, in reliance on the availability of abortion in the event that contraception should fail. The ability of women to participate equally in the economic and social life of the Nation has been facilitated by their ability to control their reproductive lives. See, *e.g.*, R. Petchesky, Abortion and Woman's Choice 109, 133, n. 7 (rev. ed. 1990). The Constitution serves human values, and while the effect of reliance on *Roe* cannot be exactly measured, neither can the certain cost of overruling *Roe* for people who have ordered their thinking and living around that case be dismissed.

## 3

No evolution of legal principle has left *Roe*'s doctrinal footings weaker than they were in 1973. No development of constitutional law since the case was decided has implicitly or explicitly left *Roe* behind as a mere survivor of obsolete constitutional thinking.

It will be recognized, of course, that *Roe* stands at an intersection of two lines of decisions, but in whichever doctrinal category one reads the case, the result for present purposes will be the same. The *Roe* Court itself placed its holding in the succession of cases most prominently exemplified by *Griswold* v. *Connecticut*, 381 U.S. 479 (1965). See *Roe*, 410 U.S., at 152–153. When it is so seen, *Roe* is clearly in no jeopardy, since subsequent constitutional developments have neither disturbed, nor do they threaten to diminish, the scope of recognized protection accorded to the liberty relating to intimate relationships, the family, and decisions about whether or not to beget or bear a child. See, *e.g.*, *Carey* v. *Population Services International*, 431 U.S. 678 (1977); *Moore* v. *East Cleveland*, 431 U.S. 494 (1977).

*Roe*, however, may be seen not only as an exemplar of *Griswold* liberty but as a rule (whether or not mistaken) of personal autonomy and bodily integrity, with doctrinal affinity to cases recognizing limits on governmental power to mandate medical treatment or to bar its rejection. If so, our cases since *Roe* accord with *Roe*'s view that a State's interest in the protection of life falls short of justifying any plenary override of individual liberty claims. *Cruzan* v. *Director, Mo. Dept. of Health*, 497 U.S. 261, 278 (1990); cf., *e.g.*, *Riggins* v. *Nevada*, 504 U.S. 127, 135 (1992); *Washington* v. *Harper*, 494 U.S. 210 (1990); see also, *e.g.*, *Rochin* v. *California*, 342 U.S. 165 (1952); *Jacobson* v. *Massachusetts*, 197 U.S. 11, 24-30 (1905).

Finally, one could classify *Roe* as *sui generis*. If the case is so viewed, then there clearly has been no erosion of its central determination. The original holding resting on the concurrence of seven Members of the Court in 1973 was expressly affirmed by a majority of six in 1983, see *Akron* v. *Akron Center for Reproductive Health, Inc.*, 462 U.S. 416 (*Akron I*), and by a majority of five in 1986, see *Thornburgh* v. *American College of Obstetricians and Gynecologists*, 476 U.S. 747, expressing adherence to the constitutional ruling despite legislative efforts in some States to test its limits. More recently, in *Webster* v. *Reproductive Health Services*, 492 U.S. 490 (1989), although two of the present authors questioned the trimester framework in a way consistent with our judgment today, see *id.*, at 518 (REHNQUIST, C.J., joined by WHITE and KENNEDY, JJ.); *id.*, at 529 (O'CONNOR, J., concurring in part and concurring in judgment), a majority of the Court either decided to reaffirm or declined to address the constitutional validity of the central holding of *Roe*. See *Webster*, 492 U.S., at 521 (REHNQUIST, C.J., joined by WHITE and KENNEDY, JJ.); *id.*, at 525–526 (O'CONNOR, J., concurring in part and concurring in judgment); *id.*, at 537, 553 (BLACKMUN, J., joined by BRENNAN and MARSHALL, JJ., concurring in part and dissenting in part); *id.*, at 561-563 (STEVENS, J., concurring in part and dissenting in part). . . .

The soundness of this prong of the *Roe* analysis is apparent from a consideration of the alternative. If indeed the woman's interest in deciding whether to bear and beget a child had not been recognized as in *Roe*, the State might as readily restrict a woman's right to choose to carry a pregnancy to term as to terminate it, to further asserted state interests in population control, or eugenics, for example. Yet *Roe* has been sensibly relied upon to counter any such suggestions. *E.g.*, *Arnold* v. *Board of Education of Escambia County, Ala.*, 880 F. 2d 305, 311 (CA11 1989) (relying upon *Roe* and concluding that government officials violate the Constitution by coercing a minor to have an abortion); *Avery* v. *County of Burke*, 660 F. 2d 111, 115 (CA4 1981) (county agency inducing teenage girl to undergo unwanted sterilization on the basis of misrepresentation that she had sickle cell trait); see also *In re Quinlan*, 70 N.J. 10, 355 A. 2d 647 (relying on *Roe* in finding a right to terminate medical treatment), cert. denied *sub nom. Garger* v. *New Jersey*, 429 U.S. 922 (1976)). In any event, because *Roe*'s scope is confined by the fact of its concern with post-conception potential life, a concern otherwise likely to be implicated only by some forms of contraception protected independently under *Griswold* and later cases, any error in *Roe* is unlikely to have serious ramifications in future cases.

### 4

We have seen how time has overtaken some of *Roe*'s factual assumptions: advances in maternal health care allow for abortions safe to the mother later in pregnancy than was true in 1973, . . . and advances in neonatal care have advanced viability to a point somewhat earlier. . . . But these facts go only to the scheme of time limits on the realization of competing interests, and the divergences from the factual premises of 1973 have no bearing on the validity of *Roe*'s central holding, that viability marks the earliest point at which the State's interest in fetal life is constitutionally adequate to justify a legislative ban on nontherapeutic abortions. The soundness or unsoundness of that constitutional judgment in no sense turns on whether viability occurs at approximately 28 weeks, as was usual at the time of *Roe*, at 23 to 24 weeks, as it sometimes does today, or at some moment even slightly earlier in pregnancy, as it may if fetal respiratory capacity can somehow be enhanced in the future. Whenever it may occur, the attainment of viability may continue to serve as the critical fact, just as it has done since *Roe* was decided; which is to say that no change in *Roe*'s factual underpinning has left its central holding obsolete, and none supports an argument for overruling it.

## 5

The sum of the precedental enquiring to this point shows *Roe*'s underpinnings un-weakened in any way affecting its central holding. While it has engendered disap-proval, it has not been unworkable. An entire generation has come of age free to assume *Roe*'s concept of liberty in defining the capacity of women to act in society, and to make reproductive decisions; no erosion of principle going to liberty or personal autonomy has left *Roe*'s central holding a doctrinal remnant; *Roe* portends no devel-opments at odds with other precedent for the analysis of personal liberty; and no changes of fact have rendered viability more or less appropriate as the point at which the balance of interests tips. Within the bounds of normal *stare decisis* analysis, then, and subject to the considerations on which it customarily turns, the stronger argument is for affirming *Roe*'s central holding, with whatever degree of personal reluctance any of us may have, not for overruling it.

## B

In a less significant case, *stare decisis* analysis could, and would, stop at the point we have reached. But the sustained and widespread debate *Roe* has provoked calls for some comparison between that case and others of comparable dimension that have responded to national controversies and taken on the impress of the controversies addressed. Only two such decisional lines from the past century present themselves for examination, and in each instance the result reached by the Court accorded with the principles we apply today.

The first example is that line of cases identified with *Lochner* v. *New York*, 198 U.S. 45 (1905), which imposed substantive limitations on legislation limiting economic auton-omy in favor of health and welfare regulation, adopting in Justice Holmes's view, the theory of laissez-faire. *Id.*, at 75 (dissenting opinion). The *Lochner* decisions were exemplified by *Adkins* v. *Children's Hospital of District of Columbia*, 261 U.S. 525 (1923), in which this Court held it to be an infringement of constitutionally protected liberty of contract to require the employers of adult women to satisfy minimum wage standards. Fourteen years later, *West Coast Hotel Co.* v. *Parrish*, 300 U.S. 379 (1937), signaled the demise of *Lochner* by overruling *Adkins*. In the meantime, the Depression had come and, with it, the lesson that seemed unmistakable to most people by 1937, that the interpretation of contractual freedom protected in *Adkins* rested on fundamen-tally false factual assumptions about the capacity of a relatively unregulated market to satisfy minimal levels of human welfare. . . . The facts upon which the earlier case had premised a constitutional resolution of social controversy had proven to be untrue, and history's demonstration of their untruth not only justified but required the new choice of constitutional principle that *West Coast Hotel* announced. Of course, it was true that the Court lost something by its misperception, or its lack of prescience, and the Court-packing crisis only magnified the loss; but the clear demonstration that the facts of economic life were different from those previously assumed warranted the repudiation of the old law.

The second comparison that 20th century history invites is with the cases employing the separate-but-equal rule for applying the Fourteenth Amendment's equal protection guarantee. They began with *Plessy* v. *Ferguson*, 163 U.S. 537 (1896), holding that legislatively mandated racial segregation in public transportation works no denial of equal protection, rejecting the argument that racial separation enforced by the legal machinery of American society treats the black race as inferior. The *Plessy* Court considered "the underlying fallacy of the plaintiff's argument to consist in the assumption that the enforced separation of the two races stamps the colored race with a badge of inferiority. If this be so, it is not by reason of anything found in the act, but solely because the colored race chooses to put that construction upon it." *Id.*, at 551. Whether, as a matter of historical fact, the Justices in the *Plessy* majority believed this or not, see *id.*, at 557, 562 (Harlan, J., dissenting), this understanding of the implication of segregation was the stated justification for the Court's opinion. But this understanding of the facts and the rule it was stated to justify were repudiated in *Brown* v. *Board of Education*, 347 U.S. 483 (1954) *(Brown I)*. . . .

The Court in *Brown* addressed these facts of life by observing that whatever may have been the understanding in *Plessy*'s time of the power of segregation to stigmatize those who were segregated with a "badge of inferiority," it was clear by 1954 that legally sanctioned segregation had just such an effect, to the point that racially separate public educational facilities were deemed inherently unequal. 347 U.S., at 494–495. Society's understanding of the facts upon which a constitutional ruling was sought in 1954 was thus fundamentally different from the basis claimed for the decision in 1896. While we think *Plessy* was wrong the day it was decided, see *Plessy, supra,* at 552–564 (Harlan, J., dissenting), we must also recognize that the *Plessy* Court's explanation for its decision was so clearly at odds with the facts apparent to the Court in 1954 that the decision to reexamine *Plessy* was on this ground alone not only justified but required.

*West Coast Hotel* and *Brown* each rested on facts, or an understanding of facts, changed from those which furnished the claimed justifications for the earlier constitutional resolutions. Each case was comprehensible as the Court's response to facts that the country could understand, or had come to understand already, but which the Court of an earlier day, as its own declarations disclosed, had not been able to perceive. As the decisions were thus comprehensible they were also defensible, not merely as the victories of one doctrinal school over another by dint of numbers (victories though they were), but as applications of constitutional principle to facts as they had not been seen by the Court before. In constitutional adjudication as elsewhere in life, changed circumstances may impose new obligations, and the thoughtful part of the Nation could accept each decision to overrule a prior case as a response to the Court's constitutional duty.

Because the cases before us present no such occasion it could be seen as no such response. Because neither the factual underpinnings of *Roe*'s central holding nor our understanding of it has changed (and because no other indication of weakened precedent has been shown), the Court could not pretend to be reexamining the prior law with any justification beyond a present doctrinal disposition to come out differently from the Court of 1973. To overrule prior law for no other reason than that would run counter to the view repeated in our cases, that a decision to overrule should rest on some special reason over and above the belief that a prior case was wrongly decided. See, *e.g., Mitchell* v. *W.T. Grant Co.*, 416 U.S. 600, 636 (1974) (Stewart, J., dissenting) ("A basic change in our membership invites the popular misconception that this institution is little different from the two political branches of the Government. No misconception could do more lasting injury to this Court and to the system of law which it is our abiding mission to serve"); *Mapp* v. *Ohio*, 367 U.S. 643, 677 (1961) (Harlan, J., dissenting).

# C

... Our analysis would not be complete, however, without explaining why overruling *Roe*'s central holding would not only reach an unjustifiable result under principles of *stare decisis*, but would seriously weaken the Court's capacity to exercise the judicial power and to function as the Supreme Court of a Nation dedicated to the rule of law. To understand why this would be so it is necessary to understand the source of this Court's authority, the conditions necessary for its preservation, and its relationship to the country's understanding of itself as a constitutional Republic.

The root of American governmental power is revealed most clearly in the instance of the power conferred by the Constitution upon the Judiciary of the United States and specifically upon this Court. As Americans of each succeeding generation are rightly told, the Court cannot buy support for its decisions by spending money and, except to a minor degree, it cannot independently coerce obedience to its decrees. The Court's power lies, rather, in its legitimacy, a product of substance and perception that shows itself in the people's acceptance of the Judiciary as fit to determine what the Nation's law means and to declare what it demands.

The underlying substance of this legitimacy is of course the warrant for the Court's decisions in the Constitution and the lesser sources of legal principle on which the Court draws. The Court must take care to speak and act in ways that allow people to accept its decisions on the terms the Court claims for them, as grounded truly in principle, not as compromises with social and political pressures having, as such, no bearing on the principled choices that the Court is obliged to make. Thus, the Court's legitimacy depends on making legally principled decisions under circumstances in which their principled character is sufficiently plausible to be accepted by the Nation. . . . However upsetting it may be to those most directly affected when one judicially derived rule replaces another, the country can accept some correction of error without necessarily questioning the legitimacy of the Court.

In two circumstances, however, the Court would almost certainly fail to receive the benefit of the doubt in overruling prior cases. There is, first, a point beyond which frequent overruling would overtax the country's belief in the Court's good faith. . . . The legitimacy of the Court would fade with the frequency of its vacillation.

That first circumstance can be described as hypothetical; the second is to the point here and now. Where, in the performance of its judicial duties, the Court decides a case in such a way as to resolve the sort of intensely divisive controversy reflected in *Roe* and those rare, comparable cases, its decision has a dimension that the resolution of the normal case does not carry. It is the dimension present whenever the Court's interpretation of the Constitution calls the contending sides of a national controversy to end their national division by accepting a common mandate rooted in the Constitution.

The Court is not asked to do this very often, having thus addressed the Nation only twice in our lifetime, in the decisions of *Brown* and *Roe*. But when the Court does act in this way, its decision requires an equally rare precedential force to counter the inevitable efforts to overturn it and to thwart its implementation. Some of those efforts may be mere unprincipled emotional reactions; others may proceed from principles worthy of profound respect. But whatever the premises of opposition may be, only the most convincing justification under accepted standards of precedent could suffice to demonstrate that a later decision overruling the first was anything but a surrender to political pressure, and an unjustified repudiation of the principle on which the Court staked its authority in the first instance. So to overrule under fire in the absence of the most compelling reason to reexamine a watershed decision would subvert the Court's legitimacy beyond any serious question. Cf. *Brown* v. *Board of Education*, 349 U.S. 294, 300 (1955) *Brown II)* ("[I]t should go without saying that the vitality of th[e] constitutional principles [announced in *Brown I*,] cannot be allowed to yield simply because of disagreement with them").

The country's loss of confidence in the Judiciary would be underscored by an equally certain and equally reasonable condemnation for another failing in overruling unnecessarily and under pressure. Some cost will be paid by anyone who approves or implements a constitutional decision where it is unpopular, or who refuses to work to undermine the decision or to force its reversal. The price may be criticism or ostracism, or it may be violence. An extra price will be paid by those who themselves disapprove of the decision's results when viewed outside of constitutional terms, but who nevertheless struggle to accept it, because they respect the rule of law. To all those who will be so tested by following, the Court implicitly undertakes to remain steadfast, lest in the end a price be paid for nothing. The promise of constancy, once given, binds its maker for as long as the power to stand by the decision survives and the understanding of the issue has not changed so fundamentally as to render the commitment obsolete. From the obligation of this promise this Court cannot and should not assume any exemption when duty requires it to decide a case in conformance with the Constitution. A willing breach of it would be nothing less than a breach of faith, and no Court that broke its faith with the people could sensibly expect credit for principle in the decision by which it did that.

It is true that diminished legitimacy may be restored, but only slowly. Unlike the political branches, a Court thus weakened could not seek to regain its position with a new mandate from the voters, and even if the Court could somehow go to the polls, the loss of its principled character could not be retrieved by the casting of so many votes. Like the character of an individual, the legitimacy of the Court must be earned over time. So, indeed, must be the character of a Nation of people who aspire to live according to the rule of law. Their belief in themselves as such a people is not readily separable from their understanding of the Court invested with the authority to decide their constitutional cases and speak before all others for their constitutional ideals. If the Court's legitimacy should be undermined, then, so would the country be in its very ability to see itself through its constitutional ideals. The Court's concern with legitimacy is not for the sake of the Court, but for the sake of the Nation to which it is responsible.

The Court's duty in the present cases is clear. In 1973, it confronted the already-divisive issue of governmental power to limit personal choice to undergo abortion, for which it provided a new resolution based on the due process guaranteed by the Fourteenth Amendment. Whether or not a new social consensus is developing on that issue, its divisiveness is no less today than in 1973, and pressure to overrule the decision, like pressure to retain it, has grown only more intense. A decision to overrule *Roe*'s essential holding under the existing circumstances would address error, if error there was, at the cost of both profound and unnecessary damage to the Court's legitimacy, and to the Nation's commitment to the rule of law. It is therefore imperative to adhere to the essence of *Roe*'s original decision, and we do so today.

— IV —

From what we have said so far it follows that it is a constitutional liberty of the woman to have some freedom to terminate her pregnancy. We conclude that the basic decision in *Roe* was based on a constitutional analysis which we cannot now repudiate. The woman's liberty is not so unlimited, however, that from the outset the State cannot show its concern for the life of the unborn, and at a later point in fetal development the State's interest in life has sufficient force so that the right of the woman to terminate the pregnancy can be restricted.

That brings us, of course, to the point where much criticism has been directed at *Roe*, a criticism that always inheres when the Court draws a specific rule from what in the Constitution is but a general standard. We conclude, however, that the urgent claims of the woman to retain the ultimate control over her destiny and her body, claims implicit in the meaning of liberty, require us to perform that function. Liberty must not be extinguished for want of a line that is clear. And it falls to us to give some real substance to the woman's liberty to determine whether to carry her pregnancy to full term.

We conclude the line should be drawn at viability, so that before that time the woman has a right to choose to terminate her pregnancy. We adhere to this principle for two reasons. First, as we have said, is the doctrine of *stare decisis*. Any judicial act of line-drawing may seem somewhat arbitrary, but *Roe* was a reasoned statement, elaborated with great care. . . .

The second reason is that the concept of viability, as we noted in *Roe*, is the time at which there is a realistic possibility of maintaining and nourishing a life outside the womb, so that the independent existence of the second life can in reason and all fairness be the object of state protection that now overrides the rights of the woman. See *Roe* v. *Wade*, 410 U.S., at 163. Consistent with other constitutional norms, legislatures may draw lines which appear arbitrary without the necessity of offering a justification. But courts may not. We must justify the lines we draw. And there is no line other than viability which is more workable. To be sure, as we have said, there may be some medical developments that affect the precise point of viability, see *supra*, at 860, but this is an imprecision within tolerable limits given that the medical community and all those who must apply its discoveries will continue to explore the matter. The viability line also has, as a practical matter, an element of fairness. In some broad sense it might be said that a woman who fails to act before viability has consented to the State's intervention on behalf of the developing child.

The woman's right to terminate her pregnancy before viability is the most central principle of *Roe* v. *Wade*. It is a rule of law and a component of liberty we cannot renounce. . . .

Yet it must be remembered that *Roe* v. *Wade* speaks with clarity in establishing not only the woman's liberty but also the State's "important and legitimate interest in potential life." *Roe, supra,* at 163. That portion of the decision in *Roe* has been given too little acknowledgment and implementation by the Court in its subsequent cases. Those cases decided that any regulation touching upon the abortion decision must survive strict scrutiny, to be sustained only if drawn in narrow terms to further a compelling state interest. See, *e.g., Akron I, supra,* at 427. Not all of the cases decided under that formulation can be reconciled with the holding in *Roe* itself that the State has legitimate interests in the health of the woman and in protecting the potential life within her. In resolving this tension, we choose to rely upon *Roe,* as against the later cases.

*Roe* has established a trimester framework to govern abortion regulations. Under this elaborate but rigid construct, almost no regulation at all is permitted during the first trimester of pregnancy; regulations designed to protect the woman's health, but not to further the State's interest in potential life, are permitted during the second trimester; and during the third trimester, when the fetus is viable, prohibitions are permitted provided the life or health of the mother is not at stake. *Roe, supra,* at 163–166. Most of our cases since *Roe* have involved the application of rules derived from the trimester framework. See, *e.g, Thornburgh* v. *American College of Obstetricians and Gynecologists, supra; Akron I, supra.*

The trimester framework no doubt was erected to ensure that the woman's right to choose not become so subordinate to the State's interest in promoting fetal life that her choice exists in theory but not in fact. We do not agree, however, that the trimester approach is necessary to accomplish this objective. A framework of this rigidity was unnecessary and in its later interpretation sometimes contradicted the State's permissible exercise of its powers.

Though the woman has a right to choose to terminate or continue her pregnancy before viability, it does not at all follow that the State is prohibited from taking steps to ensure that this choice is thoughtful and informed. Even in the earliest stages of pregnancy, the State may enact rules and regulations designed to encourage her to know that there are philosophic and social arguments of great weight that can be brought to bear in favor of continuing the pregnancy to full term and that there are procedures and institutions to allow adoption of unwanted children as well as a certain degree of state assistance if the mother chooses to raise the child herself. "'[T]he Constitution does not forbid a State or city, pursuant to democratic processes, from expressing a preference for normal childbirth.'" *Webster* v. *Reproductive Health Services,* 492 U.S., at 511 (opinion of the Court) (quoting *Poelker* v. *Doe,* 432 U.S. 519, 521 (1977)). It follows that States are free to enact laws to provide a reasonable framework for a woman to make a decision that has such profound and lasting meaning. This, too, we find consistent with *Roe*'s central premises, and indeed the inevitable consequence of our holding that the State has an interest in protecting the life of the unborn.

We reject the trimester framework, which we do not consider to be part of the essential holding of *Roe*. See *Webster* v. *Reproductive Health Services*, 492 U.S., at 518 (opinion of REHNQUIST, C.J.); *id.*, at 529 (O'CONNOR, J., concurring in part and concurring in judgment) (describing the trimester framework as "problematic"). Measures aimed at ensuring that a woman's choice contemplates the consequences for the fetus do not necessarily interfere with the right recognized in *Roe*, although those measures have been found to be inconsistent with the rigid trimester framework announced in that case. A logical reading of the central holding of *Roe* itself, and a necessary reconciliation of the liberty of the woman and the interest of the State in promoting prenatal life, require, in our view, that we abandon the trimester framework as a rigid prohibition on all pre-viability regulation aimed at the protection of fetal life. The trimester framework suffers from these basic flaws: in its formulation it misconceives the nature of the pregnant woman's interest; and in practice it undervalues the State's interest in potential life, as recognized in *Roe*.

As our jurisprudence relating to all liberties save perhaps abortion has recognized, not every law which makes a right more difficult to exercise is, *ipso facto*, an infringement of that right. An example clarifies the point. We have held that not every ballot access limitation amounts to an infringement of the right to vote. Rather, the States are granted substantial flexibility in establishing the framework within which voters choose the candidates for whom they wish to vote. *Anderson* v. *Celebrezze*, 460 U.S. 780, 788 (1983); *Norman* v. *Reed*, 502 U.S. 279 (1992).

The abortion right is similar. Numerous forms of state regulation might have the incidental effect of increasing the cost or decreasing the availability of medical care, whether for abortion or any other medical procedure. The fact that a law which serves a valid purpose, one not designed to strike at the right itself, has the incidental effect of making it more difficult or more expensive to procure an abortion cannot be enough to invalidate it. Only where state regulation imposes an undue burden on a woman's ability to make this decision does the power of the State reach into the heart of the liberty protected by the Due Process Clause. . . .

. . . Despite the protestations contained in the original *Roe* opinion to the effect that the Court was not recognizing an absolute right, 410 U.S., at 154–155, the Court's experience applying the trimester framework has led to the striking down of some abortion regulations which in no real sense deprived women of the ultimate decision. Those decisions went too far because the right recognized by *Roe* is a right "to be free from unwarranted governmental intrusion into matters so fundamentally affecting a person as the decision whether to bear or beget a child." *Eisenstadt* v. *Baird*, 405 U.S., at 453. Not all governmental intrusion is of necessity is unwarranted; and that brings us to the other basic flaw in the trimester framework: even in *Roe*'s terms, in practice it undervalues the State's interest in the potential life within the woman.

*Roe* v. *Wade* was express in its recognition of the State's important and legitimate interest[s] in preserving and protecting the health of the pregnant woman [and] in protecting the potentiality of human life." . . .

The very notion that the State has a substantial interest in potential life leads to the conclusion that not all regulations must be deemed unwarranted. Not all burdens on the right to decide whether to terminate a pregnancy will be undue. In our view, the undue burden standard is the appropriate means of reconciling the State's interest with the woman's constitutionally protected liberty. . . .

It is important to clarify what is meant by an undue burden.

A finding of an undue burden is a shorthand for the conclusion that a state regulation has the purpose or effect of placing a substantial obstacle in the path of a woman seeking an abortion of a nonviable fetus. A statute with this purpose is invalid because the means chosen by the State to further the interest in potential life must be calculated to inform the woman's free choice, not hinder it. And a statute which, while furthering the interest in potential life or some other valid state interest, has the effect of placing a substantial obstacle in the path of a woman's choice cannot be considered a permissible means of serving its legitimate ends. . . .

In our considered judgment, an undue burden is an unconstitutional burden. . . .

What is at stake is the woman's right to make the ultimate decision, not a right to be insulated from all others in doing so. Regulations which do no more than create a structural mechanism by which the State, or the parent or guardian of a minor, may express profound respect for the life of the unborn are permitted, if they are not a substantial obstacle to the woman's exercise of the right to choose. . . . Unless it has that effect on her right of choice, a state measure designed to persuade her to choose childbirth over abortion will be upheld if reasonably related to that goal. Regulations designed to foster the health of a woman seeking an abortion are valid if they do not constitute an undue burden. . . .

We give this summary:

a.  To protect the central right recognized by *Roe* v. *Wade* while at the same time accommodating the State's profound interest in potential life, we will employ the undue burden analysis as explained in this opinion. An undue burden exists, and therefore a provision of law is invalid, if its purpose or effect is to place a substantial obstacle in the path of a woman seeking an abortion before the fetus attains viability.

b.  We reject the rigid trimester framework of *Roe* v. *Wade*. To promote the State's profound interest in potential life, throughout pregnancy the State may take measures to ensure that the woman's choice is informed, and measures designed to advance this interest will not be invalidated as long as their purpose is to persuade the woman to choose childbirth over abortion. These measures must not be an undue burden on the right.

c.  As with any medical procedure, the State may enact regulations to further the health or safety of a woman seeking an abortion. Unnecessary health regulations that have the purpose or effect of presenting a substantial obstacle to a woman seeking an abortion impose an undue burden on the right.

d.  Our adoption of the undue burden analysis does not disturb the central holding of *Roe* v. *Wade*, and we reaffirm that holding. Regardless of whether exceptions are made for particular circumstances, a State may not prohibit any woman from making the ultimate decision to terminate her pregnancy before viability.

e.  We also reaffirm *Roe*'s holding that "subsequent to viability, the State in promoting its interest in the potentiality of human life may, if it chooses, regulate, and even proscribe, abortion except where it is necessary, in appropriate medical judgment, for the preservation of the life or health of the mother." *Roe* v. *Wade*, 410 U.S., at 164–165.

These principles control our assessment of the Pennsylvania statute, and we now turn to the issue of the validity of its challenged provisions.

# — V —

The Court of Appeals applied what it believed to be the undue burden standard and upheld each of the provisions except for the husband notification requirement. We agree generally with this conclusion, but refine the undue burden analysis in accordance with the principles articulated above. We now consider the separate statutory sections at issue.

# A

Because it is central to the operation of various other requirements, we begin with the statute's definition of medical emergency. Under the statute, a medical emergency is

> "[t]hat condition which, on the basis of the physician's good faith clinical judgment, so complicates the medical condition of a pregnant woman as to necessitate the immediate abortion of her pregnancy to avert her death or for which a delay will

create serious risk of substantial and irreversible impairment of a major bodily function." 18 Pa. Cons. Stat. § 3203 (1990).

. . . While the definition could be interpreted in an unconstitutional manner, the Court of Appeals stated: "[W]e read the medical emergency exception as intended by the Pennsylvania legislature to assure that compliance with its abortion regulations would not in any way pose a significant threat to the life or health of a woman." *Ibid*. As we said in *Brockett* v. *Spokane Arcades, Inc.*, 472 U.S. 491, 499–500 (1985): "Normally, . . . we defer to the construction of a state statute given it by the lower federal courts."

This "'reflect[s] our belief that district courts and courts of appeals are better schooled in and more able to interpret the laws of their respective States.'" *Frisby* v. *Schultz*, 487 U.S. 474, 482 (1988) (citation omitted). We adhere to that course today, and conclude that, as construed by the Court of Appeals, the medical emergency definition imposes no undue burden on a woman's abortion right.

# B

We next consider the informed consent requirement. 18 Pa. Cons. Stat § 3205 (1990). Except in a medical emergency, the statute requires that at least 24 hours before performing an abortion a physician inform the woman of the nature of the procedure, the health risks of the abortion and of childbirth, and the "probable gestational age of the unborn child." The physician or a qualified nonphysician must inform the woman of the availability of printed materials published by the State describing the fetus and providing information about medical assistance for childbirth, information about child support from the father, and a list of agencies which provide adoption and other services as alternatives to abortion. An abortion may not be performed unless the woman certifies in writing that she has been informed of the availability of these printed materials and has been provided them if she chooses to view them.

Our prior decisions establish that as with any medical procedure, the State may require a woman to give her written informed consent to an abortion. . . . As we have made clear, we depart from the holdings of *Akron I* and *Thornburgh* to the extent that we permit a State to further its legitimate goal of protecting the life of the unborn by enacting legislation aimed at ensuring a decision that is mature and informed, even when in so doing the State expresses a preference for childbirth over abortion. In short, requiring that the woman be informed of the availability of information relating to fetal development and the assistance available should she decide to carry the pregnancy to full term is a reasonable measure to ensure an informed choice, one which might cause the woman to choose childbirth over abortion. This requirement cannot be considered a substantial obstacle to obtaining an abortion, and, it follows, there is no undue burden.

Our prior cases also suggest that the "straitjacket," *Thornburgh, supra*, at 762 (quoting *Danforth, supra*, at 67, n. 8), of particular information which must be given in each case interferes with a constitutional right of privacy between a pregnant woman and her physician. As a preliminary matter, it is worth noting that the statute now before us does not require a physician to comply with the informed consent provisions "if he or she can demonstrate by a preponderance of the evidence, that he or she reasonably believed that furnishing the information would have resulted in a severely adverse effect on the physical or mental health of the patient." 18 Pa. Cons. Stat. § 3205 (1990). In this respect, the statute does not prevent the physician from exercising his or her medical judgment.

Whatever constitutional status the doctor-patient relation may have as a general matter, in the present context it is derivative of the woman's position. The doctor-patient relation does not underlie or override the two more general rights under which the abortion right is justified: the right to make family decisions and the right to physical autonomy. On its own, the doctor-patient relation here is entitled to the same solicitude it receives in other contexts. Thus, a requirement that a doctor give a woman certain information as part of obtaining her consent to an abortion is, for constitutional purposes, no different from a requirement that a doctor give certain specific information about any medical procedure.

All that is left of petitioners' argument is an asserted First Amendment right of a physician not to provide information about the risks of abortion, and childbirth, in a manner mandated by the State. To be sure, the physician's First Amendment rights not to speak are implicated, see *Wooley* v. *Maynard*, 430 U.S. 705 (1977), but only as part of the practice of medicine, subject to reasonable licensing and regulation by the State, cf. *Whalen* v. *Roe*, 429 U.S. 589, 603 (1977). We see no constitutional infirmity in the requirement that the physician provide the information mandated by the State here.

The Pennsylvania statute also requires us to reconsider the holding in *Akron I* that the State may not require that a physician, as opposed to a qualified assistant, provide information relevant to a woman's informed consent. 462 U.S., at 448. Since there is no evidence on this record that requiring a doctor to give the information as provided by the statute would amount in practical terms to a substantial obstacle to a woman seeking an abortion, we conclude that it is not an undue burden. Our cases reflect the fact that the Constitution gives the States broad latitude to decide that particular functions may be performed only by licensed professionals, even if an objective assessment might suggest that those same tasks could be performed by others. See

*Williamson* v. *Lee Optical of Okla., Inc.*, 348 U.S. 483 (1955). Thus, we uphold the provision as a reasonable means to ensure that the woman's consent is informed.

Our analysis of Pennsylvania's 24-hour waiting period between the provision of the information deemed necessary to informed consent and the performance of an abortion under the undue burden standard requires us to reconsider the premise behind the decision in *Akron I* invalidating a parallel requirement. In *Akron I* we said: "Nor are we convinced that the State's legitimate concern that the woman's decision be informed is reasonably served by requiring a 24-hour delay as a matter of course." 462 U.S., at 450. We consider that conclusion to be wrong. The idea that important decisions will be more informed and deliberate if they follow some period of reflection does not strike us as unreasonable, particularly where the statute directs that important information become part of the background of the decision. The statute as construed by the Court of Appeals, permits avoidance of the waiting period in the event of a medical emergency and the record evidence shows that in the vast majority of cases, a 24-hour delay does not create any appreciable . . . reasonable measure to implement the State's interest in protecting the life of the unborn, a measure that does not amount to an undue burden.

Whether the mandatory 24-hour waiting period is nonetheless invalid because in practice it is a substantial obstacle to a woman's choice to terminate her pregnancy is a closer question. The findings of fact by the District Court indicate that because of the distances many women must travel to reach an abortion provider, the practical effect will often be a delay of much more than a day because the waiting period requires that a woman seeking an abortion make at least two visits to the doctor. The District Court also found that in many instances this will increase the exposure of women seeking abortions to "the harassment and hostility of anti-abortion protesters demonstrating outside a clinic." 744 F. Supp., at 1351. As a result, the District Court found that for those women who have the fewest financial resources, those who must travel long distances, and those who have difficulty explaining their whereabouts to husbands, employers, or others, the 24-hour waiting period will be "particularly burdensome." *Id.*, at 1352.

These findings are troubling in some respects, but they do not demonstrate that the waiting period constitutes an undue burden. We do not doubt that, as the District Court held, the waiting period has the effect of "increasing the cost and risk of delay of abortions," *id.*, at 1378, but the District Court did not conclude that the increased costs and potential delays amount to substantial obstacles. . . . In light of the construction given the statute's definition of medical emergency by the Court of Appeals, and the District Court's findings, we cannot say that the waiting period imposes a real health risk.

We also disagree with the District Court's conclusion that the "particularly burdensome" effects of the waiting period on some women require its invalidation. A particular burden is not of necessity a substantial obstacle. Whether a burden falls on a particular group is a distinct inquiry from whether it is a substantial obstacle even as to the women in that group. And the District Court did not conclude that the waiting period is such an obstacle even for the women who are most burdened by it. Hence, on the record before us, and in the context of this facial challenge, we are not convinced that the 24-hour waiting period constitutes an undue burden.

We are left with the argument that the various aspects of the informed consent requirement are unconstitutional because they place barriers in the way of abortion on demand. Even the broadest reading of *Roe*, however, has not suggested that there is a constitutional right to abortion on demand. See, *e.g., Doe* v. *Bolton*, 410 U.S., at 189. Rather, the right protected by *Roe* is a right to decide to terminate a pregnancy free of undue interference by the State. Because the informed consent requirement facilitates the wise exercise of that right, it cannot be classified as an interference with the right *Roe* protects. The informed consent requirement is not an undue burden on that right.

We are left with the argument that the various aspects of the informed consent requirement are unconstitutional because they place barriers in the way of abortion on demand. Even the broadest reading of *Roe*, however, has not suggested that there is a constitutional right to abortion on demand. See, *e.g., Doe* v. *Bolton*, 410 U.S., at 189. Rather, the right protected by *Roe* is a right to decide to terminate a pregnancy free of undue interference by the State. Because the informed consent requirement facilitates the wise exercise of that right, it cannot be classified as an interference with the right *Roe* protects. The informed consent requirement is not an undue burden on that right.

Section 3209 of Pennsylvania's abortion law provides, except in cases of medical emergency, that no physician shall perform an abortion on a married woman without receiving a signed statement from the woman that she has notified her spouse that she is about to undergo an abortion. The woman has the option of providing an alternative signed statement certifying that her husband is not the man who impregnated her; that her husband could not be located; that the pregnancy is the result of spousal sexual assault which she has reported; or that the woman believes that notifying her husband will cause him or someone else to inflict bodily injury upon her. A physician who performs an abortion on a married woman without receiving the appropriate signed statement will have his or her license revoked, and is liable to the husband for damages.

The District Court heard the testimony of numerous expert witnesses, and made detailed findings of fact regarding the effect of this statute. These included:

"273. The vast majority of women consult their husbands prior to deciding to terminate their pregnancy. . . .

"279. The 'bodily injury' exception could not be invoked by a married woman whose husband, if notified, would, in her reasonable belief, threaten to (a) publicize her intent to have an abortion to family, friends or acquaintances; (b) retaliate against her in future child custody or divorce proceedings; (c) inflict psychological intimidation or emotional harm upon her, her children or other persons; (d) inflict bodily harm on other persons such as children, family members or other loved ones; or (e) use his control over finances to deprive of necessary monies for herself or her children. . . .

"281. Studies reveal that family violence occurs in two million families in the United States. This figure, however, is a conservative one that substantially understates (because battering is usually not reported until it reaches life-threatening proportions) the actual number of families affected by domestic violence. In fact, researchers estimate that one of every two women will be battered at some time in their life. . . .

"282. A wife may not elect to notify her husband of her intention to have an abortion for a variety of reasons, including the husband's illness, concern about her own health, the imminent failure of the marriage, or the husband's absolute opposition to the abortion. . . .

"283. The required filing of the spousal consent form would require plaintiff-clinics to change their counseling procedures and force women to reveal their most intimate decision-making on pain of criminal sanctions. The confidentiality of these revelations could not be guaranteed, since the woman's records are not immune from subpoena. . . .

"284. Women of all class levels, educational backgrounds, and racial, ethnic and religious groups are battered. . . .

"285. Wife-battering or abuse can take on many physical and psychological forms. The nature and scope of the battering can cover a broad range of actions and be gruesome and torturous. . . .

"286. Married women, victims of battering, have been killed in Pennsylvania and throughout the United States. . . .

"287. Battering can often involve a substantial amount of sexual abuse, including marital rape and sexual mutilation. . . .

"288. In a domestic abuse situation, it is common for the battering husband to also abuse the children in an attempt to coerce the wife. . . .

"289. Mere notification of pregnancy is frequently a flashpoint for battering and violence within the family. The number of battering incidents is high during the pregnancy and often the worst abuse can be associated with pregnancy. . . . The battering husband may deny parentage and use the pregnancy as an excuse for abuse. . . .

"290. Secrecy typically shrouds abusive families. Family members are instructed not to tell anyone, especially police or doctors, about the abuse and violence. Battering husbands often threaten their wives or her children with further abuse if she tells an outsider of the violence and tells her that nobody will believe her. A battered woman, therefore, is highly unlikely to disclose the violence against her for fear of retaliation by the abuser. . . .

"291. Even when confronted directly by medical personnel or other helping professionals, battered women often will not admit to the battering because they have not admitted to themselves that they are battered. . . .

"294. A woman in a shelter or a safe house unknown to her husband is not 'reasonably likely' to have bodily harm inflicted upon her by her batterer, however her attempt to notify her husband pursuant to section 3209 could accidentally disclose her whereabouts to her husband. Her fear of future ramifications would be realistic under the circumstances.

"295. Marital rape is rarely discussed with others or reported to law enforcement authorities, and of those reported only few are prosecuted. . . .

"296. It is common for battered women to have sexual intercourse with their husbands to avoid being battered. While this type of coercive sexual activity would be spousal sexual assault as defined by the Act, many women may not consider it to be so and others would fear disbelief. . .

"297. The marital rape exception to section 3209 cannot be claimed by women who are victims of coercive sexual behavior other than penetration. The 90-day reporting requirement of the spousal sexual assault statute, 18 Pa. Con. Stat. Ann. § 3218(c), further narrows the class of sexually abused wives who can claim the exception, since many of these women may be psychologically unable to discuss or report the rape for several years after the incident. . . .

"298. Because of the nature of the battering relationship, battered women are unlikely to avail themselves of the exceptions to section 3209 of the Act, regardless of whether the section applies to them." 744 F. Supp., at 1360–1362 (footnote omitted).

These findings are supported by studies of domestic violence. The American Medical Association (AMA) has published a summary of the recent research in this field, which indicates that in an average 12 month period in this country, approximately two million women are the victims of severe assaults by their male partners. In a 1985 survey, women reported that nearly one of every eight husbands had assaulted their wives during the past year. The AMA views these figures as "marked underestimates," because the nature of these incidents discourages women from reporting them, and because surveys typically exclude the very poor, those who do not speak English well, and women who are homeless or in institutions or hospitals when the survey is conducted. According to the AMA, [r]esearchers, on family violence agree that the true incidence of partner violence is probably *double* the above estimates; or four million severely assaulted women per year. Studies on prevalence suggest that from one-fifth to one-third of all women will be physically assaulted by a partner or ex-partner during their lifetime." AMA Council on Scientific Affairs, Violence Against Women 7 (1991) (emphasis in original). Thus on an average day in the United States, nearly 11,000 women are severely assaulted by their male partners. Many of these incidents involve sexual assault. *id.*, at 34; Shields & Hanneke, Battered Wives' Reactions to Marital Rape, in The Dark Side of Families: Current Family Violence Research 131, 144 (D. Finkelhor, R. Gelles, G. Hataling, & M. Straus eds. 1983). In families where wife-beating takes place, moreover, child abuse is often present as well. Violence Against Women, *supra*, at 12.

Other studies fill in the rest of this troubling picture. Physical violence is only the most visible form of abuse. Psychological abuse, particularly forced social and economic isolation of women, is also common. L. Walker, The . . . Why do Women Stay?, 53 J. Marriage & the Family 311 (1991). Many abused women who find temporary refuge in shelters return to their husbands, in large part because they have no other source of income. Aguirre, Why Do They Return? Abused Wives in Shelters, 30 J. Nat. Assn. of Social Workers 350, 352 (1985). Returning to one's abuser can be dangerous. Recent Federal Bureau of Investigation statistics disclose that 8.8 percent of all homicide victims in the United States are killed by their spouses. Mercy & Saltzman, Fatal Violence Among Spouses in the United States, 1976–85, 79 Am. J. Public Health 595 (1989). Thirty percent of female homicide victims are killed by their male partners. Domestic Violence: Terrorism in the Home, Hearing before the Subcommittee on Children, Family, Drugs and Alcoholism of the Senate Committee on Labor and Human Resources, 101st Cong., 2d Sess., 3 (1990).

The limited research that has been conducted with respect to notifying one's husband about an abortion, although involving samples too small to be representative, also supports the District Court's findings of fact. The vast majority of women notify their male partners of their decision to obtain an abortion. In many cases in which married women do not notify their husbands, the pregnancy is the result of an extramarital affair. Where the husband is the father, the primary reason women do not notify their husbands is that the husband and wife are experiencing marital difficulties, often accompanied by incidents of violence. Ryan & Plutzer, When Married Women Have Abortions: Spousal Notification and Marital Interaction, 51 J. Marriage & the Family 41, 44 (1989).

This information and the District Court's findings reinforce what common sense would suggest. In well-functioning marriages, spouses discuss important intimate decisions such as whether to bear a child. But there are millions of women in this country who are the victims of regular physical and psychological abuse at the hands of their husbands. Should these women become pregnant, they may have very good reasons for not wishing to inform their husbands of their decision to obtain an abortion. Many may have justifiable fears of physical abuse, but may be no less fearful of the consequences of reporting prior abuse to the Commonwealth of Pennsylvania. Many may fear devastating forms of psychological abuse from their husbands, including verbal harassment, threats of future violence, the destruction of possessions, physical confinement to the home, the withdrawal of financial support, or the disclosure of the abortion to family and friends. These methods of psychological abuse may act as even more of a deterrent to notification than the possibility of physical violence, but women who are the victims of the abuse are not exempt from § 3209's notification requirement. And many women who are pregnant as a result of sexual assaults by their husbands will be unable to avail themselves of the exception for spousal sexual assault, § 3209 (b)(3), because the exception requires that the woman have notified law enforcement authorities within 90 days of the assault, and her husband will be notified of her report once an investigation begins, § 3128(c). If anything in this field is certain, it is that victims of spousal sexual assault are extremely reluctant to report the abuse to the government; hence, a great many spousal rape victims will not be exempt from the notification requirement imposed by § 3209.

The spousal notification requirement is thus likely to prevent a significant number of women from obtaining an abortion. It does not merely make abortions a little more difficult or expensive to obtain; for many women, it will impose a substantial obstacle. We must not blind ourselves to the fact that the significant number of women who fear for their safety and the safety of their children are likely to be deterred from procuring an abortion as surely as if the Commonwealth had outlawed abortion in all cases. . . .

This conclusion is in no way inconsistent with our decisions upholding parental notification or consent requirements. See, *e. g., Akron II*, 497 U. S., at 510–519; *Bellotti v. Baird*, 443 U. S. 622 (1979) *(Bellotti II); Planned Parenthood of Central Mo. v. Danforth*, 428 U. S., at 74. Those enactments, and our judgment that they are constitutional, are based on the quite reasonable assumption that minors will benefit from consultation with their parents and that children will often not realize that their parents have their best interests at heart. We cannot adopt a parallel assumption about adult women.

We recognize that a husband has a "deep and proper concern and interest . . . in his wife's pregnancy and in the growth and development of the fetus she is carrying." *Danforth, supra,* at 69. With regard to the children he has fathered and raised, the Court has recognized his "cognizable and substantial interest in their custody. *Stanley* v. *Illinois,* 405 U. S. 645, 651–652 (1972); see also *Quilloin* v. *Walcott,* 434 U S. 246 (1978); *Caban* v. *Mohammed,* 441 U.S. 380 (1979); *Lehr* v. *Robertson,* 463 U.S. 248 (1983). If these cases concerned a State's ability to require the mother to notify the father before taking some action with respect to a living child raised by both, therefore, it would be reasonable to conclude as a general matter that the father's interest in the welfare of the child and the mother's interest are equal.

Before birth, however, the issue takes on a very different cast. It is an inescapable biological fact that state regulation with respect to the child a woman is carrying will have a far greater impact on the mother's liberty than on the father's. The effect of state regulation on a woman's protected liberty is doubly deserving of scrutiny in such a case, as the State has touched not only upon the private sphere of the family but upon the very bodily integrity of the pregnant woman. Cf. *Cruzan* v. *Director, Mo. Dept. of Health,* 497 U.S., at 281. The Court has held that "when the wife and the husband disagree on this decision, the view of only one of the two marriage partners can prevail. Inasmuch as it is the woman who physically bears the child and who "is the more directly and immediately affected by the pregnancy, as between the two, the balance weighs in her favor." *Danforth, supra,* at 71. This conclusion rests upon the basic nature of marriage and the nature of our Constitution: "[T]he marital couple is not an independent entity with a mind and heart of its own, but an association of two individuals each with a separate intellectual and emotional makeup. If the right of privacy means anything, it is the right of the *individual,* married or single, to be free from unwarranted governmental intrusion into matters so fundamentally affecting a person as the decision whether to bear or beget a child." *Eisenstadt* v. *Baird,* 405 U. S., at 453 (emphasis in original). The Constitution protects individuals, men and women alike, from unjustified state interference, even when that interference is enacted into law for the benefit of their spouses.

There was a time, not so long ago, when a different understanding of the family and of the Constitution prevailed. In *Bradwell* v. *State,* 16 Wall. 130 (1873), three Members of this Court reaffirmed the common-law principle that "a woman had no legal existence separate from her husband, who was regarded as her head and repre-sentative in the social state; and, notwithstanding some recent modifications of this civil status, many of the special rules of law flowing from and dependent upon this cardinal principle still exist in full force in most States." *Id.,* at 141 (Bradley, J., joined by Swayne and Field, JJ., concurring in judgment). Only one generation has passed since this Court observed that "woman is still regarded as the center of home and family life," with attendant "special responsibilities" that precluded full and independent legal status under the Constitution. *Hoyt* v. *Florida*, 368 U.S. 57, 62 (1961). These views, of course, are no longer consistent with our understanding of the family, the individual, or the Constitution. . . .

The husband's interest in the life of the child his wife is carrying does not permit the State to empower him with this troubling degree of authority over his wife. The contrary view leads to consequences reminiscent of the common law. A husband has no enforceable right to require a wife to advise him before she exercises her personal choices. If a husband's interest in the potential life of the child outweighs a wife's liberty, the State could require a married woman to notify her husband before she uses a post-fertilization contraceptive. Perhaps next in line would be a statute requiring pregnant married women to notify their, husbands before engaging in conduct causing risks to the fetus. After all, if the husband's interest in the fetus' safety is a sufficient predicate for state regulation, the State could reasonably conclude that pregnant wives should notify their husbands before drinking alcohol or smoking. Perhaps married women should notify their husbands before using contraceptives or before undergoing any type of surgery that may have complications affecting the husband's interest in his wife's reproductive organs. And if a husband's interest justifies notice in any of these cases, one might reasonably argue that it justifies exactly what the *Danforth* Court held it did not justify—a requirement of the husband's consent as well. A State may not give to a man the kind of dominion over his wife that parents exercise over their children.

Section 3209 embodies a view of marriage consonant with the common-law status of married women but repugnant to our present understanding of marriage and of the nature of the rights secured by the Constitution. Women do not lose their constitutionally protected liberty when they marry. The Constitution protects all individuals, male or female, Married or unmarried, from the abuse of governmental power, even where that power is employed for the supposed benefit of a member of the individual's family. These considerations confirm our conclusion that § 3209 is invalid.

# D

We next consider the parental consent provision. Except in a medical emergency, an unemancipated young woman under 18 may not obtain an abortion unless she and one of her parents (or guardian) provides informed consent as defined above. If neither a parent nor a guardian provides consent, a court may authorize the performance of an abortion upon a determination that the young woman is mature and capable of giving informed consent and has in fact given her informed consent, or that an abortion would be in her best interests.

We have been over most of this ground before. Our cases establish, and we reaffirm today, that a State may require a minor seeking an abortion to obtain the consent of a parent or guardian, provided that there is an adequate judicial bypass procedure. See, *e. g., Akron II*, 497 U. S., at 510–519; *Hodgson*, 497 U. S., at 461 (O'CONNOR, J., concurring in part and concurring in judgment in part); *id.*, at 497–501 (KENNEDY, J., concurring in judgment in part and dissenting in part); *Akron I*, 462 U. S., at 440; *Bellotti II*, 443 U. S., at 643–644 (plurality opinion). Under these precedents, in our view, the one-parent consent requirement and judicial bypass procedure are constitutional. . . .

# E

Under the recordkeeping and reporting requirements of the statute, every facility which performs abortions is required to file a report stating its name and address as well as the name and address of any related entity, such as a controlling or subsidiary organization. In the case of state-funded institutions, the information becomes public.

For each abortion performed, a report must be filed identifying: the physician (and the second physician where required); the facility; the referring physician or agency; the woman's age; the number of prior pregnancies and prior abortions she has had; gestational age; the type of abortion procedure; the date of the abortion; whether there were any pre-existing medical conditions which would complicate pregnancy; medical complications with the abortion; where applicable, the basis for the determination that the abortion was medically necessary; the weight of the aborted fetus; and whether the woman was married, and if so, whether notice was provided or the basis for the failure to give notice. Every abortion facility must also file quarterly reports showing the number of abortions performed broken down by trimester. See 18 Pa. Cons. Stat. §§ 3207, 3214 (1990). In all events, the identify of each woman who has had an abortion remains confidential.

In *Danforth*, 428 U.S., at 80, we held that recordkeeping and reporting provisions "that are reasonably directed to the preservation of maternal health and that properly respect a patient's confidentiality and privacy are permissible." We think that under this standard, all the provisions at issue here, except that relating to spousal notice, are constitutional. Although they do not relate to the State's interest in informing the woman's choice, they do relate to health. The collection of information with respect to actual patients is a vital element of medical research, and so it cannot be said that the requirements serve no purpose other than to make abortions more difficult. Nor do we find that the requirements impose a substantial obstacle to a woman's choice. At most they might increase the cost of some abortions by a slight amount. While at some point increased cost could become a substantial obstacle, there is no such showing on the record before us.

Subsection (12) of the reporting provision requires the reporting of, among other things, a married woman's "reason for failure to provide notice" to her husband. § 3214(a)(12). This provision in effect requires women, as a condition of obtaining an abortion, to provide the Commonwealth with the precise information we have already recognized that many women have pressing reasons not to reveal. Like the spousal notice requirement itself, this provision places an undue burden on a woman's choice, and must be invalidated for that reason.

## — VI —

The judgment in No. 91–902 is affirmed. The judgment in No. 91–744 is affirmed in part and reversed in part, and the case is remanded for proceedings consistent with this opinion, including consideration of the question of severability.

*It is so ordered.*

JUSTICE STEVENS, concurring in part and dissenting in part.

The portions of the Court's opinion that I have joined are more important than those with which I disagree. I shall therefore first comment on significant areas of agreement, and then explain the limited character of my disagreement.

## — I —

The Court is unquestionably correct in concluding that the doctrine of *stare decisis* has controlling significance in a case of this kind, notwithstanding an individual Justice's concerns about the merits.[1] . . . The societal costs of overruling *Roe* at this late date would be enormous. *Roe* is an integral part of a correct understanding of both the concept of liberty and the basic equality of men and women.

*Stare decisis* also provides a sufficient basis for my agreement with the joint opinion's reaffirmation of *Roe*'s post-viability analysis. Specifically, I accept the proposition that "[i]f the State is interested in protecting fetal life after viability, it may go so far as to proscribe abortion during that period, except when it is necessary to preserve the life or health of the mother." 410 U.S., at 163–164; see *ante*, at 879.

I also accept what is implicit in the Court's analysis, namely, a reaffirmation of *Roe*'s explanation of *why* the State's obligation to protect the life or health of the mother must take precedence over any duty to the unborn. The Court in *Roe* carefully considered, and rejected, the State's argument "that the fetus is a 'person' within the language and meaning of the Fourteenth Amendment." 410 U.S., at 156. After analyzing the usage of "person" in the Constitution, the Court concluded that the word "has application only postnatally." *Id.*, at 157. Commenting on the contingent property interests of the unborn that are generally represented by guardians ad litem, the Court noted: "Perfection of the interests involved, again, has generally been contingent upon live birth. In short, the unborn have never been recognized in the law as persons in the whole sense." *Id.*, at 162. Accordingly, an abortion is not "the termination of life entitled to Fourteenth Amendment protection." *Id.*, at 159. From this holding, there was no dissent, see *id.*, at 173; indeed, no Member of the Court has ever questioned this fundamental proposition. Thus, as a matter of federal constitutional law, a developing organism that is not yet a "person" does not have what is sometimes described as a "right to life." This has been and, by the Court's holding today, remains a fundamental premise of our constitutional law governing reproductive autonomy.

## — II —

My disagreement with the joint opinion begins with its understanding of the trimester framework established in *Roe*. Contrary to the suggestion of the joint opinion, *ante*, at 876, it is of a "contradiction" to recognize that the State may have a legitimate interest in potential human life and, at the same time, to conclude that that interest does not justify the regulation of abortion before viability (although other interests, such as maternal health, may). The fact that the State's interest is legitimate does not tell us when, if ever, that interest outweighs the pregnant woman's interest in personal liberty. It is appropriate, therefore, to consider more carefully the nature of the interests at stake.

First, it is clear that, in order to be legitimate, the State's interest must be secular; consistent with the First Amendment the State may not promote a theological or sectarian interest. . . . Moreover, as discussed above, the state interest in potential human life is not an interest *in loco parentis*, for the fetus is not a person.

Identifying the State's interests—which the States rarely articulate with any precision—makes clear that the interest in protecting potential life is not grounded in the Constitution. It is, instead, an indirect interest supported by both humanitarian and pragmatic concerns. Many of our citizens believe that any abortion reflects an unacceptable disrespect for potential human life and that the performance of more than a million abortions each year is intolerable; many find third-trimester abortions performed when the fetus is approaching personhood particularly offensive. The State has a legitimate interest in minimizing such offense. The State may also have a broader interest in expanding the population,[2] believing society would benefit from the services of additional productive citizens—or that the potential human lives might include the occasional Mozart of Curie. These are the kinds of concerns that comprise the State's interest in potential human life.

In counterpoise is the woman's constitutional interest in liberty. One aspect of this liberty is a right to bodily integrity, a right to control one's person. See, *e.g., Rochin* v. *California,* 342 U.S. 165 (1952); *Skinner* v. *Oklahoma ex rel. Williamson,* 316 U.S. 535 (1942). This right is neutral on the question of abortion: The constitution would be equally offended by an absolute requirement that all women undergo abortions as by an absolute prohibition on abortions. "Our whole constitutional heritage rebels at the thought of giving government the power to control men's minds." *Stanley* v. *Georgia,* 394 U.S. 557, 565 (1969). The same holds true for the power to control women's bodies.

The woman's constitutional liberty interest also involves her freedom to decide matters of the highest privacy and the most personal nature. Cf. *Whalen* v. *Roe,* 429 U.S. 589, 598–600 (1977). A woman considering abortion faces a difficult choice having serious and personal consequences of major importance to her own future—perhaps to the salvation of her own immortal soul." *Thornburgh,* 476 U.S., at 781. The authority to make such traumatic and yet empowering decisions is an element of basic human dignity. AS the joint opinion so eloquently demonstrates, a woman's decision to terminate her pregnancy is nothing less than a matter of conscience.

Weighing the State's interest in potential life and the woman's liberty interest, I agree with the joint opinion that the State may """expres[s] a preference for normal childbirth,"""" that the State may take steps to ensure that a woman's choice "is thoughtful and informed," and that "States are free to enact laws to provide a reasonable framework for a woman to make a decision that has such profound and lasting meaning." *Ante,* at 872–873. Serious questions arise, however, when a State attempts to "persuade the woman to choose childbirth over abortion." *Ante,* at 878. Decisional autonomy must limit the State's power to inject into a woman's most personal deliberations its own views of what is best. The State may promote its preferences by funding childbirth, by creating and maintaining alternatives to abortion, and by espousing the virtues of family; but it must respect the individual's freedom to make such judgments. . . .

Under this same analysis, §§ 3205(a)(1)(i) and (iii) of the Pennsylvania statute are constitutional. Those sections, which require the physician to inform a woman of the nature and risks of the abortion procedure and the medical risks of carrying to term, are neutral requirements comparable to those imposed in other medical procedures. Those sections indicate no effort by the Commonwealth to influence the woman's choice in any way. If anything, such requirements *enhance,* rather than skew, the woman's decisionmaking.

## — III —

The 24-hour waiting period required by §§ 3205(a)(1)–(2) of the Pennsylvania statute raises even more serious concerns. Such a requirement arguably furthers the Commonwealth's interests in two ways, neither of which is constitutionally permissible.

First, it may be argued that the 24-hour delay is justified by the mere fact that it is likely to reduce the number of abortions, thus furthering the Commonwealth's interest in potential life. But such an argument would justify any form of coercion that placed an obstacle in the woman's path. . . .

Second, it can more reasonably be argued that the 24-hour delay furthers the Commonwealth's interest in ensuring that the woman's decision is informed and thoughtful. But there is no evidence that the mandated delay benefits women or that it is necessary to enable the physician to convey any relevant information to the patient. The mandatory delay thus appears to rest on outmoded and unacceptable assumptions about the decisionmaking capacity of women. While there are well-established and consistently maintained reasons for the Commonwealth to view with skepticism the ability of minors to make decisions, see *Hodgson* v. *Minnesota*, 497 U.S. 417, 449 (1990), none of those reasons applies to an adult woman's decisionmaking ability. Just as we have left behind the belief that a woman must consult her husband before undertaking serious matters, see *ante*, at 895-898, so we must reject the notion that a woman is less capable of deciding matters of gravity. Cf. *Reed* v. *Reed*, 404 U.S. 71 (1971).

In the alternative, the delay requirement may be premised on the belief that the decision to terminate a pregnancy is presumptively wrong. This premise is illegitimate. Those who disagree vehemently about the legality and morality of abortion agree about one thing: The decision to terminate a pregnancy is profound and difficult. No person undertakes such a decision lightly—and States may not presume that a woman has failed to reflect adequately merely because her conclusion differs from the State's preference. A woman who has, in the privacy of her thoughts and conscience, weighed the options and made her decision cannot be forced to reconsider all, simply because the State believes she has come to the wrong conclusion.

Part of the constitutional liberty to choose is the equal dignity to which each of us is entitled. A woman who decides to terminate her pregnancy is entitled to the same respect as a woman who decides to carry the fetus to term. The mandatory waiting period denies women that equal respect.

## — IV —

In my opinion, a correct application of the "undue burden" standard leads to the same conclusion concerning the constitutionality of these requirements. A state-imposed burden on the exercise of a constitutional right is measured both by its effects and by its character: A burden may be "undue" either because the burden is too severe or because it lacks a legitimate, rational justification.

The 24-hour delay requirement fails both parts of this test. The findings of the District Court establish the severity of the burden that the 24-hour delay imposes on many pregnant women. Yet even in those cases in which the delay is not especially onerous, it is, in my opinion, "undue" because there is no evidence that such a delay serves a useful and legitimate purpose. . . .

The counseling provisions are similarly infirm. Whenever government commands private citizens to speak or to listen, careful review of the justification for that command is particularly appropriate. . . .

In light of all of these facts, I conclude that the information requirements in § 3205(a)(1)(ii) and §§ 3205(a)(2)(i)–(iii) do not serve a useful purpose and thus constitute an unnecessary—and therefore undue—burden on the woman's constitutional liberty to decide to terminate her pregnancy.

Accordingly, while I disagree with Parts IV, V–B, and V–D of the joint opinion,[3] I join the remainder of the Court's opinion.

JUSTICE BLACKMUN, concurring in part, concurring in the judgment in part, and dissenting in part.

I join Parts I, II, III, V–A, V–C, and VI of the joint opinion of JUSTICES O'CONNOR, KENNEDY, and SOUTER, *ante.*

Three years ago, in *Webster* v. *Reproductive Health Services*, 492 U.S. 490 (1989), four Members of this Court appeared poised to "cas[t] into darkness the hopes and visions of every woman in this country" who had come to believe that the Constitution guaranteed her the right to reproductive choice. *Id.*, at 557 (BLACKMUN, J., dissenting). See *id.*, at 499 (plurality opinion of REHNQUIST, C.J., joined by WHITE and KENNEDY, JJ.); *id.*, at 532 (SCALIA, J., concurring in part and concurring in judgment). All that remained between the promise of *Roe* and the darkness of the plurality was a single, flickering flame. Decisions since *Webster* gave little reason to hope that this flame would cast much light. See, *e.g., Ohio* v. *Akron Center for Reproductive Health*, 497 U.S. 502, 524

(1990) (BLACKMUN, J., dissenting). But now, just when so many expected the darkness to fall, the flame has grown bright.

I do not underestimate the significance of today's joint opinion. Yet I remain steadfast in my belief that the right to reproductive choice is entitled to the full protection afforded by this Court before *Webster*. And I fear for the darkness as four Justices anxiously await the single vote necessary to extinguish the light.

— I —

Make no mistake, the joint opinion of JUSTICES O'CONNOR, KENNEDY, and SOUTER is an act of personal courage and constitutional principle. In contrast to previous decisions in which JUSTICES O'CONNOR and KENNEDY postponed reconsideration of *Roe* v. *Wade*, 410 U.S. 113 (1973), the authors of the joint opinion today join JUSTICE STEVENS and me in concluding that "the essential holding of *Roe* v. *Wade* should be retained and once again reaffirmed." *Ante*, at 846. In brief, five Members of this Court today recognize that "the Constitution protects a woman's right to terminate her pregnancy in its early stages." *Ante*, at 844.

A fervent view of individual liberty and the force of *stare decisis* have led the Court to this conclusion. *Ante*, at 853. Today a majority reaffirms that the Due Process Clause of the Fourteenth Amendment establishes "a realm of personal liberty which the government may not enter," *ante*, at 847—a realm whose outer limits cannot be determined by interpretations of the Constitution that focus only on the specific practices of States at the time the Fourteenth Amendment was adopted. See *ante*, at 848–849. Included within this realm of liberty is "'the right of the *individual*, married or single, to be free from unwarranted governmental intrusion into matters so fundamentally affecting a person as the decision whether to bear or beget a child'" *Ante*, at 851, quoting *Eisenstadt* v. *Baird*, 405 U.S. 438, 453 (1972) (emphasis in original). "These matters, involving the most intimate and personal choices a person may make in a lifetime, choices central to personal dignity and autonomy, are *central* to the liberty protected by the Fourteenth Amendment." *Ante*, at 851 (emphasis added). Finally, the Court today recognizes that in the case of abortion, "the liberty of the woman is at stake in a sense unique to the human condition and so unique to the law. The mother who carries a child to full term is subject to anxieties, to physical constraints, to pain that only she must bear." *Ante*, at 852.

The Court's reaffirmation of *Roe*'s central holding is also based on the force of *stare decisis*. . . . What has happened today should serve as a model for the future Justices and a warning to all who have tried to turn this Court into yet another political branch.

In striking down the Pennsylvania statute's spousal notification requirement, the Court has established a framework for evaluating abortion regulations that responds to the social context of women facing issues of reproductive choice. In determining the burden imposed by the challenged regulation, the Court inquires whether the regulation's *"purpose or effect* is to place a substantial obstacle in the path of a woman seeking an abortion before the fetus attains viability.". . . And in applying its test, the Court remains sensitive to the unique role of women in the decisionmaking process. Whatever may have been the practice when the Fourteenth Amendment was adopted, the Court observes, "[w]omen do not lose their constitutionally protected liberty when they marry. The Constitution protects all individuals, male or female, married or unmarried, from the abuse of governmental power, even where that power is employed for the supposed benefit of a member of the individual's family.". . .

Lastly, while I believe that the joint opinion errs in failing to invalidate the other regulations, I am pleased that the joint opinion has not ruled out the possibility that these regulations may be shown to impose an unconstitutional burden. The joint opinion makes clear that its specific holdings are based on the insufficiency of the record before it. See, *e.g., ante,* at 885–886. I am confident that in the future evidence will be produced to show that "in a large fraction of the cases in which [these regulations are] relevant, [they] will operate as a substantial obstacle to a woman's choice to undergo an abortion." *Ante,* at 895.

# — II —

Today, no less than yesterday, the Constitution and decision of this Court require that a State's abortion restrictions be subjected to the strictest judicial scrutiny. Our precedents and the joint opinion's principles require us to subject all non-*de-minimis* abortion regulations to strict scrutiny. Under this standard, the Pennsylvania statute's provision requiring content-based counseling, a 24-hour delay, informed parental consent, and reporting of abortion-related information must be invalidated.

## A

State restrictions on abortion violate a woman's right of privacy in two ways. First, compelled continuation of a pregnancy infringes upon a woman's right to bodily integrity by imposing substantial physical intrusions and significant risks of physical harm. During pregnancy, women experience dramatic physical changes and a wide range of health consequences. Labor and delivery pose additional health risks and physical demands. In short, restrictive abortion laws force women to endure physical invasions far more substantial than those this Court has held to violate the constitutional principle of bodily integrity in other contexts. See *e.g., Winston* v. *Lee,* 470 U.S.

753 (1985) (invalidating surgical removal of bullet from murder suspect); *Rochin* v. *California*, 342 U.S. 165 (1952) (invalidating stomach pumping).

Further, when the State restricts a woman's right to terminate her pregnancy, it deprives a woman of the right to make her own decision about reproduction and family planning—critical life choices that this Court long has deemed central to the right to privacy. The decision to terminate or continue a pregnancy has no less an impact on a woman's life than decisions about contraception or marriage. 410 U.S. at 153. Because motherhood has a dramatic impact on a woman's educational prospects, employment opportunities, and self-determination, restrictive abortion laws deprive her of basic control over her life. For these reasons, "the decision whether or not to beget or bear a child" lies at "the very heart of this cluster of constitutionally protected choices." *Carey* v. *Population Services International*, 431 U.S. 678, 685 (1977).

A State's restrictions on a woman's right to terminate her pregnancy also implicate constitutional guarantees of gender equality. State restrictions on abortion compel women to continue pregnancies they otherwise might terminate. By restricting the right to terminate pregnancies, the State conscripts women's bodies into its service, forcing women to continue their pregnancies, suffer the pains of childbirth, and in most instances, provide years of maternal care. The State does not compensate women for their services; instead, it assumes that they owe this duty as a matter of course. This assumption—that women can simply be forced to accept the "natural" status and incidents of motherhood—appears to rest upon a conception of women's role that has triggered the protection of the Equal Protection Clause. See, *e.g., Mississippi Univ. for Women* v. *Hogan*, 458 U.S. 718, 724–726 (1982); *Craig* v. *Boren*, 429 U.S. 190, 198–199 (1976). The joint opinion recognizes that these assumptions about women's place in society "are no longer consistent with our understanding of the family, the individual, or the Constitution." *Ante*, at 897.

# B

The Court has held that limitations on the right of privacy are permissible only if they survive "strict" constitutional scrutiny—that is, only if the governmental entity imposing the restriction can demonstrate that the limitation is both necessary and narrowly tailored to serve a compelling governmental interest. *Griswold* v. *Connecticut*, 381 U.S. 479, 485 (1965). We have applied this principle specifically in the context of abortion regulations. *Roe* v. *Wade*, 410 U.S., at 155.

*Roe* implemented these principles through a framework that was designed "to ensure that the woman's right to choose not become so subordinate to the State's interest in promoting fetal life that her choice exists in theory but not in fact," . . .

In my view, application of this analytical framework is no less warranted than when it was approved by seven Members of this Court in *Roe*. Strict scrutiny of state limitations on reproductive choice still offers the most secure protection of the woman's right to make her own reproductive decisions, free from state coercion. No majority of this Court has ever agreed upon an alternative approach. The factual premises of the trimester framework have not been undermined, see *Webster*, 492 U.S., at 553 (BLACKMUN, J., dissenting), and the *Roe* framework is far more administrable, and far less manipulable, than the "undue burden" standard adopted by the joint opinion.

In sum, *Roe*'s requirement of strict scrutiny as implemented through a trimester framework should not be disturbed. No other approach has gained a majority, and no other is more protective of the woman's fundamental right. Lastly, no other approach properly accommodates the woman's constitutional right with the State's legitimate interests.

# C

Application of the strict scrutiny standard results in the invalidation of all the challenged provisions. Indeed, as this Court has invalidated virtually identical provisions in prior cases, *stare decisis* requires that we again strike them down. . . .

As JUSTICE STEVENS insightfully concludes, the mandatory delay rests either on outmoded or unacceptable assumptions about the decisionmaking capacity of women or the belief that the decision to terminate the pregnancy is presumptively wrong. The requirement that women consider this obvious and slanted information for an additional 24 hours contained in these provisions will only influence the woman's decision in improper ways.

Except in the case of a medical emergency, § 3206 requires a physician to obtain the informed consent of a parent or guardian before performing an abortion on an unemancipated minor or an incompetent woman. Based on evidence in the record, the District Court concluded that, in order to fulfill the informed-consent requirement, generally accepted medical principles would require an in-person visit by the parent to the facility. 744 F. Supp., at 1382. Although the Court "has recognized that the State has somewhat broader authority to regulate the activities of children than of adults," the State nevertheless must demonstrate that there is a *"significant state interest* in conditioning an abortion . . . that is not present in the case of an adult." *Danforth*, 428 U.S., at 74–75 (emphasis added). The requirement of an in-person visit would carry with it the risk of a delay of several days or possibly weeks, even where the parent is willing to consent. While the State has an interest in encouraging parental involvement in the minor's abortion decision, § 3206 is not narrowly drawn to serve that interest.

Finally, the Pennsylvania statute requires every facility performing abortions to report its activities to the Commonwealth. Pennsylvania contends that this requirement is valid under *Danforth*, in which this Court held that record-keeping and reporting requirements that are reasonably directed to the preservation of maternal health and that properly respect a patient's confidentiality are permissible. *Id.*, at 79–81. The Commonwealth attempts to justify its required reports on the ground that the public has a right to know how its tax dollars are spent. A regulation designed to inform the public about public expenditures does not further the Commonwealth's interest in protecting maternal health. Accordingly, such a regulation cannot justify a legally significant burden on a woman's right to obtain an abortion.

The confidential reports concerning the identities and medical judgment of physicians involved in abortions at first glance may seem valid, given the Commonwealth's interest in maternal health and enforcement of the Act. The District Court found, however, that, notwithstanding the confidentiality protections, many physicians particularly those who have previously discontinued performing abortions because of harassment, would refuse to refer patients to abortion clinics if their names were to appear on these reports. 744 F. Supp., at 1392. The Commonwealth has failed to show that the name of the referring physician either adds to the pool of scientific knowledge concerning abortion or is reasonably related to the Commonwealth's interest in maternal health. I therefore agree with the District Court's conclusion that the confidential reporting requirements are unconstitutional insofar as they require the name of the referring physician and the basis for his or her medical judgment.

In sum, I would affirm the judgment in No. 91–902 and reverse the judgment in No. 91-744 and remand the cases for further proceedings.

## — III —

At long last, THE CHIEF JUSTICE and those who have joined him admit it. Gone are the contentions that the issue need not be (or has not been) considered. There, on the first page, for all to see, is what was expected: "We believe that *Roe* was wrongly decided, and that it can and should be overruled consistently with our traditional approach to *stare decisis* in constitutional cases." *Post*, at 944. If there is much reason to applaud the advances made by the joint opinion today, there is far more to fear from THE CHIEF JUSTICE's opinion.

THE CHIEF JUSTICE's criticism of *Roe* follows from his stunted conception of individual liberty. While recognizing that the Due Process Clause protects more than simple physical liberty, he then goes on to construe this Court's personal-liberty cases as establishing only a laundry list of particular rights, rather than a principled account of how these particular rights are grounded in a more general right of privacy. *Post*, at 951. This constricted view is reinforced by THE CHIEF JUSTICE's exclusive reliance on tradition as a source of fundamental rights. . . .

Even more shocking than THE CHIEF JUSTICE's cramped notions of individual liberty is his complete omission of any discussion of the effects that compelled childbirth and motherhood have on women's lives. The only expression of concern with women's health is purely instrumental—for THE CHIEF JUSTICE, only women's *psychological* health is a concern, and only to the extent that he assumes that every woman who decides to have an abortion does so without serious consideration of the moral implications of her decision. *Post*, at 967–968. In short, THE CHIEF JUSTICE's view of the State's compelling interest in maternal health has less to do with health than it does with compelling women to be maternal.

Nor does THE CHIEF JUSTICE give any serious consideration to the doctrine of *stare decisis.*

THE CHIEF JUSTICE's narrow conception of individual liberty and *stare decisis* leads him to propose the same standard of review proposed by the plurality in *Webster*. "States may regulate abortion procedures in ways rationally related to a legitimate state interest. . . .

Under his standard, States can ban abortion if that ban is rationally related to a legitimate state interest—a standard which the United States calls "deferential, but not toothless." Yet when pressed at oral argument to describe the teeth, the best protection that the Solicitor General could offer to women was that a prohibition, enforced by criminal penalties, *with no exception for the life of the mother*, "could raise very serious questions." If we require a woman to risk her life for her child, what protection is offered for women who become pregnant through rape or incest? Is there anything arbitrary or capricious about a State's prohibiting the sins of the father from being visited upon his offspring?[4]

But, we are reassured, there is always the protection of the democratic process. While there is much to be praised about our democracy, our county since its founding has recognized that there are certain fundamental liberties that are not to be left to the whims of an election. A woman's right to reproductive choice is one of those fundamental liberties. Accordingly, that liberty need not seek refuge at the ballot box.

## — IV —

In one sense, the Court's approach is worlds apart from that of THE CHIEF JUSTICE and JUSTICE SCALIA. And yet, in another sense, the distance between the two approaches is short—the distance is but a single vote.

I am 83 years old. I cannot remain on this Court forever, and when I do step down, the confirmation process for my successor well may focus on the issue before us today. That I regret, may be exactly where the choice between the two worlds will be made.

CHIEF JUSTICE REHNQUIST, with whom JUSTICE WHITE, JUSTICE SCALIA, and JUSTICE THOMAS join, concurring in the judgment in part and dissenting in part.

The joint opinion, following its newly minted variation on *stare decisis*, retains the outer shell of *Roe* v. *Wade*, 410 U.S. 113 (1973), but beats a wholesale retreat from the substance of that case. We believe the *Roe* was wrongly decided, and that it can and should be overruled consistently with our traditional approach to *stare decisis* in constitutional cases. We would adopt the approach of the plurality in *Webster* v. *Reproductive Health Services*, 492 U.S. 490 (1989), and uphold the challenged provisions of the Pennsylvania statute in their entirety.

## — I —

In ruling on this litigation below, the Court of Appeals for the Third Circuit first observed that "this appeal does not directly implicate Roe; this case involves the regulation of abortions rather than their outright prohibition." 947 F. 2d 682, 687 (1991). . . . After considering the several opinions in *Webster* v. *Reproductive Health Services, supra*, and *Hodgson* v. *Minnesota*, 497 U.S. 417 (1990), the Court of appeals concluded that JUSTICE O'CONNOR's "undue burden" test was controlling, as that was the narrowest ground on which we had upheld recent abortion regulations. 947 F. 2d, at 693–697.

Applying this standard, the Court of Appeals upheld all of the challenged regulations except the one requiring a woman to notify her spouse of an intended abortion. . . . We agree with the Court of Appeals that our decision in *Roe* is not directly implicated by the Pennsylvania statute, which does not prohibit, but simply regulates, abortion. But, as the Court of Appeals found, the state of our post-Roe decisional law dealing with the regulation of abortion is confusing and uncertain, indicating that a reexamination of that line of cases is in order. Unfortunately for those who must apply this Court's decisions, the reexamination undertaken today leaves the Court no less divided than beforehand. Although they reject the trimester framework that formed the underpinning of *Roe*, JUSTICES O'CONNOR, KENNEDY, and SOUTER adopt a revised undue burden standard to analyze the challenged regulations. We conclude, however, that such an outcome is an unjustified constitutional compromise, one which leaves the Court in a position to closely scrutinize all types of abortion regulations despite the fact that it lacks the power to do so under the Constitution.

In *Roe*, the Court opined that the State "does have an important and legitimate interest in preserving and protecting the health of the pregnant woman, . . . and that it has still another important and legitimate interest in protecting the potentiality of human life." 410 U.S. at 162 (emphasis omitted). In the companion case of *Doe* v. *Bolton*, 410 U.S. 179 (1973), the Court referred to its conclusion in *Roe* "that a pregnant woman does not have an absolute constitutional right to an abortion on her demand." 410 U.S., at 189. But while the language and holdings of these cases appeared to leave States free to regulate abortion procedures in a variety of ways, later decisions based on them have found considerably less latitude for such regulations than might have been expected. . . .

Dissents in these cases expressed the view that the Court was expanding upon *Roe* in imposing ever greater restrictions on the States. See *Thornburgh* v. *American College of Obstetricians and Gynecologists*, 476 U.S., at 783 (Burger, C.J., dissenting) ("The extent to which the Court has departed from the limitations expressed in *Roe* is readily apparent"); *id.*, at 814 (WHITE, J., dissenting) ([T]he majority indiscriminately strikes down statutory provision that in no way contravene the right recognized in *Roe*"). And, when confronted with state regulations of this type in past years, the Court has become increasingly more divided: The three most recent abortion cases have not commanded a Court opinion. See *Ohio* v. *Akron Center for Reproductive Health*, 497 U.S. 502 (1990); *Hodgson* v. *Minnesota* 497 U.S. 417 (1990); *Webster* v. *Reproductive Health Services*, 492 U.S. 490 (1989). . . . This state of confusion and disagreement warrants reexamination of the "fundamental right" accorded to a woman's decision to abort a fetus in *Roe*, with its concomitant requirement that any state regulation of abortion survive "strict scrutiny." See *Payne* v. *Tennessee*, 501 U.S. 808, 827–828 (1991) (observing that reexamination of constitutional decisions is appropriate when those decisions have generated uncertainty and failed to provide clear guidance, because "correction through legislative action is practically impossible" (internal quotation marks omitted)); *Garcia* v. *San Antonio Metropolitan Transit Authority*, 469 U.S. 528, 546–547 (1985).

We have held that a liberty interest protected under the Due Process Clause of the Fourteenth Amendment will be deemed fundamental if it is "implicit in the concept of ordered liberty." *Palko* v. *Connecticut*, 302 U.S. 319, 325 (1937). Three years earlier, in *Snyder* v. *Massachusetts*, 291 U.S. 97 (1934), we referred to a "principle of justice so rooted in the traditions and conscience of our people as to be ranked as fundamental." *Id.*, at 105; see also *Michael H.* v. *Gerald D.*, 491 U.S. 110, 122 (1989) (plurality opinion) (citing the language from *Snyder*). These expressions are admittedly not precise, but our decisions implementing this notion of "fundamental" rights do not afford any more elaborate basis on which to base such a classification.

In construing the phrase "liberty" incorporated in the Due Process Clause of the Fourteenth Amendment, we have recognized that its meaning extends beyond freedom from physical restraint. In *Pierce* v. *Society of Sisters*, 268 U.S. 510 (1925), we held that it included a parent's right to send a child to private school; in *Meyer* v. *Nebraska*, 262 U.S. 390 (1923), we held that it included a right to teach a foreign language in a parochial school. Building on these cases, we have held that the term "liberty" includes a right to marry, *Loving* v. *Virginia*, 388 U.S. 1 (1967); a right to procreate, *Skinner* v. *Oklahoma ex rel. Williamson*, 316 U.S. 535 (1942); and a right to use contraceptives, *Griswold* v. *Connecticut*, 381 U.S. 479 (1965); *Eisenstadt* v. *Baird*, 405 U.S. 438 (1972). But a reading of these opinions makes clear that they do not endorse any all-encompassing "right to privacy."

In *Roe* v. *Wade*, the Court recognized a "guarantee of personal privacy" which "is broad enough to encompass a woman's decision whether or not to terminate her pregnancy." 410 U.S., at 152–153. We are now of the view that, in terming this right fundamental, the Court in *Roe* read the earlier opinions upon which it based its decision much too broadly. Unlike marriage, procreation, and contraception, abortion "involves the purposeful termination of a potential life." *Harris* v. *McRae*, 448 U.S. 297, 325 (1980). The abortion decision must therefore "be recognized as *sui generis*, different in kind from the others that the Court has protected under the rubric of personal or family privacy and autonomy." *Thornburgh* v. *American College of Obstetricians and Gynecologists, supra*, at 792 (WHITE, J., dissenting). One cannot ignore the fact that a woman is not isolated in her pregnancy, and that the decision to abort necessarily involves the destruction of a fetus. . . .

Nor do the historical traditions of the American people support the view that the right to terminate one's pregnancy is "fundamental." The common law which we inherited from England made abortion after "quickening" an offense. At the time of the adoption of the Fourteenth Amendment, statutory prohibitions or restrictions on abortion were commonplace; in 1868, at least 28 of the then-37 States and 8 Territories had statutes banning or limiting abortion. J. Mohr, Abortion in America 200 (1978). By the turn of the century virtually every State had a law prohibiting or restricting abortion on its books. By the middle of the present century, a liberalization trend had set in. But 21 of the restrictive abortion laws in effect in 1868 were still in effect in 1973 then *Roe* was decided, and an overwhelming majority of the States prohibited abortion unless necessary to preserve the life or health of the mother. *Roe* v. *Wade*, 410 U.S., at 139–140; *id.* At 176–177, n. 2 (REHNQUIST, J., dissenting). On this record, it can scarcely be said that any deeply rooted tradition of relatively unrestricted abortion in our history supported the classification of the right to abortion as "fundamental" under the Due Process Clause of the Fourteenth Amendment.

We think, therefore, both in view of this history and or our decided cases dealing with substantive liberty under the Due Process Clause, that the Court was mistaken in *Roe* when it classified a woman's decision to terminate her pregnancy as a "fundamental right" that could be abridged only in a manner which withstood "strict scrutiny." In so concluding, we repeat the observation made in *Bowers* v. *Hardwick*, 478 U.S. 186 (1986).

> "Nor are we inclined to take a more expansive view of our authority to discover new fundamental rights imbedded in the Due Process Clause. The Court is most vulnerable and comes nearest to illegitimacy when it deals with judge-made constitutional law having little or no cognizable roots in the language or design of the Constitution." *Id.*, at 194.

We believe that the sort of constitutionally imposed abortion code of the type illustrated by our decisions following *Roe* is inconsistent "with the notion of a Constitution cast in general terms, as ours is, and usually speaking in general principles, as ours does." *Webster* v. *Reproductive Health Services*, 492 U.S., at 518 (plurality opinion). The Court in *Roe* reached too far when it analogized the right to abort a fetus to the rights involved in *Pierce, Meyer, Loving,* and *Griswold,* and thereby deemed the right to abortion fundamental.

## — II —

The joint opinion of JUSTICES O'CONNOR, KENNEDY, and SOUTER cannot bring itself to say that *Roe* was correct as an original matter, but the authors are of the view that "the immediate question is not the soundness of *Roe*'s resolution of the issue, but the precedential force that must be accorded to its holding." *Ante,* at 871. Instead of claiming that *Roe* was correct as a matter of original constitutional interpretation, the opinion therefore contains an elaborate discussion of *stare decisis*. This discussion of the principle of *stare decisis* appears to be almost entirely dicta, because the joint opinion does not apply that principle in dealing with *Roe*. *Roe* decided that a woman had a fundamental right to an abortion. The joint opinion rejects that view. *Roe* decided that abortion regulations were to be subjected to "strict scrutiny" and could be justified only in the light of "compelling state interests." The joint opinion rejects that view. *Ante,* at 872–873; see *Roe* v. *Wade, supra,* at 162–164. *Roe* analyzed abortion regulation under a rigid trimester framework, a framework which has guided this Court's decisionmaking for 19 years. The joint opinion rejects that framework. *Ante,* at 873.

*Stare decisis* is defined in Black's Law Dictionary as meaning "to abide by, or adhere to, decided cases." Black's Law Dictionary 1406 (6th ed. 1990). Whatever the "central holding" of *Roe* that is left after the joint opinion finishes dissecting it is surely not the result of that principle. While purporting to adhere to precedent, the joint opinion instead revises it. *Roe* continues to exist, but only in the way a storefront on a western movie set exists: a mere facade to give the illusion of reality. Decisions following *Roe*, such as *Akron* v. *Akron Center for Reproductive Health, Inc.*, 462 U.S. 416 (1983), and *Thornburgh* v. *American College of Obstetricians and Gynecologists*, 476 U.S. 747 (1986), are frankly overruled in part under the "undue burden" standard expounded in the joint opinion. *Ante*, at 881–884.

In our view, authentic principles of *stare decisis* do not require that any portion of the reasoning in *Roe* be kept intact. "*Stare decisis* is not . . . a universal, inexorable command," especially in cases involving the interpretation of the Federal Constitution. *Burnett* v. *Coronado Oil & Gas Co.*, 285 U.S. 393, 405 (1932) (Brandeis, J., dissenting). Erroneous decisions in such constitutional cases are uniquely durable, because correction through legislative action, save for constitutional amendment, is impossible. It is therefore our duty to reconsider constitutional interpretations that "depar[t] from a proper understanding" of the Constitution. *Garcia* v. *San Antonio Metropolitan Transit Authority*, 469 U.S., at 557; see *United States* v. *Scott*, 437 U.S. 82, 101 (1978) ("'[I]n cases involving the Federal Constitution, . . . [t]he Court bows to the lessons of experience and the force of better reasoning, recognizing that the process of trial and error, so fruitful in the physical sciences, is appropriate also in the judicial function'" (quoting *Burnett* v. *Coronado Oil & Gas Co.*, supra, at 406–408 (Brandeis, J., dissenting))); *Smith* v. *Allwright*, 321 U.S. 649, 665 (1944). Our constitutional watch does not cease merely because we have spoken before on an issue; when it becomes clear that a prior constitutional interpretation is unsound we are obliged to reexamine the question. See e.g., *West Virginia Bd. of Ed.* v. *Barnette*, 319 U.S. 624, 642 (1943); *Erie R. Co.* v. *Tompkins*, 304 U.S. 64, 74–78 (1938).

The joint opinion discusses several *stare decisis* factors which, it asserts, point toward retaining a portion of *Roe*. Two of these factors are that the main "factual underpinning" of *Roe* has remained the same, and that its doctrinal foundation is no weaker now than it was in 1973. *Ante*, at 857–860. Of course, what might be called the basic facts which gave rise to *Roe* have remained the same—women become pregnant, there is a point somewhere, depending on medical technology, where a fetus becomes viable, and women give birth to children. But this is only to say that the same facts which gave rise to *Roe* will continue to give rise to similar cases. It is not a reason, in and of itself, why those cases must be decided in the same incorrect manner as was the first case to deal with the question. And surely there is no requirement, in considering whether to depart from *stare decisis* in a constitutional case, that a decision be more wrong now than it was at the time it was rendered. If that were true, the most outlandish constitutional decision could survive forever, based simply on the fact that it was no more outlandish later than it was when originally rendered.

Nor does the joint opinion faithfully follow this alleged requirement. The opinion frankly concludes that *Roe* and its progeny were wrong in failing to recognize that the State's interests in maternal health and in the protection of unborn human life exist throughout pregnancy. *Ante,* at 871–873. But there is no indication that these components of *Roe* are any more incorrect at this juncture than they were at its inception.

The joint opinion also points to the reliance interests involved in this context in its effort to explain why precedent must be followed for precedent's sake. Certainly it is true that where reliance is truly at issue, as in the case of judicial [c]onsiderations in favor of *stare decisis* are at their acme." *Payne* v. *Tennessee,* 501 U.S., at 828. But, as the joint opinion apparently agrees, *ante,* at 855–856, any traditional notion of reliance is not applicable here. The Court today cuts back on the protection afforded by *Roe,* and no one claims that this action defeats any reliance interests in the disavowed trimester framework. Similarly, reliance interests would not be diminished were the Court to go further and acknowledge the full error of *Roe,* as "reproductive planning could take virtually immediate account of" this action. *Ante,* at 856.

The joint opinion thus turns to what can only be described as an unconventional—and unconvincing—notion of reliance, a view based on the surmise that the availability of abortion since *Roe* has led to "two decades of economic and social developments" that would be undercut if the error of *Roe* were recognized. *Ante,* at 856. The joint opinion's assertion of this fact is undeveloped and totally conclusory. In fact, one cannot be sure to what economic and social developments the opinion is referring. Surely it is dubious to suggest that women have reached their "places in society" in reliance upon *Roe,* rather than as a result of their determination to obtain higher education and compete with men in the job market, and of society's increasing recognition of their ability to fill positions that were previously thought to be reserved only for men. *Ante,* at 856.

In the end, having failed to put forth any evidence to prove any true reliance, the joint opinion's argument is based solely on generalized assertions about the national psyche, on a belief that the people of this country have grown accustomed to the *Roe* decision over the last 19 years and have "ordered their thinking and living around" it. *Ante,* at 856. As an initial matter, one might inquire how the joint opinion can view the "central holding" of *Roe* as so deeply rooted in our constitutional culture, when it so casually uproots and disposes of that same decision's trimester framework. Furthermore, at various points in the past, the same could have been said about this Court's erroneous decisions that the Constitution allowed "separate but equal" treatment of minorities, see *Plessy* v. *Ferguson,* 163 U.S. 537 (1896), or that "liberty" under the Due Process Clause protected "freedom of contract," see *Adkins* v. *Children's Hospital of District of Columbia,* 261 U.S. 525 (1923); *Lochner* v. *New York,* 198 U.S. 45 (1905). The "separate but equal" doctrine lasted 58 years after *Plessy,* and *Lochner's* protection of contractual freedom lasted 32 years. However, the simple fact that a generation or more had grown used to these major decisions did not prevent the Court from correcting its errors in those cases, nor should it prevent us from correctly interpreting the Constitution here. See *Brown v. Board of Education*, 347 U.S. 483 (1954) (rejecting the "separate but equal" doctrine); *West Coast Hotel Co. v. Parrish*, 300 U.S. 379 (1937) (overruling *Adkins v. Children's Hospital, supra,* in upholding Washington's minimum wage law).

Apparently realizing that conventional *stare decisis* principles do not support its position, the joint opinion advances a belief that retaining a portion of *Roe* is necessary to protect the "legitimacy" of this Court. *Ante,* at 861–869. Because the Court must take care to render decisions "grounded truly in principle," and not simply as political and social compromises, *ante,* at 865, the joint opinion properly declares it to be this Court's duty to ignore the public criticism and protest that may arise as a result of a decision. Few would quarrel with this statement, although it may be doubted that Members of this Court, holding their tenure as they do during constitutional "good behavior," are at all likely to be intimidated by such public protests.

But the joint opinion goes on to state that when the Court "resolve[s] the sort of intensely divisive controversy reflected in *Roe* and those rare, comparable cases," its decision is exempt from reconsideration under established principles of *stare decisis* in constitutional cases. *Ante,* at 866. This is so, the joint opinion contends, because in those "intensely divisive" cases the Court has "call[ed] the contending sides of a national controversy to end their national division by accepting a common mandate rooted in the Constitution," and must therefore take special care not to be perceived as "surrender[ing] to political pressure" and continued opposition. *Ante,* at 866, 867. This is a truly novel principle, one which is contrary to both the Court's historical practice and to the Court's traditional willingness to tolerate criticism of its opinions. Under this principle, when the Court has ruled on a divisive issue, it is apparently prevented from overruling that decision for the sole reason that it was incorrect, *unless opposition to the original decision has died away.*

The first difficulty with this principle lies in its assumption that cases that are "intensely divisive" can be readily distinguished from those that are not. The question of whether a particular issue is "intensely divisive" enough to qualify for special protection is entirely subjective and dependent on the individual assumptions of the Members of this Court. In addition, because the Court's duty is to ignore public opinion and criticism on issues that come before it, its Members are in perhaps the worst position to judge whether a decision divides the Nation deeply enough to justify such uncommon protection. Although many of the Court's decisions divide the populace to a large degree, we have not previously on that account shied away from applying normal rules of *stare decisis* when urged to reconsider earlier decisions. Over the past 21 years, for example, the Court has overruled in whole or in part 34 of its previous constitutional decisions. See *Payne* v. *Tennessee, supra,* at 828–830, and n. 1 (listing cases).

The joint opinion picks out and discusses two prior Court rulings that it believes are of the "intensely divisive" variety, and concludes that they are of comparable dimension to *Roe. Ante,* at 861–864 (discussing *Lochner* v. *New York, supra,* and *Plessy* v. *Ferguson, supra*). It appears to us very odd indeed that the joint opinion chooses as benchmarks two cases in which the Court chose *not* to adhere to erroneous constitutional precedent, but instead enhanced its stature by acknowledging and correcting its error, apparently in violation of the joint opinion's "legitimacy" principle. See *West Coast Hotel Co.* v. *Parrish, supra; Brown* v. *Board of Education, supra.* One might also wonder how it is that the joint opinion puts these, and not others, in the "intensely divisive" category, and how it assumes that these are the only two lines of cases of comparable dimension to *Roe.* There is no reason to think that either *Plessy* or *Lochner* produced the sort of public protest when they were decided that *Roe* did. There were undoubtedly large segments of the bench and bar who agreed with the dissenting views in those cases, but surely that cannot be what the Court means when it uses the term "intensely divisive," or many other cases would have to be added to the list. In terms of public protest, however, *Roe,* so far as we know, was unique. But just as the Court should not respond to that sort of protest by retreating from the decision simply to allay the concerns of the protesters, it should likewise not respond by determining to adhere to the decision at all costs lest it *seem* to be retreating under fire. Public protests should not alter the normal application of *stare decisis,* lest perfectly lawful protest activity be penalized by the Court itself. . . .

The joint opinion also agrees that the Court acted properly in rejecting the doctrine of "separate but equal" in *Brown.* In fact, the opinion lauds *Brown* in comparing it to *Roe. Ante,* at 867. This is strange, in that under the opinion's "legitimacy" principle the Court would seemingly have been forced to adhere to its erroneous decision in *Plessy* because of its "intensely divisive" character. To us, adherence to *Roe* today under the guise of "legitimacy" would seem to resemble more closely adherence to *Plessy* on the same ground. Fortunately, the Court did not choose that option in Brown, and instead frankly repudiated *Plessy.* The joint opinion concludes that such repudiation was justified only because of newly discovered evidence that segregation had the effect of treating one race as inferior to another. But it can hardly be argued that this was not urged upon those who decided *Plessy,* as Justice Harlan observed in his dissent that the law at issue "puts the brand of servitude and degradation upon a large class of our fellow-citizens, our equals before the law." *Plessy* v. *Ferguson,* 163 U.S., at 562. It is clear that the same arguments made before the Court in *Brown* were made in *Plessy* as well. The Court in *Brown* simply recognized, as Justice Harlan had recognized beforehand, that the Fourteenth Amendment does not permit racial segregation. The rule of *Brown* is not tied to popular opinion about the evils of segregation; it is a judgment that the

Equal Protection Clause does not permit racial segregation, no matter whether the public might come to believe that it is beneficial. On that ground it stands, and on that ground alone the Court was justified in properly concluding that the *Plessy* Court had erred.

There is also a suggestion in the joint opinion that the propriety of overruling a "divisive" decision depends in part on whether "most people" would now agree that it should be overruled. Either the demise of opposition or its progression to substantial popular agreement apparently is required to allow the Court to reconsider a divisive decision. How such agreement would be ascertained, short of a public opinion poll, the joint opinion does not say. But surely even the suggestion is totally at war with the idea of "legitimacy" in whose name it is invoked. The Judicial Branch derives its legitimacy, not from following public opinion, but from deciding by its best lights whether legislative enactments of the popular branches of Government comport with the Constitution. The doctrine of *stare decisis* is an adjunct of this duty, and should be no more subject to the vagaries of public opinion than is the basic judicial task.

There are other reasons why the joint opinion's discussion of legitimacy is unconvincing as well. In assuming that the Court is perceived as "surrender[ing] to political pressure" when it overrules a controversial decision, *ante,* at 867, the joint opinion forgets that there are two sides to any controversy. The joint opinion asserts that, in order to protect its legitimacy, the Court must refrain from overruling a controversial decision lest it be viewed as favoring those who oppose the decision. But a decision to *adhere* to prior precedent is subject to the same criticism, for in such a case one can easily argue that the Court is responding to those who have demonstrated in favor of the original decision. The decision in *Roe* has engendered large demonstrations, including repeated marches on this Court and on Congress, both in opposition to and in support of that opinion. A decision either way on *Roe* can therefore be perceived as favoring one group or the other. But this perceived dilemma arises only if one assumes, as the joint opinion does, that the Court should make its decisions with a view toward speculative public perceptions. If one assumes instead, as the Court surely did in both *Brown* and *West Coast Hotel,* that the Court's legitimacy is enhanced by faithful interpretation of the Constitution irrespective of public opposition, such self-engendered difficulties may be put to one side. . . .

The end result of the joint opinion's paeans of praise for legitimacy is the enunciation of a brand new standard for evaluating state regulation of a woman's right to abortion—the "undue burden" standard. As indicated above, *Roe* v. *Wade* adopted a "fundamental right" standard under which state regulations could survive only if they met the requirement of "strict scrutiny." While we disagree with that standard, it at lease had a recognized basis in constitutional law at the time *Roe* was decided. The same cannot be said for the "undue burden" standard, which is created largely out of whole cloth by the authors of the joint opinion. It is a standard which even today does not command the support of a majority of this Court. And it will not, we believe, result in the sort of "simple limitation," easily applied, which the joint opinion anticipates. In sum, it is a standard which is not built to last.

In evaluating abortion regulations under that standard, judges will have to decide whether they place a "substantial obstacle" in the path of a woman seeking an abortion. In that this standard is based even more on a judge's subjective determinations than was the trimester framework, the standard will do nothing to prevent "judges from roaming at large in the constitutional field" guided only by their personal views. *Griswold* v. *Connecticut*, 381 U.S., at 502 (Harlan, J., concurring in judgment). Because the undue burden standard is plucked from nowhere, the question of what is a "substantial obstacle" to abortion will undoubtedly engender a variety of conflicting views. . . .

Furthermore, while striking down the spousal *notice* regulation, the joint opinion would uphold a parental *consent* restriction that certainly places very substantial obstacles in the path of a minor's abortion choice. The joint opinion is forthright in admitting that it draws this distinction based on a policy judgment that parents will have the best interests of their children at heart, while the same is not necessarily true of husbands as to their wives. This may or may not be a correct judgment, but it is quintessentially a legislative one. The "undue burden" inquiry does not in any way supply the distinction between parental consent and spousal consent which the joint opinion adopts. Despite the efforts of the joint opinion, the undue burden standard presents nothing more workable than the trimester framework which it discards today. Under the guise of the Constitution, this Court will still impart its own preferences on the States in the form of a complex abortion code.

The sum of the joint opinion's labors in the name of *stare decisis* and "legitimacy" is this: *Roe* v. *Wade* stands as a sort of judicial Potemkin village, which may be pointed out to passers-by as a monument to the importance of adhering to precedent. But behind the facade, an entirely new method of analysis, without any roots in constitutional law, is imported to decide the constitutionality of state laws regulating abortion. Neither *stare decisis* nor "legitimacy" are truly served by such an effort.

We have stated above our belief that the Constitution does not subject state abortion regulations to heightened scrutiny. Accordingly, we think that the correct analysis is that set forth by the plurality opinion in *Webster*. A woman's interest in having an abortion is a form of liberty protected by the Due Process Clause, but States may regulate abortion procedures in ways rationally related to a legitimate state interest. *Williamson* v. *Lee Optical of Oklahoma, Inc.*, 348 U.S. 483, 491 (1955); cf. *Stanley* v. *Illinois*,

405 U.S. 645, 651–653 (1972). With this rule in mind, we examine each of the challenged provisions.

## — III —

## A

Section 3205 of the Act imposes certain requirements related to the informed consent of a woman seeking an abortion. 18 Pa. Cons. State. § 3205 (1990). Section 3205(a)(1) requires that the referring or performing physician must inform a woman contemplating an abortion of (i) the nature of the procedure and the risks and alternatives that a reasonable patient would find material; (ii) the fetus' probable gestational age; and (iii) the medical risks involved in carrying her pregnancy to term. Section 3295(a)(2) requires a physician or a nonphysician counselor to inform the woman that (i) the state health department publishes free materials describing the fetus at different stages and listing abortion alternatives; (ii) medical assistance benefits may be available for prenatal, childbirth, and neonatal care; and (iii) the child's father is liable for child support. The Act also imposes a 24-hour waiting period between the time that the woman receives the required information and the time that the physician is allowed to perform the abortion. . . . Here Pennsylvania seeks to further its legitimate interest in obtaining informed consent by ensuring that each woman "is aware not only of the reasons for having an abortion, but also of the risks associated with an abortion and the availability of assistance that might make the alternative of normal childbirth more attractive than it might otherwise appear." *Id.*, at 798–799 (WHITE, J., dissenting).

We conclude that this provision of the statute is rationally related to the State's interest in assuring that a woman's consent to an abortion be a fully informed decision.

Section 3205(a)(1) requires a physician to disclose certain information about the abortion procedure and its risks and alternatives. This requirement is certainly no large burden, as the Court of Appeals found that "the record shows that the clinics, without exception, insist on providing this information to women before an abortion is performed." 947 F. 2d, at 703. We are of the view that this information "clearly is related to maternal health and to the State's legitimate purpose in requiring informed consent." . . . An accurate description of the gestational age of the fetus and of the risks involved in carrying a child to term helps to further both those interests and the State's legitimate interest in unborn human life. See *id.*, at 445–446, n. 37 (required disclosure of gestational age of the fetus "certainly is not objectionable"). Although petitioners contend that it is unreasonable for the State to require that a physician, as opposed to a nonphysician counselor, disclose this information, we agree with the Court of Appeals that a State "may rationally decide that physicians are better qualified than counselors to impart this information and answer questions about the medical aspects of the available alternatives." 947 F. 2d, at 704.

Section 3205(a)(2) compels the disclosure, by a physician or a counselor, of information concerning the availability of paternal child support and state-funded alternatives if the woman decides to proceed with her pregnancy. . . . We conclude that this required presentation of "balanced information" is rationally related to the State's legitimate interest in ensuring that the woman's consent is truly informed, *Thornburgh* v. *American College of Obstetricians and Gynecologists*, 476 U.S., at 830 (O'CONNOR, J., dissenting), and in addition furthers the State's interest in preserving unborn life. That the information might create some uncertainty and persuade some women to forgo abortions does not lead to the conclusion that the Constitution forbids the provision of such information. Indeed, it only demonstrates that this information might very well make a difference, and that it is therefore relevant to a woman's informed choice. Cf. *id.*, at 801 (WHITE, J., dissenting) ("[T]he ostensible objective of *Roe* v. *Wade* is not maximizing the number of abortions, but maximizing choice"). We acknowledge that in *Thornburgh* this Court struck down informed consent requirements similar to the ones at issue here. See *id.*, at 760-764. It is clear, however, that while the detailed framework of *Roe* led to the Court's invalidation of those informational requirements, they "would have been sustained under any traditional standard of judicial review, . . . or for any other surgical procedure except abortion." *Webster* v. *Reproductive Health Services*, 492 U.S., at 802 (WHITE, J., dissenting); *id.*, at 783 (BURGER, C., dissenting)). In light of our rejection of *Roe*'s "fundamental right" approach to this subject, we do not regard *Thornburgh* as controlling.

For the same reason, we do not feel bound to follow this Court's previous holding that a State's 24-hour mandatory waiting period is unconstitutional. See *Akron* v. *Akron Center for Reproductive Health, Inc., supra*, at 449–451. Petitioners are correct that such a provision will result in delays for some women that might not otherwise exist, therefore placing a burden on their liberty. But the provision in no way prohibits abortions, and the informed consent and waiting period requirements do not apply in the case of a medical emergency. See 18 Pa. Cons. Stat. §§ 3205(a), (b) (1990). We are of the view that, in providing time for reflection and reconsideration, the waiting period helps ensure that a woman's decision to abort is a well-considered one, and reasonably furthers the State's legitimate interest in maternal health and in the unborn life of the fetus. . . .

# B

In addition to providing her own informed consent, before an unemancipated woman under the age of 18 may obtain an abortion she must either furnish the consent of one of her parents, or must opt for the judicial procedure that allows her to bypass the consent requirement. Under the judicial bypass option, a minor can obtain an abortion if a state court finds that she is capable of giving her informed consent and has indeed given such consent, *or* determines that an abortion is in her best interests. Records of these court proceedings are kept confidential. The Act directs the state trial court to render a decision within three days of the woman's application, and the entire procedure, including appeal to Pennsylvania Superior Court, is to last no longer than eight business days. The parental consent requirement does not apply in the case of a medical emergency. 18 Pa. Cons. Stat. § 3206 (1990).

This provision is entirely consistent with this Court's previous decisions involving parental consent requirements. . . .

We think it beyond dispute that a State "has a strong and legitimate interest in the welfare of its young citizens, whose immaturity, inexperience, and lack of judgment may sometimes impair their ability to exercise their rights wisely." *Hodgson* v. *Minnesota*, 497 U.S., at 444 (opinion of STEVENS, J.). A requirement of parental consent to abortion, like myriad other restrictions placed upon minors in other contexts, is reasonably designed to further this important and legitimate state interest. In our view, it is entirely "rational and fair for the State to conclude that, in most instances, the family will strive to give a lonely or even terrified minor advice that is both compassionate and mature." . . . We thus conclude that Pennsylvania's parental consent requirement should be upheld.

## C

Section 3209 of the Act contains the spousal notification provision. . . .

We first emphasize that Pennsylvania has not imposed a spousal *consent* requirement of the type the Court struck down in *Planned Parenthood of Central Mo.* v. *Danforth*, 428 U.S., at 67–72. Missouri's spousal consent provision was invalidated in that case because of the Court's view that it unconstitutionally granted to the husband "a veto power exercisable for any reason whatsoever or for no reason at all." *Id.*, at 71. But the provision here involves a much less intrusive requirement of spousal *notification*, not consent. Such a law requiring only notice to the husband "does not give any third party the legal right to make the [woman's] decision for her, or to prevent her from obtaining an abortion should she choose to have one performed." . . . Because this is a facial challenge to the Act, it is insufficient for petitioners to show that the notification provision "might operate unconstitutionally under some conceivable set of circumstances." *United States* v. *Salerno*, 481 U.S. 739, 745 (1987). Thus, it is not enough for petitioners to show that, in some "worst case" circumstances, the notice provision will operate as a grant of veto power to husbands. *Ohio* v. *Akron Center for Reproductive*

*Health*, 497 U.S., at 514. Because they are making a facial challenge to the provision, they must "show that no set of circumstances exists under which the [provision] would be valid." *Ibid.* (internal quotation marks omitted). This they have failed to do.

The question before us is therefore whether the spousal notification requirement rationally furthers any legitimate state interest. We conclude that it does. First, a husband's interests in procreation within marriage and in the potential life of his unborn child are certainly substantial ones. See *Planned Parenthood of Central Mo.* v. *Danforth*, 428 U.S., at 69 ("We are not unaware of the deep and proper concern and interest that a devoted and protective husband has in his wife's pregnancy and in the growth and development of the fetus she is carrying"); *id.*, at 93 (WHITE, J., concurring in part and dissenting in part); *Skinner* v. *Oklahoma ex rel. Williamson*, 316 U.S., at 541. The State itself has legitimate interests both in protecting these interests of the father and in protecting the potential life of the fetus, and the spousal notification requirement is reasonably related to advancing those state interests. By providing that a husband will usually know of his spouse's intent to have an abortion, the provision makes it more likely that the husband will participate in deciding the fate of his unborn child, a possibility that might otherwise have been denied him. This participation might in some cases result in a decision to proceed with the pregnancy. As Judge Alito observed in his dissent below, "[t]he Pennsylvania legislature could have rationally believed that some married women are initially inclined to obtain an abortion without their husband's knowledge because of perceived problems—such as economic constraints, future plans, or the husband's previously expressed opposition—that may be obviated by discussion prior to the abortion." 947 F. 2d, at 726 (opinion concurring in part and dissenting in part).

The State also has a legitimate interest in promoting "the integrity of the marital relationship." 18 Pa. Cons. Stat. § 3209(a) (1990). This Court has previously recognized "the importance of the marital relationship in our society." *Planned Parenthood of Central Mo.* v. *Danforth, supra,* at 69. In our view, the spousal notice requirement is a rational attempt by the State to improve truthful communication between spouses and encourage collaborative decisionmaking, and thereby fosters marital integrity. See *Labine* v. *Vincent,* 401 U.S. 532, 538 (1971) ("[T]he power to make rules to establish, protect, and strengthen family life" is committed to the state legislatures). . . . The spousal notice provision will admittedly be unnecessary in some circumstances, and possibly harmful in others, but "the existence of particular cases in which a feature of a statute performs no function (or is even counterproductive) ordinarily does not render the statute unconstitutional or even constitutionally suspect." *Thornburgh* v. *American College of Obstetricians and Gynecologists,* 476 U.S., at 800 (WHITE, J., dissenting). The Pennsylvania Legislature was in a position to weigh the likely benefits of the provision against its likely adverse effects, and presumably concluded, on balance, that the provision would be beneficial. Whether this was a wise decision or not, we cannot say that it was irrational. We therefore conclude that the spousal notice provision comports with the Constitution. See *Harris* v. *McRae*, 448 U.S., at 325–326 ("It is not the mission of this Court or any other to decide whether the balance of competing interests . . . is wise social policy:).

## D

The Act also imposes various reporting requirements. . . . The District Court found that these reports are kept completely confidential. 947 F. 2d, at 716. We further conclude that these reporting requirements rationally further the State's legitimate interests in advancing the state of medical knowledge concerning maternal health and prenatal life, in gathering statistical information with respect to patients, and in ensuring compliance with other provisions of the Act.

Section 3207 of the Act requires each abortion facility to file a report with its name and address, as well as the names and addresses of any parent, subsidiary, or affiliated organizations. 18 Pa. Cons. Stat. § 3207(b) (1990). Section 3214(f) further requires each facility to file quarterly reports stating the total number of abortions performed, broken down by trimester. Both of these reports are available to the public only if the facility received state funds within the preceding 12 months. . . . As the Court of Appeals observed, "[w]hen a state provides money to a private commercial enterprise, there is a legitimate public interest in informing taxpayers who the funds are benefiting and what services the funds are supporting." 947 F. 2d, at 718. These reporting requirements rationally further this legitimate state interest.

## E

Finally, petitioners challenge the medical emergency exception provided for by the Act. The existence of a medical emergency exempts compliance with the Act's informed consent, parental consent, and spousal notice requirements. . . . We find that the interpretation of the Court of Appeals in these cases is eminently reasonable, and that the provision thus should be upheld. When a woman is faced with any condition that poses a "significant threat to [her] life or health," she is exempted form the Act's consent and notice requirements and may proceed immediately with her abortion.

## — IV —

For the reasons stated, we therefore would hold that each of the challenged provisions of the Pennsylvania statute is consistent with the Constitution. It bears emphasis that our conclusion in this regard does not carry with it any necessary approval of these regulations. Our task is, as always, to decide only whether the challenged provisions of a law comport with the United States Constitution. If, as we believe, these do, their wisdom as a matter of public policy is for the people of Pennsylvania to decide.

JUSTICE SCALIA, with whom THE CHIEF JUSTICE, JUSTICE WHITE, and JUSTICE THOMAS join, concurring in the judgment in part and dissenting in part.

My views on this matter are unchanged from those I set forth in my separate opinions in *Webster* v. *Reproductive Health Services*, 492 U.S. 490, 532 (1989) (opinion concurring in part and concurring in judgment), and *Ohio* v. *Akron Center for Reproductive Health*, 497 U.S. 502, 520 (1990) (*Akron II*) (concurring opinion). The States may, if they wish, permit abortion on demand, but the Constitution does not *require* them to do so. The permissibility of abortion, and the limitations upon it, are to be resolved like most important questions in our democracy: by citizens trying to persuade one another and then voting. As the Court acknowledges, "where reasonable people disagree the government can adopt one position or the other." *Ante,* at 851. The Court is correct in adding the qualification that this "assumes a state of affairs in which the choice does not intrude upon a protected liberty," *Ibid.*—but the crucial part of that qualification is the penultimate word. A State's choice between two positions on which reasonable people can disagree is constitutional even when (as is often the case) it intrudes upon a "liberty" in the absolute sense. Laws against bigamy, for example—with which entire societies of reasonable people disagree—intrude upon men and women's liberty to marry and live with one another. But bigamy happens not to be a liberty specially "protected" by the Constitution.

That is, quite simply, the issue in these cases: not whether the power of a woman to abort her unborn child is a "liberty" in the absolute sense; or even whether it is a liberty of great importance to many women. Of course it is both. The issue is whether it is a liberty protected by the Constitution of the United States. I am sure it is not. I reach that conclusion not because of anything so exalted as my views concerning the "concept of existence, of meaning, of the universe, and of the mystery of life." *Ibid.* Rather, I reach it for the same reason I reach the conclusion that bigamy is not constitutionally protected—because of two simple facts: (1) the Constitution says absolutely nothing about it, and (2) the long-standing traditions of American society have permitted it to be legally proscribed.[5] *Akron II, supra,* at 520 (SCALIA, J., concurring).

. . . represent my position, that "liberty" includes "only those practices, defined at the most specific level, that were protected against government interference by other rules of law when the Fourteenth Amendment was ratified," *ante,* at 847 (citing *Michael H.* v. *Gerald D.*, 491 U.S. 110, 127, n. 6 (1989) (opinion of SCALIA, J.)). That is not, however, what *Michael H.* says; it merely observes that, in defining "liberty," we may not disregard a specific, "relevant tradition protecting, or denying protection to, the asserted right," *ibid.* But the Court does not wish to be fettered by any such limitations on its preferences. The Court's statement that it is "tempting" to acknowledge the authoritativeness of tradition in order to "cur[b] the discretion of federal judges," *ante*, at 847, is of course rhetoric rather than reality; no government official is "tempted" to place restraints upon his own freedom of action, which is why Lord Acton did not say "Power tends to purify." The Court's temptation is in the quite opposite and more natural direction—towards systematically eliminating checks upon its own power; and it succumbs.

Beyond that brief summary of the essence of my position, I will not swell the United States Reports with repetition of what I have said before; and applying the rational basis test, I would uphold the Pennsylvania statute in its entirety. I must, however, respond to a few of the more outrageous arguments in today's opinion, which it is beyond human nature to leave unanswered. I shall discuss each of them under a quotation from the Court's opinion to which they pertain.

> "The inescapable fact is that adjudication of substantive due process claims may call upon the Court in interpreting the Constitution to exercise that same capacity which by tradition courts always have exercised: reasoned judgment." *Ante*, at 849.

Assuming that the question before us is to be resolved at such a level of philosophical abstraction, in such isolation from the traditions of American society, as by simply applying "reasoned judgment," I do not see how that could possibly have produced the answer the Court arrived at in *Roe v. Wade*, 410 U.S. 113 (1973). Today's opinion describes the methodology of *Roe*, quite accurately, as weighing against the woman's interest, the State's "'important and legitimate interest in protecting the potentiality of human life.'" *Ante*, at 871 (quoting *Roe, supra*, at 162). But "reasoned judgment" does not begin by begging the question, as *Roe* and subsequent cases unquestionably did by assuming that what the State is protecting is the mere "potentiality of human life." See e.g., *Roe, supra*, at 162; *Planned Parenthood of Central Mo.* v. *Danforth*, 428 U.S. 52, 61 (1976); *Colautti* v. *Franklin*, 439 U.S. 379, 386 (1979); *Akron* v. *Akron Center for Reproductive Health, Inc.*, 462 U.S. 416, 428 (1983) (*Akron I*); *Planned Parenthood Assn. of Kansas City, Mo., Inc.* v. *Ashcroft*, 462 U.S. 476, 482 (1983). The whole argument of abortion opponents is that what the Court calls the fetus and what others call the unborn child *is a human life*. Thus, whatever answer *Roe* came up with after conducting its "balancing" is bound to be wrong, unless it is correct that the human fetus is in some critical sense merely potentially human. There is of course no way to determine that as a legal matter; it is in fact a value judgment. Some societies have considered newborn children not yet human, or the incompetent elderly no longer so.

The authors of the joint opinion, of course, do not squarely contend that *Roe v. Wade* was a *correct* application of "reasoned judgment"; merely that it must be followed, because of *stare decisis*. But in their exhaustive discussion of all the factors that go into the determination of when *stare decisis* should be observed and when disregarded, they never mention "how wrong was the decision on its face?" surely, if "[t]he Court's power lies . . . in its legitimacy, a product of substance and perception," *ante,* at 805, the "substance" part of the equation demands that plain error be acknowledged and eliminated. *Roe* was plainly wrong—even on the Court's methodology of "reasoned judgment," and even more so (of course) if the proper criteria of text and tradition are applied.

The emptiness of the "reasoned judgment" that produced *Roe* is displayed in plain view by the fact that, after more than 19 years of effort by some of the brightest (and most determined) legal minds in the country, after more than 10 cases upholding abortion rights in this Court, and after dozens upon dozens of *amicus* briefs submitted in these and other cases, the best the Court can do to explain how it is that the word "liberty" *must* be thought to include the right to destroy human fetuses is to rattle off a collection of adjectives that simply decorate a value judgment and conceal a political choice. The right to abort, we are told, inheres in "liberty" because it is among "a person's most basic decisions," it involves a "most intimate and personal choic[e]," it "originate[s] within the zone of conscience and belief, it reflects "intimate views" of a "deep, personal character," it involves "intimate relationships" and notions of "personal autonomy and bodily integrity," and it concerns a particularly "'important decisio[n],'" But it is obvious to anyone applying "reasoned judgment" that the same adjectives can be applied to many forms of conduct that this Court (including one of the Justices in today's majority, see *Bowers* v. *Hardwick,* 478 U.S. 186 (1986)) has held are *not* entitled to constitutional protection—because, like abortion, they are forms of conduct that have long been criminalized in American society. Those adjectives might be applied, for example, to homosexual sodomy, polygamy, adult incest, and suicide, all of which are equally "intimate" and "deep[ly] personal" decisions involving "personal autonomy and bodily integrity," and all of which can constitutionally be proscribed because it is our unquestionable constitutional tradition that they are proscribable. It is not reasoned judgment that supports the Court's decision; only personal predilection. Justice Curtis's warning is as timely today as it was 135 years ago:

> "[W]hen a strict interpretation of the Constitution, according to the fixed rules which govern the interpretation of laws, is abandoned, and the theoretical opinions of individuals are allowed to control its meaning, we have no longer a Constitution; we are under the government of individual men, who for the time being have power to declare what the Constitution is, according to their own views of what it ought to mean." *Dred Scott* v. *Sandford,* 19 How. 393, 621 (1857) (dissenting opinion).

> "Liberty finds no refuge in a jurisprudence of doubt."

One might have feared to encounter this August and sonorous phrase in an opinion defending the real *Roe* v. *Wade,* rather than the revised version fabricated today by the authors of the joint opinion. The shortcomings of *Roe* did not include lack of clarity:

Virtually all regulation of abortion before the third trimester was invalid. But to come across this phrase in the joint opinion—which calls upon federal district judges to apply an "undue burden" standard as doubtful in application as it is unprincipled in origin—is really more than one should have to bear.

The joint opinion['s] . . . efforts at clarification make clear only that the standard is inherently manipulable and will prove hopelessly unworkable in practice.

The joint opinion explains that a state regulation imposes an "undue burden" if it "has the purpose or effect of placing a substantial obstacle in the path of a woman seeking an abortion of a nonviable fetus." An obstacle is "substantial," we are told, if it is "calculated[,] [not] to inform the woman's free choice, [but to] hinder it." This latter statement cannot possibly mean what it says. *Any* regulation of abortion that is intended to advance what the joint opinion concedes is the State's "substantial" interest in protecting unborn life will be "calculated [to] hinder" a decision to have an abortion. It thus seems more accurate to say that the joint opinion would uphold abortion regulations only if they do not *unduly* hinder the woman's decision. That, of course, brings us right back to square one: Defining an "undue burden" as an "undue hindrance" (or a "substantial obstacle") hardly "clarifies" the test. Consciously or not, the joint opinion's verbal shell game will conceal raw judicial policy choices concerning what is "appropriate" abortion legislation.

The ultimately standardless nature of the "undue burden" inquiry is a reflection of the underlying fact that the concept has no principled or coherent legal basis. . . .

The "undue burden" standard is not at all the generally applicable principle the joint opinion pretends it to be; rather, it is a unique concept created specially for these cases, to preserve some judicial foothold in this ill-gotten territory. In claiming otherwise, the three justices show their willingness to place all constitutional rights at risk in an effort to preserve what they deem the "central holding in *Roe.*"

The rootless nature of the "undue burden" standard, a phrase plucked out of context from our earlier abortion decisions, see n. 3, *supra*, is further reflected in the fact that the joint opinion finds it necessary expressly to repudiate the more narrow formulations used in JUSTICE O'CONNOR's earlier opinions. . . .

It is difficult to maintain the illusion that we are interpreting a Constitution rather than inventing one, when we amend its provisions so breezily.

Because the portion of the joint opinion adopting and describing the undue burden test provides no more useful guidance than the empty phrases discussed above, one must turn to the 23 pages applying that standard to the present facts for further guidance. In evaluating Pennsylvania's abortion law, the joint opinion relies extensively on the factual findings of the District Court, and repeatedly qualifies its conclusions by noting that they are contingent upon the record developed in these cases. Thus, the joint opinion would uphold the 24-hour waiting period contained in the Pennsylvania statute's informed consent provision. 18 Pa. Cons. Stat. § 3205 (1990), because "the record evidence shows that in the vast majority of cases, a 24-hour delay does not create any appreciable health risk," *ante,* at 885. The three Justices therefore conclude that "on the record before us, . . . we are not convinced that the 24-hour waiting period constitutes an undue burden." *Ante,* at 887. The requirement that a doctor provide the information pertinent to informed consent would also be upheld because "there is no evidence on this record that [this requirement] would amount in practical terms to a substantial obstacle to a woman seeking an abortion." *Ante,* at 884. Similarly, the joint opinion would uphold the reporting requirements of the Act, §§ 3207, 3214, because "there is no . . . showing on the record before us" that these requirements constitute a "substantial obstacle" to abortion decisions. But at the same time the opinion pointedly observes that these reporting requirements may increase the costs of abortions and that "at some point [that fact] could become a substantial obstacle." Most significantly, the joint opinion's conclusion that the spousal notice requirement of the Act, see § 3209, imposes an "undue burden" is based in large measure on the District Court's "detailed findings of fact," which the joint opinion sets out a great length.

I do not, of course, have any objection to the notion that, in applying legal principles, one should rely only upon the facts that are contained in the record or that are properly subject to judicial notice. But what is remarkable about the joint opinion's fact-intensive analysis is that it does not result in any measurable clarification of the "undue burden" standard. Rather, the approach of the joint opinion is, for the most part, simply to highlight certain facts in the record that apparently strike the three Justices as particularly significant in establishing (or refuting) the existence of an undue burden; after describing these facts, the opinion then simply announces that the provision either does or does not impose a "substantial obstacle" or an "undue burden." We do not know whether the same conclusions could have been reached on a different record, or in what respects the record would have had to differ before an opposite conclusion would have been appropriate. The inherently standardless nature of this inquiry invites the district judge to give effect to his personal preferences about abortion. By finding and relying upon the right facts, he can invalidate, it would seem, almost any abortion restriction that strikes him as "undue"—subject, of course, to the possibility of being reversed by a court of appeals or Supreme Court that is as unconstrained in reviewing his decision as he was in making it.

To the extent I can discern *any* meaningful content in the "undue burden" standard as applied in the joint opinion, it appears to be that a State may not regulate abortion in such a way as to reduce significantly its incidence. The joint opinion repeatedly emphasizes that an important factor in the "undue burden" analysis is whether the regulation "prevent[s] a significant number of women from obtaining an abortion," whether a "significant number of women ... are likely to be deterred from procuring an abortion," and whether the regulation often "deters" women from seeking abortions. We are not told, however, what forms of "deterrence" are impermissible or what degree of success in deterrence is too much to be tolerated. ...

Thus, despite flowery rhetoric about the State's "substantial" and "profound" interest in "potential human life," and criticism of *Roe* for undervaluing that interest, the joint opinion permits the State to pursue that interest only so long as it is not too successful. As JUSTICE BLACKMUN recognizes (with evident hope), *ante*, at 926, the "undue burden" standard may ultimately require the invalidation of each provision upheld today if it can be shown, on a better record, that the State is too effectively "express[ing] a preference for childbirth over abortion," *ante*, at 883. Reason finds no refuge in this jurisprudence of confusion.

> "While we appreciate the weight of the arguments ... that *Roe* should be overruled, the reservations any of us may have in reaffirming the central holding of *Roe* are outweighed by the explication of individual liberty we have given combined with the force of *stare decisis*." *Ante*, at 853

The Court's reliance upon *stare decisis* can best be described as contrived. It insists upon the necessity of adhering not to all of *Roe*, but only to what it calls the "central holding." It seems to me that *stare decisis* ought to be applied even to the doctrine of *stare decisis*, and I confess never to have heard of this new, keep-what-you-want-and-throw-away-the-rest version. I wonder whether, as applied to *Marbury* v. *Madison*, 1 Cranch 137 (1803), for example, the new version of *stare decisis* would be satisfied if we allowed courts to review the constitutionality of only those statutes that (like the one in *Marbury*) pertain to the jurisdiction of the courts.

I am certainly not in a good position to dispute that the Court *has saved* the "central holding" of *Roe*, since to do that effectively I would have to know what the Court has saved, which in turn would require me to understand (as I do not) what the "undue burden" test means. I must confess, however, that I have always thought, and I think a lot of other people have always thought, that the arbitrary trimester framework, which the Court today discards, was quite as central to *Roe* as the arbitrary viability test, which the Court today retains. It seems particularly ungrateful to carve the trimester framework out of the core of *Roe*, since its very rigidity (in sharp contrast to the utter indeterminability of the "undue burden" test) is probably the only reason the Court is able to say, in urging *stare decisis*, that *Roe* "has in no sense proven 'unworkable,'" *ante*, at 855. I suppose the Court is entitled to call a "central holding" whatever it wants to call a "central holding"—which is, come to think of it, perhaps one of the difficulties with this modified version of *stare decisis*. I thought I might note, however, that the following portions of *Roe* have not been saved:

- Under *Roe*, requiring that a woman seeking an abortion be provided truthful information about abortion before giving informed written consent is unconstitutional, if the information is designed to influence her choice. *Thornburgh*, 476 U.S., at 759–765; *Akron I*, 462 U.S., at 442–445. Under the joint opinion's "undue burden" regime (as applied today, at least) such a requirement is constitutional. *Ante*, at 881–885.

- Under *Roe*, requiring that information be provided by a doctor, rather than by nonphysican counselors, is unconstitutional. *Akron I, supra*, at 446–449. Under the "undue burden" regime (as applied today, at least) it is not. *Ante*, at 884–885.

- Under *Roe*, requiring a 24-hour waiting period between the time the woman gives her informed consent and the time of the abortion is unconstitutional. *Akron I, supra*, at 449–451. Under the "undue burden" regime (as applied today, at least) it is not. *Ante*, at 885–887.

- Under *Roe*, requiring detailed reports that include demographic data about each woman who seeks an abortion and various information about each abortion is unconstitutional. *Thornburgh, supra*, at 765–768. Under the "undue burden" regime (as applied today, at least) it generally is not. *Ante*, at 900–901.

> "Where, in the performance of its judicial duties, the Court decides a case in such as way as to resolve the sort of intensely divisive controversy reflected in *Roe* . . . , its decision has a dimension that the resolution of the normal case does not carry. It is the dimension present whenever the Court's interpretation of the Constitution calls the contending sides of a national controversy to end their national division by accepting a common mandate rooted in the Constitution.

The Court's description of the place of *Roe* in the social history of the United States is unrecognizable. Not only did *Roe* not, as the Court suggests, *resolve* the deeply divisive issue of abortion; it did more than anything else to nourish it, by elevating it to the national level where it is infinitely more difficult to resolve. National politics were not plagued by abortion protests, national abortion lobbying, or abortion marches on Congress before *Roe* v. *Wade* was decided. Profound disagreement existed among our citizens over the issue—as it does over other issues, such as the death penalty—but that disagreement was being worked out at the state level. As with many other issues, the division of sentiment within each State was not as closely balanced as it was among the population of the Nation as a whole, meaning not only that more people would be satisfied with the results of state-by-state resolution, but also that those results would be more stable. Pre-*Roe*, moreover, political compromise was possible.

*Roe*'s mandate for abortion on demand destroyed the compromises of the past, rendered compromise impossible for the future, and required the entire issue to be resolved uniformly, at the national level. At the same time, *Roe* created a vast new class of abortion consumers and abortion proponents by eliminating the moral opprobrium that had attached to the act. ("If the constitution *guarantees* abortion, how can it be bad?"—not an accurate line of thought, but a natural one.) Many favor all of those developments, and it is not for me to say that they are wrong. But to portray *Roe* as the statesmanlike "settlement" of a divisive issue, a jurisprudential Peace of Westphalia that is worth preserving, is nothing less than Orwellian. *Roe* fanned into life an issue that has inflamed our national politics in general, and has obscured with its smoke the selection of Justices to this Court in particular, ever since. And by keeping us in the abortion-umpiring business, it is the perpetuation of that disruption, rather than of any *Pax Roeana*, that the Court's new majority decrees.

> "[T]o overrule under fire ... would subvert the Court's legitimacy. ...
>
> "... to all those who will be ... tested by following the Court implicitly undertakes to remain steadfast .... The promise of constancy, once given, binds its maker for as long as the power to stand by the decision survives and ... the commitment [is not] obsolete. ...
>
> "[The American people's] belief in themselves as ... a people [who aspire to live according to the rule of law] is not readily separable from their understanding of the Court invested with the authority to decide their constitutional cases and speak before all others for their constitutional ideals. If the Court's legitimacy should be undermined, then, so would the country be in its very ability to see itself through its constitutional ideals." *Ante*, at 867–868.

The Imperial Judiciary lives. It is instructive to compare this Nietzschean vision of us unelected, life-tenured judges—leading a Volk who will be "tested by following," and whose very "belief in themselves" is mystically bound up in their "understanding" of a Court that "speak[s] before all others for their constitutional ideals"—with the somewhat more modest role envisioned for these lawyers by the Founders.

> "The judiciary ... has ... no direction either of the strength or of the wealth of the society, and can take no active resolution whatever. It may truly be said to have neither Force nor Will, but merely judgment. ..." The Federalist No. 78, pp. 393–394 (G. Wills ed. 1982).

Or again, to compare this ecstasy of a Supreme Court in which there is, especially on controversial matters, no shadow of change or hint of alteration ("There is a limit to the amount of error that can plausibly be imputed to prior Courts," *ante*, at 866), with the more democratic views of a more humble man:

"[T]he candid citizen must confess that if the policy of the Government upon vital questions affecting the whole people is to be irrevocably fixed by decisions of the Supreme Court, . . . the people will have ceased to be their own rulers, having to that extent practically resigned their Government into the hands of that eminent tribunal." A. Lincoln, First Inaugural Address (Mar. 4, 1861). Reprinted in Inaugural Addresses of the Presidents of the United States, S. Doc. No. 101–10, p. 139 (1989).

It is particularly difficult, in the circumstances of the present decision, to sit still for the Court's lengthy lecture upon the virtues of "constancy," *ante,* at 868, of "remain[ing] steadfast," *ibid.*, and adhering to "principle," *ante, passim.* Among the five Justices who purportedly adhere to *Roe*, at most three agree upon the *principle* that constitutes adherence (the joint opinion's "undue burden" standard)—and that principle is inconsistent with *Roe*. See 410 U.S., at 154–156. To make matters worse, two of the three, in order thus to remain steadfast, had to abandon previously stated positions. See n. 4, *supra*; see *supra*, at 988–990. It is beyond me how the Court expects these accommodations to be accepted "as grounded truly in principle, not as compromises with social and political pressures having, as such, no bearing on the principled choices that the Court is obliged to make." *Ante,* at 865–866. The only principle the Court "adheres" to, it seems to me, is the principle that the Court must be seen as standing by *Roe*. That is not a principle of law (which is what I thought the Court was talking about), but a principle of *Realpolitik*—and a wrong one at that.

I cannot agree with, indeed I am appalled by, the Court's suggestion that the decision whether to stand by an erroneous constitutional decision must be strongly influenced—*against* overruling, no less—by the substantial and continuing public opposition the decision has generated. The Court's judgment that any other course would "subvert the Court's legitimacy" must be another consequence of reading the error-filled history book that described the deeply divided country brought together by *Roe*. In my history book, the Court was covered with dishonor and deprived of legitimacy by *Dred Scott* v. *Sandford*, 19 How. 393 (1857), an erroneous (and widely opposed) opinion that it did not abandon, rather than by *West Coast Hotel Co.* v. *Parrish*, 300 U.S. 379 (1937), which produced the famous "switch in time" from the Court's erroneous (and widely opposed) constitutional opposition to the social measures from the New Deal. (Both *Dred Scott* and one line of the cases resisting the New Deal rested upon the concept of "substantive due process" that the Court praises and employs today. Indeed, *Dred Scott* was "very possibly the first application of substantive due process in the Supreme Court, the original precedent for *Lochner* v. *New York* and *Roe* v. *Wade*." D. Currie, The Constitution in the Supreme Court 271 (1985) (footnotes omitted).

But whether it would "subvert the Court's legitimacy" or not, the notion that we would decide a case differently from the way we otherwise would have in order to show that we can stand firm against public disapproval is frightening. . . .

Of course, as THE CHIEF JUSTICE points out, we have been subjected to what the Court calls "'political pressure'" by *both* sides of this issue. *Ante,* at 963. Maybe today's decision *not* to overrule *Roe* will be seen as buckling to pressure from *that* direction. Instead of engaging in the hopeless task of predicting public perception—a job not for lawyers but for political campaign managers—the Justices should do what is *legally* right by asking two questions: (1) Was *Roe* correctly decided? (2) Has *Roe* succeeded in producing a settled body of law? If the answer to both questions is no, *Roe* should undoubtedly be overruled.

In truth, I am as distressed as the Court is—and expressed my distress several years ago, see *Webster,* 492 U.S., at 535—about the "political pressure" directed to the Court: the marches, the mail, the protests aimed at inducing us to change our opinions. How upsetting it is, that so many of our citizens (good people, not lawless ones, on both sides of this abortion issue, and on various sides of other issues as well) think that we Justices should properly take into account their views, as though we were engaged not in ascertaining an objective law but in determining some kind of social consensus. The Court would profit, I think, from giving less attention to the *fact* of this distressing phenomenon, and more attention to the *cause* of it. That cause permeates today's opinion: a new mode of constitutional adjudication that relies not upon text and traditional practice to determine the law, but upon what the Court calls "reasoned judgment," *ante,* at 849, which turns out to be nothing but philosophical predilection and moral intuition. . . .

What makes all this relevant to the bothersome application of "political pressure" against the Court are the twin facts that the American people love democracy and the American people are not fools. As long as this Court thought (and the people thought) that we Justices were doing essentially lawyers' work up here—reading text and discerning our society's traditional understanding of that text—the public pretty must left us alone. Texts and traditions are facts to study, not convictions to demonstrate about. But if in reality our process of constitutional adjudication consists primarily of making *value judgments*; . . . then a free and intelligent people's attitude towards us can be expected to be (*ought* to be) quite different. The people know that their value judgments are quite as good as those taught in any law school—maybe better. If, indeed, the "liberties" protected by the Constitution are, as the Court says, undefined and unbounded, then the people *should* demonstrate, to protest that we do not implement *their* values instead of *ours.* Not only that, but confirmation hearings for new Justices *should* deteriorate into question-and-answer sessions in which Senators go through a list of their constituents' most favored and most disfavored alleged constitutional rights, and seek the nominee's commitment to support or oppose them. Value judgments, after all, should be voted on, not dictated; and if our Constitution has somehow accidentally committed them to the Supreme Court, at least we can have a sort of plebiscite each time a new nominee to that body is put forward. JUSTICE BLACKMUN not only regards this prospect with equanimity, he solicits it. *Ante,* at 943.

There is a poignant aspect to today's opinion. Its length, and what might be called its epic tone, suggest that its authors believe they are bringing to an end a troublesome era in the history of our Nation and of our Court. "It is the dimension" of authority, they say, to "cal[l] the contending sides of national controversy to end their national division by accepting a common mandate rooted in the Constitution."

There comes vividly to mind a portrait by Emanuel Leutze that hangs in the Harvard Law School: Roger Brook Taney, painted in 1859, the 82d year of his life, the 24th of his Chief Justiceship, the second after his opinion in *Dred Scott*. He is all in black, sitting in a shadowed red armchair, left hand resting upon a pad of paper in his lap, right hand hanging limply, almost lifelessly, beside the inner arm of the chair. He sits facing the viewer and staring straight out. There seems to be on his face, and in his deep-set eyes, an expression of profound sadness and disillusionment. Perhaps he always looked that way, even when dwelling upon the happier of his thoughts. But those of us who know how the lustre of his great Chief Justiceship came to be eclipsed by *Dred Scott* cannot help believing that he had that case—its already apparent consequences for the Court and its soon-to-be-played-out consequences for the Nation—burning on his mind. I expect that two years earlier he, too, had thought himself "call[ing] the contending sides of national controversy to end their national division by accepting a common mandate rooted in the Constitution."

It is no more realistic for us in this litigation, than it was for him in that, to think that an issue of the sort they both involved—an issue involving life and death, freedom and subjugation—can be "speedily and finally settled by the Supreme Court, as President James Buchanan in his inaugural address said the issue of slavery in the territories would be. See Inaugural Addresses of the Presidents of the United States, S. Doc. No. 101–10, p. 126 (1989). Quite to the contrary, by foreclosing all democratic outlet for the deep passions this issue arouses, by banishing the issue from the political forum that gives all participants, even the losers, the satisfaction of a fair hearing and an honest fight, by continuing the imposition of a rigid national rule instead of allowing for regional differences, the Court merely prolongs and intensifies the anguish.

We should get out of this area, where we have no right to be, and where we do neither ourselves nor the country any good by remaining.

# *Notes*

\* Together with No. 91–902, *Casey, Governor of Pennsylvania, et al,* v. *Planned Parenthood of Southeastern Pennsylvania et al.*, also on certiorari to the same court.

† Briefs of *amici curiae* were filed for the State of New York et al. by *Robert Abrams*, Attorney General of New York, *Jerry Boone*, Solicitor General, *Mary Ellen Burns*, Chief Assistant Attorney General, and *Sanford M. Cohen, Donna I. Dennis, Marjorie Fujiki,* and *Shelley B. Mayer*, Assistant Attorneys General, and *John McKernan*, Governor of Maine, and *Michael E. Carpenter*, Attorney General, *Richard Blumenthal*, Attorney General of Connecticut, *Charles M. Oberly III*, Attorney General of Delaware, *Warren Price III*, Attorney General of Hawaii, *Roland W. Burris*, Attorney General of Illinois, *Bonnie J. Campbell*, Attorney General of Iowa, *J. Joseph Curran, Jr.*, Attorney General of Maryland, *Scott Harshbarger*, Attorney General of Massachusetts, *Frankie Sue Del Papa,*, Attorney General of Nevada, *Robert J. Del Tufo*, Attorney General of New Jersey, *Tom Udall*, Attorney General of New Mexico, *Lacy H. Thornburgh*, Attorney General of North Carolina, *James E. O'Neil*, Attorney General of Rhode Island, *Dan Morales*, Attorney General of Texas, *Jeffrey L. Amestoy*, Attorney General of Vermont, and *John Payton*, Corporation Counsel of District of Columbia; for the State of Utah by *R. Paul Van Dam*, Attorney General, and *Mary Anne Q. Wood*, Special Assistant Attorney General; for the City of New York et al. by *O. Peter Sherwood, Conrad Harper, Janice Goodman, Leonard J. Koerner, Lorna Bade Goodman, Gail Rubin,* and *Julie Mertus*; for 178 Organizations by *Pamela Kartan* and *Sarah Weddington*; for Agudath Israel of America by *David Zwiebel*; for the Alan Guttmacher Institute et al. by *Colleen K. Connell* and *Dorothy B. Zimbrakos*; for the American Academy of Medical Ethics by *Joseph W. Dellapenna*; for the American Association of Prolife Obstetricians and Gynecologists et al, by *William Bentley Ball, Philip J. Murren,* and *Maura K. Quinlan*; for the American College of Obstetricians and Gynecologists et al. by *Carter G. Phillips, Ann E. Allen, Laurie R. Rockett, Joel I. Klein, Nadine Taub,* and *Sarah C. Carey*; for the American Psychological Association by *David W. Ogden*; for Texas Black Americans for Life et al. by *Thomas Patrick Monaghan, Jay Alan Sekulow, Walter M. Weber, Thomas A. Glessner, Charles E. Rice,* and *Michael J. Laird*; for the Elliot Institute for Social Sciences Research by *Stephen R. Kaufmann*; for Feminists for Life of America et al. by *Keith A. Fournier, John G. Stepanovich, Christine Smith Torre, Theodore H. Amshoff, Jr.,* and *Mary Dice Grenen*; For Focus on the Family et al. by *Stephen H. Galebach, Gregory J. Granitto, Stephen W. Reed, David L. Llewelly, Jr., Benjamin W. Bull,* and *Leonard J. Pranschke*; for the Knights of Columbus by *Carl A. Anderson*; for the Life Issues Institute by *James Bopp, Jr.,* and *Richard E. Coleson*; for the NAACP Legal Defense and Educational Fund, Inc., et al. by *Julius L. Chambers, Ronald L. Ellis,* and *Alice L. Brown*; for the National Legal Foundation by *Robert K. Skolrood*; for National Right to Life, Inc., by Messrs,. Bopp and Coleson, *Robert A. Destro,* and *A. Eric Johnston*; for the Pennsylvania Coalition Against Domestic Violence et al. by *Phyllis Gelman*; for the Rutherford Institute et al. by *Thomas W. Strahan, John W. Whitehead, Mr. Johnston, Stephen E. Hurts, Joseph Secola, Thomas S. Neuberger, J. Brian Heller, Amy Dougherty, Stanley R. Jones, David Melton, Robert R. Melnick, William Bonner, W. Charles Bundren,* and *James Knicely*; for the Southern Center for Law & Ethics by *Tony G. Miller*; for the United States Catholic Conference et al. by *Mark E. Chopko, Phillip H. Harris, Michael K. Whitehead,* and *Forest D. Montgomery*; for University Faculty for Life by *Clarke D. Forsythe* and *Victor G. Rosenblum*; for Certain American State Legislators by *Paul Benjamin Linton*; for

19 Arizona Legislators by *Ronald D. Maines;* for Representative Henry J. Hyde et al. by *Albert P. Blaustein* and *Kevin J. Todd;* for Representative Don Edwards et al. by *Walter Dellinger* and *Lloyd N. Cutler;* and for 250 American Historians by *Sylvia A. Law.*

1. It is sometimes useful to view the issue of *stare decisis* from a historical perspective. In the last 19 years, 15 Justices have confronted the basic issue presented in *Roe* v. *Wade,* 410 U.S. 113 (1973). Of those, 11 have voted as the majority does today; Chief Justice Burger, Justices Douglas, Brennan, Stewart, Marshall, and Powell, and JUSTICES BLACKMUN, O'CONNOR, KENNEDY, SOUTER, and myself. Only four—all of whom happen to be on the Court today—have reached the opposite conclusion.

2. The state interest in protecting potential life may be compared to the state interest in protecting those who seek to immigrate to this country. A contemporary example is provided by the Haitians who have risked the perils of the sea in a desperate attempt to become "persons" protected by our laws. Humanitarian and practical concerns would support a state policy allowing those persons unrestricted entry; countervailing interests in population control support a policy of limiting the entry of these potential citizens. While the state interest in population control might be sufficient to justify strict enforcement of the immigration laws, that interest would not be sufficient to overcome a woman's liberty interest. Thus, a state interest in population control could not justify a state-imposed limit on family size or, for that matter, state-mandated abortions.

3. Although I agree that a parental-consent requirement (with the appropriate bypass) is constitutional, I do not join Part V–D of the joint opinion because its approval of Pennsylvania's informed parental-consent requirement is based on the reasons given in Part V–B, with which I disagree.

4. JUSTICE SCALIA urges the Court to "get out of this area," *post,* at 1002, and leave questions regarding abortion entirely to the States, *post,* at 999–1000. Putting aside the fact that what he advocates is nothing short of an abdication by the Court of its constitutional responsibilities, JUSTICE SCALIA is uncharacteristically naive if he thinks that overruling *Roe* and holding that restrictions on a woman's right to an abortion are subject only to rational-basis review will enable the Court henceforth to avoid reviewing abortion-related issues. State efforts to regulate and prohibit abortion in a post-Roe world undoubtedly would raise a host of distinct and important constitutional questions meriting review by this Court. For example, does the Eighth Amendment impose any limits on the degree or kind of punishment a State can inflict upon physicians who perform, or women who undergo, abortions? What effect would differences among States in their approaches to abortion have on a woman's right to engage in interstate travel? Does the First Amendment permit States that choose not to criminalize abortion to ban all advertising providing information about where and how to obtain abortions?

5. The Court's suggestion, *ante,* at 847–848, that adherence to tradition would require us to uphold laws against interracial marriage is entirely wrong. Any tradition in that case was contradicted *by a text*—an Equal Protection Clause that explicitly establishes racial equality as a constitutional value. See *Loving* v. *Virginia,* 388 U.S. 1, 9 (1967) ("In the case at bar. . . . we deal with statutes containing racial classifications, and the fact of equal application does not immunize the statute from the very heavy burden of justification which the Fourteenth

Amendment has traditionally required of state statutes drawn according to race"); see also *id.*, at 13 (Stewart, J., concurring in judgment). The enterprise launched in *Roe* v. *Wade*, 410 U.S. 113 (1973), by contrast, sought to *establish*—in the teeth of a clear, contrary tradition—a value found nowhere in the constitutional text.

There is, of course, no comparable tradition barring recognition of a "liberty interest" in carrying one's child to term free from state efforts to kill it. For that reason, it does not follow that the Constitution does not protect childbirth simply because it does not protect abortion. The Court's contention, *ante*, at 859, that the only way to protect childbirth is to protect abortion shows the utter bankruptcy of constitutional analysis deprived of tradition as a validating factor. It drives one to say that the only way to protect the right to eat is to acknowledge the constitutional right to starve oneself to death.

---

**Planned Parenthood v. Casey**, 505 U.S. 833 (1973) 5–4
*editor's note:*
*Opinion authors are in bold: () indicates the party of appointing president. If the party of the justice differs from that of appointing president, then the party of the justice is listed second after the slash.*

| MAJORITY | CONCURRING | DISSENTING |
|---|---|---|
| **O'Connor** (r) | (in part and dissenting in part) | **Rehnquist** (r) |
| **Kennedy** (r) | | White (d) |
| **Souter** (r) | **Stevens** (r) | **Scalia** (r) |
| | **Blackmun** (r) | Thomas (r) |

# Washington, et al., Petitioners v. Harold Glucksberg et al.

## 521 U.S. 702 (1997)

## On Writ of Certiorari to the United States Court of Appeals for the Ninth Circuit

CHIEF JUSTICE REHNQUIST delivered the opinion of the Court.

The question presented in this case is whether Washington's prohibition against "caus[ing]" or "aid[ing]" a suicide offends the Fourteenth Amendment to the United States Constitution. We hold that it does not.

It has always been a crime to assist a suicide in the State of Washington. In 1854, Washington's first Territorial Legislature outlawed "assisting another in the commission of self murder."[1] Today, Washington law provides: "A person is guilty of promoting a suicide attempt when he knowingly causes or aids another person to attempt suicide." Wash. Rev. Code 9A.36.060(l) (1994). "Promoting a suicide attempt" is a felony, punishable by up to five years' imprisonment and up to a $10,000 fine. §§ 9A.36.060(2) and 9A.20.021(l)(c). At the same time, Washington's Natural Death Act, enacted in 1979, states that the "withholding or withdrawal of life sustaining treatment" at a patient's direction "shall not, for any purpose, constitute a suicide." Wash. Rev. Code §70.122.070(l).

Petitioners in this case are the State of Washington and its Attorney General. Respondents Harold Glucksberg, M.D., Abigail Halperin, M.D., Thomas A. Preston, M.D., and Peter Shalit, M.D., are physicians who practice in Washington. These doctors occasionally treat terminally ill, suffering patients, and declare that they would assist these patients in ending their lives if not for Washington's assisted suicide ban. In January 1994, respondents, along with three gravely ill, pseudonymous plaintiffs who have since died and Compassion in Dying, a nonprofit organization that counsels people considering physician assisted suicide, sued in the United States District Court, seeking a declaration that Wash Rev. Code 9A.36.060(l) (1994) is, on its face, unconstitutional. *Compassion in Dying* v. *Washington*, 850 F. Supp. 1454, 1459 (WD Wash. 1994).

The plaintiffs asserted "the existence of a liberty interest protected by the Fourteenth Amendment which extends to a personal choice by a mentally competent, terminally ill adult to commit physician assisted suicide." *Id.*, at 1459. Relying primarily on *Planned Parenthood* v. *Casey*, 505 U.S. 833 (1992), and *Cruzan* v. *Director, Missouri Dept. of Health*, 497 U.S. 261 (1990), the District Court agreed, 8 50 F. Supp., at 1459–1462, and concluded that Washington's assisted suicide ban is unconstitutional because it "places an undue burden on the exercise of [that] constitutionally protected liberty interest." *Id.*, at 1465. The District Court also decided that the Washington statute violated the Equal Protection Clause's requirement that "'all persons similarly situated . . . be treated alike.'" *Id.*, at 1466 (quoting *Cleburne* v. *Cleburne Living Center, Inc.*, 473 U.S. 432, 439 (1985)).

A panel of the Court of Appeals for the Ninth Circuit reversed. . . . *Compassion in Dying* v. *Washington*, 49 F. 3d 586, 591 (1995). The Ninth Circuit reheard the case en banc, reversed the panel's decision, and affirmed the District Court. *Compassion in Dying* v. *Washington*, 79 F 3d 790, 798 (1996).

We begin, as we do in all due process cases, by examining our Nation's history, legal traditions, and practices. See, *e.g.*, *Casey*, 505 U.S., at 849–850. In almost every State—indeed, in almost every western democracy—it is a crime to assist a suicide. The States' assisted suicide bans are not innovations. Rather, they are longstanding expressions of the States' commitment to the protection and preservation of all human life. *Cruzan*, 497 U.S., at 280 ("[T]he States indeed, all civilized nations demonstrate their commitment to life by treating homicide as a serious crime. Moreover, the majority of States in this country have laws imposing criminal penalties on one who assists another to commit suicide").

More specifically, for over 700 years, the Anglo American common law tradition has punished or otherwise disapproved of both suicide and assisting suicide. *Cruzan*, 497 U.S., at 294–295 (SCALIA, J., concurring). . . . For the most part, the early American colonies adopted the common law approach. . . . That suicide remained a grievous, though nonfelonious, wrong is confirmed by the fact that colonial and early state legislatures and courts did not retreat from prohibiting assisting suicide. . . .

And the prohibitions against assisting suicide never contained exceptions for those who were near death. Rather, "[t]he life of those to whom life ha[d] become a burden—of those who [were] hopelessly diseased or fatally wounded—nay, even the lives of criminals condemned to death, [were] under the protection of law, equally as the lives of those who [were] in the full tide of life's enjoyment, and anxious to continue to live." *Blackburn* v. *State*, 23 Ohio St. 146, 163 (1872); see *Bowen, supra*, at 360 (prisoner who persuaded another to commit suicide could be tried for murder, even though victim was scheduled shortly to be executed).

The earliest American statute explicitly to outlaw assisting suicide was enacted in New York in 1828, Act of Dec. 10, 1828, ch. 20, §4, 1828 N.Y. Laws 19 (codified at 2 N. Y. Rev.

Stat. pt. 4, ch. 1, tit. 2, art. 1, §7, p. 661 (1829)), and many of the new States and Territories followed New York's example. . . .

By the time the Fourteenth Amendment was ratified, it was a crime in most States to assist a suicide. In this century, the Model Penal Code also prohibited "aiding" suicide, prompting many States to enact or revise their assisted suicide bans. The Code's drafters observed that "the interests in the sanctity of life that are represented by the criminal homicide laws are threatened by one who express a willingness to participate in taking the life of another even though the act may be accomplished with the consent, or at the request, of the suicide victim." American Law Institute, Model Penal Code §210.5, Comment 5, p. 100 (Official Draft and Revised Comments 1980).

Though deeply rooted, the States' assisted suicide bans have in recent years been reexamined and, generally, reaffirmed. Because of advances in medicine and technology, Americans today are increasingly likely to die in institutions, from chronic illnesses. President's Comm'n for the Study of Ethical Problems in Medicine and Biomedical and Behavioral Research, Deciding to Forego Life Sustaining Treatment 16–18 (1983). Public concern and democratic action are therefore sharply focused on how best to protect dignity and independence at the end of life, with the result that there have been many significant changes in state laws and in the attitudes these laws reflect. Many States, for example, now permit "living wills," surrogate health care decisionmaking, and the withdrawal or refusal of life sustaining medical treatment. See *Vacco* v. *Quill, post,* at 911; 79 F. 3d, at 818–820; *People* v. *Kevorkian,* 447 Mich. 436, 478–480, and nn. 53–56, 527 N. W. 2d 714 731–732 and nn 53–56 (1994). At the same time, however, voters and legislators continue for the most part to reaffirm their States' prohibitions on assisting suicide.

The Washington statute at issue in this case., Wash. Rev. Code §9A.36.060 (1994), was enacted in 1975 as part of a revision of that State's criminal code. Four years later, Washington passed its Natural Death Act, which specifically stated that the "withholding or withdrawal of life sustaining treatment . . . shall not, for any purpose, constitute a suicide" and that "[n]othing in this chapter shall be construed to condone, authorize, or approve mercy killing. . . . " Natural Death Act, 1979 Wash. Laws, ch. 112, §§8(l), p. 11 (codified at Wash. Rev. Code §§70.122.070(l), 70.122.100 (1994)). In 1991, Washington voters rejected a ballot initiative which, had it passed, would have permitted a form of physician assisted suicide. Washington then added a provision to the Natural Death Act expressly excluding physician assisted suicide. 1992 Wash. Laws, ch. 98, §10; Wash. Rev. Code §70.122.100 (1994).

California voters rejected an assisted suicide initiative similar to Washington's in 1993. On the other hand, in 1994, voters in Oregon enacted, also through ballot initiative, that State's "Death With Dignity Act," which legalized physician assisted suicide for competent, terminally ill adults. Since the Oregon vote, many proposals to legalize assisted suicide have been and continue to be introduced in the States' legislatures, but none has been enacted. And just last year, Iowa and Rhode Island joined the overwhelming majority of States explicitly prohibiting assisted suicide. See Iowa Code Ann. §§707A.2, 707A.3 (Supp. 1997); R.I., Gen. Laws §§ 11–60–1, 11–60–3 (Supp. 1996). Also, on April 30, 1997, President Clinton signed the Federal Assisted Suicide Funding Restriction Act of 1997, which prohibits the use of federal funds in support of physician assisted suicide. Pub. L. 105–12, 111 Stat. 23 (codified at 42 U.S.C. § 14401 *el seq*).

Thus, the States are currently engaged in serious, thoughtful examinations of physician assisted suicide and other similar issues. . . .

Attitudes toward suicide itself have changed since Bracton, but our laws have consistently condemned, and continue to prohibit, assisting suicide. Despite changes in medical technology and notwithstanding an increased emphasis on the importance of end of life decisionmaking, we have not retreated from this prohibition. Against this backdrop of history, tradition, and practice, we now turn to respondents' constitutional claim.

## — II —

The Due Process Clause guarantees more than fair process, and the "liberty" it protects includes more than the absence of physical restraint. *Collins* v. *Harker Heights,* 503 U.S. 115, 125 (1992) (Due Process Clause "protects individual liberty against 'certain government actions regardless of the fairness of the procedures used to implement them'") (quoting *Daniels* v. *Williams,* 474 U.S. 327, 331 (1986)). The Clause also provides heightened protection against government interference with certain fundamental rights and liberty interests. *Reno* v. *Flores,* 507 U.S. 292, 301–30–2 (1993); *Casey,* 505 U.S., at 851. In a long line of cases, we have held that, in addition to the specific freedoms protected by the Bill of Rights, the "liberty" specially protected by the Due Process Clause includes the rights to marry, *Loving* v. *Virginia,* 388 U.S. 1 (1967); to have children, *Skinner* v. *Oklahoma ex rel. Williamson,* 316 U.S. 535 (1942); to direct the education and upbringing of one's children, *Meyer* v. *Nebraska,* 262 U.S. 390 (1923); *Pierce* v. *Society of Sisters,* 268 U.S. 510 (1925); to marital privacy, *Griswold* v. *Connecticut,* 381 U.S. 479 (1965); to use contraception, *ibid; Eisenstadt* v. *Baird,* 405 U.S. 438 (1972); to bodily integrity, *Rochin* v. *California,* 342 U.S. 165 (1952), and to abortion, *Casey, supra.* We have also assumed, and strongly suggested, that the Due Process Clause protects the traditional right to refuse unwanted lifesaving medical treatment *Cruzan,* 497 U.S. at 278–279

But we "ha[ve] always been reluctant to expand the concept of substantive due process because guideposts for responsible decisionmaking in this unchartered area are scarce and open ended." *Collins*, 503 U.S., at 125. By extending constitutional protection to an asserted right or liberty interest, we, to a great extent, place the matter outside the arena of public debate and legislative action. We must therefore "exercise the utmost care whenever we are asked to break new ground in this field," *ibid,* lest the liberty protected by the Due Process Clause be subtly transformed into the policy preferences of the members of this Court, *Moore,* 431 U.S., at 502 (plurality opinion).

Our established method of substantive due process analysis has two primary features: First, we have regularly observed that the Due Process Clause specially protects those fundamental rights and liberties which are, objectively, "deeply rooted in this Nation's history and tradition," *id.,* at 503 (plurality opinion); *Snyder* v. *Massachusetts,* 291 U.S. 97, 105 (1934) ("so rooted in the traditions and conscience of our people as to be ranked as fundamental"), and "implicit in the concept of ordered liberty," such that "neither liberty nor justice would exist if they were sacrificed," *Palko* v. *Connecticut,* 302 U.S. 319, 325, 326 (1937). Second, we have required in substantive due process cases a "careful description" of the asserted fundamental liberty interest. *Flores, supra,* at 302; *Collins, supra,* at 125; *Cruzan, supra,* at 277–278. Our Nation's history, legal traditions, and practices thus provide the crucial "guideposts for responsible decisionmaking," *Collins, supra,* at 125, that direct and restrain our exposition of the Due Process Clause. As we stated recently in *Flores,* the Fourteenth Amendment "forbids the government to infringe . . . 'fundamental' liberty interests *at all,* no matter what process is provided, unless the infringement is narrowly tailored to serve a compelling state interest." 507 U.S., at 302. . . .

Turning to the claim at issue here, the Court of Appeals stated that "[p]roperly analyzed, the first issue to be resolved is whether there is a liberty interest in determining the time and manner of one's death," 79 F. 3d, at 801, or, in other words, "[i]s there a right to die?," *id.,* at 799. Similarly, respondents assert a "liberty to choose how to die" and a right to "control of one's final days," Brief for Respondents 7, and describe the asserted liberty as "the right to choose a humane, dignified death," *id.,* at 15, and "the liberty to shape death," *id.,* at 18. As noted above, we have a tradition of carefully formulating the interest at stake in substantive due process cases. For example, although *Cruzan is* often described as a "right to die" case, see 79 F. 3d, at 799; *post,* at 9 (STEVENS, J., concurring in judgment) (*Cruzan* recognized "the more specific interest in making decisions about how to confront an imminent death"), we were, in fact, more precise: we assumed that the Constitution granted competent persons a "constitutionally protected right to refuse lifesaving hydration and nutrition." *Cruzan,* 497 U.S., at 279; *id.,* at 287 (O'CONNOR, J., concurring) ("[A] liberty interest in refusing unwanted medical treatment may be inferred from our prior decisions"). The Washington statute at issue in this case prohibits "aid[ing] another person to attempt suicide," Wash. Rev. Code §9A.36.060(l) (1994), and, thus, the question before us is whether the "liberty" specially protected by the Due Process Clause includes a right to commit suicide which itself includes a right to assistance in doing so.

We now inquire whether this asserted right has any place in our Nation's traditions. Here, as discussed above, supra, at 4–15, we are confronted with a consistent and almost universal tradition that has long rejected the asserted right, and continues explicitly to reject it today, even for terminally ill, mentally competent adults. To hold for respondents, we would have to reverse centuries of legal doctrine and practice, and strike down the considered policy choice of almost every State.

Respondents contend, however, that the liberty interest they assert is consistent with this Court's substantive due process line of cases, if not with this Nation's history and practice. Pointing to *Casey* and *Cruzan,* respondents read our jurisprudence in this area as reflecting a general tradition of "self sovereignty," Brief of Respondents 12, and as teaching that the "liberty" protected by the Due Process Clause includes "basic and intimate exercises of personal autonomy," *id.,* at 10; see *Casey,* 505 U.S., at 847 ("It is a promise of the Constitution that there is a realm of personal liberty which the government may not enter"). According to respondents, our liberty jurisprudence and the broad, individualistic principles it reflects, protects the "liberty of competent, terminally ill adults to make end of life decisions free of undue government interference." Brief for Respondents 10. The question presented in this case, however, is whether the protections of the Due Process Clause include a right to commit suicide with another's assistance. With this "careful description" of respondents' claim in mind, we turn to *Casey* and *Cruzan.*

In *Cruzan* we considered whether Nancy Beth Cruzan, who had been severely injured in an automobile accident and was in a persistive vegetative state, "ha[d] a right under the United States Constitution which would require the hospital to withdraw life sustaining treatment" at her parents' request. *Cruzan,* 497 U.S., at 269. We began with the observation that "[a]t common law, even the touching of one person by another without consent and without legal justification was a battery." *Ibid.* We then discussed the related rule that "Informed consent is generally required for medical treatment." *Ibid.* After reviewing a long line of relevant state cases, we concluded that "the common law doctrine of informed consent is viewed as generally encompassing the right of a competent individual to refuse medical treatment." *Id.,* at 277. Next, we reviewed our own cases on the subject, and stated that "[t]he principle that a competent person has a constitutionally protected liberty interest in refusing unwanted medical treatment may be inferred from our prior decisions." *Id.,* at 278. Therefore, "for purposes of [that] case, we assume[d] that the United States Constitution would grant a competent person a constitutionally protected right to refuse lifesaving hydration and nutrition." *Id.,* at 279; see *id.,* at 287 (O'CONNOR, J., concurring). We concluded that, notwithstanding this right, the Constitution permitted Missouri to require clear and convincing evidence of an incompetent patient's wishes concerning the withdrawal of life sustaining treatment. *Id.*, at 280–281.

Respondents contend that in *Cruzan* we "acknowledged that competent, dying persons have the right to direct the removal of life sustaining medical treatment and thus hasten death," Brief for Respondents 23, and that "the constitutional principle behind recognizing the patient's liberty to direct the withdrawal of artificial life support applies at least as strongly to the choice to hasten impending death by consuming lethal medication," *id.*, at 26. Similarly, the Court of Appeals concluded that "*Cruzan*, by recognizing a liberty interest that includes the refusal of artificial provision of life sustaining food and water, necessarily recognize[d] a liberty interest in hastening one's own death." 79 F. 3d, at 816.

The right assumed in *Cruzan*, however, was not simply deduced from abstract concepts of personal autonomy. Given the common law rule that forced medication was a battery, and the long legal tradition protecting the decision to refuse unwanted medical treatment, our assumption was entirely consistent with this Nation's history and constitutional traditions. The decision to commit suicide with the assistance of another may be just as personal and profound as the decision to refuse unwanted medical treatment, but it has never enjoyed similar legal protection. Indeed, the two acts are widely and reasonably regarded as quite distinct. See *Quill* v. *Vacco, post*, at 513. In *Cruzan* itself, we recognized that most States outlawed assisted suicide—and even more do today—and we certainly gave no intimation that the right to refuse unwanted medical treatment could be somehow transmuted into a right to assistance in committing suicide. 497 U.S., at 280.

Respondents also rely on *Casey*. There, the Court's opinion concluded that "the essential holding of *Roe* v. *Wade* should be retained and once again reaffirmed." *Casey*, 505 U.S., at 846 . . . the opinion discussed in some detail this Court's substantive due process tradition of interpreting the Due Process Clause to protect certain fundamental rights and "personal decisions relating to marriage, procreation, contraception, family relationships, child rearing, and education," and noted that many of those rights and liberties "involv[e] the most intimate and personal choices a person may make in a lifetime." *Id.*, at 851.

The Court's opinion in *Casey* described, in a general way and in light of our prior cases., those personal activities and decisions that this Court has identified as so deeply rooted in our history and traditions, or so fundamental to our concept of constitutionally ordered liberty, that they are protected by the Fourteenth Amendment. The opinion moved from the recognition that liberty necessarily includes freedom of conscience and belief about ultimate considerations to the observation that "though the abortion decision may originate within the zone of conscience and belief, it is more than a philosophic exercise." *Casey,* 505 U.S., at 852 (emphasis added). That many of the rights and liberties protected by the Due Process Clause sound in personal autonomy does not warrant the sweeping conclusion that any and all important, intimate, and personal decisions are so protected, *San Antonio Independent School Dist.* v. *Rodriguez,* 411 U.S. 1, 33–35 (1973), and *Casey* did not suggest otherwise.

The history of the law's treatment of assisted suicide in this country has been and continues to be one of the rejection of nearly all efforts to permit it. That being the case, our decisions lead us to conclude that the asserted "right" to assistance in committing suicide is not a fundamental liberty interest protected by the Due Process Clause. The Constitution also requires, however, that Washington's assisted suicide ban be rationally related to legitimate government interests. See *Heller* v. *Doe,* 509 U.S. 312 , 319–320 (1993); *Flores,* 507 U.S., at 305. This requirement is unquestionably met here.

First, Washington has an "unqualified interest in the preservation of human life." *Cruzan,* 497 U.S., at 282. The State's prohibition on assisted suicide, like all homicide laws, both reflects and advances its commitment to this interest. See *id.,* at 280; Model Penal Code §210.5, Comment 5, at 100. [T]he interests in the sanctity of life that are represented by the criminal homicide laws are threatened by one who expresses a willingness to participate in taking the life of another"). This interest is symbolic and aspirational as well as practical:

> "While suicide is no longer prohibited or penalized, the ban against assisted suicide and euthanasia shores up the notion of limits in human relationships. It reflects the gravity with which we view the decision to take one's own life or the life of another, and our reluctance to encourage or promote these decisions." New York Task Force 131–132.

Respondents admit that "[t]he State has a real interest in preserving the lives of those who can still contribute to society and enjoy life." Brief for Respondents 35, n. 23. The Court of Appeals also recognized Washington's interest in protecting life, but held that the "weight" of this interest depends on the "medical condition and the wishes of the person whose life is at stake." 79 F. 3d, at 817. Washington, however, has rejected this sliding scale approach and, through its assisted suicide ban, insists that all persons' lives, from beginning to end, regardless of physical or mental condition, are under the full protection of the law. See *United States* v. *Rutherford,* 442 U.S. 544, 558 (1979). Congress could reasonably have determined to protect the terminally ill, no less than other patients, from the vast range of selfstyled panaceas that inventive minds can devise"). As we have previously affirmed, the States "may properly decline to make judgments about the 'quality' of life that a particular individual may enjoy," *Cruzan,* 497 U.S., at 282. This remains true, as Cruzan makes clear, even for those who are near death.

Relatedly, all admit that suicide is a serious public health problem, especially among persons in otherwise  vulnerable groups. See Washington State Dept. of Health, Annual Summary of Vital Statistics 1991, pp. 29–30 (Oct. 1992) (suicide is a leading cause of death in Washington of those between the ages of 14 and 54); New York Task Force 10, 23–33 (suicide rate in the general population is about one percent, and suicide is especially prevalent among the young and the elderly). The State has an interest in preventing suicide, and in studying, identifying, and treating its causes. See 79 F. 3d, at 820; *id.*, at 854 (Beezer, J., dissenting) ("The state recognizes suicide as a manifestation of medical and psychological anguish"); Marzen 107–146.

Those who attempt suicide—terminally ill or not—often suffer from depression or other mental disorders. See New York Task Force 13–22, 126–128 (more than 95% of those who commit suicide had a major psychiatric illness at the time of death; among the terminally ill, uncontrolled pain is a "risk factor" because it contributes to depression), Physician Assisted Suicide and Euthanasia in the Netherlands: A Report of Chairman Charles T. Canady to the Subcommittee on the Constitution of the House Committee on the Judiciary, 104th Cong., 2d Sess., 10–11 (Comm. Print 1996), cf. Back, Wallace, Starks, & Pearlman, Physician Assisted Suicide and Euthanasia in Washington State, 275 JAMA 919, 924 (1996) ("[I]ntolerable physical symptoms are not the reason most patients request physician assisted suicide or euthanasia"). Research indicates, however, that many people who request physician assisted suicide withdraw that request if their depression and pain are treated. H. Hendin, Seduced by Death: Doctors, Patients and the Dutch Cure 24–25 (1997) (suicidal, terminally ill patients "usually respond well to treatment for depressive illness and pain medication and are then grateful to be alive"); New York Task Force 177–178. The New York Task Force, however, expressed its concern that, because depression is difficult to diagnose, physicians and medical professionals often fail to respond adequately to seriously ill patients' needs. *Id.*, at 175. Thus, legal physician assisted suicide could make it more difficult for the State to protect depressed or mentally ill persons, or those who are suffering from untreated pain, from suicidal impulses.

The State also has an interest in protecting the integrity and ethics of the medical profession. In contrast to the Court of Appeals' conclusion that "the integrity of the medical profession would [not] be threatened in any way by [physician assisted suicide]," 79 F. 3d, at 827, the American Medical Association, like many other medical and physicians' groups, has concluded that "[p]hysician assisted suicide is fundamentally incompatible with the physician's role as healer." American Medical Association, Code of Ethics §2.211 (1994). . . . And physician assisted suicide could, it is argued, undermine the trust that is essential to the doctor patient relationship by blurring the time honored line between healing and harming. . . . Next, the State has an interest in protecting vulnerable groups including the poor, the elderly, and disabled persons— from abuse, neglect, and mistakes. The Court of Appeals dismissed the State's concern that disadvantaged persons might be pressured into physician assisted suicide as "ludicrous on its face." 79 F. 3d, at 825. We have recognized, however, the real risk of subtle coercion and undue influence in end of life situations. *Cruzan,* 497 U.S., at 281. . . . If physician assisted suicide were permitted, many might resort to it to spare their families the substantial financial burden of end of life health care costs.

The State's interest here goes beyond protecting the vulnerable from coercion; it extends to protecting disabled and terminally ill people from prejudice, negative and inaccurate stereotypes, and "societal indifference." 49 F. 3 d, at 592. The State's assisted suicide ban reflects and reinforces its policy that the lives of terminally ill, disabled, and elderly people must be no less valued than the lives of the young and healthy, and that a seriously disabled person's suicidal impulses should be interpreted and treated the same way as anyone else's. See New York Task Force 101–102; Physician Assisted Suicide and Euthanasia in the Netherlands: A Report of Chairman Charles T. Canady, at 9, 20 (discussing prejudice toward the disabled and the negative messages euthanasia and assisted suicide send to handicapped patients).

Finally, the State may fear that permitting assisted suicide will start it down the path to voluntary and perhaps even involuntary euthanasia. The Court of Appeals struck down Washington's assisted suicide ban only "as applied to competent, terminally ill adults who wish to hasten their deaths by obtaining medication prescribed by their doctors." 79 F. 3d, at 838. Washington insists, however, that the impact of the court's decision will not and cannot be so limited. Brief for Petitioners 44–47. If suicide is protected as a matter of constitutional right, it is argued, "every man and woman in the United States must enjoy it." *Compassion in Dying,* 49 F. 3d, at 591; see *Kevorkian,* 447 Mich., at 470, n. 41, 527 N. W. 2d, at 727–728, n. 41. The Court of Appeals' decision, and its expansive reasoning, provide ample support for the State's concerns. The court noted, for example, that the "decision of a duly appointed surrogate decision maker is for all legal purposes the decision of the patient himself," 79 F. 3d, at 832, n. 120, that "in some instances, the patient may be unable to self administer the drugs and . . . administration by the physician . . . may be the only way the patient may be able to receive them," id, at 831 , and that not only physicians, but also family members and loved ones, will inevitably participate in assisting suicide. *Id.,* at 838, n. 140. Thus, it turns out that what is couched as a limited right to "physician assisted suicide" is likely, in effect, a much broader license, which could prove extremely difficult to police and contain. Washington's ban on assisting suicide prevents such erosion.

This concern is further supported by evidence about the practice of euthanasia in the Netherlands. The Dutch government's own study revealed that in 1990, there were 2,300 cases of voluntary euthanasia (defined as "the deliberate termination of another's life at his request"), 400 cases of assisted suicide, and more than 1,000 cases of euthanasia without an explicit request. In addition to these latter 1,000 cases, the study found an additional 4,941 cases where physicians administered lethal morphine overdoses without the patients' explicit consent. Physician Assisted Suicide and Euthanasia in the Netherlands: A Report of Chairman Charles T. Canady, at 12–13 (citing Dutch study). This study suggests that, despite the existence of various reporting procedures, euthanasia in the Netherlands has not been limited to competent, terminally ill adults who are enduring physical suffering, and that regulation of the practice may not have prevented abuses in cases involving vulnerable persons, including severely disabled neonates and elderly persons suffering from dementia. *Id.*, at 16–21: . . .

We need not weigh exactly the relative strengths of these various interests. They are unquestionably important and legitimate, and Washington's ban on assisted suicide is at least reasonably related to their promotion and protection. We therefore hold that Wash. Rev. Code §9A.36.060(l) (1994) does not violate the Fourteenth Amendment, either on its face or "as applied to competent, terminally ill adults who wish to hasten their deaths by obtaining medication prescribed by their doctors." 79 F. 3d, at 838.

Throughout the Nation, Americans are engaged in an earnest and profound debate about the morality, legality, and practicality of physician assisted suicide. Our holding permits this debate to continue, as it should in a democratic society. The decision of the en banc Court of Appeals is reversed, and the case is remanded for further proceedings consistent with this opinion.

*It is so ordered*

JUSTICE O'CONNOR, concurring.*

. . . I join the Court's opinions because I agree that there is no generalized right to "commit suicide." But respondents urge us to address the narrower question whether a mentally competent person who is experiencing great suffering has a constitutionally cognizable interest in controlling the circumstances of his or her imminent death. I see no need to reach that question in the context of the facial challenges to the New York and Washington laws at issue here. See *ante,* at 18 ("The Washington statute at issue in this case prohibits 'aid[ing] another person to attempt suicide,' . . . and, thus, the question before us is whether the 'liberty' specially protected by the Due Process Clause includes a right to commit suicide which itself includes a right to assistance in doing so"). The parties and *amici* agree that in these States a patient who is suffering from a terminal illness and who is experiencing great pain has no legal barriers to obtaining medication, from qualified physicians, to alleviate that suffering, even to the point of causing unconsciousness and hastening death. See Wash. Rev. Code §70.122.010 (1994); Brief for Petitioners in No. 95–1858, p. 15, n. 9; Brief for Respondents in No. 95–1858, p. 15. In this light, even assuming that we would recognize such an interest, I agree that the State's interests in protecting those who are not truly competent or facing imminent death, or those whose decisions to hasten death would not truly be voluntary, are sufficiently weighty to justify a prohibition against physician assisted suicide. *Ante*, at 27–30; *post*, at 11 (STEVENS, J., concurring in judgments); *post*, at 33–39 (SOUTER, J., concurring in judgment).

Every one of us at some point may be affected by our own or a family member's terminal illness. There is no reason to think the democratic process will not strike the proper balance between the interests of terminally ill, mentally competent individuals who would seek to end their suffering and the State's interests in protecting those who might seek to end life mistakenly or under pressure. As the Court recognizes, States are presently undertaking extensive and serious evaluation of physician assisted suicide and other related issues. *Ante*, at 11, 12–13; see *post*, at 36–39 (SOUTER, J., concurring in judgment). In such circumstances, "the . . . challenging task of crafting appropriate procedures for safeguarding . . . liberty interests is entrusted to the 'laboratory' of the States . . . in the first instance." *Cruzan* v. *Director, Mo. Dept. of Health*, 497 U.S. 261, 292 (1990) (O'CONNOR, J., concurring) (citing *New State Ice Co.* v. *Liebmann*, 285 U.S. 262) 311 (1932)).

JUSTICE STEVENS, concurring in the judgments.

The Court ends its opinion with the important observation that our holding today is fully consistent with a continuation of the vigorous debate about the "morality, legality, and practicality of physician assisted suicide" in a democratic society. *Ante*, at 32. I write separately to make it clear that there is also room for further debate about the limits that the Constitution places on the power of the States to punish the practice.

The morality, legality, and practicality of capital punishment have been the subject of debate for many years. In 1976, this Court upheld the constitutionality of the practice in cases coming to us from Georgia, Florida and Texas. In those cases we concluded that a State does have the power to place a lesser value on some lives than on others; there is no absolute requirement that a State treat all human life as having an equal right to preservation. . . .

Today, the Court decides that Washington's statute prohibiting assisted suicide is not invalid "on its face," that is to say, in all or most cases in which it might be applied. That holding, however, does not foreclose the possibility that some applications of the statute might well be invalid.

History and tradition provide ample support for refusing to recognize an open ended constitutional right to commit suicide. Much more than the State's paternalistic interest in protecting the individual from the irrevocable consequences of an ill advised decision motivated by temporary concerns is at stake. There is truth in John Donne's observation that "No man is an island." The State has an interest in preserving and fostering the benefits that every human being may provide to the community—a community that thrives on the exchange of ideas, expressions of affection, shared memories and humorous incidents as well as on the material contributions that its members create and support. The value to others of a person's life is far too precious to allow the individual to claim a constitutional entitlement to complete autonomy in making a decision to end that life. Thus, I fully agree with the Court that the "liberty" protected by the Due Process Clause does not include a categorical "right to commit suicide which itself includes a right to assistance in doing so." *Ante,* at 18.

But just as our conclusion that capital punishment is not always unconstitutional did not preclude later decisions holding that it is sometimes impermissibly cruel, so is it equally clear that a decision upholding a general statutory prohibition of assisted suicide does not mean that every possible application of the statute would be valid. A State, like Washington, that has authorized the death penalty and thereby has concluded that the sanctity of human life does not require that it always be preserved, must acknowledge that there are situations in which an interest in hastening death is legitimate. Indeed, not only is that interest sometimes legitimate, I am also convinced that there are times when it is entitled to constitutional protection. In most cases, the individual's constitutionally protected interest in his or her own physical autonomy, including the right to refuse unwanted medical treatment, will give way to the State's interest in preserving human life.

*Cruzan,* however, was not the normal case. Given the irreversible nature of her illness and the progressive character of her suffering, Nancy Cruzan's interest in refusing medical care was incidental to her more basic interest in controlling the manner and timing of her death. . . . . I insist that the source of Nancy Cruzan's right to refuse treatment was not just a common law rule. Rather, this right is an aspect of a far broader and more basic concept of freedom that is even older than the common law. This freedom embraces, not merely a person's right to refuse a particular kind of unwanted treatment, but also her interest in dignity, and in determining the character of the memories that will survive long after her death. In recognizing that the State's interests did not outweigh Nancy Cruzan's liberty interest in refusing medical treatment, *Cruzan* rested not simply on the common law right to refuse medical treatment, but—at least implicitly—on the even more fundamental right to make this "deeply personal decision," 497 U.S., at 289 (O'CONNOR, J., concurring).

Thus, the common law right to protection from battery, which included the right to refuse medical treatment in most circumstances, did not mark "the outer limits of the substantive sphere of liberty" that supported the Cruzan family's decision to hasten Nancy's death. *Planned Parenthood of Southeastern Pa.* v. *Casey,* 505 U.S. 833, 848 (1992).

Those limits have never been precisely defined. They are generally identified by the importance and character of the decision confronted by the individual, *Whalen* v. *Roe* 429 U.S. 589, 599–600, n. 26 (1977). Whatever the outer limits of the concept may be, it definitely includes protection for matters "central to personal dignity and autonomy." *Casey*, 505 U.S., at 851. . . .

The *Cruzan* case demonstrated that some state intrusions on the right to decide how death will be encountered are also intolerable. The now deceased plaintiffs in this action may in fact have had a liberty interest even stronger than Nancy Cruzan's because, not only were they terminally ill, they were suffering constant and severe pain. Avoiding intolerable pain and the indignity of living one's final days incapacitated and in agony is certainly "[a]t the heart of [the] liberty . . . to define one's own concept of existence, of meaning, of the universe, and of the mystery of human life." *Casey*, 505 U.S., at 851.

While I agree with the Court that *Cruzan* does not decide the issue presented by these cases, *Cruzan* did give recognition, not just to vague, unbridled notions of autonomy, but to the more specific interest in making decisions about how to confront an imminent death. Although there is no absolute right to physician assisted suicide, *Cruzan* makes it clear that some individuals who no longer have the option of deciding whether to live or to die because they are already on the threshold of death have a constitutionally protected interest that may outweigh the State's interest in preserving life at all costs. The liberty interest at stake in a case like this differs from, and is stronger than, both the common law right to refuse medical treatment and the unbridled interest in deciding whether to live or die. It is an interest in deciding how, rather than whether, a critical threshold shall be crossed.

The state interests supporting a general rule banning the practice of physician assisted suicide do not have the same force in all cases. First and foremost of these interests is the "'unqualified interest in the preservation of human life,'" *ante*, at 24, (quoting *Cruzan*, 497 U.S., at 282) which is equated with the sanctity of life,'" *ante*, at 25, (quoting the American Law Institute, Model Penal Code §210.5, Comment 5, p. 100 (Official Draft and Revised Comments 1980)). That interest not only justifies—it commands maximum protection of every individual's interest in remaining alive, which in turn commands the same protection for decisions about whether to commence or to terminate life support systems or to administer pain medication that may hasten death. Properly viewed, however, this interest is not a collective interest that should always outweigh the interests of a person who because of pain, incapacity, or sedation finds her life intolerable, but rather, an aspect of individual freedom.

Many terminally ill people find their lives meaningful even if filled with pain or dependence on others. Some find value in living through suffering; some have an abiding desire to witness particular events in their families' lives; many believe it a sin to hasten death. Individuals of different religious faiths make different judgments and choices about whether to live on under such circumstances. There are those who will want to continue aggressive treatment; those who would prefer terminal sedation; and those who will seek withdrawal from life support systems and death by gradual starvation and dehydration. Although as a general matter the State's interest in the contributions each person may make to society outweighs the person's interest in ending her life, this interest does not have the same force for a terminally ill patient faced not with the choice of whether to live, only of how to die. Allowing the individual, rather than the State, to make judgments "'about the 'quality'" of life that a particular individual may enjoy, " *ante,* at 25 (quoting *Cruzan,* 497 U.S., at 282), does not mean that the lives of terminally ill, disabled people have less value than the lives of those who are healthy, see *ante,* at 28. Rather, it gives proper recognition to the individual's interest in choosing a final chapter that accords with her life story, rather than one that demeans her values and poisons memories of her. . . .

Although, as the Court concludes today, these potential harms are sufficient to support the State's general public policy against assisted suicide, they will not always outweigh the individual liberty interest of a particular patient. Unlike the Court of Appeals, I would not say as a categorical matter that these state interests are invalid as to the entire class of terminally ill, mentally competent patients. I do not, however, foreclose the possibility that an individual plaintiff seeking to hasten her death, or a doctor whose assistance was sought, could prevail in a more particularized challenge. Future case, will determine whether I such challenge may succeed.

There remains room for vigorous debate about the outcome of particular cases that are not necessarily resolved by the opinions announced today. How such cases may be decided will depend on their specific facts. In my judgment, however, it is clear that the so called "unqualified interest in the preservation of human life," *Cruzan,* 497 U.S., at 282, *Glucksberg, ante,* at 24, is not itself sufficient to outweigh the interest in liberty that may justify the only possible means of preserving a dying patient's dignity and alleviating her intolerable suffering.

JUSTICE SOUTER, concurring in the judgment.

Three terminally ill individuals and four physicians who sometimes treat terminally ill patients brought this challenge to the Washington statute making it a crime "knowingly . . . [to] ai[d] another person to attempt suicide," Wash. Rev. Code §9A.36.060 (1994), claiming on behalf of both patients and physicians that it would violate substantive due process to enforce the statute against a doctor who acceded to a dying patient's request for a drug to be taken by the patient to commit suicide. The question is whether the statute sets up one of those "arbitrary impositions" or "purposeless restraints" at odds with the Due Process Clause of the Fourteenth Amendment. *Poe* v. *Ullman*, 367 U.S. 497, 543 (1961) (HARLAN, J., dissenting). I conclude that the statute's application to the doctors has not been shown to be unconstitutional, but I write separately to give my reasons for analyzing the substantive due process claims as I do, and for rejecting this one. . . .

When the physicians claim that the Washington law deprives them of a right falling within the scope of liberty that the Fourteenth Amendment guarantees against denial without due process of law, they are not claiming some sort of procedural defect in the process through which the statute has been enacted or is administered. Their claim, rather, is that the State has no substantively adequate justification for barring the assistance sought by the patient and sought to be offered by the physician. Thus, we are dealing with a claim to one of those rights sometimes described as rights of substantive due process and sometimes as unenumerated rights, in view of the breadth and indeterminacy of the "due process" serving as the claim's textual basis. The doctors accordingly arouse the skepticism of those who find the Due Process Clause an unduly vague or oxymoronic warrant for judicial review of substantive state law, just as they also invoke two centuries of American constitutional practice in recognizing unenumerated, substantive limits on governmental action. Although this practice has neither rested on any single textual basis nor expressed a consistent theory (or, before *Poe* v. *Ullman*, a much articulated one), a brief overview of its history is instructive on two counts. The persistence of substantive due process in our cases points to the legitimacy of the modern justification for such judicial review found in Justice Harlan's dissent in *Poe*, on which I will dwell further on, while the acknowledged failures of some of these cases point with caution to the difficulty raised by the present claim.

Before the ratification of the Fourteenth Amendment, substantive constitutional review resting on a theory of unenumerated rights occurred largely in the state courts applying state constitutions that commonly contained either due process clauses like that of the Fifth Amendment (and later the Fourteenth) or the textual antecedents of such clauses, repeating Magna Carta's guarantee of "the law of the land." On the basis of such clauses, or of general principles untethered to specific constitutional language, state courts evaluated the constitutionality of a wide range of statutes. . . .

After the ratification of the Fourteenth Amendment, with its guarantee of due process protection against the States, interpretation of the words "liberty" and "property" as used in due process clauses became a sustained enterprise, with the Court generally describing the due process criterion in converse terms of reasonableness or arbitrariness. . . .

The theory became serious, however, beginning with *Allgeyer* v. *Louisiana*, 165 U.S. 578 (1897), where the Court invalidated a Louisiana statute for excessive interference with

Fourteenth Amendment liberty to contract, *id.*, at 588–593, and offered a substantive interpretation of "liberty," that in the aftermath of the so called Lochner Era has been scaled back in some respects, but expanded in others, and never repudiated in principle. The Court said that Fourteenth Amendment liberty includes "the right of the citizen to be free in the enjoyment of all his faculties, to be free to use them in all lawful ways, to live and work where he will; to earn his livelihood by any lawful calling; to pursue any livelihood or avocation; and for that purpose to enter into all contracts which may be proper, necessary and essential to his carrying out to a successful conclusion the purposes above mentioned." *Id.*, at 589. "[W]e do not intend to hold that in no such case can the State exercise its police power," the Court added, but "[w]hen and how far such power may be legitimately exercised with regard to these subjects must be left for determination to each case as it arises." *Id.*, at 590.

Although this principle was unobjectionable, what followed for a season was, in the realm of economic legislation, the echo of *Dred Scott*. *Allegeyer* was succeeded within a decade by *Lochner* v. *New York*, 198 U.S. 45 (1905), and the era to which that case gave its name, famous now for striking down as arbitrary various sorts of economic regulations that post New Deal courts have uniformly thought constitutionally sound. Compare, *e.g.*, *id*, at 62 (finding New York's maximum hours law for bakers "unreasonable and entirely arbitrary") and *Adkins* v. *Children's Hospital of D. C.*, 261 U.S. 525, 559 (1923) (holding a minimum wage law "so clearly the product of a naked, arbitrary exercise of power that it cannot be allowed to stand under the Constitution of the United States") with *West Coast Hotel Co.* v. *Parrish*, 300 U.S. 379, 391 (1937) (overruling *Adkins* and approving a minimum wage law on the principle that regulation which is reasonable in relation to its subject and is adopted in the interests of the community is due process"). As the parentheticals here suggest, while the cases in the *Lochner* line routinely invoked a correct standard of constitutional arbitrariness review, they harbored the spirit *of Dred Scott* in their absolutist implementation of the standard they espoused. . . .

My understanding of unenumerated rights in the wake of the *Poe* dissent and subsequent cases avoids the absolutist failing of many older cases without embracing the opposite pole of equating reasonableness with past practice described at a very specific level. See *Planned Parenthood of Southeastern Pa.* v. *Casey*, 505 U.S. 833, 847, 849 (1992). That understanding begins with a concept of "ordered liberty," *Poe*, 367 U.S., at 549 (HARLAN, J.); see also *Griswold*, 381 U.S., at 500, comprising a continuum of rights to be free from "arbitrary impositions and purposeless restraints," *Poe*, 367 U.S., at 543 (HARLAN, J., dissenting). . . . it points to the importance of evaluating the claims of the parties now before us with comparable detail. For here we are faced with an individual claim not to a right on the part of just anyone to help anyone else commit suicide under any circumstances, but to the light of a narrow class to help others also in a narrow class under a set of limited circumstances. And the claimants are met with the State's assertion, among others, that rights of such narrow scope cannot be recognized without jeopardy to individuals whom the State may concededly protect through its regulations.

Respondents claim that a patient facing imminent death, who anticipates physical suffering and indignity, and is capable of responsible and voluntary choice, should have a right to a physician's assistance in providing counsel and drugs to be administered by the patient to end life promptly. Complaint ¶ 3. 1. They accordingly claim that a physician must have the corresponding right to provide such aid, contrary to the provisions of Wash. Rev. Code §9A.36.060 (1994). I do not understand the argument to rest on any assumption that rights either to suicide or to assistance in committing it are historically based as such. Respondents, rather, acknowledge the prohibition of each historically, but rely on the fact that to a substantial extent the State has repudiated that history. The result of this, respondents say, is to open the door to claims of such a patient to be accorded one of the options open to those with different, traditionally cognizable claims to autonomy in deciding how their bodies and minds should be treated.

They seek the option to obtain the services of a physician to give them the benefit of advice and medical help, which is said to enjoy a tradition so strong and so devoid of specifically countervailing state concern that denial of a physician's help in these circumstances is arbitrary when physicians are generally free to advise and aid those who exercise other rights to bodily autonomy.

The dominant western legal codes long condemned suicide and treated either its attempt or successful accomplishment as a crime, the one subjecting the individual to penalties, the other penalizing his survivors by designating the suicide's property as forfeited to the government. See 4 W. Blackstone, Commentaries *188–*189 (commenting that English law considered suicide to be "ranked . . . among the highest crimes" and deemed persuading another to commit suicide to be murder); see generally Marzen, O'Dowd, Crone, & Balch, Suicide: A Constitutional Right?, 24 Duquense L. Rev. 1, 5663 (1985). While suicide itself has generally not been considered a punishable crime in the United States, largely because the common law punishment of forfeiture was rejected as improperly penalizing an innocent family, see *id.*, at 98–99, most States have consistently punished the act of assisting a suicide as either a common law or statutory crime and some continue to view suicide as an unpunishable crime. See generally id., at 67–100, 148–242. Criminal prohibitions on such assistance remain widespread, as exemplified in the Washington statute in question here.

The principal significance of this history in the State of Washington, according to respondents, lies in its repudiation of the old tradition to the extent of eliminating the criminal suicide prohibitions. Respondents do not argue that the State's decision goes further, to imply that the State has repudiated any legitimate claim to discourage suicide or to limit its encouragement. The reasons for the decriminalization, after all, may have had more to do with difficulties of law enforcement than with a shift in the value ascribed to life in various circumstances or in the perceived legitimacy of taking one's own. See, *e.g.,* Kamisar, Physician Assisted Suicide: The Last Bridge to Active Voluntary Euthanasia, in Euthanasia Examined 225, 229 (J. Keown ed. 1995); CeloCruz, Aid in Dying: Should We Decriminalize Physician Assisted Suicide and Physician Committed Euthanasia?, 18 Am. J. L. & Med. 369, 375 (1992); Marzen, O'Dowd, Crone, & Balch 24 Duquesne L. Rev. supra, at 98–99. Thus it may indeed make sense for the State to take its hands off suicide as such, while continuing to prohibit the sort of assistance that would make its commission easier. See, *e.g.,* American Law Institute, Model Penal Code §210.5, Comment 5 (1980). Decriminalization does not, then, imply the existence of a constitutional liberty interest in suicide as such; it simply opens the door to the assertion of a cognizable liberty interest in bodily integrity and associated medical care that would otherwise have been inapposite so long as suicide, as well as assisting a suicide, was a criminal offense.

This liberty interest in bodily integrity was phrased in a general way by then Judge Cardozo when he said, "[e]very human being of adult years and sound mind has a right to determine what shall be done with his own body" in relation to his medical needs. *Schloendorff* v. *Society of New York Hospital,* 211 N. Y. 125, 129, 105 N.E. 92, 93 (1914). The familiar examples of this right derive from the common law of battery and include the right to be free from medical invasions into the body, *Cruzan* v. *Director, Mo. Dept. of Health,* 497 U.S., at 269–279, as well as a right generally to resist enforced medication, see *Washington* v. *Harper,* 494 U.S. 210, 221–222, 229 (1990). Thus "[i]t is settled now . . . that the Constitution places limits on a State's right to interfere with a person's most basic decisions about . . . bodily integrity." *Casey,* 505 U.S., at 849 (citations omitted); see also *Cruzan,* 497 U.S., at 278; *id.,* at 288 (O'Connor, J., concurring); *Washington* v. *Harper, supra,* at 221–222; *Winston* v. *Lee,* 470 U.S. 753, 761–762 (1985); *Rochin* v. *California,* 342 U.S., at 172. Constitutional recognition of the right to bodily integrity underlies the assumed right, good against the State, to require physicians to terminate artificial life support, *Cruzan, supra,* at 279 ("we assume that the United States Constitution would grant a competent person a constitutionally protected right to refuse lifesaving hydration and nutrition"), and the affirmative right to obtain medical intervention to cause abortion, see *Casey, supra,* at 857, 896; cf. *Roe* v. *Wade,* 410 U.S., at 153. It is, indeed, in the abortion cases that the most telling recognitions of the importance of bodily integrity and the concomitant tradition of medical assistance have occurred. In *Roe* v. *Wade,* the plaintiff contended that the Texas statute making it criminal for any person to "procure an abortion," *id.,* at 117, for a pregnant woman was unconstitutional insofar as it prevented her from "terminat[ing] her pregnancy by an abortion 'performed by a competent, licensed physician, under safe, clinical conditions,' " *id.*, at 120, and in striking down the statute we stressed the importance of the relationship between patient and physician, see *id.*, at 153, 156.

The analogies between the abortion cases and this one are several. Even though the State has a legitimate interest in discouraging abortion, see *Casey*, 505 U.S., at 871 (joint opinion of O'CONNOR, KENNEDY, and SOUTER, JJ.) *Roe*, 410 U.S., at 162, the Court recognized a woman's right to a physician's counsel and care. Like the decision to commit suicide, the decision to abort potential life can be made irresponsibly and under the influence of others, and yet the Court has held in the abortion cases that physicians are fit assistants. Without physician assistance in abortion, the woman's right would have too often amounted to nothing more than a right to self mutilation, and without a physician to assist in the suicide of the dying, the patient's right will often be confined to crude methods of causing death, most shocking and painful to the decedent's survivors.

There is, finally, one more reason for claiming that a physician's assistance here would fall within the accepted tradition of medical care in our society, and the abortion cases are only the most obvious illustration of the further point. While the Court has held that the performance of abortion procedures can be restricted to physicians, the Court's opinion in *Roe* recognized the doctors' role in yet another way.

For, in the course of holding that the decision to perform an abortion called for a physician's assistance, the Court recognized that the good physician is not just a mechanic of the human body whose services have no bearing on a person's moral choices, but one who does more than treat symptoms, one who ministers to the patient. See id, at 153; see also *Griswold* v. *Connecticut*, 381 U.S., at 482 ("This law operates directly on an intimate relation of husband and wife and their physician's role in one aspect of that relation"); see generally R. Cabot, Ether Day Address, Boston Medical and Surgical J. 287, 288 (1920). This idea of the physician as serving the whole person is a source of the high value traditionally placed on the medical relationship. Its value is surely as apparent here as in the abortion cases, for just as the decision about abortion is not directed to correcting some pathology, so the decision in which a dying patient seeks help is not so limited. The patients here sought not only an end to pain (which they might have had, although perhaps at the price of stupor) but an end to their short remaining lives with a dignity that they believed would be denied them by powerful pain medication, as well as by their consciousness of dependency and helplessness as they approached death. In that period when the end is imminent, they said, the decision to end life is closest to decisions that are generally accepted as proper instances of exercising autonomy over one's own body, instances recognized under the Constitution and the State's own law, instances in which the help of physicians is accepted as falling within the traditional norm.

Respondents argue that the State has in fact already recognized enough evolving examples of this tradition of patient care to demonstrate the strength of their claim. Washington, like other States, authorizes physicians to withdraw life sustaining medical treatment and artificially delivered food and water from patients who request it, even though such actions will hasten death. See Wash. Rev. Code §§70.122.110, 70.122.051 (1994); see generally Notes to Uniform Rights of the Terminally Ill Act, 9B U. L. A. 168–169 (Supp. 1997) (listing state statutes). The State permits physicians to alleviate anxiety and discomfort when withdrawing artificial life supporting devices by administering medication that will hasten death even further. And it generally permits physicians to administer medication to patients in terminal conditions when the primary intent is to alleviate pain, even when the medication is so powerful as to hasten death and the patient chooses to receive it with that understanding. See Wash. Rev. Code §70.122.010 (1994); see generally P. Rousseau, Terminal Sedation in the Care of Dying Patients, 156 Archives of Internal Medicine 1785 (1996); Truog, Berde, Mitchell, & Grier, Barbiturates in the Care of the Terminally Ill, 327 New Eng. J. Med. 1678 (1992).

The argument supporting respondents' position thus progresses through three steps of increasing forcefulness. First, it emphasizes the decriminalization of suicide. Reliance on this fact is sanctioned under the standard that looks not only to the tradition retained, but to society's occasional choices to reject traditions of the legal past. See *Poe v. Ullman*, 367 U.S., at 542 (HARLAN, J., dissenting). While the common law prohibited both suicide and aiding a suicide, with the prohibition on aiding largely justified by the primary prohibition on self inflicted death itself, see, e.g., American Law Institute, Model Penal Code §210.5, Comment 1, pp. 92–93, and n. 7 (1980), the State's rejection of the traditional treatment of the one leaves the criminality of the other open to questioning that previously would not have been appropriate. The second step in the argument is to emphasize that the State's own act of decriminalization gives a freedom of choice much like the individual's option in recognized instances of bodily autonomy. One of these, abortion, is a legal right to choose in spite of the interest a State may legitimately invoke in discouraging the practice, just as suicide is now subject to choice, despite a state interest in discouraging it. The third step is to emphasize that respondents claim a right to assistance not on the basis of some broad principle that would be subject to exceptions if that continuing interest of the State's in discouraging suicide were to be recognized at all. Respondents base their claim on the traditional right to medical care and counsel, subject to the limiting conditions of informed, responsible choice when death is imminent, conditions that support a strong analogy to rights of care in other situations in which medical counsel and assistance have been available as a matter of course. There can be no stronger claim to a physician's assistance than at the time when death is imminent, a moral judgment implied by the State's own recognition of the legitimacy of medical procedures necessarily hastening the moment of impending death.

In my judgment, the importance of the individual interest here, as within that class of "certain interests" demanding careful scrutiny of the State's contrary claim, see *Poe, supra,* at 543, cannot be gainsaid. Whether that interest might in some circumstances, or at some time, be seen as "fundamental" to the degree entitled to prevail is not, however, a conclusion that I need draw here, for I am satisfied that the State's interests described in the following section are sufficiently serious to defeat the present claim that its law is arbitrary or purposeless.

The State has put forward several interests to justify the Washington law as applied to physicians treating terminally ill patients, even those competent to make responsible choices: protecting life generally, Brief for Petitioners 33, discouraging suicide even if knowing and voluntary, *id.,* at 37–38, and protecting terminally ill patients from involuntary suicide and euthanasia, both voluntary and nonvoluntary, *id.,* at 34–35.

It is not necessary to discuss the exact strengths of the first two claims of justification in the present circumstances, for the third is dispositive for me. That third justification is different from the first two, for it addresses specific features of respondents' claim, and it opposes that claim not with a moral judgment contrary to respondents,' but with a recognized state interest in the protection of nonresponsible individuals and those who do not stand in relation either to death or to their physicians as do the patients whom respondents describe. The State claims interests in protecting patients from mistakenly and involuntarily deciding to end their lives, and in guarding against both voluntary and involuntary euthanasia. Leaving aside any difficulties in coming to a clear concept of imminent death, mistaken decisions may result from inadequate palliative care or a terminal prognosis that turns out to be err or, coercion and abuse may stem from the large medical bills that family members cannot bear or unreimbursed hospitals decline to shoulder. Voluntary and involuntary euthanasia may result once doctors are authorized to prescribe lethal medication in the first instance, for they might find it pointless to distinguish between patients who administer their own fatal drugs and those who wish not to, and their compassion for those who suffer may obscure the distinction between those who ask for death and those who may be unable to request it. The argument is that a progression would occur, obscuring the line between the ill and the dying, and between the responsible and the unduly influenced, until ultimately doctors and perhaps others would abuse a limited freedom to aid suicides by yielding to the impulse to end another's suffering under conditions going beyond the narrow limits the respondents propose. The State thus argues, essentially, that respondents' claim is not as narrow as it sounds, simply because no recognition of the interest they assert could be limited to vindicating those interests and affecting no others. The State says that the claim, in practical effect, would entail consequences that the State could, without doubt, legitimately act to prevent.

The mere assertion that the terminally sick might be pressured into suicide decisions by close friends and family members would not alone be very telling. Of course that is possible, not only because the costs of care might be more than family members could bear but simply because they might naturally wish to see an end of suffering for someone they love. But one of the points of restricting any right of assistance to physicians, would be to condition the right on an exercise of judgment by someone qualified to assess the patient's responsible capacity and detect the influence of those outside the medical relationship.

The State, however, goes further, to argue that dependence on the vigilance of physicians will not be enough. First, the lines proposed here (particularly the requirement of a knowing and voluntary decision by the patient) would be more difficult to draw than the lines that have limited other recently recognized due process rights. Limiting a state from prosecuting use of artificial contraceptives by married couples posed no practical threat to the State's capacity to regulate contraceptives in other ways that were assumed at the time of *Poe* to be legitimate; the trimester measurements of *Roe* and the viability determination of *Casey* were easy to make with a real degree of certainty. But the knowing and responsible mind is harder to assess. Second, this difficulty could become the greater by combining with another fact within the realm of plausibility, that physicians simply would not be assiduous to preserve the line. They have compassion, and those who would be willing to assist in suicide at all might be the most susceptible to the wishes of a patient, whether the patient were technically quite responsible or not. Physicians, and their hospitals, have their own financial incentives, too, in this new age of managed care. Whether acting from compassion or under some other influence, a physician who would provide a drug for a patient to administer might well go the further step of administering the drug himself, so, the barrier between assisted suicide and euthanasia could become porous, and the line between voluntary and involuntary euthanasia as well. The case for the slippery slope is fairly made out here, not because recognizing one due process right would leave a court with no principled basis to avoid recognizing another, but because there is a plausible case that the right claimed would not be readily containable by reference to facts about the mind that are matters of difficult judgment, or by gatekeepers who are subject to temptation, noble or not.

Respondents propose an answer to all this, the answer of state regulation with teeth. Legislation proposed in several States, for example, would authorize physician assisted suicide but require two qualified physicians to confirm the patient's diagnosis, prognosis, and competence; and would mandate that the patient make repeated requests witnessed by at least two others over a specified time span; and would impose reporting requirements and criminal penalties for various acts of coercion. See App. to Brief for State Legislators as *Amici Curiae* 1a–2a.

But at least at this moment there are reasons for caution in predicting the effectiveness of the teeth proposed. Respondents' proposals, as it turns out, sound much like the guidelines now in place in the Netherlands, the only place where experience with physician assisted suicide and euthanasia has yielded empirical evidence about how such regulations might affect actual practice. Dutch physicians must engage in consultation before proceeding, and must decide whether the patient's decision is voluntary, well considered, and stable, whether the request to die is enduring and made more than once, and whether the patient's future will involve unacceptable suffering. See C. Gomez, Regulating Death, 40–43 (1991). There is, however, a substantial dispute today about what the Dutch experience shows. Some commentators marshall evidence that the Dutch guidelines have in practice failed to protect patients from involuntary euthanasia and have been violated with impunity. . . .

The day may come when we can say with some assurance which side is right, but for now it is substantiality of the factual disagreement, and the alternatives for resolving it, that matter. They are, for me, dispositive of the due process claim at this time.

I take it that the basic concept of judicial review with its possible displacement of legislative judgment bars any finding that a legislature has acted arbitrarily when the following conditions are met: there is a serious factual controversy over the feasibility of recognizing the claimed right without at the same time making it impossible for the State to engage in an undoubtedly legitimate exercise of power; facts necessary to resolve the controversy are not readily ascertainable through the judicial process, but they are more readily subject to discovery through legislative factfinding and experimentation. It is assumed in this case, and must be, that a State's interest in protecting those unable to make responsible decisions and those who make no decisions at all entities the State to bar aid to any but a knowing and responsible person intending suicide, and to prohibit euthanasia. How, and how far, a State should act in that interest are judgments for the State, but the legitimacy of its action to deny a physician the option to aid any but the knowing and responsible is beyond question.

The capacity of the State to protect the others if respondents were to prevail is, however, subject to some genuine question, underscored by the responsible disagreement over the basic facts of the Dutch experience. This factual controversy is not open to a judicial resolution with any substantial degree of assurance at this time. . . .

Legislatures, on the other hand, have superior opportunities to obtain the facts necessary for a judgment about the present controversy. Not only do they have more flexible mechanisms for factfinding than the Judiciary, but their mechanisms include the power to experiment, moving forward and pulling back as facts emerge within their own jurisdictions. There is, indeed, good reason to suppose that in the absence of a judgment for respondents here, just such experimentation will be attempted in some of the States. See, *e.g.,* Ore. Rev. Stat. Ann. § § 127.800 *el seq. (Supp.* 1996); App. to Brief for State Legislators as *Amici Curiae* 1 a (listing proposed statutes).

I do not decide here what the significance might be of legislative foot dragging in ascertaining the facts going to the State's argument that the right in question could not be confined as claimed. Sometimes a court may be bound to act regardless of the institutional preferability of the political branches as forums for addressing constitutional claims. See, e.g., *Bolling* v. *Sharpe,* 347 U.S. 497 (1954). Now, it is enough to say that our examination of legislative reasonableness should consider the fact that the Legislature of the State of Washington is no more obviously at fault than this Court is in being uncertain about what would happen if respondents prevailed today. We therefore have a clear question about which institution a legislature or a court, is relatively more competent to deal with an emerging issue as to which facts currently unknown could be dispositive. The answer has to be, for the reasons already stated, that the legislative process is to be preferred.

The Court should accordingly stay its hand to allow reasonable legislative consideration. While I do not decide for all time that respondents' claim should not be recognized, I acknowledge the legislative institutional competence as the better one to deal with that claim at this time.

JUSTICE GINSBURG, concurring in the judgments.

I concur in the Court's judgments in these cases substantially for the reasons stated by JUSTICE O'CONNOR in her concurring opinion.

JUSTICE BREYER, concurring in the judgments.

I believe that JUSTICE O'CONNOR's views, which I share, have greater legal significance than the Court's opinion suggests. I join her separate opinion, except insofar as it joins the majority. And I concur in the judgments. I shall briefly explain how I differ from the Court. . . . I also agree with the Court that the critical question in both of the cases before us is whether "the 'liberty' specially protected by the Due Process Clause includes a right" of the sort that the respondents assert, *Washington* v. *Glucksberg, ante,* at 19. 1 do not agree, however, with the Court's formulation of that claimed "liberty" interest. The Court describes it as a "right to commit suicide with another's assistance." *Ante,* at 20. But I would not reject the respondents' claim without considering a different formulation, for which our legal tradition may provide greater support. That formulation would use words roughly like a "right to die with dignity." But irrespective of the exact words used, at its core would lie personal control over the manner of death, professional medical assistance, and the avoidance of unnecessary and severe physical suffering—combined. . . . I agree that one can find a "right to die with dignity" by examining the protection the law has provided for related, but not identical, interests relating to personal dignity, medical treatment, and freedom from state inflicted pain. See *Ingraham* v. *Wright,* 430 U.S. 651 (1977); *Cruzan* v. *Director, Mo. Dept. of Health,* 497 U.S. 26 (1990); *Casey, supra.*

I do not believe, however, that this Court need or now should decide whether or a not such a right is "fundamental." That is because, in my view, the avoidance of severe physical pain (connected with death) would have to comprise an essential part of any successful claim and because, as JUSTICE O'CONNOR points out, the laws before us do not force a dying person to undergo that kind of pain. *Ante,* at 2 (O'CONNOR, J., concurring). Rather, the laws of New York and of Washington do not prohibit doctors from providing patients with drugs sufficient to control pain despite the risk that those drugs themselves will kill. Cf. New York State Task Force on Life and the Law, When Death Is Sought: Assisted Suicide and Euthanasia in the Medical Context 163, n. 29 (May 1994). And under these circumstances the laws of New York and Washington would overcome any remaining significant interests and would be justified, regardless.

Medical technology, we are repeatedly told, makes the administration of pain relieving drugs sufficient, except for a very few individuals for whom the ineffectiveness of pain control medicines can mean, not pain, but the need for sedation which can end in a coma.

This legal circumstance means that the state laws before us do not infringe directly upon the (assumed) central interest (what I have called the core of the interest in dying with dignity) as, by way of contrast, the state anticontraceptive laws at issue in *Poe* did interfere with the central interest there at stake by bringing the State's police powers to bear upon the marital bedroom.

Were the legal circumstances different—for example, were state law to prevent the provision of palliative care, including the administration of drugs as needed to avoid pain at the end of life—then the law's impact upon serious and otherwise unavoidable physical pain (accompanying death) would be more directly at issue. And as Justice O'Connor suggests, the Court might have to revisit its conclusions in these cases.

## *Notes*

1. Act of Apr. 28, 1854, § 17, 1854 Wash. Laws 78 ("Every person deliberately assisting another in the commission of self murder, shall be deemed guilty of manslaughter"); see also Act of Dec. 2, 1869, §17, 1869 Wash. Laws 20 1; Act of Nov. 10, 1873, § 19, 1873 Wash. Laws 184; Criminal Code, ch. 249, §§135–136, 1909 Wash. Laws, 11th sess., 929.

2. See *Compassion in Dying* v. *Washington,* 79 F. 3d 790, 847, and nn. 10–13 (CA9 1996) (Beezer, J., dissenting) ("In total, forty four states, the District of Columbia and two territories prohibit or condemn assisted suicide") (citing statutes and cases); *Rodriguez* v. *British Columbia (Attorney General),* 107 D.L.R. (4th) 342, 404 (Can. 1993) ("[A] blanket prohibition on assisted suicide . . . is the norm among western democracies") (discussing assisted suicide

provisions in Austria, Spain, Italy, the United Kingdom, the Netherlands, Denmark, Switzerland, and France). Since the Ninth Circuit's decision, Louisiana, Rhode Island, and Iowa have enacted statutory assisted suicide bans. La. Rev. Stat. Ann. §14:32.12 (Supp. 1997); R. I. Gen. Laws §§11–60–1, 11–60–3 (Supp. 1996); Iowa Code Ann. §§707A.2, 707A.3 (Supp. 1997). For a detailed history of the States' statutes, see Marzen, O'Dowd, Crone & Balch, Suicide: A Constitutional Right?, 24 Duquesne L. Rev. 1, 148–242 (1985) (Appendix) (hereinafter Marzen).

3. Other countries are embroiled in similar debates: The Supreme Court of Canada recently rejected a claim that the Canadian Charter of Rights and Freedoms establishes a fundamental right to assisted suicide, *Rodriguez* v. *British Columbia (Attorney General)*, 107 D. L. R. (4th) 342 (1993); the British House of Lords Select Committee on Medical Ethics refused to recommend any change in Great Britain's assisted suicide prohibition, House of Lords, Session 1993–94 Report of the Select Committee on Medical Ethics, 12 Issues in Law & Med. 193, 202 (1996) ("We identify no circumstances in which assisted suicide should be permitted"); New Zealand's Parliament rejected a proposed "Death With Dignity Bill" that would have legalized physician assisted suicide in August 1995, Graeme, MPs Throw out Euthanasia Bill, The Dominion (Wellington), Aug. 17, 1995, p. 1 and the Northern Territory of Australia legalized assisted suicide and voluntary euthanasia in 1995. See Shenon, Australian Doctors Get Right to Assist Suicide, N.Y. Times, July 28, 1995, p. A8. As of February 1997, three persons had ended their lives with physician assistance in the Northern Territory. Mydans, Assisted Suicide: Australia Faces a Grim Reality, N. Y. Times, Febr. 2, 1997, p. A3. On March 24, 1997, however, the Australian Senate voted to overturn the Northern Territory's law. Thornhill, Australia Repeals Euthanasia Law, Washington Post, March 25, 1997, p. A14; see Euthanasia Laws Act 1997, No. 17, 1997 (Austl.). On the other hand, on May 20, 1997, Colombia's Constitutional Court legalized voluntary euthanasia for terminally ill people. Sentencia No. C 239/97 (Corte Constitucional, Mayo 20, 1997); see Colombia's Top Court Legalizes Euthanasia, Orlando Sentinel, May 22, 1997, p. A 18.

* Justice Ginsburg concurs in the Court's judgments substantially for the reasons stated in this opinion. Justice Breyer joins this opinion except insofar as it joins the opinions of the Court.

---

**Washington v. Glucksberg**, 521 U.S. 702 (1997) 9–0
*editor's note:*
*Opinion authors are in bold. () indicates the party of appointing president. If the party of the justice differs from that of appointing president, then the party of the justice is listed second after the slash.*

| MAJORITY | CONCURRING | DISSENTING |
|---|---|---|
| **Rehnquist** (r) | **O'Connor** (r) | |
| Scalia (r) | **Stevens** (r) | |
| Thomas (r) | **Souter** (r) | |
| Kennedy (r) | **Ginsberg** (d) | |
| | **Breyer** (d) | |

# Balancing Liberty, Constitutionalism, and Democracy

## In Theories of Constitutional Interpretation: Views from the Bench

This volume ends with selections from two prominent jurists of the late twentieth century: Chief Justice William Rehnquist and Justice William J. Brennan. These two Justices present very different views of what they believe the role of the Court should be in American society and how the Court should interpret the Constitution. In viewing our liberal, constitutional, democracy, both Justices agree that the Constitution is central to the task of the Court. Where they disagree is on the balance to be struck between liberty and democracy. Rehnquist elevates democracy to the highest good, relying solely on democratic, popular, processes to define what is good or just law and to protect the people's liberty from government tyranny. He puts forth a kind of democratic moral relativism. Brennan, on the other hand, elevates liberty to the highest good, arguing that the constitution is "a sparkling vision of the supremacy of the human dignity of every individual [and that] this vision is reflected in the very choice of democratic self-governance: the supreme value of a democracy is the presumed worth of each individual." He sees the Court's role as providing a check on democracy in the service of the protection of human dignity, recognizing that society's views of dignity evolve and change over time. These two articles provide a closing statement on the fundamental tensions that have plagued our efforts to define the proper role of the Supreme Court in our liberal constitutional, democracy—a tension that all of us must address in our evaluations of the nation's highest judicial tribunal.

# THE NOTION OF A LIVING CONSTITUTION

## William H. Rehnquist

At least one of the more than half-dozen persons nominated during the past decade to be an Associate Justice of the Supreme Court of the United States has been asked by the Senate Judiciary Committee at his confirmation hearings whether he believed in a living Constitution.[1] It is not an easy question to answer; the phrase "living Constitution" has about it a teasing imprecision that makes it a coat of many colors.

One's first reaction tends to be along the lines of public relations or ideological sex appeal, I suppose. At first blush it seems certain that a *living* Constitution is better than what must be its counterpart, a *dead* Constitution. It would seem that only a necrophile could disagree. If we could get one of the major public opinion research firms in the country to sample public opinion concerning whether the United States Constitution should be *living* or *dead,* the overwhelming majority of the responses doubtless would favor a *living* Constitution.

The phrase is really a shorthand expression that is susceptible of at least two quite different meanings. The first meaning was expressed over a half-century ago by Mr. Justice Holmes in *Missouri* v. *Holland*[2] with his customary felicity when he said:

> . . . When we are dealing with words that also are a constituent act, like the Constitution of the United States, we must realize that they have called into life a being the development of which could not have been foreseen completely by the most gifted of its begetters. It was enough for them to realize or to hope that they had created an organism; it has taken a century and has cost their successors much sweat and blood to prove that they created a nation.[3]

I shall refer to this interpretation of the phrase "living Constitution," with which scarcely anyone would disagree, as the Holmes version.

The framers of the Constitution wisely spoke in general language and left to succeeding generations the task of applying that language to the unceasingly changing

"The Notion of a Living Constitution" by U.S. Supreme Court Justice William H. Rehnquist. Published originally in 54 TEXAS LAW REVIEW 693–706 (1976). Copyright 1976 by the Texas Law Review Association. Reprinted by permission.

environment in which they would live. Those who framed, adopted, and ratified the Civil War amendments[4] to the Constitution likewise used what have been aptly described as "majestic generalities"[5] in composing the Fourteenth Amendment. Merely because a particular activity may not have existed when the Constitution was adopted, or because the framers could not have conceived of a particular method of transacting affairs, cannot mean that general language in the Constitution may not be applied to such a course of conduct. Where the framers of the Constitution have used general language, they have given latitude to those who would later interpret the instrument to make that language applicable to cases that the framers might not have foreseen.

In my reading and travels I have sensed a second connotation of the phrase "living Constitution," however, one quite different from what I have described as the Holmes version, but which certainly has gained acceptance among some parts of the legal profession. Embodied in its most naked form, it recently came to my attention in some language from a brief that had been filed in a United States District Court on behalf of state prisoners asserting that the conditions of their confinement offended the United States Constitution.

The brief urged:

> We are asking a great deal of the Court because other branches of government have abdicated their responsibility. . . . Prisoners are like other "discrete and insular" minorities for whom the Court must spread its protective umbrella because no other branch of government will do so. . . . This Court, as the voice and conscience of contemporary society, as the measure of the modern conception of human dignity, must declare that the [named prison] and all it represents offends the Constitution of the United States and will not be tolerated.

Here we have a living Constitution with a vengeance. Although the substitution of some other set of values for those, which may be derived from the language and intent of the framers is not urged in so many words, that is surely the thrust of the message. Under this brief writer's version of the living Constitution, nonelected members of the federal judiciary may address themselves to a social problem simply because other branches of government have failed or refused to do so. These same judges, responsible to no constituency whatever, are nonetheless acclaimed as "the voice and conscience of contemporary society."

If we were merely talking about a slogan that was being used to elect some candidate to office or to persuade the voters to ratify a constitutional amendment, elaborate dissection of a phrase such as "living Constitution" would probably not be warranted. What we are talking about, however, is a suggested philosophical approach to be used by the federal judiciary, and perhaps state judiciaries, in exercising the very delicate responsibility of judicial review. Under the familiar principle of judicial review, the courts in construing the Constitution are, of course, authorized to invalidate laws that have been enacted by Congress or by a state legislature but that those courts find to violate some provision of the Constitution. Nevertheless, those who have pondered the matter have always recognized that the ideal of judicial review has basically antidemocratic and antimajoritarian facets that require some justification in this Nation, which prides itself on being a self-governing representative democracy.

All who have studied law, and many who have not, are familiar with John Marshall's classic defense of judicial review in his opinion for the Court in *Marbury* v. *Madison*.[6] I will summarize very briefly the thrust of that answer, with which I fully agree, because while it supports the Holmes version of the phrase "living Constitution," it also suggests some outer limits for the brief writer's version.

The ultimate source of authority in this Nation, Marshall said, is not Congress, not the states, not for that matter the Supreme Court of the United States. The people are the ultimate source of authority; they have parceled out the authority that originally resided entirely with them by adopting the original Constitution and by later amending it. They have granted some authority to the federal government and have reserved authority not granted it to the states or to the people individually. As between the branches of the federal government, the people have given certain authority to the President, certain authority to Congress, and certain authority to the federal judiciary. In the Bill of Rights they have erected protections for specified individual rights against the actions of the federal government. From today's perspective we might add that they have placed restrictions on the authority of the state governments in the Thirteenth, Fourteenth, and Fifteenth amendments.

In addition, Marshall said that if the popular branches of government—state legislatures, the Congress, and the Presidency—are operating within the authority granted to them by the Constitution, their judgment and not that of the Court, must obviously prevail. When these branches overstep the authority given them by the Constitution, in the case of the President and the Congress, or invade protected individual rights, and a constitutional challenge to their action is raised in a lawsuit brought in federal court, the Court must prefer the Constitution to the government acts.

John Marshall's justification for judicial review makes the provision for an independent federal judiciary not only understandable but also thoroughly desirable. Since the judges will be merely interpreting an instrument framed by the people, they should be detached and objective. A mere change in public opinion since the adoption of the Constitution, unaccompanied by a constitutional amendment, should not change the meaning of the Constitution. A merely temporary majoritarian groundswell should not abrogate some individual liberty truly protected by the Constitution.

Clearly Marshall's explanation contains certain elements of either ingenuousness or ingeniousness, which tend to grow larger as our constitutional history extends over a longer period of time. The Constitution is in many of its parts obviously not a specifically worded document but one couched in general phraseology. There is obviously wide room for honest difference of opinion over the meaning of general phrases in the Constitution; any particular Justice's decision when a question arises under one of these general phrases will depend to some extent on his own philosophy of constitutional law. One may nevertheless concede all of these problems that inhere in Marshall's justification of judicial review, yet feel that his justification for nonelected judges exercising the power of judicial review is the only one consistent with democratic philosophy of representative government.

Marshall was writing at a time when the governing generation remembered well not only the deliberations of the framers of the Constitution at Philadelphia in the summer of 1787 but also the debates over the ratification of the Constitution in the 13 colonies. The often heated discussions that took place from 1787, when Delaware became the first state to ratify the Constitution,[7] until 1790, when recalcitrant Rhode Island finally joined the Union,[8] were themselves far more representative of the give-and-take of public decision making by a constituent assembly than is the ordinary enactment of a law by Congress or by a state legislature. Patrick Henry had done all he could to block ratification in Virginia,[9] and the opposition of the Clinton faction in New York had provoked Jay, Hamilton, and Madison to their brilliant effort in defense of the Constitution, the *Federalist Papers*.[10] For Marshall, writing the *Marbury* v. *Madison* opinion in 1803, the memory of the debates in which the people of the 13 colonies had participated only a few years before could well have fortified his conviction that the Constitution was, not merely in theory but in fact as well, a fundamental charter that had emanated from the people.

One senses no similar connection with a popularly adopted constituent act in what I have referred to as the brief writer's version of the living Constitution. The brief writer's version seems instead to be based upon the proposition that federal judges, perhaps judges as a whole, have a role of their own, quite independent of popular will, to play in solving society's problems. Once we have abandoned the idea that the authority of the courts to declare laws unconstitutional is somehow tied to the language of the Constitution that the people adopted, a judiciary exercising the power of judicial review appears in a quite different light. Judges then are no longer the keepers of the covenant; instead they are a small group of fortunately situated people with a roving commission to second-guess Congress, state legislatures, and state and federal administrative officers concerning what is best for the country. Surely there is no justification for a third legislative branch in the federal government, and there is even less justification for a federal legislative branch's reviewing on a policy basis the laws enacted by the legislatures of the 50 states. Even if one were to disagree with me on this point, the members of a third branch of the federal legislature at least ought to be elected by and responsible to constituencies, just as in the case of the other two branches of Congress. If there is going to be a council of revision, it ought to have at least some connection with popular feeling. Its members either ought to stand for reelection on occasion, or their terms should expire and they should be allowed to continue serving only if reappointed by a popularly elected Chief Executive and confirmed by a popularly elected Senate.

The brief writer's version of the living Constitution is seldom presented in its most naked form, but is instead usually dressed in more attractive garb. The argument in favor of this approach generally begins with a sophisticated wink—why pretend that there is any ascertainable content to the general phrases of the Constitution as they are written since, after all, judges constantly disagree about their meaning? We are all familiar with Chief Justice Hughes's famous aphorism that "We are under a Constitution, but the Constitution is what the judges say it is."[11] We all know the basis of Marshall's justification for judicial review, the argument runs, but it is necessary only to keep the window dressing in place. Any sophisticated student of the subject knows that judges need not limit themselves to the intent of the framers, which is very difficult to determine in any event. Because of the general language used in the Constitution, judges should not hesitate to use their authority to make the Constitution relevant and useful in solving the problems of modern society. The brief writer's version of the living Constitution envisions all of the above conclusions.

At least three serious difficulties flaw the brief writer's version of the living Constitution. First, it misconceives the nature of the Constitution, which was designed to enable the popularly elected branches of government, not the judicial branch, to keep the country abreast of the times. Second, the brief writer's version ignores the Supreme Court's disastrous experiences when in the past it embraced contemporary, fashionable notions of what a living Constitution should contain. Third, however socially desirable the goals sought to be advanced by the brief writer's version, advancing them through a freewheeling, nonelected judiciary is quite unacceptable in a democratic society.

It seems to me that it is almost impossible, after reading the record of the Founding Fathers' debates in Philadelphia, to conclude that they intended the Constitution itself to suggest answers to the manifold problems that they knew would confront succeeding generations. The Constitution that they drafted was indeed intended to endure indefinitely, but the reason for this very well-founded hope was the general language by which national authority was granted to Congress and the Presidency. These two branches were to furnish the motive power within the federal system, which was in turn to coexist with the state governments; the elements of government having a popular constituency were looked to for the solution of the numerous and varied problems that the future would bring. Limitations were indeed placed upon both federal and state governments in the form of both a division of powers and express protection for individual rights. These limitations, however, were not themselves designed to solve the problems of the future, but were instead designed to make certain that the constituent branches, when *they* attempted to solve those problems, should not transgress these fundamental limitations.

Although the Civil War Amendments were designed more as broad limitations on the authority of state governments, they too were enacted in response to practices that the lately seceded states engaged in to discriminate against and mistreat the newly emancipated freed men. To the extent that the language of these amendments is general, the courts are of course warranted in giving them an application coextensive with their language. Nevertheless, I greatly doubt that even men like Thad Stevens and John Bingham, leaders of the radical Republicans in Congress, would have thought any portion of the Civil War Amendments, except section five of the Fourteenth Amendment,[12] was designed to solve problems that society might confront a century later. I think they would have said that those amendments were designed to prevent abuses from ever recurring in which the states had engaged prior to that time.

The second difficulty with the brief writer's version of the living Constitution lies in its inattention to—or rejection of—the Supreme Court's historical experience gleaned from similar forays into problem solving.

Although the phrase "living Constitution" may not have been used during the nineteenth century and the first half of this century, the idea represented by the brief writer's version was very much in evidence during both periods. The apogee of the living Constitution doctrine during the nineteenth century was the Supreme Court's decision in *Dred Scott v. Sandford*.[13] In that case the question at issue was the status of a Negro who had been carried by his master from a slave state into a territory made free by the Missouri Compromise. Although thereafter taken back to a slave state, Dred Scott claimed that upon previously reaching free soil he had been forever emancipated. The Court, speaking through Chief Justice Taney, held that Congress was without power to legislate upon the issue of slavery even in a territory governed by it, and that therefore Dred Scott had never become free. Congress, the Court held, was virtually powerless to check or limit the spread of the institution of slavery.

The history of this country for some 30 years before the *Dred* Scott decision demonstrates the bitter frustration which that decision brought to large elements of the population who opposed any expansion of slavery. In 1820 when Maine was seeking

654   ★   *Balancing Liberty, Constitutionalism, and Democracy*

admission as a free state and Missouri as a slave state, a fight over the expansion of slavery engulfed the national legislative halls and resulted in the Missouri Compromise,[14] which forever banned slavery from those territories lying north of a line drawn through the southern boundary of Missouri.[15] This was a victory for the antislavery forces in the North, but the Southerners were prepared to live with it. At the time of the Mexican War in 1846, Representative David Wilmot of Pennsylvania introduced a bill, later known as the Wilmot Proviso,[16] that would have precluded the opening to slavery of any territory acquired as a result of the Mexican War.[17] This proposed amendment to the Missouri Compromise was hotly debated for years both in and out of Congress.[18] Finally in 1854 Senator Stephen A. Douglas shepherded through Congress the Kansas-Nebraska Act,[19] which in effect repealed the Missouri Compromise and enacted into law the principle of "squatter sovereignty": the people in each of the new territories would decide whether or not to permit slavery.[20] The enactment of this bill was, of course, a victory for the proslavery forces in Congress and a defeat for those opposed to the expansion of slavery. The great majority of the antislavery groups, as strongly as they felt about the matter, were still willing to live with the decision of Congress.[21] They were not willing, however, to live with the *Dred Scott* decision.

The Court in *Dred Scott* decided that all of the agitation and debate in Congress over the Missouri Compromise in 1820, over the Wilmot Proviso a generation later, and over the Kansas-Nebraska Act in 1854 had amounted to absolutely nothing. It was, in the words of Macbeth, "A tale told by an idiot, full of sound and fury, signifying nothing."[22] According to the Court, the decision had never been one that Congress was entitled to make; it was one that the Court alone, in construing the Constitution, was empowered to make.

The frustration of the citizenry, who had thought themselves charged with the responsibility for making such decisions, is well expressed in Abraham Lincoln's First Inaugural Address:

> [T]he candid citizen must confess that if the policy of the government, upon vital questions affecting the whole people, is to be irrevocably fixed by decisions of the Supreme Court, the instant they are made, in ordinary litigation between parties in personal actions, the people will have ceased to be their own rulers, having to that extent practically resigned their government into the hands of that eminent tribunal.[23]

The *Dred Scott* decision, of course, was repealed in fact as a result of the Civil War and in law by the Civil War Amendments. The injury to the reputation of the Supreme Court that resulted from the *Dred Scott* decision, however, took more than a generation to heal. Indeed, newspaper accounts long after the *Dred Scott* decision bristled with attacks on the Court, and particularly on Chief Justice Taney, unequalled in their bitterness even to this day.

The brief writer's version of the living Constitution made its next appearance, almost as dramatically as its first, shortly after the turn of the century in *Lochner* v. *New York.* [24] The name of the case is a household word to those who have studied constitutional law, and it is one of the handful of cases in which a dissenting opinion has been overwhelmingly vindicated by the passage of time. In *Lochner* a New York law that limited to ten the maximum number of hours per day that could be worked by bakery employees was assailed on the ground that it deprived the bakery employer of liberty without due process of law. A majority of the Court held the New York maximum hour law unconstitutional, saying, "Statutes of the nature of that under review, limiting the hours in which grown and intelligent men may labor to earn their living, are mere meddlesome interferences with the rights of the individual. . . ."[25]

The Fourteenth Amendment, of course, said nothing about any freedom to make contracts upon terms that one thought best, but there was a very substantial body of opinion outside the Constitution at the time of *Lochner* that subscribed to the general philosophy of social Darwinism as embodied in the writing of Herbert Spencer in England and William Graham Sumner in this country. It may have occurred to some of the Justices who made up a majority in *Lochner*, hopefully subconsciously rather than consciously, that since this philosophy appeared eminently sound and since the language in the due process clause was sufficiently general not to rule out its inclusion, why not strike a blow for the cause? The answer, which has been vindicated by time, came in the dissent of Mr. Justice Holmes:

> [A] constitution is not intended to embody a particular economic theory, whether of paternalism and the organic relation of the citizen to the state or of *laissez faire*. It is made for people of fundamentally differing views, and the accident of our finding certain opinions natural and familiar or novel and even shocking ought not to conclude our judgment upon the question whether statutes embodying them conflict with the Constitution of the United States.[26]

One reads the history of these episodes in the Supreme Court to little purpose if he does not conclude that prior experimentation with the brief writer's expansive notion of a living Constitution has done the Court little credit. There remain today those, such as wrote the brief from which I quoted, who appear to cleave nevertheless to the view that the experiments of the Taney Court before the Civil War, and of the Fuller and Taft Courts in the first part of this century, ended in failure not because they sought to bring into the Constitution a principle that the great majority of objective scholars would have to conclude was not there but because they sought to bring into the Constitution the *wrong* extraconstitutional principle. This school of thought appears to feel that while added protection for slave owners was clearly unacceptable and safeguards for businessmen threatened with ever-expanding state regulation were not desirable, expansion of the protection accorded to individual liberties against the state or to the interest of "discrete and insular" minorities,[27] such as prisoners, must stand on a quite different, more favored footing. To the extent, of course, that such a distinction may legitimately be derived from the Constitution itself, these latter principles do indeed stand on an entirely different footing. To the extent that one must, however, go beyond even a generously fair reading of the language and intent of that document in order to subsume these principles, it seems to me that they are not really distinguishable from those espoused in *Dred Scott* and *Lochner*.

The third difficulty with the brief writer's notion of the living Constitution is that it seems to ignore totally the nature of political value judgments in a democratic society. If such a society adopts a constitution and incorporates in that constitution safeguards for individual liberty, these safeguards indeed do take on a generalized moral rightness or goodness. They assume a general social acceptance neither because of any intrinsic worth nor because of any unique origins in someone's idea of natural justice but instead simply because they have been incorporated in a constitution by the people. Within the limits of our Constitution, the representatives of the people and the executive branches of the state and national governments enact laws. The laws that emerge after a typical political struggle in which various individual value judgments are debated likewise take on a form of moral goodness because they have been enacted into positive law. It is the fact of their enactment that gives them whatever moral claim they have upon us as a society, however, and not any independent virtue they may have in any particular citizen's own scale of values.

Beyond the Constitution and the laws in our society, there simply is no basis other than the individual conscience of the citizen that may serve as a platform for the launching of moral judgments. There is no conceivable way in which I can logically demonstrate to you that the judgments of my conscience are superior to the judgments of your conscience, and vice versa. Many of us necessarily feel strongly and deeply about our own moral judgments, but they remain only personal moral judgments until in some way given the sanction of law.

As Mr. Justice Holmes said in his famous essay on natural law:

> Certitude is not the test of certainty. We have been cocksure of many things that were not so. . . . One cannot be wrenched from the rocky crevices into which one is thrown for many years without feeling that one is attacked in one's life. What we most love and revere generally is determined by early associations. I love granite rocks and barberry bushes, no doubt because with them were my earliest joys that reach back through the past eternity of my life. But while one's experience thus makes certain preferences dogmatic for oneself, recognition of how they came to be so leaves one able to see that others, poor souls, may be equally dogmatic about something else. And this again means skepticism.[28]

This is not to say that individual moral judgments ought not to afford a springboard for action in society, for indeed they are without doubt the most common and most powerful wellsprings for action when one believes that questions of right and wrong are involved. Representative government is predicated upon the idea that one who feels deeply upon a question as a matter of conscience will seek out others of like view or will attempt to persuade others who do not initially share that view. When adherents to the belief become sufficiently numerous, he will have the necessary armaments required in a democratic society to press his views upon the elected representatives of the people, and to have them embodied into positive law.

Should a person fail to persuade the legislature, or should he feel that a legislative victory would be insufficient because of its potential for future reversal, he may seek to run the more difficult gauntlet of amending the Constitution to embody the view that he espouses. Success in amending the Constitution would, of course, preclude succeeding transient majorities in the legislature from tampering with the principle formerly added to the Constitution.

The brief writer's version of the living Constitution, in the last analysis, is a formula for an end run around popular government. To the extent that it makes possible an individual's persuading one or more appointed federal judges to impose on other individuals a rule of conduct that the popularly elected branches of government would not have enacted and the voters have not and would not have embodied in the Constitution, the brief writer's version of the living Constitution is genuinely corrosive of the fundamental values of our democratic society.

## *Notes*

1. See *Hearings on Nominations of William H. Rehnquist and Lewis F. Powell, Jr., Before the Senate Committee on the Judiciary*, 92d Cong., 1st Sess., 87 (1971).

2. 252 U.S. 416 (1920).

3. Ibid., at 433.

4. U.S. Constitution, Amendments XIII, XIV, and XV.

5. *Fay* v. *New York*, 332 U.S. 261, 282 (1947) (Jackson, J.).

6. 5 U.S. (I Cranch) 137 (1803).

7. F. Thorpe, *A Constitutional History of the American People*, Vol. 2, 18 (New York: Harper & Bros., 1898).

8. Ibid., at 191.

9. Ibid., at 81, 91–95.

10. Ibid., at 134–139.

11. C. Hughes, *Addresses and Papers of Charles Evans Hughes* 139 (New York: Putman's, 1908).

12. "The Congress shall have power to enforce, by appropriate legislation, the provisions of this article." U.S. Constitution, Amendment XIV, 5.

13. 60 U.S. (19 How.) 393 (1857).

14. Act of 6 March 1820, ch. 22, 3 Stat. 545.

15. See Thorpe, supra note 7, at 366–377 and 433.

16. Act of 19 June 1862, ch. III, 12 Stat. 432.

17. Thorpe, supra note 7, at 430.

18. Ibid., at 430–432.

19. Act of 30 May 1854, ch. 59, 10 Stat. 277.

20. See Thorpe, supra note 7, at 518–521.

21. Ibid., at 536–542.

22. Shakespeare, *Macbeth*, V.v. 19.

23. First Inaugural Address by Abraham Lincoln, 4 March 1861, in A. Lincoln, *Complete Works of Abraham Lincoln* 171–172, ed. by J. Nicolay (1894).

24. 198 U.S. 45 (1905)

25. Ibid., at 61.

26. Ibid., at 75–76 (Holmes, J., dis. op.).

27. *United States* v. *Carolene Products Co.*, 304 U.S. 144, 152 n.4 (1938).

28. Oliver W. Holmes, "Natural Law," in *Collected Legal Papers* 310, 311 (New York: Peter Smith, 1920).

# THE CONSTITUTION OF THE UNITED STATES: CONTEMPORARY RATIFICATION

## William J. Brennan, Jr.

I am deeply grateful for the invitation to participate in the "Text and Teaching" symposium. This rare opportunity to explore classic texts with participants of such wisdom, acumen and insight as those who have preceded and will follow me to this podium is indeed exhilarating. But it is also humbling. Even to approximate the

The speech entitled "The Constitution of the United States: Contemporary Ratification" delivered by U.S. Supreme Court Justice William J. Brennan, Jr. on October 12, 1985 at the Text and Teaching Symposium at Georgetown University in Washington D.C. Reprinted by permission of the author.

standards of excellence of these vigorous and graceful intellects is a daunting task. I am honored that you have afforded me this opportunity to try.

It will perhaps not surprise you that the text I have chosen for exploration is the amended Constitution of the United States, which, of course, entrenches the Bill of Rights and the Civil War amendments, and draws sustenance from the bedrock principles of another great text, the Magna Carta. So fashioned, the Constitution embodies the aspiration to social justice, brotherhood, and human dignity that brought this nation into being. The Declaration of Independence, the Constitution and the Bill of Rights solemnly committed the United States to be a country where the dignity and rights of all persons were equal before all authority. In all candor we must concede that part of this egalitarianism in America has been more pretension than realized fact. But we are an aspiring people, a people with faith in progress. Our amended Constitution is the lodestar for our aspirations. Like every text worth reading, it is not crystalline. The phrasing is broad and the limitations of its provisions are not clearly marked. Its majestic generalities and ennobling pronouncements are both luminous and obscure. This ambiguity of course calls forth interpretation, the interaction of reader and text. The encounter with the Constitutional text has been, in many senses, my life's work.

My approach to this text may differ from the approach of other participants in this symposium to their texts. Yet such differences may themselves stimulate reflection about what it is we do when we "interpret" a text. Thus I will attempt to elucidate my approach to the text as well as my substantive interpretation.

Perhaps the foremost difference is the fact that my encounters with the constitutional text are not purely or even primarily introspective; the Constitution cannot be for me simply a contemplative haven for private moral reflection. My relation to this great text is inescapably public. That is not to say that my reading of the text is not a personal reading, only that the personal reading perforce occurs in a public context, and is open to critical scrutiny from all quarters.

The Constitution is fundamentally a public text—the monumental charter of a government and a people—and a Justice of the Supreme Court must apply it to resolve public controversies. For, from our beginnings, a most important consequence of the constitutionally created separation of powers has been the American habit, extraordinary to other democracies, of casting social, economic, philosophical and political questions in the form of law suits, in an attempt to secure ultimate resolution by the Supreme Court. In this way, important aspects of the most fundamental issues confronting our democracy may finally arrive in the Supreme Court for judicial determination. Not infrequently, these are the issues upon which contemporary society is most deeply divided. They arouse our deepest emotions. The main burden of my twenty-nine Terms on the Supreme Court has thus been to wrestle with the Constitution in this heightened public context, to draw meaning from the text in order to resolve public controversies.

Two other aspects of my relation to this text warrant mention. First, constitutional interpretation for a federal judge is, for the most part, obligatory. When litigants approach the bar of court to adjudicate a constitutional dispute, they may justifiably demand an answer. Judges cannot avoid a definitive interpretation because they feel unable to, or would prefer not to, penetrate to the full meaning of the Constitution's provisions. Unlike literary critics, judges cannot merely savor the tensions or revel in the ambiguities inhering in the text—judges must resolve them.

Second, consequences flow from a Justice's interpretation in a direct and immediate way. A judicial decision respecting the incompatibility of Jim Crow with a constitutional guarantee of equality is not simply a contemplative exercise in defining the shape of a just society. It is an order supported by the full coercive power of the State that the present society change in a fundamental aspect. Under such circumstances the process of deciding can be a lonely, troubling experience for fallible human beings conscious that their best may not be adequate to the challenge. We Justices are certainly aware that we are not final because we are infallible; we know that we are infallible only because we are final. One does not forget how much may depend on the decision. More than the litigants may be affected. The course of vital social, economic and political currents may be directed.

These three defining characteristics of my relation to the constitutional text—its public nature, obligatory character, and consequentialist aspect—cannot help but influence the way I read that text. When Justices interpret the Constitution they speak for their community, not for themselves alone. The act of interpretation must be undertaken with full consciousness that it is, in a very real sense, the community's interpretation that is sought. Justices are not platonic guardians appointed to wield authority according to their personal moral predilections. Precisely because coercive force must attend any judicial decision to countermand the will of a contemporary majority, the Justices must render constitutional interpretations that are received as legitimate. The source of legitimacy is, of course, a wellspring of controversy in legal and political circles. At the core of the debate is what the late Yale Law School professor Alexander Bickel labeled "the counter-majoritarian difficulty." Our commitment to self-governance in a representative democracy must be reconciled with vesting in electorally unaccountable Justices the power to invalidate the expressed desires of representative bodies on the ground of inconsistency with higher law. Because judicial power resides in the authority to give meaning to the Constitution, the debate is really a debate about how to read the text, about constraints on what is legitimate interpretation.

There are those who find legitimacy in fidelity to what they call "the intentions of the Framers." In its most doctrinaire incarnation, this view demands that Justices discern exactly what the Framers thought about the question under consideration and simply follow that intention in resolving the case before them. It is a view that feigns self-effacing deference to the specific judgments of those who forged our original social compact. But in truth it is little more than arrogance cloaked as humility. It is arrogant to pretend that from our vantage we can gauge accurately the intent of the Framers on application of principle to specific, contemporary questions. All too often, sources of potential enlightenment such as records of the ratification debates provide sparse or ambiguous evidence of the original intention. Typically, all that can be gleaned is that the Framers themselves did not agree about the application or meaning of particular constitutional provisions, and hid their differences in cloaks of generality. Indeed, it is far from clear whose intention is relevant—that of the drafters, the congressional disputants, or the ratifiers in the states?—or even whether the idea of an original intention is a coherent way of thinking about a jointly drafted document drawing its authority from a general assent of the states. And apart from the problematic nature of the sources, our distance of two centuries cannot but work as a prism refracting all we perceive. One cannot help but speculate that the chorus of lamentations calling for interpretation faithful to "original intention"—and proposing nullification of interpretations that fail this quick litmus test—must inevitably come from persons who have no familiarity with the historical record.

Perhaps most importantly, while proponents of this facile historicism justify it as a depoliticization of the judiciary, the political underpinnings of such a choice should not escape notice. A position that upholds constitutional claims only if they were within the specific contemplation of the Framers in effect establishes a presumption of resolving textual ambiguities against the claim of constitutional right. It is far from clear what justifies such a presumption against claims of right. Nothing intrinsic in the nature of interpretation—if there is such a thing as the "nature" of interpretation— commands such a passive approach to ambiguity. This is a choice no less political than any other; it expresses antipathy to claims of the minority to rights against the majority. Those who would restrict claims of right to the values of 1789 specifically articulated in the Constitution turn a blind eye to social progress and eschew adaptation of overarching principles to changes of social circumstance.

Another, perhaps more sophisticated, response to the potential power of judicial interpretation stresses democratic theory: because ours is a government of the people's elected representatives, substantive value choices should by and large be left to them. This view emphasizes not the transcendent historical authority of the framers but the predominant contemporary authority of the elected branches of government. Yet it has similar consequences for the nature of proper judicial interpretation. Faith in the majoritarian process counsels restraint. Even under more expansive formulations of this approach, judicial review is appropriate only to the extent of ensuring that our democratic process functions smoothly. Thus, for example, we would protect freedom of speech merely to ensure that the people are heard by their representatives, rather than as a separate, substantive value. When, by contrast, society tosses up to the Supreme Court a dispute that would require invalidation of a legislature's substantive policy choice, the Court generally would stay its hand because the Constitution was meant as a plan of government and not as an embodiment of fundamental substantive values.

The view that all matters of substantive policy should be resolved through the majoritarian process has appeal under some circumstances, but I think it ultimately will not do. Unabashed enshrinement of majority will would permit the imposition of a social caste system or wholesale confiscation of property so long as a majority of the authorized legislative body, fairly elected, approved. Our Constitution could not abide such a situation. It is the very purpose of a Constitution—and particularly of the Bill of Rights—to declare certain values transcendent, beyond the reach of temporary political majorities. The majoritarian process cannot be expected to rectify claims of minority right that arise as a response to the outcomes of that very majoritarian process. As James Madison put it:

> "The prescriptions in favor of liberty ought to be levelled against that quarter where the greatest danger lies, namely, that which possesses the highest prerogative of power. But this is not found in either the Executive or Legislative departments of Government, but in the body of the people, operating by the majority against the minority." (I Annals 437).

Faith in democracy is one thing, blind faith quite another. Those who drafted our Constitution understood the difference. One cannot read the text without admitting that it embodies substantive value choices; it places certain values beyond the power of any legislature. Obvious are the separation of powers; the privilege of the Writ of Habeas Corpus; prohibition of Bills of Attainder and ex post facto laws; prohibition of cruel and unusual punishments; the requirement of just compensation for official taking of property; the prohibition of laws tending to establish religion or enjoining the free exercise of religion; and, since the Civil War, the banishment of slavery and official race discrimination. With respect to at least such principles, we simply have not constituted ourselves as strict utilitarians. While the Constitution may be amended, such amendments require an immense effort by the People as a whole.

To remain faithful to the content of the Constitution, therefore, an approach to interpreting the text must account for the existence of these substantive value choices, and must accept the ambiguity inherent in the effort to apply them to modern circumstances. The Framers discerned fundamental principles through struggles against particular malefactions of the Crown; the struggle shapes the particular contours of the articulated principles. But our acceptance of the fundamental principles has not and should not bind us to those precise, at times anachronistic, contours. Successive generations of Americans have continued to respect these fundamental choices and adopt them as their own guide to evaluating quite different historical practices. Each generation has the choice to overrule or add to the fundamental principles enunciated by the Framers; the Constitution can be amended or it can be ignored. Yet with respect to its fundamental principles, the text has suffered neither fate. Thus, if I may borrow the words of an esteemed predecessor, Justice Robert Jackson, the burden of judicial interpretation is to translate "the majestic generalities of the Bill of Rights, conceived as part of the pattern of liberal government in the eighteenth century, into concrete restraints on officials dealing with the problems of the twentieth century." (Barnette, 319 U.S. at 639).

We current Justices read the Constitution in the only way that we can: as Twentieth Century Americans. We look to the history of the time of framing and to the intervening history of interpretation. But the ultimate question must be, what do the words of the text mean in our time. For the genius of the Constitution rests not in any static meaning it might have had in a world that is dead and gone, but in the adaptability of its great principles to cope with current problems and current needs. What the constitutional fundamentals meant to the wisdom of other times cannot be their measure to the vision of our time. Similarly, what those fundamentals mean for us, our descendants will learn, cannot be the measure to the vision of their time. This realization is not, I assure you, a novel one of my own creation. Permit me to quote from one of the opinions of our Court, *Weems v. United States*, 217 U.S. 349, written nearly a century ago:

> "Time works changes, brings into existence new conditions and purposes. Therefore, a principle to be vital must be capable of wider application than the mischief which gave it birth. This is peculiarly true of constitutions. They are not ephemeral enactments, designed to meet passing occasions. They are, to use the words of Chief Justice John Marshall, 'designed to approach immortality as nearly as human institutions can approach it.' The future is their care and provision for events of good and bad tendencies of which no prophesy can be made. In the application of a constitution, therefore, our contemplation cannot be only of what has been, but of what may be."

Interpretation must account for the transformative purpose of the text. Our Constitution was not intended to preserve a preexisting society but to make a new one, to put in place new principles that the prior political community had not sufficiently recognized. Thus, for example, when we interpret the Civil War Amendments to the charter—abolishing slavery, guaranteeing blacks equality under law, and guarantee-

664 ★ Balancing Liberty, Constitutionalism, and Democracy

ing blacks the right to vote—we must remember that those who put them in place had no desire to enshrine the status quo. Their goal was to make over their world, to eliminate all vestige of slave caste.

Having discussed at some length how I, as a Supreme Court Justice, interact with this text, I think it time to turn to the fruits of this discourse. For the Constitution is a sublime oration on the dignity of man, a bold commitment by a people to the ideal of libertarian dignity protected through law. Some reflection is perhaps required before this can be seen.

The Constitution on its face is, in large measure, a structuring text, a blueprint for government. And when the text is not prescribing the form of government it is limiting the powers of that government. The original document, before addition of any of the amendments, does not speak primarily of the rights of man, but of the abilities and disabilities of government. When one reflects upon the text's preoccupation with the scope of government as well as its shape, however, one comes to understand that what this text is about is the relationship of the individual and the state. The text marks the metes and bounds of official authority and individual autonomy. When one studies the boundary that the text marks out, one gets a sense of the vision of the individual embodied in the Constitution.

As augmented by the Bill of Rights and the Civil War Amendments, this text is a sparkling vision of the supremacy of the human dignity of every individual. This vision is reflected in the very choice of democratic self-governance: the supreme value of a democracy is the presumed worth of each individual. And this vision manifests itself most dramatically in the specific prohibitions of the Bill of Rights, a term which I henceforth will apply to describe not only the original first eight amendments, but the Civil War amendments as well. It is a vision that has guided us as a people throughout our history, although the precise rules by which we have protected fundamental human dignity have been transformed over time in response to both transformations of social condition and evolution of our concepts of human dignity.

Until the end of the nineteenth century, freedom and dignity in our country found meaningful protection in the institution of real property. In a society still largely agricultural, a piece of land provided men not just with sustenance but with the means of economic independence, a necessary precondition of political independence and expression. Not surprisingly, property relationships formed the heart of litigation and of legal practice, and lawyers and judges tended to think stable property relationships the highest aim of the law.

But the days when common law property relationships dominated litigation and legal practice are past. To a growing extent economic existence now depends on less certain relationships with government—licenses, employment, contracts, subsidies, unemployment benefits, tax exemptions, welfare and the like. Government participation in the economic existence of individuals is pervasive and deep. Administrative matters and other dealings with government are at the epicenter of the exploding law. We turn to government and to the law for controls which would never have been expected or tolerated before this century, when a man's answer to economic oppression or difficulty was to move two hundred miles west. Now hundreds of thousands of Americans live entire lives without any real prospect of the dignity and autonomy that ownership of real property could confer. Protection of the human dignity of such citizens requires a much modified view of the proper relationship of individual and state.

In general, problems of the relationship of the citizen with government have multiplied and thus have engendered some of the most important constitutional issues of the day. As government acts ever more deeply upon those areas of our lives once marked "private," there is an even greater need to see that individual rights are not curtailed or cheapened in the interest of what may temporarily appear to be the "public good." And as government continues in its role of provider for so many of our disadvantaged citizens, there is an even greater need to ensure that government act with integrity and consistency in its dealings with these citizens. To put this another way, the possibilities for collision between government activity and individual rights will increase as the power and authority of government itself expands, and this growth, in turn, heightens the need for constant vigilance at the collision points. If our free society is to endure, those who govern must recognize human dignity and accept the enforcement of constitutional limitations on their power conceived by the Framers to be necessary to preserve that dignity and the air of freedom which is our proudest heritage. Such recognition will not come from a technical understanding of the organs of government, or the new forms of wealth they administer. It requires something different, something deeper—a personal confrontation with the well springs of our society. Solutions of constitutional questions from that perspective have become the great challenge of the modern era. All the talk in the last half-decade about shrinking the government does not alter this reality or the challenge it imposes. The modern activist state is a concomitant of the complexity of modern society; it is inevitably with us. We must meet the challenge rather than wish it were not before us.

The challenge is essentially, of course, one to the capacity of our constitutional structure to foster and protect the freedom, the dignity, and the rights of all persons within our borders, which it is the great design of the Constitution to secure. During the time of my public service this challenge has largely taken shape within the confines of the interpretive question whether the specific guarantees of the Bill of Rights operate as restraints on the power of State government. We recognize the Bill of Rights as the primary source of express information as to what is meant by constitutional liberty. The safeguards enshrined in it are deeply etched in the foundation of America's freedoms. Each is a protection with centuries of history behind it, often dearly bought with the blood and lives of people determined to prevent oppression by their rulers. The first eight Amendments, however, were added to the Constitution to operate solely against federal power. It was not until the Thirteenth and Fourteenth Amendments were added, in 1865 and 1868, in response to a demand for national protection against abuses of state power, that the Constitution could be interpreted to require application of the first eight amendments to the states.

It was in particular the Fourteenth Amendment's guarantee that no person be deprived of life, liberty or property without process of law that led us to apply many of the specific guarantees of the Bill of Rights to the States. In my judgment, Justice Cardozo best captured the reasoning that brought us to such decisions when he described what the Court has done as a process by which the guarantees "have been taken over from the earlier articles of the federal bill of rights and brought within the Fourteenth Amendment by a process of absorption . . . [that] has had its source in the belief that neither liberty nor justice would exist if [those guarantees] . . . were sacrificed." (Palko, 302 U.S., at 326). But this process of absorption was neither swift nor steady. As late as 1922 only the Fifth Amendment guarantee of just compensation for official taking of property had been given force against the states. Between then and 1956 only the First Amendment guarantees of speech and conscience and the Fourth Amendment ban of unreasonable searches and had been incorporated—the latter, however, without the exclusionary rule to give it force. As late as 1961, I could stand before a distinguished assemblage of the bar at New York University's James Madison Lecture and list the following as guarantees that had not been thought to be sufficiently fundamental to the protection of human dignity so as to be enforced against the states: the prohibition of cruel and unusual punishments, the right against self-incrimination, the right to assistance of counsel in a trial, the right to confront witnesses, the right to compulsory process, the right not to be placed in jeopardy of life or limb more than once upon accusation of a crime, the right not to have illegally obtained evidence introduced at a criminal trial, and the right to a jury of one's peers.

The history of the quarter century following that Madison Lecture need not be told in great detail. Suffice it to say that each of the guarantees listed above has been recognized as a fundamental aspect of ordered liberty. Of course, the above catalogue encompasses only the rights of the criminally accused, those caught, rightly or wrongly, in the maw of the criminal justice system. But it has been well said that there is no better test of a society than how it treats those accused of transgressing against it. Indeed, it is because we recognize that incarceration strips a man of his dignity that we demand strict adherence to fair procedure and proof of guilt beyond a reasonable doubt before taking such a drastic step. These requirements are, as Justice Harlan once said, "bottomed on a fundamental value determination of our society that it is far worse to convict an innocent man than to let a guilty man go free." (Winship, 397 U.S., at 372).

There is no worse injustice than wrongly to strip a man of his dignity. And our adherence to the constitutional vision of human dignity is so strict that even after convicting a person according to these stringent standards, we demand that his dignity be infringed only to the extent appropriate to the crime and never by means of wanton infliction of pain or deprivation. I interpret the Constitution plainly to embody these fundamental values.

Of course the constitutional vision of human dignity has, in this past quarter century, infused far more than our decisions about the process. Recognition of the principle of "one person, one vote" as a constitutional one redeems the promise of self-governance by affirming the essential dignity of every citizen in the right to equal participation in the democratic process. Recognition of so-called "new property" rights in those receiving government entitlements affirms the essential dignity of the least fortunate among us by demanding that government treat with decency, integrity and consistency those dependent on its benefits for their very survival. After all, a legislative majority initially decides to create governmental entitlements; the Constitution's Due Process Clause merely provides protection for entitlements thought necessary by society as a whole. Such due process rights prohibit government from imposing the devil's bargain of bartering away human dignity for human sustenance. Likewise, recognition of full equality for women—equal protection of the laws—ensures that gender has no bearing on claims to human dignity.

Recognition of broad and deep rights of expression and of conscience reaffirm the vision of human dignity in many ways. They too redeem the promise of self-governance by facilitating—indeed demanding—robust, uninhibited and wide-open debate on issues of public importance. Such public debate is of course vital to the development and dissemination of political ideas. As importantly, robust public discussion is the crucible in which personal political convictions are forged. In our democracy, such discussion is a political duty; it is the essence of self government. The constitutional vision of human dignity rejects the possibility of political orthodoxy imposed from above; it respects the right of each individual to form and to expresses political judgments, however far they may deviate from the mainstream and however unsettling they might be to the powerful or the elite. Recognition of these rights of expression and conscience also frees up the private space for both intellectual and spiritual development free of government dominance, either blatant or subtle. Justice Brandeis put it so well sixty years ago when he wrote: "Those who won our independence believed that the final end of the State was to make men free to develop their faculties; and that in its government the deliberative forces should prevail over the arbitrary. They valued liberty both as an end and as a means." (Whitney, 274 U.S., at 375).

I do not mean to suggest that we have in the last quarter century achieved a comprehensive definition of the constitutional ideal of human dignity. We are still striving toward that goal, and doubtless it will be an eternal quest. For if the interaction of this Justice and the constitutional text over the years confirms any single proposition, it is that the demands of human dignity will never cease to evolve.

Indeed, I cannot in good conscience refrain from mention of one grave and crucial respect in which we continue, in my judgment, to fall short of the constitutional vision of human dignity. It is in our continued tolerance of State-administered execution as a form of punishment. I make it a practice not to comment on the constitutional issues that come before the Court, but my position on this issue, of course, has been for some time fixed and immutable. I think I can venture some thoughts on this particular subject without transgressing my usual guideline too severely.

As I interpret the Constitution, capital punishment is under all circumstances cruel and unusual punishment prohibited by the Eighth and Fourteenth Amendments. This is a position of which I imagine you are not unaware. Much discussion of the merits of capital punishment has in recent years focused on the potential arbitrariness that attends its administration, and I have no doubt that such arbitrariness is a grave wrong. But for me, the wrong of capital punishment transcends such procedural issues. As I have said in my opinions, I view the Eighth Amendment's probition of cruel and unusual punishments as embodying to a unique degree moral principles that substantively restrain the punishments our civilized society may impose on those persons who transgress its laws. Foremost among the moral principles recognized in our cases and inherent in the prohibition is the primary principle that the State, even as it punishes, must treat its citizens in a manner consistent with their intrinsic worth as human beings. A punishment must not be so severe as to be utterly and irreversibly degrading to the very essence of human dignity. Death for whatever crime and under all circumstances is a truly awesome punishment. The calculated killing of a human being by the State involves, by its very nature, an absolute denial of the executed person's humanity. The most vile murder does not, in my view, release the State from constitutional restraints on the destruction of human dignity. Yet an executed person has lost the very right to have rights, now or ever. For me, then, the fatal constitutional infirmity of capital punishment is that it treats members of the human race as nonhumans, as objects to be toyed with and discarded. It is, indeed, "cruel and unusual." It is thus inconsistent with the fundamental premise of the Clause that even the most base criminal remains a human being possessed of some potential, at least, for common human dignity.

This is an interpretation to which a majority of my fellow Justices—not to mention, it would seem, a majority of my fellow countrymen—does not subscribe. Perhaps you find my adherence to it, and my recurrent publication of it, simply contrary, tiresome, or quixotic. Or perhaps you see in it a refusal to abide by the judicial principle of *stare decisis*, obedience to precedent. In my judgment, however, the unique interpretive role of the Supreme Court with respect to the Constitution demands some flexibility with respect to the call of *stare decisis*. Because we are the last word on the meaning of the Constitution, our views must be subject to revision over time, or the Constitution falls captive, again, to the anachronistic views of long-gone generations. I mentioned earlier the judge's role in seeking out the community's interpretation of the Constitutional text. Yet, again in my judgment, when a Justice perceives an interpretation of the text to have departed so far from its essential meaning, that Justice is bound, by a larger constitutional duty to the community, to expose the departure and point toward a different path. On this issue, the death penalty, I hope to embody a community striving for human dignity for all, although perhaps not yet arrived.

You have doubtless observed that this description of my personal encounter with the constitutional text has in large portion been a discussion of public developments in constitutional doctrine over the past quarter century. That, as I suggested at the outset, is inevitable because my interpretive career has demanded a public reading of the text. This public encounter with the text, however, has been a profound source of personal inspiration. The vision of human dignity embodied there is deeply moving. It is timeless. It has inspired Americans for two centuries and it will continue to inspire as it continues to evolve. That evolutionary process is inevitable and, indeed, it is the true interpretive genius of the text.

If we are to be as a shining city upon a hill, it will be because of our ceaseless pursuit of the constitutional ideal of human dignity. For the political and legal ideals that form the foundation of much that is best in American institutions—ideals jealously preserved and guarded throughout our history—still form the vital force in creative political thought and activity within the nation today. As we adapt our institutions to the ever-changing conditions of national and international life, those ideals of human dignity—liberty and justice for all individuals—will continue to inspire and guide us because they are entrenched in our Constitution. The Constitution with its Bill of Rights thus has a bright future, as well as a glorious past, for its spirit is inherent in the aspirations of our people.